Northern Sun, Southern Moon

Northern Sun, Southern Moon
Europe's Reinvention of Jazz

Mike Heffley

Yale University Press
New Haven and London

The past is never dead. It's not even past.
— William Faulkner

In Memoriam

Peter Kowald
Joachim-Ernst Berendt
Peter Niklas Wilson
Steve Lacy

Set in AGaramond by SNP Best-set Typesetter Ltd, Hong Kong
Printed in Great Britain by Cambridge University Press

Library of Congress Control Number: 2005920690
A catalogue record for this book is available from the British Library.

Contents

Acknowledgments

Heartfelt thanks go to all those in Europe who helped to make this study what it is. First, to the people at Deutscher Akademie Austauschdienst (DAAD, the German Ministry of Academic Exchange), for their interest and investment in, and logistical assistance of, my research in Germany, Austria, and the Czech Republic. I am honored and proud to have been granted their support.

Most of all, I thank the musicians whose work ignited this one, and who helped with so much openness and attention to its development: Albert Mangelsdorff, Vinko Globokar, Günter Hampel, Joachim Kühn, Peter Brötzmann, Peter Kowald, Alexander von Schlippenbach, Sven-Åke Johansson, Ulrich Gumpert, Günter Sommer, Conrad Bauer, Ernst-Ludwig Petrovsky, Uschi Brüning, Johannes Bauer, Wolfgang Fuchs, Paul Lovens, Axel Dörner, Evan Parker, Fred Van Hove, and Tony Oxley. While the space and other constraints of this book prevented some of them from getting the attention they deserve from me, that can be found in my dissertation (Heffley 2000), easily accessible through my website (almatour.org).

Over the fifteen-year span of our collaboration, I have garnered many reasons to acknowledge the influence of Wesleyan University Professor of Music Anthony Braxton – as musician, academic mentor, friend – on my life and work. My association with him opened the doors of his long-time European colleagues and friends to my interviews with them. Professor Braxton has consistently offered his trust and support through our long periods of both close contact and more distant interactions. My gratitude for both – the personal fellowship and the permission to drift apart back into our own separate paths without any sense of disorienting rift – is immeasurable.

Next round of thanks go to the other mentors and colleagues who have contributed to this work: Lewis and Clark College Professor of Music Franya Berkman, whose monograph on Alice Coltrane (see Bibliography) progressed as my own did, providing us both a context as neighbors to cultivate a collegial camaraderie and friendship that helped us both (certainly me) endure our similar tasks through to their completions; and Yale University's Musser Professor of Anthropology, African American Studies, Music, and American Studies John Szwed, for his insightful and encouraging responses to my drafts as the work evolved.

Pianist/composer/scholar Ursel Schlicht, Harvard Professor of African American Music Ingrid Monson, trombonist and Columbia Professor of Music George Lewis, Loyola University of Chicago Professor of History Lewis Erenberg, Darmstadt Jazz-Institut Director Wolfram Knauer, and journalist and scholar John Corbett engaged in informal give-and-take with me at conferences that informed my thinking and influenced the final results.

Wesleyan University, my doctoral alma mater, is an internationally renowned center of world music. Its attraction of the best and brightest in music and music scholarship from everywhere on the planet ensured that my investigations of faraway places and people were always tempered and fed by the informed and human touches of people connected to them as home and kin, while to me as friend and colleague. Wesleyan graduate students Claudia Van Herm and Bastien Heim helped me with German translations; Junko Oba with my Japanese material; Mark Slobin, University of Minnesota Professor of Music Mirjana Lausevic (from Bosnia), and (Polish) Ph.D. candidate Marzanna Poplawska with aspects of my Eastern European studies; Wesleyan Professor of Music and Director of East Asian Studies Su Zheng, and Korean composer/improviser/scholar Jin hi Kim, with insights into Mongolian and Korean music, respectively.

My German teacher was Wesleyan Professor of German Krishna Winston, American translator of novelists Günter Grass and Peter Handke. Her tutelage in the language launched me into the world of German-language discourse that makes this study so fresh to its English-language readers. Wesleyan Professor of Intellectual History Cecilia Miller and Wesleyan Professors of Music Mark Slobin, Su Zheng, Jon Barlow, Neely Bruce, and Eric Charry, and (visiting Columbia Professor of Philosophy) Lydia Gehr provided my project, both in their classes and out, with much valuable historical information and insight, and a full scholarly toolkit.

Dagmar Gebers was my first German contact and my gateway to all the others; she opened her home to me during my first visit to Berlin, then helped me find a more permanent arrangement for the duration of my stay there. Her proficiency in English got me off to a much stronger start than I could have initiated alone. Her friendship and help has won my undying gratitude.

Dagmar's photographs of the musicians presented by FMP have become historic works of art in their own right (view them all, and an essay on her work, at www.fmp-label.de). Likewise, French photojournalist Gérard Rouy's work (see more at www.shef.ac.uk/misc/rec/ps/efi/ehome.html), gracing the book's jacket and inner pages, is that of one who has been there and engaged with this music from its beginning. I am honoured and proud to have their contributions.

Special thanks also go to Panajota Tserkesi, who opened her home as well, for four months, to a lodger she trusted on faith much more than sight. For her patience with our language difficulties, her help with daily life, and her intelligent and genuine friendship I will also be forever grateful.

Thanks go out to Gerlinde Koschik for her help with my Wuppertal and Düsseldorf contacts, and her help in crucial practical matters.

I am also grateful to the Nationalgalerie Berlin and Sotheby's of London for permission to reproduce their historic paintings.

I am grateful to Berlin's seminal label Free Music Production (FMP) founder and long-time manager Jost Gebers, for sharing his time and his stock of recordings and publications so generously, and in such gracious settings; and to his office manager Dieter Hahne, for his similar cooperation. Thanks too to David Radlauer, for sharing with me his radio broadcast interviews with German jazz buff and record collector Ray Taubert; and to Dale MacBride, for use of his extensive collection of recordings.

During the time devoted to the writing and editing, from 2000 through 2004, I was blessed with housing and employment situations that were warmly personal and stress-free in nature – something that made a potentially dry and lonely experience one grounded in pleasant daily life. Cecilia Miller shared her beautiful home with me, as did Margaret Phillips, both as landladies, housemates, and kind and considerate friends. Wesleyan Ph.D. candidate and Fulbright scholar Amelia Ingram was another classy housemate through much of this time. Jazz pianist and scholar Noah Baerman and his wife, artist Kate Ten Eyck, gave me a great year in a cozy, quiet part of their house; and Peter and Jennifer Hadley, also Wesleyan music colleagues, with their children Emma, Thomas, and Sonya turned the first floor of their three-story Victorian country home over to me. All of these situations felt like elegant writer's retreats.

Thanks go to Don Gondek, a Glastonbury, Connecticut housepainter with a master's reputation among his clientele, who took me on as an apprentice when I wanted to balance my writing work with physical rather than the academic labor of being a Rutgers University Writing Instructor. He kept me healthily, happily busy and well paid when many in his shoes would have lost patience with my learning curve, while teaching me as much about human decency as he did about excellence of craftsmanship.

Yale University Press editors Harry Haskell, Robert Baldock, and especially Sandy Chapman and Barbara Massam would be showered with the gratitude of this book's readers were their roles in its final draft as public as its author's. They certainly have all of my appreciation.

Inexpressible gratitude abides and ever increases toward the elders in my family – my late mother, Mary Herrera; my father, Wayne Heffley; my aunt, Jaylene Sutton; and my late uncle, Wesley Sutton – for their crucial roles in preparing me for the journey resulting in this study.

Last (for emphasis only), thanks to my daughter Geneva Angine Heffley for her adult love and respect, after the long odyssey from her birth to her ripest moments with me on the planet. She has been my motivation, inspiration, and muse in many deep ways, as this study (of improvisation as an issue of childhood and myth, and of parent traditions, among other things) subliminally displays.

Mike Heffley
2004

Introduction

Now Was the Time

"There is only one history," said Karl Marx, famously, to take his stand against the disciplinary splitting of the one history into histories of politics, economics, philosophy, art, music, etc. . . . There is only one history, but there are many different ways to explain it.

Ekkehard Jost ("Reflections on Jazz History")[1]

The One History

Anyone who subscribed to *Down Beat* and other jazz magazines from around 1959 through the 1960s, as I did, remembers the shock resounding through their pages. The American press's reaction to what it called "free jazz" bespoke a riot of controversy in the headlines alone: "Avant-Garde: A Plea for Sanity," "New Jazz – Black, Angry, and Hard to Understand," "Jazz is Mugged by 'New Thing.'" They signaled heated debate, denunciations of the music as one of anger, hate, self-destruction, social anarchy, charlatanism, racial enmity . . . and scandalized countercharges of Eurocentric racism, ignorance, and insensitivity, white America clutching at its threatened power.

The battle raged as hotly in the musician community itself, and not solely down racial lines. Trumpeter Miles Davis dismissed the new music's nominal godfather, saxophonist Ornette Coleman, as "psychologically screwed up," and cursed its pianist-pioneer Cecil Taylor as one who "couldn't play"; vibraphonist Cal Tjader called Taylor "a heart attack waiting to happen"; altosaxophonist Phil Woods called fellow altoist Anthony Braxton a "primitive" with an ego, someone who was crazy to think he could play that horn.[2]

When I began my research for this study of that music's impact in Europe, I pondered with a sense of déjà vu more recent headlines from the American press: "The Sound of Sameness: Why European Jazz Musicians Hate Modern American Jazz," and "Europeans Cut In With a New Jazz Sound And Beat."[3] These stories, which provoked many passionate reader responses, were new to this press, indicating what it saw as a burgeoning trend away from American jazz as yesterday's news, and toward its hottest torchbearers in Europe. Yet that trend had begun some forty years ago, and I had watched it grow since then in British, French, and German accounts of free jazz in Europe and America.

"Northern Sun, Southern Moon" is an image representative of my central concern with the Western side of jazz's European–African parentage. It evokes the northern countries spanning from Western Europe to Russia, distinguishing them from their more Mediterranean cousins. American jazz's Eurasian roots are as deep as its African ones; its Western and African sources, whatever their separate identities and conflicts, are parents sharing equally visceral, original, and unique bonds with their one child. European jazz is no more a foreign echo of its American source than the latter is of European music.

Europe's move away from imitation of American jazz and into its own originality was, like its African-American model, effected by a coup of improvisation over composition. This coup had been preparing and positioning itself in America's music throughout the twentieth century, and it made its decisive moves in the free-jazz movement of the 1960s – a liberation *of* as much as *from*, especially in its European versions, Western music history and principles.

"Jazz" the word, of course, has been invented and reinvented all along, like the music it tags, always controversially. I will use it here with little such fuss, in simple acceptance of that historical and continued usage. Finally, since Ornette Coleman's New York debut in 1959, the explanations of "free" have been as controversial as those of "jazz" – but I will stay with that word too, for the same faithfulness and convenience, and for the many layers of meaning it will yield. Both words, separately and together, have been employed much less problematically in European than in American discourse. By the end of the book, what they do and do not mean here will be clear.[4]

So called, free jazz emerged in late 1950s/early 1960s America, along with the Civil Rights/Black Power movements, as an African-American challenge of Western aesthetic and social premises. Waxing with the passions of those times, the music then waned in America's limelight with the country's turn from social unrest and youthful idealism to the less public individualism and conservatism of the Nixon years, giving way in the 1970s to the more market-driven "Fusion" (of jazz and rock) music. That gave way in turn, with the 1980s rise of a black middle class and a globalized music industry, to an even more media-and-market-driven promotion of pre-free-jazz styles, the so-called "neocon(servative)" school ascribed to trumpeter Wynton Marsalis.

The returns on those investments continue to compound pre-free jazz's cultural capital up to this time, through its institutionalization in public performing arts venues, marketing and programming, and funding; and in music education, mass media, and music journalism and scholarship. In the wake of that mainstreaming, scholars and critics have historicized "free jazz," most disparagingly, as a failed musical and economic experiment and a cultural–political cul-de-sac; or, less so, as something still too new (after forty years) and/or eccentric – or, conversely, by now too dated, though still forging on at the margins – to have found its purchase in mainstream American culture.[5]

The music under the "free-jazz" rubric – that of Ornette Coleman, Cecil Taylor, Albert Ayler, John Coltrane, Sun Ra and their bands, to name the major pioneers with the most impact in Europe – ignited the jazz scenes there in the mid-to-late 1960s. The subsequent free-jazz movement in their countries was as linked to the events and spirit of the 1968 student protests and riots in Paris and Berlin (the "'68ers") as it was to new assertions of black identity in America.[6] The racial conflict specific to the United States translated in Europe to an international radical leftism – one with a youthful white more than an angry black face – hostile to Western imperialistic capitalism and faux-culture. In Soviet-controlled Eastern Europe, it translated to liberatory resistance (also youthful, more than politically ideological) to Communist regimes.

European jazz had always labored in the shadow of its African-American parent. Under the latter's free-jazz shadow, however, some European musicians grasped the spirit of that parentage fully enough to free themselves from the role of slavish imitators, to initiate new approaches and sounds appropriate to their own personal and collective lives. Like their mentors, they did so through a spontaneous improvisation theoretically free of the diatonic/chromatic and metric systems governing harmony, melody, and rhythm of both pre-free jazz and other Western music, both "high" (art) and "low" (popular entertainment). These are the musicians of our focus, the voices in this pan-European network of what came to be called in the German-language press the *erste Stunde* (first hours) of Europe's *Emanzipation* from American jazz.

The music these Europeans launched then, and have developed since, has moved so far away from its parent idioms – Western art music, including the American Experimentalists from Charles Ives to John Cage, and American jazz – that its initial free-jazz handle has gradually given way to the more wide open, less jazz-specific descriptor "new and improvised music." (The "new" has generally distinguished the compositional/conceptual from the improvisational/performative aspects of the music.) This music has survived and grown from the radical fringes of European jazz into a categorical status that "bop," "early jazz," and "swing" (thanks largely to Marsalis et al.) enjoy in America (and, still, in Europe). It has established the gestures of spontaneous improvisation and idiosyncratic composition not as dated, edgy eccentricities, but as musical and cultural gestures resonant with the mainstream of Europe's one history.

Indeed, this period, far from being an historical dead end, marked the turn in European jazz that moved beyond stylistic shift to sea change, a turn crucial to its individuation from America. Over time, the music has taken on a strength and confidence – even a certain amount of crowing – that is sounding off beyond its local scenes and language barriers, commanding attention in the global arena. European improvised music now carries musical and cultural information and implications as potentially vital, edifying, and new to American music and culture as jazz was to Europe in the twentieth century, or as Western classical (especially German) music was to America in the nineteenth.

My looks at this history are drawn primarily from the untranslated German and French texts that documented it as it emerged, and by more current retrospectives. English translations of such sources come next in priority, followed last by the American, Canadian, British, and Australian work to which English-language readers have had most access. Besides the obvious peek behind the veil of other languages, a big part of my agenda here is to right an imbalance in international discourse on jazz. (To that end, incidentally, I encourage the most serious readers to pay special attention to the endnotes, for that is where the most direct conversation between me and my non-English-language sources takes place.) Most German and French writers, and many readers, read English fluently, and are as familiar with American news and discourse about jazz as are we Americans. For us to remain so out of touch with them and their untranslated work on both American and European music is professionally embarrassing, to say the least; to say the most, it is intellectually, culturally, and psychologically perilous.

The feedback provided by many of these sources itself helped to define and develop the music's identity in Europe as it emerged, just as earlier generations of European jazz scholars (especially the French Hugues Panassié, Charles Delauney, and André Hodeir) helped define and develop jazz in America. Part of European free jazz's identity has been a "serious amateurism," as opposed to a (musically) frivolous or (commercially) compromised professionalism, an amateurism inherited from the history of jazz in Europe generally.[7] Many of the best writers and scholars on the music there have also been avid players, and/or have been involved with the presentation and promotion of the music as it emerged and unfolded. This fact, for my money, translates into more insight and authority than I have encountered in their English-language counterparts, especially on the subject of this study. My European colleagues have a record of service to the music that has contributed substantially to the greater presence in Europe not only of the newly "emancipated" European players, but of their African-American heroes and peers as well, as will be discussed.

Other Explanations

The faithfulness of the many explanations of jazz's "one history" to it has been contested in print since they started appearing. These contests arose from those between white and black American cultures, and between American and European cultures – contests of worldviews and aesthetics, shaped by internal and interacting social, political, and religious dynamics.

The transatlantic conversations about jazz have been revisited, revived, and reframed by recent retrospectives; those conversations have also expanded and deepened in the process.[8] The European and the black and white American sources of these retrospectives corroboratively inform the following summary:

- European music critics in the 1920s, mostly French and English, woke Americans up to the value of jazz beyond its American contexts. They put a Western high-cultural stamp of approval on the music qua Western music, for its integration of musical elements – composition, performance, rhythm, harmony and melody, expressive nuance and ornament – and for its integration of those elements with the people playing, hearing, and dancing to the music;
- their narrative: African-American culture gave birth to this American integration because of its roots outside of, and continued exclusion from, a racist society; paradoxically, the European cradle of that society was more receptive than its American cousin to the genius and soul, and the black bodies, creating the music. Europe purged itself of its own racist and classist history by hosting the music and its makers with grace and respect not found in America, and through two world wars significantly fought against said history;[9]
- white American (Jazz Age) writers about the music, by comparison, were ignorant, shallow, insensitive hacks whose work seldom rose above adolescent froth; or, alternatively, they were imitation Europeans, Europhiliac elitists, talking down to and about the music, at least in the early years. Eventually, however, they matured into a mind and voice able to match, then to challenge, their European models and colleagues as themselves wrongheaded, condescending, out of touch with American reality;
- the black Americans at the center of this story did not ply their own minds and voices to its body of print until the 1960s, concurrent with their more general rise as a people in the Civil Rights and subsequent movements.[10] When they did, it was usually to rebuke, scorn, disagree with, correct, and upstage the white voices that had defined and dominated the conversation for so long;[11]
- those white speakers (their new generation, both American and European) listened to those black voices, and a new wave of literature – mostly (unlike before) academic – reassessed the conversation from its beginnings, made room for (even deferred to and built upon) both the new and unearthed older black voices, expanding the conversation to link with still other voices, from other rooms of culture, arts, and letters.[12]

Broadly speaking, then, we have an American jazz discourse launched and shaped by French scholars; seized and reshaped, mainstreamed out of academia, by European-American journalists and scholars; seized and reshaped again, still in that mainstream, by African-American public intellectuals;[13] adjusting its tack accordingly back on the French side;[14] then shifting away again from public into more insular academic discourse, especially in (both black and white) America.

From the first translations of Panassié up to the late 1950s/early 1960s, articles and books on jazz were most typically projects of the mainstream commercial press. Some houses specialized in music (e.g., Schirmer), some were music-specific divisions of more general catalogues (e.g., DaCapo), but many were simply offering the jazz side of American public intellectual life (e.g., Morrow, Doubleday, Knopf, among others). Since those years, the arena has shifted increasingly to academic presses, and to academia as ivory tower or ghetto, depending on an author's place in its pecking order.

This shift represents a double-edged sword to those of us working in and on the music. On the one hand, the range and quality of information is better. Widely varying in backgrounds and concerns, this scholarship falls within the same post-Romantic tradition that spawned French and German anthropology, which gave rise to American ethnomusicology, cultural studies (especially those that break down the high–low divide), later identity (primarily black, at first, then women's, queer, and other ethnic) studies, and current jazz studies (the latter with some ongoing overlap in the public realm, inherited from jazz fanzine journalism).

On the other hand, aside from a few jazz-politically correct voices (Stanley Crouch, Gary Giddins, Marsalis, magnified through Ken Burns), we do not see the authors of these post-1960s' studies, nor most of their subjects, interviewed or discussed on, say, Charlie Rose, or even Book TV, as a rule. They are well received and read in their own academic professional conference and publishing networks, but even those who write regularly for magazines and newspapers of general and special public interest are more likely than before to find an academic publisher to collect and offer their work in book form. This implies (accurately, I suggest) that the Americentric journalistic-cum-critical context, which arose in responsive counter to the European academic one of Panassié and Hodeir by the 1950s, has been subsumed by the latter. It remains black- and white-Americentric in content, perhaps, but Eurocentric, even Europhiliac, in deep historical context, language, and affect.

Having come of age and matured with this conversation, I found myself increasingly drawn to its European voices.[15] They piqued my interest in the rest of the conversation across the pond that had been going on out of my earshot throughout the twentieth century, especially its second half. They all had a wider and deeper take on the music and issues I cared about than I found in America. They were refreshingly detached from the American commercial, political, and cultural contexts I found hostile to, exploitive of, and/or cold to that music and those issues. They piqued my interest – in the way, say, de Tocqueville has piqued that of American readers – in both American and Western music as major tributaries among others feeding the new and improvised music I was involved with. In the process, they ignited my interest in Europe. I see this study as my reciprocal gesture to those Europeans who have served the American scene and discourses so well.

Having immersed myself in them (this study's sources) most recently, I have come to see the American discourse at a new remove. It strikes me now as an extension of Western history stemming from the birth of the nation itself during the foments of Enlightenment thought and Revolution, and the subsequent (largely reactive) Romanticism of the nineteenth century. Panassié's rapture was for a local (black) ethnic purity standing up against the soulless (white) oppression of Empire – much as German Romanticism itself stood for soul and local

culture and place against Napoleon.[16] The rise of African identity in America –
beyond the cruelties of the melting pot, reaching even to claim the primacies of
place peculiar to the hardwon strengths of an underdog – is a similar assertion of
the Romantic against the Enlightenment spirit; as is, finally, the development
of an American identity itself, incorporating while honoring all such local/
racial/ethnic groups, contradistinct from classist Europe (and from its American
simulacrum, voiced by the melting-pot and capitalist narratives that have masked
its classism).

As we proceed through this study, it will become clear why I have come to
review the American jazz discourse through the Enlightenment–Romantic lenses:
they bring into focus the common global ground shared by American and European cultures and histories. As Anthony Braxton once said, "Europe has never
forgotten her history, because she is her history." (We will see that this becomes
increasingly true the farther east in Europe one goes.) The spectacle of jazz in
twentieth-century Europe, and of its individuation from its American parent, is
most clearly discerned in the context of the two centuries prior.

And, I find, these lenses bring into focus many more details that tell me why,
when I ponder the courses and discourses of the music in America, I am so
reminded of the clashes of small powers challenging great ones, becoming great
ones themselves, then meeting at Yalta after their bloody clashes in order to divide
spoils, draw borders, define doctrines, and establish their rule over the powers still
standing small.

This Explainer

This study is the fruit of a lifelong personal and professional engagement; the
history of that engagement is intertwined with the larger one I explain. My own
voice and concerns dominate enough here that you need to know certain things
about me.

My professional engagements with this music are those of a musician working
in it from the late 1960s through the mid-1990s (mostly nonprofessionally since
then); a journalist writing about it from the mid-1970s to the present; and a scholar
of it from the early 1990s to the present. My interest in jazz's Western aspects stems
from my curiosity, after much education in and exposure to African-American
history and issues, about my own European–American (mostly German and Irish)
heritage.

My grandfather and uncle worked in the postwar shipyards of my home town
of Richmond, California, a town mentioned in one recent jazz study as

> the site of an inordinate number of clubs and taverns featuring blues players
> catering to the after-hours enjoyment of the Black shipyard workers who had
> recently arrived from the South. Shipyard worker Diana Wilson recalls that
> the blues spots were small, underfunded operations and many had women

managers . . . The Richmond 'blues joints' were reminiscent of the small Jazz Age cabarets in *Chicago*; and there was also a similarity in the larger establishments.[17]

I played in some of my first jam sessions in some of those clubs, and in those that also featured jazz, later. My emphasis of "Chicago" in the citation reflects several affinities pertaining here. My initiation as a player into the "new" jazz then came through a circle of players clustered around bassist-reedsman Donald "Rafael" Garrett, cofounder with Muhal Richard Abrams of the Association for the Advancement of Creative Musicians (AACM) in Chicago, and an important presence in San Francisco's free-jazz scene. From the rise of that scene to its moments of fame in the jazz press, through its shift, around the mid-1970s, to the margins of same, I was mentored by and/or played with some of its preeminent figures: people who had played and recorded with John Coltrane, Eric Dolphy, Ornette Coleman, Cecil Taylor, and Steve Lacy; later, people such as Andrew Hill, Mal Waldron, Oliver Lake, Roswell Rudd, and others; and people involved with founding such organizations as the Black Artists Group (BAG) in St. Louis. My longest and most important such association is with a Chicagoan, Anthony Braxton.[18]

I grew up surrounded by plenty of African-, Asian-, and Latin-American people; as my interest in the music grew, so did my interest in these (mostly, naturally enough, African-American) circles. That interest and environment socialized me into a milieu that was unusually multiracial and musical. I formed jazz groups large and small, with the help of older professionals, to play at high school and other concerts I organized. I wrote and arranged pieces – poetry and music along the lines of the Charles Mingus and Miles Davis records I liked at the time – to record for demo tapes. I won a scholarship from *Down Beat* magazine to attend a summer semester at the Berklee School of Music in Boston, where I learned more about the conventions of jazz composing and arranging and improvising.

The liberal paradigm of nonviolent, Christian civil disobedience and integration gave way in the flash of those years to Marxist and other secular-revolutionary, separatist rhetoric, to the Islam of Malcolm X, to black national-ism – all embracing and exalting, rather than supplicating for, blackness; all attack-ing, or at least snubbing, whiteness-as-ally. The music began to reflect that shift. By the mid-1970s, I had made some changes too. I moved out of my San Fran-cisco home base and my novitiate-musician stage; married and had a daughter in Eugene, Oregon; and turned from the tense streets of the urban 1960s to the more bucolic Pacific Northwest. I formed my own small groups and played the local clubs-and-concert circuit. Through my jazz gigs and freelance journalism about the music, I developed a strong presence in my local and regional scenes through-out the '70s and '80s.

Most of my public performances were in more or less mainstream contexts. I could play the blues and American songbook standards in my sleep with the best of them, following the usual drill of tune/improvised solos/conversational improvisations ("trading-fours")/tune, until it felt like the nine-to-five routine of any deathly boring day job. The alternative to that – forging an original repertoire and style and taking it down the road to fish bigger waters – did not appeal to me, for various reasons.

So, in 1988, I incorporated a nonprofit with a mission to commission new works and performances by internationally celebrated cutting-edge musicians, in collaboration with my local colleagues. Dr. Bernard Dobroski, then dean of the University of Oregon School of Music, now of Northwestern University School of Music (also a Chicago native), helped me launch the first project, with Anthony Braxton, which led to my Northwest Creative Orchestra's CD of his music. Under Braxton's direction, *Eugene (1989)*[19] garnered great reviews and ratings in the American and European jazz press.

My association with Braxton led me through a Master's degree in Music/Arts Administration (Antioch University, 1993) and a Ph.D. in Ethnomusicology (Wesleyan University, 2000), where I worked as his graduate teaching assistant from 1993 to 1996, played in his bands, and co-incorporated with him his own nonprofit, the Tri-Centric Foundation. Managing the latter, I won grants for and helped produce several more major performances of his music in several New York City venues throughout those years. Besides the "post-jazz" course of that music, I also worked in the "new music" side of Wesleyan and the Northeast on projects with composers such as Alvin Lucier and Christian Wolff, performed and recorded music by John Cage, and performed and recorded my own electronic music.

Recounting this history leads me to wonder: how and why have I found the musical gestures of free improvisation and chance, and composition facilitating them, so compelling? How, in the face of my maturation from youth to middle age, and of the changes in my American society from the 1960s to the present? Why, when that society (exceptions proving the rule) has found them so relatively uninteresting, problematic, irrelevant? What has my payoff been, what the problem for society? What developmental results – in my own personal growth and identity, in the music, in the social context of both – have come of this long engagement?

These questions to myself shaped my interviews with the European musicians of my focus here. What musical and social fruits had their gestures borne in Europe, turning the honeymoon with critics and public there into a workable marriage, in contrast to the stormier and less legitimized American version of that relationship? What peculiarly German-historical and social forces contributed to this success, leading to Germany's reputation in the larger European music press then as "the land of free jazz" (even in the former East Germany, where the wrong kind of "jazz," as in Nazi times, could lead one to prison)? Were parallel Western-musical/historical issues in America weighted unduly with the minstrelsies of race, generation (American cult of youth, and ageist disrespect), and gender that buried their more broadly Western cultural (social, political) implications? Did those issues and implications develop more on their own terms in European scenes freer of that American weight? What roles do nature and culture respectively play in the dynamics of race, class, power, violence, generation, gender, and sexuality at the fore of free jazz's history and historiography?

My interest in European scenes started with recordings I had heard in Eugene throughout the '70s and '80s from my friend Dale MacBride's extensive collection. Initially, my interest was in those that featured Braxton, who from the beginning, like most of his African-American colleagues in what he calls "creative music," found the bulk of his work and audience in Europe. My later close involvement with Braxton's music led me deeper into European scenes.

I remember Dale's oft-avowed opinion, echoed by many of the articles I read in *Cadence, Coda* and other magazines then, that European improvised music was carrying the (African-) American jazz tradition – which Dale (who is white) knew and loved as well as I – on to new fulfillments of its promises. I also recall the complete lack of interest in it, even annoyed dismissal of it, on the part of my two closest African-American Oregon friends, also serious, informed music people. Actually, it was what felt alien in this music to me, some shockingly so, that drew me to it: a prevalence of thin, tinny harshness of tone, so many nervous runs away from pulse, phrasing and inflections that often struck me as simply ugly or cold, bizarre distortions of what I knew as "jazz." What were its fans and players hearing in it? And, again, the interest in African history so many of my African-American friends were pursuing then provoked my own curiosity about the ancestors and cousins of my own European-American culture.

I also remember feeling throughout the years from mid-1960s to early 1970s, apparently like many others my age then, that I might well be living through a time of fundamental social change on a global scale, and might be among its generational vanguard. I had penetrated and understood music, the one area of my most passionate interest, enough to have a sense of what was so portentous about the changes it was undergoing, and of why they were so, however frightening, confusing, or meaningless they may have looked to the less engaged. That sense informed my other, less intense engagement with political and social change, aligned me, however naively, with the liberalism and leftism surrounding both African-American and European protest movements then.

Like novelist Doris Lessing's "good terrorist," and like most intelligent, thinking, sensitive, and moral people throughout the world, I felt, I assumed that Marx and, even more, the major anarchist writers had been on the right track, however short of ideal. I assumed that Americans from the founding fathers on had talked the talk but not walked the walk, and that now the chickens were indeed (per Malcolm X) coming home to roost, as the oppressed peoples of the world were rising to throw off the racist, colonialist, imperialist Western yokes to seize their own justice and dignity. I felt allied with such people from my own position as white insider born to that unjust regime, shaking off its death with the rest of my generation's life force of youth and health . . .

If that sounds naive and grandiose, then it captures well the spirit of the times. It was the kind of feeling that fueled the ardor and romance both of Black Power movements and of their white counterparts, as the initial nonviolent resistance

moved into threats against both property and life. Like most of my erstwhile comrades, I stopped short of taking up arms and doing harm before naivety passed –
but the maturity it passed to is not inconsistent with those youthful experiences,
intuitions, or insights. It is more like a fruit of growth and refinement, subsuming and surpassing more than renouncing or repenting them.

Reading interviews, and conducting my own, with the first-hour *Emanzipation*
players in Western Europe, and with their peers then on the other side of the Iron
Curtain, I often recalled my own experience of those years, in the Berkeley/San
Francisco center of many of its storms. The relationship the Europeans had forged
between art and politics, with the former at the fore, reminded me of the one my
peers and I had then. Musicians often have an immediate grasp of forces, concepts, and relationships that political programs and gestures manifest more dimly,
with less enduring depth. The art can last, grow, satisfy for life, after the politics
burn out and fade. Or, as Jost Gebers, one of the German *Emanzipators* discussed
later, put it, "The truth of the music was stranger than the fiction of those
politics."

This Explanation

European art music in America and jazz in Europe have long been, and remain,
powerful influences on each host culture and economy. Both traditions reflect both
psychological and social order, as well as the passions that challenge and change
both. French economist and cultural theorist Jacques Attali framed music history
in the West as rooted in a primal, murderous violence that has served the imposition and maintenance, as well as the overthrow, of social orders. His countrymen Phillipe Carles and Jean-Louis Comolli framed jazz history so, seeing in free
jazz a definitive moment in the power struggles of American racial politics.[20]

My concerns here lie in the deep connections between the "free" rubric of
the music and the Western-historical charge behind the word. To abstract the
one history (of jazz) as pithily as a French scholar might: the common
mythological ground of African-American music up to the free-jazz moments is
the age-old struggle between "power-over" and "power-of" bodies. This is an
obvious, and not a new observation; jazz studies from early to current have run
with the theme of the "subaltern" cultural voice asserting itself effectively through
the mainstream culture's music to complicate the basic assumptions of both music
and culture.[21]

The point of more interest here, however, is that it was not so long ago that
the northern Europeans themselves were the barbarians and outsiders to Western
civilization. Wherever there is classist hierarchy there is a subaltern voice, and if
history had not made it a black one in America, the West would have invented
another one (as indeed it did, several of them, in Europe). We will consider the
ways in which the musicians of the *Emanzipation* empowered, as did the African-
Americans from whom they took their cues, such disempowered voices.

Free jazz's pioneers – first in African-American, then in European circles – asserted that empowerment more directly than did their forbears. America's assertion featured (the power-of) black personal and social bodies contesting (the power-over them of) white ones, both American and more widely Western. Europe's version featured (the power-of) European bodies contesting (the power-over them of) their own states, civilizations, histories, traditions – and of American, including African-American, culture and music.

The free-jazz movements in America and Europe feature both alliances and adversities between their bodies: blackness asserted itself against whiteness in America in the very act of asserting itself as simply, fully, and freely human, through specific musical strategies. Those strategies included burning through and up systems that were millennia in the making, systems musical (diatonic, modal, metric – tonal hierarchies of pitch, rhythmic hierarchies of meter), social (classist, high art above low entertainment, hierarchies of bodies and instruments established by their performance roles), and mythological (Judeo-Christian hierarchies of creator over creation; and ancient-Greek-cum-modern-secular hierarchies of mind over body, of theory and composition over experience and performance). Free jazz's deconstructive and reconstructive strategies were grounded in clear understanding of the Western musical paradigm as a homological reflection of Western history and social order, and they featured evocations of the personal, the primal, the archaic, of prehistorical and ahistorical, along with non-Western historical grounds for new systems, functions, and mythoi. In doing so, they explicated what their pre-free jazz precursors had, by comparison, only implied, however effectively.

The first power-of assertions of free jazz in Europe included the phrase, in more than one voice ahead, "kill the fathers" – from psychology, the image the Oedipus story gave Sigmund Freud, of (among other things) people maturing by taking responsibility for themselves from their overlords. That image suggests two propositions that give definition to the power-of/power-over drama in history and culture: one, that such spiritual parricide is an inevitable process in the natural and healthy development of a body that the wise "fathers" will not fear or resist, but endure, encourage, and recognize as in their own long-term best interests; and two, that there is a higher, deeper order and authority than that of the "father's" power-over that the "children" call on to assert their power-of.

To get the real-world sense of both of these counterintuitive propositions, consider how the so-called "avant-garde" jazz expressions from 1950s–'60s America and Europe were progressively marked by reaches back to the archaic as much as forward to the new. Some examples:

• George Russell's and Miles Davis's turn to Greek modes sent former West German trombonist Albert Mangelsdorff and others in Europe to the early Western music that preceded and gave rise in the West to equal-tempered diatonicism, a deconstructive step back in time and music on both sides of the Atlantic;

- the Black Power movement (as explained by Carles and Comolli) cued the conscientious turn of East German musicians Günter Sommer and Ulrich Gumpert to their own medieval European musical roots and identity, in their aversion to being thieves of black identity and history in the music;
- John Coltrane's later (post-*A Love Supreme*) music reminded us of the ancient and still timely Indian, Asian, and African grounds of the Old World's more recent Western (post-Christian) music culture, nudging English saxophonist Evan Parker and his Dutch, Danish, Belgian, and German colleagues on to the groundbreaking recording of "first-hour" European free jazz, *Machine Gun*;
- Ornette Coleman's idiosyncratic treatment of the blues evoked a musical and real time free of Western meter and song form, recalling both the African *jali's* (storyteller's) narrations to the freely streaming musical accompaniment of a stringed instrument and Western music's own development of such instruments as accompaniments to voices speaking and singing both freely and in (poetic) meter;
- Coleman's bandmate trumpeter Don Cherry built his post-Coleman career (largely in Europe) around a search for what he called "primal music" in the world's traditions; his close work with the French free-music collectives we will examine overlapped with their own "imaginary folklore" of Europe, a conceit akin to the Afroasiatic Edens imagined by American players Pharoah Sanders, the Art Ensemble of Chicago, Julius Hemphill, and others;
- Sun Ra invoked ancient Egypt for musicosmic mythology, and for theatrical spectacles recalling the ancient Greek concept of *mousike* – "multimedia" ritual and ceremonial events in which gods and humans met, events coming to Greece by way of the East and West then, from Asia and North Africa[22] – inspiring the first also-groundbreaking recording *Globe Unity* by Alexander von Schlippenbach's pan-European Globe Unity Orchestra;
- the motto of the Art Ensemble of Chicago was "Great Black Music, from Ancient to Future";
- German saxophonist Peter Brötzmann's and his Dutch colleagues pianist Misha Mengelberg's and percussionist Han Bennink's involvement with the Fluxus movement of the 1960s was premised on a conscious turn away from Western history to global archaism through folk/shamanistic roots, as was German bassist Peter Kowald's connections to Japanese traditional musicians and *butoh* dancers and Greek, Korean, Mongolian, and other traditional musics;
- Anthony Braxton's neologism "Tri-Axium," as defined by his *Tri-Axium Writings*, conceived of the present drawing on the past to shape the future; his own "Ghost Trance" series of compositions draw on traditional Native American music and history.

These few among many such examples suggest the thick tangle between them, and between them and their common musico-mythological roots and terrain. My focus here is on the European examples for their suggestion of deep Eurasian roots underpinning European improvised music's place in global culture today.

Those examples are far more examined by my German and French sources than by my English-language colleagues. Among the German sources, one merits special attention here for its role in translating, for German readers, essays by scholars from most Western and Eastern European languages on the histories of their respective national jazz scenes: *That's Jazz: Der Sound des 20. Jahrhunderts*; Klaus Wolbert (ed.): Darmstadt, Germany: Verlag Jürgen Häusser, 1997 – referred to henceforth as Wolbert. It is also worth mining for the peculiarly European angles of interest in and emphases on the European influences on nineteenth-century American music that led up to jazz. Our glances at both of those offerings will tell us much about the one history as explained here.

This study's center of gravity falls to Germany for several reasons. German musicians were responsible for the first pan-European coalition of jazz scenes, in the *Emanzipation*'s first most groundbreaking and internationally important recordings. German literature on that phenomenon is more extensive and more often based in the broader current of Western intellectual history than its French, English, or Italian counterparts (though they too have their moments, also glimpsed here). Germany's history as the Cold War-torn country models in microcosm the broader West vs. East geopolitics of the European jazz scenes that reshaped the sociopolitical implications of "free" there; and Berlin's concert and recording concern Freie Musik Produktion (FMP) has played a leading role among similar European brokers in the international development of the *Emanzipation* gestures over the entire time from their "first hours" to the present. Finally, recent studies similar to this one have showcased the comparable Dutch, French, English, and Russian scenes.[23] Mine adds to them a focus on the one I find the most interesting, especially during the decades at the center of my focus (1960s–'70s).

More broadly, German music has been the most recent torchbearer (from the Baroque era on) of Western music history's long march. It has embodied the Western extremes of good and evil, especially during those centuries of America's history, through the lineage of the Bachs, Handel, Haydn, Mozart, Beethoven, Wagner, Brahms, Mahler, Schoenberg, Webern, and Stockhausen. J. S. Bach and the last three impinge directly on the work of some artists discussed later, and on European improvised music in general; the others have been invoked as racial/cultural standard-bearers by the German and other Eurasian state-repressors of jazz. The spirituality, mythos, and intellect of Western tradition, as well as its dark sides of racism, classism, and imperialism, and its ongoing struggles to reform itself, have all been shaped by German culture and music, and Germany's strong voice in European free jazz is part of that historical continuum.

It is that continuum, both its good and bad sides, that African Americans have had to engage most overtly to forge their own most ambitious music, in a North American musical milieu more defined in fundamental ways by German than by French or Spanish, or even Italian or English strains.[24] That German continuum has been most deeply impacted in its turn by African-American music, as well as by the historical realities of racism, genocide, and occupation that resonate in

Germany with the African-American experience of slavery, oppression, and struggle for the American dream.

I saw for myself the truth of Braxton's remark about Europe's living historical memory, cited above, on my 1997 trip to interview and record performances by the musicians of my focus. I saw it while walking down a busy street in Konstanz, lined with statues depicting the city's lineage of bishops dating roughly to the time of the Rhenish mystics (Hildegard of Bingen, Meister Eckhardt), about 1100; in Dresden, where Günter Sommer showed me the huge mural depicting his own Saxon lineage stretching back over the millennium on the centuries-old civic center building; in Grimma, near Bach's home city of Leipzig, with Swedish drummer Sven-Åke Johansson, where he performed in a building with a foundation laid in Roman-imperial times; in Vienna, where the 638-year-old St. Stephen's Cathedral towered over the Dixieland band playing for tourists in its shadow. The art and culture of the New in such places cannot help but refer to that of the Old, even when it seems to move on from the past most completely, because the shock, or simply the newness alone, is always proportionate to the degree of outrage it commits on, or imputes to, the Old.

This unbroken history, as material/visceral to Europeans as it is (by comparison) academic to Americans, surely explains why much of the European discourse engaged here discusses (American, but especially European) jazz in the context of Western musical, cultural, and intellectual histories more than has its American counterpart (which has often been both anti-European and anti-intellectual, as though the two were the same, in its approaches). In international academic discourse, American jazz studies have focused (albeit often by inappropriately Europhiliac criteria) on African roots and African-American fruits of the music, and on the identity politics of race and gender in the light of Americentric twentieth-century anthropological and cultural studies. European scholars – who historically initiated and set the tone for those same American studies, a "whiteness of voice and perspective" that dominated until the free-jazz years – are more interested lately in what the music has meant to them as an import, and in their own domestic versions of it. They are more interested in both in the contexts of their own various national and larger Eurasian histories.[25]

European discourse on its own jazz has a more secular and recent focus than that suggested by the reaches back to the mythico-historical listed above. That focus is rooted in the nineteenth-century's post-Enlightenment rise of the "grand narratives" of history and culture – of Hegel, Marx, Darwin, Freud, Nietzsche, even the Bible (then newly critiqued by German scholars) as the mythos underpinning both white and black American histories. The twentieth-century extensions of those narratives, into wars both on and off European soil, shaped European improvised music's contexts and tenor, even as slavery, segregation, and the Civil Rights movement shaped American jazz and free jazz. Europe's grand narratives of history became relevant and timely in the free-jazz years to the black critical and musical communities that took them on directly with their own critiques and adaptations, in music and music criticism as in other arts and letters.[26]

Having centralized and foregrounded German discursive voices as most pertinent to my explanation of the broader Eurasian *Emanzipation*'s "one history," I would point out the more diffuse and backgrounded force of the French sources. As already noted, French scholarship has given jazz the European light of most influence on the shape and course of later American jazz studies; it has also provided the more general academic-interdisciplinary theoretical framework for all discussion of culture, including music. Ethnomusicology, and (more recently) jazz studies, have proven themselves worthy participants in that discussion, launched by the linguistic structuralism of Ferdinand Saussure, extended into narrative and myth and kinship systems by Claude Lévi-Strauss, then further into the more dynamic narratology of Roland Barthes and the semanalysis of Julia Kristeva. Readers familiar with this twentieth-century (mostly French) discussion will recognize echoes of, specifically, Emile Durkheim and his torchbearers, Jacques Lacan, Jean-François Lyotard, Jacques Derrida, and Michel Foucault in these pages.

There are two senses in which I am decidedly not centralizing and foregrounding these sources, and two in which my backgrounding of them bolsters the strength and clarity of my more German-discursive foreground. The first negative: I do not enlist them as high-theoretical authorities to elevate some cultural phenomenon that would be, by implication, more prosaic without their illumination. Such enlistment would be, in my context, unseemly Francophiliacademic careerism. All the more so for the second negative: even as intellectuals, their work derives from the earlier Germans, from Marx and Hegel to Freud and Nietzsche to Husserl, Heidegger, and others who speak more directly to the European sources of jazz in America, and to the distinctively European voices of post-1960s European jazz.[27]

The first positive: the approaches and methods of the French scholars are timelier to and wider in current discourse. Thus my intertextual looks at paintings, literature, theater, history, and philosophy to illuminate musical issues; the use of binary constructs such as chapter six's Fig. 6:1; the juxtaposition of voices as disparate as J. S. Bach's and Ornette Coleman's in chapter one; the thick mesh of my own and my subject's voices in chapter four; and, generally, the co-creative rather than merely expository approach to my subject all owe much to the French methodologies mentioned above.

The second positive: some of those sources underpinning my narrative date from the period of my focus. For example, Jacques Chailley's history of Western harmony resonates better than would much more recent work with the history I explain because it was written contemporaneously with the unfolding of the latter (this is also true of the German Curt Sachs's work). Bassist Peter Kowald had Barthes on his bookshelf, and drummer Günter Sommer had Sachs; what they read as they worked often sheds more light on that work than what scholars or musicians might be reading and writing (thinking) now.

The Biggest History

It is tempting to process the European literature on European improvised music into my own "grand narrative" here, simply because that literature is, again, so directly tied to Western intellectual history. Truer to our present moments (and, I think, even to those that spawned, and those later framed by, the grand narratives, and to the spirit of the grand narrative approach itself) is the discourse of so-called "big history," which looks at the most local/specific phenomena of culture as points on the most vast temporal and geographical continua of both nature and culture, tracing the connections between the two.[28]

Merely to mention such an interpretive approach is enough to suggest the deep historical/mythical roots of the power-of/power-over dialectic immediately evident in free jazz and receptions thereof, and to suggest the timeless and timely connections therein. If I were to construct the narrative they imply, I would start with the historical migration of bodies from their tropical cradle in Africa outward to the rest of the world; the evolutionary changes in the biology of their bodies (into "races") wrought by diverse environments and genes; the varieties of culture (gender, family, and social arrangements) those dispersions and changes brought about; the different worldviews, ideas of what was holy or unholy about life and death, sex and violence; the various religious myths and later philosophical rationales they bore; the rise of civilizations through agriculture and literacy, and the philosophical and social hierarchies and powers that emerged therefrom; civilization's clashes and mergers with its outsiders and rivals; the revisions of its administration, and of its cultural and religious mythoi, throughout that flux.

I would zoom in from that overview's scope to the deep musical traditions of the pre-civilized northern Europeans and the sub-Saharan Africans whose descendants came together in North America, and to their respective relationships to the musical traditions of the Mediterranean civilization that lay between them. I would chart their co-creation of music in America, would consider the Western-historical moments of Renaissance, Reformation, Enlightenment, and Romanticism for their relationship to African- and European-American realities in the nineteenth century. I would look at the rise of jazz as part of the ancient dialectic between power-of and power-over, would chart the music's spread from America to Europe and its impacts there, finally bringing into focus the details of my study.[29] Having presented those details, I would theorize and explain free jazz's breakaway from its traditional Western musical moorings, through spontaneous improvisation and idiosyncratic composition, as the body's primal quest to find its own logic and freedom – the power of itself – in its harmony with a biocosmic reality (nature) that overrides and overwrites the power over itself of its fellow bodies (culture). I would argue this biological wisdom as *con*scripting this cosmic harmony not by *pre*scribing it musically but by *a*scribing to the body a music from the world which the cosmos had already *in*scribed on it. I would say that that microcosmic body's own scripting and scribing of this cosmic harmony then effects a social harmony between itself and others, a balance between power-over and power-of such that they become one and the same, to universal, never-ending delight . . .

(There, I said it! But that is what I *would* rather than *do* say, because no one can will or do such utopia [Greek for "nowhere"] alone. But again, in a book about a utopic moment in a music's history, just as in that music itself – a meditation, a conceit of the imagination – anything is possible. And since that particular utopic moment features many examples of reaches back to such mythological and primal *Urgrunde*, and out to such transcendent cosmos, at least this short nod to the possibility of this "big history" is, I think, suggestive of a real "somewhere.")

A Littler History

Western civilization has challenged its own classist histories and social orders all along, as much as – and more effectively than – its victims and enemies have done. The fall of monarchies and rise of democracies comprise something like a two-century revolutionary war playing itself out over the northern latitudes, one that directly shaped the music at issue here, coming to something like a conclusion in that music's aura and wake, as will be demonstrated later. The inception of America itself against the *ancien régime*, as also its Civil War over slavery, and its twentieth-century wars against totalitarian and dictatorial regimes, are aspects of this larger conflict.

Conversely, Western classism's non-Western victims and enemies have colluded with it to resist such challenges to its order from any quarter within or without, for the same payoffs. Think not only of the figure of the successful Uncle Tom, but also the phenomenon of prejudice based on skin color in the black community itself. For that matter, go back to the African and Arab slave traders who helped their European counterparts. Also, the most liberatory – we are sounding the depths of "free" here – assertions of whiteness have come from the top down as often as from the bottom up, out of interests other than universal brotherhood. Like Western liberatory moves from the Magna Carta to the Russian Revolution, these were often espoused and practiced by power players only a rung or two down the social ladder from the rulers they challenged. Their revolutionary plans as often meant little more than *faux* or token freedoms, if any, to those on the rungs below them, and all too often such tokens proved sufficient to their purposes.[30]

This pattern too has had its jazz-historical face. The tension between "hot" (Afro-improvisatory) and "legit" (Euro-schooled) styles of black and Creole musicians in early New Orleans, on up through "hot" vs. "sweet," "authentic traditional" vs. "commercial swing," "moldy fig" vs. "bop" vs. "cool," to "out" (free) vs. "inside" (mainstream) jazz has been discussed as a running contest between power-of black (and some white) and power-over white (and some black) bodies. The power-over group has often consolidated its wins more by feigning or granting small concessions to, buying off, dumbing down, or otherwise redefining the power-of than by resorting to repression as strong as their greater power.[31] Some of the pre-free Europeans discussed later – the culture police serving both post-Romantic (German and Italian) and post-Enlightenment (Russian) totalitarianisms – tried such repression, and failed as resoundingly as did the Prohibitionists in America. On the other hand, those small and false and token concessions coming from the top down as control mechanisms have sometimes gone far, in the right hands, at the right times. This complex tangle called "free" in its musical specifics, for what they say about the complexities of their social contexts, is considered closely later.

The more bottom-up liberatory assertion of blackness in free jazz found its closest matches in key alliances with European, along with its more usual drag and bane in American, whiteness. Through such alliances, European whiteness found its own self-deliverance from the classism that had served America as well as it had savaged Europe – along with new opportunities for enmity and suspicion. If African-American post-free players had just cause to suspect rhetoric such as "emancipation" and "kill the fathers" in the context of European post-free playing, they also had cause to see their music being taken "as seriously as their lives" (to borrow from British writer Valerie Wilmer) by the European sources of an American whiteness that had become more reflexively inclined to reduce both music and lives to minstrelsy.

Parts I and II cover the roughly three decades (1950–80) of the *Emanzipation*'s history and its impacts in both Western and Eastern Europe. As the roles and rules of improvisation and composition begin morphing into a sea change in Western music, the nature and definition of improvisation, and its relationship with composition, are called into question in chapter one. It surveys the first sporadic stirrings of freedom from conventionally scripted form, meter, genre, and harmony and melody in American jazz improvisation and composition, as explored by musicians such as Lennie Tristano, Charles Mingus, Miles Davis, George Russell, and others in the 1950s and '60s; it scans European composers and jazz musicians for their similar gestures. It considers the gradual changes, both musical and social, in the relationship between improvisation and composition in jazz, between the determined and chanced in contemporary art music, and between American and European jazz in that time. It ends with a close comparison between Ornette Coleman and J. S. Bach through the former's musical relationship with pianist Joachim Kühn, a native of Bach's Leipzig and, like Coleman in America, the seminal catalyst of a free-jazz movement in his country.

Chapter two focuses on the responses of Western European musicians to the music of Coleman, Coltrane, Ayler, Taylor, and others, noting the unprecedented departures from imitations of America in their various national scenes, and how those scenes spoke with one another. This chapter builds on a notion (put forth by German jazz historian Gunther Joppig) of jazz as Western music's new center, and explores the ways it had developed and was now flowering as such. Situating the musical within and around the social history (of the 68ers, the student riots in France and their radical-left, anti-American activism throughout the next decade), it looks at the new ways of improvising and composing for improvisers forged by the Europeans, with the help of their African-American mentors and colleagues.

Chapter three focuses on former West Germany, where the scenes above came together in free jazz's more international network. It looks closely at the work of vibraphonist-reedsman Günter Hampel; at saxophonist Peter Brötzmann and bassist Peter Kowald, for their standout presences in the Wuppertal scene; and at the Globe Unity Orchestra (GUO) formed by Cologne pianist Alexander von Schlippenbach. It sees in the emergence of the GUO a full and fertile merger of the diversity of scenes and players examined in chapter two, and a synthesis of the jazz and composition traditions in Europe that successfully fulfilled the promise of its many precursive starts in both America and Europe. Jazz's traditional premise of improvisation on a compositional platform is reversed, improvisation taking the foundational role. Improvisation and composition, and American and European jazz, then strike a balance in the musical developments of the *Emanzipation* that equalizes their formerly disparate weights. The ancient dialectic of (composed) power-over as definitive and (improvised) power-of as derivative is seen in this musical shift to strike its own syncretic (anarchic, classless) symmetry, from asymmetrical (hierarchical, classist) conflict.

Chapter four chronicles the difficult but ultimately successful attempts of the Western and Eastern European scenes to make inroads into each other. It examines the role the Western European *Emanzipation* played through the Eastern scenes in undermining Communist repression specifically of jazz, and the grassroots rise in the East against Communist rule, paying particular attention to its musical manifestations (more rooted in European tradition, less Americanized, than the West). The focus narrows and deepens from wide views of Russia, Czechoslovakia, and Poland to East Germany, where the music moved from marginal pariah to rock-star status in a few short years.

What began in America as both contest and concourse between black and white continued in Western Europe more as one between American and European identities; it developed in the Eastern bloc as a youth movement that successfully challenged a repressive old guard. Whereas their Western and American counterparts had merely gestured toward a political as well as a musical paradigm shift, the free-jazz torchbearers in Soviet Russia and East Germany saw their music play a part in bringing down the political power it contested.

Part III considers improvised music as a global phenomenon transcending its European and African (American) roots. Chapter five selectively scans the years since those first hours of the *Emanzipation*. It looks at the turn of European improvisers to more collaborations with Americans, now as equals rather than "sidemen"; to more collaborations with composers and performers in the "new music" as well as the "jazz" side of improvised music; and to collaborations with musicians, writers, theater people, visual artists, and dancers from traditions outside the Americentric "jazz" rubric. It considers the impact wrought by the fall of Communism, especially in East Germany, on the music in both East and West. All of these new collaborations and contexts are seen to forge a kind of post-jazz improvisatory lingua franca approaching the German idea of *Weltmusik* – a universal music – more than the postmodern pastiche signaled by the commercial "world music" marketing category.

Within the traditional framework of ethnomusicological discourse, this is where the story gets most interesting. In the early years of our discipline, when the first field recordings of Native American, Asian, and African traditional musics were first possible and being made, "classical" music was studied through scores, and jazz was ignored by music scholars as shallow popular entertainment, neither "high" nor "authentically" traditional. "Comparative musicology" was what the first assessments of the latter fell under, using recordings to construct yet more "scores" (transcriptions) to study. European jazz was the lowest part of that Western mass pop culture the first comparative musicologists shunned, as a cheap imitation of America's most shallow and vulgar. Yet it is the genre – through which American jazz and European art music have set forth their deepest musical, historical, philosophical, and political thought – that we have taken utterly seriously here, in its current connections with those same "others" first contacted.

Chapter six raises questions of how to analyze the new musical terrain, how to historicize, theorize, politicize, and situate it philosophically, pedagogically, and personally. (A note about analysis: my many close discussions of recorded musical events serve the function graphic transcriptions usually do in studies such as this. In chapter six, I do construct such transcriptions, including conventional notation, to represent one recording. I have saved this until this final chapter because it also proffers a new approach to such analyses and their methodologies, one targeting this new music and its issues, which I needed to define before analyzing. My verbal descriptions – ideally, read to the recordings described – function for me as closer revelations of the music itself. Because I am a player of such music, my writing is shaped by it, in cadence, syntax, imagery and emphases. Long practice in listening to, playing, and writing about it has brought me to a zone of comfort and strength when discussing it so. Graphic depictions, by comparison, are usually only looks through shards of a broken glass darkly.) The scholarly paradigm of objective science, hard and soft, shifts to one of subjective artistry on a par with that of the music studied; Warlike hierarchy in aesthetics, society, and philosophy shifts to Erotic anarchy, via a turn to the archaic; performativity shifts to improvisativity in the educational arena; and personal power-of trumps impersonal power-over in all those shifts.

The déjà vu I opened with has another dimension. The current tensions in the world remind many of us who came of age in the 1960s of the overshadowing dread of nuclear war with Russia, or of unpredictable acts of violence led by young black and/or white militants in America and/or Europe. As visceral as that dread, we recall the desperate hope that sparked the surges of Eros and its various "freedoms" to counter the cruel and stupid madnesses of War. My meditation on that earlier time will inevitably speak to the one we are all living now, and, I hope, usefully illuminate it.

The Indo-European root of "free" (*prijos*) is the same as that of "friend," and "kin"; its ultimate implication is indeed a global family, a world without enemies, a self with no "others." Black and white, man and woman, old and young, this

Holy or that, this Religion or that, East and West, North and South, America and Europe, the West and the Rest can all shake away as the tricks of perception they have been all along, all while the music endures and grows as the agent of the shaking.

What else might shake away here?

Emancipation I: From Hierarchy

Class is the one big social force that keeps dropping out of the national discourse. We talk about race, we talk about gender. Class is inside race, it's inside gender. I am just really trying to put it back on the table without dropping the other things.

Sherry Beth Ortner

To me, socialism is to try to find social ways of sharing. That's all. And to replace the dependence upon authority with the principle of sharing. Because it's very likely that there would be much more for everybody, thousands and more times for everybody if things were shared. We're living like dogs from all the competing.

Jack Smith[1]

One

Mangelsdorff, Kühn, Globokar: Three Ways Back and Out

Etymologically, *compose* means simply "put together"; it comes, via Old French *composer*, from *compos-*, the perfect stem of Latin *compônere*, and *pônere* "place, put," source of English *position*. Amongst its many descendants and derivatives are *compound, component . . . composite . . .* and *compost*.
— *Dictionary of Word Origins* (Ayto [1990: 128])

It would be no exaggeration to state that up until the nineteen-sixties practically the entire repertory of Western art music was based on written tradition.
— Joaquim Benítez (1986)

Etymologically, if you improvise something, it is because it has not been "provided" for in advance. The word comes via French *improviser* from the Italian adjective *improviso* "extempore," a descendant of Latin *improvisus* "unforeseen." . . . (The closely related *improvident* "not providing for the future" preserves even more closely the sense of its Latin original.)
— *Dictionary of Word Origins* (Ayto [1990: 296])

. . . in any but the most blinkered view of the world's music, composition looks to be a very rare strain, heretical in both practice and theory. Improvisation is a basic instinct, an essential force in sustaining life. Without it nothing survives. As sources of creativity they are hardly comparable.
— Derek Bailey (1980: 140)

A French writer characterized the American free-jazz movement of the 1960s as the successful vision quest of a whole culture, the coming-of-age of African America into adulthood, an eschewal of Western "training wheels" and a responsible, risky embrace of creative potential and power both musical and sociocultural: *freedom from impression, freedom to grow*.[2]

An African-American musician put it rather this way: "We're on the eve of the complete fall of Western ideas and life values. We're in the process of developing more meaningful values, and our music is a direct expression of this . . ." *freedom from oppression, freedom to show.*[3]

A German writer described the 1950s as German jazz's *Klauser* – a student's comprehensive exam – the American jazz idiom being its school and professor. He marked 1960 as the beginning of the *Emanzipation*, in which the music and musicians moved away from that (mostly African-) American shadow and into a sense of themselves: *freedom from impression, freedom to know.*[4]

A German musician claimed that free jazz was much more than a passing stylistic trend time-bound to the 1960s; it was also not primarily a protest music, reacting against convention with no proactive integrity of its own. It was, rather, a point in the development of jazz similar to the shift Schoenberg and the Second Viennese School of composers effected for Western composition/tradition, part of its historical dialectic intrinsic to a "tendency of materials" in their natural evolutionary process: *freedom as progression, freedom to grow.*[5]

These sweeping statements about the development of "Western music" and "jazz" are reflected in individual musicians. The music of (formerly West) German trombonist Albert Mangelsdorff leads us to the ancient Greek modes at the birth of notated Western music; the work of (formerly East) German pianist Joachim Kühn, via his collaboration with Ornette Coleman, evokes the historical shift from the modal to the diatonic-chromatic that accompanied the rise of the West as a world power; and the music of Slovenian trombonist and composer Vinko Globokar brings us to the subsumption of the diatonic-chromatic system by some of the elements, from both inside and outside Western music – timbre, rhythm, musical time, improvisation – that system had organized.

The historical forest this chapter surveys is marked by the seminal roles of these three trees in shaping that forest's current moments. Before we hike its trails, a scan of its root system . . .

Saxon Fanfares

Gunther Joppig's essay in Wolbert ("From Wind Quintet to Big Band," 1997: 9–22) traces the popularity of the French wind quintet and Prussian military bands in nineteenth-century Europe and America to the twentieth century's jazz combos and big bands. In doing so, he proffers the notion that this historical shift of instrumentation – from strings to winds, and from melody and harmony instruments to percussion instruments – came with a concurrent shift of Western music's intellectual history.

Drawing on Czech-born Viennese aesthetician Eduard Hanslick's report of an 1867 concert in Paris, Joppig conveys the shock Adolphe Sax's newly invented saxophone was to ears attuned to Beethoven's world. Hanslick discusses the rise of the French wind quintet as an alternative to the string quartet tradition, and its expansion through military ensembles throughout the first half of the nineteenth century; he voices concern about the influence thereof on compositional standards for concert and theater music. His play on the saxophone's name compares it with a Saxon fanfare: something coarse, loud, and primitive, an instrument he likens to "workmen's tools." He is both amazed and disturbed by the force of the fourteen-man band he had heard play the new instruments. He acknowledges the players' virtuosity, but worries about the damage such proficiency on such gross media might do to the subtler dimensions of the composer's art.

In America, military bands widened and popularized the larger European repertoire by taking it out of the concert halls and into the parks and streets (a natural setting for both their volume and American populism). Joppig cites an 1889 American report from *Harper's Weekly* to document the ratio there of German musicians as ten-to-one.[6] Italians were second in number, French very scarce, and Americans themselves only beginning to appear. As these popular sounds were increasingly desired in more intimate and enclosed social settings, the instrumentation was parsed into smaller formations, of French, Berliner, and American arrays. Both Berliner and American – the two most alike – contained a piano, two violins, a cello, flute, clarinet, cornet and drums (only the Berliner also contained trombone, viola, and bass).

The first drumkits were assembled, to simulate in one player the Prussian marching band's percussion section. Gradually, the subtlest and most flexible instruments (violins, flutes) were replaced by stronger, louder winds, as the rhythmic aspects ruled dancers. (Creole clarinetist Sidney Bechet gets Joppig's honorable mention for introducing the soprano saxophone into early jazz formations.)

After tracing this instrumentation's development through early jazz into that of the Swing Era's big bands, Joppig recalls Hanslick's feeling that virtuosity on saxophones, trombones, and trumpets was something amazing, bizarre, and unsettling. Strings, flutes, oboes, and keyboards were the rightful province of such subtlety of expression; percussion virtuosity did not even cross Hanslick's mind. Yet, Joppig notes, the technical virtuosity for which Hanslick feared instead evolved on these more powerful, less delicate horns, as well as on the basses and drums, in jazz. Likewise, Joppig concludes, the art of composition Hanslick wanted to protect was instead developed and revitalized by jazz's ascent, especially through improvisation and rhythm (as opposed to the scored orchestration of patterns of chromatic pitches, both melodic and harmonic, Western composition's traditional parlance; Joppig posits improvisation and rhythm not as challenges to or subsets of composition so much as aspects of its art, theoretically musical equals of scored melody and harmony).

Hanslick was shocked, in large part, by the upstart assertion of a low against a high European class – certainly a major cultural trope of his time, and an assertion reenacted by nineteenth- and twentieth-century African Americans against the same Western hierarchy, in its racist cast. His shock bespoke several ways of looking at the world in his world, some handed down from the West's ancient Greek and Judeo-Christian beginnings, others at the most modern edge of his day, and all associated directly with the music he knew so well and feared for.

Two of those ways considered here are ancient, two modern (then). They form European lenses through which to look at Europe's new and improvised music of the last forty years, even as they have helped to shape Western music history, including its "jazz."

The Holy, Religion, Eros, and War

The first of the two ancient tropes is instrumental symbolism. Stringed instruments had evolved in the West from the post-Pythagorean science of vibrating strings' naturally occurring pitch relations, primarily as accompaniments to the declaiming-singing voice; reedless woodwinds, from archaic bone and wooden flutes to modern church organs, embodied the same rationalized – from the root of "to cut," as in the division of the string into "ratios" – relations, in finger holes and stops, adjusting the vibration of a column of air rather than a string. The composer "put together" his vision of the cosmic order of these physics – what the medieval theoretician Boethius called *musica mundana,* or "music of the world," nature – into a composition (*musica humana,* in culture) to be played or sung by a performer (*musica instrumentalis,* actual sounded music). This paradigm was enjoying its full Western bloom in Hanslick's time and place.

In contrast to this Holy- (mystical, magical) cum-Religious (rational, narrative, literate) union with an orderly cosmos sounded by the Pythagorean monochord, early brass, reed, and struck instruments were associated with the chaos of Eros and War, for their blood-stirring timbres, volume, and rhythms.[7] The capitalized words signal the second ancient trope, and are used here as general theoretical rubrics for the history ahead. The second ancient trope, sprung from the primal realities of the first, is the governing power of the Holy and Religion (faith, mind, thought – composition) over the powers of Eros and War (sense, body, act – performance), in musical as in social order.

I call the rational "Religious" because religions – from the Latin *ligare,* the root of "ligament," meaning "to tie together" – are rationales of mystery. I do not use the word to single out specific religions for praise or criticism, although its exoteric sense covers such religions that pertain to our story (Christianity both black and white, mostly, and the various sectarian, occult, and other religious engagements that are part of the history of, especially, black American artists and thinkers looking beyond the West in the free-jazz years). Religion here will rather refer to the mental process of explaining the one mystery, then mistaking that explanation for definition (religion as idolatry; as with Marx's "one history," the Holy is the one mystery, begging many explanations). In the West, particularly, such explanations are literate ones; Jews, Christians, and Muslims are all "people of the Book," as are, via literacy, the modern torchbearers of Greek scientific rationalism itself.

I call that one mystery, before Religion explains it, "the Holy" to denote its nature as pure potential, unconflicted and undivided, in and beyond natural and social worlds. Again, I am not asserting some specific notion of holiness of my own here, some defined truth over and against my "Religion;" I am using the word to signal the sense of the good and sacred people experience before they explain or rationalize it. As Religion produces only one of many possible explanations of the one mystery, the Holy is only one of many possible experiences of it (for example, Eros or War as good or evil, depending on the perspective).

Lest we romanticize either the Holy or Religion at the expense of each other – nature, physicality, is inherently good, the rational mind is invasively bad, ever problematic; or, conversely, nature is a mess the rational mind must clean up – I recall both life and death as defined by both Eros and War. In our human cultures as in our animal natures, there are (theoretically) good and bad deaths, lives, victories, and defeats – plays of power – in both Eros and War.

Most exoterically, here, Eros is the contested and contesting force evident in the challenges African-American music has posed to Western culture's Puritan-Victorian sexual mores and morals (and hypocrisies). The music's history in brothels, clubs, and dance halls formed the real-world contexts of that challenge; the different (from American and each other) European receptions, understandings, and versions of that history will be our more central concern.

More esoterically, Eros covers not only mating practices but, more generally, the process of negotiation, compromise, and syncretism between bodies within a culture, and between them and those outside their culture: Eros as optimistic social glue, even in asymmetrical power relations; the force that constantly levels and reshapes the playing field for everyone in it, that seduces rather than coerces everyone to it, and that delivers on the promises of its seductions.[8]

Like Eros, War has its exoteric cultural expressions and esoteric intellectual dimensions in our story of this music. For examples of the first, the American Revolution effectively launched a two-century civil war for equality between northern-latitude rulers and their subjects stretching from Russia through Europe to America; the American Civil War effected the Emancipation of African-American slaves; and the outbreak of the First World War brought the closing down of Storyville (New Orleans' Red Light district) and subsequent migration of its musicians to Chicago and New York. It also brought James Reese Europe's 369th U.S. Hellfighters Infantry Band to England and France, launching the first major European engagement with what would become "jazz" there. The Second World War had comparable impacts on the shape of jazz's developments in both America and Europe, and the Cold War and Vietnam War provided such social/historical contexts for the European music of our focus.

As a term of recent Western intellectual history, War stems from the Hobbesian sense of the state of nature. It covers here all impositions of violent force to assert one party's agenda or identity over another's, eschewing the Eros of negotiation, compromise, syncretism. As such, it covers wars between nations, police and military repression within them, colonialism, imperialism; it also covers the bottom-up counters to those, in revolutions and revolts, or coercive assertions of, rather than Erotic seductions by, subaltern identities.[9]

Jazz lore has seen the latter in the smiling stage personae of Louis Armstrong, Duke Ellington, and many others – indeed, in such personae of entertainers and artists crafted for those they served as masters throughout history. The more angry affect of Charles Mingus, or the arrogant-to-contemptuous one of Miles Davis (both resonant with the Romantic affect of, classically, Beethoven), rather signal War. The free-jazz movement itself fell more under War than Eros, in the militant and separatist rhetoric associated with it, even at its most truly spiritually erotic (for example, the way John Coltrane's music was read by some white critics as "hateful," or hijacked by black and white leftists around their own militant political agendas.[10] As will be demonstrated, there were similar projections upon European players).

What is a good death in Eros? Received, any not willfully or carelessly caused; inflicted, self-sacrifice for some good, self-defense, or defense of another. What is a good death in War? One received, or inflicted, in a just cause. A bad death? One received, or inflicted, in an unjust cause. These abstractions have concrete examples in jazz lore too – mostly of (good) selfless devotion in the face of neglect and persecution, or of (bad) self-destruction – but these will be discussed later, after the final pieces of this theoretical staging.

Eros and War have been visceral forces at both surface and heart of both Western and African-American music history. No less so the Holy and Religion, when we recall the spirit and (Northern European Protestant) charter of the (North American) black church in jazz, and the turns away from Western religion and toward occult and mystical professions of other stamps associated with free jazz.[11] In short, Western music history is marked by an instatement of the mental (both rational and mystical, sometimes at odds, more often in collusion, as Church and State) at the seat of governance over the bodily forces of Eros and War. It is also marked by uprisings of the latter two forces against that governance, in their rewrites of its charters and reforms of its spirit. The history explained here is thick with these dynamics, and their rubrics will cut through real-world details to the chase of the heart of what they are.

The King is Dead, Long Die the King

All of which brings us to the two tropes contemporary to Hanslick, and at the root of (his countryman, our contemporary) Joppig's explanation of jazz's one history. They are the sociopolitical movements of liberalism versus royalism, and the intellectual movements of Romanticism versus Enlightenment. Their ready-made rubrics will also frame and inform our look at European new-and-improvised music, as indeed they do much of the European academic and journalistic-critical discourses thereon.

Liberalism, conceived as freedom (especially of trade) from monarchic rule, did not spring forth full blown in Hanslick's time. Apropos of the "free" rubric, modern liberalism (stemming from the Latin word for "free," *liber*) is a political philosophy with roots in ancient Greek scientific rationalism, then enlisted by Enlightenment and Romantic thinkers, especially nineteenth-century Germans, for their agendas.[12] Liberalism's social reflection of Greek thought's mind-over-body hierarchy lay in the freedom of citizens/nobles who were liberated from the demands of mundane work, by the service of their slaves/subjects, to cultivate the liberal arts and letters. All of this, of course, undergirds the history of slavery in America, in the Old World before it, and the liberationist charge in "free" jazz.

The spectacle of large outdoor nineteenth-century American military bands and smaller indoor versions of them playing arrangements of Bach, Handel, Beethoven, Gluck, Cherubini, and Verdi, along with the marches and popular music of the time, reflected the post-Enlightenment reach of the bourgeoisie for that same freedom (one resting on subjugation and enslavement). As *nouveau riche* European and American merchants, industrialists, and landed gentry began to live (and war, and rule) more like the nobles they usurped, and as the working classes began, with increasing boldness and pride, to dream and fight their ways into a middle class, the coarser, louder, more militant brass and saxophones began to replace the more effete violins, flutes, clarinets, and oboes, and the drums served more as rallying calls to preserve or challenge the social order within, and to expand its new empowerment without.[13]

As wide-ranging and as Afrocentric as it is, American jazz history has played itself out primarily on this Western class-upheaving, martial-instrumental field: trumpets, trombones, and saxophones – power horns, the "workman's tools" – rising from the bottom and margins of the orchestra to the top and center in marching and jazz bands. The bowed and chordal stringed instruments fell from the top and center (as violin family and piano) to the marginal bottom (as the "rhythm section's" piano, guitar, banjo, and bass, sole survivor of the violin family). The drums, moving from marginal-to-absent (in the orchestra) to center-to-foreground (in marching and jazz bands), shaped all other musical elements (instrumentation, voicings, harmony, melody, dynamics, attack, timbre) in the group.

Joppig's suggestion is that the results of this reversal of that ancient hierarchy's order (mind/soul over body), through its instrumental symbolism and musical elements (rhythm and improvisation usurping melodic/harmonic composition), embodied a teleological thrust, not a regression, of Western music, in the music born in America to the name of "jazz."

Albert Mangelsdorff: Trombone Archaisms

To this day it remains unexplained how modal key signature, which shaped the foundation of European musicality from the early Middle Ages until the 16th century, appeared in American jazz of the '50s as material for improvisation. Neither the church sounds nor even the Indian Raga model can have been, because of historical reasons, direct sources for Coltrane and Miles Davis.[14]

Albert Mangelsdorff was born in the city of Frankfurt-am-Main, in the German state of Hessen, on 5 September, 1928. He took up the trombone in 1948, and by

1955 he was voted Musician of the Year in Germany. His Frankfurt All-Stars Quintett, with saxophonist Joki Freund, established the cool/West Coast sound of the German mainstream in the late '50s and early '60s; it and the Hessian radio studio jazz ensemble and the International Youth Band of German All Stars – all led by or showcasing Mangelsdorff – began to move that sound into the international arena through tours and broadcasts, including the 1958 appearance at the Newport Jazz Festival that led to a contract with Columbia Records.[15]

The quintets Mangelsdorff led in the early 1960s produced his first distinctive early small-group recordings, including those that opened a door onto the later free-jazz and jazz-with-world-music movements. His solo work and his collaborations with the younger generation of the *Emanzipation* established him as a force in that movement. He won a bevy of awards, including Best Trombonist in the World from *Melody Maker* (1977) and *Jazz Forum* (1978), and has remained active in the German Jazz Musicians' Union, in the studio, on the road, in the best jazz venues, and in the German music schools as a workshop/ensemble leader. In 1995, he took over the artistic directorship of the annual Berlin Jazz Days, now called JazzFest Berlin.

"After being a rather conventional jazz musician for many years," he tells me, "I was still also interested in free improvisation, almost from the beginning of my career." In his 70s as we speak, Mangelsdorff is a lean man, his wire-rimmed glasses and thin, gray hair suggesting an elderly schoolteacher. "Lennie Tristano's piece 'Intuition' meant a lot to us. It gave us the idea of doing free improvisation in a group. We played a lot of Tristano-like music in our groups at that time, only for a public performance we wouldn't dare. I don't know why, maybe we didn't trust ourselves – and even from Tristano and his companions, you didn't hear anything else, just that one composition – or rather a collective, spontaneous composition."[16]

Having been asked by Americans why so many Europeans were good sidemen but never leaders, Mangelsdorff eventually responded with his 1963 album *Tensions,* so titled to signal his eschewal of the stagnant complacency of the epigonal. The album was internationally significant as the first in a series of recordings of German musicians issued by Berlin agent Horst Lippmann for the American label CBS. Mangelsdorff wrote in the liner notes:

Every art form is an expression of its time and a reflection of its world. The jazz musician in Europe should therefore not play forever like a black musician in New York or Chicago, he shouldn't try to and one shouldn't expect him to, because his problems are simply different and his life's sphere subject to different forces . . . I believe that many European jazz musicians don't make use of [jazz's] freedom enough to express themselves, their personalities – they are in awe of the musical models of their idols . . . [But] what most American jazz musicians have that we Europeans don't is simply originality . . . too few European musicians think to develop their own creative personality, to really break free from the mold and use the freedom jazz offers them.

Musically, this first such offering from Mangelsdorff included both the conventional and the "free" of that time – an open bass solo, a static section (free of steady pulse), a collective free improvisation – but the overall concept of the LP was what was most important about it. It served as a platform from which the next such gestures extended, with Mangelsdorff's 1967 tour of Asia and subsequent recording *Jazz Now Ramwong*: much more modal playing over both static and walking bass sections, pianoless sections, all as self-explorations and self-conscious departures from "straight" American jazz conventions of harmonic development.

One of the album's tracks, "Es sungen drei Engel" (Song of the Three Angels), was built from a song sung at the Battle of Lechfeld between German Christians and Magyar (Hungarian) pagans, one of many such that took place throughout northern Europe between 950 and 1010, resulting in Christianity's upper hand. Berendt writes this about it on the liner notes to the CD reissue of the LP:

> Albert plays a German folksong from medieval times when many of our songs were "modal." "Song of the Three Angels" was originally a fighting song . . . However, in the thirteenth century it came to be sung as a Christmas carol; Paul Hindemith wove the song into his opera *Mathis der Maler*. Roland Kirk and Benny Golson took it from the opera with the mistaken idea that it was an original theme by Hindemith. Over the course of many months, Albert transformed it into a piece of music completely his own – a kind of "Old-German soul waltz," complete with all the fascinating collective improvising so typical of all the Mangelsdorff groups.

The whole LP was conceived as a musical impression of Asian cultures (that is, as similarly modal, only Western) Mangelsdorff's quintet had visited on a tour sponsored by the Goethe Institute.[17] It marked the trombonist's turn away from unreflective adherence to American jazz conventions and, taking cues from similar turns by Coltrane, Davis, and Lateef, toward his own European roots shared with other Eurasian traditions. Through modalism, the improvisatory freedom in such gestures came from the abandonment of the metrical and diatonic-chromatic structures of song forms repeating cyclically as platforms; pulse could proceed in solos with no reference to the form of a song (including its number of measures), and harmony could be engaged as an unchanging chord (as sonority, not the "function" of development as defined by Common Practice).[18]

While the other, younger players who came after Mangelsdorff preceded him into an *Emanzipation* unmoored even more (from modes and regular pulse), his history in the mainstream led him as naturally to join them as John Coltrane's led him to join forces with his younger counterparts in America. He tells me:

> At a certain moment, maybe 1970 or so, my group decided not to use compositions any more, but just go on stage and improvise freely. I got so fanatic about playing free that I didn't want to play any written compositions; spontaneous composition was the thing for me then, and that lasted a few years.

After that, I started thinking about my narrow devotion to spontaneous freedom, and I realized that it was too much a one-track thing, and it was spoiling another talent I had, for making interesting compositions – which I didn't do for two or three years, didn't write one composition; free improvisation, free composition was the thing then for me. I still think that free jazz is a logical consequence of the whole jazz tradition, even though I don't play it every day.

German musicologist Ekkehard Jost's *Free Jazz* (1994 [1975]), released in English a decade before Litweiler's (1984, and the first comparable American) account of the same subject, addresses the musical specifics, in Western terms, of the music's African-American initiators. Jost's narrative: the free-jazz pioneers, while all African American and all rooted as much in their social as their musical contexts, were of most interest to Europe for the sheerly musical changes they brought to the Western table. While they did indeed "free" their music from Western compositional conventions through improvisation, they established new conventions to govern it, which were not beyond the analytical and theoretical grasp of conventional Western music scholarship, whatever the mystification surrounding it at the time.

Jost's succession of chapters reflects, roughly, the chronology of the major American players and their recordings. The first, "John Coltrane and modal playing," explains modalism as more than a nearly related scalar alternative to functional chordal harmony, noting that it was also a shift from motion and development to stasis and trance.[19] This move from active to static was the first fundamental formal change that set the stage for deconstructing and reconstructing the Western system of Common Practice harmony through jazz.[20] Although it was adopted and developed by African-Americans, it was a Western-rooted strategy with a deep historical charge in Europe.

The common ground of both modal and diatonic-chromatic harmony – indeed, of all such systems of scaled octaves – is the harmonic overtone series.[21] It constitutes the natural hierarchy of intervals and their pitched markers (the notes of a scale) that the West would chart most literately, then dismantle, both most rationally (the French Impressionists, the Second Viennese School) and most extra-rationally (the American Independents and the European post-serial composers). The hierarchy these melodic flows spell out is rooted in the harmonic moment of any and every sound: the harmonic overtone series is an acoustic phenomenon, charted for the Western world by Pythagoras and his heirs, which spans, roughly, the comfortable human hearing range.

French theorist Jacques Chailley conceived this relationship between harmonic moment and the West's unfolding of it into temporal flows as a history that has itself unfolded as a progression from a masculine bottom to a feminine top of that range. More roots . . .

From Modal Melody to Diatonic Harmony and Back Again

A first step towards the conquest of harmony was made when it was realized that a man and a woman thinking they are singing in unison are really singing an octave apart.[22]

The Greek word for "octave" is *diapason,* which denotes "by all," used to signal the performance of a melody by both men and women. French musicologist Jacques Chailley envisioned (in 1951) Western harmony developing historically from that "unison" as a gradual unpacking of the overtone series discovered on the Pythagorean monochord.

Certain historical periods and places, Fig. 1.1 shows, favor certain intervals over others. This is a true reading of Western harmonic development, but without my qualifiers its narrative is of the Western world distinguishing itself from a "primitive" one, first by divining this secret order in sound, then by shaping a uniquely Western vertical – harmonic – matrix directly from that order's vibrational frequency's design from its simplest lowest to its most complex highest octave ranges. It is something like the construction of an architectural monument in sound, a pyramid, or a sphinx, based on sound principles of design and engineering, spanning centuries in the making.

My alterations spin that narrative into one pertaining more here. "Primal," "Urgrund," and "archaic" all reflect timelier, less chauvinistic understandings of

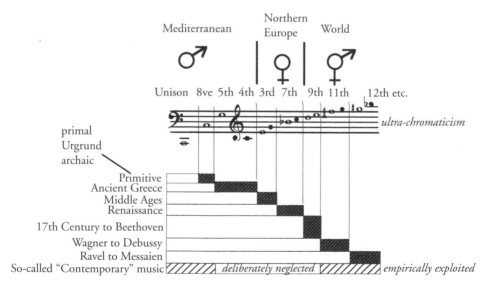

Fig. 1.1 All but the gender symbols and geographical allusions at the top, and the words added to the left of "Primitive," constitute Chailley's original design (1951: 23). My additions of those build on his narrative.

Chailley's "primitive." The "primal" in Don Cherry's quest has already been noted. The German prefix *Ur-* is reminiscent of the name of the ancient city in modern Iraq that stands in historical consciousness as symbolically foundational to the beginning of civilizations built around both agriculture and monotheism (Abraham came out of Ur, then of the Chaldees). German musicologist Friedrich Schenker unearthed the *Urlinie*, or the melody lines over which Western harmonic movement had developed. Finally, "archaic" stems from the Greek word *archē*, for "first principles."

It should be clear by now that we are looking for some sort of *Urgrund* to which our musical paradigm shift has directed itself, from the grounds of hierarchically pitched and metered matrices of sound and rhythm. Chailley's depiction of his own historical moment, by his chart's bottom line, suggests such a shift as a turn back as much as forward in time, somehow. The rise of what was first called the "primitive" in twentieth-century arts and letters, especially jazz, has been much observed and discussed.[23] As already noted, this study falls naturally into that conversation.

The gender symbols and geographic descriptors flag a geocultural history with a gendered face that complements the Western-rational one of Chailley's narrative. The male symbol over the first two eras, through ancient Greece, signals two things, sited in the Mediterranean world of antiquity: a phallocentric patriarchy that systematized Eros into power plays between dominant penetrating men and subdominant penetrated women, youth, and other men; and another such hierarchy, in music, spawned by this cradle of Western democracy.

The intervals of the first octave broken by overtones, the second one up on Chailley's chart, are the unison, fifth, and fourth – the tonic, dominant, and subdominant. The pitches spelling out those intervals were considered the stable, strong ones in melody lines, points of attraction to which the less stable "passing" tones gravitated. When polyphony began in the West, they were the notes and intervals that could move in parallel, making a single sonority as integrated as that of a single voice. They formed the I-IV-V root motion and its inversions at the heart of (later) Common Practice harmony, itself the topography of both Schenker's *Urlinie* and the blues, and much other folk and popular music. Finally, they were located by Western music notation, as they appear in Chailley's chart, on the bass clef, which, in the four-part harmonic grid, is the realm of the specifically male voices of bass and tenor. Modalism ruled then, as did the men (at least the ones who did).

The female symbol covers, roughly, the rise of the West – more precisely, the North – coinciding with the decline of antiquity. Or, again more precisely, it covers the subsumption of Mediterranean by northern Eurasian civilization spanning from Spain and France northward through England to Scandinavia, and eastward through Germany to Russia. Women had more power and status in those Germanic/Celtic/Slavic tribal entries into Mediterranean civilization, and that fact translated in the new Christian empire into the cult of Mary and Marian theology, and the theology of romantic and courtly love.[24]

It also translated into the option of celibacy as a passion and freedom from the breeder's destiny (for both sexes); and, later, the Reformation's openness to married and (still later) female clergy. Women monarchs figured large in the West's rise as a world power, and by the time "the free" began to storm the *ancien régime*, she was a woman ("lady liberty"), in both France and America. The dark side of all this – witch burnings and other expressions and degrees of patriarchal power-over – bespeaks in kind the light's brightness.

Again, this cultural history had its harmonic correlates. If the male era foundational to Western patriarchy formed the *Urgrund* of the *dia*-tonic – the open string's one tone divided judiciously, rationally, into the (tetrachordal) melodic flows of the scaled octave – its female follow-up laid the *triadic* down over its baseline. The triadic, as practiced beyond the civilized pale, was then a prime strategy whereby different voices sang in harmony.[25]

Scholarship on both Western music and jazz history suggests that harmony developed in the pre-civilized tribal world through a common practice of stacking thirds within the pentatonic scale; that civilization, spreading from east to west in a wedge between northern Europe and sub-Saharan Africa, rather developed melodies favoring the fourth and fifth and shunning the third, associating it both with weakness and with that barbarism beyond its pale; that Europe's diatonic triadicism rose and developed as a compromise between those two worlds of tribal and civilized; and that the sub-Saharan vestiges of the tribal "thirdness" met up with its now-assimilated northern European counterparts in the Americas, to negotiate there the new such compromise of "jazz."[26] Western harmony began largely as the compromise between civilized-rationalized-melodic modalism and barbaric-traditional-harmonic triadicism.

This history of Western music's Greek scientific and cultural template is a fine example of the nature/nurture dynamic at work: nature (the overtone series) is there to explore and reveal, the truth as a good; but we are part of nature, and that part we are twists and teases and tortures its truth and good to make them tell a thousand different tales, for better or worse. The tritone (bop's famous flatted fifth) belongs to the Devil until we get around to redeeming it for God; and the hierarchy of our harmonic matrix justifies the mastery of one human body over another as true and good, in the way its king/god (tonic) demands the service of its queen/devotee (dominant), its prince/ss (subdominant youth), its subjects (thirds), and lowliest serfs (seconds) – not to mention its "justifiably" forced labor and/or expendable bodies (those offenders outside the diatonic system altogether – the chromatic notes-between-the-notes – the captives of foreign wars, the heretics, criminals, and slaves) until that "Great Chain of Being's" weakest links sing louder in that matrix than its own "natural" truth, pushing the envelope to show the way through the natural to the greater (nurtured) truth of empowerment of the formerly powerless (tones, bodies).[27]

Key to our story is what Ornette Coleman, John Coltrane, and their European colleagues would do with all of this. Suffice it to say here that this much of Western harmonic history spells out the blues, with the male rock (of fifths, fourths, and octaves) moving in the bass and the female role chording those stacked thirds statically over the bass motion in her treble clef, voiced by alto and soprano. At which point, having established their hierarchical arrangement as stable, Western man and woman moved up to the next octave (Chailley's chart's fourth), and out into the rest of the world, a move that is discussed in more detail later.

Joachim Kühn: Free At Last, At First

While he was staying with Miles [Davis], [Paul] Buckmaster often practiced the Prelude to Bach's Cello Suite No. 1, and Miles loved it, and asked him to work it into something for him to play. Though Buckmaster never did anything with it, Miles' interest in the Prelude shows that he could be drawn to music that was primarily made up of rhythm, texture, color, and structure and was without a real melody as such. This is all the more interesting because Miles later said that Bach made him hear what Ornette Coleman meant by "harmolodics" – a system by which all instruments of a group are liberated to solo simultaneously.[28]

Most jazz musicians follow maps to improvise. I prefer musicians who are seeking something freer, easier, more enjoyable. The main thing that makes towards music perfection is the will to make it better instantly.

– Ornette Coleman[29]

One might metaphorically call Coleman the "Bach of free jazz," not only for his central role and influence but for the nature of his musical strategies themselves. Having suggested that the free-jazz years marked the first real African-American departures from the Western paradigm as a source for improvisational platforms, and a decisive assertion of black over white identity in the music, I have nonetheless – inevitably? – set myself up to explain that departure as the West's own self-transformation, and white identity's fullest flowering therein too.

The details of Coleman's innovations and place in the music's American discourse over time since then are documented well;[30] and a scan of index entries of his name in sources covering the European scenes then reveals the extent and details of his impact and influence there.[31] My contribution to that conversation is a look at his collaboration with Joachim Kühn, and at their common ground in Bach and the Baroque.

Coleman's system of harmolodics, as described to Shipton, resonates (synchronistically, not derivatively) with that of Bach and the German Baroque on fundamental levels. Jost explains Coleman's approach to composing his own tunes and improvising on them as a step past modalism's retention of tonal hierarchy, down the same path from diatonic harmony-driven to melody-driven invention: still tonal, in the way such invention is anchored and dominated by a central tone, but chromatically flexible, as compared with modalism's fixed relation to diatonic structure.[32] The modes, after all, are simply one step back in music history from diatonic harmony; the root tone of each mode is a step in the major diatonic scale, and the notes of each mode's scale are likewise those of the major scale, using each as root tone in succession.

Coleman freed himself from those constraints by allowing himself any tone in the chromatic scale for a root, and also for any melodies composed or improvised against it. While most of those he did choose resembled conventional harmony, especially in his early years, they were marked from the beginning by their freedom to leap around the scale at his will, and to resolve or not resolve conventionally (hierarchically) in their melodic-harmonic patternings.[33]

Joachim Kühn is the very picture of the stereotypical German Romantic artist, with his leonine hair, elegant clothes, and rugged-refined good looks. Like Vinko Globokar (discussed later), he spent much of his life in France after growing up behind the Iron Curtain, in East Germany; also like Globokar, he is as much the composer as the improviser, only more in the jazz-traditional than the new-music side of things. His visceral and living connection with Western music history ignited in his formative years in response to Coleman's first recordings.

The thrust of Kühn's innovation was primarily time-based: from conventional playing, he moved away from regular meter and its formations into a free treatment of pulse, a move redolent of the Romantic practice of rubato time; from group sync to independent, or two-against-one (heterarchical) lines; and from regular harmony to experimental alterations of it. Pure sound effects (mostly in the percussion, and inside the piano) emerged, solo cadenzas of completely free playing alternated with collective improvisations and clearly orchestrated sections.

Kühn's breakthrough into the "free" came when he was only nineteen, and deeply moved by his first exposure to Coleman. I spoke with him, in fact, a block or two from Coleman's New York studio, where they were practicing together for an upcoming date with Coleman's group and the (Moroccan) Master Musicians of Joujouka. "I first heard about Ornette in my home town of Leipzig, around 1959 or 60," he recalls.

> East Germany wasn't a place where jazz was accepted as a profession, in general, but since my brother was a jazz musician I started at an early age, with early jazz. I knew even then that playing forever over chord changes just couldn't be it. So I got my brother to send me one of Ornette's early records. From the first few bars I knew instantly that I could spend my life with this guy. I had already started composing my own music, and when I heard Ornette, it was like my confirmation.
>
> Then, just three years ago I was working in Paris, and my agent became friends with him, and he was often at her house, writing pieces or something. One day she did a blindfold test with him, and played him one of my records, and said "you should play with this man." He liked it, said okay. So, some forty years after I first heard him I got the chance to play with him. A dream come true.

I ask him about his approach to the piano with this master who played for so long without a piano, without chords.

"It's not really about chord changes," he says. "Sometimes Ornette likes to put his own chords into his compositions, sometimes very simple ones, sometimes complex. But ninety per cent of the time it's just a matter of playing sounds more than chords." (About Kühn's work with him then, Coleman said: "Most jazz pianists play in a 'pop' style – that's to say, they play chords as you would do for a singer . . . they're always put in a situation to be support. None of the pianists I use play like that . . . Joachim Kühn plays in a style that's almost orchestral in the way he improvises. With him the chordal structure is there, but much freer than in a set sequence – it's almost a new format."[34])

Kühn's first trio, following Coleman's lead, took the first East German step away from diatonic-metric conventions and into an area that would overtake and dominate its musical culture for the next two decades, in a way that free-jazz musicians in both Western Europe and America could only wildly dream about. He was only twenty when he did this, and twenty-two when he defected. He opened one door, then went through another one.

Kühn expresses strong feelings, as do Mangelsdorff and West Germany's first *Emanzipation* figure Günter Hampel, about free improvisation as the height of, not an escape from, traditional Western musicianship. He also expresses opinions about America's "sad" commodification and commercialization of pre-1960s' jazz styles, and about the necessity for each musician to forge new and personal expressions. That said, he is as traditional as Wynton Marsalis, in his thick engagement with German Baroque, and his disdain of unschooled players (his love of Coleman, also like Marsalis's, obviously signals his disdain too for those many who have counted Coleman among the unschooled).

"It's been true since the '60s," he says, "that in our music there were three or four people from each country doing something, so we all got connected somehow. And it was good for doing self-initiating kinds of things on the business end, and for bringing out our individual identities from which to play. On the other hand, it opened the door up to a lot of people who didn't know anything about music, about the saxophone or whatever they played. But you have to know everything about music, basically, in order to play free. I think I can hear it when a person is just blowing without that foundation."

As with his youthful passion for Coleman's music, Kühn's even earlier, just-as-personal involvement with Bach also flowered in his maturity to collaboration with the source, in a sense. Poetically, his more traditional use of the word "confirmation" – a bop-charged term (a famous Charlie Parker title) he used in connection with Coleman's music – works for his connection to Bach (the apotheosis of whose music system flowered with a vengeance in bop). When we spoke, Kühn was involved with a project with the same church choir Bach wrote for (the Thomannerchor), in collaboration with the man who held the position Bach held (Georg Christoph Biller, the sixteenth Thomaskantoren after Bach), in the Thomaskirche in Leipzig. The choir sang Bach, Kühn improvised against it.

This is the church where I myself had my Confirmation [he tells me]. I grew up in this church, and learned that music and was playing classical piano until I was seventeen or eighteen. And, of course, as I got into jazz I saw that Bach was as important to the art of improvisation as anything, even the blues. For me it was never a conflict, being German and dealing with this music.

Music doesn't know any race, music doesn't know any jealousy; there may be some caught up in those things, but not the best. Also, as black as it is, jazz has very much the European influence. When you analyze Bach, for example . . . it's just like pure jazz, what he did, even down to some of the improvisations.

Bach's Blues

Kühn's invocation of Bach brings us back to Chailley's chart. His "17th century to Beethoven" covers Bach's German Baroque through the first Viennese School through the Romantics, an idea that requires further discussion before my juxta-position of male and female symbols onto that era/pitch range can be explored.

The move of winds and percussion instruments to the foreground in Europe, usurping strings and voices singing texts – as in nineteenth-century America, to serve dance – also occurs at this point. Brandenburg cornetist Bartholomäus Prae-torius published in 1616 a collection of dance suites under the tutelage of the Elizabethan English composer William Brade – the first Berlin court Kapellmeis-ter to be an instrumentalist rather than choral director. His addition of stringed instruments to the brass-heavy, military-style orchestra served to raise rather than overshadow the musical and social functions of the winds, elevating the folk dance tunes that culminated in the music of Bach and Handel. These tunes were short, rhythmically symmetrical, and improvisationally varied when repeated – thus the origin of the symmetrical, periodic expressions of theme and variation that would define the shift from vocal to instrumental music (and from southern to northern Europe, and from sanctimonious Latin and Germanic voices and texts to dancing bodies and vernacular liturgies and more secular texts). This shift would dominate formal construction and improvisation, including that of (pre-free) jazz, for the next three centuries.[35]

Perhaps the quickest way to cut through historic accretions to the Germanic thread of musical thought being traced here is to turn to a contemporary theorist with one foot solidly in the thousand-year (roughly speaking) diatonic (and founding) moment of that thought, and the other as solidly in the not-quite-hundred-year (Western) musical moments succeeding and going beyond it – atonal heterarchy as offspring of tonal hierarchy – and paralleling jazz. Allen Forte's (1982) introduction to the work of Heinrich Schenker serves here as a quick expo-sition of Western polyphony as an explication of the horizontal's (melody's) impli-cations for the vertical (harmony), and that as the Western heart of the blues.[36]

Forte discusses the system of "species counterpoint" devised by Bach's con-temporary Johann Joseph Fux as the basis on which Schenker elaborated his own analytical work. Fux developed five sets (the "species") of rules governing the leading of one or more voices against a *cantus firmus*; Schenker went down the same lines to develop his *Urlinie*, the melodic (horizontal) unfolding he saw as the "bass line" from which Western vertical music derives.

To characterize and detail their bodies of work any more than that would take us too far afield here, but that much makes the point that their most Germanic of contributions to Western musical thought are themselves characterized by a conception of harmony as an issue of melody, not the other way around. Neither theorist starts with a system of harmonic rules that determine how to lead voices against a fixed melody. Rather, that (horizontal) melody itself is fixed according to the ancient conventions ordering intervals hierarchically within the octave, and all subsequent melodies (the different parts, or voices) are constructed to reflect that same hierarchy vertically (harmonically): unisons, octaves, and fourths and fifths are still regarded as primary, strongest, stablest; thirds and seconds and their respective inversions (sixths and sevenths), still as less so.

In other words, monodic melody sounding in flow time is primary; polyphonic harmony sounding in moment time is secondary. Grounding the vertical in the horizontal so is to ground the transcendent in the immanent as much as the immanent is grounded in the transcendent, no more, no less. Precursors of jazz's early stride piano style confirmed this primacy of melody by playing the melody in the left hand and ornamenting – "beautifying" – it with arpeggiated chords in the right, reflecting the way stringed instruments had evolved in the West to complement the singing voice.[37] As the French wind quintet and Prussian military band reversed orchestral hierarchies of instruments in the nineteenth century, the stride pianists would reverse this particular Western usage of left and right hands.

What are the philosophical and social implications of this musical history? That Plato's emphasis on the transcendent – the Greek source of the West's mind-over-body dualism – was never wrong, precisely, but rather, ultimately, misplaced. Transcendence and immanence can never constitute other than what modern physics calls a "tangled hierarchy" – one in which the up and down positions are never more than a function of perception. The West's "Great Chain of Being," from highest immaterial God to lowest material organism, is a paradigm that freezes the transcendent over the immanent; its social reflections have similarly frozen rulers over ruled. Both aspects of the paradigm have always proven themselves to be flying in the face of reality.

The challenge to the Baroque composer was to make the richest vertical moments possible out of two or more equally rich horizontal lines, "rich" being defined by the same hierarchical criteria of pitch relations on both axes, and the balance of vertical and horizontal reflecting that between the transcendent and immanent. The I-IV-V melodic pattern is simply the key landmark (from Chailley's second octave, that of the Western male voice) defining those criteria; it is also the quartal musical emphasis that distinguished Mediterranean civilization from both the northern European and sub-Saharan African tertial traditions that came together later in North America.

In other words, it is the doorbell of the Big House (civilization), deconstructed and reconstructed first by the northern Europeans (relatively uncivilized until around the time Western polyphony began, largely as a move by the Church to contain and control, having failed to force every voice to conform to the one melody of the plainchant), then by the (also forcibly Western-civilized) African Americans. It was a force to be reckoned with on its own hierarchical terms in both cases, but by no means an immutable one.

Ornette's More-than-Blues

Some of Coleman's own words about this Western/rational aspect of his system corroborate and illuminate in retrospect Jost's 1974 explanation of it. They also place it squarely in the Western music-historical discourse we are engaging:

> Most song forms have a harmonic structure known as ii-v-i in Western music . . . in harmelodic [*sic*] structure, the ii-v-i structures are spread out in three basic changes, the major 7th, the minor 7th, and a minor sound. *In other words, you have a major sound, a minor sound, and a dominant sound.* But in harmelodics those sounds are three individual chords that consist of the whole total of 12 pitches in Western musics. (1982)
>
> The word "improvise" is supposed to mean something that's not there that you bring there. In jazz, it's when a person can change his will and thought at the moment he wants to do it. The same twelve notes support all kinds of different performances – there must be something in those twelve notes that lets each individual be free. (1997)[38]

Here we have another definition of freedom, straight from the "free jazz" source's mouth: the freedom to be spontaneous by systematic design, and that design as Western (equal-tempered chromatic).

However, if Coleman's engine of such freedom on the sheerly mechanical level of note selection was driven by chromatic melody more than diatonic harmony, more radically it was also driven by an imperative of inspiration and emotional self-expression – a conscious move to thwart the temptation to hide behind rational formal constraints. Coleman advised his bandmates to use his tunes as igniters of their feelings, then to use those feelings rather than the rational plan of the composition to direct their improvisations (the spirit rather than the letter, the improvising body rather than the mental map – the Holy rather than the Religion – of the music).[39] Finally, he systematically allowed for the phenomenon of group interaction in the process, including the group's power to go beyond the composer's parameters.[40]

The most profound and bold part of this threefold liberation – from modal-diatonic hierarchy to chromatic democracy of pitch, from mental map to inspiration, from one composer-player-leader to interactive group – is the trust and respect it grants to emotion and inspiration. The rational aspects and checks and balances of the system are designed to serve, even force, spontaneity, in the assumption that the improvising body has something it can draw on that is more powerful, more providential, even more orderly in the end than any rational/ religious script. Freedom from, in, and to form – form in this case being Coleman's own system, clearly Western, and just as clearly effecting and serving black liberation and identity, on both personal and collective levels – converge, balance together dynamically.[41]

From Bach to Coleman

Historical literature on jazz and free jazz has sometimes cast the music, specifically, the music of Ornette Coleman, as ugly, primitive, and backward by Western aesthetic standards. The very term "Baroque," as also the earlier "Gothic," was similarly conceived as part of the rhetoric of Romanic civilization about Germanic barbarism. The upsurge of the Gothic at the beginning of the last millennium – musically, in polyphony before it was officially assimilated and metered – was named after the Goths by Romanic humanists contemptuous of its barbaric disregard for their classical learning. The "Baroque" period, which included a reassertion of all that was called Gothic as a backlash against Renaissance humanism, was also described so by those humanists

> as a term of abuse. The word may be derived either from the Portuguese *barocco,* meaning an irregularly shaped pearl (in which sense it is still used by jewelers) or, as is perhaps more likely, from *baroco,* a scholastic term coined as a mnemonic aid for a tortuous argument in logic. As used by late 18th-century art critics, it signified "absurd," "willful," "grotesque" – in other words, a wanton defiance of the classical rules.[42]

Table 1.1.

Bach/Baroque	Coleman/Free Jazz
Protestantism	Black church (Protestant)
Lutheran chorale	spiritual, gospel, blues
post-Thirty Years War, German reconstruction	post-slavery, segregation, Civil Rights movement
death of Roman Catholic, birth of Northern Protestant, identity	death of blackness-as-second-class whiteness, birth of new black identity as definitive
rise from German-local to global (European/Western) cultural power	rise from African-American local to global (American) cultural power

The period of the Baroque – roughly 1600 to 1750 (when Bach died) – marked the rise in the West of both absolutist power and the ideals of individual liberty, a double-edged sword that extends to our own moment. Absolute power had always been around in one form or another, but its hyper-inflation in both hostile and cooperative responses to the reaches for individual rights and liberties became the irony of modernity that endures.[43]

It is an irony, as we are seeing, very much at the heart of the musical issues: ecstasy and a sense of divinely just order both develop from a casting-off of traditional moorings, but so do conflict, anxiety, and confusion, and with them the impulse to control the chaos with impositions of will – by force, in a pinch – or with passive regressions to said moorings. The historical conditions from which free jazz emerged – via rebellious blackness and youth in America, and rebellious youth in Europe – have the same profile of outsiders to an Establishment feeling their claim as potential insiders thereto betrayed. Like the good Catholic Martin Luther, or the Prophet Mohammed, they started in good-faith acceptance of the promise and ideals of that Establishment, tasted them as lies and hypocrisy, then set about trying to make them true for themselves and the world.

The "land in the middle" of Europe (Germany) has always been a battleground. It has no natural bordering defenses; its feudal lordships, like their tribal-chief predecessors, established themselves early and well for sheer survival. They learned to suffer, as well as inflict on their neighbors, the worst of the many ravages of wars their princes fought with each other and with other Europeans for imperial power. The culmination of this violent history came with the Thirty Years War (1618–48), a watershed German trauma that wiped out half the country (about nine million people), triggered the first big wave of German emigration to America, and set Prussia (especially hard hit) on its militaristic path.[44]

> A great lassitude descended on the towns and villages and countryside devastated by the Thirty Years War. There was a sense of exhaustion which gradually transformed itself into an introspective obsession with the immediate vicinity. People's horizons shrank and the life of the village became the widest world of many Germans. While the rest of Europe pushed back new frontiers beyond the seas, the Germans retreated into themselves.
>
> Gradually this introspection of the towns and villages of the Holy Roman Empire turned into a sense of contentment and achievement. Local prosperity returned and under the patronage of the princes and prince bishops in a myriad of ecclesiastical and hereditary states, music and literature developed and blossomed. The strong sense of local identity born of the defeatism and the futility of the Thirty Years War became a source of pride and psychological contentment.[45]

I would add that that sense – captured uniquely by the German word *Heimat*, which translates into the much less emotionally charged and meaningful "homeland" – also goes far toward explaining the German states' susceptibility to, as well as their cynicism about, a centralized power. Empire had always been there, and Germany's grassroots could not escape its machinations if it wanted to, which it often didn't; but it could and did let them play themselves out, self-destruct, and survive them and thrive.

The history of the West German part of its *Emanzipation* – the site, in fact, of the pan-European one – concretely reflects this dual German identity: the two parts of Empire (Prussian aristocracy, in the Berlin scene) and eclectic-radical grassroots (in the Ruhr Valley town of Wuppertal, near the Rhinelands). Both locales figure large in the birth of the *Emanzipation*, as well as of nineteenth-century American pre-jazz culture. It was the Protestant church music born and nurtured in Saxony-Anhalt (very near Berlin) to spread throughout the world, combined with the heartland's folk and burgher traditions of amateur music-making, that fed the Celtic-Germanic ground of North American soil for its part of the European/African garden (in marked contrast to the Romanic-Germanic *Catholic* ground in the Creole and South American parts of that garden). And as we've seen, it was Prussia's marching bands, its drums and horns (including the newly invented saxophone), that infused American popular music with its power and energy throughout the nineteenth and into the twentieth centuries, giving Europe's martial affect and shape to much of the instrumentation, orchestration, and spirit of jazz. It was Berlin's status as a major European cosmopolis that fostered the importation and spread of jazz in Germany and from there to much of the rest of Eurasia.

It was also East Berlin that hosted another unique and equally potent bloom on this German branch, and it was Joachim Kühn who, like Coleman in America, more or less cultivated that flower singlehandedly. Historical conditions thus meet personal profile to make for a certain kind of musical power, synchronistically similar in these two men and their worlds.

I do not presume with this comparison to characterize the individual personalities or psychologies of Bach or Coleman so much as draw on their least personal biographical and demographical information, and on the affects widely perceived in their musical personae – with the suggestion that those affects, even more than their respective geniuses as musical system builders, are what made their work so powerful.[46]

Johann Sebastian Bach lost his parents at an early age. As an adult, he lost his first wife and several children; he then remarried and had many other children.

Table 1.2

Bach/Baroque	Coleman/Free Jazz
Affect: introvert, unworldly, provincial church, aesthetically conservative, not modern	Affect: innocent, naif, rustic, blues-folk more than urban-jazz

He worked in relative isolation from the Enlightenment musical and intellectual trend of his time in a succession of often frustrating and demanding positions as organist (with a legendary reputation as an improviser), teacher, conductor, and composer in Weimar and Leipzig. His orientation was to the past in his time, to the medieval German mysticism of Johannes Tauler, and to the first flush of Lutheranism. The deaths and births in his family can be seen as linking his music to the larger collective German death and resurrection (religious, cultural, and physical, in the Thirty Years War) from which Protestantism was born. The imagery of death in the religious poetry set by so much of Bach's music links it to medieval mysticism, but the music itself is full of as much joy as melancholy, suggesting (with much of the texts) death as Christ's redemptive, resurrective gift, or simply a natural and inevitable part of life not to be dreaded by the pious. All of this, as also Germany's isolation from Mediterranean culture and society, and Bach's personal isolation, fostered the conditions underlying his work that link it emotionally, mythically, psychologically, as well as intellectually (as already noted), to the blues.

Coleman's professional career has been similarly checkered and fertile, owing in part to similar personality and social dynamics. He came up in relative isolation from urban jazz scenes and social-cultural elite, developed something strong enough to match and challenge the premises of same, kept "the country" in him throughout his subsequent labors to deliver that "something" to that "civilization," and met with enough professional and social hostility or indifference, along with the respect and acclaim, to make his actual daily and yearly toil as an artist much less the smooth, rewarding sail enjoyed by many less significant voices around him.

Coleman's integration of the rural blues into his sound and style is widely acknowledged; that, and the reach back to a pre-diatonic approach to tonality and melodic invention noted here, bespeak a "radical conservatism" similar to Bach's. The most poignant extremes of both joy and sorrow, also widely recognized and acknowledged in the blues, characterize Coleman's compositions and his improvisations thereon. (This similarity of isolation from the world leading, through genius, to a new world, also reminds me of something I heard of Max Roach saying, that jazz itself developed the way it did because white America excluded and neglected black America, left it to its own devices.) Again, historical conditions thus meet personal profile to make for a certain kind of musical power, synchronistically similar in these two men and their worlds.

Table 1.3

Bach/Baroque	Coleman/Free Jazz
shift from modal to well-tempered, Rameau's "common practice," a new Western identity (Germanic, Northern)	shift from jazz's neo-modal to the harmolodic variation on the same principle, and a new Western identity (African-American/pan-African)

It is necessary here to anchor the two separate musical aspects just discussed –
"architecture" (system) and "affect" (feeling) – to their own musical ground
in Western intellectual history. German Baroque music theorists and
composers occupied various parts of a spectrum between medieval and
Enlightenment/Romantic precepts. The former centered on abstract and objective mathematical and philosophical aspects, the latter on the more subjective (and
then-recent) "doctrine of temperaments and affections." This doctrine held music
as an expression of different emotional states themselves generated by different
types of bodies (sanguine, choleric, phlegmatic, and so on) – not appropriated
from nature, as medievalists would have it – and of different environments (conceived as collectives, literal "cultures" of such "organisms," therefore also distinguished by their particular physical-affective traits).[47]

The work of the medievalists led to such practical innovations as Andreas
Werckmeister's tuning system for equal temperament, in 1691. Many Coleman
scholars have included the departure from equal temperament among his various
"innovations,"[48] but that is true only on the level of "just intonation" (his is often
ornamentally wide of the ideal mathematical mark, not "just"). In principle, as
discussed, he embraces dodecaphonism, and equal temperament is by definition
the rationalization, defying the natural hierarchy of acoustic proportions, of the
octave into twelve equal parts.

More deeply, it is also the relocation of both shell and soul of the music from
nature's field to culture's garden of sound. Modes originated as arrangements of
the natural acoustic order, and were conceived to be mutually exclusive frameworks with distinct, sometimes clashing characters. (For example, Plato preferred
the Dorian over the Phrygian mode as more conducive to psychological and social
peace; the Lydian mode referred to a specific place; some Indian ragas serve
morning, others evening "energies"; major keys signal happiness, minor ones
sadness. All "performers" in such modes are entranced and possessed by, conveying more than creating, the affects of these modes.) Equal temperament's North-
ern/Western European "justification" of these clashes allowed for a theoretical
linkage – modulation – between the previous disjuncts ("diatonic" signals this new
relationship between those monotonic fields, "dia" denoting "through," to connect
them). It did so through the agency of the controlling body-mind that orders scales
into mobile, relativized "keys" – any scale can be constructed on any pitch – rather
than locking them into tonal vibrations with naturally intrinsic characters, of
hierarchical structure.[49]

The move to justify the modes so – like the cultivation of humanistic rationalism and democracy in the cultures of gods and kings – was one of those many
human (particularly Western) engagements with the external world motivated by
the convenience of, control over, or simple curiosity about the possibilities for per-
sonal-cultural expression and growth in a field hitherto less amenable to those
things. The body finds itself or its others oppressed, shorted, or thwarted by the
world; it then seizes the authority of that world, to re-author it to rather serve the
body.[50]

Table 1.4

Bach/Baroque	Coleman/Free Jazz
instruments as extensions of voice more than of music system	instruments as extensions of voice more than of music system

Bach's music is medievally conceived in the mathematical architecture its polyphony displays, but every turn in that architecture sounds a poetry as human as the deepest folk song, as the blues resonates in the "architectural" sophistication of jazz, especially that of Coleman and Coltrane. Bach's vocal lines evince some of the same traits for which his foremother Hildegard of Bingen's were criticized, often given more to the daring, sometimes harsh leaps of the German language itself than to the gentle flows of Italian and French, or even English, by comparison. These very traits are those for which his instrumental music has been universally praised (Lang [1941: 503]), albeit sometimes questioned by players as to its playability. They are also traits that marked the similar challenges of the compositional and improvisational styles of Charles Mingus and Eric Dolphy, as well as Coleman and Coltrane, and Cecil Taylor and (later) Anthony Braxton.

One of the first directions early Baroque music took was from predominantly vocal into instrumental music, which was largely developed in the dance-suite forms marked by symmetrical periodicity and variations on a theme. Bach's instrumental music was the apotheosis of this Baroque impulse to develop the instruments. As important as his work to the development of the chromatic scale in diatonic harmony was the service these newly fortified instrumental voices offered to words in poetic-dramatic action. Instruments began to be grouped for their tone-color effects, fugal potentials, and rival displays of virtuosity; the concept of playing in concert (i.e., together) emerged. The drama of religious texts and other poetry informed the structures and textures of music, and the instrumental music took on the role of rendering the process of the passions and forces produced by and producing the drama rendered by the text.[51]

Hartman (1991) succinctly locates Coleman's source of lyricism and feeling, even originality, in his voice (extended by the sax), after seeking it unsuccessfully in the musical texts of his compositions. Coleman's disengagements of African-American musical vernacular from European generative grammar let it roam freely through his own personal roots and patches of rhythmic and melodic free association, some of them more African than American, some more "folk" and "blues" than "jazz," some more American than Western, some more his own voice than anything else.

The significance of his system, then, lay more in its effectiveness in awakening and providing a fertile field for his freely roaming voice – just as Bach's system proved more valuable, over time, as a field on which the many subsequent voices of Western music could plant themselves and grow. This is very different from

Table 1.5

Bach/Baroque	Coleman/Free Jazz
nature of polyphonic-monophonic relationship	from solo to group free improvisation

something like "total serialism," or "socially conscious" art (propaganda, religious or secular), where the body/mind rather serves the system. (It is also a rational answer to charges of charlatanism leveled by rationalists who disparage harmolodics as a shuck-and-jive simulation of literacy by a non-literate genius, charges Coleman's erstwhile protégé Anthony Braxton has also often had to field.)

Jost's description of Coleman's recording *Free Jazz* (1960) and its relationship to Coltrane's *Ascension* (1965, clearly influenced by *Free Jazz*, and a major catalyst for the late '60s *Emanzipation* players) is a good European entry point into the dynamic between individual and group play in both, and that dynamic's resonance with Baroque music.[52]

> In the collective improvisations of *Free Jazz*, the contributions of each and every improviser have a certain melodic life of their own; motivic connections and dove-tailing of the various parts create a polyphonic web of interactions. In *Ascension*, on the other hand, the parts contribute above all to the formation of changing sound structures, in which the individual usually has only a secondary importance. Quite plainly, the central idea is not to produce a network of inter-woven independent melodic lines, but dense sound complexes.
>
> Melody-plus-motives on the one hand; tone-color structures on the other; the antithesis these two principles represent gives rise to problems that go far beyond the immediate comparison of *Free Jazz* and *Ascension* . . . The increasing trend in collective improvisation (especially in larger groups) toward playing with tone color and away from motivic improvisation, is probably due in some measure to the extraordinary effect *Ascension* had on late Sixties' jazz.[53]

In describing *Free Jazz* as a democracy and polyphony of melodies and motives more than of timbres and sound masses, and *Ascension* as a collective of individuals all somewhat less than the sum of their efforts, Jost signals something about the European reception of, and musical responses to, both Coleman and late Coltrane. Coleman was not the shock to European musicians and audiences that he was to Americans, and was seen instead more as the latest bright light (after Charlie Parker) in the mainstream jazz tradition. His tunes and improvisations, his rhythm section, did not depart as far from harmonic and metric convention as (according to his own theoretical lights) they could have, and as European and American art music already had; and he was clearly a leader setting the musical stage, not a collectivist (*Free Jazz* being the exception). Coltrane's step beyond the chromatic and metric matrices into sheer sound was more the breakthrough to the "energy" music Europeans would shape for themselves, in collectives.[54]

This suggests that, again, Coleman's affect – his voice, his off-key sound – was perhaps more the issue than his system, for better or worse, in America. His was the song of the black manchild at (free) play in the (supposedly unfree) fields of the lord. Coltrane's departure from the chromatic scale through collective manipulations of it massaged it into a single mass of sound defined more by unmetered timbre, texture, and volume than by loosely metered and tuned pitch relations. This approach mirrored that made by Schoenberg and developed by others since him in Europe, and took that African-American free play out of the older (tyrannical master's) and into the newer (liberal master's) Western harmonic field.

In any case, taken together rather than contrasted, as Jost treated them, both seminal recordings fit under Bach's Baroque umbrella as described by Lang:

> The specific formal principle of the baroque is the statement of the "basic affection" and its subsequent exploitation by continuous expansion. This means that the basic affection (which does not necessarily express any concrete idea or notion) must be stated in the most pregnant and concentrated manner – the fugue theme – for the rest of the musical composition depends on it. The baroque sonata does not have contrasting themes as used by the symphonists of the classic era, for it is concerned with the exploitation of one affection which would be weakened and disturbed by additional material, introducing a different state of mind, idea, or affection . . . Once a fugue or a concerto gets under way, it brooks no obstacle, ignores challenges, refuses to pause until it reaches its destination, which is the end; the material is exhausted. Thus baroque form gives free rein to the artist's imagination . . . Viewed from the conventional angle of formal theories (usually labeled "classical," although with little justification), this baroque unfolding of music seems essentially formless, always reaching out for wider expanses and never ending . . . (1941: 443)

The "basic affection," conveyed by the "fugue theme," the "essentially formless" variations on that theme, the intense focus and energy, and the infinite reach all describe the open-ended jam sessions that characterized the free-jazz movement's "first hours" in the late 1960s.

This single-minded tunnel vision is the perfect vehicle for fascistic chauvinism excluding all dissent, one fed by both the Enlightenment tendency to totalitarianism and Romanticism's equal passion for the infinite and universal mixed dangerously with its cult of local rather than global identity, and its subsequent cult of the genius composer hero (the charismatic dictator) peopled by musical serfs interpreting his work for passive audiences. However, it is mitigated in Coleman's system (as also in Cecil Taylor's and, incidentally, in Braxton's) by another crucial component: the allowance of other creative participants to overrule the parameters (the "basic affection") laid down by the composer, an allowance, as will be demonstrated, less brooked by even the most "liberal" composers, such as Cage and Stockhausen.

The *Emanzipation* in European free jazz had a particularly urgent need for this gift; it got its musical culture back in touch with the spirit of the Baroque score

– sketchy, open, like a jazz lead sheet, not the overdetermining *Werk* of the two hundred years prior to 1950. European improvisers were also well positioned to function spontaneously as a leaderless collective by virtue of a long historical development of the arts of both polyphony and orchestration.[55]

The bundling and bonding of modes by equal temperament gave, in principle, Western polyphony the force and flexibility of the single voice – the (monophonically) "unified field" of Chailley's primal unison, paving the way for the completely democratic network of the twelve pitches to come through Schoenberg. Coleman's harmolodics gave the African-American – and (of more universal import) the personal – voice (affect) access to that previously exclusive Western field. Charlie Parker and John Coltrane – as, indeed, all the "jazz" masters from Jelly Roll Morton and Louis Armstrong on – brought the same voice to the same table. But Coleman's voice instigated a redesign of that table.

After the modalism brought to jazz by George Russell, Miles Davis, Coltrane, and others, Coleman's approach mirrored the Baroque consolidation of modalism's system and subject – of medievalist objective acoustic science (underpinning harmony) and the body's subjectivity (motivating melody) – fusing them literally in the word "harmolodic." It was as if the jazz modalists had reached back to a musical moment before the West had quite distinguished itself from the Rest, there to find respite from the increasingly oppressive presence of those moments since it had done so. Coleman then seized that moment to distinguish his African-American identity from that of the West by both a systemic and an affective design necessarily shaped, as was Bach's, by what came before him.

What formerly served the needs of Germanic over Mediterranean bodies, then, Coleman used to serve his African-American body over Germanic (post-Romanic Western) ones. It was a musical move akin to Bishop Desmond Tutu's, or Martin Luther King's (or, again, Martin Luther's): an honest, human application of an oppressor's religious myth and system to shame its hypocritical professors into the ideals they professed. Its privileging of melody over harmony set it on the shelf next to Fux and Schenker, at the heart rather than the skin of Western music.

Given the penchant (examined ahead) in both French and East German post-free scenes for European folk and early Western as well as for contemporary art music and for Coleman, and given Coleman's associations with country blues as well as atonal Third Stream pieces, it is interesting that Kühn expresses little interest in either as source material. He thought instead that "It's more important to write your own music . . . If it's working like it should, you shouldn't even be able to tell the difference between composition and improvisation in performance. The compositional aspect serves as a platform, but it does go in both directions. Sometimes the best way to make a piece is to start with nothing, no ideas, then let the improvisation lead it into a composition. Many of the pieces I've made with the trio start out that way."

This organic meld of composition and improvisation implies similar fusions of everything else discussed here as different in nature and often clashing – black and white music in America, European and American traditions and identities, harmony and melody, different instruments, pitched and unpitched sound, metered and unmetered pulse. The Coleman–Kühn duo is a sterling example of symmetrical Eros agenting these marriages beyond all hint of their asymmetrical Wars.

Ornette Coleman and Joachim Kühn/Colors: Live from Leipzig

The eight tracks of this CD are 6-to-10-minute duo performances of eight Coleman tunes, recorded live at the Leipzig Opera during the twentieth anniversary of the *Leipziger JazzTage* (Leipzig Jazz Days) on 31 August, 1996. The gameplan is generally to play the tune together, sometimes at the beginning and/or end, sometimes somewhere in the middle, of an open improvisation. In the middle of the performance (tracks 3 and 4) Coleman intersperses his alto sax playing with a brief flurry on trumpet and violin, respectively. These take the music to its least melodic and chromatically pitched, its most rhythmically flexible, and its most atonal, for Kühn, and most "noisy" – dirty smears rather than clean phrases of discrete notes – for Coleman. (Recalling Chailley's chart, one can easily relegate most of the concert to the first four octaves' worth of overtones and intervals comprising chromaticism, and these momentary digressions to the next octave up, where such discretion acoustically blurs in the winds and the strings.)

The first thing that strikes one familiar with both of these artists' histories is the significance of Coleman duetting with a pianist at all. It is not without precedent, but it is a departure from the concept of the early work that made his mark.[56] His piano-less quartets had their forerunners too – most notably, from the West Coast Cool groups so big in 1950s' Germany – but his own omission of the instrument was a radically obvious eschewal of Western harmonic paradigm and convention in the one instrument that houses and sounds it by design.

Coleman's tunes and improvisational style, however, did remain close to that design in their chromatic palette, however loose the brush strokes that palette has fueled. And this particular pianist had developed his free style in his formative years in direct reaction to Coleman's early recordings. Here they both are, Coleman in his 70s, Kühn not far behind, their powers and lines well established and forged by now. The result is a real slice of the vision and spirit of their musics, separate and together.

The first piece, "Faxing," is a lively if ginger dance to stake out every bit of the chromatic grid. The players nudge each other with conversational phrases, playful cries and clever turns, childlike experiments, inventions. When it all culminates in a unison melody played with the least restraint and most relish, what is composed and what was improvised declares itself immediately, in a wonder at the reversal of their usual platform-catharsis roles.

Kühn, especially in "House of Stained Glass" and "Night Plans," suggests an Andrew Hill-ish concept, more than the usual European claim on Cecil Taylor's laser-like approach: melodic and contrapuntal dance giving way to jagged rhythm and phrasing of stark, dark chords, clusters at the liminal edge of Coleman's triadic envelope, fragments of broken mirrors, each gleaming, mercurial, and murky, that gradually fall into place on a plane. The mind moves from open and facile to open and unknowing, a cloud bearing rain.

The rain comes, with flashes of lightning in "Refills," then balmy downpour in "Story Writing." The trumpet in the former tops off vulnerable a cappella sax figures that skip and trip into sudden unexpected destination tones, and piano responses that hit and miss them; tonality need not be "deliberately neglected" if one is free to wander on and off its old trails at whim. The trumpet blurs their lines, and the piano helps it do so, just as it proactively helped the sax blaze its new ones. Coleman's solo opening of "Refills" is echoed by Kühn's solo piano launch of "Story Writing," joined briefly by the sax to sound the tune, then left alone again, to shift radically to another solo, stormed just as radically by the rhythmic sawing of the violin.

The rain swells to a free-rhythmic patter of notes in "Three Ways to One," and recedes through "Passion Culture" into a final visit to the more chordal sonorities of tracks "House of Stained Glass," "Story Writing," and "Night Plans." The final track, "Cyber Cyber," returns to the opening gavotte of free play, only now with the gusto of a victory celebration instead of the tentative steps of the first dance.

Coleman escapes the sterile perfection of system, even his own, by peppering it with little cries up his saxophone's register. Neither Eduard Hanslick nor Adolphe Sax himself could have imagined the poignant, vocal beauty this "ugly" instrument would someday sing. Kühn's chords suggest that Bach, the spinner of lines and joy whom his contemporaries thought so thorny and old-fashioned, might easily have imagined it.

Vinko Globokar: Modern Times

Chailley's third octave spans the Age of Exploration, covering the spread of Europe to the Americas; his fourth covers its nineteenth- and twentieth-century global expansion as colonizers and rulers, and all the clashes of cultures and ideas that that history encompasses. Musically, the fourth octave stakes out the intervals of the major and minor second as now stable, as indeed they physically become in that range (as brass players know viscerally), and as the French Impressionists and German Dodecophanists made them systemically (first through the whole-tone, then through the chromatic scale, respectively). All twelve tones are thus delivered from their previous diatonic hierarchy to a chromatic equality. (As Schoenberg put it: "Dissonances . . . are merely more remote consonances in the series of overtones."[57])

Albert Mangelsdorff's description, above, of free improvisation as "spontaneous, collective" and "free" composition resonates with the "fantasy" and "free composition" (noted through Schenker) of earlier Western art music. It also mirrors Vinko Globokar's account of the same move, from the contemporary composer's rather than the jazz improviser's side. Globokar described to me one of his groups that specialized in free improvisation, the quartet New Phonic Art, as "musicians who were playing all this other music, from this culture of ours, until one day we decided that we no longer needed a composer."

When German identity began to coalesce around the idea of political unification of its states, the nationalist stirrings extended to music: Beethoven's first wave of Romanticism, the passionate embrace of the world as a whole, of the universals, seemed to be finding concrete form in this new birth into a family of nations. German music ripened from there through Mahler and Schoenberg into what seemed as much a birth of the new as a passing of the old. The public and its leaders turned outward more than inward, as at other times in German history, and their fascination with "others" stemmed from a desire to inform their own emerging "self."

It was in this atmosphere of post-Romantic openness that all of Europe, starting with France and Czechoslovakia, but especially Germany, first took jazz into its own "serious" musical discourse. Hunkemöller traces the first European compositions with African-American stamps to Debussy, then notes that those most influenced by the music were, first, the generation born between 1900 and 1907, to debut their work in 1922–31; and, second, those born in the 1920s, to make a strong showing in the 1960s. The first group included Ernst Krenek, William Walton, Kurt Weill, Mátyás Seiber,[58] Michael Tippett, and Dmitri Shostakovitch; the second included György Ligeti, Hans Werner Henze (to mention those best known outside Europe; he might also have mentioned Karlheinz Stockhausen), and others of Globokar's generation.[59]

The two-generational phases of this reception and assimilation were, first, perception and incorporation of African-American music as folk art (gospel, blues, ragtime, boogie-woogie, dance music) to be characterized/caricatured compositionally; and then postwar treatments of it more as something to converge with than to portray, as the serialist and later free-jazz styles and artists overlapped.

The earlier cultural semantics of jazz centered on modernity, the urban, the declassé, decadence, cynicism, the grotesque, the vulgar; later came wit, the proletarian cry, exotica, vitality, and freedom. These associations led to new concepts of sound, which ripened from metonymic sound-iconography to a new model of partnership, which in turn benefited European composers in terms of seriousness, competence, and (especially) spontaneity (that is, when they converged with rather than portrayed the music, they had to deal with improvisation, rhythm, and form in less clichéd ways, even as the improvisers had to retrain their own bodies' ingrained habits of jazz riffs and licks).[60]

Globokar has a reputation both as a jazz/free-jazz improviser of seminal influence (especially for trombonists) and a notable composer of new European art music (especially for the trombone). His parents emigrated in 1929 from Slovenia to France, where he was born in 1934. In 1947, the family returned to Slovenia, where he was educated in the Communist school system. The Yugoslavian government sent him to the Paris Conservatory to study and train to become a professor and teacher of the trombone in Ljubljana; he managed to extend his studies and eventually gain French citizenship. His work as a musician led him to travel throughout Europe and the United States all his life. Today he lives in Berlin (where he also lived from 1964 to 1968, during the early free-jazz years), retains French citizenship, and works as a teacher part of the year in Italy.

He started New Phonic Art in 1968 with saxophonist Michel Portal and percussionist Jean-Pierre Drouet (both French) and Carlos Alsina (an Argentinian composer who played keyboards and piano). The group specialized in free improvisation and played some two hundred concerts throughout Germany and France between 1969 and 1982. Globokar was also part of the legendary team at the Institute de Recherche et de Coordination Acoustique/Musique (IRCAM) in Paris, headed by Pierre Boulez in 1973. His track record in both "new" and "improvised" music authorizes him to speak about the relationship between improvisation and composition from a more conventionally formal (and informed) perspective than most of his peers on one or the other sides. He spoke to me about it in his Berlin apartment, touching on the social and psycho-physical aspects of the improvising body, and its relationship to composition.

I had two paths into the '60s: I knew all those composers, like Berio, Stockhausen, and Kagel, I played their music as an interpreter. I was in Stockhausen's group that did the first performances of his *Aus den Sieben Tagen* (*From the Seven Days*). I started to improvise also, but I was already improvising in jazz, so it was much easier.

When I compose, I am from this European school, which is rational, very structuralist and so on. So the improvisation is something necessary for your health. But as a composer, I ask this: what do you get as a composer from an improvisation, what are the useful consequences? I think it's on two levels.

One is to see how the behavior of musicians goes – how they interact, how they carry themselves. I tried to do a kind of interrogation of these processes, through imitation, or following someone, or doing the opposite of what someone was doing, or developing an idea, or to have a contradictory attitude and propose something completely different, etc. So these categories that you can track in an improvisation, you can also use them in composition.[61]

The second level is the way an improviser struggles with an instrument. Of course, that's not a problem if you simply construct a vocabulary of personal clichés; I avoid this, so that I never work at home on any kind of prepared structures. When I improvise, I try to go on with what I have to do in the moment. This means that the mind is always faster than the instrument, and that provokes different accidents, and in these accidents you can find material for composition.

And in Europe, in the compositional field, you now had the element of chance, which also came from America, from John Cage. It's not improvisation, but let's say it's a process of deconstruction of things. Then the aleatorical techniques, where the composer still writes out certain elements, but the ways of handling them in performance are left to the musicians. Then the graphical devices that began to appear, through Ligeti and others, in notation in the '60s; then the music consisting only of verbal instructions, such as Stockhausen's.[62]

I would say that in the '60s there was an explosion of language . . . Before the '60s you still had kind of a common spine, to which you could refer. This was serial music.

Serial music is so named because of its systemic connection with Schoenberg (it is music constructed on a "series" of chromatic pitches, the tone row). A working definition of postserial music, here, is that which shifts the center of generation from pitch relationships to other musical elements, such as timbre, texture, dynamics, rhythm, chance, or improvisation.

Hans Kumpf's (1975/1981) book *Postserial Music and Free Jazz*[63] starts with a short historical look at jazz as a music that from its beginnings was something warm, hot – an immediate folk music, oral-traditional, an organic bodily expression – engaging (sometimes confronting, sometimes courting) something cool or cold, in European literate-traditional formalism. Free jazz's overlaps with serial and postserial music are simply the most current manifestations of that engagement. The music has oscillated between its hot and cool tendencies, starting with the dialectic expressed by the Armstrong–Henderson and the Paul Whiteman groups, moving similarly through the Swing, Bop, and Cool eras. Free jazz – certainly in America, and especially in Germany – made its appearance as a "hot" expression. Kumpf sees it as something of a full circle back to the very hottest (most African) beginnings.

Like Globokar, Kumpf points out the importance of the player's relationship to his/her instrument: there must be a total physical fusion; the mental – emotional, psychological, spiritual – expressions must unfold within that physical context, wherein what comes out of the mind immediately comes out of the instrument (through the body playing it), and what comes out of the instrument is always what is happening in the body-mind.[64]

Given that, Kumpf finds it useful to think analytically and theoretically about breath and heartbeat: the arc of a breath determines the shape and contour, the development, the duration of sounds and phrases for wind players; the heartbeat (and by implication other such organic rhythms) provides the *Urgrund* for discussions of pulse, rhythm, periodicity. In European tradition, he claims, such an aesthetic and praxis resonate mostly with those of the Romantic period, for its ground in nature more than culture.[65]

The act of music-making, especially free improvisation, demands a continuous self-fulfillment and development of one's highest (and most unblocked, most accessible) potential; the entire human being, in all personal and collective contexts, is called upon to find its unfoldment in the terms of the art; there is no question of role-playing – of "performance," in the sense that both cultural theorists and interpreters of pieces and genres use the word.

The sociopolitical implications of this fact were seen in the zealously and overtly expressed agenda of both French and German musicians and intellectuals when free jazz took center stage in the days of the 1968 student riots. The persecution of the music by various totalitarian states – and the neglect, or the attempt to contain, control, or dismiss it in less violent but no less threatening ways that occurs in the capitalist West – becomes more readily understandable when the connection between the abstract and the concrete is made, and when one understands who has an interest in keeping them divided, as Kumpf observes.

His synopses of "New Music," "Free Jazz," and "Postserial Music" sketch musical and music-historical ground stressing the intertwined destinies of new and improvised music, especially from the 1960s, and their juxtapositions. He presents seven key characteristics, outlined in a 1969 lecture by the composer Ulrich Süsse, drawn from the works of Cage, Henri Pousseur, Luciano Berio, Krzysztof Penderecki, Mauricio Kagel, Luigi Nono, Earle Brown, Anestis Logothetis, Stockhausen, Gottfried Michael Koenig, and Murray Schafer: the aleatoric, static "sound painting," musical theater, structure (organic, not prescribed by a paradigmatic system), graphic notation for improvisation, electronic music (with "musique concrète," or taped pieces), and group improvisations.

Table 1.6

	Free jazz	Postserial music
	the process (energy)	the product (the work)
	emotional	rational
	intensity	cool
	spontaneity	construction
	linear phrase	structure-/material process
dynamic	loud, organically evolving	quiet, sudden differences
tempo	fast, driving, pulsing	slow, static, no pulse
rhythm	also organic, unfolding in an arc	sudden differences, contrasts
articulation	mostly legato	varies, much staccato
instruments	mostly wind (breath) & percussion (heart)	strings, peripheral percussion
pitch	subjective, imprecise	objective, precise
composer/interpreter relationship	usually the same person	usually different people
way out of musical impasse	emotional expression	through the composer's material
fixed composition	usually only for ensemble sections	mostly flexible
variety of fixed codes	often orally transmitted by composer, and flexible	explicit, on the score

Kumpf follows his description of the two musical discourses with a structuralist comparison between them (Table 1.6), one that shows clearly the hot–cool dynamic (1975/1981: 14–16). His appellation of the dyad as Dionysian-Apollonian (echoing Schoenberg's "Apollonian Evaluation of a Dionysian Epoch")[66] signals his own deep Western-historical/mythological siting of it. His quick rundowns of both the German and English scenes, seen with an eye for groups and artists who seemed to cross the line between free jazz and postserial music into some workable synthesis, read very much like glances at something in the early stages of its process. He seems to see more of such fusion in the English scene (his section on it is longer, he reflects more), and his German examples have more of the misbegotten "Third Stream" feel to them, and look now similarly dated and transient. (In fact, since his book, more English–German confluence has occurred, through the work and collaborations of the next generation of German improvisers such as trumpeter Axel Dörner and reedsman Wolfgang Fuchs.[67])

Back to Globokar

"Then [the music] exploded into so many different directions," (from serialism) Globokar continues. "So in the '60s I expressed myself with the word 'we,' because I was part of groups: *we* had projects, etc. Thirty years later I express my identity only with the word 'I.' Who is then the person who uses the word 'we?' These are only groups who want to defend and promote something commercially. So you have groups dedicated to schools of composing, such as 'the new simplicity,' 'the new complexity,' 'the neo-romantics.' They are groups proposing something, but they are not projects with utopian character. They are projects with an agenda to say, 'this is the truth.' This phenomenon holds no interest for me. If you look into each country, you see some people composing, researching something on their own, not monumental, but experimental things."[68]

Bert Noglik, a critic from the former East Germany, also looks at the clashes, overlaps, and syntheses of the improvisational and compositional aspects between jazz and this century's European art music.[69] He muses over the dynamics between internally generated (freedom in form) and externally provoked (freedom to form) change in musical/cultural paradigms (the Second Viennese School is an example of the former, jazz in Europe of the latter). The promises of free jazz, he claims, emerged as possible solutions to problems posed earlier by Western composers (for examples, he invokes composer Ferruccio Busoni's critique of the conceptual limits set by a succession of motives, and Schoenberg's exhaustion of the chromatic scale). Noglik, like Globokar, sees in John Cage the link between such pushes of the European envelope and free jazz, with one foot in (Cage's erstwhile mentor) Schoenberg's world and the rest of his body on the foreign terrain of the American West Coast, with its Asian influences. Anton von Webern, Stockhausen, Berio, Iannis Xenakis, Olivier Messaien, Witold Lutoslawski, Penderecki, Kagel, Ligeti, the aleatory music of the 1950s: Noglik mentions and/or cites from these as having as direct a bearing as Cecil Taylor and Albert Ayler on much of European free jazz and improvised music.

This from German free-jazz trombonist Günter Christmann is just one example of many expressions of that connection: "[T]he cohesion possible to music was never demonstrated, in my opinion, more clearly than by Webern . . . His work gave me the desire to play, as much as possible, only the most essential tones. In this regard his music has been an enormous blessing to me" (Noglik, in Wolbert [1997: 527]). What Christmann expresses here, as is obvious with many post-*Emanzipation* improvisers who turn to new compositional options, is the deliverance from the cyclical repetition of hierarchical pitch patterns playing out their power relations – which improvisation had to bear before free jazz – and to an ocean of sound whose play of currents is virtually infinite, where improvisation can "simply swim," as Christmann put it. Schoenberg's *Klangfarbemelodie* (literally, melodies made from sound colors rather than pitches; functionally, something like hocketing) principles, and their later development into timbral-textural and unpitched "noise" (*Geräusch*) music by composers as expressive ends rather than effects, became important for improvisers as means. So optioned, they suggest that any ("modern") compositional system or idiom could be similarly used, as part of a necessarily disunified field, without being dogmatically adhered to. A jazz lick could give way to noise to *Sprechgesäng* to silence to melody to environmental noise, as desired in the moment. The way for something like what Braxton calls the "affinity principle" – subjective taste, attraction, intention, decision – was thus cleared to develop as the unifying force in improvised music, replacing that of paradigmatic system. "Musical identity was allowed a certain self-knowing/constant element within each [such non-idiomatic] expression; the question of assimilation versus variability of materials became thus moot. In the tension between identifiable quality of personal expression and unforeseen results lay new possibilities for the development of improvised music" (Noglik, in Wolbert [1997]: 527).

Noglik cites Cage's comments about the Western composer's relationship with percussion music being the entry point to a liberation from pitched to unpitched music, and from there to *Geräusch* music, once the rhythmic structure as meaning-matrix is left behind; he (Noglik) explains Cecil Taylor's pianisms as rich convergences between jazz tradition and this percussive/rhythmic-to-noise approach. He mentions Americans Richard Teitelbaum and George Lewis for their improvisational convergences with electronic new music in the more jazz-traditional backgrounds of their collaborations with Steve Lacy and Anthony Braxton.

Interesting from an American point of view is Noglik's discussion and citations relating to the controversy over how and to what degree composition and improvisation, in this particular scene's convergences, are alike and/or different, and how they bear the stamp of, respectively, European and African-American influences.

• Is improvisation really "instant composing" and composing "frozen improvisation," or are they two qualitatively different processes?[70]

- Is European composition the fruit of a long historical process not yet granted (African-) American jazz improvisation, thus beyond personal-emotional rhythmic-tonal (gross-body-based) expression and into one that is transpersonal-cerebral arhythmic-atonal (subtler-body-based)?

Noglik sees the gross as a healthy balance to the subtle expression, but even to frame such a comparison to explain how much more naturally suited European improvisers are to incorporating new-music influences into the improvisational flow of the jazz idiom than are African-Americans (as he does, and as several of the European musicians I interviewed did) brings an element to the composition/improvisation discussion begging attention here:

- is the proper understanding of the relationship of a body's heartbeat to its central nervous system really one of gross to subtle? are some *chakras*, to put it another way, really "lower" than others? can the "high" ones be healthy if the "low" ones are not, and vice versa?[71]
- correlatively, is the problem with social hierarchy solved not by forcing and institutionalizing egalitarianism but by seeing that all parts are healthy, equally valued, forced on no one, and have synergetic access to all other parts?
- is the development of a (literate) composition tradition indeed teleologically contingent on a backgrounding oral-aural cultural history, such as the West's, as Noglik suggests? or can it spring forth haphazardly and sporadically to serve rather than subsume the growth of the oral-aural tradition?[72]
- is the role of personal identity and its idiosyncratic intentions what is crucial to the development of a sophisticated improvisation, as opposed to the desirability of the subsumption of such identity and intentions (as proposed and demonstrated by Cage) in the development of a sophisticated composition?

We will return to these questions in chapter six. Noglik's own conclusion is that the internal change-generator of new composed music and the external one of free-jazz improvisation have brought European music and culture to a rich field of problems and possibilities that bind them more deeply and faster than anything either could have encountered without the other.

Globokar's body of work evinces his fascination with words, and the voice, and the connections of both with music. His account of how his music has come to depend heavily on narrative, a dramatic impetus behind the music, led me to ask him how it drew from his Yugoslavian roots. "I did two works on Yugoslavian folklore. One is *Kolo*, for trombone, and one is *Étude for Folklora*. The tradition of the bards is poetical, more than musical, improvisation. It was very interesting, for instance, during the war. The musicians called the *guslars* originally improvised on texts describing the historical wars with the Turks. During the war, in '40–'45, they started to improvise long epics about what Tito did!" he laughs.[73]

The modern nationalism rooted in Romanticism has become intolerable in some European quarters (especially Germany), benign in others (especially Scandinavia). Globokar, like most Germans, is keenly sensitive to its problems in the home of his birth (Slovenia, the Balkans).

I am a person whose identity doesn't really come from something like nationality . . . There are musicians who are flags for their country; I am not a flag. I
was living eight years in Yugoslavia, here now for thirteen years, born in France,
came back and lived there for thirty, thirty-five years, then I was in the States
quite a lot, and lately Italy every month for five days. So if you ask me what I
am, I can only respond that I am communicating only with individuals in my
work. I never sit and drink a coffee with a nation.

Nonetheless, with the *Emanzipation*, national styles did emerge from what had
previously been a more or less pan-European imitation of American music, even
as the first pan-European collaborative network of the previously less linked
national scenes also emerged. The *Emanzipation* was a "think local, act global"
movement away from the hegemony of both jazz and Western music, a movement that European scholarship has discussed most recently in terms of, again, its
nineteenth-century roots.

Two

Italy, Scandinavia, England, Holland, France: Five Ways In

Be careful when you write. These are real people who have given their real lives, sweat and tears for this music.

– Dagmar Gebers

I had an experience at a performance by Cecil Taylor in Berlin that echoed the shock of the free-jazz movement's first hours, some four decades earlier. For that matter, it echoed the shock African-American music has been to many in the West all along.

Taylor was leading a band of ten American and European musicians, booked in a midsized hall for FMP's 1996 Total Music Meeting. He began by emerging from behind the stage's back curtain while the house was completely dark. We discerned his presence only through the sound he vocalized, an animal-like, growling mutter spiked with occasional little cries. We gradually sensed him in the darkness as he stumbled around the cluster of instruments on stands, making his noises.

Then his bandmates started trickling in, in similar fashion. Within five minutes, all were milling about so as if they could not find a thing, vocalizing like several different species of wild beasts converging on a nighttime watering hole, eventually ending up at their stations. They picked up their instruments as if, indeed, animals encountering them for the first time, making rough noises that gradually coalesced into more obviously human patterns. (The musicians later told me the game plan for the event was a series of solos, duos, and other combinations, mixed in with full group play, all of which was unprescribed improvisation, and much of which departed from even that loose plan in the spirit of the entrance.)[1]

My own reception of these opening moments, informed by long exposure to Taylor's music, prepared me to expect anything that involved improvisational dance and vocal-verbal behavior, loosely defined, as well as piano playing. More broadly, what he and the others had just done called to mind two Eurasian schools of performance that have had close collaborative ties with the European improvisers of the *Emanzipation*. One was the Fluxus movement, born in the 1960s from the visual arts scenes in Europe, especially strong in Germany and Holland, as well as Korea.[2] The other was the Japanese *butoh* dance movement dating back to the 1950s, some of the elder founders and later members of which started working with European improvisers in more recent decades.[3]

What both movements have in common is what might be called an aesthetic of the ugly and the archaic: both were conceived in reaction against cultures felt to be so refined, mannered, "beautified," and ritualized as to be intolerably repressive of healthy personal and social bodies. Both were also reactions against the imposition of Western (American) culture through war and occupation; and both professed and evinced a conscious quest to reconnect with a primal animistic-shamanistic identity that preceded the rise of civilization's great religious and secular systems, namely the Confucianism, Buddhism, Judeo-Christianity, Capitalism, and Communism most pertinent to their respective situations.

The results of this aesthetic in performance were improvised expressions of bodies defying conventions of beauty, propriety, nobility – expressions often unsentimentally sexual, often overtly mimicking animals, often irrational, in both movement and voice. Being aware of all this, and assuming the famously well-read Taylor was too, I pondered his performance in its light.

Eerily, the band's opening moves had a mirror image in the audience. Four people arriving late, two attractive young women and two men, one young and one elderly, all dressed for a formal evening out, picked their way in the dark through the crowd. They irritated many in the audience as they navigated clumsily through aisles seating an overflow of bodies, fans trying to concentrate on Taylor. When they finally got to their seats in the back, right in front of me, they listened for a few moments, conferred, then exasperated the people around them again by getting up and leaving as disruptively as they entered.

The synchronicity of this slapstick made me wonder if they were plants Taylor had put in the audience to reflect what he was doing on stage, to make a statement that would show this passive flock of concertizers, so worshipful of his escapades, their true colors when exactly the same activity had no bourgeois stamp of approval for the eccentricity of "artistic genius," safely caged in the Romantic ritual of a "performance." As it turned out, when I met them at the bar downstairs, they were very nice, intelligent, cultured, casual fans of mainstream jazz, and it was their first time hearing Cecil Taylor – and they absolutely hated his music and the persona they perceived him projecting. The younger man and his partner were Finnish, the older man and his young lady friend were, respectively, German and Polish, and all spoke a little English.

Expressing no overt racism, they explained their intensely negative reaction to the music in terms of good and evil, describing Taylor as a devil producing evil music. They saw him enthralling his younger protégés (all white – and the young man alluded to white Americans as a populace spawned by the losers and outcasts of European civilization) with his evil charisma. I responded that, as an American from a pluralistic society, I had to refrain from immediate demonization of others as the natural response to such feelings. Our conversation went on to such mutual demonizations (mostly interracial, often between the "civilized holy" and the "barbaric unholy") that had taken place, in both American and European history, and the genocides and murders that had resulted from them. These people reminded me of the music's real power. They had experienced insult and injury, and had not found the emotional distance, surrender, or new life beyond that shock that the music also delivered. American pluralism cultivates open minds and tolerance, but often by reducing real (threatening) power and meaning to a mélange of spectacles that relativize each other out of their primal thrusts (and threats).[4] The four friends reminded me of a danger and passion I had come to take for granted, to forget.

For their part, however, a little emotional distancing and perspective was just what was called for. They left feeling less threatened when I suggested that Taylor's persona and music were simply the marks of one man among many, marks that had a right to their place on the planet despite the negative reactions they might provoke in other quarters, marks they (and all) could take or leave without feeling obliged either to support or suppress.

The synchronicity between Taylor's opening and the four friends' own entrance to the concert, complete with the two provocations of hostility thereat (Taylor provoked them, they provoked the audience, both unintentionally), stands for me as a reflection of the West talking to itself through the African-American voices of the free-jazz pioneers: nonwhite to white, "low" white to "high" white, woman to man, "God's" people to "Satan's" (variously cast), rage to outrage, in America. In Europe, that piece of American theater translated to the Eurasian histories of tribal outsider against imperial(ized) insider, peasant against noble, worker against capitalist – and, in the *Emanzipation*, anarchist against hierarchist.

The clash between the hostility of these four and the audience's reverent/controlling embrace of Taylor as Romantic hero also reminded me of the vehement conflicts between, mostly, white jazz fans and scholars in both Europe and America, from the very beginning and all along, over what constitutes "pure" and "authentic" jazz: "black," with "black" well defined by "white," and kept in its place. This, as opposed to "black's" supposed sell-out concessions to commercialism; or black's claim not only on the performer's/improviser's/power-of's place in the food chain, but also on the composer's/manager's/power-over's place (read: "black laying claim to white's place").

The point is not about the intellectual-aesthetical abstractions of style bound to time and place and art form so much as about physical-social phenomena handed down viscerally and subliminally through generations of bodies.[5] A correct understanding of what transpires in the makers and hearers of this music may conceivably be a matter of life and death, or, at least, health and sickness, in the personal and social bodies.

Overview

In 1955, every Western European jazz scene was undeniably derived from imported American artists and recordings, the occasional exceptional talent proving the rule.

By 1975, those scenes had all come into their own distinct national identities and musical terrains, and strong senses of individuation from American jazz. The line between amateur and professional had blurred, along with that between composed and improvised, and serious and popular; the line between recorded and live had become contested in new ways; and the line between the group and the individual had been redrawn, to centralize subjectivity and thus capture the personal as the political. Joppig's notion of the Western composer's art shifting from the manipulations of pitch patterns for string-topped, wind-bottomed orchestras and chamber groups to the improvisations and rhythms of wind-topped, string-bottomed jazz big bands came to full bloom on Western European soil.

Furthermore, that musical revolution unfolded in the same bodies, logics, and passions as a global social-political one, burning on the line between Eros and War, to take on the unHoly classist Religion underpinning racism, colonialism, imperialism, sexism, and all-around power-overism from the inside of its Beast's own youth. And if the classless, cooperatively prosperous global utopia that was supposed to replace all rapine exploitation and evil on earth failed to materialize, at least some of the effects of many of the visionary actors, musicians included, felt no less dramatic, at the time. Things did change, in both Western and Eastern worlds, in ways that arguably added up to one big victory of Eros over (apocalyptic) War.

With the sensibilities of a modern German, Jost (1997: 501) pointedly disavows a chauvinistic reading of these new European identities, some of which expressed themselves as militantly as their black American counterparts. The militant nationalisms of earlier decades were still too fresh in memory, no one wanted to think about an upsurge of some pan-European, teutonic soul coalition, even from the left. Nevertheless, the distinguishing traits of national scenes were distinct enough to quickly become stereotypes. To describe the three strongest identities:

- the English became known as "sound researchers," introverted collectivists cultivating an aesthetic, both musical and social, of quiet anarchism, static and non-hierarchical in both *Gestalt* and sound;
- the Dutch were the louder anarchists, the humorists, the ironists, the rugged individualists and musical gamesters/tricksters radicalized around their own folk and music theater traditions, nudged by the Fluxus movement to provide a grassroots populist (if also intellectually esoteric) alternative to both commercial pop-schlock and pompous classical *Kultur*;
- the Germans were the "energy" players, picking up on the most intense and improvisatorily streaming aspects of American free jazz, including their emotional affects (of aggressive political protest, in the West, and rapturous, often melancholy, spiritual reverence, in the East). Indeed, Germany was the scene that most attracted labels of "white power" to match the "black power" cry from America.

The fact that these differences in national personae flowered in response to the different free-jazz voices was clear proof that "free" did not mean "blank slate," that there was something still there to replace the mental maps of "jazz" being left behind. It was something like the ethnic identities of Balkan peoples re-emerging after the fall of Communism, but, as was also true of African-Americans reaching for their own pre-American roots, none of these new assertions of European identity could properly be seen as simple regression to some past self, long repressed and now reclaimed. They were rather identities forged under the restraints and constraints of earlier American and European jazz, now bursting free.

The recordings of the time, partial and narrow a chronicle though they are, reflect the rise of the "free" in Europe's own scenes. As seen with Globokar and Mangelsdorff, these had the feel more of sporadic nudges against the envelope than of critical mass reaching the tipping point; free improvisation and composition were still more like scouting forays away from, than systemic revolution of, the center. In France, pianist Martial Solal and pianist-bandleader Jef Gilson; in Great Britain, saxophonist Joe Harriott, pianist-composer John Dankworth, pianist Stan Tracey, Scottish composer David Mack, trumpeter Ian Carr, pianist-composer Michael Garrick; in Italy, Giorgio Gaslini; in Poland, Krzysztof Komeda and Tomasz Stanko; and in Scandinavia, saxophonists Lars Gullin and Bernt Rosengren, and trombonist Eje Thelin are some who began to forge improvisational and compositional styles and voices rooted in Europe rather than America, and/or to shift the compositional platforms from American blues, show tunes and standards to other folk and concert material closer to their homes.[6]

Jost and most other writers on European free-jazz history generally agree that alto saxophonist Joe Harriott was its original voice. A black Jamaican immigrant to London in 1951, he was the first European to develop anything comparable with what Ornette Coleman and Cecil Taylor were doing in America, and he did it independently and unaware of them, at around the same time. His memory calls up the presence of the "Black Atlantic," with which Western European countries have an historical relationship, through colonialism, more akin to the visceral one American whites and blacks share than is Europe's own very different historical relationship with African-Americans.[7] Harriott had led standard bop groups throughout the 1950s, then started experimenting, in his quintet of exceptionally educated and skilled bandmates, with free-form, free-time, a-tonal spontaneity. His three LPs from 1960 to 1963 enjoyed great critical and popular success in both Europe and America.[8]

Sadly, Harriott proved to be about half a decade ahead of his time, at least for Britain. He continued working – mainly in collaboration with some of his old bandmates and with classical Indian musicians, in their "Indo-Jazz" fusion projects – making his last recording in 1969.[9] By then, he had abandoned his earlier free-form approach, and had spoken critically (in 1963) of what he saw as Europe's slavish devotion to American models. The more widespread combustion of European recordings following Harriott's musical boldness took place between 1966 and 1968, and they were indeed more an echo of and response to the Americans than was Harriott, or than they were to him. But those from England were arguably the most radical, in their anti-American tenor, an expression of English purism reacting to capitalistic decadence.[10]

England's pre-free scene is closest to America's in its socioeconomic dynamics. Unlike other countries, where political or cultural criteria would be this music's making or breaking locally, if records did not sell in England, their music did not take. England also had the closest home-grown version of American race relations, from its Caribbean and South African links, fostering the emergence of that first real European free voice. But its black identity fell shy of the bigger impact of the American Civil Rights and Black Nationalist movements and the correlative fore-grounding of free jazz as an expressive vehicle of same, just as England had always fallen shy of the direst frays of the Continent's wars, both class and military. Still, Harriott might be called the Django Reinhardt of European free jazz, for his solid grounding in both Western music fundamentals and jazz so independently of America.[11] His outspoken position as such set the tone for England's later sharp turn from America to the keeping of its own counsel.

Bibliographer John Gray's exhaustive documentation of articles, books, and other media published in several languages from 1959 to 1991 on the free-jazz movement in America and Europe captures in a single reference the thirty-year stream of that literature and history. In doing so, it also sites the American/English-language literature on the music within the larger Western dis-course on it in other languages. Even a quick scan of Gray reveals European popular, specialist, and academic presses, compared with their American counter-parts, to be more closely knit. It also reveals a perception of the free-jazz move-ment in Europe as itself more closely knit with both mainstream jazz and the larger cultural discourses, with more writers who played, and players who wrote about, the music – many as serious amateurs, rather than people trying to make their living by their music. In stark contrast to the American scene, Gray's data evince little if any adversarial relationship between players and press in Europe, or between "out" (avant-garde) and "straight" (conventional) players. Accordingly, European discourse pays more serious attention, especially to issues of both theory and praxis, to both the music and its role in the culture.

The French and German sources on their national scenes have no good English-language counterparts, so I will pay most attention to them here. The German sources on Europe as a whole, I think, are best; and those on England and Holland have excellent English-language counterparts, so I will touch on them more cur-sorily.[12] The details I choose are those most pertinent to Europe as a whole, and to the musical and cultural issues explored here.

Italy: Un/Conscious Winds

My personal connections to the Italian scene are through the two recordings with Anthony Braxton on which I played trombone.[13] More broadly, they are through the very language of Western music's notation of its performance dynamics (volume, phrasing, tempo, and so forth) every music student learns. Even the German music of the last three centuries, which I have described as the recent Western torchbearer, drew its inspiration and power from Italian culture and music, starting with rulers such as Frederick the Great (Berlin) and August the Strong (Dresden), around the time of my country's gestation and birth, and of my ancestors' (1735) migration to it from their Black Forest homeland of Württemburg.

Pianist-composer Giorgio Gaslini is cited by Italian jazz historian Luca Cerchiari (1997) as a major embodiment of the quest for an Italian meld between jazz and art music traditions. Gaslini's 1957 *Tempo e relazione* for octet, debuted at the San Remo Jazz Festival, Cerchiari calls the first synthesis of jazz and serial music techniques in Europe.[14] Gaslini's example in this and similar work stands out from an otherwise rather undistinguished *Emanzipation* scene, and prompts Cerchiari's discussion of "conscious" and "unconscious" approaches to improvised music.[15]

The author's "Unconsciousness" is revealed by the musician who masters a style without a "perception of its sense," either musically or socially, and without a sense of how it can be changed, or of how or why or whether it should be. He lists Jelly Roll Morton, Duke Ellington, Charlie Parker, Dizzy Gillespie, George Russell, Charles Mingus, Eric Dolphy, Anthony Braxton, and James Newton as examples of African-American masters "conscious" of these things, challenging and changing European aesthetics so as not to be "victimized" by their implications, either personally or socially. Even "unconscious" players – such as the still-derivative, imitative European jazz stylist engaging the American idiom – will display the elements of their own cultures' different backgrounds, but the "conscious" ones know how to strike just the right balance between the idiom imposed and the idiosyncracies, composed or improvised, that signify his or her own identity. Italian jazz, then, is best when it displays its own such awareness and mastery, in a seamless expression that avoids the "Third Stream" trap of bundling without bonding conflicting elements.

As in the more northerly cultures, some Italian critics saw (both approvingly and not) only African-American jazz as "real," and Italian jazz only as imitative. Cerchiari sees the influence of such critics holding so strong in the decades after the Second World War, bolstered by the press and presenters there, that when the free-jazz craze grew throughout Europe in the 1970s, Italian locals adhered to the same tradition of imitation (think "spaghetti westerns") – now of Ornette Coleman, Archie Shepp, Albert Ayler, and Cecil Taylor – when their other European colleagues were striking out with their own voices.

After Gaslini, Cerchiari lists a dozen or so, all wind players, who span the two generations from pre-free up into free eras and demonstrate this distinctively Italian aesthetic.[16] (Some of these players – Enrico Rava, Gianluigi Torvesi – did make a strong showing in the first hours of the *Emanzipation*, as will be discussed.) After describing the scene as a whole in the 1970s as still too derivative, he compares it at its best to Wayne Shorter's "harmonic ambivalence," "chiaroscuro-coloring," and "characteristically Lydian" tonality, along with metrical asymmetry, all serving a "deep European poetic" set against the framework of post-bop and post-cool American styles. The use of folk melodies, from Sardinia, Sicily and elsewhere is more common, conceptually reminiscent of (his example) John Coltrane's rendition of the English folk song "Greensleeves."

In the early 1980s, these trends took conscious form in the Rocella Jonica Festival, conceived as a meeting place for jazz and Mediterranean culture. When this scene does finally blossom more strongly in the groups, it blossoms into something like what the English free scene might have been had its Gil Evans-like "high" orchestrations set the tone for its improvised music more than did its "low" influences from within, and the German ones from without.[17]

Cerchiari's parting glance covers the two labels I recorded on, and similar enterprises, calling them a part of a rich and vital grassroots business milieu that nonetheless should have more official state support, in recognition of the music's integral value to the culture. His assessment applies equally to most European post-free scenes: economically self-reliant labors of love for all concerned, and stronger as such than their American counterparts, as well as in the official support, however slight, they do attract. His plea for more official support rests on an assertion of the music as deeply Italian, much as jazz activists in America have pled its central American identity as just cause for elevation of its official status. In America, the success of that plea for pre-free has been at the expense of post-free jazz; and the greater success of post-free scenes in Europe, modest though it is, has lifted the American musicians in its circles on its own rising tide.

Scandinavia: First Contacts

Europe's northernmost venues had the distinction of hosting and recording some of the first European performances of the American free-jazz groundbreakers. Cecil Taylor played the Jazzhouse Montmartre in Copenhagen with Albert Ayler and Sunny Murray in 1962; the same year, Archie Shepp and Bill Dixon played in Helsinki, Finland. Ayler, who had spent several years in Europe in the army, made his first recordings in Denmark with Swedish and Danish sidemen (a musical mismatch by all accounts, dampening Ayler's interest in future such collaborations). Litweiler (1984: 156) hears "nineteenth-century European nursery rhymes" in the folk themes of Ayler's major recording *Ghosts*.

The Scandinavian scenes of these years and since emerged as a kind of Nordic microcosm of the Continental *Emanzipation;* Jost and other writers on the subject generally leave them out of the list of "strongest free scenes." Like France, their long and relatively strong history as hosts to African-Americans arguably positioned them more to provide well-informed sidemen to the leads of those guests than to cultivate their own local or pan-European versions of "free." Still, one might add to the thumbnail descriptions of the three most prominent national scenes above (England, Holland, Germany) something like "the folkish, lyrical, Nordic-Romantic sound," as presented by distinctive exceptions to the sideman rule. From Lars Gullin to Jan Johansson to Jan Garbarek, it is a sound and style with particular traction in Europe's post-*Emanzipation* branches into world music.

Denmark

Oslo, Stockholm, and Copenhagen, like Berlin, Paris, and Amsterdam, got early and ongoing exposure to jazz through their importance on shipping and, later, airline routes. The nearest northern neighbor to Germany, and southernmost of the three Scandinavian countries, Denmark had a steamship line to America, and enjoyed much concourse with the German scenes until Germany banned foreign musicians in 1931. Likewise, it had a rich exchange in American recordings, beginning in 1919 with the Original Dixieland Jazzband, until 1932 foreign exchange restrictions. By the late 1930s, some internationally famous soloists had emerged from Copenhagen's cosmopolitan milieu, most notably violinist Svend Asmussen. Its major airport brought in American musicians before German occupation, some of whom stayed. Even during occupation, the Odeon label cornered the European market for jazz recordings.

Along with Cecil Taylor's group in 1962, Montmartre hosted numerous touring jazz artists throughout the 1960s. Kenny Drew, Dexter Gordon, and Ben Webster moved to Copenhagen, and many young Danish musicians, such as alto saxophonists Franz Beckerleeand and Karsten Vogel, turned to playing free jazz. For the most part, however, the jazz-rock-fusion scene proved to be more influential in Scandinavia than in countries to the south, as it also would do in England and East Germany. More than in the latter two, that influence would grow and endure, along with the world-music connections, to contribute to Scandinavia's distinct identity in Europe's general individuation from America, and the later blooming of same. Trumpeter Palle Mikkelborg and keyboardist Kenneth Knudsen would bring the fusion with rock to term, as Norwegian Jan Garbarek would the local/global, folk/early-Western/free synthesis.

From 1960, the all-amateur status of Danish jazz musicians changed to professional, albeit short of a full-time living wage. From the Kenton-style big band led by Ib Glindeman came the neo-bop Jazzkvintet '60, whose members would also be the source of studio hires by the state-supported Radio Jazz Group, which lasted from 1961 to 1986. Bassist Nils-Henning Ørsted Pedersen and Mikkelborg were two from this generation and scene who would become strong presences in the transatlantic post-*Emanzipation* circles, especially Pedersen, for his work with Cecil Taylor and Anthony Braxton. Pianist-composer Finn Savery had a Third Stream group, and Danish percussionist Marilyn Mazur played with Miles Davis and Wayne Shorter.

Alto saxophonist John Tchicai had the most impact in the circles of our concern. He was born in Copenhagen, in 1936, to a Congolese father and Danish mother. He started playing violin as a child, switched to alto saxophone and clarinet at sixteen, and studied at the Conservatory of Music in Aarhus, Denmark, for two years. He moved to New York City in 1962, and recorded with John Coltrane on *Ascension*, Albert Ayler on *New York Eye and Ear Control*, and co-founded his own groups, New York Contemporary Five and the New York Art Quartet, establishing himself as one of the main voices in the new music jazz bore then. He moved back to Denmark in 1966 and co-founded Cadentia Nova Danica in 1967 to give voice to the music there. Since 1991, he has lived and taught in California.

Copenhagen's counterpart to Boston's Berklee College of Music, the Danish Rhythmic Conservatory, was established in 1986 (still, some of the best new musicians, such as pianist Ben Besiakov and guitarist Jacob Fischer, are self-taught). Throw in the annual Copenhagen Jazz Festival, begun in 1979, and the Copenhagen Jazzhouse (1991), and the Danish jazz scene's current health and hopeful future would seem amply sketched. However, Wiedemann's (1997) survey of Denmark's jazz scene from 1960 (much like Cerchiari's of Italy) paints one rich in contributions of individual players to the international scene, but poorer than other European countries in its home base, in terms of general social and official support.

Sweden

Westin's (1997) picture of Swedish jazz history suggests that it, like Denmark's, is more interesting for its sociological than its musical dynamics. That said, he sees its relative isolation as fertile for the development of a distinctly European identity in the one soloist its generally high valuation of technical and artistic virtuosity produced, baritone saxophonist Lars Gullin. Gullin's (1950s) "folkloristic, romantic" lyricism – similar to the impact Norwegian saxophonist Jan Garbarek would have in later decades – Westin acknowledges as signaling to the outside world a uniquely "Swedish" jazz, but he sees it as more the expression of an original personality apart from the herd than as the herd's mouthpiece. (Of course, that kind of synchronicity between personal and cultural identity is just what we are fishing for in these waters.) More Tristano-cool than Parker-bop inspired, Gullin collaborated with many Americans in Sweden, for the Swedish label Metronome and others.

As the rock revolution waxed, jazz-as-dance music waned, along with official support for it; the least radical jazz scenes were the hardest hit. The tough times the 1960s posed for Swedish players, true to their history, produced some tough go-getters, including those who turned to free improvisation for their part in the wider *Emanzipation*. Two from the 1950s' mainstream scene were noteworthy for their artistic integrity through that hardship, and for their music's engagement with the changes in jazz then: tenor saxophonist Bernt Rosengren and trombonist Eje Thelin, both leaders of their own small groups. They were already positioned at home and throughout Europe to be heard, and both incorporated free improvisation into their music then, briefly, returning to their mainstream roots in the 1970s.

Of most interest here is drummer Sven-Åke Johansson, who moved to France to work as a mainstream jazz drummer there, and went on to become a major voice in European improvised music. Among his peers, he matured into one of a few elder statesmen of the music who extended his role as first-hour innovator into a mentoring collaboration with the new generation of players, eschewing the rest on his own youth's laurels.

More characteristic of Scandinavian identity in this music, in the tradition of Lars Gullin, was pianist Jan Johansson's "Jazz på svenska" (Jazz in Swedish), a treatment of Swedish folk melodies that was more idiosyncratically original than imitatively American in approach. Johansson also began collaborating with symphony orchestras, choirs, and chamber groups, a new and provocative move at the time. Older musicians such as Arne Domnérus and Putte Wickman then began playing in churches; and jazz composers such as Bengt Hallberg, pianist Nils Lindberg, and bassist Georg Riedel wrote various pieces hard to place in a genre. These all bespoke a trend of jazz's move from club-and-restaurant to concert contexts, and thus to some of the cultural status and support formerly accorded only classical music.

Part of that new status included a place in music schools, such as the College of Music in Göteborg. As jazz became a Conservatory repertory art ranging from early to modern styles, lively forums such as the Nefertiti Jazz Club in Göteborg and an international autumn jazz festival in Umeå, a northern university city, joined Stockholm's Fasching club as parts of Sweden's scene. Virtuoso players and canny, facile composers, mostly in the post-bop modal-chromatic vein of John Coltrane, soon outnumbered local opportunities, thus traveled more than other European musicians. Bassist Palle Danielson, with the world-music connections of the Rena Rama quartet; and pianist Per Henrik Wallin, with a style attracting descriptors such as "intuitive," "idiosyncratic," "eclectic," "spontaneous," and "original" are two examples of such master craftsmen with fingers in the winds of musical change blowing then. A new generation of players with roots in rock would shape the scene in the 1970s and beyond.

A motif of this chapter's overview of the national scenes that flowered in the *Emanzipation* is the phenomenon of the big bands and collectives. I look at them with the same heightened interest I have in trombonists, because of my experience playing in and organizing them. When I did my first project in the late 1980s with such a band in my own Pacific Northwest region, a reviewer in Seattle's *Earshot* magazine wrote, "Picture yourself in a perfect jazz world where every city with 100,000-plus inhabitants has a resident orchestra that can play the music of visiting composers like Anthony Braxton, Carla Bley, or George Russell. Sound unlikely?"[18] His words convey how unusual such a "perfect jazz world" was next to the American reality. In Europe, however, the amateur tradition had created a milieu much more like the reviewer's wistful dream. When the free-jazz movement presented Europe with the chance to self-actualize as a culture in jazz, this milieu was the perfect soil for the flowering of local, self-determining collectives and initiatives of recording and performing.

I tend to see these groups in the light of Joppig's notion that the soul of the art of Western music migrated from the symphony orchestra and chamber group into the jazz big band and smaller combos, both as musical ensembles and as microcosmic reflections of their societies. Their proliferation by the hundreds in Sweden's grassroots network of amateur local scenes proved the healthiest outlets for the plethora of formally educated and trained players and composer-arrangers who would otherwise have been "all dressed up with no place to go." Such bands – exemplified by the best known Tolvan Big Band, in Malmö – played a sophisticated original repertoire as well as stock American charts, featured guest professionals as soloists, and evinced a pride and joy in the art that was essentially out of any professionalist, commercialist, or elitist loop.

Norway

As in East Germany's Zentral Quartett (discussed later), Norway's free scene revolved around a "Big Four" – bandmates Jan Garbarek, Terje Rypdal, Arild Andersen, and Jon Christensen – as the players most key to a distinctively Norwegian sound. Garbarek had grown up listening avidly to Coltrane, which led him to the three Coltrane torchbearers most noted for their combination of folkish melodicism and phrasing and rich, expressive timbral palette (Albert Ayler, Archie Shepp, and Pharoah Sanders). Combined with Coltrane's interest in world music, this early influence steeped the Norwegian tenor player in the possibilities of the saxophone's voice and the jazz musician's access to material. After he sat in with George Russell's band at the Molde Festival, at age eighteen in 1965, the American bandleader hired him. By 1970, he was thoroughly schooled in Russell's "Lydian Chromatic Concept of Tonal Organization," the foundational theoretical abstract of American jazz's neo-modalism.

In a classic example of individuation worthy of the Scandinavian Romantic precedent of original genius giving birth simultaneously to personal idiosyncracy and to the sound of a people and their place (think Sibelius, Nielsen, and Lars Gullin), Garbarek responded to these initial formative influences with his own statement, which effectively launched his career beyond their shadows. *Afric Pepperbird*, recorded in Oslo in 1970, was one of the first releases on German Manfred Eicher's ECM label; it was followed two years later by *Triptykon*, a trio with Arild Andersen and Edward Vesala. The "Nordic sound" eventually came to signify ECM.

By that point, Garbarek had turned the rubato melodic and timbral raptures and dramas of Albert Ayler's trio into his own treatments of Norwegian folk music, echoing from its native's point of view Ayler's similar dips in the European-folk well. The resulting sound and style would accommodate well subsequent influences from rock and fusion, world music, and experimental groups such as the AACM and the German free players. (Its evocation of northern broodiness had a special cachet in my home region of the Pacific Northwest throughout the 1970s and '80s, through Garbarek's collaborations with pianist Keith Jarrett and with Ralph Towner, guitarist in the group Oregon.)

Manfred Eicher's ECM catalogue has defined a European aesthetic of the Nordic Romantic meeting the Eurasian primal no better expressed than by Garbarek. The saxophonist's Norwegian roots led him from his initial engagement with American jazz to something older and other, and closer to home:

> I started with Coltrane's 'Countdown', in which there are a lot of notes. I copied that and then had to 'weed my garden', you know? It was like one abstraction was being piled upon another: contact was being lost to where the music came from.
>
> Norway's isolation has preserved much of its extremely old melodies and extremely archaic ways of singing. It was very important for me to listen to folk music from all over the world, but especially from Norway. You might say I live in a spiritual neighborhood which is scattered geographically.

Garbarek recorded *Rosensfole* with traditional singer Agnes Buen Garnås: "The ornaments she is using in her music sound Middle Eastern Turkish or Arabic in a way. This really fascinates me, the connection between Norwegian music and that of India via the Balkans and Asia Minor . . . I found the most 'exotic' music right in my own backyard."[19]

The double album *Rites* begins with sounds Garbarek taped in an Indian village. It includes a tribute to Don Cherry, who turned Garbarek's first attention to folk music as improvisational platform. Nordic folk traditions underpin "It's High Time" and "Her Wild Ways," and Georgian conductor-singer Jansug Kakhidze performs his "The Moon Over Mtatsminda" with the Tbilisi Symphony Orchestra. Garbarek's saxophone blankets the voices of the Norwegian choir Sølvguttene on "We Are the Stars," a setting of a Native American poem. The album's music was performed on tour in 1998 in Germany, Austria, Hungary, France and the United Kingdom. Much like Joachim Kühn with the choir in Bach's Leipzig church, Garbarek has also collaborated with the Hilliard Ensemble, improvising to its performance of early Western music.

Taken together, the Scandinavian scenes are interesting for their blend of British and German influences, see-sawing to the fore and back through the flux of history and persons. Their gender, generational, and racial dynamics all played out more overtly, transparently there; their grasps and assertions of their own national-cultural identity in the music have been similarly more straightforward and balanced than elsewhere in points southerly. Their contributions to the larger pan-European expression of that identity have been major, in players such as drummer Sven-Åke Johansson and Jan Garbarek and their younger torchbearers. It seems fitting that they were among the first to host the major new voices of Ornette Coleman, Archie Shepp, Albert Ayler, and Cecil Taylor, thus introducing them to the rest of Europe.[20]

Holland: Rugged Thinking Men (Ur-New Yorkers, Ur-Harlemites)

> Dutch music is always about the strong idea, associated with the remarkable individual. And about clarity. In some way the musical activity serves to illustrate the idea of the remarkable man.
>
> – Evan Parker (in Whitehead [1998: 46])

Whitehead (1998) will tell you all you want to know about the details of the Dutch scene. I will give you my take on Dutch writer/producer/radio host Michiel de Ruyter's thumbnail sketch in German, highlighting the voices these "remarkable men" brought to the pan-European arenas of Germany's Globe Unity Orchestra and FMP label, and the Western-musical and social issues driving their history.

By 1957, the Amsterdam jazz scene was split between the echoes of American bop and cool styles. In 1958, the first recordings by Cecil Taylor (*Looking Ahead*) and Ornette Coleman (*Something Else*) hit town. A few entrenched players grasped them, but mostly the younger ones, who quickly categorized them under the traditional Western "avant-garde" rubric: the "new thing" was simply the next stylistic phase of an art form, as bop and cool had been earlier . . . nothing exclusively "African-American," nothing distinctively "European" or "Dutch," in theory, at first.

Twenty-one-year-old drummer Pierre Courbois started the Original Dutch Free Jazz Group (it was that) in the eastern city of Arnhem, but its impact was relatively parochial, minus recordings. The Theo Loevendie Three LP *Stairs* featured contemporary classical bassist Maarten van Regteren Altena, and drummer Johnny Engels playing Turkish rhythm patterns under composer/reedsman/pianist Loevendie's modal and timbral echoes of Coltrane, Dolphy, and Coleman. The rhythmic elements in bass and drums corroborate Joppig's view of rhythm and improvisation superseding harmony and melody in jazz, here with their decidedly European voices.

The Dutch free scene would develop very much as a man's game, but nerdy more than macho, something like the audience Dave Brubeck attracted. This, in contrast to an especially strong showing of women – similar to neighboring queendoms of Sweden and England – in its pre-free history. Rita Reys, Babs Pronk, and Anny Xhofleer, all singers, had established themselves as substantially (and as unusually, for their time in Europe) as Americans such as Billie Holiday and Ella Fitzgerald and their foremothers. (Was the Dutch man's new-and-improvised game driven to "kill the mothers"?)

Bandleader Boy Edgar took full practical advantage of Amsterdam's thick exposure to live American jazz greats, modeling his own big band on Duke Ellington's: much group play worked out on the fly, little on paper, sectional riffs memorized and led by Edgar or someone else's whim. Edgar had a hungry ear for modern sounds and experiments – singers Abbey Lincoln and Nina Simone, and altoist Eric Dolphy were among his guests – and Willem Breuker and other pillars of the *Emanzipation* years in Holland started out with him. The new-music (as well as a world-music ethnic) cast to such jazz avant-gardism came through Edgar's temporary replacement as leader, composer-saxophonist Theo Leovendie – again, a personality comparable with Brubeck and his redoubtable alto saxophonist, Paul Desmond. Leovendie had a love for Turkish music, and thus worked often with Eastern meters and scales, founding his own group Consort in 1968 to further his own music.

Pianist Misha Mengelberg, drummer Han Bennink, and saxophonist Willem Breuker would become the key players in the Dutch free story. Mengelberg was twenty-four when his trio won the Loosdrechts Jazz Competition, in 1959. He had grown up steeped in classical and contemporary art music and jazz, had heard the work of John Cage at Darmstadt by 1958, and was developing his jazz style in the footsteps of American pianists Thelonious Monk, Herbie Nichols, and Brubeck.[21] His quartet with alto saxophonist Piet Noordjik, Bennink, and Jacques Schols on bass was, by the mid-1960s, one of Holland's best jazz groups on the international scene. Its rhythm section had recorded with Eric Dolphy on *Last Date* in 1964, just before Dolphy's death in Berlin (Mengelberg spoke of Dolphy's harmonic "simplicity" much as he did of Art Tatum's); and in 1966 the quartet was invited to play at the Newport Jazz Festival. All but the bassist also recorded some live radio broadcasts with Ayler bassist Gary Peacock in that year. Direct connections with major emerging American free voices were thus solid as the Dutch scene found its own things to say.

When he started playing his own repertoire exclusively, Mengelberg, with his German colleagues from Wuppertal, was involved with the Fluxus people and aesthetic of the time: musical games including chance and the organic, along with the kind of self-asserting improvisation Cage and others eschewed (and the Germans asserted with a vengeance; Mengelberg is closer to the English improvisers, in that sense). Cecil Taylor's 1967 visit, says Whitehead, suggested to Mengelberg how free improvisation and experimental composition could really work together, two areas he had worked in separately before that. He was reaching beyond modalism, beyond Coleman's idiosyncratic tunesmithing, beyond strict atonality, seeing all those as part of something like "the death of jazz."

Noordjik dropped out as the music "went out," to be replaced by thirty-three-year-old Willem Breuker, in 1967. Like Mengelberg, Breuker was as much composer as improviser, though more the autodidact than formally trained, more the man of action than the contemplative philosopher Mengelberg was, and more the music-theater performer than the esoteric avant-gardist. Growing up listening to Schoenberg, Bartók, and Count Basie, Breuker's persona as a composer is most obviously informed by Charles Ives, whose musical juxtapositions of art and life were hot stock elsewhere in the European free scenes, most clearly in Peter Kowald's projects with the Globe Unity Orchestra in Wuppertal.

Han Bennink is a drummer – fired up first by Max Roach and Kenny Clarke, then by Sunny Murray – who can swing like a grandfather clock and jump in and out of time in any and all directions on a moment's notice. He did both relentlessly as the group struck out for its own music beyond the jazz and contemporary-music boxes. With Mengelberg and Breuker, he formed the Instant Composers Pool (ICP) in 1967, adding to the musical discourse forging itself around the blurring borders between the planned and the unplanned in music.[22]

Breuker left in 1973 to form his own Kollektief, a group of free players for which he wrote and orchestrated more closely than usual for most such groups then, and few such since (some of Braxton's groups are notably similar in that way). Bennink went on to play mostly spontaneous duos with as many frontline players on the international scene as possible, and Mengelberg was instrumental in initiating official support and promotion for jazz and improvised music in Holland through institutions such as BIM (the Union of Improvising Musicians, 1971), SJIN (Stichting Jazz [and Geïmproviseerde Muziek] in Nederland), and STEIM (Studio for Electro-Instrumental Music). The ICP label and that of Breuker's BV-Haast put out the recordings that put the Dutch free scene on the map. Interestingly, the ICP trio itself never recorded, except in larger formations built around it.

Whitehead notes that:

> There are a number of traits peculiar to Dutch improvised music, not all of them on this list: an ability to abstract from the music of American jazz masters; an impulse toward theater, role play, humor and ironic distance from one's own creations; killer chops that make all the horsing possible, the virtuosity that assures any fuck-up is deliberate; a certain clunkiness Louis Andriessen calls "lousy Dutch wooden-shoe timing" (1998: 4–5).

I would add that, especially in Mengelberg, there is in Dutch improvised music an aversion to trance, or the spiritual rapture pervading much from America and taken up by much of Europe elsewhere, particularly East Germany and Norway. Mengelberg dismissed Coltrane's "snake-charming" music, was more attuned to Dadaism and Surrealism, and more to the musical idea than its experience in performance (although, on the other hand, he liked what the later flamingly Romantic pianist Keith Jarrett was then doing in Coltrane-influenced saxophonist Charles Lloyd's group). One cannot imagine the Dutch players hooking up with, for examples, the Moroccan *gnawa* musicians Peter Brötzmann joined in the 1990s, or the Tuvan or Greek musicians of Peter Kowald's later circles, all traditional voices steeped in the practice of music for its trance potential. Composer Louis Andriessen, with his words about Taoism, comes closest to anything overtly mystical that Whitehead reports (15) from Holland.

Kees van Baaren, a composer who directed the Royal Conservatory in the Hague when Mengelberg was a student there, was the part of the latter's circle who embodied its link with the larger Western tradition. Whitehead (14–15) describes him as a gentle anarchist, and a champion of serial music, which had generally been disfavored in Holland (Mengelberg [in Whitehead 1998: 49] reports a mutual interest with John Tchicai in "Africanizing the 12-tone row," but more through Webern than Schoenberg – i.e., more impressionistically than systematically – again, a Stravinsky-ish penchant for the game and pastiche, for detachment and irony over the deadly serious Schoenbergian deconstruction and reconstruction of the totalizing system). Van Baaren's pedagogy around tonal music framed it as a dead, albeit important tradition (as Mengelberg felt about "jazz"), but with that was also a sense of Western music that was continually dying and resurrecting, not stopping with any one "death." He presented Palestrinian counterpoint as akin to serial music, in the way the polyphony of melodies developed in relation to each other (much like Coleman's harmolodics), rather than by some underlying harmonically hierarchic plan.

A more visceral, less cerebral link to Western tradition – only one such example of many European improvisers – is pianist Leo Cuypers. Whitehead relays Cuyper's childhood immersion in classical tradition via his church-composer grandfather. Cuyper's description of learning to mimic the styles of Bach and Mozart as a seven-year-old singer echoes similar reports of American jazz musicians with hymns in the black church, as does his later pattern of learning and making music more by ear than by reading it. It was a background common to many of the musicians discussed here.

Michel Waisvisz is Holland's major contributor of electronics to European improvised music. Electronic music as a European avant-gardism started out very much more oriented to product (*das Werk*) than process than did its acoustic counterparts, largely because of the way the technology developed. Waisvisz in Holland, Keith Rowe in England, and Richard Teitelbaum in Italy's Musica Elettronica Vita moved the medium from taped pieces to live performances; George Lewis developed it to interact with his solo trombone work; Wolfgang Fuchs, with fellow Germans Georg Katzer and Thomas Lehn, and Englishman Tom Leed; and Evan Parker would further develop this area of the music, which has come to flourish.

Mengelberg's statement that "all music is political" characterizes the Dutch scene, according to Jost (in Wolbert 1997: 508), but if so, it does so more subtly – culturally more than socially – than English, French, or German free scenes. Mengelberg's own musical persona seems more playful than political, but it is rooted in the Surrealist/Dadaist tradition of the intellectual manifesto reactive to the high culture of all the social and philosophical hierarchies at issue here. His notion of "construction," Fluxus-inspired, stems from the idea of all system and structure in art as ephemeral, transient, female more than male – like the ad hoc "city" assembled by nomads for a specific function at a set time (indeed, like the temporary couplings of x chromosomes that define femaleness), rather than those built by and for power to endure (like the unchanging and ever embattled y).

Breuker, who started out as fiery and serious as Brötzmann on *Machine Gun*, went on to lead something more like a circus band with his Kollektief – something only post-free improvisers could perform in, yet diverging from the dead earnestness of the loud German and delicate English strains that were both almost as dogmatically spontaneous and anarchic as their pre-free predecessors were orchestrated and hierarchic. The Instant Composing Pool, for all its solid fusion of esoteric improvisation and new-music games of composition, shared with other Dutch initiatives and voices an ethic of offering an alternative popular music to counter that of commercial mass culture. Whitehead (1998: 60) cites Breuker shrugging off the May '68 student uprising in France as something the Dutch had foreshadowed in '64 or '65, thus as hanging back from it in spirit to something of their own. Likewise, bassist Arjen Gorter describes the thick tangle of music with theatrical contexts as well established in Amsterdam throughout the '60s before the first reports of the AACM's stagings of same in America.

The subtlety and depth of this Dutch *Emanzipation* identity has endured since those first hours, and resonates so with the latest blooms in the Eastern scenes of a couple of decades later, when the political had to be both subtle and deep, as well as socially efficacious. For now, it serves well as the entry point into the more overtly political dynamics of the other Western scenes (England, France, Germany), which, if they fell short of the transitions to utopia they clamored for, nonetheless ignited quite effectively their kindred movements in the Eastern bloc.

England: The Queen is Alive, Long Live the Queen

With Chailley's chart, in chapter one, I gave an archetypal female face to the northern European peoples who forged "the West" out of their mergers with Mediterranean civilization. The British Island countries evoke that face in music history as suggestively as the Continental ones do its male counterpart.

Figure 2.1 is Joppig's way of conveying the world from which American music's European side developed. The painter, Joseph Danhauser, was a Viennese portraitist generally regarded as producing sentimental depictions of his society. He shows us men – stout-looking, responsibly bourgeois men of action, reading (intellectual) men, passively contemplative (cloaked in the chair) and passionately creative (Liszt at the piano) men, worshiping at the shrine of music, its icon the bust of a man (Beethoven). Farthest from our point of view, the storm clouds frame this music/man with their darkness and light – the *Sturm und Drang* of Romanticism, the sun sunken (into cold, dark, industrialized iron, just above music's/man's head) in the West (toward the New World). Nearest to us, a woman is rapt at the player's feet, her own face hidden in her devotion to the music/man.

In these essentials, an Austro-Hungarian-German sense of the West emerges that is crucially different from that conveyed by figure 2.2, and by the art of the previous hundred years out of America and England (American culture's more overt Germanic influence).[23] In it, music-making seems unmanly, music makers are mostly women. A casual observer might wonder whether they are the thralls, birds in gilded cages, or the lion tamers, Victoria's angels doing their duty of civilizing men. In any case, whether submitting or manipulating at their keyboards, they are rarely seen at the feet of a man who is playing, nor is a man usually seen at the keyboard (when a male is, it is usually a feminine boy).

The Greek-rooted hierarchical classism characterized by male dominance and master–slave relationships, a mind-over-body rationalism that translated into man-over-woman and man-over-boy power plays and paradigms – all made virtual religion through both the process and products of Western literacy–took different

Fig. 2.1 Gunther Joppig (in Wolbert [1997]: 9) characterizes this 1840 Viennese painting as an illustration of "European Music Culture." (Josef Danhauser, *Liszt am Flügel*, courtesy of the Nationalgalerie, Berlin.)

Fig. 2.2 Leppert (1993: 164) describes this depiction of a Victorian English music lesson as a cultivated ritual of female domesticity. (George Dunlop Leslie, *Home Sweet Home*, oil on canvas. Private collection. Photo courtesy of Sotheby's, London.)

shapes in the Continental and the British Island countries exerting most influence in nineteenth-century America.

Continental Romanticism emerged as a re-embrace of nature, including the mystique of place, the local, and the body, as the supreme goods. This was a turn away from the legacies of Platonic idealism, otherworldly theism, and Enlightenment rationalism and universalism that had mistrusted that goodness, abstracted or conscripted it to serve the agendas of church, science, civilization, and/or empire. Romanticism emerged in France, but weakly; ignited and waxed, differently, in Germany and England; then found a marginal but increasingly important niche in America. In patriarchal German lands, it was a preservation of local identities against Napoleonic imperialism; in more matriarchal England, it reacted to the grossness of its own industrialization and capitalism; and in America's countercultural (and English-descended) forefathers, beginning with the spirit of Thomas Jefferson, it moved through Walt Whitman, Ralph Waldo Emerson, and Henry David Thoreau against that same Anglo-Saxon grossness overtaking America. New England composer Charles Ives and German-American author Henry Miller picked up its torch to become the European-American forefathers linked most directly in spirit and influence, through the Beat generation of writers and the American Experimentalist composers, to the *Emanzipation*, which comprised assertions and coalitions of European local identities against the hegemony of American culture, even when the latter was more loved than hated.

The most widespread, grassroots influence of Romanticism came through literature, which was more accessible than its counterparts in painting and music. German Romantic literature is a male affair; its English counterpart reflects the greater presence of women with their male peers, as in society as a whole (contrast William Blake's marriage-grounded version of the Romantic mythos with Goethe's unrequited-love, and recall Mary Wollstonecraft, Jane Austen, and the early women's rights movements in England). Both the Enlightenment and Romanticism also re-embraced the potential and sanctity of the individual, of democratic and humanistic ideals, over the classist hierarchy of the *ancien régime*. Enlightenment (in France, America, and later Russia, disastrously) from the top down, Romanticism (in German and Italian nationalism, also disastrously) from the bottom up.

But again, as reconnections with ancient Greece, both intellectual movements also continued to tolerate and perpetuate the social realities, albeit with more tension, that tainted those ideals from their beginnings. Both would spawn oppressions and tyrannies, the former in the form of totalitarian systems and exploitive superpowers, the latter in autocratic, militant dictators. The two-century civil war spanning the northern latitudes from Russia to America can be seen, most optimistically and least cynically, as these two forces checking and balancing each other.

The most patriarchal and literate (Austro-Hungarian-German) aspects of Western music culture comprised, with the French and Italian opera presence in

New Orleans, the high-cultural, seized by the low martial, side of American music's development into jazz-as-art. The music's more predominantly low-cultural (and more woman-friendly and oral-traditional) cast came more through the British (Scottish, Irish, English) folk and music-hall/medicine-show influences on the development of the blues and other rural American folk and urban popular musics black and white. It also came through the prevalence of the piano as both an amateur pastime of middle-class women and a staple of saloons, brothels, music and dance halls, and other "low" venues (jazz-as-entertainment).[24]

To contrast this European male-high/female-low context with jazz's Creole/African parentage, one might glance at the slave songs in America of the same period – by birds in decidedly ungilded cages, as well as a few gilded ones – and recall the matriarchal cast of African-American culture, embodied in women such as Marie Laveau, and personified later by many seminal gospel, blues, and jazz singers (and some pianists): Lil Hardin Armstrong, Mamie Smith, Ma Rainey, Bessie Smith, Billie Holiday, to mention a few of the best known.[25]

These women have few counterparts in the development of European jazz, reflecting the larger point here that while male dominance has been a feature of the classism inscribed in both Western music and jazz, it has generally been more effectively subverted in American than European jazz. Women, mostly African-American, account for roughly ten per cent of the entries in *Grove's Dictionary of Jazz*, non-American women for something more like one per cent of those, and those mostly from the 1950s on. This is not to say that women have not found ways to sing and play, both professionally and otherwise, when they have wanted to, all along, so much as that they have rarely made it into the histories or commercial arenas.

Annette Hauber (1997b) makes this point with her opening lines, and defies it by mentioning little known names in the same paragraph with "Ella," "Billie," and "Sarah." She chooses American women who played typically "masculine" instruments – all other than voice, harp, and piano, which, furthermore, are not as atypical for men – sometimes in famous male-led bands. She attributes the rule these exceptions prove in jazz directly to the exclusion of women from church and court (high) music from the Middle Ages to the seventeenth century, when opera and concert stages began opening up to them.

The women Hauber chose as a cross section of current notable voices in the whole spectrum of international jazz include some but not all who play parts in the particular *Emanzipation* histories surveyed here.[26] Most of her post-free group are singers. While this statistic reflects jazz's conventional relegation of women to the vocalist's role, what stands out about these women is how radically they have extended, from jazz phrasing and scat singing, the range and techniques of the female voice as an instrument. Much as their European male colleagues did for the trombone,[27] these singers – (see p. 323, n. 26 for first names) Galas, Nichols, Dudziak, Tippet, Namtchylak, Brüning, and Lee (the only [African-] American among them, and the late wife of German vibraphonist/reedsman Günter

Hampel, one of the early groundbreakers of the *Emanzipation*) – showed how far and wide beyond conventional parameters they could go.

The next most-represented instrument among them is the piano (four are pianists, only half the number of singers). One of them (Jutta Hipp) was an international German star in the 1950s who played with Charles Mingus and others in New York; her Tristano-inspired style in that context directly foreshadowed the free-jazz years. Two (Carla Bley and Aki Takase) are also composers-arrangers and leaders or coleaders of major big bands; and the other (Schweitzer) is a soloist and frequent collaborator with others, and leader of small groups that helped to school some of the most important men of the first hours of the *Emanzipation*, in which she was a seminal voice herself. French bassist Joelle Léandre, Korean *komungo* player-composer Jin hi Kim, and Danish percussionist Marilyn Mazur round off those in the circles of our focus.

By contrast, Hauber's look at the women who play in a more mainstream style, and who are more or less contemporary with those above, reveals no vocalists, six pianists, one saxophonist, one trumpeter, one flautist, one trombonist, and one drummer. All of this suggests a certain view of women's liberation in both pre-free and free jazz, through one European woman's eyes: it is spreading gradually from a traditional status quo of singers and pianists to the more male-dominated instruments, in pre-free jazz; and, dramatically, back to the actual voices of women, radically altered, in post-free-jazz (especially Eurasian) improvised music.

This increase of European women in the music in the 1950s slightly precedes the emergence of the contemporary women's movement and feminist discourse, which are reflected in the music history since then. Accordingly, as we consider the women who most helped shape the *Emanzipation* in Europe, and at their growing presence in improvised music, the points of most interest will be their continued rarity even relative to their also-rare American counterparts; their relatively strongest presence in England as resonant with the character of the British influences on African-American music; and the character of that music's impact in England, shaping its strong voice in the *Emanzipation* (as also in blues and rock) in the particular ways it did.[28]

The mixed gender symbol I put above the most recent centuries of Chailley's timeline of Western harmonic development extends the logic begun here in several ways. It suggests the mixture of DNA that is offspring in the "jazz" born from Europe and Africa in America. It also suggests the integration and balance of male and female forces; by implication, such a balance goes to the heart of all power-over classism, in its primal unit. The roots of civilization begin with human power over the mother of all mothers, in agriculture; over animals, including selective breeding and castration, for forced labor as much as for food; over the bodies of women, children, and less powerful men, all of whom came to fall prey to the same sort of manipulations and fates as the rest of the nature being civilized. Such thoughts hearken back to those on the "big history" behind jazz, still all too raw in American memory. I bring them up again to underscore the foundational role of gender in classism, and to note some aspects of its musical expressions different, though intertwined, between America and Europe.

Racism, again, has been the face of Western classism more crucial to most histories, both American and European, of jazz.[29] But sexism is the deeper *Urgrund* common to all the music at issue here in both Eurasia and the Americas, and racism is especially less relevant to jazz, especially free jazz, in Europe. But again, the word "sexism" is inadequate to what it is describing, in the same way "racism" falls short of the complexities of "minstrelsy." "Gender minstrelsy," in the music reflecting the culture, is the most fertile phenomenon we can attach to our symbol.

Think of the strategies of feminization and infantilization power employs over its objects. The lone words "bitch" and "boy," as insults spat by a bully at males and females (as "girls") of any age, race, or social status, say it all: neutral biological descriptors are enlisted to define power-over as the alpha male commanding all women as mates and all men as rivals for them, subdued (until a "boy" finally bucks the king off his throne, to take his turn in the same power-over place). With that in mind, consider the ways the one history continued to unfold in America and Europe.

Pitches and Bitches, Boys and Noise

Tracing this gender minstrelsy down the English side that developed through jazz-as-entertainment more than as art music, two things come to mind: it has enjoyed its own arena of feminine power, posing an alternative to the patriarchal one; and that arena is nonetheless in the one-down position to the male realm in the larger arena of Western classism.

After ceding its American colonies, England managed to skirt the violent class warfare happening elsewhere in Europe, through liberal-democratic reforms that kept the monarchy intact as decisively as Continental royals put such reforms down. England's monarchs never enjoyed the absolutism of France and the rest of Continental Europe, but they were relatively free of war on their turf, which was home to the industrial revolution, the Socialist philosophy and movement, and the modern women's movements. This mix of sustained monarchy and democratic reform might be compared with the old Southern patrician's fantasy about a happy plantation: the master (king or queen) is there to serve and make the slaves (subjects) happy to serve and make him or her happy, all within the classist order (think of Robert Altman's film *Gosford Park* as an image of the well-run English manor as Southern plantation).

On the one hand, women could look up to a figurehead of power – the same archetype, for that matter, that African-American singers and keyboardists drew on to construct their own personae, as "Empress of the Blues" (Bessie Smith), "Lady Day" (Billie Holiday), or "Queen of the Organ" (Shirley Scott) – a numinosity rooted in England's first queen regnant Mary Tudor and many since. On the other hand, from Victoria on, that power has voluntarily deferred to the patriarchal status quo, in exchange for some concessions of the British imperial power then waxing in the world (Victorianism was in fact more like Albertism; it was the prince who was paternalistically prudish and protective of the family order and decorum). This was classism's amelioration of the social upheaval most peculiar to England, the women's rights movements that emerged there around the turn of the nineteenth century, which led directly to the rise of their American counterparts, in tandem (again, often conflicting) with the rise of Abolitionism. The Victorian Romanticization of women – the virgin/whore syndrome – proved as effective a classist undercut of egalitarian gender and generational relations as did the slave block, sharecropper farm, ghetto, prison, or the (unextended) nuclear family home itself.

Both the power and the compromise in this Western social history of gender and generational roles have been mirrored by symbols of African-American womanhood both strong and longsuffering – from activists such as Harriet Tubman and Sojourner Truth, to the strong mothers holding the family together through the failures of its fathers, to the "wild women" who both made their ways in the man's world and bore the scars and constraints it put on them. Think of two archetypes of this mix of strength and pathos, Bessie Smith and Billie Holiday: a natural strength and genius bearing as much power and charisma as anyone, male or female, and gross mistreatment and neglect at the hands of men, or of a man's world, by virtue of that very power.

The tension between the power and the compromise produced, in music, a "female eunuch," to borrow from Germaine Greer: the figure of the diva emerged in nineteenth-century America as a feature of the newly commercialized Italian opera packaging itself for international consumption. She was a direct descendant of the male castrati of the former century, and adopted both the power and powerlessness of his character: over-the-top femininity, siren and erotic fool's gold, silly child and bird in a gilded cage all at once.[30]

One can read the Euro-patriarchal grooming/appropriation of African-American music and manhood for high American mainstreaming – that is, for whatever exploitation of blackness whiteness has perpetrated – in the Romanticization of the lone male blues singer (post-slavery, the black-as-oppressed/defiant, the aura behind later Romantic-phallic Heroes of rock);[31] of itinerant saloon piano man (post-Emancipation, the black-as-liberated/genius, leading to later Romantic-cerebral Heroes such as Art Tatum and Thelonious Monk, installed [mostly posthumously, when profits can accrue more to the exploiter than the exploited] on the thrones formerly held by Chopin and Liszt); and of male jazz soloists and bandleaders as "stars" (Romantic Heroes in the tradition of Paganini – or, as Leppert sees them, "artistic freaks," whose aura of hyper- [or, conversely, wounded] masculinity comes at the cost of the manhood it caricatures[32]).

Let's ponder these performance personae of (male) "artistic freak" and (female) "diva" as minstrelsies of gender inherited by and pervading pre-free jazz and literature thereon, and consider how they were challenged by free jazz, both American and European.

Fools Set Free

Leppert recalls a Western view of music, stretching from Plato to contemporary conservative scholar Allen Bloom, as a feminine and castrating force, for good or ill, one put in its subservient place by the alpha males of patriarchy (per both paintings above, differently). His "artistic freak" is a figure grounded in the court fool, the eunuch guarding the sultan's harem, the Italian *castrati*. As English literature scholar Gary Taylor (2000) has reminded us recently, such figures are by no means without power, even erotic and political power.

Jazz cognoscenti are familiar with the way this tradition has played out through American racial minstrelsy, in the personae of artists from Louis Armstrong (as Uncle Tom) to Lester Young (as effeminately vulnerable) to Miles Davis (as machismo and sensitivity both courting pathetic extremes), as also through Little Richard, James Brown, Prince, Michael Jackson, and others. The macho swagger and strut, as much as the queenly falsetto and swish, have delineated the artistic freak's role in jazz, bearing much of its social as well as its musical charge. Kept in its place, it has served the agenda of white hetero male dominance (make the fools sing and dance, sweat and writhe and scream for your profit and amusement, even magnification); threatening to go too far, it has challenged that dominance.

One of Europe's most famous critical takes on this syndrome was Theodor Adorno on jazz, most overtly in his contempt for Armstrong as, indeed, a castrated male.[33] His was a Western position echoed by the (conservative) culture police and policies in Germany and the Soviet Union, by both Nazis and Communists, key (as in America, anti-erotic as much as political) parts of the history ahead. The "good cop" to that "bad cop" shows in the (liberal) phenomenon of the "white Negro" (to borrow from Norman Mailer), in which white masculinity succumbs to the sirens of the black artistic freak's gender minstrelsy and, rather than simply leveling the playing field, assumes a submissive posture that distracts from his dominant position. Signs of this can be seen in some details of the French (as in the Italian) *Emanzipation* scenes, echoing American patterns of liberal praise, reward, and honor that mask control and containment of black by white powers and identities.

I am suggesting these performance contexts as those shaping the history of pre-free jazz in America, and of American black and white professional (business as well as artistic) identities in the music. What is interesting about the different development of pre-free jazz in Europe is the way its scenes were generally polarized between, on the one hand, professional dance bands or symphonic appropriations of jazz that upheld white European gender and cultural norms by favoring Eurocentric over Afrocentric models, from Paul Whiteman to Lennie Tristano – and those as securely fixed within either the low-cultural niche of dancing-and-dining or the high-cultural one of composed concertizing – and, on the other hand, amateur societies where they explored their notions of "hot," "black," "authentic" jazz as a "primitive" art form, or folk music (the legacy of Romanticism's interest in the "pure" "folk" roots of "corrupt" civilization).

Both professional and amateur contexts, so cast, cordoned off the pain and confusion, as well as the deeper psychological and social threats and promises, of
America's serious minstrelsies, of gender, race, and youth (the black as "boy," and
woman as "girl," premised on youth as the elder's property or servant or even rising
heir apparent, rather than a free person in his or her own right, a premise directly
challenged by 1960s' youth movements). This gender/generational stability held
even when the men of the *Emanzipation* began to carry and present themselves as
originals rather than imitators, and were received so in the press: the star system
was decidedly replaced there by the collective (more on this ahead), and
Romantic Heroism clearly became a source of embarrassment more than allure.
Youth as a class was valorized as seizing its freedom and integrity from the venal
agendas of its elders; the young and old guards of the jazz communities clashed
less, cooperated more, and more quickly, than in America. The few women in
those scenes did not stand out for their gender, functioning (like Melba Liston in
America, for example) more as "one of the guys," in the "guy thing."[34]

That is not to say that the alpha-fe/male star system was not challenged first by
the African-American creators of the music, specifically by the overt collectives
(AACM, BAG, NYCO). At the same time, the old gender minstrelsy continued
to play itself out through some of the most seminal players as part of the norms
they were confounding: Sun Ra's untrumpeted but uncovered homosexuality
extended the court jester archetype into that of ancient hermaphroditic mystery;
Ornette Coleman's comments about the stream of sexual invitations his performances elicited, and his turn away from the role of black stud on the block in his
words about castration, signaled both the power of the role still holding sway and
his unease with it; and Cecil Taylor's gayness has conveyed, like Ra's, detachment
from, more than reactive pandering to, the loop of the straight white alpha male
game.[35]

Generally, the turn free jazz brought to the music's performance personae has
served to defuse glaring polarizations and imbalances of power, including those of
patriarchal heterosexuality as normative. The different expressions of manhood
and womanhood by the players embodying free and post-free jazz, whatever their
sexual profile, contrast starkly with even their closest pre-free predecessors for their
redirection of the erotic charge from a problematic public to a safer private place.
It is a move similar to the one in 1980s' Russian jazz, which enjoyed its own version
of the *Emanzipation* in large part by finally eschewing political expressions in the
music altogether, after frustrating decades of trying to make music and cultural
policy, per Plato and Party line, conform. Giving up that dream is what made it
come most true. Likewise, walking away from the problems Eros had accrued in
jazz was what began to solve them, and to unlock the power they had been
choking.[36]

England: Quiet Anarchy

The postcolonial mix in Holland and England of Indian, African, and Caribbean voices could well have brought their free scenes a predominantly "Black Atlantic" identity to match the African-American one in those first colonies that later became New York and New England. The work of both Joe Harriott and South African pianist Chris McGregor and their bands clearly suggested the potential of this identity. More "English" and "Dutch" both in the pan-European *Emanzipation* mix, however, has been the coterie of improvisers and experimental composers emerging from, rather than drawn into, the culture.[37]

London's Little Theater Club was to this emergence what Minton's in New York was to bop. Around its house band the Spontaneous Music Ensemble (SME), it functioned from 1966 as a research laboratory for the cultivation of the English sound: more ascetic than ecstatic; live and improvised electronics rather than taped *musique concrète*, or executions of tape loops; a balance of winds, strings, and percussion more than an assertion of one at the expense of the others; and a dogged, even dogmatic, eschewal of traditional harmony and melody and meter.[38]

Trumpeter Ian Carr is another of those musicians-who-write (privileged here) among such sources. His 1969 group Nucleus was the first jazz-rock/electronic fusion group in Europe, post-Miles Davis; previously he had worked with saxophonist Don Rendall and pianist Michael Garrick on his own original (not American) repertoire in their quintet. Carr's *Music Outside* (1973) is a definitive look at the early British/European scene, giving much space to close musically and broader culturally literate portraits of its main artists.

Carr's complaint about the general neglect suffered by the British artists, compared with their counterparts on the Continent, resonates tellingly with that suffered by their African-American counterparts in the similar commercial, linguistic, and Anglo cultural milieu of North America, only without the racial aspect. He cites Coleridge to convey his central point:

> The darkest despotisms on the Continent have done more for the growth and elevation of the fine arts than the English government. A great musical composer in Germany and Italy is a great man in society, and a real dignity and rank are universally conceded to him . . . In this country there is no general reverence for the fine arts; and the sordid spirit of a money-amassing philosophy would meet any proposition for the fostering of art, in a general and extended sense, with the commercial maxim – Laissez-faire. (vi)

Carr cites German radio as recognizing jazz as the third major Western genre, an equal with the others, and laments that the British free players get more exposure and support there than at home.[39]

Supporting this point, and contrasting starkly with both the activity in Great Britain and the amount of print Germany devoted to its own smaller free-jazz scene from the beginning, the English-language coverage of the British free-jazz scene is scant until the 1980s.[40] The journal *The Wire* began in 1982, and went on to become one of the major international commercial publications covering the post-free-jazz (new and improvised) scene both in Europe and internationally. (It has since become more integrated into the music industry, much like *Rolling Stone* magazine developed with rock.)

Ansell's piece on the British scene for *The Wire*, three years later (around the time of Litweiler's [1984] and the major German retrospectives on Europe, by Jost [1987] and Berendt [1986]), begins to historicize it, presaging Wickes's recent (1999) comprehensive history. It depicts the British players of the 1960s as having used "free jazz as merely a developmental stage to a yet more radical form of music making" (1985c: 27). Ansell writes of the "first generation" that

> These musicians took what they perceived to be the central values of the new Black American music – most notably its vibrant assertion of the qualities of spontaneity and co-operation and its fundamental relevance to the cultural and historical position of its creators – and reshaped the music to suit their own needs. In doing so they incorporated elements derived from the European traditions, most notably certain aspects inherent in Stockhausen's intuitive works. (1985c: 27)

Carr sees four watershed groups in this early wave: AMM, composer Cornelius Cardew, saxophonist Lou Gare, guitarist Keith Rowe, and drummer Eddie Prevost in a group with the most overt link to the European and American avant-garde concert music (rather than the jazz) community, including the Sonic Arts Union (with Alvin Lucier and his circle), and Musica Elettronica Vita (MEV, featuring Richard Teitelbaum);[41] the People Band, whose agenda was mainly to blur distinctions between performers and audience; Spontaneous Music Ensemble (SME), John Stevens's group that moved away from their original jazz impulse into a Cage-ian universe of small, refined sounds; and the Music Improvisation Company, forerunner of Incus, on a similar conceptual track with SME but into a more dynamic, varied and active sound world, and with active ties to the more free-jazz sides of the *Emanzipation* elsewhere in Europe.

To those, one could add Mike Westbrook's idiosyncratic, symphonic sorts of pieces for big bands designed to showcase conspicuously original (not imitation American) improvisers, such as baritone saxophonist John Surman; and Barry Guy's London Jazz Composers Orchestra, led by a classical bassist/composer who had also developed himself as an improviser, which was and has been a deeply graceful meld of the new and the improvised, in fine English tradition (although it has been based in France for much of its career).[42]

Ansell notes a generational split in the scene, using the example of the first generation's Musicians' Co-op's evolution and regrouping into the London Musicians' Collective as a change from relatively international (strong ties to American jazz tradition) to relatively isolationist (which, as it happened, foregrounded the blurring of audience-performer distinctions stressed by the People Band, then splintered off into groups much more aligned with the rock than the jazz tradition).

Articles on some of the key figures and groups did appear throughout the 1970s – the time when the music in Europe came into its own as it began to drift from the American center stage – in a few short-lived journals (*Musics, Impetus: New Music*) and in the mainstream *Melody Maker*. *Coda* writer Peter Riley's "Incus Records" (1979) is a full and thoughtful look at the longest-lasting and farthest-reaching of the English free-jazz associations, and the one with the most vital contributions to the larger European *Emanzipation*. Evan Parker, Derek Bailey, and long-time house drummer at Ronnie Scott's Tony Oxley (with financial help from journalist Michael Walters) started Incus in 1970, around the same time as similar collectives in West Germany, France, and Holland.

Deconstructing the Star System and Commodified Recordings, Reconstructing Anarchy

This is a good place to mention the general shift from the star system to the collective that marked this time. It was a shift that implicated both post-Enlightenment and post-Romantic replacements (including that of American liberal capitalism) of Royal and Ecclesiastic patronage of the arts as flawed in their retentions of monarchy's centralization of charisma, despite their populist faces. In other words, there were still powers paying the pipers to play (more than to play to, or for) the people.

Volunteer associations advocating and acting for racial and musical equality are an American tradition dating from the Abolitionists and the Colored Opera Company of the eighteenth and nineteenth centuries; they are also something of a German bourgeois tradition indicating the respectably conscientious civic mind. (Thus, upper-middle-class youth of Weimar Germany formed jazz clubs, or associations, that effectively signaled their informed, cultivated taste and cultural cosmopolitanism – a strike against them when the Nazis took over.) Generally, while it has been true that more government monies have been available in Europe than America for arts and artists clearly not commercially viable, they have not been that much greater. A grassroots network of activist fans and musicians has been the main international and local support of the music since the beginning.[43]

Various versions of the self-determined musician's co-op, of course, also comprised the option in which African Americans had placed their hopes to get around their American dilemma of dependence on the music industry and its commercial criteria. Philosophically and aesthetically, they also marked a shift away from hierarchical structures supporting a "star" (instrument, voice, person) or leader with "sidemen." In the spirit of James Reese Europe's Clef Club, right on up to the Association for the Advancement of Creative Musicians, Black Artists Group, the New York Composers' Guild, and others, African-American musicians had oscillated between the mainstream labels and their own independent alternatives, with varying degrees of commitment and success.[44]

Oddly, FMP is the single European co-op listed in Gray's "The Jazz Collectives," one that has endured and played a seminal and prolific role in producing, presenting, and recording international artists. FMP provided work for the Incus people, and each group distributed the others' recordings in its native country (though practical difficulties eventually quenched that), an alliance that Evan Parker sheds light on. At a festival in Nickelsdorff, Austria, Parker told me

> I brought the idea for Incus back from sort of watching [FMP cofounder Peter] Brötzmann . . . I think it was like a baptism of fire when I met him for the first time. I was playing then in a more English kind of way, but it just didn't hold up to that level of intensity and physical commitment, of acoustic strength and robustness, of the *Machine Gun* record. Peter was important in all kinds of different ways. I was hugely encouraged by his total comittment. He was doing everything that I wanted to do: playing fulltime, making records, dealing with the problems.

As alternatives to establishment music enterprises, collectives such as FMP and Incus posited both new recording aesthetics and new social agendas. Both aesthetics and agendas overlapped, in the shadow of Walter Benjamin and the Frankfurt School theorists' problems with recording technology and mass culture, leading to the brand of indictments thereof (of market-driven canonizations of pre-free jazz as "America's classical music," and appropriations of "world music" as a Western-framed genre) peculiar to Europeans. Incus was one of the least commercial and most musically radical such alternatives, formed in the European center closest to America's music-industrial empire.[45]

Hearkening back to the theme of resistance to American hegemony and decadence, Riley recalls the situation of the British/international recording industry in the late 1960s:

> Vast fortunes had been won and lost in the rock explosion at such an alarming rate that record promoters were quite frenetically trying to keep pace with the music. By the end of the decade, rock itself was trying out all sorts of new formats, so that the big-label promoters, completely lost in this sudden profusion of new styles, became willing to give almost anything a try. One result of this was the commercial market's brief flirtation with improvised music. The music itself had been in existence since about the mid-sixties in Britain as a very advanced, and almost audience-less practice of totally free improvisation – not entirely jazz-derived nor anything-else-derived (Incus is evidence of this). (1979: 4)

Incus took an archival approach to recording that FMP would parallel, an interesting one in light of their shared philosophy of spontaneous improvisation. Their problem with recording as conventionally practiced was not, in the tradition of criticism running from Benjamin through John Cage, that it was a dead simulation of live musical experience; it was rather that a market-driven (meaning, often, an artificially hyped product-driven) recording industry robbed the music's creators of creative control and recontextualized it as a commodity expendable according to the flux of commerce.[46]

From a musician's (or scholar's, or fan's) point of view, the development and evolution of music over time is a centrally fascinating aspect of the creative process, and one accessible only after the fact of creation, in the recording (indeed, the recording helps to agent the process). Both FMP and Incus have archives of recorded live performances (as opposed to studio work), most of which have emerged on the labels. (This, of course, situates their mission in a direct line with traditional ethnomusicological use of archival recordings.)

Apropos of this issue, German musicologist Batel's (1978) title conveys his direct grasp of "Free Jazz as Intensive Form of Sociomusical Communication." He compares free with pre-free jazz's reflection of sociocultural dynamics. In pre-free, a fixed plan (the mental "map" Ornette Coleman said most musicians follow) is memorized and internalized by players and informed hearers, and referred to in improvisations, in recognitions and judgments, worked and milked for new ideas and for new angles on old ideas. This is a picture of Platonic hierarchy, in that an abstract ideal is the source of all concrete things taking place, and is the standard for judging them. It might also be seen as a musical picture of Cartesian-Newtonian science, of Western theology, and of Western Enlightenment social philosophy, all for its hierarchical balance between transcendent ideals (laws of nature, the traits of God, the rule of law – Religion) and its countless immanent manifestations (nature itself, a godly universe, the society determined and maintained by mutable legislation – the Holy).

Free jazz, by contrast, is truer to the post-Romantic Einsteinian scientific paradigm, to a spirituality of immanence rather than transcendence, and a workable, responsibly responsive anarchism (one defined as self-rule that also accounts for the interests and well-being of the collective). There is no predetermined plan or ideal to guide, live up to, or judge by; each player is both center and periphery of the circle, its microcosm more than its cog; each hearer is receiving, perceiving, and conceiving the web of sound – the musical *Ding an sich* – immediately and directly as a whole, rather than as a specific articulation or development of a general abstraction. This is a view of physical, spiritual/psychological, and social realities that is both terrifying and exhilarating, redolent with faith in a void that is a plenum, the source of all order, rather than simply the absence of any.

When meaning is so much less obvious, so much more transient and elusive – and so much more dire and urgent – the roles of presentation and recording contexts, interpretations, and critical inquiry intensify. Of most interest here is the picture of the most direct exchange of such information taking place in an interactive and small, chamber-type context; recordings and broadcast media are shown as mediations that simulate, via commodified musical objects, such smallness.

This suits the drive from functionalism to formalism described by Viennese anthropologist Wolfgang Suppan (1973): a concept of art evolving from the decoration of the functional, the way a piece of pottery on display as an aesthetic object has evolved in perception and use from a simple to an elegant, then finally simply a formal, bowl (intended for the wall rather than the table). It does not say anything about improvisation's resistance to such a drive seen throughout the jazz tradition (and Western tradition, for that matter), until Suppan's last sentences, citing his own source, Lorenzian cultural ethologist Otto König: "Extreme specialization develops in every system on a foundation, and with the safeguards, of extreme primitiveness . . . The way to one's daily bread, the precision of a hot band's rhythm, or the programmed operations of a computer – *all are created from the balance of primitive forms* (61; my emphasis).

Supann ends with the speculation that this view would be a useful entry point into a reception and analysis of free jazz that would force and suggest a revision of our relationship with music (one addressed in chapter six).

Batel observes that the workable anarchy is first the local one, not the mass, or simulated or fragmented mass, experience. He suggests the potential of a global version of that local workable anarchy, in macrocosm. The suggestion is that, for the abovementioned (post-Romantic) free-jazz paradigm, smaller is better, smallest sometimes best; that for anarchy to be workable, each person has to cultivate him or herself not only as a microcosm rather than a cog, but also as an interactor (creator, improviser) rather than an actor (interpreter, performer).[47]

An argument could be made for the recording's potential contribution to "responsible anarchy" offered by this particular music (specifically in the area of reception). The act of listening in an audience to a musical event is centralized in time and space; the event is placed there by the musicians, and the audience must take it in there, en masse, on those terms. More interactive possibilities open up between listeners and players (not to mention between listening players) when the event can be placed in whatever time and space each audience member, or new listener, chooses for it. This privacy, mobility, mutability that recordings bring to the fixed imbalances (especially that between a collection [and collective] of passive listeners and active players in a nineteenth-century Romantic ritual) of the concert situation is perhaps one of the most fitting arguments against the only-live purists for recordings and/or broadcasts (including today's Internet ones) of improvised music.

Another aspect of Incus as fresh as its recording aesthetic, and as shared in common with both German and African-American collectives, was its radical leftist utopic, internationalist political rhetoric and agenda – the European version of black nationalist spirit in the music – woven into the very fabric of its aesthetics:

> In the announcement issued with *Incus 1* Evan Parker briefly associated the enterprise with a leftist theoretic implying that the musician-controlled company was a political act parallel to the anarchic societal model provided by the combination of musicians into a free improvisation group. He quoted Aldous Huxley:
>
> Only a large-scale popular movement towards decentralisation and self-help can arrest the present tendency towards statism.

And G. D. H. Cole's *The Meaning of Industrial Freedom*:

Men will act together in the full consciousness of their mutual dependence: but they will act for themselves. Their liberty will not be given them from above: they will take it on their own behalf. (Riley [1979: 4])

Combined with German critic Wilhelm Liefland's maxim widely applied in Europe to its free-jazz movement in 1968 – "Against capitalism, on the field of capitalism" – this fabric extends the "think global, act local" motto more to "think utopic, act utopic": start living your life as though the world was already in the (your) utopic state.

Riley goes on to compare Incus with FMP, noting that (by that time) the musicians who started the latter had turned its management over to the non-player among them, Jost Gebers. This turn too reflects the pragmatic health many of the American musicians displayed when they forsook '60s idealism for later opportunism, given FMP's long survival and robust production, compared with Incus. It also suggests that the initial idealism (of the musicians who have continued to grow from it) was in fact more realistic, at its core, than it looked – and that it was too "out" to become "sellout" because of a little thing like maturity.

France: Rise of the Monautarchy

The sociopolitical context of American free jazz was sketched in Gray's opening chronology of key musical and social events – starting with the 1954 Supreme Court decision ruling segregation of schools unconstitutional, followed by the 1955 death of Charlie Parker – as a pan-African liberatory one. It could be matched by a similar chronology of European student and other leftism at the time, woven in with the *Emanzipation* music history leading up to and erupting in 1968.[48]

The French/Parisian free scene resembled the first bloom of early nineteenth-century German/Berlin Romanticism: a heady mix of almost equal parts literature, music, philosophy and politics in an all-around intellectual foment shaded more by the mystical than the rational. This birthplace of both Enlightenment and Romantic movements seemed relieved to be delivered from the whiteface mask of Enlightenment universalism – from its classical aesthetics of "the good" and "beauty," in musical terms – and to a Romantic comfort with nature and local identity. Accordingly, it read in African-American gestures deflations of Wagnerian bombast, then developed its own original gestures down such lines – lighter, jollier than the sources – even as the Germans gravitated to and built on the extremes of intensity and energy.

Paris's tradition as the center of Continental Western European civilization, combined with its similar status as the major destination for American jazz expatriates, would seem to suggest it as the prime candidate for the leadership of Europe's coming-of-age in the jazz discourse. Besides being that cradle of both Enlightenment and Romanticism, it saw the first American-style grassroots overthrow of the monarchy, which spilled into New Orleans through the Napoleonic version of the old *code noir* (democratic and antiracist, for its time).[49] Its opera, compared with the self-full melodrama of its Italian and German counterparts, gave early jazz the cool, light affect that would take it so far both in and out of America. Its aesthetic of *beauté* prevailed in the piano stylings immediately preceding stride (recall the example of Eubie Blake "beautifying" a left-hand melody with right-hand arpeggios, suggesting a harp accompanying a voice). France was also the source of the first internationally influential jazz scholarship, and of much of the music's dissemination throughout Europe.

To characterize the French free scenes before surveying their details, they did produce – specifically in response to the examples of Ornette Coleman, John Coltrane, Cecil Taylor, Albert Ayler, Archie Shepp, and, later, AACM and Black Artist Group (BAG) luminaries Don Cherry and Sun Ra bassist Alan Silva – excellent individual musicians, some of whom played important roles outside their country, in the *Emanzipation's internationale*.[50] However, they comprised a national voice more insular, less distinctive and provocative in terms of international impact and musical radicalism, than did their Dutch, German, English, and even Scandinavian colleagues.

True to its cosmopolitan roots and character, France had a bit of everything in its musical mix – folk, jazz, classical-composed, and new-experimental pop – often in the same players and groups. The result, again, suggests more than it delivers: it suggests a breakdown of genre walls that implies a dissolution of class walls, but it delivers rather a facile skating on the surfaces of each genre, a Third Stream-ish experiment that reconfirms distance and difference between them more than it evokes deep common ground. Cecil Taylor with Mary Lou Williams, Sun Ra with John Cage, or Sonny Rollins with the Rolling Stones are some examples of mismatches on record, however interesting, familiar to American cognoscenti that suggest the neither-fish-nor-fowl feeling of much of French improvised music. This is not to disparage its unique moments. Its evocations of French *chanson* and Basque traditional material resonate with Ornette Coleman's similar evocations of the country blues, and its "imaginary folklore" with the evocations of a mythic Africa sounded by Coltrane, Sun Ra, Pharoah Sanders, Julius Hemphill, John Carter, and others.

The French ways of working with their traditional folk, popular, and art musics resemble aspects of the Dutch scene, but, again, the results have had less impact outside their own country. Their variously motivated reasons for not recording for an international audience contributed to that. The nature of their music itself – introverted, redolent of Impressionism, existential – is also a contributing factor. Another has been an ideological devotion to the local and live, and to long-lived groups growing a local identity, more than to the globetrotting freelancer's opportunism.

Jost's view of the post-free French identity in the larger European *Emanzipation* is that it is more overshadowed by African America than are other countries, owing to France's longstanding role as host to same. That said, he pegs it to three aspects: a foundation of melody rather than harmony, in the *chanson* tradition, syncing up with Coleman's melodic approach; the mythologization of its folk tradition, mentioned above; and a meld of those two with contemporary composition, with a result of something like Rempel's stage two of European treatments of non-Western influences ("liberalism"), falling short of the stage three "openness" to fundamental paradigm shift (see p. 317, note 60).

The French reception of free jazz might also be characterized as one marked more by the power of "letters" than of "arts." Even the music scene's engagement and direction with the music can be read, overall, as one more weighted to the literate, rational aspects of Western music – melody, systems of pitch arrangement, much as the Scandinavian responses – than were its English, German, and even Dutch counterparts. The results of that, naturally enough, resemble Scandinavia's in the development of a distinctly French free style and sound that stood more as a stand-alone microcosm of the larger European "emancipated" identity than as a major presence in that European macrocosm. It also, for the same musical reasons, compares with Italy's responses to free jazz, in its sense of itself as a center of arts and letters to which others come, and follow, rather than the reverse (even when the reverse may be true). What is certain about the *Emanzipation* is that it was ignited by jazz and free jazz in Europe. The European scenes that fell to its leading edges were those inclined to use their own bases as springboards and hosts to other scenes, more than as newly planted private gardens to tend.

If the above characterization belies my personal bias for other *Emanzipation* scenes, more sympathetic is my interest in the French collectives and big bands as most akin to my own experience with ensembles of creative virtuosi, each equipped to captain his or her own musical universe, both alone and with others. This interest shines by the light of Joppig's notion, recurrently motivating the drive of this study, of jazz (wind) ensembles large and small usurping orchestral and chamber (string) groups as Western music's then-current central arenas of musical and social thought, rendering the classical ensembles as philosophically and culturally (if not socially) marginal, rather than the more commonly assumed reverse. All that said, France stands as an interesting case study of what might have been the leading voice in the *Emanzipation*, and why it was not.

The Good, the Black, and the Ugly

While Paris was slow in receiving and discovering Coleman and other free-jazz giants, it became from 1965 to 1970 an important city for them all, then for a later second wave (Marion Brown, Anthony Braxton, Frank Wright, Steve Lacy, the Art Ensemble of Chicago, Sun Ra and their bandmates). Paris served them for the same reasons as it had their predecessors in earlier decades – better money, opportunity, and reception – as well as for a few new ones.

For the musicians, escape from an increasingly hostile and tense society at home was a relief more acute than ever; more positively, they felt they had something new and important, particularly for the world beyond America, and were eager to connect with curious and sympathetic audiences, harder to find at home. The French jazz scene and public, for their part, were primed and positioned to be just such an audience.

Among the other European scenes, France arguably had the richest integration of jazz with its other arts and letters, and with its society's politics. Jazz had become familiar to all classes there, and was an object of contemporary interdisciplinary scholarly interest built on a tradition of the first such from Panassié on, through the journal *Le Cahiers du Jazz*, started in 1959. The literati – writers, screenwriters, playwrights – were especially interested in the issues the music raised for them, and provided the first free jazz with some of its most serious, comprehensive, and multifaceted critical reception and reflection.[51]

As the idea of an "avant-garde" emerged – which was the French rubric first attached to the music in America too, before Baraka, Shepp, and others situated it more specifically in liberatory and militant black identity – French musicians and other artists and intellectuals were uniquely open and interested in developing it down their own lines. For the musicians, those lines were, at first, more of a revamping of tradition by relatively seasoned players well steeped in it than by radical young turks, often not only untrained but disdaining training, crying "out with the old and in with the new."

Strong individual voices led the charge in responding to the strong individual voices of Coleman and the others of the first wave of free. André Hodeir's role as both scholar and composer was similar to that of Gunther Schuller's in America's Third Stream: syncretic, universalist, inclined to merge rather than choose one over the other of the poles of race, nationality, identity, or aesthetics (of improvisation over composition, or high over low). Pianist Martial Solal had also developed specific musical strategies ("discontinuity" and "evasion") to neutralize and/or alter convention, as the modalists, Third Streamers, Mingus, Coleman, and Taylor were doing. The first free-jazz moments, in short, were simply drops in a roiling whitewater of public consciousness open to and avidly exploring change and innovation, rather than reacting to it defensively or perplexedly.

This openness moved all European jazz musicians to turn with increasing interest to their own contemporary art music, particularly for its least rational aspects. That is, while they were intellectually interested in the systems and languages of atonality, they were more viscerally engaging the new potentials of rhythm and timbre to express their own emotional and physical energies, long harnessed to Western agendas and norms. If it was not clear that Coleman's or Shepp's voices, their signature sounds on the saxophone, were more the vehicles not only of expressiveness but also of invention than were the more abstract composition or improvisation of notes, it certainly became so with Albert Ayler, whose playing prompted an aesthetic debate in print about the dialectic between "the beautiful" and "the ugly." This was a conversation, joined in German some years later by Berendt, that went to the heart of the recent histories of both countries in the Second World War.[52] It signaled something more emotional than the merely aesthetic differences between sweet-cool-white and hot-bop-black in America.

Longstanding conventions of *musicalité* – sonority, melodic lyricism, structural clarity, tasteful variance of dynamics and tempo – remained unchallenged by jazz in French criticism up to and including the boppers. For all their timbral and temporal gutsiness and harmonic-melodic inventiveness, the excitement in musicians from Duke Ellington to Lester Young to Charlie Parker lay more in the way they massaged these criteria of musicality from within, pushing their envelopes suggestively, signifying on and through them more than cutting their Gordian knots with a blow. That field of expression itself was enlarged when Ayler's such blow included much that convention would have called *laideur* (ugliness), the opposite of the above criteria (American critics revealed their similar value base with their "anti-jazz" charges against Coltrane, Coleman, and others).

The philosophical behind the aesthetic tension here: if the criteria for *musicalité* all serve a larger context of some sort of evil, and their opposites for *laideur* one of an opposing good, how can the one be "beauty" and the other "ugliness?" The dichotomy was expressed initially between France's own art music (and mainstream jazz as its progeny) and American free jazz, a dialectic the French grappled with in a reach for their own "freedom" in European identity.

French musicians (Michel Portal, Jean-Louis Chautemps, François Tusques, Bernard Vitet, Barney Wilen) spoke of Coleman and his peers as having liberated them from the prison of rigid fixed paradigm. The French free players, more than seeing in Ayler's power the spirituality he himself expressed when he said his music "tried to help each human being to awaken in himself new outlooks on life," saw it as a successful enlargement of the musically expressive field from its former rigid hierarchy of criteria for beauty and ugliness.[53] As Joachim Kühn's bassist Jacques Thollot observed, "A musician doesn't make only beautiful things. Who can say that of all that happens in the world around us where we live what inspires beauty? If he is sincere, a musician can't limit his talent to beauty . . . which is sometimes a distraction from bawling, and that can also be beautiful (Cotro, 1999: 58). Kühn himself stated that "It is important for me to express truly the feelings like love, hatred, rage, peace, impressions, visible things, to express them musically in free music . . . It is not only a question of musical order – that is obvious enough. This free music brings new meaning to beauty" (58).

The impact of Ornette Coleman's first records in Europe was perhaps most like that of Louis Armstrong's in Sweden some thirty years earlier. At a single stroke then and there, Armstrong had changed the name of the Western game from European to American; Coleman, as instantly, reversed that. His own musical disengagements from that game cued the Europeans playing it to walk away from it too – from superpower American back to their own European identities.

Old Dogs, New Tricks

Cotro's presentation of the post-Coleman scene in France suggests three phases: the direct responses by established mainstream players to the "new thing's" musical innovations; the leaderless collectives of a younger generation of players more directly engaged with their African-American colleagues (the second wave mentioned above, including Braxton's trio with Leroy Jenkins and Leo Smith; BAG, Don Cherry, Alan Silva, AEC, and AACM), but also more focused on forging distinctively French/European identities; and the big bands initiated by prominent African-American free players as collaborations of many French and American voices, marked more than the smaller collectives by utopian, global unity-in-diversity than by local identity.

The established musicians of the first phase had heard recordings by, and followed the press and local criticism on, Coleman between 1960 and 1963. In interviews with French magazines, Coleman made comments about his music – "our music," and "I'm myself, I'm home," and "a music of interior thought" – that French musicians and intelligentsia embraced not as the curiosities of an "other" so much as lights at the end of their own tunneling quest for identity. Some had begun responding in kind with their own music a few years before Coleman came in person, in 1965. The tenor of all their remarks (as also about Cherry, Eric Dolphy, Archie Shepp, Pharoah Sanders, and Sunny Murray, later) revolved around the existential heroism and action of the music, the valorization of subjectivity, the idea that a new door had opened in the music that enabled other new openings. The musical specifics of Coleman's work almost seem secondary to his impact in those philosophic and social dimensions.

Many of those most directly associated with "free" in France began in Jef Gilson's bands. A pianist-composer born in 1926, Gilson was by the 1950s an established bandleader somewhat along the lines of Duke Ellington, Stan Kenton, Bob Graettinger, Charles Mingus, Gil Evans, or Don Ellis, in the sense that he liked to experiment as one with solid grounding in tradition, to expand on rather than defy conventions of melody-harmony and meter. He was comfortable with free improvisation, but not swept away by it as by some new religion so much as open to its usefulness as one of many musical options in the larger project of orchestrating and arranging pieces notable for making new and complex ideas sound inevitable and natural, and for incorporating and showcasing well a multitude of strong idiosyncratic voices.

Gilson's recordings *Enfin!, Oeil Vision, A Free Call From France,*[54] *A New Call From France, Le Concert à la MJC Colombes,* and *Le Massacre du Printemps* (an homage to Stravinsky after his death), released between 1962 and 1971, feature meters beyond the standard 3/4 and 4/4, harmonic refinements along the lines of André Hodeir, generous helpings of Indian and Asian musical gestures, fresh lower-register timbres; two basses, one playing outside the walking-bass box; soloists overdubbed to play duets with themselves; free improvisations within organized structures; chromatic and modal treatments of harmony and melody; breakups of rhythm in and out of pulse, or melodies and sounds in and out of silences; flexible rather than fixed tempi; clear traces of African-American influences (Ayler, Coleman, Shepp) in phrasing, construction, and timbral declamations of soloists; electronics; and totally free collective improvisation. Over the

course of these, Gilson moved, something like Sun Ra, from precursor to full participant in the French brand of free jazz. His bands comprised a Who's Who
of the French scene both pre- and post-free: Vitet, Wilen, Chautemps, Portal,
François Jeanneau, Henri Texier, Jacques Thollot, Bernard Lubat, and Jean-
François Jenny-Clarke.

Portal was already a pillar of the French scene when free jazz hit it. Born in
1935, he had established himself in the 1950s, like his New Phonic Art bandmate
Vinko Globokar, as an interpreter of contemporary composition. His classical
training and work in jazz and pop rounded out his diverse base.

Cotro's five-point summary of Portal's influence (which the author deems one
of European free's most significant between 1969 and 1976) shows how easily analyzable he is on Western terms. It lies in:

- the power of his "festive ostinato" (or "vamp" in American jazz), a melodic and
  rhythmic pattern crafted to stimulate free improvisation through indefinitely
  cycling repetition. It is a device that evokes the primal and ritualistic, the reptilian brain, via the stasis of non-developing modes and undifferentiated pulse,
  only with a melodically-rhythmically elaborated platform. Portal's particular
  focuses suggested French *chanson* (Edith Piaf, Charles Trénet) and Basque traditional music, and thoughtful manipulations of dynamics;
- explorations of timbral possibilities, especially in the lower registers, through
  wide-ranging, dense, and unconventional instrumentation. This device suggested France's new-music (composed) influence of the time;
- forms that were modular, additive, sprawling grand unifiers of different styles,
  sounds, and unrelated musical events, rather than the linear, self-referring little
  pieces of song craftsmanship wrought by German cabaret composers (Hans
  Eisler, Kurt Weill), or Americans such as Thelonious Monk or even Ornette
  Coleman;
- themes and motifs used to launch free improvisation, without shaping it like a
  template; and
- collective more than solo improvisations.

Portal's voice is one that naturally embodied *musicalité* rather than *laideur*. His
words in interview in 1997 (Cotro [1999: 133–5]), while seeming to belie the "light-
ness" in French free, also suggest possible reasons for it. He looks back on his years
of spontaneity and experimentalism as on a wild and brilliant youth not entirely
misspent, but certainly as spent, limited, an object of nostalgia. He expresses mixed
feelings about French "free" drawing on both new music and free jazz, a sense that
it knew itself as neither really one nor the other, nor anything more definite issuing
from both. He also expresses mixed feelings about the difference between composition and improvisation, and recorded and live music . . . but mostly between
black and white identities.

"Free" for him was certainly more than a lark, but was more so compared with
Coleman, or Sunny Murray, or Taylor, or Braxton. On the one hand, he states
outright that jazz had a certain *négritude* in it, and that he had full access to it

("when I play it, I am black" [131]); of free jazz, he says its essence is that of "collective intensity," similarly invoked through sound. On the other hand:

> The drama, for us, is that we play a stolen music. It is a black music, born in a precise context, in reaction to a precise political and ideological situation. A context and situation that are not ours . . . And then to make a revolutionary music, in France . . . The Black had something that condensed all that against which one could revolt: the white American and his culture. We, what can we attack so? Sure, the motives of revolt are there, but it's all a blur, surrounding us, streaming by, all is a hand-me-down, distorted. (61)

These words first saw print in May of 1968, when the French students were doing their best to match the gravitas, focus, and passion of their African-American counterparts in militancy.

Like Portal, Jean-Louis Chautemps was already a seasoned/trained player (b. 1931) who met the free head on when it came to France. He had been prepared for it. In 1951, around the time of Lenny Tristano's experiments, Chautemps and cornetist Jean Liesse had improvised spontaneously with drummer Robert Barnet, but also with mixed feelings. In an interview with Cotro he said "I was not really excited by the thing: I participated more out of politeness than real conviction . . . I had just, finally, learned to play chord changes without getting lost, and I wasn't all that excited about forcing myself to leave this hard-won skill behind. Also, I didn't really have the ears to pull it off with the confidence of Jean Liesse" (142).

Chautemps made up for that initial ambivalence by forming a piano-less trio with bassist Guy Pedersen and drummer Daniel Humair. Although the trio never recorded – partly as a gesture of artistic integrity in the face of commercialism (the luxury of the idealistic, serious amateur, of the old aristocrat), partly because "no one ever offered to record us, we would have had to do it ourselves" (143]) – some radio broadcasts of their performances exist. Their titles signal a European claim on jazz.[55] The sound is reminiscent of Sonny Rollins's acknowledged influence, a churn of free-ranging blowing, unconstrained by strict adherence to form and tempo but still working with an identifiable theme and groove.

Chautemps expresses a relationship with "free" linked to European precedents rather than Coleman's first recordings: André Breton and the surrealists, Nietszche. He sees "free" as a musical window onto the "primordial foundations of being," those underpinning all the world's musical traditions, not only jazz and Western art music, though those were at first the sites of the most burning issues. On the more personal level, he invokes both psychoanalysis and surrealism, compares the process of free improvisation with automatic writing, and with "talking therapy's" "free association." His association of free jazz with both free verse and the Free Speech Movement at the University of California at Berkeley convey his literary-cum-political sense of the music's aesthetic.

He even disparagingly describes Coleman's system of harmolodics as a "swindle" (*escroquerie*), suggesting that it is something of a theoretical façade erected around free improvisation and unnotated compositions to give them the respectability of literate criteria. (If that were true, Chautemps, Portal, and other early French free players might be charged with a similarly transient and opportunistic flirtation with free improvisation, falling short of taking it seriously enough to fashion their own systems and vocabularies out of the freedom, as have Coleman, Braxton, Taylor, and others.)

Saxophonist Barney Wilen came to prominence in the 1950s as sideman to American bop visitors and expatriates such as Roy Haynes, Bud Powell, Dizzy Gillespie, Thelonious Monk, and Miles Davis. He retreated from jazz around the same time as did Sonny Rollins, in the early 1960s, then came back with a trio (with drummer Henri Texier, alternating with Jean-François Jenny-Clark, and bassist Jacques Thollot) that quickly established itself as a major player in the emergence of French free. Wilen's distinctive contribution turned out to be his use of electronics, and of multimedia spectacles and literary texts to contextualize a peculiarly French exercise of the free-jazz options.

Cotro's description of Wilen's *Zodiac Suite* (1966) resonates with Jost's of French free as a whole as light, facile, more playful than serious. More serious, and more generally European than locally French, was Wilen's (1967) "total spectacle" of taped electronics, film projections, light show and live music called *The Tragic Destiny of Lorenzo Bandini*, released on disc in 1968. Its theme (the death of an Italian race car driver), its literary treatment thereof, its media, its new-music devices (aleatoric, dodecaphonic, *musique concrète*) all moved its free-jazz core away from the African-American mythos and identity.[56]

> In France, we are not confronted with the same problems. We have virtually no racial problem. Our problems consist rather in the harassments of administrative order or commercial variety of departments that govern us. One can get angry over these things, but they're also not as grave as the situation of Mr. Archie Shepp or Mr. Albert Ayler. (Wilen, 1967, cited in Cotro [1999: 61–2])

Pianist François Tusques, unlike those mentioned so far, made his debut as a free player exclusively, with no previous history as a mainstream player. He also expressed both Coleman's influence and his own response to it more blatantly and politically than did those colleagues. His 1965 LP *Free Jazz*, followed in 1967 by *Le Nouveau Jazz*, with Portal, trumpeter Bernard Vitet, bassist Bernard Guerin, and Wilen on the second, sans Guerin, came out right around the time of Coleman's first European concert. The titles alone suggest theft, but Jost – no easy critic, especially of derivative dilettantes – writes that the LP succeeded as a "synthesis of recognizable influences nonetheless organized in a personal musical language" (Cotro [1999: 96]). The overall sound presents an integrated loose weave – through diatonic, modal, and atonal skeins – of the written and composed articulated clearly along the lines of Coleman, Mingus, and Taylor. It distinguishes itself by an organic clarity of both the composed and the collective, unmuddied by the soloist or bandleader's ego, or by free improvisation's thrashings. The music is conspicuously balanced, transparent, supple, especially in its statements and changes of rhythm and tempo. *Le Nouveau Jazz*, featuring Wilen, went from the Colemanish to the Taylorish, from the "jazz" to the "new music" side of things, with its lack of swing and prevailing atonality.

Tusques echoed Coleman's words too ("music of interior thought"), almost verbatim, in print three years later when discussing his own music: it was a technique to explore the unconscious, identity, on both personal and French-cultural levels. Tusques, among this whole cadre of such explorers, was the only overt ideologue; he insisted that creative musicians should also be responsible intellectuals, indeed, dogmatic Maoist Marxists. Though such stands were rewarded with general *simpatico*, most musicians would shy away from being any sort of "Party men." The black testimony of the music in the United States inspired, in its French counterparts, a general rather than partisan sense of the artist as the conscience of his society: freedom from theory (ideology), but also to praxis (action). In Tusques's case, the mixed feelings his colleagues expressed translated into a critique of the black American free players as leaders in some ways, but also as in need of Western intellectual guidance:

> For people like Sunny Murray, Clifford Thornton, Don Cherry, the music is a truly important thing. It is they who have created this music. It is normal to place oneself under their direction. They have much more motivation to play than we . . . But all that is confused, ill formulated . . . The problem is that musicians are not intellectuals, at least not solely. (1972, in Cotro [1999: 61–2])

Intellectuals

Two books came out of France around the time of the statements cited above, both also clearly portraying the dynamic of African Americans as heavyweights and French as lightweights in the same sport. *Free Jazz, Black Power* (Jean-Louis Comolli and Philippe Carles, 1971) covered the American free-jazz movement not as a Western "avant-garde" but as an expression of anti-Western, pan-African militancy; and *The Action-Image of Society* (Willener, 1970) presented the student riots as an expression of the West's own youth naturally allied with that black militancy, through its own revolutionary spirit. Willener's placement of a chapter called "Free Jazz" in his study of the May 1968 student uprisings captures well, from the French intelligentsia's point of view, both the import of the music to the student movement and its place among the other arts and letters informing and motivating it, in the moments they were current.

By far the biggest influence of the two on European jazz musicians outside France, Comolli and Carles produced a study from the point of view of a Continental philosopher/social critic. It corroborated the political protests voiced by Americans then on behalf of the music – Baraka, Backus, Kofsky – but it has stood the test of time better. It seems no stretch for these writers to frame the "free jazz" of "black power" as a cry coming straight from the first engagements of Africa with the West, of outrage and insistence on inclusion in its utopian freedom from and dismantling of age-old tyranny. At the same time, it problematizes the idea of black music as being Western as much as African at its core; it thus paints both black and white identities into essentialist corners they can never really escape. Black cries must always fall on deaf (or distorting) white ears, white minds and bodies will never really "get" black ones.

The book's next-to-last chapter, "Fragments of Free," spells out thoroughly the musical components of this black power, the same ones in the same ways concerning us here – the "democratization" of instruments, of the composed and the improvised, of individual and collective, of pulses and pitches, the turn to the primal as authentic, away from the civilized as corrupt – but white and black identities themselves remain frozen in eternal, mutual remonstrance.

As the title signals, the book would be of interest to a reader versed in Marxist thought; a dash of Sartre and Gênét would not hurt either, to start constructing a characteristically French sense of "négritude's" vital challenge to "whiteness" in the international cultural arena, through this music. In contrast to Brit Valerie Wilmer's (1977) look at the same music and players, one does get a sense of the musicians as "others" here, albeit others with whom the reader is exhorted to come to terms. On the down side, the book can be criticized much as has been white guilt and liberalism in general: it romanticizes the "otherness" and the oppression of African Americans, and, at worst, has a hidden agenda, half-unconscious, to perpetuate it.[57]

Three reliable and different witnesses report amateurism (in the bad sense) rampant in the French free scene. Joachim Kühn is one among many musicians and critics who bemoaned the lack of musicianship among free players; and Carles/Comolli and Willener both commented on the peurile conformism, in hippy face, masked as its opposite: all primal scream and bashing drums, unrelenting intensity of volume and rhythm gone meaningless, clichéd iconoclasm.

Willener is one of many who demur at Berendt's idea (which found its way into the opening of the *Grove Dictionary of Jazz's* essay on "Jazz") of the development of jazz as a centurial recapitulation of a millennium of Western music, likening the blues to plainchant and free jazz to twentieth-century post-diatonic musics. Still, the undue Eurocentrism in that projection that Willener and others criticize is in fact part of our concern here with European views, interests in, and treatments of African-American music.

I see in African America's quick mastery of and steps beyond Western music principles an instructive example of people acting under fire to learn and do what they must to get what they need and want. It is an example telling of the similar absorption and transformation of jazz carried out by the northern cultures jazz had conquered, and occupied, less oppressively and violently, but no less thoroughly, after the violence and tyrannies Eurasia had wrought on itself.

Small Bands of Brothers

The French collectives that emerged as solutions to the problem of free-as-dead-end permitted a "liberty more real, because organized." The organization the collectives brought, in fact, can be seen as one of France's strongest contributions to *Emanzipation*, one it holds in common with later Russian music, and with Braxton's *oeuvre*. It is one that flies in the face of the German and English "kill the father" spirit, one closer to the Dutch and Scandinavian. It is one where the long enmeshment with African Americans in Paris proved more the asset than the challenge to French individuation from them.

Hearkening back to the different views on the different natures of improvised and composed music discussed in chapter one, the French collectives can be viewed through the Eros/War lenses. Those dominating the pan-European *Emanzipation* (Germany, England, Holland) were arguably most defined as improvisers with an almost dogmatic eschewal of the composed. Incus embodies this dictum most consistently, in a way Germany would not match until Wolfgang Fuchs's King Übü Orchestrü a generation later. Hearkening forward to the next chapter, although the Globe Unity Orchestra (GUO), especially the Wuppertalian contingent, was much more spontaneous than orchestrated, it did have its occasional collaborations with contemporary composers, and its own sporadic, ad hoc road maps to facilitate the spontaneity; and Holland's Instant Composing Pool (ICP) came out of a new-music as much as a jazz and pop background. After the flush of the first hours, both GUO and ICP would morph into new large and smaller splinter groups that would fall back on traditional orchestrations; but at first, in the wake of Taylor, late Coltrane, and Ayler, they were storming the Old with all colors of the New flying. War, then, between the improvised and the composed, with the former conquering the latter as decisively as the reverse had been the case for two hundred years prior.

The French collectives, as their Russian counterparts would do later, demonstrated rather an Erotic fusion of free improvisation and the composed, and of black American and white Eurasian identities. Their second wave of French free players was a marked shift from the prominent player, schooled in one or more conventional genres and charging ahead into the unknown, to collectives of players organizing themselves around sounds and aesthetics variously more specific, conscious, and intentional than those of sheer open spontaneity. The latter had quickly proven as limited an aesthetic as was the total control afforded by notated music, giving rise to a hundred expressions of cliché and conformism for every one of originality and skill.[58]

Around 1970, that second phase unfolded: collectives formed around specific musical games and strategies rather than groups led and lit by a stellar player's genius and charisma. They were more proactively constructive than reactively deconstructive, in distinctive ways; they were more enduring constellations than shifting collaborations, by design, to the end of growing more profound music. In large part, this turn was a clear reassertion of the "beautiful" in Western music that "the ugly" of free jazz had called into question. As already noted, even the players who responded to Coleman and Ayler most viscerally had mixed feelings about the free approach. It was not long before they and everyone were fed up with the unrelenting monotone of loudness, nervousness, Aylerish folksiness. What had started as an earthshaking sea change was fast degenerating into a small stylistic box less and less worthy of the attention it initially grabbed.

The way Cotro distinguishes between *les collectifs* and *les big bands* reads like a distinction between small, locally focused chamber ensembles – laboratories for the development of a certain concept/spirit/sound – and sprawling, spectacular, universalist symphonic reflections of society. Both categories, read so, again give flesh to Joppig's notion of jazz as the flowering of Western music. Indeed, they embody quite neatly the difference between the informal collectives – of family and friends – and the formal ones of chartered cities and states, nations and civilizations. As such, they give us just as rich a metaphor for the peculiarly French blossoming of one cultural identity (European) from another (African-American).

Cohelmec, Perception, Dharma, and The Free Jazz Workshop de Lyon (FJWL) are the collectives most famously associated with French free jazz's second wave; and Don Cherry's Eternal Rhythm Orchestra, Alan Silva's Celestial Communication Orchestra, and Manuel Villarroel's Machi Oul were the major big bands of that moment. Each of the collectives was exclusively European, most were exclusively French. The big bands were rather constellations of French and North and South American players, two led by bandmates of the first African-American originators of the music, one by a Chilean pianist, respectively.

Cohelmec's name is a combination of the first few letters of its four core players' last names (saxophonist Jean Cohen, pianist Dominique Elbaz, and brothers François [bass] and Jean-Louis [drums, vibes] Mêchali). Recalling the common etymology of "free" and "friend" is Cohelmec's "collective" explanation of what made its free improvisation good, when it was good: "we play as we do because it gives us pleasure to play together" (Cotro [1999: 168]). It was the most famous of the free-jazz collectives because it played abroad (at Montreux and Newport festivals) and in unticketed concerts in Parisian public squares and gardens the most. Jean-Louis characterizes his group as "more modern" than Perception, and more of a rupture with jazz tradition than Dharma, aligning its aesthetic most closely with FJWL (François: "eclectic, not extremists, anchored in Western tradition"). Cotro (169) likens Cohelmec's eclectic collaging of musical materials – melodies and harmonies, original and variously genre-traditional rhythms, sonorities, dynamics – and theatrical flare to the similar work then of Sun Ra, the Art Ensemble of Chicago (AEC), and Anthony Braxton. Less musicologically, he describes it as an expression of joyous liberation of youth from the old monolithic gray of the venal elders. The politics were still anarcho-leftist, but now more creative and individual than partisan and dogmatic.

Perception was a quartet of similar instrumentation, with Yochk'o ("Jeff") Seffer on saxes, Siegried Kessler on piano, Didier Levallet on bass, and Jean-My Truong on drums. Its range was less experimental – generally modal, lyrical, most influenced by John Coltrane and Bélà Bartók, with free improvisations always launched by a complete melody – but it also resembled groups such as the AEC and the AACM for its clear collective identity and lack of instrumental-personal hierarchy therein, even with the standard quartet. Levallet likens the spirit of this and other free-jazz collectives to that of rock groups of the time, which typically created leaderless collective identities with such panache and imagination.

Dharma ("right action") formed with the express mission to bridge the gap between artists and public inherent in the post-Romantic concert ritual, thus doing most of its public playing in academic and amateur associative rather than commercial venues. Its members were art activists, pedagogues, entrepreneurs at the grassroots community level. All the original players (Jean-François [Jef] Sicard and Gérard Coppéré, reeds; Patricio Villarroel, keyboards; Michel Gladieux, bass; and Jacques Mahieux, drums) were born between 1944 and 1948, and lived in the same house in Nanterre together during the 1970s.

Dharma shared with its fellow quartets a spirit of the celebratory freedom of youth culture from Western elders, and to the traditions of India, Indonesia, and Asia. All of the collectives expressed this spirit musically through loose improvisations on written melodies, both (improvised and written) exploring a variety of *ludique* (playful, game-like) devices and influences – tempo rubato, atonality, bathetic timbral-tonal gestures and drama, modalism – drawing heavily on Coltrane, Miles Davis, Herbie Hancock, and Chick Corea. The latter three especially signaled a strong leaning toward the fusion gestures of the electric Miles bands, for their resonance with the electricity of the international cult of youth emblematized most by Jimi Hendrix.

Guitarist Gerard Marais, a later member of the group, gives a special nod to Anthony Braxton. After getting his first big inspiration from the example of Albert Ayler to "Do your own music!" (advice Marais calls "universalist"), Marais found in Braxton's trio with Leo Smith and Leroy Jenkins, then in Paris, a more accessible model of the same genus as Ayler, Taylor, and Ra, but without the force of the same distant, intimidating blackness emanating from pre-free giants such as Monk, Mingus, or Coltrane. As Evan Parker also put it to me, Braxton was more like a "hero in the same room" as Marais and his peers, one who engaged white Europeans on their own Western terms, and invited them on his own black American terms without awkwardness or coercion. Again, this translated into Dharma as a site of "creative coexistence" between the written/orchestrated and the improvised, always open and in process (as, indeed, is true of Braxton's work).

The Free Jazz Workshop of Lyon (bassist Jean Bolcato, reedsman Maurice Merle, trumpeter Jean Méreu, drummer Pierre Guyon, originally) started in 1967, became the Workshop de Lyon in 1976, and remains active as the oldest French jazz group, and the most widely traveled (to just about everywhere except the United States). Its spinoff group, l'Association à la Recherche d'un Folklore Imaginaire (ARFI), as its name signals, formed around the mission "to defend improvisation, to diffuse the various musics and to give the musical means to whomever is ready to consecrate them to establish a new folklore . . . created by the art and ritual of improvisation and spectacle" (Cotro 1999: 194).

Like Dharma, Workshop de Lyon started as a co-op of art activists/pedagogues running their own label. They were perhaps a bit more ideologically declarative about the music's free aesthetic and its sociopolitical correlate of leaderless anarchy. Their faith (and action) in the viability of both corroborated the idea of free "improvisation" being, in fact, a "composition" of something provided (see the citations opening chapter one). "On the melodic plan," writes Cotro, about a 5/4–4/4 riff by ARFI he pegs to Breton folk dance, "this color derives from a mélange of traditional and folkloric elements appropriated by scholarly tradition. Diatonicism, chromaticism and pentatonicism coexist thus in the ear, creating a perpetual hesitation between tonality and modality" (197).

Part of this thrust, shared by both groups, was manifest through their common eschewal of piano or guitar, and embrace of only acoustical instruments (bass, percussion, brass, and reeds), modeled after the AACM and the Jazz Composers' Orchestra. Melody and percussion and timbre are thus the delimiting landmarks of a musical terrain free of the harmonic matrices of chordal instruments. Sounds imitating those of natural settings (birds in the woods, wind in the trees) are favored, as is the "choral hymnique"; all notions of "soloist" and "accompanist," or leader and sidemen, are as stripped away in the musical interactions between individuals and group as in its aesthetic professions.

Reedsman Louis Sclavis, very much the Michel Portal torchbearer, brings the composer's as well as the improviser's sensibilities to the shape of the collective play. Christian Rollet's spontaneous rhythmic play blurs with the labyrinthine accented melodies of archaic folk dance to suggest a real connection with something primal, while simultaneously reminding us of the intrinsically mythical (and ever more present than past) nature of all such primal "realities."

The collectives arose after the first wave's shock of *laideur* similarly to the *Empfindsamkeit* after Baroque, or Impressionism after Romanticism; or, closer, the African-American collectives in Chicago, St. Louis, and New York after the *Sturm und Drang* of the first free-jazz marathons of Coleman and Coltrane: Jost's third phase of the *Emanzipation* (see p. 126), *après la deluge* kinds of things, each with its own personality. Each had its own way of redeeming and extending freedom from Baroque-like compulsion, by organizing it when entropy was setting in. All were generally less organized around the vision and charisma of a "remarkable man," more around musical games and philosophical positions.

The following words of Perception bassist Didier Levallet express well the sense that the Western fathers had been killed, and the way was clear to claim his own freedom's mandates: "With the advent of free jazz, *the breakdown of forms believed to be eternal opened the door to all possibilities*. There were no longer typical 'jazz' themes so much as propositions that allowed each to develop his own language. In fact, the lesson the 'new music' taught us was to finally become ourselves" (61–2; my emphasis).

The French collectives as a whole define French free identity as familial/clannish, ideological, young, mythical, and populist without being anti-intellectual, local and longlasting more than traveling and ad hoc, but mostly, and most importantly and distinctively, as a re-embrace of the very criteria of *beauté, rationalité, musicalité* and *clarté* that the initial shock of the *laideur* attributed to African-American identity so effectively challenged. New compositional approaches designed to liberate individual more than group expression privileged coherence, stability, clarity over density and energy; they spawned writing and analysis, all in palpable reaction against the muddy catharses of collective free improvisation that had initially held sway. The collectives left such "freedom" behind as a cliché, by expanding on visual and humor components, and by signifying on their own Western and French traditions high and low, rather than trying to avoid or deconstruct them.

The word "utopic" crops up often in Cotro's interviewees' own descriptions of their musical projects, looking back on those years (Vinko Globokar's dismissal of current movements as lacking that quality, for example, seems peculiarly associated with French free). The same names – Chick Corea, Anthony Braxton, Art Ensemble of Chicago, Association for the Advancement of Creative Musicians, Archie Shepp, Milford Graves, Ornette Coleman, Don Cherry, Steve Lacy, Sunny Murray, and Cecil Taylor – were also readily acknowledged not as "fathers" to "kill," but as the models and masters who lit the way to the peculiarly French gestures, different though they often were in sounds and approach.

Big Bands of Brothers

This story of the first French engagements with free jazz lends itself in its conclusion to the discussion that forms the crux of this book.

It is a small but, let us say, alchemically critical step from chamber-sized ensembles to big bands that improvise collectively without the conventional scripts, and organize themselves non-hierarchically, without leaders and section leaders.[59] It is the step where the musical issues discussed here shift from social abstracts to social concretes; where the informal, primal levels of friendship, family, clan, kinship, and orality – the Holy – suddenly meet the prime moment of formality, the chartered, the legal, the literate – Religion – and with it the keenest taste for organizational hierarchy.

Archē, again, is Greek for "first principles." The first principle of all culture is nature, specifically human nature. The individual bodies making music – rooted in pan-species strategies to mate, to define and defend territory, to entrance and train the brain to dance and transcend – comprise the *archē* of the collective, social body making it. *Hier* (god) signals an organization of those principles by a force higher than them; *a[n]-*, at the opposite extreme, denotes simple negation of the idea of any organization of the first principles (implying they need one imposed by that higher force, lacking their own).

The study of big bands from early jazz to the free-jazz years and beyond is a study in new ways of ordering the *archē*, ways best suited by a few new prefixes: *heterarchy, monautarchy,* and *panarchy.* These concepts speak loudly to Joppig's vision of the jazz big band as the twentieth-century center of Western music's intellectual history, and that as a reflection of its cultural and social ones.

Return to Jost's comparative analysis of Coleman's *Free Jazz* and Coltrane's *Ascension.* Each of the two sessions' personnels was more like a small French collective, or an amalgamation of a couple of them, than it was like the French big bands, or even like Sun Ra's Arkestra, the quintessential prototype of those bands. Summarizing the musical approach of both recordings, along with that of Cecil Taylor's groups, Jost writes:

> A new type of group improvisation emerges in which melodic-motivic evolution gives way to the molding of a total sound. For Ornette Coleman (*Free Jazz*), the various parts have an "intellectual" influence on one another, resulting in a collective "conversation"; for Cecil Taylor the collective is mainly led by *one* player who acts in accordance with constructionist principles; in *Ascension*, however, the macro-structures of the total sound are more important than the microstructures of the parts. (1994: 94)

These three descriptions correlate with my heterarchy, monautarchy, and panarchy, respectively. The first example, *Free Jazz*, most closely resembles the various approaches of the French collectives: the informal oral exchanges and communions of families, clans, tribe. Coleman abdicates his role as crafter of tunes that usually lead his "jazz," to "free" it from even them in this session, doing all his musical thinking out loud in spontaneous improvisation with the rest of the band.

In comparing and contrasting the qualities and natures of French collectives with those of French big bands, Cotro notes the function of both as social microcosms. The collectives were, as noted, little versions of utopia, effecting all the deconstructions and reconstructions of social hierarchy and roles effectively, easily, variously, and unproblematically. The promise of the big band is that of an arena of more power and connection between such little utopias, to make one big one: more of all the same freedoms, collective communions, immoderations of emotion and musical thought, rereadings of tradition. The problem, of course, is that the bigger in number and more diverse in options, the less those things can be achieved without a change in organization – like the string quartet that can rely on its own ears and body language to shape and direct the communal reading of a piece, but needs a conductor and section leaders when it disperses into the orchestra.

Cotro indicts the "steeped in tradition and highly hierarchical" nature of the big band, as well as its greater logistical (scheduling, financial) impracticalities, as the two main liabilities blocking it as a viable vehicle for the "freedom" staked out by individuals and small groups by that time. The second problem, as he notes, has generally been addressed by foregoing the idea of a regularly rehearsing and performing ensemble in favor of ad hoc coalitions of smaller groups and individuals for something like a meeting of nomads at one time and place for a

gathering of musical traders, socializers, athletes, and aesthetes. Money and opportunity fall into place for a project, phone calls are made, maybe a rehearsal or two,
sometimes little more than warm ups and game plans, and the fact that most
players have done other such projects together often before is the glue that gives
their free-for-alls cohesion.

Beyond that basic of heterarchical organization lies the pattern of Jost's second
analysis, of Cecil Taylor's improvisational approach, and it resembles, more than
the collectives, the big bands he discusses. Again, each was led (as also the European Free Jazz Group in Frankfurt, by Art Ensemble of Chicago trumpeter Lester
Bowie, in 1970) by a non-French player, three of them African-Americans associated with the music's American stars and pioneers. That shared aspect begs a discussion of that second approach as generally taken by many other such well-known
players.

"Monautarchy" suggests an organizing principle that comes into play when the
heterarchy of free play stalls or breaks down, either because the group gets too
large to support it, or because the vision or energy fails it. A monautarch is not
quite a monarch, not quite an autarch. A monarch would be the traditional leader
of the traditional hierarchy – in the history of the big band, figures such as Frank
Johnson, James Reese Europe, Duke Ellington, Count Basie, Dizzy Gillespie,
Lionel Hampton, Charles Mingus, Gil Evans, and Jef Gilson. Such leaders are like
CEOs and artists both – they hire and fire, get the gigs, enforce discipline when
necessary, design the music (even when delegating its design to other composers-
arrangers-players, and even when their hands are more light than heavy – it's their
band, their aesthetic, their identity). Once this organization is embraced, freedom
(in its form) is as possible there as anywhere. If all agree that the king's love of his
subjects and good stewardship of his holdings mitigates the problem of tyranny;
that the subjects' love of their place on the great chain of being, and their humble
service to those above and below them frees them from servitude, and to service;
and that freedom and fulfillment lie in resting content or climbing or descending
the ladder as one can and/or will, then the system need never be challenged, never
impugned as intrinsically tyrannous (only contingently so, in the wrong hands),
never changed. An "autarch" suggests the administrator of a rigid system, with the
same absolute power of the monarch, but without the personal charisma.

A monautarchy is more democratic, while retaining the unifying symbolism of
a figurehead. Don Cherry's project, for example, was the fruit of a loose convocation of French, other European, and American players who comprised a pool
of individuals and smaller groups accustomed to shifting collaborations and sporadic projects.[60] Cherry assumes and/or is handed the leadership billing as a reward
for the dues he paid in service of another leader's (composer's, organizer's) vision
(Ornette Coleman's); and he takes advantage of the opportunity to further his
own such, which in his case was direct engagement with Asian and African
rhythms and tonal-timbral textures and colors.

That 1968 big band event served as something of a launching pad for Cherry's
subsequent career as a leading voice in free-jazz/world-music encounters. It was

less the launching of a permanent group fixed under his personal and musical control than it was a band of brothers putting themselves at his disposal for the moment to honor and further his designs. The bandmates benefit from their association with him and his vision, and any one of them may well call in the favor of their own service to lead their own such initiative in the future, in which he might serve as bandmate under their name and leadership, to further their creative vision.

This is probably the most typical way of pulling off post-free big-band projects to get them around the economic challenges of maintaining an ongoing group, and the social ones of hierarchy Cotro mentions. Cecil Taylor, Anthony Braxton, and Butch Morris are a few examples of monautarchs – leaders with real authority who lead as guests more often than as steady employers running an ongoing institution – who have mined this approach to great effect.

Most significant to the French story at that point was the monautarchic formation of Alan Silva. A bassist who brought to the table years of experience playing with Shepp, Taylor, Bill Dixon, Sunny Murray, Ayler, and especially Sun Ra, from 1965 to 1970, Silva's vision for the Celestial Communication Orchestra was by his own account an extension of Ra's. Nonetheless, his organization and leadership style was, according to Cotro, "free of the propositions of the musical patrimony of black America" inevitable with Ra.

The Celestial Communication Orchestra was, like most post-Ra big bands challenging the big-band social and musical hierarchies, an amalgamation of individuals and collectives already well acquainted and seasoned teammates in free improvisation and effective orchestrations thereof. It included, over the course of one recording a year from 1969 to 1971, Americans in Paris then (Anthony Braxton, Leroy Jenkins, Archie Shepp, Grachan Moncur III, Dave Burrell, Robin Kenyatta, Oliver Johnson, and others; Art Ensemble of Chicago members Malachi Favors, Lester Bowie, Joseph Jarman, Roscoe Mitchell, as well as Don Moyé; Steve Lacy band members Irene Abei, Bobby Few, Kent Carter, Jerome Cooper) and French and other European players on the scene (Portal, Beb Guérin, Claude Delcloo, Tusques, Vitet, Kühn, and others).[61]

The overarching principle re-ordering the sheerly musical organization was that of an undifferentiated sound continuum, a kaleidoscopic carpet of sounds and rhythms, not of notes and their relations, nor of meter or tempi. From that primal sound – the collective picture of Chailley's first octave, the unbroken OM (the primal cosmic sound as chanted by Buddhist monks) between the pedal tone and its first overtones, and its correlative historical mythos of the world from which the West began to emerge – various differentiations emerge, to have their moments and then re-submerge, but they are not the rational differentiations that characterized Western music, at least not teleologically so. That is, melodic gestures, riffs, rhythmic patterns, individual soloists would come and go, but never usurp the primacy of the sound mass. "Energy and stasis" replaced the linear temporality of "fast and slow," and the unscripted symmetries and periodicities of real, biological time replaced the scripted ones of metered time.

This was not the land of the scaled octave, nor of the divided pulse; it matched rather the bottom line of, again, Chailley's chart, with its "deliberate neglect" of Western history and system, and its mining of the first-octave primal past for its fifth-octave primal present and future; it re-established all three of those temporal divisions (and the middle three octaves bearing the chromatic intervals) as part of the unity of the timeless Now.

The traditional use of different instruments to produce different timbral and rhythmic textures and harmonic sonorities was not buried by the collective drone; the piano distinguished itself in chords sustained and repeated, the brass in melodic motifs, the saxophones and violins in cries and smears of sound, but none of this escaped or shaped the OM so much as rang and blew in the upper reaches of its wind. Likewise the solos; all were virtuosi, but none stood forth as embodiments of the Great Man theory of history, or as voices of enlightenment, power, or authority to the inchoate masses.

Silva's own words about his role in that as, one might say, facilitator of collaboration between leaderless clans more than leader of sections with leaders, show the monautarchy as designed to cancel itself out even as it cancels out hierarchy:

> I think that this experience of collective music demands an adaptation, because it is necessary to absolutely abandon that to which one has become habituated. I don't wish to say that jazz has never been collective before this, but it was always directed by individual forces. Now, with the orchestra I would like to see, it is the collective forces that direct. This will be a music based on the relationships between human beings and sounds. That is my conception of a leader today. (Cotro [1999: 213–14])

For its part, the collective Silva monautarchically launched succeeded in its own quest for a distinctly French identity in the music. As Cotro states:

> Let us brave an image: the concert of the Celestial Communication Orchestra of December 29, 1970 was for us, in its spectacular reach, like an immense group therapy of free jazz in France. The conflicts and contradictions that it harbored (foreground/background, soloist/group, repetition/variation, problems of duration and the physical resistance of the listener . . .) crystallized definitively most of the questions raised by the "free" in a large ensemble. (212)

Again, all of this paints a picture very different from the "kill the fathers" spirit sounding out of England and Germany. Departing for a moment from the heter-/monaut-/pan-archy sequence begun above, a comparison between Sun Ra's Arkestra and the Celestial Communication Orchestra illuminates a face of the larger Eurasian (both Western and Eastern blocs) *Emanzipation* that might have been – Erotically more than Martially, synchronistically holistic more than religiously panarchic – instead of the one that was.

Sun Ra's roots were in the old big bands of his first boss Fletcher Henderson's day. He had always voiced admiration for Western civilization's hierarchical organizational discipline, had achieved his own brand and measure of it in his band, a more or less permanent community very much organized around his person and vision. The more sheerly musical organization of that group represented a transformation of the traditional big-band (hierarchical) sword to a ploughshare, all under the monarchic rule of its leader. From that clearly African-American patrimony of the musical paradigm shift (to large-ensemble free), to the same terrain staked out by Silva's and Cherry's mixes of America and France, is a big-band version of the same shift on the level of the smaller collectives, as described by Gerard Marais about Anthony Braxton's trio, above. The fathers did not have to be killed, since the brothers wore so lightly their primacy of place.

Jost's description of the three new improvisational approaches does not include an idea of progressive development between them, but such an idea does emerge if his description is applied to these different ensembles. Silva's description of leadership facilitating its own obsolescence in the deft invocation of collective forces reflects Jost's description of Coltrane's approach in *Ascension*, and also what I am calling panarchy. The "pan-" signals a unity that the "heter-" lacks, and which the "monaut-" limits to an individual. It is the unity of the *archē* working together in concert and order without any top-down governance. The panarchic stage reflects Marx's vision of the socialist utopia following the transitional dictatorship of the proletariat (a monautarchy of a class rather than a person). Finally, that third stage also resembles the Christian church, launched by its monautarchic founder to then run on the steam of its panarchic Holy Spirit.

With his recording *A Love Supreme*, Coltrane had engaged the West fully on both such mythical/religious and musical levels, in the way Ornette Coleman did (see chapter one). That is, he divined and matched the Judeo-Christian heart of it, its origin as a melody setting a religious text; and he engaged and commanded the Greco-Roman mind of it, in playing out that melody in all twelve keys, and all twelve notes, all much as Coleman did with his system of harmolodics.[62]

Coltrane had also, before *Ascension*, engaged traditions beyond the West's, from Africa and India, in his way. In his latest recordings, after *Ascension*, he was most like Ra, floating free of Western and then other earthly roots, and looking to the stars and future. Cotro's accounts (and the sounds) of Silva's and Cherry's big bands read very much like the farthest reaches and highest crown of France's free scenes in its first full flush of *Emanzipation*; we do not sense them playing the sidemen to those leaders. Both bands thus present visions of Eros rather than War, for their banding of American and French brothers; neither presented assertions of French/European identity coming to life by killing its fathers, black or white.

Coleman, Coltrane, and Ra, in themselves and through their protégés, had an effect on France something like Martin Luther King's in America – Erotically syncretic, integrationist. Albert Ayler and Cecil Taylor, by contrast, were something more Warlike, Ayler on an emotional and Taylor on an intellectual level. They sounded the Malcolm X to the King swung and sung by the other three. Their deconstructions of the West were more radical and uncompromising, more intense and singleminded. Taylor did not swing; he responded to Western power's down beat with his own damn down beat, toe to toe. He responded to contemporary

Western composition with the full power of its own vocabulary, to make his own new black statements of rhythm and sound. Ayler did not temper his cries and melodies with Western systems of rhythm and pitch, he just gave them his fullest voice.

The small and large collectives in both West and East Germany were as German as those in France were French, but they were also pan-European, and non-American, in a way those in France were not. In spirit and sound, they were more about the Ayler and Taylor side of things.

Emancipation II: To Panarchy

Everything is coming out into the open now . . . the old and the new are coming out to battle.

– Nikolai Gogol, 1848

Three

Hampel, Brötzmann, von Schlippenbach: Panarchy Rising

The Dutch are more intellectual: "Before you start, know your ideals." The
Germans: "I go into the deep. Follow me."
                                              – Leo Cuypers (Whitehead 1998: 43)

Paris and Berlin have been the Continental jazz centers embodying, respectively,
Eros and War, first as hosts, then as cultivators of the music in their own rights.
When it came to matters of change in Europe, Germany was Malcolm X to
France's Martin Luther King, Jr. If France became introspective and ultimately
Erotic in its response to American free jazz's *laideur*, West Germany's response was
to match the latter, sometimes sound for sound, like white brothers in arms who
would rather make ugly War than pretty Love. German introversion itself had
been Expressionistic rather than Impressionistic, and twice as intense as French
(literally, if whole-tone and chromatic scales can be used as measures). It included
no history of France's romanticization of *négritude*, and it had no problem, especially after Nazism, breaking free from either the (low) folkish or the (high) *musicalité* so dear to France. Its "kill the fathers" had two targets, American-jazz and
Western-classical musical patrimonies; it saw both as part of the same classist
and/or imposed identity, and it wanted the liberation both dangled before it but
would not deliver without a fight.

That said, those roles were reversed in the respective literatures about the music.
French discourse about African-American free jazz, as discussed, is more War than
Eros. Whether speaking on behalf of the righteous African-American cause
(Willener, Carles and Comolli, some of the musicians) or of the French response
of *beauté* to African-American *laideur*, the discourse about the music is marked
by *la différence* more than by the syncretism of the musical practice itself. In that,
the discourse on the free is in line with France's pre-free jazz literature, both
Panassié's stress on the distinction between the black and the white and Hodeir's
on that between "jazz" and "non-jazz."[1]

Germany, on the other hand, has historically discussed jazz as a branch
of Western music more than as an imported exoticism, and Jost and Berendt
have remained true to that tradition in their explanations of both American

and European free jazz.[2] Yet as Erotic (syncretic, both racially and musically) in approach as this discourse has been, the German musical practice has developed more out of a need to find its own voice than to blend with the American ones, in the end. Jazz found not only a tolerant, or mildly interested reception in Weimar Germany, but a genuine musical and cultural rapport surpassing anything else in Europe.[3] The vitriol with which the Nazis suppressed and persecuted it was a measure of the real popularity it enjoyed, and the real threat it posed. Whether Germans loved or hated it, they understood it as a powerful, serious force.

The point of most interest here, then, is Germany's hate as the flip side of a love unmatched elsewhere. Germany took jazz as seriously as it did on both its own and on German terms, understanding its implications for German and European culture. It was the European site – of Bach, Beethoven, Wagner, Mahler, Schoenberg – in which a musical discussion about merging the two traditions of West and Africa should have taken place, and did take place. It was the most logical European site not only for an intellectual discourse but for the most visceral one possible, taking place on the primal level of "blood and soil" (a body in its geographical and cultural place), identity and myth, of universals and ultimates concerning the future of the world and the human race.[4]

German jazz artists have exhibited the same life-or-death sense of "serious play" that has marked the European composer-improviser tradition from Bach through Stockhausen (with his aspirations to "cosmic" music). When German jazz finally found its own voice beyond the American shadow, in the 1960s, it went farther off into uncharted terrain of rhythm, sound experimentation, and energetic improvisation, and with more zeal, than any other European jazz scene, matching and often extending the gestures of its African-American models.

Racism as Classism

Race has been the more frightening face of class than have gender or generation in America, simply because people have been contesting openly with each other for the music's identity, both in practice and in print, more as blacks and whites than as men and women or – as in Europe – as young and old. The American racial contest flared in the music and time of the free-jazz years, when jazz scholarship's first major African-American voices joined what had previously been almost exclusively a European and European-American discourse.[5]

My suggestion of the free-jazz movement as one that ignited Western and Eastern European (more than European-American) white musical identities in proportion to its assertion of non-Western, even anti-Western black musical identity, finds a pithy and clarifying resonance with some words from a discourse on race spanning from the 1930s to the time of the *Emanzipation*, but removed from the American jazz discourse's muddier waters.

Négritude was a French literary and philosophical movement conceived to assert and promote pride in African history and culture. One of its originators was Leopold Senghor, a Senegalese poet who studied literature at the Sorbonne in Paris, served as a French army officer imprisoned by the Germans in the Second World War, went on to lead Senegal's struggle for independence from France, and became its first president in 1960, serving until 1980. The movement served as one of the models for the turns black American intellectuals took, with the end of colonialism, into Black Pride, Black History, Black Arts and their more political expressions during the American free-jazz years. *Négritude's* discursive patrimony extends through those times to the more recent diasporic studies of our own.

Of interest here are its words about music and Germany. Senghor writes,

And I find, in the land of the Germans, as it were echoes of the things I encounter in my night, of the expressive expressions of ideas and inexpressible feelings that churn within my mind, my heart. I discover, in their philosophy, as it were a *vision*: better, a feeling; better still, a *knowledge of the profundity in things*. But the philosophers are not who captures and seizes my attention; no more than do the linguists, when that knowledge articulated falls upon my ears. It is rather the musicians, and above all the German Romantics. Without doubt, they are the easiest to hear, to *feel*. But if that is so, it is also simply because they speak to me the *same language as my own soul*, where Germans and black Africans meet. (1968: 10)

In keeping with the connections made last chapter, between German and English Romanticism and the historical experience of African Americans, I read in these words something that applies beyond "Germany" to "the West," and beyond "Africa" to "African America": they express the process of what I read here (also broadly) as Eros subsuming War. They suggest how black and white identities can flower completely on each other's soil in the very act of flowering so on their own, even at odds with each other. This removes all disturbing notions of power-playing identity theft, or appropriation – of African-American music as perpetually doomed to minstrelsy, or to the irrelevance of a reactive recapitulation of some Eurocentered source (a point to keep in mind as we hold up pre-free American jazz to just that light); or of European jazz as perpetually doomed to its version of the same fate, under the Afrocentered original. It replaces such notions with a clear vision of the real common ground.

Négritude et Germanisme (Senghor's title) stare at each other on the spent battlefield of their joint history in both Old and New Worlds like a couple of worn warriors who have come to an intimate bond through fighting and surviving each other. This hard-won intimacy and equality is certainly mirrored in the musical collaborations and shared vernacular of the European artists discussed here with both Africans and African Americans.

I would further extend Senghor's "Germanism" through "the West," to *Négritude's* counterpart in "whiteness." A newer academic discourse than *Négritude*, whiteness has emerged from it and the wake of succeeding ethnic-identity studies, as we realized that the unnamed "we" naming all "others" was in fact itself just another "other," however effectively disguised as the neutral, universal touchstone of "self" against which all "others" were to be assessed and defined.[6]

Again, jazz historiography's own version of these discourses is reflected in the "hot-sweet" then "hot-cool" dialectic starting with assertions of jazz-as-white by groups and artists such as the Original Dixieland Jazz Band, Paul Whiteman, Bix Beiderbecke, and the white Chicagoans Benny Goodman, Lennie Tristano, or Stan Kenton – all in one way or another premised on the idea, spoken or implied, that the energy of black expression is somehow too rough and raw, reflexive rather than reflective, parochially black in a universally white world, in need of improvement by white refinement before attaining universality.

In the free-jazz moments, however, any suggestion of such a contest gives way to the retrospective dominance of jazz-as-black all along, and certainly so in those moments. Who possibly could have played the "great white hope," or even a close runner-up, to Ornette Coleman, Albert Ayler, or John Coltrane? Certainly no Americans; the few whites as much in the free-jazz vanguard as they were clearly in "sidemen" or otherwise marginal roles, such as those played by Coleman's white bassists.[7]

It seems significant and obvious, then, that this period in the music is the one associated with the emergence and assertion of an undeniably Afrocentric identity in America, and a pan-African one abroad; a turn away from, or through and beyond, American pop-music conventions and Western music tradition and principles to those of the rest of the world (including America's own underground of maverick experimental composers, from Charles Ives through John Cage), and/or those of African-American invention; and an engagement thereas with European culture as a Western artistic and professional context and arena more viable and fertile than America's.[8]

It also seems as significant and obvious that Europe, especially Germany, was able at that point, in direct response to that wave of *Négritude*, finally to find its own voice of "whiteness," beyond that of white supremacy/Western hegemony or its African-American reflections (European players had to individuate from African-American identity as much as from their own Western tradition). If any hints of that new-and-improved voice could formerly be heard in artists such as Beiderbecke, Goodman, Tristano, or Jimmy Giuffre, it was now speaking up through free-jazz players in Europe.

Moreover, in doing so, like its African-American models, it recast the "rough-black/refined-white" dialectic in retrospect. Its own turn toward not "civilizing" refinement but rather to even rawer and rougher fire and heat and improvisatory reaches reminded us that although "hot-cool" has often enough run down racial lines, "cool" was no more "white" than were Lester Young, John Lewis, or Miles Davis, and "hot" no more "black" than Europeans such as Peter Brötzmann, Han Bennink, or Willem Breuker.

Even the racial difference between American and European early free scenes was not necessarily polarizing, and certainly not in the case of FMP – arguably the most chauvinistically European of *Emanzipation* player collectives – whose artists have always collaborated with, and whose company has supported, an international, interracial cast. The "white" and "black" identities that can be inferred from the musical attributes of artists such as Cecil Taylor and his many European collaborators have proven as often as not the source of complementary thrusts and parries comprising a fruitful match of equals, more than of an African-American "father" being challenged or deferred to by his European "sons." Some European post-free artists, such as flugelhornist Franz Koglmann, have been discussed in the more conventional terms of a whiteness distinct (in either a one-up or a one-down way) from blackness.[9] On the whole, though, American and European scholars both have so discussed them less than American scholars (both black and white) have discussed African-American musicians in terms of blackness.[10]

These musings clear the path to let considerations of classism and the musical mythoi that ground it contextualize those of race, as also of gender and generation; and to let them lead in turn to a consideration of American jazz as Western music's own self-liberatory deconstruction of classism (albeit a reflexive one provoked by black self-liberation), and of European jazz as a reflective response to that deconstruction.

Pre-free Germany

Until the outbreak of the First World War, Berlin was the German locus of a network of European cities that provided a lucrative market for a booming export economy, including the business of performances, sheet music, then recordings. The presence of live American jazz in Germany effectively began after the war's initial export of it to England and France. Unlike those countries, with their older national cultures centered in capitals and relatively marginalized elsewhere, Germany's new nationhood comprised many different centers, each distinct from the other in character, culture, and politics. Berlin was clearly the cosmopolitan equivalent of Paris and London, and, arguably, embraced and engaged jazz even more deeply and honestly than they during the Weimar years – but the music was not so well received elsewhere in the country.

With the 1933 ascent of the National Socialists, a racist campaign against jazz as degenerate and dangerous resulted, with the onset of war, in American jazz activity on the Continent drying up completely. Instead of dying off, though, jazz "became the emblem of freedom, democracy, individualism . . . of rebellion against repression and conformity. While American musicians in Europe were only indirectly present through the media of radio and records, local musicians were free to develop their own seriously sincere interpretations."[11]

The Nazis themselves developed such interpretations, motivated by the impulse to "Aryanize" the music. Thus Germans continued to produce and record their own versions of jazz, as dance music, for domestic and foreign consumption (including propaganda consumption, in the case of Charlie and His Orchestra),[12] while officially going for the jugular of what they considered decadent about it in its "non-Aryan" forms.

The bebop movement in America as defined by Charlie Parker, Dizzy Gillespie, and Thelonious Monk did not take root in Germany until hard bop caught on in the 1960s; the Cool school as defined by Lennie Tristano's groups and the West Coast sound had a much more dominant presence. There were some exceptions to this rule. One was the band of one of the first European bop violinists. Helmut Zacharias's idiosyncratic engagement of bop's musical innovations defined the first widely broadcast instance of German bebop as a drumless string-band, chamber-type phenomenon suggesting a hybrid of Monk's cabaret sound and the more European roots of Django Reinhardt and Stephan Grapelli. Along with his violin, Zacharias's groups featured instruments distinct to northern European tradition, such as the harpsichord, and bell and chime and string and piping sounds. These sounds suggested a European revival of those formerly high-traditional instruments that the low power horns and drums of jazz had usurped. The rhythm is not wooden or mechanical or stiff, but jumpy and nervous – something like a reversal of the behind-the-beat Basie style. The effect is one of the manic cheer and insipid sentimentality one might associate with Lawrence Welk, or (ironically) with a David Lynch movie – or, again, with a (no irony) Sun Ra foray into the world of Les Baxter or Walt Disney.[13] Some of this music also bears a strong resemblance to the sound of Western swing coming out of Texas at the time, recalling the German-immigrant accordionists who helped launch the Tex-Mex style.[14]

The first active German jazz label after the war was Amiga, based in the Soviet sector. It captured a 1948 appearance by Rex Stewart and his All-Star Band, the first postwar visit by an American, and one that had a big impact on jazz history there, one extending to our moments.[15] Two (of six) recordings from this performance convey the nature of that impact. The title of one, "Lindy's Blues," refers to the major Berlin thoroughfare Unter den Linden, where Prussian history abounds. The slow tempo of this piece suggests two kinds of physical space. Unter den Linden in its prewar state was a picture of space filled with history, including the Linden trees themselves, favored by aristocracy from the Baroque era on. In its postwar state, photos of it in ruin and rubble show that same space stripped of that history.

Stewart's slow blues conceptualizes both types of space in time; his amazingly vocal style of trumpet improvisation defines the denuded space much as Count Basie or Jay McShann's bands defined the American heartland space as a fertile cultural void with the potential to be filled through sheer human will and imagination – a stark contrast to the space defined by urban culture's enthrallment to history. Stewart dances on the rubble much like German-American writer Henry Miller did with his words on the whole idea of Western civilization, put down by itself at the moment of one of its most murderously self-destructive reaches.

The second of the Stewart recordings, "Old Woman Blues," features his vocalizations and words as well as that poignantly vocal trumpet style. His mixture of European nursery rhyme and blues riffs goes right to the heart of the real-life conditions of postwar Berliners living, like the (his lyric's) old woman in the shoe and the man who's been drinking all night long, right on the edge of existence.

A harmonica-vocal group, the Mundharmonika-Trio Harmonie, released "St. Louis Blues," also in 1948, a response to the blues the sophisticated Ellingtonian Stewart was signifying on, that matched its African-American identity with an unalloyed German genuineness. The harmonica sound and hint of a Jew's harp suggests country blues at the gutsiest level, and the bass harmonica suggests the quintessentially German sound of the accordion, all making for a direct conversation between the Mississippi Delta, New Orleans, and the North Sea folk.

When Germany officially divided into East and West, in 1949, the history too began its development down two very different social and musical tracks. One thing they shared, however, was governance of a land divided into smaller states, as well as zoned by the two occupying powers. This return to decentralization gave rise to a network of broadcast stations important enough to have their own resident orchestras. Jost writes, "In this way, the paradoxical situation developed that in no two other Western European lands could so many big bands be established as in war-ravaged Germany, in both East and West" (in Wolbert [1997: 367]). The style that emerged was a mix of all the styles heard on American and British Forces Networks: swing, bar music, boogie-woogie, bop, all in the frameworks of popular dance bands. If Joppig's vision of the jazz big band replacing the symphony orchestra in Western music's evolution were actualized anywhere in Europe, Germany looked to be the most likely place at this point.

Berlin was the undisputed center of jazz musicians and public after the war, even as it was before. The difference between the two times, however, was that before the war were many (mostly Jewish) managers, booking agents, and international music production and booking agencies, as well as a press and critical community. These were gone now. They would emerge later elsewhere in West Germany, but even more in surrounding Germanic countries (Holland, Switzerland, Belgium, Denmark), and in America. Alfred Lion and Francis Wolf were Jewish emigrants from Berlin who cofounded Blue Note Records, which, in turn, broadcast over the Voice of America, helped shape the coming-of-age of many *Emanzipation* players, most notably here East German pianist Ulrich Gumpert.[16]

The term "Golden Age," like "Emancipation," is telling, coming from the Germans themselves. Postwar, pre-1960s' jazz enjoyed a Golden Age because the music was finally allowed to take its place in Germany with much more personal contact with American musicians, as it had already done elsewhere in Europe. In the Weimar days it had been an exotic American import; the literature on it from that time evinces a struggle to come to terms with its rhythmic, improvisational, and timbral aspects on the terms of Germany's own classical and popular music traditions. During the years of National Socialism, it became an underground force. Now it could make itself comfortable to seek its own level in the domestic and international performance and recording networks, and in the extensive and effective domestic broadcast system. The musicians themselves could relax and explore and develop what they could make of this American idiom, how they could assimilate and alter it for their own needs and purposes.

During the closing years of the 1950s, their "Golden Age" dimmed. The Jazz Föderation, like many unions, had shifted in the perception of many players from its grassroots advocacy role to an unwelcome policing one. In 1958, the producers of Jazz-Festival Frankfurt decided not to produce it in 1959, owing to lack of interest and new musical developments to showcase. In 1960, however, new stirrings did arise. Albert Mangelsdorff's star rose, as did drummer Hartwig Bartz's, both of whom Berendt identifies as ingenious originals. He marks 1960 as the beginning of the *Emanzipation*, in which the music and musicians moved into a sense of themselves as such too.

Free Germany

> 1968 was the year of the big band, a time when we met with our friends to play like crazy people.
>
> – Peter Brötzmann

> It is music which literally charges you with hate, I can't listen to it. I want to set everything ablaze or hack it all to pieces after I've listened to Brötzmann for awhile.
>
> – Attila Zoller[17]

The term *Emanzipation* was first introduced by Berendt (1986) in conjunction with the recording widely hailed by the German jazz press as the first of German free jazz, vibist-reedsman Günter Hampel's 1965 *Heartplants*.[18] Berendt qualifies his use of the term with the reminder that emancipation was realized through the very American musical idiom from which it declared freedom. He nonetheless accepts that paradox, along with the full force of the word, and goes on to argue the aspects of the *Emanzipation* that made it truly so in Europe.

He begins by asserting it to be an emancipation from and to several things: from American jazz, from the Western art music tradition, and from the international music industry; and to non-Western music traditions, to early Western (medieval, folk) traditions, and to a social as well as a musical liberation. He nods at the five Americans without whom "European free jazz would be unthinkable": Charles Mingus, Cecil Taylor, Ornette Coleman, Elvin Jones, and John Coltrane.

In his 1987 book *Europas Jazz 1960–1980*, Jost traces three stages in the *Emanzipation*'s unfolding: a transitional phase of tentative departures from bebop conventions, represented by Hampel's *Heartplants*; a coalescence of diverse pan-European groups and musical elements into the *unification* of West German pianist-bandleader Alexander von Schlippenbach's Globe Unity Orchestra; and a splintering from that into a conscious pursuit of diversity of idiosyncratic gestures.

(Notice the reversal this is of the pattern in France, of a similar transitional period followed by small French groups that then coalesce into international big bands.)

Jost's later (1997) explanation of the *Emanzipation* sees two general trends in American free jazz that shaped its European counterparts: a musical one, a shift from multivoiced styles (bop, cool) to many different styles of voices (that is, Coleman, Taylor, Coltrane, Shepp, and Ayler diverged much more radically than did Charlie Parker, Miles Davis, Dizzy Gillespie, and their colleagues); and a social one, as the anti-American/Western politicization of the African-American music spoke to the similarly angry European youth, much as it did to some European-American youth. Both impetuses cued the emergences of distinct personal and national sounds and styles where before had been one more or less homogeneous European imitation of American jazz.

Günter Hampel: Breakthrough

Like Globokar and Kühn, Günter Hampel broke out of his local German scenes, played much in France, then in America, where he took up a second residence in New York in 1969. His own initial model was the Modern Jazz Quartet – formal attire, high-cultural airs – and he found that when juke boxes began to replace live musicians in German clubs in the late 1950s, he could keep his competitive edge by writing his own charts.

"Compared to my later work, with [his band] Galaxie Dream, *Heartplants* is still very clumsy. But it's like a baby who starts to walk and always falls down at first," Hampel tells me in his Manhattan apartment.

> We already were established in the European circles as the first band that used our own heritage to make jazz music. We were the first European band playing, for instance, a piece by Béla Bartók; and we used what you called free jazz as a way to understand a musical area where the twelve-tone system would be at home with us. That system was an extension of what came before, not so much the radical break that most people see. It was essential; it came at the beginning of the century, when other cultural aesthetics, other things were going on, and Schoenberg was just a master at putting it into a system, a theory, so that we all could hear it.

Hampel's description of growing up wild on the postwar streets of his home city Göttingen, of being influenced in his formative years by African-American GIs who exposed him to jazz, was echoed by many other European, especially West German (nearest to so many United States army bases), musicians of his generation.

> We were re-entering a place that the two world wars had swept under the rug: the freedom of expression. Every time you have a war, it finishes off everything that was there before. We were just lucky to be the first generation coming out

of the wars that was allowed to do things people are no longer allowed to do even these days. We were left to our own devices, there was no one saying to our generation, do this, do that – because we were left out, on the streets, and once we had gotten out there and played our own music, we became stronger and stronger in playing it.

Hampel met *Heartplants* pianist Alexander von Schlippenbach in Cologne, where the latter attended the "first school for jazz in Europe," the Köln Hochschule für Musik. "Since he was officially registered there, I used to go with him to his classes. Then we would sneak out of those classes and go to the part of the department where the new music was being taught, by Stockhausen, and Kagel. I visited Stockhausen's house many times, played music with his kids, had conversations . . ."

Stockhausen's "intuitive music" rested on the composer's dictum to musicians to play "free" in various ways. The problem with it, something Globokar also critiqued from experience, was the tyranny of the composer. Having "liberally" bestowed freedom on his players, the composer would reserve the right to declare which "free" improvisations "worked" and which did not. This aesthetic gatekeeping was effectively overthrown (in theory, if not always in practice) by the approaches of Globokar's (French) New Sonic Arts, the (pan-European) Globe Unity Orchestra, the (Dutch) Instant Composers Pool, the (English) Incus and Company groups, and, later, Wolfgang Fuchs's (German) King Übü Orchestrü, to name the premier among post-free European groups forging an art of unscripted, uncensored collective improvisation.

Von Schlippenbach was the player in Hampel's group showing the most obvious influences from the Americans Berendt named as most significant to European free, especially Taylor, Coleman, and Coltrane. He wrote two of the five tunes on *Heartplants*, the most adventurous, as well as the most conventionally skillful.

The first one is the title track, a fleet modal tune in 6/8 reminiscent of early Miles Davis or Dave Brubeck, with an introduction that varies between 9- and 8-beat measures. Players such as Brubeck and Coltrane then were exploring the rhythms of non-Western musical systems; those from Turkey, or the Balkans, were exotic in the United States, but as much the next-door neighbors to the Germans as Latin rhythms have been to American jazz. Von Schlippenbach's writing and improvising are thoroughly informed by conventional technique and theory, specifically as defined by Charlie Parker and Thelonious Monk, exploring the rhythmic possibilities of phase-shifting in the way they displaced the accents of musical phrasing within a symmetrical metrical framework. Also evident is the restraint and romantic lyricism of Euro-tinged American pianists such as John Lewis and Bill Evans, something less apparent in his edgier playing on other cuts, and in his later work.

In bassist Buschi Niebergall's "No Arrows," the pianist stretches out more, into clusters that suggest the beginning of a Cecil Taylor influence and looser runs suggesting Coleman, though the bedrock of jazz drive and swing is still a constant under this free-bop approach. "Iron Perception," von Schlippenbach's other tune, has the most "out" playing. It opens with a free-for-all that moves into a written part that emphasizes the roiling bass notes the pianist would come to develop, almost like a drummer, in his later free playing. It goes out as it begins, with more open interplay.

Like Mangelsdorff's recordings around the same time, *Heartplants* does not sound as groundbreaking now as it was perceived to be then. The first steps away from conventional sounds, small as they were, were informed by much bigger steps away from conventional to idiosyncratic system and theory.

To me, twenty-five years later, Hampel said,

> In Germany, if you really think about it, we are just another state of the United States. The war was lost, we were occupied, still are; our politics are connected with American politics. I think it's wonderful, because we still have our own traditional culture and concepts, and they are healthy and alive too. But this multi-kulti thing in America is really the future of our planet – to put all of our resources together. Good grief, we don't need leaders anymore, we just need common sense, to find out that all human beings have the right to be here and sing and live, and we don't have to be slaves of anything or anyone.

Those last words hearken back to the "responsible anarchy" of Batel's take on free jazz (chapter two); in light of our more recent refinements on *archē*, they suggest an American monautarchy gliding seamlessly into a European panarchy through Hampel's first German gestures of *Emanzipation*, one with global as well as local aspirations.

"Music as Communicative Teamwork" is a (1973) conversation between Hampel and German musicologist Dietrich Noll. Hampel states that the music categories imposed by the culture and the marketplace – E-Musik (*Ernst*, high, serious music), U-Musik (*Unterhaltungs*, low, popular music), jazz, and experimental – under which his work had to labor were not conducive to proper understanding and sustainable support.

Hampel tells Noll he has developed his new music out of a grounding and training in traditional expressions, from "Dixieland" on. He likens his new composing style to that of a quarterback in football: he transmits certain musical impulses to his fellow players so that they may run with them into certain zones. Their musicianship generates its own rules in the spontaneous creation of the music, allowing each player (and listener) to bring his or her own rules to the music; the musical event is an expression and mining of the one soul shared by players and audience. The game's only spoilsports are the commercial powers that make or break musical artists according to their own unmusical agenda. Hampel says it is a time of the breaking down of borders between islands (of culture, and music), and that his music will both get people in touch with their own islands, and wake up their interest in others. He relates proudly an (unnamed) American musician's declaration to him that he (as a European) had truly developed his own music. He asserts free jazz over pop music as much more the communicative, less narcissistic, more fulfilling and challenging process for all concerned. He says that his and his (free-jazz) colleagues' music has been hailed as a picture of a new society, that politicians and statesmen could learn much from musicians.

Hampel went on to develop his later music and groups largely around this aesthetic. His career has been marked more by organic collaborations and associations with the American scene than have those of his Europeans colleagues who would strike out more radically into music seen as distinctively European for one reason or another, especially that of his bandmate von Schlippenbach, soon after *Heartplants.* Hampel himself used the words "transitional figure" when explaining to me his role in those years. His importance – like that of Mangelsdorff, Coleman, Kühn, and Globokar – has in large part been defined by his history as an opener of doors through which others could go to open still more doors, and by his endurance as a vital and active player.

Free at Jost

Ekkehard Jost is an inveterate, even compulsive, maker of pithy lists. Whether summing up the contributions and issues of the American free-jazz pioneers, the distinguishing traits of their European counterparts, or the blow-by-blow components of a single musical event, he likes to sketch the essentials he sees in their details as concisely and precisely as an inventory taker. Taking a cue from his methodology, I would summarize the contents of his now-classic *Free Jazz* so:

(1) The continuing dialectic between improvisation and composition (in the bands of Charles Mingus and Sun Ra – two classic matches for Joppig's vision of the jazz big band as Western music's flagship) led to freedom from the harmonic conventions determining melody, leading to experiments with melodic inventions that determined new approaches to harmony (John Coltrane, George Russell, Ornette Coleman); thence

(2) to freedom from tonal centers and hierarchies, leading to pantonal, atonal arrangements of pitch (Cecil Taylor, Sun Ra, the Chicagoans); then

(3) to freedom from metered time and pulse, leading to an open range of rhythmic options (Coltrane, Elvin Jones, the Chicagoans, Taylor, Ra); then

(4) to freedom from the timbral and tonal conventions of equal temperament, leading to a range of "dirtier" timbres and intonations (Coltrane, Ayler, Coleman, Shepp); then

(5) to freedom from syntactical interpretations of pitched sound, leading to subjective divinations of unpitched sound (Coltrane, Ayler, Chicagoans); and

(6) to freedom from instrumental conventions and roles, leading to new ones as they served all the above.

This snapshot became a bit more generalized in his 1997 essay in Wolbert on the same history. There he characterizes the musical terrain charted by the Americans as:

(1) a shift from rules to spontaneity,
(2) group interplay,
(3) collective, non-hierarchy,
(4) sound-color improvisation, a-melodic,
(5) energy/intensity as ecstasy,
(6) world-musical interplay, and
(7) social-political-economic issues.

At the same time, he prioritizes *Free Jazz's* original assemblage of the movers and shakers of all this into a clear primacy of two of them: Ornette Coleman and Cecil Taylor. They stand in retrospect as something like the Romulus and Remus of the free, the first openers of doors through which the other luminaries then went to go down their own idiosyncratic paths. Coleman was the grassroots, bottom-up genius forging his style far from the East Coast urban milieu of jazz-as-high-art, a Texas blues and R&B player who eschewed the equation of post-bop harmonic complexity with intellectualism in favor of folkish melodies and heartfelt emotion. That approach matured into its later sophistications and reaches into the *klangfarblich* and unmetered rhythmic grounds it shared with other new music from elsewhere, but it never lost those roots in the blues.

Taylor, by contrast, came up in the New York heart of jazz's thickest confluences with mainstream American music culture both high and low, black and white. He had his own serious engagements with European composers such as Bartók, Stravinsky, and Schoenberg, whose music, he said, he wanted "to serve new energy in black music" (Jost 1973: 67). Jost's chapter on Taylor captured in clear musical terms what brought his music closest to contemporary Western art music, and what made it a vital part of the jazz tradition: the "new energy" was a function of Taylor's concepts of rhythm and musical time.

Throughout this study, we have been contemplating meter as governor-gone-tyrant, jazz swing as a reactive strategy of dancing around meter without breaking free of it, and "free jazz" as including that breakaway freedom from meter. In places around the world where Western culture has moved in to dominate some other one, the musical hybrids that emerge invariably include a Western side that defines the down beat, and another that defines and mines patterns of upbeats and offbeats that oppose that definition, even while deriving life and identity from it. (For that matter, the same phenomenon is found within the West, between its ruling and ruled classes and concepts.) Coleman and even Coltrane continued to root their freer music in this reality, even as they also regularly reached beyond it; the Western down beat remained the center of gravity to and from which free flights returned and relaunched.

Taylor, more than his peers, defied this fundament of the groove, to claim the downbeat and its force for his own ground. As Jost suggests with his comparisons,

Taylor's simplest phrases inhabit the rhythmic universe of a Bach Toccata, and they morph as he works them improvisationally into the proactive polyrhythms of a Bartók or Stravinsky. When he works them to his fullest, they take on the even greater rhythmic complexity and energy of the best jazz, as generated by Tatum, Monk, or Powell, but they do so without relying on the symbiosis of "swing" to "time." Taylor steps from the power-of side of the jazz looking glass to the power-over one, asserting the down beat as its own swing. Something schizophrenic about black music and culture – du Bois's "double soul" – vanishes in the single-mindedness of his stalkings and attacks.[19]

Moreover, as a pianist, Taylor covered the territory Coleman shunned at first, that of Western harmony. Coleman's "harmolodics" was still a chromatic affair, but one snaking down the horizontal lines of unconventional melody, rather than up the vertical architecture of conventional harmony. Taylor had to deal with both sheerly by virtue of his instrument, and the way he did so evinced as total a claim on Western power as did his claim on the down beat. His fondness for Dave Brubeck's style of block chording lay in the sonorities it achieved, not in their modulatory development. He appropriated that influence and the more sophisticated versions of it in twentieth-century composers to develop his own "harmonic poetry" (Jost's charming term).

Such poetry put Taylor naturally in the company of composers going beyond Wagner's relentless harmonic suspense, beginning with Debussy and extending through Schoenberg to Stockhausen and all the others who developed their own such harmonic poetries during jazz's first century. This preference for sonority, texture, over function in harmony also put Taylor back at the first hours of Western harmony itself, when it too was still about sonority (such as that of the parallel fifths of civilization's early organum, and the "twinning" thirds of the northern tribes then beyond the civilized pale) rather than hierarchical function. As with his rhythmic aspects, Taylor's harmonic poetry went beyond that enounced by the West's reactive others, into his own heights and depths. And, again, it opened the door especially for those who would orchestrate collective free improvisations for the largest (most harmonically potent) ensembles.

All this is a simple recapitulation, plus my own insight, of one German writer's insight into and particular interest in the American creators of this music. It pertains to this book through the varying impacts of the different voices in the range of national scenes. Once we make Coleman and Taylor the two banks of a river that flows through Coltrane, Ra, Shepp, Ayler and others later, we see how some national scenes fall more naturally to one bank or bend than another, according to their histories and identities.

Without making too much of those loose orientations, it is safe to say the more syncretic-Erotic influences of Coleman/Coltrane (Great Britain) and Coleman/Ra (France) were superseded in West Germany by the more martial Ayler/Taylor impact. Taylor has loomed especially larger there, from the beginning and through the years to the present, although Coltrane, in his *Ascension* project, had an equal impact, at first and historically, especially on the Wuppertal scene, and for the same trait as Taylor's "energy" treatment of rhythm and time.

Jost's description of *Ascension* – "the macro-structures of the total sound are more important than the microstructures of the parts" (1974: 94) – describes the step beyond the monautarchy of the provisional leader into the true collective, which was the principle informing the formation of the Globe Unity Orchestra. But that influence was fleeting, Taylor's enduring. Coltrane ignited the West Germans, English, and Dutch more at that point than any earlier, and all earlier points were more steeped in the ground shared in common with Coleman's system – tonal syntax, meter, and the connections of these to language and speech, blues and gospel. From *Ascension* on, Coltrane had more in common with Ayler and Ra, for their timbral drama and cosmic allusions. Ayler was quite important to the Wuppertalians and their Dutch and English comrades; and Taylor, after Coleman and Ra, to von Schlippenbach and his bandmates. Taylor's influence went to the high-culture side of German musical thought, and Ayler's more to the working-class culture of Wuppertal's Ruhr Valley.

Pan-European Emanzipation*: Whiteness as Friend, or Same Old Foe?*

The recordings seen by English-, German- and French-language press as most representative of Jost's "stage two" of the *Emanzipation* include those discussed next: German saxophonist Peter Brötzmann's *Machine Gun* and *For Adolphe Sax*; and the Globe Unity Orchestra's *Globe Unity*, and *European Echoes*, not least for their inclusion of the other national free-jazz scenes in their personnel.

Several things distinguish these recordings from the stage-one transitional gestures of Hampel and his bandmates. On the one hand, they reflect their African-American influences in such a way as to beg the question of appropriation rather than homage (to what degree might they be, yet again, blatant derivations posing as original statements?). On the other, they were perceived and received in both European and North American presses as original rather than derivative enough to beg the question of what made them so.[20] Finally, unlike any stage-one recordings, they were as associated with anti-American political and cultural sentiments as were their African-American counterparts, and provoked in Europe the same vehement zeal either for or against their free-jazz approach and its resulting sound and spirit.

This new aspect of the European scene was part of a general love–hate dynamic between the Europeans and their African-American models and peers. Wuppertal bassist Peter Kowald's term "kill the fathers" targeted the African-American masters the Europeans loved but felt they finally had to individuate from (Globokar also used it in reference to European composers, and Jost called it "spiritual parricide"). The European jazz musicians saw the Americans, even their fellow up-and-coming young peers, treated and paid like stars in Europe, while they and their fellow Europeans were second-billed or not working at all. Some, especially in England, spoke bitterly in the press about American cultural decadence, political and cultural imperialism, and commercialism as undermining the music and its potential impact. At the same time, African Americans such as Don Cherry, Frank Wright, Anthony Braxton, and others were regular collaborators and friends with the European players, who were acknowledged by the creators of even the most Eurocentric of the new musical gestures to have been crucially influential, per Berendt and Jost, Coleman, Coltrane, Ayler, Taylor, and Ra.

It would be easy enough to make a case for European whiteness as foe rather than friend. As AACM luminary and long-time player on the European scenes, trombonist George Lewis, has noted, *Machine Gun* can be heard as a blatant imitation of Coltrane's *Ascension*.[21] Also, some of the anti-American/pro-European remarks about musical aesthetics made by both European musicians and critics can be read as echoes from jazz's earlier days, to the effect that African-American jazz was raw material to be cleaned up and civilized by European refinements. (For example, several of the Europeans I interviewed felt their Western music tradition imbued them with a more informed sense of how to spontaneously improvise sophisticated form and structure, and that African-American strengths lay in the other areas of rhythm-based individual intensity and energy that they should stick to, as though it were their "place."[22]) *Machine Gun* remains the classic iconic expression of Peter Brötzmann's signature sound and style. To some, again, it conveyed the aggressive, wild, harsh sound of the warrior on the rampage, a threat to all that was about humanity and order in music; to others, the same wild cry represented a healthy barbarism that took Europe back to its primal roots, revitalized it after its long oppression by its own civilization and history.

To situate the musical-historical moments of both Brötzmann's and von Schlippenbach's first hours in the question of white appropriation of black music, consider Thelonious Monk's oft-quoted (possibly apocryphal) remark that he and his fellow bop pioneers were motivated in part by the desire to forge a music that would be impossible for white musicians to imitate. That notion was arguably better served by the advent of free jazz, when Western song forms and other fundamental conventions used as platforms for improvisation were left behind. Still, it is a War impulse that inevitably gives way to Eros, as fire does to water (or to self-consumption). The interesting question to pose here is that even if *Machine Gun* is a direct theft of *Ascension*, more so even than a comparable French gesture that might include collaboration with African-American players themselves, is it at the same time more original and profound, in the same way Bob Dylan's appropriations of and spins on Woody Guthrie and Charley Patton are more original and profound than are those of others who might have collaborated with them or learned at their feet?

After reading many European articles, and talking to many of the African-American and European musicians at the heart of this issue, my sense is that the European musicians themselves have no conflicts about the two aspects of "love and hate"; they see themselves indeed as sons and daughters who love and honor their "fathers" best by becoming their own men and women. The press on the subject has its own agendas, with which the musicians usually reflexively align their interests – and the American press differs from the European, with the American playing up the music's European aspects as the "new-and-improved," and the European stressing African-American influences, in a bid to give the European innovations authority. In addition, the most recent concerns of African-American musicians such as George Lewis and Anthony Braxton, both long-time players in the European scene, are that the innovators still living and active get their due as such in terms of work or recognition, and that that be more than lip service or token bandwagon spots as opening acts (such as British rock groups, for example, gave people such as Muddy Waters or B. B. King).

Unlike the free scenes surveyed in the last chapter, which sketched the first hours of the German *Emanzipation*, the focus now is on Europe as a whole. Both *Globe Unity* and Brötzmann's own small-group recordings fall into Jost's "second stage" of the *Emanzipation*, which came to be tagged in the German music press the *Kaputtspielphase*.[23]

Jost characterized the *Kaputtspielphase* so:

(1) what composition there is proceeds idiomatically through the various creative processes of individuals, rather than through a single common paradigm or system, and then in clear subservience to free improvisation;

(2) definite pitch as the stable element of musical organization is abandoned, now favoring unstable sound patterns. A structural distinction is achieved mainly by using collective variation of the parameters of the sound register, density and loudness;

(3) the latter happens spontaneously, as a result of the group process, is not orchestrated by the composer-arranger-leader; development processes are being led, somewhat inevitably, toward a limit where individual musical events cannot be strictly identified as such but combine to become a diffuse, intensive totality;

(4) the concept and structuring of time moves from one in which "swing" was the guiding principle to one in which a very fast pulse (his example here is 300–350 quarter notes per minute) typically prevailed; and

(5) instrumental techniques are idiosyncratically conceived and developed to convey one's own voice and vision. In the hands of a "real" musician, these come across as innovative, inventive, and expressive; in players with less talent or authority, they come off as charlatanism and inadequacy – the difference between the Emperor having no clothes and clothes so fine that only the keenest eye can see them. (1987: 57–8)

Litweiler saw the European free scene welcoming its African-American mentors, leading to much more work and acceptance than they found in America. He also saw in it an evolution of personal voices that cast them as "the first internationally important European jazz generations . . . The currents of their own cultures provide them with inspirations and background that are at least as vital to them as the jazz tradition" (1984: 241). He then nodded to Brötzmann, Han Bennink,

Fred Van Hove, and the Globe Unity Orchestra (GUO) players as *the* torch-bearers of Albert Ayler and other free masters.

Our "stage two" recordings by those players compare well with the first record-ings of Ornette Coleman, for their initial and enduring capture of a new musical sound and ground, and for the impact they had on the press and continuing critical discourse in Europe. Those under Brötzmann's name (*Machine Gun, For Adolphe Sax*) were released after but recorded before von Schlippenbach's *Globe Unity*.[24] The personnel of the small and large groups combined comprised a coalition of French, Italian, Swiss, German, English, Dutch, Belgian, and Scan-dinavian players (one of the first free-jazz steps out of nationally isolated scenes). The impact of these recordings and musicians was to fulfill the sociomusical impli-cations just considered, through *Heartplants* and the other "transitional" record-ings, in the rawer and more volatile contexts of late-1960s Europe.

"Why So Much Free Jazz? Questions of Sociological Relevance" is a subhead-ing of Berendt's conclusion to his (1986) book's chapter "German Jazz and the Emancipation (1961–1973)." He points out that Germany has a reputation in the international music press as being the land of free jazz in Europe; moreover, it is often reported so in a negative light: a music of "hate" all too resonant with the image of the "berserker Hun."[25] Citing also "a French journalist" on the subject, Berendt reports a general amazement in the European community that entire festivals were devoted to free jazz in Germany, at a time when one concert was an almost impossible sell elsewhere.

He broaches a reason for this by positing a self-evident relationship between melody and society. The more intact and homogeneous the society, the less broken its art music's relationship to melody. The more distant and critical a generation of musicians from its society as a whole, the more in opposition to the music "that the people sing, that the society represents," will the new music be. He asserts that the Germans have a tradition of self-criticism dating back to Goethe, one reach-ing its strongest pitch after the Second World War. Free jazz, although an African-American expression of social protest of this sort, proved in that very fact the vehicle most suited to Germany's need to exorcise its deep, oft-sublimated self-alienation and to struggle with its collective demons, to protest its dilemma and break free of it.[26] (The East German musicians inherited no such dilemma. Their Soviet social conditioning steered them more into antifascist pride than guilt over a Nazi past. They were thus more comfortable drawing on German tradition and its Ur-melodies/harmonies, especially triadicism, for their own syntheses with jazz.) African-American music had exorcised its participants' deep alienation from white society, through humor, satire, irony, sheer fun, naked grief, and spirituality, and the entire emotional spectrum, as well as the more reactive deconstruction-then-reconstruction of melody and everything else.[27]

Musically, German free jazz scans as a reaction, on the one hand, against the deadly, compulsive chauvinism of Nazism (and its official exaltation of a "teutonic" folk-melodic tradition over its repression of atonality and "foreign" rhythms) and, on the other, against the perceived slavish imitation of American jazz. Is free jazz in Germany – Berendt is careful only to ask, not assert – a magnified reflection of the larger society by a small portion of it both more awake and less safe and secure (therefore all the more motivated to express fear, and protest, and alternatives) than the rest?

Peter Brötzmann (Improvisation)

The German thing is about the music as expression of a way of life. On-stage, off-stage, it's all one thing: an intensity of experience which has to be communicated. Obviously Peter embodies that. There's no doubt that Brötzmann was a sort of beacon or central focus for the freer approach.

– Evan Parker[28]

Peter Brötzmann started out as a painter with a fan's/amateur's taste for early jazz. He worked as an assistant to the Korean Fluxus artist Nam June Paik, helping to produce one of their first exhibits, at the Gallerie Parnasse in Wuppertal, a town that he described to me as "a very artificial thing." We are sitting in his Wuppertal apartment building's sheltered courtyard, surrounded by his paintings on the walls, circa 1997. It is a few blocks from Peter Kowald's house; the men have been neighbors so since their first hours in the music. Brötzmann is short and stocky, with cropped hair, trim beard, and a gentle air and manner.

It's really a row of villages along the Wupper River. Then, to please Kaiser Wilhelm, they built up the Schwebebahn [a hanging overground train], and then they thought, "Okay, we are not just villages anymore, we have to be a proper city," with this new "Wupper Valley" name. So this town has no center, in a way.

We have had interesting people living here at any given moment [artist Joseph Beuys and dancer Pina Bausch among them] very strong-minded, some of them not looking left or right, just doing their things. And we had a lot of quite rich bankers here who were very, very open, and they looked around for art – like the Impressionists and Expressionists and all from that era. So our museum, for example – the Von der Heydt – is named after one of these guys. It has a lot of really beautiful art from the early years of the century in stock – it's too small to show, but they have it. So this town does have something special.

It was well known before the first and second wars as the town with the most religious sects. You have different churches, not only the Catholic and Protestant but all kinds of small shit . . . so the people here are kind of different from others. It's all mixed up.

You even have two roots of language here. You have the Western part, that of the Rhine people – from Köln, and Dusseldorf – and the Barmen, in the east, goes more to the woods and is a bit more rough language, toward Westfalen. But of course through the war and after the war it's all mixed up. You find from time to time old people in the bar just talking original dialect, but they are passing away.

Brötzmann told me that the main impact living in that town had on the shaping of his music was that it gave him permission to sidestep the boxes of formal conservatory training and mainstream jazz conventions, to see his music as part of the Fluxus approach to aesthetics (overlapping with one of its major American collaborators, composer John Cage), which embraced every sound as potentially musical; and to ply that to the energy and openness of both the free-jazz movement and the spirit of radical-leftist student activism in the 1960s – art as politics as anti-*Kultur*.[29] He also told me that his ideal then and now was to play with a sound so big and dirty that one note implied within it all the notes in the octave – Chailley's first-octave OM of the overtone series – as a rainbow contains all the colors of the spectrum, and as a painting contains the flow of its creation process in the moment of its frame.[30]

The network with other national scenes grew with the emergence of the German one from its beginnings. "When I first moved to Wuppertal, the collaboration with Peter Kowald was the most important thing. In 1966 we formed our trio with the Swedish drummer Sven-Åke Johansson. At that time I already had a lot of connections with the Dutch scene – Misha Mengelberg, and, a little bit later, Han Bennink and Willem Breuker – and Peter was a little more oriented to the English scene, so he went over a little more often than I to visit Johnny Stevens, Derek Bailey, these guys from the very early hour of improvised music."

Both *Machine Gun* and *For Adolphe Sax* were first produced out of Brötzmann's earnings as a graphic artist, then released later by FMP. *Machine Gun* has the title track on the whole of side A, and two tracks on side B, "Responsible" and "Music for Han Bennink." The title track is attributed to Brötzmann, "Responsible" to Belgian pianist Fred Van Hove, and "Music for Han Bennink" to Willem Breuker. The A side's sound echoes the title, with its short staccato bursts of drums and horns (Brötzmann told me the title came from Don Cherry's description of his sound); the reeds have that buzzing, noisy quality of the tin drum, the colloquial German name for the Prussian military snare, which both jazz and novelist Günter Grass brought to the attention of the world.

If *Ascension* bears the aura of Coltrane's burgeoning spiritual quest against the backdrop of Malcolm X's Muslim and Martin Luther King's Christian versions of same, *Machine Gun* recalls rather the Prussian military roots of jazz. Those roots are aligned here in solidarity with, rather than against, black militancy, and with the spirit of the Surrealist's idea of the ultimate act of art being terrorism (André Breton's notion of the firing of a pistol into a crowd – an image with a timeliness we will return to).

Several things are noteworthy. First, the opening is divided into two distinct braids of sounds: that of Brötzmann's and Breuker's two rough tenors shooting out their Morse-code-like messages with Johansson's heavy snare, without much thought for pitch distinctions, and plenty for nervous, barking rhythm and rough, loud sound; and that of Evan Parker stringing pitches together into chains of sound that rattle with other discrete pitches on the piano, and more hierarchically metered, swinging rhythmic layers in the drumkit, both accurately suggesting

Parker's and Johansson's connections with the mainstream jazz tradition of the time. The presence of Fred Van Hove's piano itself is natural enough here – these moments of Parker soloing over a rhythm section recall the spirit and sound of Coltrane's quartet – but when Brötzmann comes back in with his savage cries, blowing away all the fancy pitch and stick and finger work going on in these jazz moments, the piano's role and voice immediately comes into question.

Again, pianos were eschewed in many of the American groups from Ornette Coleman on, as too rigid and limited to the Western chromatic-harmonic matrix. Cecil Taylor was an exception, and always more a solo/leader voice, even in groups, than part of a band. By contrast, here in one of the major European debuts in the free-jazz arena, a piano is rolling along and finding its way and voice right there with the horns and drums. Von Schlippenbach's equally pioneering role would affirm and develop this inclusion.

The last thing that stands out as something that distinguishes this from comparable American recordings of the time (Coltrane's *Ascension*, Coleman's *Free Jazz*, or Albert Ayler's records) is that the regular but flexible rhythm of the breath, of the lungs – not the also-regular but more fixed rhythm of the heart, such as in jazz, where keeping the beat, the time, and doing it artfully, is the desired goal – is the overarching framework surrounding the more restless, irregular and quicker ones of the fingers and limbs.

The oscillation here between Brötzmann's unmetered cry and Parker's Coltrane-like sheets of sound with a rhythm section evokes for me a conversation between the barbaric German spirit of the Northern forests and his Anglo-Saxon counterpart in Britain, more tempered by the Roman and Celtic civilizations – or, less broadly, between the saxophone player from Wuppertal who had sound pictures to paint that were only marginally concerned with the American jazz (syntactical) conventions his fellow Europeans were laboring under, and the saxophone player from England who was still working from his own greater enmeshment in those conventions, and would struggle so away from them successfully in direct proportion to the influence of his German colleague.

"Responsible" is an interesting track to consider, because an alternate take of it was included on the CD reissue, revealing it as an orchestration of collective free blowing rather than a spontaneously articulated form. As a form, it is a mix of suite and Ives-like collage. In the opening, we can hear a quick turnover of statements – opening cymbal roll, repeating bass vamp, overlaid by a second bassist and second drummer, leading into a brief collective jam, leading in turn to one note held and repeated by Brötzmann, becoming one of his solo statements, fading abruptly to a slow, open foray into basses, piano, and percussion, into which Parker gradually insinuates himself.

The net effect is of a musical experience marked by the most extreme intensity of catharsis and wild abandon, but also by a clear governance in time, a dispassionate decision to realize that intensity and catharsis and freedom in a variety of musical situations, each relatively brief in scope, marked by self-editing. The orchestrated gestures are posited as places to surround with little improvised ornaments that trigger other predetermined melodic phrases and/or full-blown solo or collective jams. Both irony and unabashed fun abound. Also, unlike the *For Adolphe Sax* trio's imbalance between percussive and wind instruments, this larger group strikes and expands that balance from the trio's tangled hierarchy of instruments and voices to a more or less constant collective voice and mind speaking through all the different players in turn.

The whole record stands as a convocation of northern European scenes that developed as distinctly from each other as they did cooperatively. The Dutch approach of orchestrated suites of melodic escapades of irony and humor that Breuker went on to make his own; Bennink's expansion from percussion instruments into the surrounding environment as a percussion instrument; the more delicate, introverted sound surfaces Parker's English circle explored; and, of course, the full-throttle cries and energy of Brötzmann and the Germans are all in the mix here.

Jost's obsession with summary lists is challenged most starkly by the utter eschewal of musical codes in *For Adolphe Sax* (Brötzmann refers to it as *Morning Glory*, a working title it had at its pre-release inception). His opening strategy for meeting that challenge is contrast – an 1849 citation from Heitor Berlioz about the then newly invented saxophone's sound, followed by a contrasting depiction of Brötzmann's sound as off the scale of that original voice. Jost declares the recording to be "from A to Z freely improvised music, which knows neither a tonal center nor a regular rhythm and which ignores every standard of composition." He quotes Brötzmann as claiming the "individuality of the musician" and the "collaboration of musicianships" as being, respectively, system (of creation) and form (of the resulting music). Feeling, tolerance, and personally interactive sensitivity are further specified as the group's "glue."

While giving this its due, Jost nonetheless analyzes as he can and as suits him. He notes the recording's three different "pieces," with titles, with Brötzmann's byline.[31] He then tackles the music itself by talking in terms of the three instruments' voices and roles – trios, and which instrument therein dominates, duos, solos, and so on – as the small group's natural analytical framework. He proceeds to discuss the work on those terms, moving through the individual stylists and their interactions, asserting it as "the first German, actually the first European jazz recording, that followed the consequences of a concept of total improvisation."

My interest in this recording lies in the way it takes us more to the heart of the Wuppertal matter (as opposed to the broader European echo of America still sounding in *Machine Gun*). Although released after the latter, it was produced first, by the bare-bones trio of Brötzmann, Kowald, and Johansson. Like a string quartet, its intimate size makes for a clear window onto the musical thought behind it.

It opens with a relaxed interaction between the instruments, a heterarchical discourse in which no one stands out. That quickly changes around the different physical natures of the instruments. Brötzmann's sax sounds, unlike Johansson's drums and Kowald's bass, begin and arc and end with the breath; Johansson's percussion, unlike Kowald's bass, can better match, in volume and timbre and the bite of phrasing, Brötzmann's sax; Kowald's pizzicato bass can sound a plucked, reverberating unmetered pulse in a sphere of sound unlike both, as unlimited by the breath and pitch as the drums, while as able as the sax to pitch his sounds.

What fast takes shape, then, is a duo between sax and drums that reverses the traditional concept of horn stringing notes and phrases over a bedrock of metered rhythm. Here the bottom line is that of the sax, waxing and waning with the breath, with the drums responding to it with an overlay of fills that spar and dance with its blowing, and fuel its silences with more rhythmic food for its thought. The bass notes float both sonically and rhythmically distant from that duo, suggesting a pulse several temporal layers removed from the duo's longtone cries, clashes, and chatter.

Having defined and explored these relationship dynamics, the trio shifts to a duo between the bass and drums. Johansson immediately quiets down, de-intensifies to strike the acoustic parity most natural to the bass. That opens the way for Kowald to up his activity, which leads him to walk more traditionally; a more defined and regular pulse comes to the fore, though still not marked by the traditionally timekeeping drums. Finally, the bass drops out, and Johansson takes a rather conventional post-bop solo. We've moved from the most "out" rhythmic concept in full trio, to more inside without the horn, to most inside by drums alone.

Then the process recycles itself, spiraling up to a new level. The trio in full engages a second time, with less tentative foreplay, less haphazard thrashing and more flowing synchronicity; we experience the same free play now informed by the residual short-term memory of its first excursion, and all sound more in tandem with each other and with some plan. Johansson proves bolder in his solo this time, running along and building on the momentum of Brötzmann's lead after it stops, rather than reverting to convention and cliché. Kowald grabs his bow and ventures into closer contact with Brötzmann's most keening, unpitched cries; Johansson responds immediately so as to let that sound come forth. In all, the effort of an open, close listening reveals pattern and proportion, units and sequences of analysis that compare perfectly with anything that might have been scripted in advance. A less open, less close listening would easily report only random noodling, however intense, suggesting that analysis and theory of freely improvised music is at least half projection, like the pictures seen in a Rorschach ink blot (something I address in chapter six).

Berendt never worked out the answer to his question "Why So Much Free Jazz?" in Germany, but he did, in discussing Brötzmann, embrace the "teutonicism" in German free jazz as an expression of "white power" that best matched in Europe the "black power" expressed by African Americans (and others from the "Black Atlantic"). He pegged this to "West Germany's industrial powerhouse," the Ruhr Valley region around Wuppertal, as one source of the musical energy and sound in these players. (In the nineteenth century, the Ruhr was something like the American South, with an agricultural economy and peasant populace. That working class morphed with industrialism into factory workers, with accordingly anti-elitist, radical leftist political views.)

Having considered, via European-American Litweiler, these West Germans as Europe's "great white hope" in the musical discourse of black liberation, it is necessary to consider how the proposition holds up in the political one.

The '68ers

The FMP folks in West Germany have always had a pretty political angle on things, judging from their literature. Not really socialist or anti-socialist. More utopian-socialist, egalitarian. Yeah, all those guys at FMP have better connections to Eastern Germany than to the Western state . . .

– Ernst-Ludwig Petrovsky[32]

I don't think the political developments of the time really had that much to do with the evolution of the music in any deep sense. They certainly provided a vehicle for its development – that I believe – but the truth of the music is, I think, stranger than the fiction of those politics . . .

– Jost Gebers[33]

German publications about jazz, from the first instructional materials of Baresel and Seiber in the 1920s to Ekkehard Jost's analyses of free jazz, have been more concerned with the musical than the social or political issues it has raised. They have been so in contrast to other Western European countries, especially France; and when they do go beyond musical issues, they tend toward the metaphysical – philosophical, spiritual, and occult – more than (except in former East Germany) the social, cultural, or political. The West German *Emanzipators* were clearly not detached from the political issues and passions of their time, but their revolutionary fervor was focused more on the music than on the politics.

Quinke's article for *Musik und Bildung*, subtitled "Musical and Social Emancipation," provides a substantial history of FMP to its date (1977), with an emphasis on the sociocultural implications. He describes the emergence and rise of FMP in the context of the "student unrest and street riots occurring in the Western world from Berlin to Paris to Berkeley . . . The only art relevant to the new consciousness was that which was a means of political agitation" (1977: 556). He saw the Western music-culture-industry as an arm of Western oppression; the access all voices have to the free market he saw as the oppressor's Achilles heel:

A subsidiary of Deutsche Grammophon in Germany presents black musicians such as Archie Shepp, whose music has an overt anti-white, anti-capitalistic battle cry (e.g., "Attica Blues"). As long as such socially critical music comes through such large recording firms is exactly as long as it makes them a profit. (556)

If there was or is such a soft spot, it is one that time has by no means proven fatally vulnerable, in either the United States or Western Europe. The most that can be said is that in Germany, thanks to West Berlin's status as a West German showcase of free enterprise (ironically, thus heavily subsidized by Bonn), even of countercultural freedom, FMP has managed to make more of its situation, in terms of producing alternative performances and recordings for a niche market, than have its American counterparts.

Another German chronicler of the European free-jazz scene as it emerged, the late poet Wilhelm Liefland, spontaneously made a cardboard sign for the first Total Music Meeting (TMM) in November, 1968, at the Berlin club Quasimodo: "In the midst of capitalism, playing against capitalism starting out . . . double entrance price for jazz critics" (in Forst, 1983: unnumbered pages).

Again, the most documented activism of the musicians was more cultural than political. Forst, and Wood (both 1983) describe the defections of players well established by then (Manfred Schoof, Gerd Dudek, Alexander von Schlippenbach) to the company of their more radical younger counterparts (Peter Brötzmann, Peter Kowald), and away from mainstream venues in Cologne and Berlin to their ad hoc alternative concerts nearby. These were clearly protests, as well as ploys to siphon off audiences. Their impact on the jazz scene was comparable to the Newport Rebel Festival Charles Mingus led in opposition to George Wein's Newport Jazz Festival, in 1960.

> Even though they did not regard their music as a political weapon . . . the almost euphoric political atmosphere caused European musicians to ponder such concepts as exploitation, manipulation and monopoly. While tens of thousands in Berlin participated in blockading the Springer [German corporate] concerns and in closing the Sorbonne in Paris, the Free Jazz musicians began their march against the institutions in unspectacular and quite small groups. (Forst [1983])

Forst reports that the first TMM was well attended, and did indeed, as intended, siphon audience members off from the mainstream festival, as well as some critics and visiting American celebrities, including Americans Sonny Sharrock and Pharoah Sanders, and Brits John McLaughlin, Evan Parker, and Paul Rutherford. The second TMM took place in a Berlin bar called the Litfab, then moved to the Quartier Latin[34] in 1970 (and again, in 1991, to the Podewil in East Berlin, where I saw my 1996 Cecil Taylor concerts). The 1970 move brought it even closer to the Philharmonic Hall (site of the Berlin Jazz Days), thus facilitating its draw of audience and critics.

What started as a reactive gesture of protest against the Jazz Days quickly turned into a proactive alternative to it, and eventually even a collaborative supplement. In 1975, the city's cultural ministry began to help finance the TMM, and the two festivals began sharing audience and musicians in a cooperative way. Pianist George Gruntz, the musical director of the Berlin Jazz Festival said, "With you music is made. With us it can only be performed."[35]

Old guard helping new guard – one of the key factors in the continuation of FMP's first flush of success in the German jazz scene, rather than the more American experience of relegation to a generation-bound cultural moment that came and went. And now Mangelsdorff himself is director of the Berlin Jazz Days, and the premier elder statesman of all German jazz.

I asked Jost Gebers about the relationship between the student protest movement and the music. "I think it comes down to individual personal histories that vary," he said.

There is a wide spectrum that spans an avid communist such as Paul Rutherford to his conservative opposite in von Schlippenbach. They all had the musical approach and vocabulary in common, on the one hand, but their own various political pursuits on the other.

Naturally, that said, there was more of an ideal and spirit of collectivity and unity in those times than later, but it quickly became obvious that it would not function so smoothly and simply, with artists, because they are always focused on their own individual careers more than the interests of any collective. They must do their own job, not FMP's, and that has been the problem throughout this whole history.

One might say it has also been the problem, yet unresolved, throughout the history of the West, at home and abroad. The most radical attempts to resolve it took place in the East, where the focus from 1917 on was decidedly more on the interests of the collective than those of the individual. Accordingly, the most radical counterfoci of the musicians on their own individual careers there, as we will see, achieved an efficacy as agent for sociopolitical change that made their Western counterparts look like shadowplays about revolution, rather than the thing itself.

"I started a kind of jazz club at my school," Brötzmann tells me:

I was about thirteen or so, and I played to records by Kid Ory and Benny Goodman, Louis Armstrong and the Hot Five, all kinds of records. But eventually, of course, I realized that I wasn't a black man, wasn't even an American, that I had my culture here.

For me, jazz had a kind of political meaning, because in my very early youth I was already very left wing, and connected to the Communist Party – naive, of course, but genuine. Then Vietnam started up; Korea was just over, and to deal with jazz music was a way to be on the right side in the war between the poor and the rich, the black and the white – well, we didn't have that particular problem, but, you know, the worldwide class struggle and so on.

Free Jazz is the "Utopia of a creative socialization . . . the musically expressed quest to make living together bearable," Forst presents as the words of "some critics." He goes on with his own words: "Indeed, in its best moments this music actually transcends the free and merely intuitively bound collectivity of musicians, encompasses the audience, is felt, understood and is then perhaps in reality the 'fiction of a socialist society.'"

While associating the spirit of FMP with the student protest movement, Forst takes care not to similarly associate it with what he saw as the "music as a political weapon" of African-American players (interestingly, in the light of previous chapters' observations of French jazz studies, and of the impact their book had on East Germans, he makes this distinction in reference to his French colleagues' Comolli and Carles's *Free Jazz, Black Power*). Shoemaker, on the other hand, broadens rather than restricts the comparison, and actually likens FMP's relationship with leftist politics to that of African-American artists with black nationalism:

> Essential to this analysis is the concept of Germany being a divided country occupied by two opposing armies, each, in the course of forty years, establishing a self-perpetuating political status quo for its sector. So entrenched is the idea of a permanently divided Germany within the respective strategic establishments in Washington and Moscow that a movement "from below" – a people's movement – for reunification is theorized to be a flashpoint for theater warfare that would, presumably, escalate to nuclear proportions. (1985: 22)

He reports an interview with FMP artists von Schlippenbach, Mangelsdorff, and Paul Lovens in 1983, when American Pershing missiles were being deployed throughout Western Europe. The musicians protested this for its use of Germany as an arena of global confrontation – the old land-in-the-middle syndrome, now on a global scale, between the white Western and Eastern, individualist and collectivist, tribes of the northern latitudes – which, as Reunification would also do, drained the political and economic structures of their former support of the arts.

That drain resulted, in 1984, in FMP's halting of its fifteen-year-old recording operations. Shoemaker suggests that the Reagan-allied Kohl administration knew that it was cutting off potential political opposition as well as its cultural correlatives. He argues that if recording started up again in spite of cuts, it would have to improve its United States distribution, its reprinting policy, and its graduated artist royalty scales (into "a way of doing more for less, particularly for the emerging musician," the support of whom became an increasingly crucial part of FMP's mission and staying power over the years).

Alexander von Schlippenbach (Composition)

> My influences actually begin with Oscar Peterson, widening through Bud Powell to Thelonious Monk. These influences were timely to certain stages in my playing, except for Monk's, which still plays a role. Then, of course, later Cecil Taylor played a deciding role, influencing my work as a whole. I have also always been involved with composition, have myself, over time, written many

pieces. Ultimately my goal is to integrate what I learned of the classical discipline as a student with my work as a jazz musician . . .

– Alexander von Schlippenbach[36]

Alexander von Schlippenbach is one of those pianist-leaders of a big band of wind players in the grand tradition of James Reese Europe, Ellington, Basie, and Ra, who work the music-making spectrum from solo keyboard to largest ensemble, stamping the public roar of the latter with the whispered thought of the former (note the similarity of his professional goal to Cecil Taylor's words about bringing new energy to black music from contemporary Western composers). Wrote one scholar for his international readership in 1982:

> It's to a considerable extent due to the work of pianist-composer Alexander von Schlippenbach that people nowadays talk of independent European styles of jazz, and even of "European jazz." The West German's composition "Globe Unity," written for the orchestra of the same name in 1966, has gone down in the annals of jazz history as a seminal work combining new music techniques and free improvisation. At the time there was nothing similar – even in the homeland of jazz, the United States – which could have opened up such radical paths. (Thiem [1982: 44])

Perhaps it makes more sense to say that there was nothing similar that could have effected what the GUO effected in Europe, for and by Europeans, both in its first hours and for many subsequent years.

Von Schlippenbach was born in Berlin, but moved with his family to Budapest, where he lived until the age of five. The Second World War triggered a move back to Germany, where he grew up in a mountain village in Bavaria. At sixteen he went to Cologne to take up his music education, then moved back to Berlin in 1970, where he has remained. Unlike the Rhinelanders and the East Germans with whom he would later work, and like Globokar, von Schlippenbach's start was more broadly European, less personally rooted in *die Heimat*.

Like Kühn, von Schlippenbach credits Ornette Coleman for the primary nudge from his bop to his free style; for the same reason – the beat – von Schlippenbach's more radical countrymen (even the older Mangelsdorff) overlooked Coleman in favour of Coltrane, Ayler, and Taylor. "When we were still boppers we had more in common with today's free jazz than with bop. The crucial part, that did make up our strongest link to bop, was the ongoing tempo, which from the first we got from Ornette Coleman. The rhythmic conception in our playing as a whole was strongly influenced by Coleman" (Noglik 1981: 101).

His piano playing from those first post-bop moments, however, does indeed show more the "deciding influence" of Cecil Taylor, in its move away from that ongoing tempo, and away from boppish free play and into clusters, noise, and atonality. What can be said in hindsight is that von Schlippenbach managed to stake out the most radical free-jazz stretches of the time in the framework of his orchestrations and pianisms for the band without losing his roots in pre-free jazz.

This synthesis – by no means a common one – played out both in the GUO recordings following *Globe Unity*, and its later incarnation as the Berlin Contemporary Jazz Orchestra; and in the solo and small-group projects ranging from conservative jazz repertoire to full centralization and cultivation of unscripted improvisation. The result over time has been to contextualize the *Emanzipation* years and all their musical landmarks as part of the larger Western music history in Europe and the Americas, not as some historical-musical cul-de-sac spawned by maverick spirits. "Looking back, you could even say that Globe Unity resulted from a combination of the Schoof Quintet and the Brötzmann trio of that time. In those days they were the most interesting groups playing exactly the kind of music I had in mind. So following my own concept, I put together this lineup in 1966 and wrote a composition to fit this frame" (Noglik [1981: 45]).

The "composition to fit this frame" was "Globe Unity," filling one side of the LP by the same name. Von Schlippenbach's liner notes evoke both Sun Ra's mind and the original mystic spirit of Pythagorean sound-and-number magic, before it was reduced to acoustics and mathematics by the no less rational but much less ecstatic among the Greeks. His notes also cover well, as do his later words about it, the aspect of rhythm Joppig paired with improvisation, in attributing to jazz the reborn soul of Western music:

> *The sphericity of time: that means a world of universal musical connections.* Player and composer, in jazz embodied in the same person from the very beginning, create intricate connections, whose primary formal principle is *unity*. The cosmic eye at the middle and at the periphery of the sphere sees the structures simultaneously from all sides. Out of the sphere's divine indifference, the solos burst forth with a gesture of revolt. They form arches after life's likeness. Rhythm is the breath of the world. Sound is fire, water, earth, air. Behind . . . its colored screen a figure glows phosphorescent in pure, inviolable beauty. This music is the world of the orchestra. Fourteen European musicians of the last jazz generation have realized with admirable discipline and utmost exertion the idea of playing free-tone jazz with a big orchestra. By their reaction to the scores, which consisted almost exclusively of directions for improvisations derived from certain principles and ciphers, they demonstrated the finest intuitive grasp of music. They were attuned to the new sounds and illuminated their dynamic properties. By their ability to grasp graphically drawn structures, to improvise with available groups of notes and interval dispositions, as well as to play strictly written phrases absolutely freely, they opened up a world of fascinating possibilities for such orchestras. With such an orchestra, in which spirit resists all musical subservience, Paul Klee's vision becomes possible: "One takes leave of the mundane and is transported to a realm beyond, which can be one total affirmation."

The sounds of Indian and other non-Western traditional musics are part of this realm beyond. In Berendt's part of the liner notes, the OM of Chailley's primal first octave – a unity along the lines of Stockhausen's "cosmic music," Cherry's "primal music," Coltrane's "universal music," or Braxton's "composite reality" – is wedded with the formalized tumbling strain, an octave divided by thirds, something rooted deeply in Northern European tribal musics:

> Schlippenbach explains that the piece takes its title from the revolving sphere of the earth, from movement constantly returning to where it has begun. Everything in the music is developed from a twelve note row, dominated by a third. The solos, uninhibitedly individual as they may be, are closely related one to the other, so that each, rather than appear a separate performance, constitutes a part of the whole.

The GUO was the *crème de la crème* of West European free players, changing in personnel slightly between performances/recordings around the West German core. Over the course of its three major LPs and two singles to that date, it featured, with its core of the Brötzmann/Kowald and von Schlippenbach/Schoof forces, fellow West Germans Willi Lietzman, Hugh Steinmetz, Gerd Dudek, Kris Wanders, Günter Hampel, Karl Berger, Buschi Niebergall, Jackie Liebezeit, Günter Christmann, Mani Neumeier, and Albert Mangelsdorff; Claude Deron (French), Enrico Rava (Italian), Paul Rutherford, Evan Parker, and Derek Bailey (all three English), Pierre Favre, Iréne Schweizer (both Swiss), Fred Van Hove (Belgian), Arjen Gorter, Willem Breuker, Han Bennink, and Peter Bennink (all four Dutch), and Kenny Wheeler (Canadian in England). Perhaps this mix of people – all of whom had either played together much already in smaller combinations, or had performed and recorded in the free idiom enough to know each other's work and how to situate their own in the ensemble – explains the musical success of the group in spite of its difficulties.

The traits behind that success: GUO is a band of leaders, all virtuoso soloists as well as ensemble players; it can play both the compositions put to it by those of its members or guests who want to orchestrate free improvisations (von Schlippenbach, Breuker, Steve Lacy, Anthony Braxton) as well as the collective free improvisations with little or no orchestration favored by others (Parker, Brötzmann, also von Schlippenbach). It is a non-hierarchical collective organizationally too, with Kowald managing technical details, and von Schlippenbach acting as musical director – "but the other musicians have the same rights as them" (Rouy, 1976).

As seen from Brötzmann's musical tastes, the more radically improvisatory voices in the GUO – clear reactions against the European legacy of composers dictating their visions down the food chain to interpreters – made this democracy no foregone success. In response to Noglik asking him how he dealt with the tensions in leading a musical democracy of a band full of leaders, von Schlippenbach said,

> Take for example two very different players of the same instrument, Gerd Dudek and Evan Parker. Both bring contrasting but complementary presences to the collaboration. Naturally this makes for musical variation from case to case. To one event Albert Mangelsdorff will bring more than Günter Christ-

mann; in another Christmann or Paul Rutherford will move naturally to the foreground. One can never foresee this, it depends on many factors. However, I am convinced that these differences work out to a balance and equilibrium between voices more than a hierarchy of leaders and followers, in the end. (1981: 107–8)

This philosophy would face some challenges; von Schlippenbach was decidedly not in the tradition of J. R. Europe-through-Ra (or even Cecil Taylor, or Ornette Coleman, apart from *Free Jazz*) in terms of his leadership style, which was more along the lines of Alan Silva's words (see p. 114). He would share his composing/conducting duties with other band members and guests regularly, sometimes supporting gestures quite different from his own (such as Kowald's, discussed ahead).

The Keyboard behind the Composer

The "deciding influence" of Cecil Taylor shows itself most directly in von Schlippenbach's percussive attack and approach, and his chromatic palette. When Thiem suggested to him that "jazz critics often maintain that too much of the jazz feeling is lost in twelve-tone improvisation," he responded,

> That all depends on how much command the musician has of the twelve-tone scale with which he intends to improvise and how far he is capable of improvising. It's also possible to think of a jazz improvisation with a very slow measure and very few tones. This does not necessarily mean that it is of poorer quality than a fast one. So, this whole assertion cannot be maintained . . . I'm an admirer of Arnold Schoenberg, and I've dealt with his theory of harmony . . . It was all quite a logical development. (1982: 45)

On the other hand, also a logical development was that of his composer's vision from (in the grand tradition of James Reese Europe, Ellington, Basie and Ra) his hands-on work as a pianist, and (also in that tradition) from the work of his fellow instrumentalists, at least as much as from abstract theoretical formal training.

Noglik remarked that "this [jazz] impetus is itself rooted in the world of composition. A jazz musician modifies at the most a predetermined structure in large part as a classical musician simply plays it" (1981: 113).

In response, von Schlippenbach extends that "modifies" to factor in an improviser's deep self-expression, style, and individualism; an ensemble's range of sound and potential for creative play; and sounds from nature (shades of the "tumbling strain"; see p. 289). He characterizes the GUO as an ensemble of improvisers that was also a rich field for the serious composer. He describes his own twelve-tone improvisations as something more than scripted, plowed into his fingers by his mind over time, so set to run free in play with his bandmates.

Von Schlippenbach traces this hands-on incorporation of Schoenberg's dodecaphony (an approach Taylor was the first to fully exploit in jazz) to his work with his trio with Evan Parker and drummer Paul Lovens. His words in interview are telling, both about the nature of processing even the most challenging theoretical system through the improvising body rather than mental maps, and about the relationship of small to large freely improvising groups.

He stresses that the group never rehearses, just starts playing its concerts. He says this spontaneous intimacy developed musical processes that became the engine driving the similarly free play of the larger GUO.[37] He describes how it was Evan Parker's playing that shaped his own chromatic palette:

> He can split up the melody somehow, in different motives, and go on with them in ways reminiscent of minimal music, the way he repeats phrases and uses circular breathing. It took me awhile to find things to do with that, but as I've developed my sort of twelve-tone system of improvising, which comes out of the structure of the piano – six notes for one hand and six notes for the other, each a tone-row – we can work together on certain tempos and pitch overlays in a very interesting, interactive way. What happens in my hands relates, in other words, to his circular breathing structures.[38]

Von Schlippenbach's erstwhile employer Günter Hampel described to me the early stride pianists in terms of the collision of African drumming and a chromatic instrument, right around the time of Schoenberg's leveling and foregrounding of the chromatic scale. I muse over Cecil Taylor as a torchbearer of that collision, and the looming presence he's been behind FMP's European roster, and the way that presence has kept cropping up in my own study despite my decision to focus on a handful of European "first-hour" players. Indeed, as I've mused over the trombone – along with the fretless string instruments and the human voice, the least chromatically designed of the typical jazz-free/jazz instruments – I muse over the piano's greater integration and diversity in the European than in the American early free-jazz scene.

"Kill the Pianos!"

> Piano is maybe the most technical of all instruments. The tradition of the instrument, not just the jazz piano tradition – it's a very big literature of technique and exercises. It might be hard to get out of it . . . but it's the same with most instruments. There were many things to discover on trombone, say, which you can't do with a piano. Apart from prepared piano, but I've stopped that now.[39] I think there are still big possibilities to play things that have never been played.
>
> – Alexander von Schlippenbach

Von Schlippenbach's single solo LP for FMP (*Solo Piano*), or any other of the labels I've found him on, is significant for the post-free-jazz gesture it is of the keyboard virtuoso tradition starting with Bach and developing through Beethoven and his pupil Czerny, carried through Chopin and especially Liszt. It brings us full circle here to Joppig's (Danhauser's, p. 81) picture thereof (as Günter Sommer will soon bring us back to Prussian drums).

Much of this tradition provided the piano music on which the great American jazz pianists, whatever their background, cut their teeth for over a century, and still do. It is the tradition running through the *Sturm und Drang* Romantics, stressing the techniques of ecstatic rapture. Out of the technical and into the theoretical realm, it is the approach to harmony that starts with the German Baroque and spirals through Beethoven (especially in his late string quartets) into Schoenberg's tightly wound pieces for piano and voice. Its key descriptors are "intensity," "energy," and "harmony," more than "melody," revealing the musical moment's inner workings and mysteries as if looking at it from above or below, at its verticality, even while boring relentlessly through its horizon of flowing time.

Von Schlippenbach's grounding in this German Baroque lies in the sense that rhythm is the great motivator of all the great patterns of pitch. It is something that began floating away with the French influence Germany took in at the turn of the nineteenth century, but came back in force with jazz – specifically, here, in the persons of Bach fanatic Fats Waller, Art Tatum, and (von Schlippenbach's youthful favorite) Oscar Peterson. The rhythmic platform stretches unchanged from Bach through those recent players – a few simple meters in a few simple forms – in keeping with their close connection to dance. The excitement the jazz greats brought to those meters and forms lay in the greater variation they brought to both pitch and pulse. Monk put that variation at the heart of his concept, winding down the ultimately facile gesture of dazzling technique – which is to move through time so fast that the horizontal blurs itself into the vertical contour it suggests, as a strummed guitar chord sounds like a chord rather than the succession of plucked notes it really is. Monk figured out a way to stuff rather than spin time's flow into its moment.

As influential as Monk was on Von Schlippenbach, however, in *Solo Piano* he clearly goes in the Oscar Peterson direction – spurred on, no doubt, largely by Cecil Taylor's own brand of fancy fingering – but perhaps even more by the force of his own tradition and training, and the transformations they underwent in jazz, especially free jazz. The dialectic between rhythm and harmony generated from the German Baroque through jazz is in this recording too, only the interest lies in the attempt to centralize rhythms that traditionally would have been accents or ornamentations on an underlying simple pulse, and to centralize pitches that would have similarly referenced diatonic or chromatic matrices.

Even though the piano is a chromatic instrument, and even though we hear patches of diatonic and chromatic patterning come through here and there, the name of the game at this point is to make a music out of such patches, not within them. Pitches simply cannot be seen as matrices of musical meaning here any more, nor even phrases. The instrument here happens to be chromatic, but the music being made on it is as full of the throaty repetitive cries of Brötzmann's or Evan Parker's, where the manipulation of pitch is more repetitive and random than systematic, something for color and texture more than syntactical complexity.

Miles Davis is often quoted as saying he turned to the cool approach in the '50s because "the music was getting too thick"; von Schlippenbach's solo recording sounds a hundred times thicker than *Heartplants*, but in fact it is a hundred times simpler in its conception. Von Schlippenbach had learned all he could about melodically and harmonically syntactical music; it was in his body, in his brain and hands; it was internalized and revealed in his spontaneity more than carefully prescribed, rehearsed, then performed. The performance here rather lies in the quest to go beyond what was encoded in the body, and to express that quest as the meaning of the music. And that quest's musical embodiment can be expressed at least this specifically: it is based on the idea that it will best proceed and unfold from the body's dreaming logic, its sub- and super-conscious logics, rather than its waking, rational, willfully circumscribed logic. All of this, of course, is the very picture of German Romanticism's reach through the finite for the infinite in music.

The series of several shortish improvised duets between von Schlippenbach and fellow pianist Martin Theurer, *Rondo Brilliante*, likewise bespeaks classically trained, skilled pianists. These duets, also like the solo, are premised on the maximization of musical elements – notes, rhythms, volume, speed – as imparting the desired musical event. The strategy of the series as a whole is also obviously to pace and ration several discrete events, rather than to present one wending flow; and to vary the sound terrains and musical ideas explored between each piece, but to keep them relatively consistent within each.

Jonathan Kramer's pithy discussions (1978, 1988) of the development of "moment form" in twentieth-century European art music hit close to home here. Stockhausen, moment form's progenitor, himself spoke of it as born under the constant threat of wartime attack, an elemental sound untempered by civilization's restraints or optimism about a future to plan for (Stockhausen [1989: 94]). The move from form as tonality's unfolding of pitch and metric relationships to sound's physical demarcations of duration was a move from time's horizon as flow to a theoretically infinite succession of vertical eternal Nows. But, once cracked as a totalizing system, metered time still has a place as one paint on the palette, in the work of von Schlippenbach, Kowald, and others.

Kramer's concept of "cumulative listening," its influence on the perception of musical time, and the importance of proportional durations of musical time all speak directly to these piano duets. Their musical content is best understood in terms of conventional analysis as examples of moment forms: self-contained, non-teleological, non-referential musical events. They vary from each other in surface aspects that could be graphed, but with events as thick and busy as these duos are, there is no payoff worth the effort of gathering the information. Even assuming such a harvest was effortless – say, a MIDI transcription of every note, and a computer analysis of the whole for selected parameters, patterns and aspects – the result would be the equivalent of musical fingerprints, idiolects, profiles of indi-

viduals and group interactions that would carry whole a body of information conceived and crafted for the ear in real time, translated into a representation crafted
and conceived for the eye, in the fixed media of analysis. These are gestures of
improvisers, not of composers or interpreters. From the jazz side of this music's
parentage comes the lust and vitality of immediate proactive engagement, of
muscular energy and full-fledged individuated, self-expressive ego, whether it is
asserting itself with or without restraint (again, dance, not text). Stockhausen's
Momentforme is consistent with the immediate reality of dance, and with the
cosmic, timeless reaches of the Romantics.

How should we receive as listeners this music that seems made so completely
for its players alone? For me, it is as an engagement between the human
organism and its own potential in a chosen area, valuable for inciting and inspiring other such bodies to go and do likewise. This is slightly different from a similar
moment-form event generated by a composer for players. In that case, the attention is drawn more to an idea and its expression. It might expand our horizons as
to what is possible in life, but it does not draw us into real compulsive-obsessive
identification and action quite as viscerally. If one were a painter, especially at the
stage of a work where one is striving to find its identity, this is music that might
be the most fruitful aid and stimulus to the process. It encourages one to get
physical with one's tools and media, to delight in them as ends in themselves,
whatever means they might develop into therefrom.

The strategy for the first duo emerges after a couple of listenings, and is the
same that one hears in German Baroque's single-minded pursuit of one musical
affect to its exhaustion, or in Coltrane's *Ascension*, or in Cecil Taylor's solo work:
start with something simple and obvious, something every listener can grasp and
track; repeat it and work it through permutations of gradually increasing complexity and intensity, fly above it improvisationally without losing the thread, and
ebb and flow as many times as necessary to creating the sense not of discrete (and
discreet) phrases, but of a roaring stream. The skill in both executing and tracking this lies simply in staying with its initial impulse and premise, so that even
during the most cathartic, climactic floods, you can go in and out of it as you
will, and end it gracefully.

The recording as a whole is amenable to the value Kramer places on cumulative listening as an analytical tool. What at first sounds like sensory overload gradually sorts itself out over repeated listenings. Fast lines, dense textures and rhythms
all become more discernible against the backdrop of an implied pulse or pulses;
traces of familiar influences – such as, here, Monk, Peterson, or Stockhausen's
piano music – suggest themselves. One can even see a track developing into something like a playable aural notation, as it becomes so memorized that it could be
played to by ear. What gets played is the text of a texture, in which the author
can both write and read his or her own life as does one who throws and reads the
I Ching, or tea leaves.

In other words, this music in Europe has perhaps stretched farther, or in different ways, down the extremes of the spectrum of instrumental concept design,

those at the most Dionysian/wind/unpitched-noise end (Chailley's first and fifth octaves) and that at the most Apollonian-Pythagorean/scientific/mathematical/pitched-noise end (Chailley's second through fourth octaves).

> Von Schlippenbach isn't very involved in the vast structural heights that obsess [Cecil] Taylor. He paces himself quite thoughtfully through a piece of playing: in duet with [Sven-Åke] Johansson on records like *Kung Bore*, the interplay is definite and emotionally direct. His piano voicings are sometimes stripped away to [Carla] Bley-like essentials, as in their vicious rumination of *Over the Rainbow*; mostly they're a skilful balance of curt, stabbing patterns, hectoring speedball rushes and sober, schematic interludes. Some performances, like the fascinating *Drive*, create a tangible long form out of the collision. (Noglik [1981: 10])

I found just such a "tangible long form" and "collision" in a duet with one of Taylor's most copasetic drummers, Sunny Murray, recorded as *Smoke*. This balance between the vertical moment and horizontal flow I attribute to von Schlippenbach's fast hold on and embrace of the jazz-traditional premise of tension sustained between palpable pulse and departures from it, and between pitch and rhythm – contradistinct from many of his European colleagues' radical embrace of only the vertical dimension of sound in stasis.

Evolution of the GUO

European Echoes was recorded in Bremen in 1969, a year after *Machine Gun* and two years after *For Adolphe Sax*. In keeping with the pattern of accretion of players and scenes and styles of the first two recordings, here at least four different cells are represented, totaling a band of sixteen, under trumpeter Manfred Schoof's leadership. There's Brötzmann's contingent with Fred Van Hove, Bennink and Kowald; the trio with pianist Iréne Schweitzer and drummer Pierre Favre that Kowald also played in; Evan Parker's Incus group from England, with trombonist Paul Rutherford and guitarist Derek Bailey; and Schoof's group with von Schlippenbach on piano, Gerd Dudek on tenor sax, Buschi Niebergall on bass. Trumpeters Enrico Rava and Hugh Steinmetz, and bassist Arjen Gorter round out the group. One immediately discerns the influence of the von Schlippenbach–Schoof group with its compositional and close-to-conventional post-bop approach. Lines suggestive of Ornette Coleman set off free-blowing.

The title of this LP was interpreted by at least one German jazz critic as signaling something derivative, a European response to the American free-jazz statements of the time. Although each side is an unbroken cut – actually one 30-minute session divided into two sides – both show the same episodic approach of dividing the music into shorter subsets of free playing by different soloists and combinations. The same high pitch of speed and intensity is held throughout, opening with the full band sound, then giving ample spaces to a succession of multiple solos, as it were, the first being by the three pianists von Schlippenbach, Van Hove, and Schweitzer; the second by drummers Favre and Bennink; and the third by bassists Gorter, Kowald and Niebergall – all of whom form something like a three-layered carpet of rhythm, noise, and low tone textures over which various horn players blow, and come together to play occasional riffs in sync.

The overall sound here – owing mostly to that unusually thick carpet of percussion and strings, including pianos – is smoother and more high-octane than the first two, in effect something that strikes the ear as both longer-reaching in its power, and more deeply grounded in its source, while also more fluid in its arrangement of episodes and transitions between them.

The piano trio comprises one of the unique aspects of the early European free jazz, both in sound and role. What we hear on this record – largely shaped by von Schlippenbach's clustery, fast-glissando percussive playing, from the sound of it, is a placement of the piano (or several pianos, *à la* James Reese Europe's response to the Russian *balalaika* orchestra) at the core of a sound that is chromatic, but not exclusively or centrally so; and of a rhythm that is never metric, thus never requiring a piano for anything like comping, but is certainly percussive and pulsive.

The history of the GUO after its first cathartic eruptions is a little study in how Jost's five descriptions of the *Kaputtspielphase*, above, played out in practice. Von Schlippenbach told me, "We've always had contact with *Ernst-Musik* composers, since the beginning, but it's always been a very occasional thing, too, nothing so important." But a glance at the literature covering those years also suggests his past hopes for a different outcome. He himself wrote in 1975,

> If we in the GUO had the opportunity to work with art music composers, to have enough money to rehearse with orchestras for a week, I think you would see the art of free improvisation go much farther and wider than it has so far into the common cultural discourse, and into composed art music. The improvisational tradition from jazz has the musical potential to go where art music goes in terms of pitch relationships, technique and so on, with the added emotional components in the sound and feeling we bring to it, both from the jazz tradition and from our individual personal voices (12–13).

With the LP *Hamburg '74*, von Schlippenbach and Schoof both took a step toward a closer integration of compositional and improvisational strategies and sound worlds. The two were commissioned by the Norddeutsch Rundfunk (NDR) in Hamburg to compose a piece to be performed by the GUO and the NDR's resident choir. Taking off from a patriotic hymn called "The City of Hamburg in the Elbe Meadow," they produced what von Schlippenbach called a satirical *oratorium* in seven parts for choir, orchestra, and soloists. His liner notes seem conspicuously tongue-in-cheek and formally reverential at the same time, as though he were reveling in the shock of the humor of the juxtaposition of a classically oriented choir and the free-jazz rowdies of the GUO. "The choral parts were in part spontaneous, and to some degree reflective of the improvisatory processes of the GUO players" (Noglik [1981: 114–15]).

The choir's regular conductor was given instructions from the score, and von Schlippenbach led and played with the band. The result, as orchestrated as it was, was in a way much wilder, the spontaneous parts much keener in detail and variety than many wide-open free jams the band typically had done alone. Von Schlippenbach used the choir to set up sound events for the GUO to bounce off of, the GUO sent musical signals to trigger scored choral statements, and the two played off each other in increasingly interactive repartee. The personal and musical influence of Polish composer Krzysztof Penderecki is obvious in the vocal glissandi and chattering sections.

After a time of inactivity owing to the difficulties of time and money, the recordings *Live in Wuppertal* (1973) and *Jahrmarkt* (1975–6) marked something of a resurrection of the GUO at the time. True to the spirit of democratic monautarchy, they also marked a turn from von Schlippenbach's and toward Kowald's vision as a composer, a vision reflecting the Ives–Cage more than the Schoenberg–Penderecki lineage. Von Schlippenbach's contribution was a tribute to one of America's seminal beneficiaries of the French opera tradition.

> At that time [of the first Wuppertal Workshop, in 1973] I began to make pieces different from the partly graphically scored, partly serially organized pieces I'd been doing, using instead simple themes and song forms. That was when I wrote a piece based on Jelly Roll Morton's "Wolverine Blues." I had written so many such short heads for small groups before that I wanted to try something similar for the large group. At the same time, we began to play entirely improvised sets, to contrast with the through-composed pieces. This was a very important development, because it was actually our way of organizing possibilities for improvisation. It was more or less totally drained, this whole idea of mastering a definite form. We recognized then that our development undoubtedly leaned in the direction of total improvisation. That was the result of continual group activity in which individual players worked their own styles unto ever greater realizations of their own musical potential and energy. This energy was that of the players themselves. (Von Schlippenbach [1975: 11–12])

Live in Wuppertal features several short compositional statements, most framing and setting the tone and feel of free improvisations, some standing alone. "Wolverine Blues" opens side one, and something reminiscent of a Prussian march from the same period as Jelly Roll Morton's ends it. In between are pieces similarly suggestive of the style of a place and time or folk. The second track evokes the Balkans with both rhythm and scales, as does the fourth; they sandwich something that is heavily reminiscent of Coltrane's *Africa Brass* LP. The fifth could be a Russian lament, with a Turkish interlude. The "Bavarian Calypso" reflects the popularity of, perhaps particularly the Dutch interest in, that Caribbean sound at the time. Sometimes the band has the feel of Dizzy Gillespie's, when he used it to explore Afro-Cuban music: stretches of the "other's" rhythmic and melodic patterns punctuated by flights into post-bop big-band chords.

I found an interesting exercise in stripping away all the improvised and leaving all the written parts, sequencing them into a CD track of their own. The result reveals a kinship with a composer such as Ernst Krenek, with his opera *Jonny Spielt Auf*. This side is the most composed and arranged of the early GUO records, and it does not have any of the feel of someone like Stan Kenton, Bob Graettinger, or even Charles Mingus; overdetermination is not something von Schlippenbach would ever be accused of. It does suggest a kind of benign, even affectionate nod by the players to the material, not a condescension so much as a kindly salute from those whose serious jazz dues are paid in full and whose credentials as hip and creative intellectuals are well established (think of the treatments of Spanish classics by Gil Evans and Miles Davis). The high-energy cathartic jams are still in the mix, but so are these other things from both German-traditional and from neighboring traditional idioms.

If side one is primarily von Schlippenbach's statements on traditional material, side two is Kowald's. After an opening featuring his alpenhorn as a call to primal arms, and Peter Bennink's bagpipes similarly signifying on the pristine triadicism of Germanic tradition, the whole side turns into a lava flow of free playing.

As its title suggests, *Jahrmarkt* ("annual market") is conceived as a sort of Ives-like (also very Braxtonian) collage of the different sound worlds one encounters strolling through a public festival, where different bands are stationed throughout the one big space. It was also Kowald's brainchild, done in Wuppertal and featuring actual local groups outside the jazz and free-jazz sphere of FMP, juxtaposed with various FMP artists doing their own various things.

As we round the corner, the Wupperspatzen, an accordion orchestra, plays its own well-determined music in contrast to free improvisations, as does an organ grinder and a Greek folk music group down the block. We pass the wandering Rom or Turkish accordionist, and the free-jazz saxophonist and trombonist encountering each other, in Thelonious Monk's "Straight, No Chaser." There are no last words in this dualog; it develops its patchwork quilt through time with more such episodes, including a snatch of Charlie Parker's "Anthropology", of Miles Davis's "Milestones," a patch of blues, along with the most out, hardcore free-blowing, incoherent chatter, tangos, ballads, beerhall accordion and clarinet, straight and hard bop heads and blues running together like hot chocolate syrup over smooth vanilla ice cream.

The impact of the LP obviously lies in the studio mix of events that happened in several different tape recorders. It stands as an early example of the kind of studio art Kowald mentioned as preferable to live recordings for home listening, even as it was also spun from one of the more radical of the GUO's live public Wuppertal community events.

The extensions by Ornette Coleman and Cecil Taylor of the jazz improviser into the classical composer's realm led eventually into the concept of spontaneous, unprescribed improvisation as "instant composition." When von Schlippenbach merges what he organically, idiosyncratically develops in the context of a small group (the Schoof Quintet, then the trio with Parker and Lovens) with those body-based gestures similarly cultivated by the Brötzmann trio and its Dutch, Belgian, Scandinavian, and English collaborators, the GUO comes about: a collective driven by a nucleus of (orally/aurally) autodidactic, radical free improvisers, and (literate) schooled, trained musicians.

A certain dialectic is set up between these two circles: von Schlippenbach brings to the table German music tradition, including both American and German jazz at this point, in the voice of the cosmopolitan, formally trained European, a typical Berliner (and, as the "von" in his name signals, an aristocrat); Brötzmann and the Wuppertalians and their other national contacts rather represent the decentralized local grassroots working man, the rowdy radical at odds with the nobility and its history and culture. For the two to start forging their very different musics independently and then merge in the successful way they did is a picture of Globe Unity indeed, one in many ways uniquely German, as much in its clashes as in its synthesis. In fact, one might read it as rather the "Class Unity" the West needed to forge for itself before unifying with the rest of the world.

Evidence shows off the band's ability to follow the leads of guest "monautarchs" and soloists. It fills side one with a composition by guest artist Steve Lacy. The band improvises an atonal counterpoint in classic traditional German style that goes on for quite some time, and recurs when Lacy reappears as a soloist on a later track. It is almost as if the GUO players were leaving behind the raucous, full-throttle, sometimes sloppy way they might have played at home alone amongst themselves to be politely deferential to their guest artist. They do take off their gloves, in the person of Evan Parker – von Schlippenbach's English partner with Paul Lovens in free crime – once they get into the piece.

Side two features a piece by Misha Mengelberg, von Schlippenbach's fellow pianist-composer and all-around mastermind of the Dutch scene. Besides showing the GUO as at home with that influence as with their own German energy sound, it shows yet another aspect of the mix of composition and improvisation explored here. Mengelberg's title "Alexander's Marschbefehl," which roughly translates as "Alexander's Failed March," resonates both with von Schlippenbach's name and the classic "Alexander's Ragtime Band." Here's where one gets a taste of the jabbing humor and gamesmanship alluded to so often in connection with the Dutch improviser's scene; the longish, rambling improvisation following the theme builds and mutates around loose references to its pitches and rhythms. Von Schlippenbach's solo piano moments tip Mengelberg's hand as a composer, with its tight blocky harmonies, quirky rhythms and harmonies, and short, pithy phrasing: a perfect example of why and how Monk looms so large in the European free-jazz scene. Indeed, this long rumination by the GUO over Mengelberg's musical universe very effectively sets up, as did Lacy's piece for that matter, the exiting statement of the title track, Monk's tune "Evidence," arranged by von Schlippenbach, and performed largely by Monk's old bandmate Lacy.

Into the Valley sports the same band as *Evidence*, volume two to its volume one, both billed as the Globe Unity Special. It is a lean version of what is already a band of virtuoso players, reaching for the singular plateau shaped by the addition of Lacy and Mangelsdorff to the core of regulars Kenny Wheeler, Evan Parker, Paul Rutherford, Gerd Dudek, and Kowald, von Schlippenbach, and Lovens. It is essentially an open session of free-blowing designed to showcase the solo improvising of the members and their deftness in short collective jams.

In keeping with the trend of featured guests on the last few records glimpsed, *Pearls* features appearances by Albert Mangelsdorff, Anthony Braxton, and Enrico Rava. Like *Into the Valley*, it seems primarily to be an opportunity for the players to share the various sound worlds and expressions they had developed as solo improvisers and orchestraters of same. The concept of drive and push and energy is not always so de rigueur here, though it does come and go on the LP. More distinctive to it, however, is the procession of statements floating almost lazily down the sonic stream: Paul Lovens's and Evan Parker's attraction to the extremes of the high register, suggestive of metal birds, or friction between glaciers and earth; the duos between voice and horn developed in both Mangelsdorff's and Rutherford's trombone work; Kowald's fondness of Ives in his use of collage technique, and the low throat singing gleaned from his Mongolian travels; von Schlippenbach's solo piano style, here showing particularly the thought it milked from both Monk and Schoenberg.

All in all, this is a very meditative LP. It had been almost ten years since the first GUO recording, with which the players had opened up a new area and era of the music, from Europe to the rest of the world with love. They had not played or recorded all that often, and now they were having a conference, taking a little care to show their most serious peers how the new music had been brewing in them, what it might be up to. This almost nostalgic feeling culminated in a sweet rendition of godfather Monk's ballad "Ruby, My Dear," featuring the GUO's longtime comrade-in-arms in their revolution, Herr Braxton playing solo alto.

Four

Gumpert, Sommer, Bauer, Petrovsky: Panarchy Spreading

If we cannot conquer the communist world with weapons, we will do it with the jazz trumpet.

— British Field Marshal B. L. Montgomery

In music, too, one should ask why men, as soon as they are free, get the feeling that *things must be put into good order* . . . They imagine that order must be imposed on freedom from the outside, that it must be restrained rather than allowed to organize itself, without obeying any heteronome criterion, which would mutilate what demands to develop itself freely.

— Theodor Adorno, 1967[1]

When I began my quest for a Germanic identity in this music, the fall of Rome to the Germanic tribes seemed as primally poetic a place in recorded history as one could start (indeed, it was the only beginning recorded by Western letters). In my mind, Germany was part of this civilization called "the West," and "the East" another world entirely.

Actually being in Europe, however, reminded me of John Szwed's image of the "jazz landscape":[2] a map of America more defined by New Orleans, Chicago, New York, Kansas City, and Philadelphia — places significant to jazz history, lore, and mythos — than by its various geopolitical entities local and larger. For such a map, the ethnic/racial, tribal, civic, and regional identities defined by the music would constitute the demographic. Thus, for example, the music histories of New Orleans and Chicago would be crucially tied to the dynamics of the French, Creole, Eastern European, and other groups, and the migration of southern blacks northward. One would want to recall and understand this mix and migration for their parts in the development of a musical aesthetic/expression that was ongoing, current in its life and development, whereas one might leave them in the museum of a history that was long past if one's focus were politics, economics, sociology, or even history itself. This map of the American jazz landscape became a sort of template for the new map I wanted to draw, of the Eurasian jazz landscape. Thus I might think of Paris as a kind of New Orleans if I wanted to find an historical entry point of the music from which it moved to other points in time, space, and aesthetics. I might think of Berlin, London, Amsterdam, or Wuppertal as cities where distinctively "white European" sounds grew, as counterparts to Chicago, Detroit, or Kansas City, the grounds of distinctively "black American" expressions. Russian history and culture were dawning on me now, in the terms of my particular work, as the more primal, deeper *Urgrund* of whiteness and the West, a ground that, as I had seen German history and culture to be, was also a still-living root.

However, before my interviews, my mental counterpart to America and its history was Western Europe and its history; after my interviews – with the West Germans, for their contacts and influences that extend to Japan, eastward; and with the East Germans, for their similar contacts as well as their closer ties to Russia (as Petrovsky's name signals, his family background is Russian) – and after the sights and sounds of East Berlin and other Eastern cities I visited, with their Russian war memorials and street names, my working mental map had expanded to encompass the whole of Eurasia as the entity to consider. That entity was the counterpart of the American whole I knew so well as a whole, with Western Europe as only one of its regions – the New to its Old – albeit the one where the music I knew both originated (as "Western music," exported) and re-originated (as "jazz," imported).

When I had first considered ancient tribal names and other descriptors for their current semantic charges as "barbarian," sometimes specifically Teutonic barbarian – the Berserker, the Hun, the Vandal, the Goth – Germanicism was my sole focus; now the also still-current word "Caucasian" added itself to that list, to remind me of the Caucasus mountains and steppes, from which the waves of Aryans on horseback swept across the continent from north to south as conquerors millennia before the Germanic tribes moved down into Western Europe. It was this part of the world where the first Aryan conquests of the Rest began millennia before Christ; where the first Russian dynasty, around the time of that first-millennial (C.E.) birth of the West, was founded in Kiev by the Viking family Rurik; where the very word for "slave" was born, from the Slavs those eastward-sailing Germanics captured and traded up and down the Volga River to the Black Sea. I recalled that the Prussians were themselves originally a Slavic tribe, and that the Slavic credentials as "barbaric horde" were as impeccable as those of the Vandals, Goths, Huns, and other Germanic and allied tribes at the gates of Rome when Slavs inhabited the Berlin region (indeed, they were all cousins in the Aryan clans, and familially and culturally enmeshed in Russia). The Old World imperial–cultural axis of Russia, Prussia, and Austria was still intact as recently as the quarter of a millennium ago when the democratic New World rose to its day in the West – close to the time Joppig chose to start his explanation of jazz history – and it remained a force to be reckoned with in its twentieth-century borders, battles, and détentes.

An understanding of such history is necessary in order to demonstrate how disparate were the people – Russians, Finns, Englanders, Greeks, and Italians – who became, simply, "white people" in racist nineteenth-century America; just as all the tribes from the African continent became "black people." Going back and out so far is, in history's mythical terms, a way to connect with that differentiation's opposite – with its pre-, rather than post-, stage. It was only as recently as the last century or two, since the revolutions and falls of monarchies, that this entity known as "the West" had become such a force in the world, so distinct from "the Rest." And, in the geopolitics that defined those words, West had prevailed and imposed its influences and agendas on the Rest, including the East.

Western music history is itself rooted in the East, albeit even more circuitously than the route made here from jazz back through Romantic and Classical to Baroque styles, to Lutheran chorale to medieval modalism, organum, and plainchant. Accordingly, it is no surprise to see jazz take hold in Russia (or to see the Russian seedings of jazz in America) in much the same way as it did in Western Europe throughout the twentieth century. No surprise, then, to see it sprout a distinctively Russian flower from Western pollination, one reflecting its own terrain's history and topos.

When we say that Western music is rooted in the East, we are talking more about Byzantium than ancient Asian or Indian civilizations. While it is true that ancient Indian (because also Aryan) history spells out the virtual template for Western classism – in its misogyny and caste system, as well as its musical system of ragas (hierarchies of pitch ratios) and talas (hierarchies of metered rhythmic divisions) – it stands at a remove from its younger Western cousins, as do Asian cultures. Keeping with the project of mining archaeo-musical "digs" for the roots of "free," we look rather to the Byzantine East for its part of cultural/tribal ground in common with the West: ancient Mediterranean civilization, through the Greek Orthodox Church, and tribal northern Europe, through that first Russian dynasty founded by Vikings.

A number of sheerly geo-musical trends linked that West to that East around the end of the first millennium, when they began to move toward their modern incarnations:

- the replacement in French, English, and German churches of hydraulic by wind organs (in 750) from Byzantium; the arrival in Europe, through the Arabs, of kettle drums and trumpets (in 942); and of the harp (in 1050), also from Byzantium. These instruments are rational, erotic, and martial, chinks in the armor of Western plainchant's exclusion of them all. Conversely, around the same time, the Slavs themselves were just becoming Christianized, were taking on the Byzantine liturgy and chant, unaccompanied by instruments; they eschewed polyphony until the sixteenth century;
- both ancient Greek and early medieval European and later Russian music cultures practiced a mono/hetero-phonic, improvisatory performance on oral-traditional, free-rhythmical incantations bound up with texts and ritual, idealizing skill in singing and playing not as personal invention but as faithful significations (however personally artful) on something listeners already knew

and understood, shared in common and expected. Gregorian chant was the Western flowering, via Rome, from roughly the sixth to the tenth century, of this tradition established more directly from Greece in Byzantium. We see its Eastern character (one that extends through John Cage) in its placement of humanity at the selfless service of a greater fate and force (the Greek *logos*): here is the formal ritual-in-writ (the score, the chart, the text, the work – the logic, the axiom, the law, the state, the fate, the church, the scripture, the scientific-hypothetical "truth" of nature), learn it, work it, actualize its potential on the temporal horizon, lose and find your voice and soul in it, don't mess with it – the mandate of "top" to "down," "high" to "low," "hier-" to "-archy;" of "composers" to "players" (and audiences), of "schools" and "genres" to their "stylists," of gods and gurus to their disciples, of tradition to its heirs to this day. We know, of course, that many in the West did learn and lose and find their soul in, as well as mess with (improvise, redefine, restructure), "it": the Latin sequences and tropes of this time were interpolations of new text and melody from the bottom up onto the chant liturgy imposed from the top down;

- we also know that the pentatonic scale and polyphony were characteristics compatible with northern European tribal music cultures and that both were associated, in the eyes of Mediterranean scholastics, with the licentiousness and idolatry of Greco-Roman paganism, were thus threats to social order as much as to aesthetic or intellectual sensibilities. Gregorianism's revisioning of Old Roman chant looks much, for its intervallic leaps of thirds, like an appropriation of pentatonicism for the Catholic agenda, as does, later, the church's similar appropriation of polyphony;[3]

- finally, we know that when polyphony did officially replace monophonic chant in the Western churches, it did so by fixing the formerly free-flowing melody in time, making it a *cantus firmus*, assigning (in 1050) the first time values to musical notes.[4] The original one melody was now measured – mensural, metered – because if two disparate and diverging voices were to be in sync in time's flow, they had to forgo their respective immediacies and mediate where (when) to meet and move together. Both pentatonic and polyphonic strategies were at once concessions to power-of and assertions of power-over, strategies to contain and order, hierarchically, a mix of civilized and barbaric – the seed of that paradoxical (but understandable) mix of increasing democracy and individual rights and freedoms enforced by increasingly absolute power, peculiar to both the Enlightenment West and its Russian counterpart, through the (Jewish) German Karl Marx.

Peter the Great's eighteenth-century Westernization of Russia led it through the same Italian and French opera stationed in New Orleans by the early twentieth century. Western composers and performers mingled in Russian court life well into the nineteenth century, and Russian composers processed and developed their own native folk and religious materials through their own studies in the West. A nationalistic Russian style emerged through opera that was closer to theater, with its use of continuous recitative (spoken rather than sung sections), than its Western template, until Schoenberg's *Sprechgesäng*. Russia's free-jazz scene would accordingly orient itself – much like Sun Ra, the Art Ensemble of Chicago, and the AACM and its individual luminaries such as Henry Threadgill and Anthony Braxton – around the multimedia spectacle reminiscent of Greek *mousike* and "noise."[5]

Both Orientalism and modalism flavor Russian more than Western composition tradition, albeit through Rempel's "liberal" (meaning superficial, not "open"; see chapter one) *démarche*, one Russia acquired from the West. Indeed, Westernizers (internationalists) and Slavophiles (nationalists) formed an Enlightenment–Romanticism kind of contest begun with Peter the Great's project, and played out in full force through the reception of jazz in Russia.

In 1917, with the closing of the New Orleans red light district of Storyville, then-nascent jazz moved out of New Orleans to points north and then to points European with America's entry into the First World War. Also in 1917 came Russia's version of the same post-Enlightenment "killing of the fathers" that had been carried out by the American and French Revolutions. This international, two-century revolutionary war (1776–1989) between the northern Eurasian royal family network and its liberal sons and daughters entered its direst and bloodiest phase, if all Russian casualties of wars and revolutions from 1917 on are counted. After the October Revolution that year, many composers and performers left Russia for the West, to regale its music world with the soul and spectacle of Moscow and St. Petersburg.[6] Most notable here is Stravinsky's most deft turn to the archaic, with *Le Sacre du Printemps*.[7]

As in its earlier Western conflagrations, the revolt in Russia was sparked by educated and empowered liberal ideologues taking over the leadership of the masses, more than by the masses themselves (as opposed, for example, to the relatively peaceful revolutions in South Africa, East Germany, Poland, Czechoslovakia, and, later, Russia itself). And as the music of the most oppressed and/or radicalized parts of such leadership's post-Revolutionary societies in first America and then Western Europe exposed that fact and suggested the path beyond it, so would the same music in the Communist world, born when the music was born on the other side of the planet.

One might think that the music created by oppressed black Americans, then adopted by disaffected European and white American youth with radical leftist leanings, would have found its most hospitable soil in the Communist state that was ideologically based on creating a classless, egalitarian society. In some ways, it did; the music's Russian champions from early on embraced it less as an exotic import and more as a revolutionary, proletarian music immediately translatable for the Russian masses, via Russian musicians. Jazz also curried some official favor in the Eastern bloc right after the Second World War for that reason, but the Cold War nipped that sympathy in the bud. In fact, the music was taken up by the youth in the East as the clarion call to freedom from the repressive state, and as the generationally recurring theme of Russian youth looking to the West for its hip modernity. Jazz succeeded as both, not merely protesting or resisting, but overcoming and changing the state's power over it.

Virtually all of the musicians I spoke to, while musicians first and foremost (and now middle-aged men recalling their more naive youth), shared a leftist history to some degree. Evan Parker, hailing from Socialism's country of origin (and Karl Marx's 1848 host country), spoke eloquently about the music's sociopolitical implications and how they translated from West to East:

> Having been introduced to anarchist political philosophies as a student, and finding the arguments that Bakunin had with Marx back there before the first Internationale, it's quite obvious that the seeds of the downfall of Communism were predictable, foreseeable; that whole centralist, statist model was wrong . . . I was always more interested in the anarchist-socialist life than the Marxist one. I think it's very interesting that in this same thirty-year period [of the free-jazz history from its first hours] we saw the collapse of the Marxist model, while the anarcho-syndicalist movement is still quietly plugging away in France and also in bits of Spain. It will remain, in a way, a kind of conscience for the left.

Parker recalls feeling "slightly used" by East German presenters eager to totter the regime, by showing Eastern audiences how wild and crazy the Western musicians were allowed to be. "The whole musicians' community was always critical of everything, of both sides, and always eager to see positive as well," he says.

> We played in East Germany a lot, and it may be that in the bigger picture we were slightly used. I can think of several situations where money was freely available to go somewhere where the regime was tottering a little bit, and it was almost like our function was just to nudge things, to make people think "wow, they can do that in the West." In a way, the response to the music was much more intense in East Germany than it was in West Germany. I think it was perceived as having this kind of symbolic quality of personal freedom, liberty and all of that. They weren't looking at the music for its equally strong possibility for representing collectivity, solidarity, comradeship; they didn't want to see that, they wanted to see the other side.

In retrospect, the 1960s' convergence of idealistic youth and history reads like a failed revolution in the West, both in America and Europe, albeit to different degrees. The radicals in America gave way to enough nonviolent change, or failure of it, to give way to a reaffirmation of the status quo, in the rise of a black middle class and in a white reabsorption of baby-boomer leftism into politics and business as usual (much of it in academia, where much of it started) for their adulthood. In Europe, the social movement signaled by the May 1968 student revolts took root more in the political and social machinery it challenged, and developed into a more integrated presence there over time.[8] The Western protest movements that failed to live up to their initial revolutionary rhetoric read most interestingly

in retrospect as something that succeeded against those Communist regimes, ironically, professing the same rhetoric.

Russia

Starr's comprehensive 1983 study of Russian jazz was reissued in 1994 with a new
final chapter called "Emancipation and Pluralism, 1980–1990." That edition
followed Leo Feigin's 1985 collection of essays, articles and reviews by various parties
privy to the Russian scene, called *Russian Jazz, New Identity*. Combined, they
suggest Russia and its former Soviet satellites as the site of the freshest flowering of
the musical thought begun with the meeting of Africa and Eurasia in America.

Most interesting here is the fact that what Starr calls the "two revolutions"
(birthing jazz and the Soviet Union) did not meet on the deep level of their respective agendas until the 1960s, when black nationalists engaged Marxism overtly for
their own purposes, and when Soviet *dhjaz* culture joined its European counterparts in beginning to break free from both American musical identity and its
own ideological straitjackets.[9] Up to the 1960s, "Russian jazz" meant swing dance
bands after the American–British model, including much "light" music (much as
pre-free American big-band jazz, though steeped in the black tradition that would
shortly emancipate it). Most players were conservatory trained, good technicians
with little "jazz" feeling; most bands had only two or three real improvisers,
and those were strictly circumscribed, the exceptions proving the rule. The level
of musical quality was generally low until Stalin's death loosened tight cultural
rules.

As Germany's intolerance provided America with the founders of Blue Note
Records, Russia's gave it Joseph Schillinger. This young Russian, who came of
age in the literate and experimental milieu of post-Revolutionary avant-gardism,
would have a direct impact on the course of American jazz in his turn, including
that of my own serious amateurism in the 1960s. I first heard of the "Schillinger
system" as a new student at the Berklee School of Music, in 1965. The school was
founded in 1945 by MIT-trained engineer and pianist-arranger Lawrence Berk,
and was called the Schillinger House of Music until it became Berklee, in 1954.

Born in 1896 in Kharkov, Schillinger was a composer and pianist who came up
in the 1920s in the thick of jazz-as-modernism as explored in the St. Petersburg
Conservatory. His passions were mysticism, theosophy, Scriabin, and the ancient
musical cultures of the Caucasus, where he did ethnographic work. He also collaborated on early electronic music with Lev Theremin.[10]

Like Blue Note's Alfred Lion and Francis Wolf, Schillinger might be likened to
the German scientists who defected from the Nazis to help the Americans
build the atomic bomb. He gave a lecture in Leningrad's State Academic Capella
(Russia's equivalent of Carnegie Hall then) on "The Jazz Band and the Music of
the Future." It was a thoughtful, passionate argument for the importance of
improvisation and other performance practices that distinguished jazz from clas-

sical music. He nodded at the problem of vulgar American materialism, but said it did not detract from jazz's real popular appeal. This, he said, made it *the* answer for the Communist call for a "music for the masses."

He was initially ignored and subsequently suspected. In embracing the ethos and spirit of jazz on the deep level that he did, he was stepping dangerously beyond the ken of the Communist cultural policies then coming into their own first shapes. Appropriation of jazz's musical skin by composers such as Milhaud and Stravinsky was one thing; seeing it as the music of the future that left European tradition behind as a past was another. After a few unpleasant interrogations, Schillinger decided to move to New York. Once there, he had as much impact on the course of American jazz as he had hoped to have on Russian.

He became an habitué of all the major jazz spots, especially the Cotton Club. He was active as both lecturer and performer, with Leopold Stokowski's New York and other major symphony orchestras. His book *The Mathematical Basis of the Arts*, published in 1949, developed an analytical-theoretical approach to music that centralized rhythm. It influenced American musicians including Glenn Miller, George Gershwin, Benny Goodman, Tommy Dorsey, Eubie Blake, Gerry Mulligan, Quincy Jones, and John Lewis and the Modern Jazz Quartet, among others, as well as the curriculum of the Berklee School at its inception. It is no exaggeration to say that Schillinger was to American jazz performance practice and theory what Hugues Panassié and André Hodeir were to American jazz scholarship.

The official hostility that caused Schillinger to defect took on a clout similar to that of Nazism in Germany, with Russia's first cultural revolution in October of 1928, and its first Five-Year Plan around the same time. War trumped Eros in Stalin's conscription of Culture against all threats, real or perceived, to his power and agendas. While Nazi repression of jazz in Germany was racist in spirit and letter, Communist Partisans despised it as the music of the capitalist enemies of the people and their revolution.

Interestingly, in light of the idea of jazz as a child of Africa and Europe, the Association of Proletarian Musicians attacked the music through its Western more than its African parentage, via a backhanded compliment to the latter. In *The Art of Contemporary Europe* (1926), Ivan Matsa declared compositional and harmonic sophistication to be beyond jazz, but compared its "unexpected internal strength and strict rhythmic unity" with the best of nineteenth-century classical music. In context, this was a charge of guilt by association with the tainted classist aesthetics of Czarist Russia.

At War with Eros

Novelist Maxim Gorky dealt the decisive blow against the music, with his 1928 essay in *Pravda* "On the Music of the Gross." Gorky had been lionized by both Western and Russian literati as a voice of the proletariat, but his voice in this essay is more that of an old lion growling at the vitality of the younger cats annoying him. He characterized jazz as a degradation of sex from the heights of human love and spirit to the depths of mindless, soulless animality; he saw it as the new opiate of the masses, dispensed to replace the Christian religion Marx had critiqued as such, by the money-changing powers of the capitalist world. He charged not the blacks but the whites with this vulgarization of Eros, for their prurient exploitation and consumption of black music, the cause of their own eventual demise in decadence. By contrast, he saw the music's makers, along with other true proletariats, reaping eventual victory.

Later, when the Party led by Stalin got more seriously into its purges, it sharpened its lines of definition between the good and the banned. As it tried to manufacture its own alternative to the banned – such as The State Jazz Orchestra of the USSR – it brooked fewer challenges from more popular private competitors. This was bad for the vitality and creativity of the music in its traditional strongholds of major Russian cities, but good for the scenes in the satellite republics. Since the "jazz problem" had finally been resolved by the tried and true tactic of official assimilation and neutering, state-sponsored ensembles were allowed to spring up in the non-Russian Caucasus, the Muslim south, and the Baltic states of Estonia, Latvia, and Lithuania. These and other Soviet republics were much freer of the strictures prevailing in Moscow and Leningrad, and would function as the most fertile soil for the growth of distinctive native ethnic expressions that Russian jazz would mine to renew itself after Stalin's death in 1953.

The ups and downs of jazz in the Soviet Union can be traced in part to those of the relationship between East and West. Immediately following the Second World War, Russian liberation of Nazi-controlled cities was typically accompanied by performances of *dhjazes*, playing dozens of choruses of popular Glenn Miller tunes; and the healthiest scene in Berlin, then, was in the Soviet sector. The sudden freeze of the Cold War, predictably, quickly institutionalized the elements unsympathetic to the music.

This two-century revolutionary war between the nationalist and internationalist powers-over of the northern peoples was coming to its head in the Eastern bloc. The post-Enlightenment Communist dictators sensed it as surely as had the post-Romantic Fascist and Nazi counterparts they had defeated; they responded to jazz with the same War-like top-down repression, one dogged by the same bottom-up Erotic impulses coming from all quarters of their own society. Stalin denied the reality of those impulses by ramping up the existent aversions to jazz to the level of official paranoia about its perceived threat to social order and quality, as if it were a plot to poison the world from the Western top down, rather than the grassroots phenomenon it really was everywhere.

Andrei Zhdanov was Stalin's chief of enforcement against the musicians. His *Zhdanovschina* cultural edicts of 1947–8 cracked down on Russian composers perceived as too Western (modern, jazzy in some way), and jazz itself went out that window. Socialist realism embraced Paul Robeson (who himself denounced jazz as decadent and debased, an insult to the true Negro art of gospel and spirituals), but not Louis Armstrong and his musical godchildren. People who used to love jazz to the point of rebellion now passively accepted this crackdown because they were older, tired of war, and just wanted peace.

The aesthetic police came out against musical specifics: flatted-fifth chords, vibrato and mutes in brass, dirty timbres, blues thirds and sevenths, pizzicato bass, and drumkits were all suspect, and saxophones actually banned in 1949. All were associated with animal instinct unleashed, including capitalist greed. The Komsomol (ministry of youth affairs) brigades, much like the Chinese Red Guard later, enforced all this most zealously, showing the darker face of the spirit of youth, a spirit more typically behind the threat the music posed.

Whereas cool jazz reigned in Western Europe and most of the Baltic states, bop caught on in Moscow and Leningrad and the Central Asian state of Baku in the late '50s and early '60s. The art of improvisation at breakneck speeds was seized upon as the engine driving the private, subjective, inner life by musicians and fans disaffected with the state-scripted and controlled public one. The "style-hunters" (*stiliagi*) – "parasitic" dropouts shunning social responsibility for naked self-indulgence, in the eyes of officialdom – grew under the mythos of Charlie Parker into a youth cult, if not quite the full-blown (Beat) culture it was in the West. They were bent on exploring not shallow trends but their own subconscious psyches. "If the earliest jazz music embodied the anarchist's dream of individual freedom with a minimum of social constraints, bop pushed that freedom to its logical extreme," writes Starr (1994: 242–3). Willis Conover's Voice of America broadcast of Music USA, launched in 1955, provided the musical material for hundreds of groups to perform in universities, workers' clubs, and culture houses throughout the USSR.

In the increased openness following Stalin's death, this bop-tinged youth movement did flower into a big business both on and off the books. Private and official presenters/producers cultivated the music with an acceptance unshadowed by the former hostilities and paranoia, starting with the 1957 VI World Youth Festival held in Moscow. Visiting foreign jazz groups performed alongside Russian bands in a gathering of some 30,000 teenagers and young adults from around the world. Naturally, some of Stalin's old guard were still voicing disdain for the sexualism and animalism of the decadent Western sounds, but the world's foot had gotten in the Russian door.

Of the two musical components – rhythm and improvisation – Joppig saw usurping melody and harmony at the center of Western music, the weakest aspect of Russian performers of American bop was rhythm, the strongest improvisation. Their country's musical predecessors had already shown themselves to be colorful, able orchestrators; improvisation, long soloing over endless chord changes, even if it was self-indulgent and awkward, was avidly dispensed and consumed in this culture starving for freedom of self-expression. Horn players – trumpeters and saxophonists – were the stars and virtuosi of the day; drummers suffered from lack of contact with American sources, until the late 1960s.

Big bands – again, because of state sponsorship, and the collectivist ethic – throve in the 1950s. While most were musically unimportant kitschy imitations of

American bands, the few that excelled did so in proportion to their desire to unearth and perform arrangements by Stan Kenton, Charles Mingus, and others that they could only get by wanting them badly enough to transcribe them off recordings. This atmosphere made for a kind of natural selection of Russian players who cared about the music the most, and were forced to foster their own original music in isolation from its American sources.

The national success of the music itself mitigated any associations of it with juvenile delinquency. While the first wave of *stiliagi* had given way to less "parasitic" younger versions, the latter were still sometimes uncomfortably aloof from official culture. When the problem of juvenile delinquency increased, even as the music associated with it kept gaining respectability, the Komsomol instituted "Jazz Cafés," first in Moscow, then Leningrad, Riga, Kiev, and elsewhere. Unlike many such co-optational gestures by such powers, they were well received by musicians and audiences both, as the Party intended. Artists and intellectuals of every sort could eat and drink alcohol from 5 p.m. to midnight, to the accompaniment of standup comedians and the best of Soviet jazz players. It was this viable brand of healthy Soviet jazz culture that was in place when the culmination of Soviet pre-free jazz flowered.

Starr dates this flowering to 1965–7, after the Khrushchev administration, which had again suppressed the music for a few years, shutting down or changing the Jazz Cafés. It manifested in tandem with acceptance of other liberalized expressions in literature and economics; lectures on jazz history and aesthetics by accomplished Russian and Estonian musicians and scholars enjoyed a grassroots popularity in small towns and factories, with audiences numbering in the thousands. A huge collective translation project to publish in Russian all major jazz studies in all languages was undertaken by a network of volunteer aficionados, producing some 7,000 single-spaced pages in thirty-five volumes.

All of this took place during the "first hours" of the *Emanzipation* in Western Europe, as it happened – but Russia's own version of that would not come for another couple of decades, and when it did it would be as proportionately more radical, both musically and socially, as the history leading up to it was mixed with such promise and problems. A hint of the shape it would take, even more decidedly than in Western Europe, lay in the Russian reaction to the rise of black nationalism in American musicians such as Art Blakey, Sonny Rollins, and Charles Mingus. Starr paints this reaction in the same shades and shape as those of Fluxus and *butoh*, in nearby Korea and Japan:

> Soviet musicians studying this current realized that beyond ethnic identity, the essence of "soul" was the sophisticated exploration of primitive folk motifs and tonalities. By plunging into their own folk sources with this purpose in mind, the jazzmen of the USSR participated in the international current . . . But, for the most part, the turn to ethnicity had none of the ideological content with which the American black nationalists imbued it. Soviet musicians were well informed on the spirit of racial exclusivity in America at the time but rejected

it. Tovmasian, an Armenian, pioneered the exploitation of Russian folk themes, while Zubov, a Russian, was, along with Babaev, among the first to explore Central Asian folklore. If there is any ideological content in this quest, it is in the rejection of a blandly technological Soviet monoculture in favor of a richly textured primitive past. (Starr. 1994: 280)

Starr also reports an untranslated book that goes to the heart of this study's premises. Leningrad philosopher and jazz buff Efim Barban's *Black Music, White Freedom*, he writes, is "nothing less than an aesthetic and sociological analysis of modern jazz in the context of the entire history of music in the West . . ." (306).

Barban dismisses racial-cultural explanations of free jazz's challenges to Western sensitivities and sensibilities, seeing the "true cause of the public's aversion to all forms of avant-garde jazz is that they constitute a fundamental revolution in music and aesthetics, an upheaval so vast in scope that it can be compared with only two other breakthroughs in Western music in the past one thousand years, namely, the discovery of the principles of key and of dodecaphony" (cited by Starr, 306).

Barban's study offers a theoretical foundation for both the personal and social value of bop and free jazz: its "sensual, spontaneous and ecstatic" nature, combined with "great complexity and formal sophistication," made it the new, healthy alternative to previous high art in the West, which was inherently ascetic and undemocratic.

Eros Unmasked

I characterized the summary above, of Starr's history of pre-free jazz in Soviet Russia, as a war with Eros. At first reading, notwithstanding the eloquent grousing of one Great Man (Gorky), it scans like just another version of the same xenophobic war white Americans waged against black Americans, and European *Emanzipators* waged against American hegemony. Russia's resistance to the music looks similarly like a beleaguered "self" threatened by some encroaching "other." But the xenophobia on all three fronts becomes a red herring on closer examination. Eros emerges as the heart of the matter across the board, after much hiding in plain sight.

Conveniently synchronistic to this thesis, (the American) Starr's contribution to Wolbert (1997; in German) comprises one essay on his research area (jazz in the Soviet Union [463–8]), and one on New Orleans (79–102) that foregrounds the issue of Eros in the early jazz there. He paints the music then as cosmopolitan, Creole, multicultural urban and (musically) literate rather than folk/Afrocentric/oral; and as non-Puritanic/Victorian Catholic rather than (anti-erotic) Protestant.[11] More specific to the European view of Eros as an issue of the music, what he conveys about that is something that endured as distinct from America's view throughout the rest of the century, into the *Emanzipation*.

"In the nineteenth century, European visitors were often struck by the prudery of American culture," writes Starr (1997b: 88) under the subheading "The Invasion of Eros." The wording of the historical fliers advertising New Orleans brothels, and the photos (82), suggest erotica more than pornography: Eros-respectful, cultured establishments, bracingly free of the air of sleaze and sin that still imbues American culture, no less in its glibly "guilt-free" pop culture than in the guilt-fed edge of its porn culture.

To cut again to the free-jazz moments for the relevance thereto of this and similar clashes between expression and repression of Eros in jazz history, we do not see as direct a connection as we may with class in gender, generation, and race – neither musicians nor writers about them, in either America or Europe, made as much out of free jazz's erotic implications as they did out of its racial, social, and political ones – but remember that this was the era of "free love" as well as "free jazz." The sexual revolutions in white America (1920s' Jazz Age, postwar 1940s–50s [baby boom], 1960s) have largely been inspired by black music and culture, however misread, stereotyped, and projected upon they may have been. Indeed, beyond the ambiguities of purely instrumental music and self-censoring euphemisms for popular consumption, the vast number of blues lyrics, from that genre's beginnings to its spread from exclusively black to more broadly white and non-American consumption, have centered on the themes of sex and love, working out a narrative thereon that defied and overcame, over time, the post-Puritan American repression of Eros.[12]

For our purposes, the most noteworthy aspect of this history lies in expression over repression of Eros as part of some larger assertions: the syncretism between African-American and European traditions that finally led to the full individuation of the latter from the former, and to a pan-European syncretism of previously separate scenes in the *Emanzipation*; and the shift from top-down social-aesthetic impositions on cultural paradigms, from mental maps and scripts that mediated the body, to the body's own bottom-up (its immediate improvisations, un- mapped/scripted) authority over itself and its expressions. This goes to an important issue packed in the "free" rubric under examination here: the difference between, if you will, love and license.

The *Emanzipation*, like its African-American models, may have burst the gates of various strictures and repressions in a cathartically and blindly reactive way at first, in part, in some – but the majority of its voices were either thoroughly grounded and trained in the musical "rules" they were breaking, or were conscientiously grounding and training themselves in new sets of rules and gameplans to play by, to take them beyond the flash of the blind thrash-against. Virtually all so-called "free" improvisers I have worked with or talked to have taken pains to make this clear, resenting any implication that their art is a merely reflexive flight by the seat of the pants. Just as the spirit of "free love" of the time was conceived more as a liberation from unhealthy sexual arrangements or hypocrisies than as the contained and transient riot of Carnival "chaos" against the ever-dominant and enduring Lent "order," so was the music called "free" conceived more as the freedom to right and revamp a wrong social-musical situation than as a chance to perpetuate its potency by raving impotently (or even potently) against it.[13]

If, as Starr writes, much of Europe was free of America's Puritan legacy, it was accordingly free of the need to reflexively defy it. However, Europe's own brands of repression of Eros, by War – in wars national, ideological, cultural, class, and racial, all at once – marked it in some countries more than others, to the various musical outcomes we survey. Russia's history with the music is the one that most reveals the red herrings in the histories of American and Western European jazz. As noted, the issue of race in America drew attention away from the more crucial one of class, identified by the dramatic diminishing of race as a social issue in European jazz, both imported and domestic.

With some stark exceptions, jazz jittered class-war more than race-war nerves in Western Europe: the vulgar, callow New of Modernity rudely usurping the once treasured and hallowed Old, Hanslick's shock at the saxophone rippling its waves down the generations.[14] Americans, both black and white, brought over a music Eurasia had to reckon with, much as blacks in America had had to reckon with Northern/Western Eurasian music. With the American race war more or less out of the picture, the tension was between high and low cultural identities. The formerly noble, seasoned, refined now looked lifeless and elitist; the formerly low and shallow became vital, healthy, egalitarian.

By contrast, Russia had neither the same racist nor classist baggage, at least none left unpacked by Revolution, which had rationalized, dogmatized, and institutionalized clear social positions about the evils of racism, classism, and capitalism in the West; good Communists could not object to the music on any such grounds. In the socialist utopia, all races and classes and both genders were comrades; and traditional morality, both religious and secular, no longer had the authority church and state had brought to it.

Gorky's problem with the music thus stands free of rationales for disgust and enmity that had obscured the nature of the core issue in the West. He did not hate it, xenophobically, because it was "black" (read: any "other") and he was "white" (read: any "self"); he did not hate it, elitistically, because it was "common" and he was "noble" (by birth, and/or socially); he did not hate it, dogmatically, because it offended a Communist version of religious moralism, or because it offended such moralism itself. He hated it subjectively, viscerally, like a skilled player of a finely tuned instrument of Eros who hates less skilled players of less well-tuned instruments.

I dwell on Gorky because his ideological detachment from the red herrings of American racism, Western classism, and the millennia of Judeo-Christian moral authority imply that his disgust and enmity, permitted its freest expression, is closest to that experienced in the West. Westerners could deny the real nature of their aversion when they could call it a racism or classism that could be unlearned; Gorky, as a modern Russian Revolutionary had unlearned those, but still felt the aversion. The constraints of the mystical had been loosed from governance over Eros, but those of his own mindful body had not been. When that now clearly subjective, arbitrary governance was translated from one private body to its public collective, the authority of the rational took on a weight that was too much in reach, and not enough in grasp – hence socialist realism.

The real conflict the music (allied with rock) forced in Russia, East Germany, and elsewhere was between the elders and the youth, for whom Eros, not the state, was the undeniable birthright. It may have looked like a contest between social-ist realism and all other aesthetics, or between high and low culture, or between a national self and international others, along the way; but the force that really brought down both Berlin Wall and Iron Curtain was, as it was in America and Europe, the Eros of youth winning the War waged by "the fathers" to use and abuse Eros's energy. That victory led to later flowerings of ethnic expressions burst free from the monoculture, and of improvisations and compositions free of the monoculture's centrist prescriptions and controls.

While these are discussed in more detail later, it is necessary now to reconnect with the *Emanzipation* unfolding in the West at its points of entry to the USSR's own Western fronts. The cities of Warsaw and Prague were, if you will, the Midwest to Russia's East – the Chicago and Detroit to Moscow-as-New York – as London, Paris, and Berlin were its West. The Polish and Czechoslovakian scenes are more noteworthy, much like Scandinavia, for contributing important voices to the international stage than for producing national styles that helped to set that stage. East Germany is, rather, the most interesting example of that.

Poland

Poland's literature on its scene is scant, especially considering its leadership in the Eastern bloc, and its names well known abroad: trumpeter Tomasz Stanko, the late pianist Krzysztof Komeda, violinist Michał Urbaniak, and vocalist Urszula Dudziak, are four major post-free voices; alto saxophonist Zbigniew Namysłowski, violinist Zbigniew Siefert, and pianist Adam Makowicz are three more recent ones. Berendt called Poland the leader of Eastern European jazz after the second of its international Jazz Festivals in Sopot, in 1957.[15] Its Jazz Jamboree, in Warsaw, pro-vided the other major forum for that part of the world for Americans and Euro-peans to play and mingle. The East German players discussed later made their first big splash outside their own country there.

Poland's first jazz group was started in 1923 by saxophonist Zygmunt Karasiński. He had worked in Berlin with an early American Dixieland group (Harry Spiler's Orchestra) in Europe. Drawing on a mix of German and Polish locals in Gdańsk he brought the group to his home city of Warsaw. The band led a profusion of similar groups, initially mixes of foreigners and locals and soon a prevalence of Poles, that brought the Chicago style – one with national/personal as well as musical ties to Poland – into the night life and budding sound film industry of Warsaw. One of the first European academic articles on the "new dance music" came out in 1927, by pianist and educator Professor Zbigniew Drzewiecki, in the only issue of a publication called *Jazz* – a sympathetic argument for the value and health of the music's "primitivism."

Many Jewish musicians emigrated to Poland after the Nazis took over Germany in 1933. Trumpeter Ady Rosner led a swing band that provided the next big model for other Polish groups. He was called both the "Polish Harry James" and the "white Louis Armstrong," and might also be described as the Gil Evans of his time, with his original instrumentations and voicings, interesting arrangements and tone colors. Nazi occupation then scattered some bands to the Soviet Union, and at least one (Szal, led by Franisjek Witkowski) to the United States. Those who stayed played more locally to shrunken underground audiences; some (such as bandleader Bromislaw Stasiak) died in Auschwitz.

The dance bands started up again openly in Cracow and Lodz, removed from the Warsaw ruin. The YMCA clubs in all three cities provided the first venues for the more amateur ("authentic") scene, and in May 1947 in Warsaw, writer and jazz buff Leopold Tyrmand (Brodowski reports [1997: 450]) initiated the first so-called "jazz concert," billed as a "jam session." The white swing bands of Glenn Miller, Harry James, and Benny Goodman were the most popular, and all American pop music was considered "jazz." The YMCA clubs played an important role in launching Poland's postwar scene, but they shut down suddenly in 1949 when Stalin's *Zhdanovschina* edicts defined jazz as "bourgeois, decadent, suspicious, and harmful." (The YMCA itself had an air of Western upper-middle-class elitism in Poland.)

So began the "catacomb" period, a word recruited from early Christianity by several East European jazz scenes to describe the underground character forced upon them. The band Melomani was this generation's answer to Stalin's edicts. Formed by five students from Cracow and Lodz, it functioned something like a Modern Jazz Quartet of its time and place, foregrounding a stylistic purity and an assertion of the music's parity with the arts of high culture. It was this spirit that led to the first and oldest Polish jazz festival, the Cracow All-Souls Jazz Festival, which in its turn furthered Melomani's career to the point where it was the flagship group for the first national festival in Sopot, begun in the wake of de-Stalinization, in 1957.

Also cast in the Modern Jazz Quartet/Gerry Mulligan mold was pianist Krzysztof Komeda's sextet, the first Polish combo devoted exclusively to modern jazz. Komeda would don the mantle of Melomani's good fight for the music in Poland on international stages, where he would shine as a leading light from his country through the free-jazz years. It was this late-1950s' period when Poland took its lead for jazz and for contact with the West in Eastern Europe, moving from the catacomb to what Tyrmand called the "frenetic period, when jazz was no less popular than rock music would later be" (Brodowski [1997: 451]). The Jazz Jamboree, begun in 1958 in Warsaw when the International Festival on the Baltic Sea was shut down, surpassed even Sopot as an international stage.

The magazine *Jazz* started in 1955 and ran for twenty-two years. It catalyzed the organization of the Polish Federation of Jazzclubs in 1958, which in turn led to the 1964 Polish Jazz Federation and the 1969 Polish Jazz Society. Brodowski calls them among the "most dynamic jazz organizations in the world, which in great measure helped the emergence of the European (now International) Jazz Federation" (451).

All of this made for a European scene rich in its own tradition, cultural infrastructure, and hardwon identity, as well as richly nourished by visiting American masters. Komeda made a name writing film music (Roman Polanski's *The Knife in the Water* and *Rosemary's Baby*, among others), not only for himself but for a new Polish style of modern jazz – Slavic-melodic, romantic, Chopinesque (Namyslowski and Stanko, Komeda's bandmates, are the sax and trumpet voices, respectively, associated with this sound in their own post-Komeda work; pianist Brad Mehldau is a young American player clearly in their debt). Komeda incorporated the contemporary composing techniques of clusters and aleatoric structure, putting himself into the *Emanzipation* currents of the time. His 1965 LP *Astigmatic* put him on the international map as one of the important new European originals. His quintet also included Albert Mangelsdorff's West German bassist, Günter Lenz, and Swedish drummer Rune Carlsson. His untimely death in 1969 left an aura to his life as a Polish jazz legend, much in the way Charlie Parker's, Clifford Brown's, and John Coltrane's deaths did for them.

Andrzej Trzaskowski was another pianist innovator, heavily influenced by Horace Silver and hard bop, as well as by the Polish enthusiasm of the time for jazz as high art. His group with Namyslowski and Michał Urbaniak played American festivals in Washington, D.C. and Newport. In 1963 he debuted a Third Stream work featuring trumpeter Don Ellis, and in 1965 formed Quintett Free Jazz. Like Komeda, he went on to a career in film and theater production, as well as a jazz theory educator. (A pattern begins to emerge here; the Eastern scenes comprise people involved with literature and spectacle more than in the West, where the aesthetic is more *Musik an sich*. The pattern holds in East German and Russian free scenes, as will be discussed.)

Brodowski calls Tomasz Stanko Europe's first overtly "free jazz" group leader, with his Jazz Darings quartet in 1962 (as I write in 2003, Stanko is making his New York club debut, some forty years after his first international splash in the 1960s). It was a major force in Poland until 1974, after which Stanko himself was a major voice there and internationally, with collaborations including Westerners such as David Holland, Reggie Workman, and Cecil Taylor.

The success of Polish jazz holding steady and waxing through the free-jazz years positioned it to penetrate the international, especially the American, market with players who were perhaps cosmopolitan first, Polish (albeit a strong) second. Urbaniak and Dudziak made strong impressions as originals in fusion bands, including some of Miles Davis's; Makowicz, on the invitation of John Hammond, played Carnegie Hall in 1977, coupling a Tatumesque technique with his own standards-like compositions.[16]

Poland developed through years of repression with strong ties and access to the West, especially America. This rendered it a strong presence in Eastern Europe, but also one at a remove from the efforts of others striving to be heard. Günter Sommer told me the Jazz Jamboree was the big break for his group Synopsis to be heard outside of East Germany, let alone in the Eastern bloc as a whole. He also said that Polish musicians were generally too engaged abroad already – and that as originally "Polish" as much as, let us say, epigonally "American" – to have much incentive to form the kind of ad hoc network with fellow Eastern scenes that their Western counterparts were forming to escape the much nearer American shadow.

Czechoslovakia

Czech jazz history is similar to Poland's, in its successful cultivation of a national identity rooted solidly in both jazz and European art music traditions, balanced with compromise with both American capitalist and Soviet Communist culture industries and agendas. Like Poland's, its jazz scene has enjoyed strong organizational and educational support – its leading voices are known for high-level musicianship, conservatory-certified – albeit more overshadowed by the state. Those voices also stand out in the fields of theater, film, literature, and high-tech fusion music during the *Emanzipation* years – which, again like Poland (and the rest of the U.S.S.R.), were politically easier to sidestep than to stand with, anti-Western in tenor though they were.

Early Czech exposure to American music, domestic dance bands, and avantgardism with art music unfolded much as elsewhere. Emil Burian – a composer, playwright, poet, and conductor – translated W. C. Handy's blues lyrics and sang them in a voice blending Louis Armstrong's gruffness with French *chanson*. In 1928, his book *Jazz* was one of the first in Europe on the subject, along with Baresel's in Germany. Prague was one of those major European urban centers with a musical intelligentsia initiating solid ties between contemporary art music and a vital local dance band scene.

Jaroslaw Ježek (1906–42) mined this potential in a career that embodied the distinctly Eastern aspects of theater, East European folk, and art music all in a healthy marriage of equals with the best of the American music of the day. A Prague Conservatory-trained composer, Ježek wrote several works that drew on or included jazz-band instruments and sounds, including a big dose of Duke Ellington. He was the musical director of the Liberated Theater, something of a student's lark, begun in 1927, which matured into an outspoken political theater with an antifascist, left-wing satirical style and agenda throughout the rise of Hitler. Before it was closed in 1938 – when Ježek was forced to flee with his senior staff to the United States, where he died – it was the *Urgrund* of a Czech jazz scene that would continue to regard its founder as a strong and revered father. Dorůžka has noted that: "In a certain sense, Ježek was a forerunner of many later European trends in which the borders of jazz were widened beyond their blackmusical origins by elements of a country's native tradition" (1997: 455).

This strong start sustained the Czech scene as one bearing an air of protest and resistance through the Nazi denigrations of the music. Guitarist Gustav Vicherek was yanked offstage by the SS and sent to a concentration camp for singing "Tiger Rag" too much like Louis Armstrong. A "swing kids" kind of uppity youth movement developed around the big bands of Karel Vlach (Prague), and Gustav Brom (Brno). They were schooled by the best of Benny Goodman, Chick Webb, Woody Herman, Glenn Miller, Stan Kenton, and Count Basie, and endured until the early 1960s, spinning off small combos that developed virtuoso improvisers. One, pianist Jiri Verberger, John Hammond called "a white Negro" when the two met in Prague after the war.

Prague's and the country's scene grew even more robust after the war, even with the advent of *Zhdanovschina*. Everything best about the postwar years as a Golden Age for European jazz – a national network of well-organized big bands in touch with the American sophistication of Stan Kenton, Miles Davis, and Gil Evans; a grassroots amateur scene of clubs, contests, and festivals for both traditional and modern styles; small groups to develop improvisation – happened here, in spite of repressive policy, sheerly on the strength of the musical culture. Some prominent players left, of course, and the "Dixie revival" generally had an easier time socially (as proletarian) than did bop or cool, until the 1960s, but "progressive" bands such as Ladislav Habert's, and "hot accordionist" Kamil Behounek's, and small modern combos such as Rhythm 47 nurtured many individual artists who would put voice and face to jazz as a Czech expression (one was Dr. Jan Hammer, violist and bassist, and father to Jan Hammer, Jr. of *Miami Vice* soundtrack fame). Generally, able hands held the strong Czech jazz fort down through the worst of the Stalinized years, until around 1960, when reedsman-bandleader Karl Krautgartner was able to play the system to good advantage.

When Krautgartner led what was essentially one band under the names of both Dance Orchestra and Jazz Orchestra to present music programs over the Czech state radio broadcast system, it was the first time jazz as a genre was legitimized and facilitated, rather than vilified and repressed, by official culture machinery. It was the kind of foot in the door that opened the music to the only allowable source of financial and social support, the government. As such, it was part of an international trend toward government support of commercially unviable art, recalling the United States's National Endowment for the Arts launched in 1965. The shift of the cultural categorizing of jazz to high rather than low would be a strategy European jazz activists in several countries during that time – West and East Germany, the Netherlands, Belgium – would pursue to help fund and promote especially post-*Emanzipation* improvised music as a serious and original art form, up from a derivation of imported commercial entertainment. Nonetheless, the criteria for respect continued to reside in compositional rather than improvisational aspects, so the Czech jazz scene tended to foreground technically perfect composers-arrangers first, and technically brilliant improvisers only in the frameworks of those principals.

Accordingly, after the Prague International Jazz Festival started in 1964, the focus for its first three years was on Third Stream, jazzy "new music," fully scored. It was part of a vibrant scene in that decade, one fully meshed as the purview of a significant twentieth-century global art form with the rest of the culture. A telling example of that enmeshment would be trumpeter Loco Deczi, whose group Jazz Cellula would bring a macho, hard-bop sound to the effete chamber music city, in part on the strength of his pianist Karel Ruzicka, who won several prizes as a Slavically lyrical composer, rather than player, in the Monaco Jazz Composition Contest.

The impact of the Western student uprisings of 1968 – coinciding closely with the Russian invasion of Czechoslovakia – was to weaken the mutual trust and support that had been subtly forged between officialdom and the music community. The perceived spirit of barbarism and anarchy in free jazz rekindled old suspicions about jazz generally, especially as a medium for youthful rebellion, along with rock, punk, and new wave as they emerged. Krautgartner, only the most prominent among others, left the country as the repressive winds started blowing again. The Musicians' Union started its Jazz Section in 1969 to institute the annual Prague Jazz Days festival, a largely amateur forum with a New Wave-theater aura, for modern to avant-garde jazz and new and improvised music. The festival never enjoyed state support, and ceased in 1980. The Jazz Section turned its activities to the more suspiciously nonconformist paintings and theoretical manifestos of radical fringe groups in the arts, and officialdom washed its hands of their provocations by dissolving the Musician's Union in 1984. In 1987, several members of the old Jazz Section were jailed for several months for continuing some of their activities that had become unsanctioned.

As in Russia, all this looked from the outside more like partisan purging than deep antipathy to the music itself – although who was defining "jazz," and how, was clearly a real concern to the authorities – because the government immediately allowed the formation of a new amateur association, the Czech Jazz Society, a network of twenty festivals organized in a strict national framework. With it also began an immediately popular summer course of training for jazz musicians, the first such in the country.

Doružka compares the health of this revamped '80s' scene to that of the pre-1968 '60s' – a government move that, like the Russian Komsomol Jazz Cafés, arguably improved the quality and state of the music, from a certain aesthetic as well as the obvious political point of view. Indeed, it resonates interestingly to its capitalist counterpart in the United States around the same time, the well corporate-financed and promoted neo-con movement associated with Wynton Marsalis and Stanley Crouch: same eschewal of post-'60s' free and post-'70s' pop-rock-jazz fusion, same revival of traditional jazz and earlier big-band styles, same official cultural red seal of approval (and disapproval of the "purged" elements and their ways). The fact that we in the West know such names as Miroslav Vitous (bass), Alan Vitous (percussion), Jan Hammer (keyboards), and Jiri Stivin (reeds) stems more from their work as freelancing expatriates than as representatives of that official Czech scene then.

Stivin perhaps came closest to something like a Czech *Emanzipation* voice standing out from the international sideman crowd. After studying film at the Prague Conservatory, then music with John Dankworth at London's Royal Academy of Music, he returned to Prague and became involved as a flautist with Baroque music, new music, improvised music, and other styles in a notably eclectic career. Cultivating this garden with free improvisation, he developed what Dorůžka calls a "global music in Czech." His duo with guitarist Rudolf Dasek was often the house band in West Berlin's Blue Note club in the 1970s, and was well known and respected as an original contribution to the European jazz world then. This and a couple of other post-free groups, including cellist Vojtěch Havel's Trio, managed to work, if often as professionals only outside the country, and mostly as amateurs at home (again, not unlike the "out" black and white players in America then). As a rule, the aggressive, always-angry, anti-*Kultur* affect of the German and (all that, but also humorous) Dutch free jazz then found scant purchase in Czechoslovakia. There, conventional conservatory musicianship was the standard, even for those who pursued the "free."

As in the Western scenes, then, it again fell to (the former East) Germany to contribute the lynchpin to the *Emanzipation* components assembling themselves. Russia would follow suit later with its own strong showing, but throughout the 1970s and into the 1980s, East Germany's players would express like no other in the Eastern bloc the dynamic pervading it between the music, its state suppressors and champions, and its own captive audience, and that dynamic's role in the larger dismantling of the totalitarian system from within. Their voices were both inspired and heard outside their country through West Berlin's FMP manager Jost Gebers's courageously persistent campaign to get the major Western players into East Germany, and to get the East Germans out on record and live for Western audiences.

East German Balladeers

The free-jazz movement in East Germany was more popular than in any other Soviet satellite of the time. The leftist West Germans longed to see their music as a popular, grassroots expression seizing center stage, to be on the right side of history, even one of its agents, when the quixotic dream of the complete collapse of the capitalist Beast came true. The East German players actually experienced something very much like that, but after their play was done and their theater collapsed, they found themselves on the wrong side of history.

The word "totalitarian," above, cues a meditation here on some actors in Western and Eastern cultural politics and musical aesthetics, and their overlaps in German music culture's roots on both sides of the Berlin Wall: Theodor Adorno, Hanns Eisler, and Arnold Schoenberg. Adorno is most familiar to English-language jazz scholars for his (1963) essay "On Jazz – The Perennial Problem." Those scholars, when they have not pointedly ignored him, have usually taken him to task for "not getting" jazz, for glossing over it (or the commercial entertainment he mistook as it) as sensationalistic, superficial, and pretentious; and for dismissing its luminaries and devotees as psychologically and/or even sexually stunted or perverse.[17] To Americans, especially – brought up on jazz as the most intellectually, emotionally, and physically liberating music of an oppressed black or repressed white people's victorious struggle – it has usually been Adorno who seemed more the wrongheaded one.

Here, however, we should remember why he had enough influence to matter in the first place. He was not a typical racist–classist reactionary lashing out at the music in blind prejudice; he was a darling of the German New Left in the 1960s, part of the intellectual milieu that spawned the '68ers. His (1973) work on his modern music of choice – the Second Viennese School of composition – provoked a stir similar to his words on jazz, for their strong polemics defending the aesthetic of Schoenberg against that of Stravinsky. His was a stand, like so much of the "free" encountered here, for the deep primal, in preference to an unmoored, merely reactive avant-garde.

When Medieval German composer Hildegard of Bingen created her traditionally monophonic ouevre, monophony was giving way to polyphony in the (church's) imperial culture around her. When Bach created his polyphonic work, polyphony as contrapuntal art was giving way in that same (secularized aristocratic) culture to an instatement of melody based on a homophonic harmonic matrix below it (as in the *Lied*, and symphony, and the American songbook). It was Schoenberg who would tangle the hierarchies of both mode and key back to a contrapuntal polyphony of equal voices, each built from a monophonic melodic base (the tone row), all within the post-Romantic framework of the symphonic and *Lieder* tradition.

As were the innovations of Hildegard and Bach, Schoenberg's was a backward gesture, through Romanticism (which had essentially crested in the first part of the nineteenth century) to Medievalism (music as cosmic science), through the tenets of an established art (like Hildegard through Gregorianism, and Bach through the Lutheran chorale). It was thus against rather than with the trends of the times, which were arguably issuing from Paris through the Impressionists to Stravinsky to the Dadaists; and from American composers Charles Ives and Henry Cowell, independently of and obscurely to Europe.

Schoenberg's radical summing up of polyphony on the chromatic level and beyond its pitched distinctions altogether (in *Sprechgesäng*) was, in keeping with the liberal impulse, a unification and dynamic balancing of elements that were previously both constrained and hierarchical, by comparison. He redeemed the tradition's promise, did away with it by mastering it and taking it to a new level.[18] As difficult as it is to imagine either Bach (Brandenburg Concerti notwithstanding) or Coltrane providing the soundtrack to imperialistic, militant fascism/statism, it is even more so to imagine Schoenberg doing so. The hypnotic command of a central tone subordinating and defining all others; of regular, repeated rhythmic patterns inducing trance and directing motion; of the singing-orating rather than the normal speaking voice imbues these musical devices with the qualities intrinsically conducive to the marshalling and manipulations of power relations. Conversely, a would-be dictator is on slippery ground indeed trying to get the masses' blood boiling behind him to a piece by Schoenberg.[19]

More to the point, a would-be advertising/PR person for a major corporation doing her bit to celebrate and perpetuate the current economic-cultural status quo is more at home in the pastiche culture of postmodernism itself, founded more on the musical concepts signaled by the prefixes "poly-," or "hetero-" applied most naturally to Stravinsky and Ives, than on that of the "a-," or the "pan-" better matching Schoenberg. The former are about the loose juxtaposition of the divided many onto a field unsystematically (which is not to say chaotically) manipulated by the composer; the latter is about their unification into a field defined and enlivened by the process of that unification itself, systematically transcending what the prefixes above (as also "post-") fix.

This inaccessibility of Schoenberg's music has often enough been described as the rarefied esoterica of an overly refined, culturally elitist tradition, self-obsessed, neurotically introverted.[20] But the more one studies this man and his music, the picture that emerges is rather of someone plumbing the secrets of a tradition sheerly for their musical information – not for any perceived historical, cultural, social, or national-racial privilege or prestige associated with it – and then joining his own personal contribution to that tradition. The source of the alienation generated by the sound itself then looks more like a discomfort with the idea and actuality of the individual personality breaking through to its own voice's universal level – "expressionistically" – rather than subjugating that voice to the momentum and machinations of that tradition as something abstract and above and beyond it. In Schoenberg's case, it was a matter of Judeo-Christian Germanity wrapping up and leaving behind a tradition that had run its course in life, in stark contrast to Kaiser Wilhelm's and Führer Hitler's coeval Germania, trying to ride that spirit like Hildegard's dragon, to a misbegotten glory.

Still, Adorno's stand with Schoenberg links back to the word "totalitarian." While he was as solidly antifascist as antijazz (he wrote *The Authoritarian Personality* and was a refugee from Hitler's persecutions), so was he clearly a pro-totalizer intellectually, opposed to what he saw as an unprincipled, unoriginal, vulgar pastiche of style driven by blind panderers leading blind consumers of bland culture mass produced and disbursed through a recording technology and industry that robbed living music of its soul. Pro-totalizer, because he saw in the music of Schoenberg an integrated system grounded in and true to the same tradition it was revolutionizing from within (it is a small step to compare Schoenberg's system with Marx's and Lenin's, for its top-down legislation of the egalitarianism of chromatic pitches).

In all of this, although he died in 1969 in probable ignorance of the free-jazz movements happening around him then, Adorno's work resonates with several of the characteristics of their histories in both America and Western Europe. It also presages both the purely musical traits of the music and its social contexts in East Germany from its ascension in the 1970s, and those in Russia a decade or so later, because:

- Adorno's aversion to what he called jazz had had its echoes all along within the American scene he disdained from without – the traditionalist critiques of swing, and then bop, as ersatz sellouts to the marketplace – which came to a head in the Marx-inflected Black Nationalism of the 1960s. "Out" and "free" players saw themselves much as Adorno saw Bach, Beethoven, and Schoenberg, as the real thing, in contrast to "straight" and "inside," the jazz version of (per Adorno) Stravinsky's sellout turn to neoclassicism;
- Adorno's aversion to Louis Armstrong as a "castrated male" was matched by the bop generation's aspersions on Armstrong as an Uncle Tom – or, more specifically to our story, by the most militant of the post-free black American players seeing Toms in their elders as a class. Adorno's aversion is also reminiscent of the European *Emanzipators* (especially the English) who scorned American jazz peers as marketplace sellouts, even those they respected as musicians (for example, Sonny Rollins);
- Adorno's aversion to recording technology – something like some traditional cultures' dislike of photography as a capture of its subject's soul – mirrors a general ambivalence about recording in both European and American new and improvised music, a strong preference for the live event;
- Adorno's preference for "totality" over "pastiche" is in sync with what Braxton calls the superiority of a "restructuralist" over a "stylist," of "composite reality" and the "universal music" as desirable and attainable; and, more generally, with the post-free aesthetic, rooted in jazz's valuation of individual voice and spin on genre conventions, that values individual creation of a total system of music-making over flitting cannibalizations of existing styles from everywhere and everywhen (for example, the neocon jazz scene, or Stravinsky's neoclassicism). It is also in sync with my picture of Baroque, Romanticism, Coltrane, and *Kaputtspielphase* as unified fields with more bottom-up power and primacy than *Empfindsamkeit*, Enlightenment, and neocon jazz capitalizations on such power, premised as the latter are on containing it in a top-down governance of that power's aggregates, managed and relativized into neutrality;
- Adorno's preference for revolution from within rather than overthrow from without – as the German student in Paris saw in the *Négerball* (see note 14, p. 332) an invasion of civilization by barbarians; as whites in Europe and America, especially the Americans during the free-jazz years, generally have feared such invasion; and as much of the world, including Europe, fears from America now – is echoed by the seminal example of Alexander von Schlippenbach and the Globe Unity Orchestra's debut and reception. Von Schlippenbach,

unlike some of his more raucous Dutch and Wuppertalian colleagues, was no enemy of *Kultur*, was indeed a great friend particularly to the music of Schoenberg and his protégés.

The fact that such grassroots, unpretentious, earthy, and palpably non-elitist musical spirits as the German jazz musicians in 1960s Berlin would find with Schoenberg's music a happy affinity for their own undeniably spontaneous, robust, vital expressions argues loudly (as does Braxton's similar response) for Schoenberg's "inaccessibility" as more a problem on the side of reception than on that of a self-indulgent, introverted composer (*pace* Eisler).

There is something Augustinian about Adorno: criticize the paganism of your beloved Rome, coax it out of the City of Man into the City of God, but do not open the gates for the barbarians to come in and sack it. He had chosen his side in the two-century revolutionary war – its nonviolent Cold War phase allowed him the luxury of warring with ideas against his own side, even though the conclusive victory in his embrace of Schoenberg was bittersweet, seeing in it as he did a death of something he hated (bourgeois culture), but not the new life of something he longed for (socialist utopia).

All of this becomes more complex when we move from a West critiquing itself (almost literally to death) toward a resolution of its problems in the musical terms Adorno employed. It becomes still more so when we move across the Wall to Adorno's closest counterpart in Marxism and music theory, Hanns Eisler. Eisler shared many of Adorno's critical perspectives, but moved beyond the latter's gloomy sympathies with Schoenberg's alienation from the society (indeed, the civilization) he served so faithfully. Like Adorno, Eisler saw Schoenberg's work as the death rattle of a declining bourgeoisie, but rather than go down with that ship and its captain, he turned his back on both to let them drown in their accidents of history, choosing for his part to make another kind of music for another kind of world.

Eisler's work and shadow loomed large for the East German post-free scene. Actually, it cast itself into the West in some of the first American instigations of the free scene there, when pianist, composer, and bandleader Carla Bley (one of the new jazz's central voices) and trumpeter Mike Mantler toured Europe with some of Europe's up-and-coming free players, and recorded a project of treatments of Eisler material. Eisler's association with the *Gebrauchmusik* composers already removed him from Adorno's exaltation of alienation from mass culture as the real innovator's logical fate.[21] All the East Germans I spoke with praised him as a moral hero for putting his strong musical talent at the service of his society, sincerely rather than cynically.

Peter Kowald, like Brötzmann and most other West Germans discussed here, never did feel as alienated from Eastern tradition as they did from their own; whatever about the East that could inform or be informed by him had done and been so all along.

I always felt that the East German musicians had a little different quality of identity than the West German musicians had; it had to do with how they were

Fig. 1   Albert Mangelsdorff, 1985. Photo: Dagmar Gebers.

Fig. 2   Joachim Kühn, 1991. Photo: Gérard Rouy.

Fig. 3   Vinko Globokar, 1987. Photo: Dagmar Gebers.

Fig. 4   Cecil Taylor, 1996. Photo: Dagmar Gebers.

Fig. 5   Evan Parker, 1997. Photo: Dagmar Gebers.

Fig. 6   Günter Hampel, 1981. Photo: Gérard Rouy.

Fig. 7   Peter Brötzmann, 1997. Photo: Dagmar Gebers.

Fig. 8   Peter Kowald, 1999. Photo: Gérard Rouy.

Fig. 9   Alexander von Schlippenbach, 1973. Photo: Dagmar Gebers.

Fig. 10   Peter Kowald, Anthony Braxton, Evan Parker, 1974. Photo: Gérard Rouy.

Fig. 11   Paul Lovens, 1990. Photo: Dagmar Gebers.

Fig. 12   Ulrich Gumpert, 1992. Photo: Dagmar Gebers.

Fig. 13   Ernst-Ludwig Petrovsky, 1998. Photo: Dagmar Gebers.

Fig. 14   Conrad Bauer, 1979.
Photo: Dagmar Gebers.

Fig. 15   Johannes Bauer,
1998. Photo: Dagmar Gebers.

Fig. 16   Günter Sommer,
2004. Photo: Gérard Rouy.

brought up, but also with certain identifications they felt with Brecht and Eisler as musicians. Many of them knew Eisler, and he was there in their time; they identified with him in many ways, so that's an interesting thing. It is very interesting the way he did marches; they're never really left-left-left *foot*, there's always something off. And he has a lot of jazz influences in his songs, especially after he went to America; some of them sound like the jazz of the '30s. I think he was a very clever and a very moral man.

Adorno's influence, in contrast to Eisler's (which comes under focus later in connection with one of his torchbearers, Ulrich Gumpert), was even in those first *Emanzipation* hours fast becoming one of historical more than vital interest to the Eastern free players, much the same as it was for Western jazz scholars. Nonetheless, had Adorno lived long enough to write a book lauding the ways the free-jazz movement in both America and Europe addressed concerns and righted wrongs he had declared throughout his life, his warmest and highest regard might have been for the East German scene, Eisler's defection from Schoenberg notwithstanding. Reasons for this include

- its reverence for the same classical tradition Adorno revered, its ability to signify on rather than break with same, its political remove from the "corruption" of the mass American culture Adorno hated;
- its deep treatment of hymnal material – something akin to the passion of a Coltrane built on black church music, or Bach on Protestantism, or late Schoenberg on Judaism – as opposed to the shallow lack of commitment to same of the ironic pasticheur (the Dutch and West Germans come to mind, as do the French);
- its similar embrace of medieval folk music – like Schoenberg, tapping pre-Enlightenment organization/rationalization of pitches, forging the modern out of the archaic (something, again, Western free and new-music scenes found more problematic, at least at first);
- its general orientation toward Ornette Coleman more than Cecil Taylor and late Coltrane, for Coleman's closer cleaving to triadic diatonicism/chromaticism (thus to Schoenberg more than, say, early Stravinsky, Varèse, or Cage) and to the Cool-jazz history.

Following a German article von Schlippenbach wrote about the music he was involved with, shortly after it had just made its big splash in Europe, is a sidebar containing a quote from Adorno on jazz – his famous criticism of its glib, smoke-and-mirrors effects that passed for innovation and improvisation, its monotonous beat and static nature, its basically orchestrated "spontaneity" and "ephemerality," and its market-driven nature. Whether von Schlippenbach or an editor placed the citation to complement his piece, its effect is that of a valid and true criticism that has been addressed successfully by the European free-jazz turn in jazz's historical dialectic.[22]

East German Blues

Berendt distinguishes between East and West scenes in Germany by noting that "jazz was always . . . a proletarian music," and that East and North Berliners were more proletarian than the South's and West's upper and middle classes. Perhaps for that reason, the music escaped Stalin's most vicious persecutions when it fell out of favor, falling more to an official freeze-out. The foremost artists, such as pianist Jutta Hipp and Joachim Kühn's brother Rolf, eventually left East for West Berlin while they still could, for the greater opportunity and friendlier atmosphere of the music there.

The healthiest broadcast and recording activity certainly came first from the Soviet Sector, with the first postwar radio programming from its Berliner Rund-funk, in 1946, followed in January of 1947 by the first recordings on the Amiga label. Amiga's production of trumpeter Rex Stewart's July 1948 sessions, mentioned in chapter two, documented one of the first postwar collaborations between an important American player and the Berlin locals.

By 1950, Soviet Party edicts were officially binding in the East. Jazz clubs were closed down, and jam sessions officially banned. Jazz musicians who played pro-fessionally had to play a conservative style of dance music; anything else had to be pursued as a private, amateur hobby. In 1958, the Party ordered that only forty per cent of all songs performed professionally could be from the West. As in Nazi Germany, there was an overlap between jazz as practiced in private by its afi-cionados and the music the authorities desired and needed for popular entertain-ment and social functions. There was also a stronger mix of sheerly ideological feelings in the East. The same sort of repressive bans of the same sort of musical gestures came with the same subjective and slippery attempts to subvert and enforce as in Nazi times.

Noglik's citation of one musician of the period conveys a sense of the typical experience of his colleagues:

> It wasn't long before we started experiencing some sort of repression – now here, now there. It culminated in an incident when the *Volkspolizei* came in on a dance we played one night. The orchestra was banned from playing any more because of "musical incitements of the audience" or something like that. We couldn't play at all for two or three months. Then someone sent us an accor-dion player around from the union to sort of function as our supervisor, and under him we could play again. (1996: 208)

Articles of the time, also cited by Noglik (208–9) convey the official and unof-ficial disdain for jazz. In an article in the *National-Zeitung* of Berlin on 11 August 1950, composer Jean-Kurt Forest called for "a dance music that is not influenced by American imperialism. It must be rooted in folk song, because that is the root of melody. In American dance music the melody is both clichéd and torn, like life in general there. Dance music must have a bright, light rhythm. Its model? The Strauss waltz." Ernst Meyer wrote in his *Musik im Zeitgeschehen*, published in

Berlin in 1952, "Jazz has from the first moments of its early period been appropriated by the American entertainment industry to churn out profits on a mass market. The current 'Boogie-Woogie' is a channel through which the barbaric American poison threatens to deaden the worker's brain. This threat is as dangerous as a military attack of poison gas . . ." (162). Even stronger in his opinion was Ludwig-Richard Müller, who in *Musik und Gesellschaft*, published in Berlin in 1955, declared that "The culture of imperialism is . . . a stupid culture, and an essential achievement of this cultural stupidity is modern-day jazz" (4).

In such a climate, the following from Eisler – also no friend of jazz or American political culture – sounds sympathetic:

> Whether jazz can help us or not, I don't know; I only know that it can shame us. Our popular music lacks the good fortune of great talent. A lack of talent, with or without jazz, is its own reality. The level of our popular music is intellectually low. And even at its worst, jazz still carries something of the real human cry of the oppressed black. If I had to choose between the most basic jazz song and one of our rotten tangos . . . I would choose jazz.[23]

Trading Fours

The core of the East German free scene was a quartet, first called Synopsis, later the Zentral Quartett. It comprised pianist-composer Ulrich Gumpert, the most directly influenced by Eisler's songcrafting; alto saxophonist Ernst-Ludwig Petrovsky, like Albert Mangelsdorff an older and established mainstream player who gave his strong voice to the new music emerging; drummer Günter Sommer, who apprenticed with cutting edge bandleaders of Petrovsky's caliber; and trombonist Conrad Bauer, who started as a rock singer with a large youth audience which he brought to free jazz and Synopsis when he crossed over, becoming the first East German full-time professional jazz player.

Synopsis made a surprisingly strong international debut in 1973 at the Warsaw Jazz Jamboree, playing totally spontaneous acoustic music: "a first serious high point for Free Jazz in the GDR [German Democratic Republic] – a point which was nevertheless achieved only by chance. It was also the first visible sign of a new stage of development which was based on significant qualitative and quantitative changes" (Reichelt [1980: 21]). Such changes lay in the group's decision to use traditional German materials (mostly Medieval and folk) and aesthetics (lyrical, melodic, from the Romantic period) as the springboard, along the lines of Ornette Coleman's melodies, into free improvisation. They did this without the Western sense of sarcasm or irony, more with respect and affection. Unlike the West Germans, for them it was a reassertion, not a denial, of local identity beyond that imposed by the Russian occupiers, and of European roots that matched the African roots unearthed by their heroes from America. Each of these four got their starts with four other players who should be mentioned in the same breath as Eisler, for their foundational roles in the shape of the music from the 1970s on: Eberhard Weise, Kurt Henkel, Manfred Schulze, and Friedhelm Schönfeld.

Eberhard Weise

Petrovsky is the most direct source of information about his first employer and long-time friend. "I learned jazz first through records – Tristano, Konitz – at the same time I got to know Eberhard Weise, a trombonist at that time in a small theater in Güstrow. He provided my first big push into the discipline of music, though unfortunately he didn't get much chance to play the jazz he loved."

Big bands prevailed as dance groups, but the group in which Petrovsky started his long and interesting career was more than that. Weise switched from trombone to piano, and formed his own dance band. Petrovsky shared Weise's passion for the cool modern jazz of Miles Davis's Capitol Orchestra, and helped him shape the band's sound along those lines. Noglik reports him saying that:

> The Eberhard Weise Orchestra is the serious and genuine jazz expression of . . . young people who are earnest about their music, and who see in the face of bourgeois existence only a superficial nod to their engagement with musical and spiritual problems . . . With Eberhard Weise, we bravely forged through. We developed a true broadcast sound which we also brought to our dance engagements such that we could play one popular song for an hour, in a style that was distinctly ours. The audience was often enough appalled, and often we played such engagements one time only as a result, which naturally lowered our income. Colleagues who had families to support scraped by in a marginal existence. (1996: 211)

In 1997, at the Franz Josef Hotel in Vienna, former servant quarters for the Emperor, Petrovsky tells me not about mere neglect, but the constant threat of jail Weise and others labored under:

> Unless one wanted to play rock music . . . dance music was the closest compromise to playing jazz. We had big problems in all of these bands, because we always wanted only to play jazz. My colleagues found their only security there then, because jazz was politically problematic. The groups that later had the chance to become successful, such as our own Zentral Quartett, all came out of this popular music background of necessity . . . Cool jazz had absolutely no chance; there were always these petty officials ready to charge you with playing decadent music. I had a good friend who played good jazz [Weise] but it was flirting with prison if you tried to play it on the job. I remember drum solos in these bands, just a chorus or two, that were dynamite – but no one ever heard them, and they had to constantly make sure that no one really would.

Petrovsky and his wife, singer Uschi Brüning, spoke at a Darmstadt Jazzforum about the turnaround in the way the East German press's cultural discourse represented jazz.[24] Petrovsky's reading of the Party newspaper *SED-Zeitung Sächsische Zeitung* 1958 coverage of one of his gigs with Weise showed jazz in a good light (the preview presented it in politically correct terms as an "outcry against racism"), a mixed light (the review was a chestnut of fence-sitting, to cover all bases), and a bad light (an article by a Party official argued that the band should be fined for the decadent music they had played). Petrovsky then read and commented on the letter of acceptance he wrote to the "Congress of Popular Arts" in 1989, before the Wall fell, when they gave him his *Nationalpreis*. These were the mischievous jabs of the targeted "problem" who has learned to laugh far beyond the tears and turmoil.

Kurt Henkel

Jost states that the West's cathartic *Kaputtspielphase* of high-energy power-playing was only partially matched in the East, which held to a comparatively conservative central aesthetic, expressed through a variety of musical syndromes. He discusses *Just for Fun*, recorded with Petrovsky's quartet (with trombonist Conrad Bauer replacing the usual [trumpeter] Heinz Becker, bassist Klaus Koch, and drummer Wolfgang Winkler, all seasoned studio professionals) as the closest example of an East German *Kaputtspielphase* expression: more restrained and edited (in performance, not on tape), less monochromatically intense than Brötzmann's *Machine Gun*, yet also showing the influence of the latter.

Other of Jost's descriptions – a comparison of Bauer to trombonist Roswell Rudd, a description of a piece as a marriage of English (quiet) and Wuppertalian (loud, Ruhr Valley) styles, observing the bassist and drummer alternating between conventional and free patterns – add up to a picture of a style with one foot in tradition and one stepping gingerly out of it, in contrast to the headlong rushing plunge taken in the West. Similarly, Jost's portrait of Gumpert – of his fascination with German folk music, his sense of the need for connection to such roots, along with the obvious links to peers such as von Schlippenbach and Cecil Taylor – situates the East's free scene as more grounded in tradition.

Dresden, when Günter Sommer and Conrad Bauer were growing up there, Noglik calls a particularly vital city for swing bands. Here, as in Leipzig and other centers removed from Berlin's mixed influences, emerged between 1945 and 1949 the Stalinist culture politics that would define jazz in the East as, like all modern art, an expression of bourgeois decadence. Still, again, the abundantly recorded and danced-to music of the time tells its own contrary tale.

Kurt Henkel's was the leading band after the war. Its 1948 recording of "Rolly's Bebop" is notable for being the first major hit by a German big band in the new bop style. Even more notable is the tune's composer and clarinet soloist, Rolf Kühn. Henkel's 1950 version of "Cherokee" shows what the Germans had a mind to do with the influence of bands such as Woody Herman's and Stan Kenton's. Both evince the hot edge and jumpy, nervous beat and tone characterizing jazz in Germany then.

Those traits take a clear turn to their opposites over the course of the 1950s. The slow time and open space of Rex Stewart's statements seem prescient in retrospect, with the almost absolute pervasiveness of Cool and West Coast to the exclusion of Bop and East Coast in both East and West Germany. Jazz had finally taken root as an established part of the domestic music culture, thanks to the healthily decentralized network of city radio broadcast stations, many with their own resident studio big bands. With the breezy, sly, and slinky motion of '50s' cool jazz, this country on both sides of the Iron Curtain seemed to relax and fall into that American groove first dug by Count Basie – a perfect one for the cultural and economic complacency that marked the 1950s in both America and Europe, after all the carnage and deprivation of war.

These years are still widely known by German jazz historians as an extension of the imitation of Americans that would not change until the mid-1960s, and in many ways they are clearly that. At the same time, they show us the beginning of an alternate jazz universe, in which the players and styles widely regarded in American jazz studies as idiomatically "white," and also marginal to the central African-American work of Charlie Parker and the New York founders of bop, are rather the central voices defining the mainstream.

The Dresdner Tanzsinfoniker was one of the bands instrumental in making jazz reputable in East Germany throughout the '50s. What is interesting about its orchestration of Gerry Mulligan's piece "Walking Shoes," and its own "Teddy Blues," is that both were released in 1962, months after the Berlin Wall went up. The schizophrenic policy of official condemnation coupled with pragmatic indulgence that Hitler and Göbbels had exercised was now in place under Khrushchev and his East German government officials.

While the situation for live performances in private clubs and public institutional venues was still restrictive and policed, the radio broadcasting networks sported a few friends of jazz in high places who were instrumental in showcasing and recording adventurous musicians. The latter would strike out through free jazz with a vengeance, both musically and socially, that would explode the music's laid-back, almost corny affect at this point. After postwar years of relatively little exposure to American jazz, and a gradual awakening to it through its growing presence in Czechoslovakia and Poland, its East German audience gradually grew interested in what their own compatriots were doing with the music. A series of major concerts in Dresden, in 1965–6, featured Western guests.[25]

Rolf Reichelt, a long-time employee with the GDR Rundfunk, names Manfred Schulze and Friedhelm Schönfeld as the two most important voices to break the "Eisler-Monk-Folklore-Weill" syndrome. (This was a commonly used term referring to the combined influence of composers Kurt Weill and Hanns Eisler, choreographer Egon Monk, and folk music on the Communist music culture trying to offer an alternative to American hegemony. It signaled a socialist-realist kind of stereotype.) Reichelt claims that syndrome was only a part of the whole picture, one including the important work of saxophonist Schönfeld's trio with Günter Sommer, and reedsman Schulze, with whom Petrovsky and Gumpert both worked, separately.

Manfred Schulze

Reichelt names Schulze as the one who truly started breaking free from the "dra-maturgical" conventions he sees as rather having only loosened and expanded through the others following in the wake of Joachim Kühn.[26] Jost (1987) cites Schulze's Berliner Improvisations Quartetts as one of the most important in the 1970s for its chamber-music communicativity in interaction, and in dynamic balance of composition and improvisation (and its use of text and vocalism, which are generally more prevalent in GDR and Russian than in Western scenes).

Already, in the mid-1960s, Schulze's description of his work signaled what freedom from "dramaturgy" meant in his musical terms: "I am interested in sound structures and planes of sound and not in choruses with resolved harmonies . . . The improvising musician is free to make variations not only on one model but can himself choose from various models" (Reichelt [1980: 2]). Nevertheless, a sense of conscious, disciplined intent was still at the fore: "I have always been surprised that our music has been classified as Free Jazz. We never play 'free' in the sense of playing without prerequisites or uncoordinated, for the manipulation and varying of such models demands from the performers a high degree of discipline. It is not easy to find capable players for this music" (20). Schulze's experimental wind quintet, featuring Petrovsky and others in 1969, was marked by a direct reference to one of its primary models: "Before the rehearsals I played a recording of Schoenberg's wind quintet – then things went a bit better" (21).

Reichelt gave Schulze much print "because his too-little represented music, while it does not fit exactly in the jazz category, is to be regarded as the first really individual improvisational music of the GDR Avantgarde" (21). It is a strong link back to Joppig's image of Western music (for its affinity with Schoenberg over the socialist-realist norm) shifting from strings to winds with the invention of the sax-ophone; it extends Joppig's notion of Western music's shift from orchestral and chamber ensembles to American then European jazz formations, on into the post-free collectives.

The Manfred-Ludwig-Sextett, led by Petrovsky, was originally co-led by fellow reedsman Schulze. It was conceived more in the spirit of the hard bop sound then current than the earlier cool sound. Its 1964 Amiga LP *Jazz with Dorothy Ellison and the Manfred-Ludwig-Sextett* featured a black American singer from Atlanta, Georgia singing jazz standards and the Ray Charles hits of the time. The four tracks penned by Petrovsky (out of sixteen) best exemplify what the band did best on its own then, and what Petrovsky's role in that was. They show how sheer musi-cianship can bridge the gap between a style for which German players had more affinity and exposure and experience – the Cool school – and the newer, more foreign hard-bop sound demanding their serious attention at that point.

Schulze's wind-quintet legacy continued in Petrovsky's work with contempo-rary composers, which has itself continued apace with the latter's more conven-tional jazz and free-jazz work. The relationship between contemporary composers and jazz players laboring in the dance-band straitjacket was closer and more rele-vant to their mutual time and place than with their counterparts in the West, for the most part. Contemporary composers could both affirm and challenge the Party lines both more overtly and more subtly than could writers, playwrights, or painters. Eisler was the archetypally "politically correct" socialist composer; by contrast, Noglik mentions a 1956 composition by Friwi Steinberg, *Fragen* (*Questions*), performed by the Modern Sextet of the Dresden Dance Orchestra as an example of a composer paying his own idiosyncratic homage to the sheerly musical devices of cool-jazz orchestrations, reflecting an ambiguous social statement that will never reveal itself either as one of "bourgeois decadence" or as one of successful appropriation and redirection of the enemy's language (indeed, Noglik sees it as a foreshadowing of the West German free-jazz *Emanzipation* from the American model).

The 1976 FMP release *Number Six: Two Compositions for Improvisers* was a scored piece by East German composer Hans Rempel for his all-star octet featuring Heinz Becker and Joachim Graswurm on trumpets, Bauer on trombone, Petrovsky and Schönfeld on reeds, Rempel on piano, Klaus Koch on bass, and Sommer on drums.[27] The compositional approach is to alternate sections of notated pitches with the players' well-developed free-improvisational gestures. It shows both how much at home these players, so at home with jazz and free jazz, could also be with realizing a new-music composer's vision for their skills, and how much at home Rempel was in that role. A musical setting such as this, originally broadcast in 1974 on the East German radio network, came with none of the politically suspect associations clinging to jazz and free jazz in the then-not-too-distant past, and with none of the charges of unsuccessful hybrid that Third Stream events often provoked in the West.

When I was in Berlin, Petrovsky did a twenty-year anniversary re-creation of his performance, with the Berlin Philharmonic, of East German composer Friedrich Schenker's piece *Electrization*. This was also a scored piece, for the orchestra, fronted by Petrovsky's improvising trio. The compositional approach in this case also drew clear lines between written and improvised sections, but as the composed provided a new-music carpet over which the improvised could be spontaneous, very reminiscent of Braxton, the resulting meld blurred those lines in the ear (recall Joachim Kühn's words about this result as desirable). This suggests that a composer's task when writing for a particular improviser is akin to composing in a particular form. A sonata is a sonata, a 32-bar standard a 32-bar standard, however different may be the composers who write them. Similarly, a piece written for Petrovsky by two different composers who really hear and care about how he plays should bring those composers onto some common ground, past the idiosyncracies of their independent approaches. Petrovsky himself says that:

> There are very few composers who have what jazz offers . . . Often in an hour of improvised music, all but two minutes can be mostly bullshit, but those two minutes are so fantastic that it's worth it. It is something no composer could ever write, and no player could ever play twice. This is what makes this music so important.

But the composer who is good enough can set up something that takes the improviser beyond his own clichés, gives him musical information and structure, a spiritual dimension, a philosophical dimension, that is really a great human thing, I must say. The composer's tradition throughout Germany is very important. I have experienced great inspiration from my work with composer friends, not only in the music we make together but in my private conversations with them as well.

Petrovsky expresses his preference for his East German composer colleagues, for their sensitivity to his own role as an improviser, over composers such as Lutoslawski and Penderecki, who, he feels, appropriated more than collaboratively incorporated the improviser's sound world and process.

Friedhelm Schönfeld

Joachim Kühn was the first to play free, but no one really understood it at the time. It was my musical relationship with Joachim Kühn that began my own original style's development. Kühn practiced day and night, and brought an intensity and a sense of calling to it that only a few musicians do. When I visited Leipzig, I always had my saxophone, and even though I only played with him a few times, I always learned a lot.

– Ernst-Ludwig Petrovsky

When Joachim Kühn left the scene he launched after only two years, his mantle passed to saxophonist Friedhelm Schönfeld's trio with Kühn's bassist Klaus Koch and drummer Günter Sommer. Reichelt calls it "the first stable group of New Jazz in the GDR" (1980: 19). Sommer's recollection of his experience gives some insight into the character of the Eastern differences from many more wide-open Western experiments:

In the early days I was told I should play more freely and finally forget 4/4 time and all those things – but I hadn't yet any experience in listening to others. So, finally, I tried to understand and to fulfill the demands made on me and I got away from the regular beat. On the other hand, we did, however, play regular pieces – between them we were asked to play "free." All that confused me a lot. So totally free, without a piece, without melody, without rhythm – that just didn't work. It was a case of seeking and trying out. (20)

Schönfeld expressed similar concerns about the tension between "freedom" and "structure." His 1967 radio broadcasts featured titles that signal the musical processes he was working ("Wandering Beat," "Cesura," "Mixtures"). He voiced both the need then to escape from cliché and restrictive convention, and the difficulty of breaking out of what he had practiced for years. He first broached the latter by writing twelve-tone pieces, then trying to improvise with them. "The exact conception was born from the intention to verify or check everything. One still had inhibitions about doing anything in a simply intuitive way," he said about this period (Reichelt [1980: 20]).

Schönfeld said his mission – an uphill battle all the way – had been to counter the official culture's dismissal of jazz as a decadent capitalist expression and to assert it as a probing, honest and critical one that both West and East needed for different reasons. He said his struggle had not been that of a starving artist, nor had he been persecuted or harassed, simply frozen out, ignored in the cultural discourse.[28]

By 1972, after much work, the trio had effectively stretched convention a bit at a time, ending at their peak with a style that opened more than abandoned or ignored convention. "The arrangements remain recognizable, to be sure, but do not act as incitation to playing and are, rather, as *dramaturgical linking together*, and which nevertheless no longer has any 'corset' or cramped character. Günter Sommer plays in freely pulsating fashion, the starts become emotionally and intuitively activated, and close interaction is real and intensive 'Powerplay'" (20) (emphasis mine; Sommer would speak much in our interviews about the ongoing importance of this dramaturgical quality, one the East Germans would return to after having stepped away from it – something like what the French and the Russians did with *beauté*).

Sommer gave me a rare 1968 Amiga LP called *Jazz: Jazz-Gedichte von Jens Gerlach*, which he dismissed as a relatively unimportant example of his early work. However, besides neatly showcasing Schönfeld's compositional and improvisational versatility and command, it foreshadows the shape of the Eastern version of the West German musical miracle of *Emanzipation* in several telling ways.

Two LP sides unbroken by separate tracks, its thirteen musical and poetic vignettes encapsulate different styles and periods by invoking thirteen different names from the beginning to the then-current cast of American blues and jazz legend. The first noteworthy thing is the tribute itself. I know of no such overt homage of this sort from West German jazz scenes of the time, and it would be hard to imagine. The West European players certainly had the same sort of avid passion for and knowledge of American jazz and its lore, but the shadow of same loomed closer to home for them; their urge was rather to dissociate from America, black and white both, and to find their own original paths. A few years later, that would relax; Alex von Schlippenbach, always adamant about his jazz roots and credentials, would record with Globe Unity and Steve Lacy the latter's arrangement of Thelonious Monk's tune "Evidence," and his own arrangement of Jelly Roll Morton's "Wolverine Blues." Years later, he and others from the West would do such tribute projects more frequently, but in these "first hours" they were the exception for Western post-free-jazz players.

East Germans were not only less worried about being seen as imitators of Americans, they were also less guilt-ridden about their own German history. Their language had never been put down in favor of English, in the music scene, and their connection to the high German musical tradition of composition was seen not so much as a burden of history to leave behind, as in the West, as it was a source of musical material and ideas.

While this particular recording is nothing more unusual than a concept album by very talented players and writers, it gives us a version of jazz history proactively Afrocentric in its posture, in the way its poetry (Jen Gerlach's) romanticizes the music's heroes and heroines (Blind Boy Fuller, Henry Baltimore Zeno, Bessie Smith, Pinetop Perkins, Joseph Leon Rappolo, Billie Holiday, Chick Webb, Charlie Parker, Miles Davis, Lennie Tristano), at a time when such a view was on the rise among African-Americans themselves. The LP situates the music, which was always associated in the Communist world with both the freedom from oppression and the championing of the downtrodden, as well as with American imperialism and capitalist faux culture, with the pro-underdog rather than the pro-decadent spin, thus securing its place in East German society. And, most importantly, it presents this politically correct solidarity with Afrocentrism in German poetic and musical terms, suggesting its own original statements to come, a few years later than its Western counterparts (who were in the process of start- ing up FMP at this point), by framing jazz history in a way that would lead nat- urally into German musical and social history by way of visceral personal analogy.[29]

Dialogue with West, Via FMP

Following in the tradition of playwright Bertolt Brecht and composer Kurt Weill, East Germany's free-jazz scene has had close ties with its counterpart in theater. In 1965, a series of regular concerts called *Jazz in der Kammer* (Jazz in the Chamber) was launched by a group of East Berlin actors who were also jazz fans, in the Deutsches Theater Kammerspiele. Joachim Kühn's trio opened the 112 con- certs the series would present until March 1979, when it ended.

Linzer explains the group's professed goal for the series:

> to create a permanent podium for Jazz, one that had not existed in Berlin up to that time, to popularize and to promote Jazz, to present the national scene as well as to engage international representatives of contemporary Jazz. (After 100 concerts, the result was: more than 350 musicians from 20 countries had been guest-performers at the "Kammer") ... The history of "Jazz in der Kammer" as a focus and equally an orienting factor in the development of a national scene: there, GDR musicians presented their then newest produc- tions; there, they experimented with new "casts" for their bands in a workshop fashion; there was a center, a place to meet – and, increasingly, a place to meet with those foreign musicians who later became important for the developing of a national school. (1980: 15)

Jost calls Ulrich Gumpert's Workshop Band, a large ensemble begun in 1972 comprising players from both sides of the Wall, a "sociomusical" experiment with positive results.[30] By 1978, he writes, the group had transcended its members' conceptual and stylistic conflicts to forge a heterogeneous sound and approach, the fruitful synthesis of which lay in its "wide variety of ways in which to realize the interweaving of composition and free improvisation" (Jost [1987: 264]). The breadth and depth of thematic material derived from European and other folk musics combined with the energy and inventiveness of the West to provide fresh expressions. Some familiar comparisons might include Miles Davis's and Gil Evans's treatment of Spanish classical music, or Dizzy Gillespie's of Afro-Cuban music, or Chris MacGregor's South African and free-jazz crossbreeds. A further development of this workshop situation was, again, a move back to some elements of bop (mostly rhythm and phrasing) with some elements of free jazz (mostly pantonal pitch patterns).

The Workshop Band was the Eastern formation most naturally comparable with the Globe Unity Orchestra. Its personnel varied, and it was typically smaller than the GUO. The first FMP release of the band, *Unter Anderem: 'N Tango für Gitti*, in 1978, featured Petrovsky, Gumpert, Sommer, Bauer, trumpeter Heinz Becker, altoist Manfred Hering, tenorist Iri Antonow, and bassist Klaus Koch. Like the GUO, it showcased the pianisms and composing-arranging of its nominal leader, and it showcased the improvisations, both conventionally couched and free, of virtuoso players. Unlike the GUO, however, it was much tidier and more formal in its overall concept and sound. If especially its core of principals, the Synopsis players, were as adventurous and skilled on their instruments as their Western counterparts, the composer's script was much more unapologetically conventional than the GUO's. (One might think of the Charles Mingus Workshop Band as compared to Sun Ra's Arkestra for a sense of the difference in sound.) The distinguishing traits of most interest here include charted sections reminiscent of German brass bands blowing over drones, that peculiarly Mexican or Latin American feel Gumpert's horn and rhythm lines often have, the classic Blue Note hard bop and funk sound he loved so much, the tango that seems as East German as it does Argentinian – all of which were New World imports with strong German influences in their own roots – a touch of Ornette Coleman's triadic melodicism, and the personal voices of a pantheon of hot soloists.

Regarding the Coleman influence, the common thread at the center of all these traits, one rather marginal to the GUO, is the concept of the triadically scaled octave, often minor, whether in modes suggestive of various folk musics, or the diatonic modulations of jazz or art music. It is what New York pianist Borah Bergman (who has a large dose of it in his own playing) calls "the East German blues," and is indeed closer to African-American blues than much of what comes from Western Europe. Musically, it may be more transparent and conservative in its devices than the latter, but it effects much more evocation of Germany's connections with Slavic culture, with the grim melancholy of Stalinist history, with something deep and ancient, as the blues evokes the history of slavery and oppression: the broken-hearted dreams of a risen proletariat and an international socialist utopia that come from this part of the world. Petrovsky the Russian sings it, Sommer the Saxon, and all those other East German comrades who brought it to the West as a badge of honor before the Wall fell. Now they sing it more or less in private, for their ears only, with a bittersweet nostalgia for an erased world. If I ever felt like the stereotypical anthropological fieldworker witnessing history sweeping a culture away, it was with these and other East Germans. But that change is superficial; in the depth of things, this music itself signals a spirit bound to outlast and swallow, somehow or other, the one that seems to have overcome it. It signals a healthy symbiosis between East and West, the former providing depth, substance, and grounding, the latter vitality, mercurial energy, wit, and imagination, to a uniquely German expression.

In 1973, the sixty-first *Jazz in der Kammer* concert featured the Swiss pianist Irène Schweitzer's Quartet (with Rüdiger Carl, Arjen Gorter, and Heinrich Hock). Musically, this was nothing vastly different from the other concerts, but it was the first accomplished by FMP's "still unofficial" negotiations. On Jost Gebers's initiative, informal club sessions, and later (official) concert and workshop situations, teamed the most prominent FMP musicians from several Western countries with their East German peers. This influx had the most impact on the Eastern players themselves, as well as providing the Westerners with a larger, more enthusiastic, better-paying, and (literally) more captive audience than they had in the West.

Sommer's recollection of these first exchanges is typical of the other reports the East Germans gave me:

> We were not allowed to go out, we couldn't go to the West but they came to us, and this was a very, very important and great moment for me. This was the moment I came to know Evan Parker, Paul Rutherford, Derek Bailey, Irène Schweizer, Paul Lovens, Peter Brötzmann, Peter Kowald, Günter Christmann, Detlef Schonenberg, Steve Lacy, Alex von Schlippenbach – and nearly all the West German musicians of the free jazz scene came to us, and we played together. Some of them I still have a very close personal friendship with, like Peter Kowald; he came to visit me with his family, stayed at my place for holidays. Alexander von Schlippenbach came for holidays, and we had a very good private relationship also.

Gebers gained through his contact with Rolf Reichelt the purchase of licenses for tapes to release in the West "for a thousand marks or so . . . not very much money."[31] Between 1973 and 1980, FMP put out twelve recordings of East German artists, most drawn from those archived broadcasts. Gebers persisted in flooding the redoubtable East German bureaucracy with continued requests for the allowable one-day passes, which most people would simply find too daunting. After that relationship between FMP and the GDR solidified, East German players became available for FMP-initiated projects.

Beginning in 1978, FMP organized concerts with GDR musicians in the West, and in 1979 coproduced with the GDR state record company VEB Deutsche Schallplatten the first of a series of recordings released simultaneously in both East and West. Over time, FMP recordings of Western players established a presence in the East German broadcasts, and the East German players one in the FMP catalog. In that year too, the first Peitz Jazz Workshop took place, in a small town near Cottbus. Peitz developed into the most important GDR center outside Berlin for its six to eight concerts and workshops annually. Its producer, Uli Blobel, expanded it into GDR tours, exposing the country as a whole to many collaborations between East and West.

In the United States, as noted, the free-jazz movement developed in tandem with the formation of nonprofit advocacy organizations, both private and governmental, conceived as alternatives to the commercial system. In Western Europe, both private patronage and cultural ministries supported the music, albeit sporadically and sparely. In the GDR, there was no commercial system – no night clubs, no recording companies – except the state-run concerns (broadcast system, official-culture agencies), which afforded relatively few opportunities for musicians to work outside of classical or popular music. Jazz as a special art found the majority of its activities through just such private alliances as had organized Kammer and Peitz – associations of fans, local groups, and individuals devoted to organizing local performances in institutions (universities, colleges and professional schools, cultural centers), mass meetings or gatherings, and industrial plant functions.

As a result of the grassroots development of the jazz scene, and of a past history of suspect status, official TV and recording media, journalism, and academia had little part in the music's indigenous blossoming there. The radio system's support of the music was an exception to the rule. In 1979, thanks to that support, a report from the Committee for Popular Music and Entertainment finally broke the ice of thirty years of official freeze-out.

FMP's relationship with the East German players resonates with the historical and cultural dynamics in the immediately postwar differences between the more proletarian musical culture of the Soviet sector and the international show-business one of the West; and with those between the brashly, nervously experimental American jazz and avant-garde art music free scene of the West around 1960 and its more German- (with other ethnic, such as Balkan- and Turkish-) traditional counterpart in the East.

In West Germany, the musicians were alienated from their folk roots because of the confrontation with Nazi history forced by the Allies' occupation; the Russian occupiers rather distinguished and distanced their German subjects from the Western "fascists." Both occupiers set the stage for the Germans to want to find their own identity unshadowed by either.[32] For West Germans, the earlier the material, the less problematic it was historically, and the more common musical ground it shared with other cultures. Albert Mangelsdorff's turn to early Western music was matched in the East by Rolf Kühn and his brother Joachim with their recording of similar material around the same time.[33] East Germans accepted undeniable roots, but deconstructed them freely, with irony, parody, gusto, yet also with affection and respect.

Even though the song is played to death with moods of anger, naiveté, solemnity and authority, it cannot be killed. Maybe it is not meant to be . . . When I hear Gumpert and Sommer being played, I recall Prussia and Heinrich Heine, Kurt Tocholsky and the Weimar Republic . . . With an ever more towering spirit, the pompous pretentions of solidified tradition are blown away, yielding to a hint of aging Prussia in the music of jazz annihilation . . . The way into modern jazz is prepared here for the Schoenberg/Eisler concept from the truth of musical thought. March and waltz are dissected and dispersed, their phraseology no longer of use; a sunrise of endless light in C major which, with a twist of hopeful irony, refused to set and in reality is played as majestically as all musical sunrises and moments of enlightenment in the history of music. (Engelhardt [1980: 37])

Reichelt – the jazz-friendly radio broadcaster who sold his tapes to Jost Gebers for FMP release – recalls the brief but intense period Gumpert refers to as the GDR's version of the West's cathartic *Kaputtspielphase.* He sees the influx of Western players at the time as a stimulus, but not generative of this phase, which he sees as already fading with the release of Synopsis's *Auf der Elbe schwimmt ein rosa Krokodil* (*In the Elbe Swims a Red Crocodile*),[34] with its "open structures and occasionally even . . . a certain reinstatement of melodic balance and motivic development" (1980: 21).

Just For Fun is one of those broadcast tapes. It is an LP's worth of completely spontaneous improvisation (by Petrovsky, Gumpert, and Sommer) marked by the same formations of short statements succeeding each other with clear, abrupt shifts of texture crafted by tempo, volume, timbre, instrumental voices, and combinations. Overall, it is somewhat more subdued in its intensity than the West German sounds (of Brötzmann et al.) it echoes, leaning more toward the delicate, spacey English style at times, and toward a lot of fleet tumbling and twittering strains around a looming, often droning tonal center, and triadic texture both major and minor. That said, all players are as intent on exploring the farthest reaches of their instruments' potential for any and every sound, and Sommer is usually more horizontal in his forward driving motion than are the Western percussion standard-bearers Paul Lovens, Tony Oxley, or Han Bennink most of the time.

The Old Song, released in 1973, opens with Sommer playing on his own piece called "Ein Holz für Angelika" ("A Wood for Angelika") on the marimba. This short statement stands as a kind of microcosm of his whole approach to percussion, one of pitched sounds (more on which ahead). It is followed by Gumpert's insistence on the major triad as musical field, saxophonist Manfred Hering's more vocal and Dionysian extensions of that field, backed by Sommer now letting loose with his thunderous Saxon handling of the drumkit, including his own vocalizations of the tonal field. This short piece, for all those elements, is an emblem of the Eastern roots of the free-jazz concept.

That deconstruction of the major scale gets wider and rangier. Side two develops in a way that is always interesting to me when it happens in free improvisation. The trio continues to play around with this ghost of the major triad so long that we feel they will never get out of it; then they start to thrash their way out of it so radically that we are sure they have forgotten all about it – except that they have also played it long enough that it continues to echo in our mind as we listen to them thrash. Every so often their wild free play throws out a phrase or a timing that is in sync with the echo in our mind of the long lost major chord, but that could be, must be, we feel, coincidence. Then, for a climax, they return to that major triad, suggesting it had continued to echo in their minds too, that they were blowing on it all along, even when blowing away from it – and perhaps, in doing so, even evoking it in our memory. It is a magical thing about this music.

At the end of this long thrash, it comes back to a spin on the old song of the major chord personal to the chemistry between Sommer and Gumpert, who are long-time close friends. Sommer's idea for his percussion array was to pitch its components to function almost as storytellers, in the deepest Eurasian tradition of music as an aspect of drama, or the African one of talking drums. Gumpert engages that concept by preparing his piano to function itself more like a pitched percussion instrument, as both John Cage and Cecil Taylor conceived it in their respective ways.

The move from one major chord to its chromatic permutations, cited in this prepared piano's rambling modulations – as in the history of Western music – is, we are reminded, just another version of the old tumbling strain of thirds within one octave (see p. 288). This side, a virtual suite of six short variations on this theme, is ushered out by the lead of a solo by the one drummer we survey here who consciously signifies on that theme.

Alienation from one's own self thus provokes a search and discovery of new life in the killing of that self quite different, but no less effective, than that undertaken in the West (Engelhardt cites Brecht as an advocate of alienation's value as a spur to fruitful self-criticism). Indeed, these recordings might stand for the firm reconstruction of something the West Germans had deconstructed with such gusto.

Even more pointed and specific to its emerging style and identity in the free milieu was Synopsis's use of old hymns (the *rosa Krokodil* LP is a classic early example). This developed into a more frequent, recognizable category of composed pieces on which they improvised. Jost says this use of folk material and hymns became almost a stereotypical image of East German free jazz, but that, however important it was to Synopsis, it was only so as their way of developing as improvisers. As they kept one foot in tradition and one in exploration so carefully, so, he says, did they always keep one in individual and one in collective expressions when they played together (as opposed to the West German collective sounds that, following Coltrane's lead in *Ascension*, often swallowed up their individual components, unto a whole greater than their sum).

Overall, the West Germans' almost dogmatic avoidance (Chailley's "deliberate neglect") of melody, tonality, and regular pulse was not so keen in the East. Jost characterizes Petrovsky's style as a flexibility between whatever extremes it might approach. Following the clarinetist's development from that "first hour," he sees it turning from what was, for all its conservatism (compared with the West), nonetheless a distinctly Eurocentric (his word) jazz-traditional style, especially in its more swinging rhythm. The European voice is not subsumed by this turn to African-American jazz roots, but alternately fused with and set against it in various ways.

Petrovsky himself told me how impressed he had been by von Schlippenbach and the other players from the West when first hearing their music in 1973.

They were much farther along than us musically because they had no political constraints, they could always play what they wanted. The problems with that I didn't see at first, only much later; at first, they were very important to us, because they were free, and they played that freedom, musicalized it. Naturally, they had another path than we did. We were also playing free, as well as somewhat oppositionally [to the state]; for them, there was nothing to oppose, people either listened to them or not.

And not that many did, in the West; and many of those would respond with enthusiastic applause, all the while thinking "this free jazz is a passing fad, it could be a little softer, much of it is simply dreadful sounding." It was something people affected to seem intellectual, or revolutionary in their thinking at that time. So it dawned on me eventually that there was a lot of the lie, of phoniness in this scene. The first jazz musicians had no time for phoniness; they simply had to play what they lived out of their horns, without a lot of clever tricks. My life in the music has been very different from what I see now. There is too much commercialism.

Free jazz emerges in the West, okay, well and good – but there the goal is to sell it in the market place. But as much and deeply as the art may survive and flourish, even its most well known practitioners enjoy no great success. Peter Brötzmann is perhaps the best example of what success this music offers; his recordings have always sold the best. Perhaps not in the beginning, but later he became almost a cult hero. And that surely, in this case, stems from nothing other than the seriousness and discipline and dedication that drives this music, not from hype. He is also a very talented painter, perhaps as good as a musician. He is almost like a philosopher, a very intelligent person.

The 1980 recording *Snapshot*, a collection of performances recorded for FMP at one of its own three-day concert events (Free Music Workshop) in August of 1979, functioned as a calling card for "Jazz aus der DDR" into the international arena. The booklet of articles accompanying it features the writers from whom my own shot of the East German free scene is snapped. This recording is long out of print, thus hard to find even in Germany.

Wilhelm Liefland was a West German writer who chronicled brilliantly the *Emanzipation* as it unfolded there, before committing suicide at a tragically young age. His piece for *Snapshot* opens the series with its author's signature mix of sociopolitical, philosophical, poetic, and musicological impressions, "Theorizing was the result of reflection and, since 1968, of political agitation (secondary to music). The music came from the musicians. In linguistic terms, music is a tautology; it denotes itself. However language may illustrate this, it never is identical with music. Specifically American and, even more, German Jazz critics have been suffering to date from this never quite comprehended distinction" (1980: 6).

Liefland cites from an East German book handed to him by Petrovsky at the *Snapshot* event. The excerpts from Günter Mayer's *World View – View of Notes. On the Dialectics of Musical Material* convey, in classic high-German and Marxist rhetoric, a picture of East German free jazz as a politically correct force allied with its "Anti-Imperialist, Democratic and Socialist forces" (6) in Western countries: "In brief: modern Free and Post-Free has been emancipated from American supremacy, in the FRG [West Germany] and Western Europe as well as in the GDR" (6).

Mayer-via-Liefland goes on to paint a picture of GDR jazz history as comprising three essential trends: "popular-democratic," the music of the proletariat it was in the beginning and never stopped being; "commercialized-snobbish," a post-Second World War aspect shunned and sometimes banned as Western decadence; and a conscious gesture of "progressive" and full-blown musical aesthetics in the mainstream of Western art music and Democratic Socialism.

Virtually every East German player I interviewed expressed derisive contempt, in one way or another, for the self-serving hypocrisy of Party officials, knowing firsthand the repression and ignorance of their music it could mask. On the other hand, having effectively freed themselves from its grip, they also had no illusions about its Western counterparts, in equally shallow and self-serving capitalist-style attitudes (toward "jazz" as America's stepchild, born to learn how to sing and dance for the grown-ups in power, and to inherit their wealth only if they also learn the deepest rules of minstrelsy, to play ball in the marketplace). If anything, the Reunification put them in the position, like other East German intelligentsia, of speaking up for the positive aspects of life in a society in which they had more than once walked a fine line between being "progressive" and "subversive" elements.

Liefland's own whimsy here captures the sense of the absurd most of the artists themselves express:

> The Positivist in his armchair:
> What's correct, is correct.
> The Hegelian in his armchair:
> Is it right or am I right or are the facts unpleasant?
> Percussionist Baby Sommer at his instrument:
> Hombre! Come out!
> Alex at the press conference:
> Shit! . . .
> The skeptical utopian in his armchair:

What does not exist now still can become . . .
A German Jazz critic:
    Lo, all there is came to you by ME, saith the Lord Zabidoo. (7)

The same whimsy also captures the wonder and hope transcending that sense of the absurd:

I also believe a bit in laws of nature and historic processes. But with the Arts it's a bit different. Western dialectics, by the way, is nothing but a dualism of competition. Capital requires much more planning than the humanist idea of communism. But both systems become repressive once they forget about the real human being. We, we play the blues, or free instrumental expression. It's no mere outlet. It's creation and goes all the way . . .

    . . . Socratic Question: Why, o Alcibiades, do the projects of Free Music and dialectical materialism with its political forms of expressing both Socialism and Anarchy often come so excitingly close?

    Why shouldn't they, o Socrates? (9)

Ulrich Gumpert: From Blue Notes to Passion Plays

We improvised there, and somehow in our improvisation suddenly some riffs developed that then became fixed, stayed in my mind. It was a careless love.
                                                                    – Ulrich Gumpert

Ulrich Gumpert's neighborhood lies just against the Eastern side of where the Berlin Wall stood by the Spree River; its Friedrichstraße Station was the major checkpoint for all train travel between East and West. The Friedrichstadt Palast, dating back to the late eighteenth century and newly renovated as a glitzy venue for commercial live shows, remains the center of a part of the city traditionally devoted to arts and entertainment (mostly the latter, as the name of Gumpert's street attests). His building is one of those run-down edifices that almost look abandoned (until one gets inside, where they are restored and elegant), in a small cul-de-sac called Am Zirkus (On the Circus) in this half-decayed, half-revived district.

Recalling much that I had read and heard from others about the quality and strength of tradition and education that had endured in the East in general, and was reflected specifically in even its most adventurous arts, I ask Gumpert about his relationship to tradition.

Well, the tradition has always been in my consciousness, but actually more as the European than my own local tradition. For example, Manfred Schulze's music was out of the tradition of the [French] wind quintet; and it is actually so that if he weren't so conscious of that tradition he wouldn't have been as serious a player as he was.

I started playing the french horn as a student in Weimar. I played there only three years, then they put me out. I had some problems with Marxism and Leninism. For every field of study, that was the main focus, and it had to be sharp. Then I started to play Dixieland, because the jazz music in the early '60s was forbidden, but Dixieland was okay. Student clubs were allowed to form to play it, but it was very rigid. And in Weimar the music school was very Stalinistic, and the real jazz music was too free, too liberated; it wasn't allowed.

Along with french horn, Gumpert started out on tuba, trombone, and euphonium, and saw his brass techniques as having an influence on his piano phrasing. He told me his influences were primarily reed players – Charlie Parker, John Coltrane, Ornette Coleman, and Archie Shepp – as well as pianists Thelonious Monk and Cecil Taylor. (Again, the rule of horns, winds, even in the piano man, as with von Schlippenbach and his GUO.)

Gumpert spoke to Noglik (1978) of a turn to European folk music by himself and other East German jazz players-composers as a way to avoid imitating or selling out to American jazz. But he also saw the neo-Romanticism (of Keith Jarrett, then) as "dangerous,"[35] preferred Cecil Taylor as a soloist, called his own music's Romantic elements ironic. Piano-stylistic differences (the "how") were not as important to him as the "what" of the music.

He chose for himself the "what" that was "free" and "new" music, but also questioned what that "what" really meant. He pieced together from such questioning a sense of his own role as being that of a contemporary musician working new things out of the *Gestalt* and media of jazz;[36] he saw playing from structure as part of the "free" *Gestalt*. For him, that freedom was an opening and increase of musical options, not an abandonment of them, as forged by Monk, Taylor, Willem Breuker and Misha Mengelberg, and modern art music in the East (Eisler) and West. He felt a responsibility to, not aloofness from, his audience.

All of this bespoke a modern German distrust, both East and West, of the ideas of Romanticism, "the folk," and art for art's sake, for the hells their good intentions had paved the way to in recent history. It also conveyed the strong dose of textual content and context his work would take on in the '80s and '90s, in setting libretti, theater, and poetry to his composed and improvised music. He praised his countrymen Brecht and Eisler for making art relevant to their people; he nodded to John Coltrane as a bridge back to European (for him) modalism, that of the oldest folk roots, not more recent ones (he was careful to make that distinction, skirting the pre-nationalistic project of the Brothers Grimm). The jazz tradition for him offered a method, the European tradition a statement. He valued jazz as reflective of society and culture; he had close affinity with *E-Musik* (*Ernst*, or serious music) composers, and performance techniques. For him, body, eye contact, audience rapport, show-theatrical elements, were all part of the "free jazz" concept.

Most of our own conversation, two decades later, centered on the social context of his role as a musician. The success he had enjoyed through the 1970s and '80s, set against his post-Reunification frustration in finding enough work, affirmed the idea that at least some post-free musicians depend at least as much for their iden-tity – not just outer persona, but the inner identity that generates motivation and direction – on the sociocultural context as on an abstract aesthetic or personal self-image. In that sense, his art and its situation resembled those of much African-American music, but further consideration suggests it as more a matter of personal temperament. We cannot imagine Coltrane's music outside the context of African-American historical identity, however clearly it transcends it, nor Bach outside German Baroque, nor Schoenberg outside Viennese Romanticism, in the same way we can imagine, I suggest, Handel's (outside German), or Stravinsky's (outside Russian or French), or Braxton's (outside both African-American and Western tra-ditions).[37]

I asked whether his reading of Comolli and Carles's *Free Jazz, Black Power* made him look to his own German roots for inspiration rather than to black America, as it had his good friend Günter Sommer.

> Very much so. It made us distance ourselves from the American influence – not the music, we've always listened to that – but just to grasp our own social sit-uation here. It made us mine the potential of jazz as a gesture of resistance. It forced us to politicize, rather than just musicalize, our lives more.
>
> In 1976 – you've heard of Wolf Biermann? This story, of his expatriation? Many of us signed a petition against that action, which was a polarizing event for us here. The effect of it contributed to our growing awareness that we had political positions sheerly by virtue of the music we were involved with.[38]

"But that was all very long ago, and now all is in order" – his laugh is benign but dripping with irony – "it's the past." Of course, the past often looms larger than the passing cruelties of historical absurdities. Again, more than one East German expressed to me the sense of Orwellian surrealism they experienced in the West's single-minded view of their Eastern history as something that the fall of the Wall had simply erased. It felt no less absurd than the equally bizarre sense of reality they endured before the Wall fell.

I saw Gumpert perform a block away from his apartment at the Berliner Ensemble theater, Brecht's old home stage, and one of Berlin's historical land-marks, with its round sign that resembles the Mercedes-Benz logo.[39] The occasion was a Brecht tribute, in which Gumpert's part was a solo improvisation on East German music by Eisler. He made sure I understood that this was more a com-munity duty than a typical gig, something he half-apologetically dismissed as mar-ginal to his more serious musical life. For my purposes, however, it was of great interest as an example of the peculiarly East German-jazz significations on Eisler's music about which so much has been written.[40]

Gumpert told me that as a composer and pianist he was motivated by social concerns, but that this was more in terms of the words and the people who wrote them: "Musically, I do recall the influence of Carla Bley. She did a project involv-ing the work of Eisler and Kurt Weill, and Charlie Haden too participated.[41] And Eisler was very out of favor in the GDR at the time." (He was very in favor with the Western left then, because of his associations with socialist ideals, was an inspiration to jazz musicians, through his well-crafted tunes, even as most disagreed with his socialist realism.)

As we watch my recording of his Eisler gig Gumpert tells me that the opening piece, "On Suicide," is a text is by Brecht that had for East Germans another level of meaning that has endured to this day. He starts to recite the text, then looks through his materials for a copy of it, then reads it in German:

> Murky evenings should not be,
> nor high bridges over water;
> these are no good.
> The whole winter is no good,
> for in the face of this misery
> the people throw away their unbearable lives.

I am still enchanted with this performance exuding those "East German blues," and curious about his embarrassed diffidence about it. I ask him to relate it to the blues from America. He tells me:

The writer Joachim-Ernst Berendt was the promoter for the big Folk-Blues Festival in Europe, and in '65 they came for the first time to East Berlin. The concert was here in the old Friedrichstadt Palast. So the people heard their first live blues here en masse then: Memphis Slim, Willie Dixon, John Lee Hooker. Most of the rock bands were still forbidden here, but the blues bands were the exception because they were politically correct, the music of an oppressed class.[42] Naturally, there were many intellectuals here who were fans of the new rock music – very many Jimi Hendrix fans, for example. They were part of an underground distribution network of recordings, nothing legal, and whatever could get through on the radio, Voice of America and so on.

For me it was a universal language. I hear it, and I know exactly what it means, quite well. I had read a lot about it, and actually it was just received as a universal language that we used in our own situation. Naturally we didn't understand the words, necessarily, but that didn't matter. We had also been prepared for them through our exposure to Dixieland.

My first experience with modern jazz was through a radio show that played all the new Blue Note recordings every day [recall Blue Note's Berlin progeniture] from NDR [Hamburg, Western] broadcasts, not GDR [Eastern]. Bobby Timmons, Jimmy Smith – great stuff, also blues-tinged, all through the '60s. Then I started to try it, because I heard so much from these other keyboard players.

In a sudden digression that seems significantly synchronistic for its spontaneous linkage of the spirits of the blues and Hanns Eisler's songs, Gumpert points to the videotape still playing in the background. "You know, this song is by Eisler. It's an incredible song, called "Lenin." It's like a hymn to Lenin; but I play it more in the gospel style. The original is . . ." he goes to the piano and plays something that sounds to me like a Russian military march; he tells me it's an "old German folk song."

Aus teutschem Landen – a title spelled in old German, translated as *From German Lands* – is Gumpert's series of pieces based on early German folk song. Its boisterous rhythms and collective blowing might have been something Mingus would have pulled off had he been born in this time and place.[43]

"Of course, 1972, the time of *Aus teutschem Landen*," he tells me, "was also the time Jost Gebers first came to the East; we met for those sessions at the Melodie Klub, which was part of this huge building that had been a part of the entertainment complex of the old Friedrichstadt Palast. Göbbels had wanted to resurrect it into a spectacular theater for the Third Reich, but luckily that never happened.

"That record brought us a renewed respect here in the East as serious artists. People saw it as an expression of distinctly Eastern, as opposed to Western jazz," he concedes, "but for me, there was no such thing as GDR jazz. We lived in the GDR and we played that music, so okay, GDR jazz. But for the public it became a sort of standard of a GDR music. Which was okay, but not our real intention. In fact, it was also somewhat subversive. Actually, we had nothing to do with this East German state." He makes sure I understand.

Gumpert's most far-reaching work as a composer/bandleader has been in collaboration with poets and playwrights from the vital theater scene grown up around his neighborhood's Deutsches Theatre (the home of the *Jazz in der Kammer* series). The international journal *Contemporary Theatre Review* devoted a 1995 issue to, as it was titled, *No-Man's Land: East German Drama After the Wall*. Editor David Robinson's introduction summarized its subject so:

> More than any other artistic form, theater embodied and fulfilled the GDR's ambition to surpass the West in cultural as well as political consciousness. The presence and influence of Bertolt Brecht in the early 1950s, the formative years of the East German state and its cultural policies, guaranteed that its theater would command world attention, setting a pattern of innovation and social critique that would outlast the GDR itself . . .

By the 1980s, GDR dramatists such as Heiner Müller and Christoph Hein were acknowledged to be among the most important dramatic voices of the German stage, with Müller in particular acclaimed as Germany's preeminent postmodern playwright (Robinson [1995: 1, 6]).

Gumpert's close collaborations in this scene have included Müller (on *Hamlet Machine*), Thomas Brasch, and Jochen Berg, all of whom have been central to it in varying degrees.[44] His setting of Brasch's poems under the title *Hahnenkopf*[45] conjoin Eisler-type cabaret, mainstream, and free jazz with the text and its singers' voices. The text itself (which Gumpert says irritated the Stasi [East German secret police] when the piece was performed in the late 1970s) is about the brutally suppressed Peasant's Revolt of 1525 in South Germany.

One of its lines, "ein Vertrag ist ein Stuck Papier," translates as "a contract is just a piece of paper." It resonates with the same dramas played out in nineteenth-century America between the Native Americans and Europeans, and between Dust Bowl farmers and bankers later, as immortalized by Woody Guthrie's line "some men rob you with a shotgun, others with a fountain pen." The East German literati, most powerfully in its playwrights, lyricists, and librettists, had established themselves as populists wielding words as swords against a state they felt was betraying the socialist contract in both letter and spirit. The applications of jazz and free-jazz sound tracks and effects to this history suggest a deep (more than an East) German solidarity with the victims of American power. Petrovsky's saxophone cry, for example, is associated with the revolting peasants in the same way American clarinetist John Carter associated his own sound with African and African-American slaves in his similarly theatrical project.[46]

Jochen Berg's career reflects the quintessentially East German mixture of venerable and revered tradition that is also perpetual alienation. He was the third in the lineage of the Deutsche Theatre's house playwrights, preceded by Brecht and Müller. He wrote several plays throughout the 1970s for its Berliner Ensemble, serving in his official capacity from 1974 to 1990 – yet none of them was ever actually staged in East Germany, with the one exception involving Gumpert. A long-time friend, Gumpert first worked with Berg on his 1972 unpublished play *Dave*, about alienated youth in the GDR. Berg's work was also produced in West German theaters in Stuttgart and Wuppertal, and Gumpert composed the music for Berg's American debut, the New York premier of his opera *Die Engel*.

As Brasch drew on German history for his political statement, Berg drew on the Western mythos of the Bible's Book of Revelation for his (about the pain of Germany's division). As with the first hours of the East German free-jazz players themselves, primal German roots are unearthed as still living and timely currency for the present, in a way not seen in the West Germans. The text is brief, and Gumpert's orchestrations are spare. The opera almost feels Native American, in its poetry of primal images and its repetitively insistent, simple musical framework. It also recalls the operas, the Ghost Trance and earlier music by Anthony Braxton that I had performed over the last ten years – complexities evolving from and returning to simplicities, in both music and libretti.[47]

Especially pertinent here is the way both literary and musical patterns hearken back to themes struck in the first recordings by Gumpert et al., tying them together in a new level of expression. As we are seeing, the deep history of the major triad and diatonic scale was embraced by the East Germans as a ground for their own obsessive signifyings on it, as if on a mode. That background keeps us from quickly pigeonholing Gumpert's more recent strategy as a composer as derivatively minimalistic. If anything, it reminds us of the debt the American minimalists owe to the Eisler–Brecht–Weill cabaret theater tradition, and the source of the even deeper roots of sheer triadic diatonicism in general from which the American minimalists themselves clearly derive. Gumpert's minimalist framework here is, like Berg's Christian imagery, the assertion of a home turf that had been so thoroughly appropriated and reworked in so many senses as to make the original look like a copy.

Günter Sommer: The Saxon Angles

The influence of the free players from the West . . . was more their example
than their actual music; by going their own way they encouraged us to do the
same, and it has been both a similar and different way.

– Günter Sommer (in Noglik [1981: 323])

Günter "Baby" Sommer, Gumpert's closest and oldest friend of the Zentral Quartett four, traces his Saxon ancestry into the mists of history in his home city of
Dresden. He reports with pride the way he stood up to school and state authorities in his teenage years to avoid being herded into training and professions other
than the life in music he wanted, passing auditions and exams at the Carla Maria
von Weber School of Music against great (political, not musical) odds. Now he is
the recently hired head of its Jazz and Pop Department, with solidly established
credentials as a pillar of German jazz – something like Kowald's official status in
the West[48] – after years of notoriety as the free-jazz wild man through the GDR
years. He travels to music departments across the United States as a guest artist
and scholar, collaborates with author Günter Grass on highly popular recordings
of readings with improvised music, and is generally professionally comfortable in
the Reunification situation that has been so much more difficult for most of his
colleagues in the music.

As it was for all of those colleagues, the successful transport of Western FMP
artists to the East was a defining moment for Sommer's musical career. His descriptions of encounters with Evan Parker, Cecil Taylor, and, especially, fellow drummer
Han Bennink, suggest in musical terms the nature of the disorientation widely
reported decades later as the dilemma Reunification brought to the East as a
whole: "With my Eastern colleagues, I always had a clear role to play, as the
rhythmic support of the group, one who would sometimes goad it on – but
mostly there were always pauses the others took which I would fill up with
my own statements. With these Western players there was no pause, no place for
statements."

As he said this, I was reminded of the way the feel and rhythm of European
culture had contrastively heightened my awareness of American energy as superficial mania. Reading about and observing the sweep of global capitalist, pop, and
political culture in the American mold and flesh here was like seeing shoots of
new ivy begin their crawl over an old building. If the building were not there, the
ivy would simply constitute the landscape; since it was, the ivy might seem the
vital, active force in its moment, but would in the end be shaped to the building
in a way that would enhance the latter's aesthetic, with venerability. (In other
words, as the West spreads to the East, it is bound eventually to become, as much
as overcome, the East.)[49]

Saxony, Prussia embodied the building; the Western players, by comparison,
were more like the ivy, not in a parasitic so much as a complementary way. Sheerly
by dint of history – including that of the emigration to America from mostly

western and southern states – West Germans were more infused with the restless, uprooted aspect of Germanity; the Easterners had rather been forced to oversee the old building, to redeem its humanity from the tyrants.

Sommer goes on to explain to me in more detail his experience of playing in duo with Cecil Taylor.

> Cecil is so tightly sealed into his own music that . . . one must listen to him for a long time, until one begins to discover the slowness in the midst of the speed.
>
> The first time you hear it, it sounds so quick [he sings a fast scat] and there are so many notes, you feel like you can't really connect with any of them. But when I had the chance not only to listen to but to play with Cecil, then I discovered that in this whirlwind of tempo, there is also a slowness. It's like classical études for the piano; we have so many lightning-quick études, but structurally all those notes are just subdivisions of quarter notes from the melody – eighth, triplet, sixteenth and so on ornamenting a slower, simpler line. I could see that he was using structures. At first I couldn't hear all these notes; after our second meeting, I realized there was a logical system in his approach. Many musicians wouldn't feel it necessary to play all the possible per-mutations of one note's duration, but that's what he did. I felt his system was just to use certain material – for example, an interval window, such as an octave or a fifth – and to play all the notes in there, not just once but repeatedly, many times. This determined the music as static, built on one unmoving point [he sings fast figures dancing around a single note]. All these little notes, without any development, just on one point, and then another later. So it's kind of like being slow by playing fast.

This is also a perfect description of Curt Sachs's "tumbling strain" (more on which in chapter six), adding to my sense of a distinct and perhaps deeper bond (than in the West) between East German and African American cultures that needed further exploration. This slow thing – what I called the building, what we might also call the Old, next to the New, more nervous ivy – is something that music can preserve in its depths, like a time capsule, or an archaeological dig, until conditions are such that it becomes relevant and useful for, again, overtly surface purposes: the cantus firmus from which Western meter, harmony, and counter-point derived; Schenker's *Urlinie*; Charles Seeger's (1940) words about folk music as bearer of deep-historical information; the field hollers and blues and later "Afro-isms" that emerged from jazz in the 1960s, after the music's beginnings as a "Negro-inflected" European-style society/dance music. One could develop a whole study of the dual aspect of New complexities as the overlay of some Old simplic-ity, showing how some parts and players of music history served the New, others the Old, still others both, somehow.

When Sommer tells me about his own encounter with the French book *Free Jazz, Black Power* – his feelings of guilt over "stealing" black music, and his con-fusion over what to do about them – he describes the epiphany of identity it triggered. "From that moment I was listening deeply into myself and . . . there is a big part of the marching tradition in my body, in my stomach, because I played in a marching band when I was young. There is something Pr-r-r-russian!" He says the word "Pr-r-r-r-EUssisch!" with rolled-R gusto, then sings "R-r-r-r-r-u-u-u-mp! gong gada . . . r-r-r-r-u-u-ump da-ga dada!" . . . lusty, syncopated, strong. "From my childhood, you know. Something of that is still in the music. So I played my new things with the same energy as I previously spent on playing time. Only it did sound different from the West Germans, because we began to realize that we had something unique to us, which was Saxon, Thuringian, Medieval music. And that not as nostalgia, but with our new consciousness, as material we could work improvisationally. Finished forms, pieces, that we took apart and put together again in a totally new shape."

The first practical step toward his own music came with Sommer's trio with saxophonist Friedhelm Schönfeld and bassist Klaus Koch, then with the Selb-Viert quartet with Petrovsky and trumpeter Heinz Becker. He began to depart from the straight-ahead swing of hard bop, of hierarchical beats in bars of steady pulse and symmetrical meter into his first way with the new (in 1966) "free" style. One of his most unique signature attributes, however, came out of his historical situation. "At this time in the East, you couldn't buy good drumkits," he says, "so I decided to build my own. This was a very, very, very important point for me. I collected very old drums, tympanis that were a hundred years old, and eight-year-old snares, and huge bass drums, and I used, like Han Bennink, all metal and other materials that I could find to produce noises." Sommer approached his first important international gig with his homemade kit with some trepidation about how they would be received by his American peers, so much better equipped with their high-end gear from Ludwig and Gretsch. They were received by all with wonder and delight. "That happened enough times with others that I felt sure this was my way to be unique, to sound different and have a different melody in my playing to distinguish me from the others. From then on I was quite proud of all my old-fashioned stuff."

Sommer told Noglik that he was very interested in the percussion music of many non-Western cultures but not so interested in that of Western music traditions.[50] I wondered what interest all this early Western music held for an experienced jazz drummer. His answer — that his early musical training on accordion, trumpet, and piano laid a foundation of melody and harmony for his work as a percussionist — brings us to another signature part of his style. "My stomach is full of harmonies and melodies. When I play drums, it is always about" [he sings some lines like a scat singer, a string of varied pitches sung percussively] "it's not like" [scats again, but all on one pitch]. "Always melody and those things, and I use, especially in solo concerts, all tuned drums, so I can play chords with my drums."[51]

His journey to his deepest Western roots thus equipped and mapped, Sommer began it mindful of the motives and approaches of others who had taken it that he felt fell short or wide of his own musical marks.

One was through Gunther Schuller and his Third Stream music. Here he had Charles Mingus and Miles Davis and all of these wonderful black American artists and blues tradition, and I thought "Why is this idiot trying to play European music in such a context?" I think that now, out of the ground of both traditions – the American, with its Afro-American background, and the European, with our classical symphonic background – that we, on the one hand, can each do something unique. But when we try to create a synthesis, we cannot thus suddenly play like Americans and they can not suddenly start playing like us. It doesn't work.

His passion for American jazz had led him to "deliberately neglect" his own European tradition; The Third Stream movement, for all its disappointing results, did serve to redirect him to that tradition, to consider the ways the two traditions might work together better. Jazz, he reasoned, had served his youthful need to reactively rebel against his repressive society; as he matured into a more informed and articulate political consciousness, he needed to acknowledge African-American musical gestures as peculiar to their needs, and to recognize his own different situation, and how his music might speak to it.

How could we, with all that we had developed in European music culture, develop something of a worthy response to American jazz culture? And that was the moment when I, with Ulrich Gumpert, began to dig around in German soil. Just as America had the blues, we felt, so have we ancient German folk music, Prussian marches. We tried, then, to forge a new concept and practice of playing with these folk and grassroots traditions. One element was the material from the Middle Ages.

Such material was not politically suspect; indeed, a case could be made for its cultural-political support.

On another front, the contemporary music composers working next to Sommer at his home university in Dresden, the Carla Maria von Weber School of Music, also enjoyed strong official support, as the current moments of the great classical tradition. "Content attracted the attention of the politicians," he says.

They perceived rock music as motivated very clearly by a political position, and jazz by a political background, and these things overshadowed the music's formal interest or qualities. If, however, the rhythmic field is rearranged in a fresh way, or the music is presented onstage unconventionally, or if the score is made not with notes but graphics – such innovations in themselves cannot be censored as capitalist expressions, or socialist either. Hanns Eisler always wrote about such things, but one really can't read such motives into aesthetics.[52] So we are a nation with a great musical tradition that could bear much innovation, but only within the clear realm of a formal musical evolution free of suspicious political context.

Sommer's turn away from American jazz was not a turn away from other musical traditions, and it was not a rejection of American post-free players who were themselves turning away from America and toward European improvisers as colleagues. He found Anthony Braxton's music of interest for its meld of African-American and European traits, and formed a trio with Braxton's fellow AACM colleague and long-time bandmate trumpeter Wadada Leo Smith, with Peter Kowald on bass. "The other direction in black American culture, through Wynton Marsalis, is of no interest to me," he says. "I think that the period of jazz we grew up with is really over. Jazz, in a way, has become a music like Baroque, or Classical, something historical you might want to play. In the next century, I think, jazz will be played like we play the music of the last century."

The improvisation of form is an aspect of Sommer's mature music that he attributes to his European composer's tradition. He describes such form building as the "dramaturgy" he brings to the improvisational moment, around which he structures the "semantic information" of his gestures. "Earlier I did not do this – improvisation was at first a freeing from such order – but for many years this consciousness of form-building has been in my improvisations," he tells me.

> In 1976, I started playing with a church organ player named Hans-Gunther Wauer. He's really educated in the pure classical tradition of pedagogy on how to play the organ. And he was interested in improvising. We made many LPs and CDs; and he always brought a great sense of form to our improvisations. They were like little classical symphonies, with the overture, themes and variations, submotifs, reprise, and ending. None of this was ever planned verbally before playing, it was just his natural way. All these steps in our free playing brought home to me very clearly that, one way or another, free improvisation was not free from rules and order. I decided from this experience that I too had that background to make such form, deep with me, in my stomach, a very classical sort of *Urgrund*. It had slept, but at this moment I was working with a person who was using all this material, and I felt, "Yes!" And from this moment I have preferred to play, to structure my improvisation in this German way of thinking dramaturgically about music.

Such form-building later developed from close engagements with theater, dance, and literature, in collaborations with practitioners of those arts and in his own study and consumption of them.[53] "For example, when I play with Inge [German dancer Inge Mißmahl, with whom he has worked often] the information that I receive from her is not music, neither music nor words nor any sound, but just energy of movement; I have to know something about the arc of a movement and what its counterpart is in beats, duration, triplets, sixteenth notes, or what phrase I can put in this window of the motion's time."

Sommer introduced himself to Günter Grass by declaring "I am Oskar" (the hero of *The Tin Drum*). The two men became close friends and recorded duets of the author reading and the musician improvising. "When I started to work with Günter Grass I came to know for the first time what energy was in the speaking as opposed to the singing voice. I had to study his own personal cadence and pace, and pitch fluctuations. Writers seldom consider the elements a musician brings to the mix, but we have to think of the ones they bring, with their reading."

This relationship between words and music is at the heart of Western music, before the dance of Baroque, in Medieval texts of chants that had already then been passed down orally for centuries. In Medieval plainchant, form grew out of the expansions of breath; the phrases chanted got longer and longer until the singer was hyperventilating, in trance. In the music Sommer and I know best – in the African-American voices of Coltrane, Cecil Taylor, and Braxton, specifically – language has shaped improvisation and composition, in three different ways, on just as deep a level. Sommer recognizes that connection in both its similarities and differences:

> There are only a few musicians in Europe who have all these qualities of the African-American musicians we've talked about, like drive, or groove, or swing, or all these special things. When our trio recorded *Touch the Earth*, and *If You Want the Pearl, You Have to Break the Shell*, in 1980, I was very surprised that Leo Smith – a very dark black man, with dreadlocks – played like a European, contemporary-music educated musician. No blues at all, no timing at all – and I felt like the black drummer, the black jazz musician, compared to him. There are only a few American musicians with a sense for European forms – symphony forms, classical forms. Leo Smith is one of them; Anthony Braxton is one of them. I believe they are able to compose a piece that uses this European form language.
>
> But what I miss – this is a question for me – I don't know if they are able to use their form knowledge in their improvisations. I have to confess that I doubt it. Leo uses a language of European classical material, contemporary of course, as a part – so he takes apart the structure of European composition – of dramaturgy – and, in a way, it is a fragmentation of the language, not the entire language.

Knowing how long and hard the road was from the free, cathartic, and experimental gestures of the 1960s to the creation of full-blown idiosyncratic systems in those two examples, and recalling Sommer's admission that his own form-building came later in his work too, I ask him if he thought one must stick with the free-improvisational approach and process for a long time before getting to its real power and potential.

> That is a good question. I think everyone starts out with a position, a bottom line, from which they begin to improvise. This improvisational capacity should be encouraged from childhood and nurtured, and helped, without burdening it at first with questions of structure, or of musical dramaturgy – all of these things should come later. When one wants to make music professionally, then one must know somewhat more. But it should be from the beginning – in elementary school, through high school, in the university, in practice at home, in private lessons – that people should improvise. Improvisation affords us the

only possibility to learn about and develop the *informal* side of life, without the order that is imposed by the disciplines education brings. Improvisation is thus for me a vital part of the general development of a society; it is for me an important matter.[54]

[He speaks intensely here, from the heart.] How would society develop with such a relationship with improvisation? Or, from the other side, in an autocratic, authoritarian society, is such a relationship with improvisation possible? Does it thrive only in a society that is like a park, where all the trees and flowers grow naturally, without design, and can it find no such home in a society where all is rigid and determined, like a garden? So to return to your question, I think it is essential that everyone be allowed and encouraged to improvise, however far or whatever direction they take it, whether they are ultimately musicians or not.

A *New York Times* editorial said in September 1996:

The easterners' underlying problem may be less financial than psychological. While the Czechs and Poles are proud to be building their new nations, victorious over Communism, each new day reminds eastern Germans that they lost the cold war and must defer to the victors. The most powerful position any easterner holds in Germany today is provincial governor. To many in eastern Germany, closing a factory is not a necessary economic adjustment but a cruel penalty of capitalism. East Germans thought of themselves as the stars of the Socialist economy. Now they are told their work was second-rate. Even if Dresden became as rich as Düsseldorf overnight, many eastern Germans would resent a process that seems to them less a marriage than an adoption.

Sommer is not one of the East Germans suffering the shock of Reunification so acutely; he has his teaching position. More to the point, he also has a gregarious go-getter's personality, has taken his own destiny in hand from the beginning. He says, and I believe him, that he would continue to find ways to work and live as a freelance musician even without his teaching job.

He is keenly aware of the problem more generally, of course. As we drove from Dresden to Konstanz, he pointed to the surrounding area, "just as one of many examples," that had been thriving before the Change (the fall of the Berlin Wall) around a local industry of light-bulb manufacturing. Instead of recognizing whatever success was already established in the East, the ministers from Bonn and their business counterparts simply threw out all babies with all bathwater and redrew the socioeconomic along with the geopolitical map, and that (naturally) according to their own interests and agendas, disenfranchising individual East Germans and the society as a whole. Widespread cynicism and bitterness about this in both East and West is harbored by many with the leftist-intellectual orientation and background most of the musicians share. Sommer's friend Günter Grass is one of the most outspoken critics of the situation.[55]

As for the musicians, their experience was that of underdogs who had bucked the system from the inside effectively enough to have had, from the 1970s to the

Change, a period of real stardom, both inside and outside their country. Inside, they had walked the political tightrope into positions of public acclaim and official cultural power; outside, when they could get out, they were received as exotic voices from another world, testaments to the power of the music under duress. After the Change, all that was moot. The East was flooded with the commerce of the global music industry, for which the audiences there were as starved as for the rest of the West; and elsewhere, the cachet of rebels protesting oppression was no more. Their situation was very much like that of the free-jazz pioneers in America after the rise of the neocon young turks in the mid-1980s there.

Sommer's next words echo Jost Gebers's on this subject, about the need for public support of cultural expressions that aren't commercially viable.

> I think that in this moment it is a duty of a town or the state to support more creative things, because it's not necessary to put money where the capitalists are already doing it. It's nonsense when official money goes to such events, as it often does. One must be anxious that the small things, the grassrooots which is the basis for all culture, such as our improvised music, or small theater, such as the Kitchen or the Knitting Factory in New York – we have such things in Dresden, but they work with all their energy and go to the state, which says, "No, we must spend our money on restoring the Frauenkirche."[56] It's sad . . . The political powers don't understand how important these grassroot networks are.

In America, the shift in *Gestalten* from jazz/free jazz/improvised music as "popular music" to "art form" has posed a confutation and challenge of the "high" and "low" categories all along. From the mix of Carnegie Hall and other such concerts offered from James Reese Europe through Duke Ellington through Benny Goodman on up to Wynton Marsalis, Anthony Braxton, and Cecil Taylor, jazz and its tributaries have claimed their position (and piece of the pie) as the "high" Western art music in whatever way they could along the way, usually right in tandem with carving out whatever pieces they also could in the more commercial, social-recreational "popular" ("low") venues and studio packages.

In West Germany and similar Western European scenes, this mix of social contexts has been similar and different: same double front of "high" and "low," only each is more officially defined, and that outside the context of America's black–white racial dynamic. Thus in Holland, as noted, Maarten van Regteren Altena, one of the premier bassists of European improvised music, has kept himself much busier and more supported as a "composer" than he would have by declaring himself an "improviser." The money and the classy venues and the professional respect of the bourgeois/academic culture are there for the former, and the little amateur associations of fans and the night club and other grassroots forums for the working players are there for the latter. That pattern is more or less the same throughout both Western and Eastern Europe.

In West Germany, of course, this high–low official split was expressed in the *U-Musik/E-Musik* division, with most of the money for *Kultur* going to the latter.

That is why it was so significant for Jost Gebers to get FMP categorized as the latter, and rightly so, sheerly on aesthetic grounds. However, had improvised music traditionally been considered the "high" end of the art form, and composed the "low," FMP would have fallen naturally under the *E-Musik* heading, and would thus have had no incentive to seek reclassification – point being that it did seek reclassification self-interestedly more than aesthetic-idealistically or ideologically.

The East German working-out of this cultural, political, and economic conundrum, in regard to its domestic jazz, had its own interesting twist: since the players who pushed for political respectability and social support for jazz were the country's successful "Dance and Popular Music" artists, they effectively negotiated from a position of power and influence to get the music accepted, not by bringing it to the mountain but by bringing the mountain to it. Petrovsky described this process with panache, in his acceptance speech at a 1989 ceremony awarding him a national prize for his work in jazz, by examining the nuance in the shift not of jazz from *U-Musik* to *E-Musik* categories, but of the *Unterhaltungs* category itself from "popular music" (*Unterhaltungsmusik*) to "popular arts" (*Unterhaltungskünste*).

In principle, had the GDR continued, this would have paved the way for an official confutation of the high–low hierarchy that would have put "folk," "popular," and "art" music all within the fold of a seamless cultural policy (they would all be popular "arts") – something akin to the unofficial institution of the Jazz Department at Lincoln Center in the late '90s, and similarly prestigious but unofficial recognitions of jazz and its tributaries as high culture (unofficial because not established as part of a government cultural policy – for example, the awards of Pulitzer and MacArthur prizes in recent years to artists and intellectuals ranging the jazz/new-music spectrum from Marsalis and Crouch to Taylor and Braxton).

Sommer declares that despite the difficulties and changing society, he will not give in to commercialism. For example, he says that:

> Fifteen years ago or more, they came out with these drum pads, this electronic drum kit. And all of the world's percussion players used these pads – black rubber pads, with an amplification system and all this. I thought, "My God, is this the end of the real drum playing?" And for a moment I was thinking, "Shall I use it also? Shall I try to use these drum pads? Shall I electrify my drumkit?" To be "in" with what was happening, I should have done it; but my deep inner instinct said no. "Even if you have to be the last person on earth who uses an acoustic drumkit, natural volume and so on, you will do it."
>
> ... I found after a year of playing my concerts that people liked it; that people are still interested, really, in hearing how a sound, how music is being made not by the engineer who is off the stage somewhere, they want to see and to hear how you form the tone, how you produce, how you create the music – handmade things, you know. Very soon, I believed again in my way of drumming and using my very old stuff, so I could survive – and all these

drummers who used these drumkits, after two, or three, or five years, it was over.

Günter Sommer's quintessential signature trait is, arguably, one that says much about the value and nature of improvised music as a whole, and about its relationship to composition.

> Our improvising music is as important in this time as when we used it as a protest, as a destruction against established forms. But the music, the form, the way we play it, today should be a little bit different than in the '60s. When in the '60s I used a big bunch of material, I used it haphazardly on the stage, threw things around without any sense of control, wooden and metal things. But today, the way to improvise is with a structure, more control, but also to discriminate. I sift through and select this sound to go with that one, and that with another, and that is more highly personally controlled. It's about learning to structure, to dramatize, and something about one's own inner sense of discipline, and of control. After thirty-five years of ordering such materials, of improvising music out of them, you have a big arsenal, a big amount of material, of course. And now, for me it is time, really, to let some space into the material, to give the material some ability to breathe.

Conrad Bauer: Full-time Free

Petrovsky's work stands in East German history as an elevation of jazz-as-popular to jazz-as-art not least for its collaborations with composers. Sommer and Gumpert, having first developed something of a "German soul" in the music, made a crossover from the jazz to the rock audiences, through their fusion band SOK, which affected a similar widening of exposure and public along the way into the free-jazz splash of Synopsis. But it was Conrad Bauer who, arguably, pulled off the most dramatic shift, in terms of widening free-jazz's audience and official support.

Bauer is the one among these four middle-aged children of the free who still has the long hair. His youthful look resembled that of a sleepy version of actor Jon Voigt; his blond pony tail is graying, and he wears his age well. Like Sommer among the four Zentral Quartett players, he is handling the post-Change situation well too, finding work both at home and abroad with less floundering than many of his colleagues.

As a guitarist, singer, and songwriter in the GDR rock scene, Bauer came from celebrity in an area of popular music that was more popular than dance music or mainstream jazz, in the 1970s. When he switched to trombone in Synopsis, the most radical free-jazz group of the time and place, not only did he bring his wide audience with him, he also gave them something there that they devoured as if it were the real meal, to the previous appetizers. (His move might be compared with a mini-version of the Beatles disbanding, and John Lennon successfully attracting their previous mass audience to his collaboration with Yoko Ono, to merge it with her existing little avant-garde audience.) One of Bauer's claims to GDR fame (mentioned often in the German music press) was his success as the first professional musician to make his living playing only free jazz, no commercial dance or mainstream jazz gigs.

Bauer was born in Halle, 4 July 1943. He went to school with Sommer in Dresden, at Carla Maria von Weber, and began his career as a trombonist with the Manfred-Ludwig sextet (1968–70) and Modern Soul (1970–73). He formed the free-jazz quartet Exis in 1971, then Fez (1974–7),[57] then other small groups. He played with Ulrich Gumpert's Workshop Band and Synopsis (reformed as the Zentral Quartett in 1984). From 1976 he has done concerts and recordings as a soloist. In 1982 he formed the quartet DoppelMoppel with his brother Johannes (also a trombonist), and guitarists Uwe Kropinski and Helmut "Joe" Sachse.[58] He has also worked throughout Europe with Han Bennink, Derek Bailey, George Lewis, Borah Bergman, and others. His most recent activities – besides the Zentral Quartett, DoppelMoppel, and various ad hoc duos – include solo work with an electronic attachment to his horn that delays and distorts the sound, duo projects with his playwright-actor partner Walfriede Schmitt, and regular visits to Canadian festivals as featured soloist and/or guest in pick-up groups of free improvisers.

In the above history, the groups Modern Soul (Petrovsky's) and Fez functioned somewhat as transition groups between the pop-rock audience and the radical free jazz of Synopsis. Bauer's words to Noglik about his development as a musician in these (often overlapping) band situations, coupled with the update of our interview, narrate the development of a musical personality keenly attuned to the social processes of mass public entertainment (on the stringed instrument accompanied voice) gradually shifting that attunement to the more introspective ones of the individual plumbing of his own psychophysical depths (on the quintessential wind voice of War) for expression.[59]

Mindful of the solo recordings Bauer went on to make after years with groups, I ask him why he decided to develop a solo approach to the trombone after so many years of working teams up to play. He replies that:

> It was my way of forging a style for myself that was independent of the groups I had been working in and continued to work in. I started branching out from scalar to *Geräuschmusik*, to better match what Uwe was doing on guitar. This got me into circular breathing [a technique of inhaling through the nose while exhaling through the mouth to keep a continuous tone sounding] which I had been doing in private a long time, but never really had much chance to use in my mainstream bands. This all fortified both my group and solo playing at the time . . .
>
> It was also that time that I decided to play only free jazz, and not worry about my livelihood as before. I was the first in this dance band scene to make that move. Then Uli and Baby, in the group SOK, left that behind, and we all came together with Petrovsky to form Synopsis. That was '73, when we had our

big debut at the Jazz Jamboree in Poland. We were able to draw on the audiences we had had in Fez and SOK to get attention for Synopsis. It was all the same continuum. I did very many concerts outside of the GDR throughout this decade . . . It was naturally a time that gave me the chance to develop my professionalism to a much greater degree.

The musical developments that took place from Fez to Synopsis bespeak a thoughtful, not a blindly reactive, reconstruction of the collective to better serve the needs of the individuals. Unlike the approach described by Alexander von Schlippenbach for his trio, or Vinko Globokar with New Phonic Art, and many other such groups – no rehearsals, always spontaneous – Fez members would write pieces for the group to work on for three to six months before playing them in public. The rehearsal period would be a collective process of memorizing and working over a tune so thoroughly that it would move from scripted to free play through sheer saturation of familiarity. No one, in either band or audience, could know what surprises spontaneous improvisation would bring to such a piece the hundredth time it was presented. This process, of course, is very much like the forging of "head" charts in American pre-free bands large and small, from Count Basie to Sun Ra to John Coltrane and many others.

Composition and improvisation were understood as musical means to the ends of both individual psychic and collective social health, not as ideological ends in themselves to be served at the expense of either aspect of that health. In this collective-heavy context, "free" is defined as a cooperative rather than lone quest for individuation and its new identities:

> Free music in general, understood as freely improvised, unprescribed playing, whether done by jazz or classical players, makes for the most honest and direct kind of musical collaborative process, in my opinion. The time of free jazz's beginning here is not long ago. Even with Fez we always try to play free, though we aren't a "free-jazz" group. In that context, playing free means developing a sound and style that is uniquely Fez . . . Fez has been an expression of its time; it should also therefore give its time new expressions back. (Noglik [1978: 19])

By contrast, Synopsis made its 1973 breakthrough in Poland with a completely spontaneous set, and served as the vehicle through which its four members would develop themselves as free improvisers together and with colleagues at large. Bauer, among all I spoke to, seemed to use the word "family" the most to describe what I have tagged Eros – a bond of kinship in the music that also resonates with the aforementioned Indo-European root of "free" (*prijos*, kin, dear one). He has played in a wide range of ad hoc, one-time groups and situations as a freelancer, as well as in a few longstanding groups with intimates friends and relatives. His most recent groups are equal mixes of preconceived ideas and open explorations. Recalling Vinko Globokar's rule about improvising only once with new people, to avoid falling into cliché, I ask Bauer what he does to keep things fresh and interesting in such "family" dynamics.

It is difficult to do a tour with such a group. A group like DoppelMoppel, after two gigs or so, the clichés do start coming. When you see that happening, you simply have to play something else against them, to break free of them. You have to always keep probing for what is really the new.

But then, if I play with the Zentral Quartett four or five times, then come back to DoppelMoppel for another concert, it will be fresh again. It's always fresh when you make something you haven't made before together. It is the struggle of the body to constantly renew itself, to find something it's never found before. That said, it's also good when one knows one's fellows for a long time, and have a history of experiences of many such different new musical discoveries together; it brings a certain dramaturgy, like a composition, to the mix.

Actually, what we call improvised music is no longer strictly so; free jazz really was spontaneously improvised, collectively, interactively; but what we've come to know as "improvised music" is really thought out, for the most part, by each person playing it, a hundred, or a thousand times rehearsed; a certain position has been established, and a sense of form worked out.

Bauer's words here pick up where Sommer's left off in my mind: what does it mean to improvise form? All Western-trained musicians know what it is to compose within a prescribed form, and to compose new forms; all jazz musicians know what it is to improvise within forms, and all free improvisers know about playing free of forms. What in these Europeans was taking place when they spoke of improvising forms, and how did it relate to their history and culture?

That can vary widely, but as an example, with DoppelMoppel, in the beginning we tried to play concert pieces. For my part, I hoped to avoid what you hear often in free music: the music begins, everyone just blows for maybe a half-hour or forty minutes, then it stops, people clap, there's a pause, then you repeat the process, and that's it. For me, that lacks the sense I like of good form. One can have a piece that begins and ends in a set period of time, but not be constrained by that; you just play the piece until a closure sort of organically presents itself, then you wrap it up, whether it's seven, ten, or twenty minutes. But as a player, you have the feeling that you are operating more as a composer, making similar decisions about material with a shape.

So then form as I understand it, and I think I speak for the others in DoppelMoppel, is when even in our free play we hit upon a clear, certain idea, work it together communicatively, maybe bring in other equally clear ideas to the mix, and either go with and leave the other behind, or juxtapose the two. We go in and out of things, depart from an area then return to it; and, when the band is really playing that way well, we somehow bring it to an end in a way that ties up all the lines we've laid out there.

It isn't something that happens every time, but it is an example, really, of the classic German fugal development, and theme and variations, and so on, only happening in the realm of improvisation rather than composing. There have been many improvised pieces that stand as gems of instant composition.

Form as variety, not repetitive ritual; themes and their variations threaded together by whatever interrelationships the memory at play can manage to see and express on the fly, like a juggler handling many objects. The intensity and single-mindedness of the Baroque – the one affect, plumbed to exhaustion – combined with the overview and relativism, freedom from obsessive compulsion, of *Empfindsamkeit* classicism, the quiltmaking of music.

Bauer has established his presence as a post-GDR player in North America (both Canadian and American venues and recording outlets) as well as in the German home turf he prefers. Two CDs from the 1990s clearly present themselves to an international more than a European audience.

The Konrad Bauer Trio is a French-Canadian recording of a 1992 concert at the Victoriaville festival, released in 1993 on the indie label Victo. It has a direct American appeal in its packaging, with liner notes by well-known American jazz critic Art Lange giving a well-penned lesson on the history of the jazz trombone in both America and Europe, and on the members of the trio (Kowald and Sommer), presumably to readers who may need the information more than Europeans. (New York-based Cadence Records distributes many European labels in the United States and Canada, but most are unmistakably European imports.) The billing of Bauer as the leader of the trio is itself an American strategy, unlikely to be seen, especially between these three leaders, in European counterpart contexts. This trio's live performance does showcase the trombonist both as player and as slightly more foregrounded leader (he got the gig). We notice here the continued presence of the old song, the diatonic triad, in the full flower of the extended techniques Bauer had developed for himself in his solo work.

Joachim Kühn's 1997 CD *Generations from East Germany* features Bauer with his long-time bandmate guitarist Uwe Kropinski, alto saxophonist Volker Schlott, bassist Klaus Koch, and Kühn's brother Rolf on clarinet. The title is apt; Rolf got out of the Soviet sector in the 1950s, well before the Wall went up; Joachim defected in 1963 when it did; we have seen the course of Bauer and his colleagues who stayed; and Kropinski is a younger post-Wall player. The CD has ten tracks, averaging about six or seven minutes each; they are titled pieces with composer bylines, mostly Kühn's alone or with one or two of the others. Some sound clearly worked out, either written or orchestrated platforms for improvisation, others just as clearly spontaneous and open.

This CD is very much the fruit of old friends and family coming together to express something that, despite their shared command of jazz's international lingua franca, inevitably reveals the personal roots and GDR history and aesthetics they also share. There is the austere, darkly brooding quality; there is a melancholy resignation, much like the one Ornette Coleman captures so well in his melodies and tone. There is the combination of wide open collective free play and mathematical rigor and technical facility one might associate with the Tristano-Konitz-Marsh lineage, or Bach. There is that droning central tone that feels like the hush and awe of holy ground.

Another pair of CDs from around the same time reflects as clearly the other, more local and European sides of Bauer's live performances at home, aimed for European more than international audiences. The first, *Bauer Bauer* (1995), offers as neat a juxtaposition of both military and ecclesiastical histories in Europe. Ostensibly a trombone duo between Conrad and brother Johannes in a Leipzig war memorial building, it is really a trio, with the acoustic space itself playing the third part. Noglik's liner notes articulate the significance of this ensemble:

> Conrad and Johannes Bauer already learned how to make use of the musical aspects of rooms while they were playing in churches . . . In September 1993 there was a duo concert . . . in the room inside the monument, which has an echo that can be heard for up to twenty seconds . . . Although architecturally speaking, the structure radiates a rather somber monumental atmosphere (it was erected 100 years after the Battle of October 1813, when the united forces conquered Napoleon I's), the improvised music is free of any ideology, it does away with associations concerning anything warlike or pompous, the musicians are able to reinterpret the historical connotations of the atmosphere into something pleasurable and creative.

Johannes's background itself reflects this juxtaposition of War, the Holy, and Religion. The younger (by ten years) Bauer learned trombone from his brother, then encountered his next major influence:

> After my student days, I had to serve in the military, and played then in a marching band . . . The music was dreadful, but the experience was very interesting. This German, Prussian march music had an outrageous intensity, a monstrous intensity, and that made a big impression on me. These marches went on and on endlessly, repeating the form as many times as necessary to fill the time of your motion, which of course had a function quite apart from the music. It was perhaps the opposite of a good string quartet's clarity, something that lacks the power of good free jazz. Peter Brötzmann's intensity, or Alex Schlippenbach's Globe Unity Orchestra, provided me with the only experiences that could match it.

He adds that "Jazz was not really the music that originally got to me in youth . . . My father was a preacher, and in our house was only church music, the early Baroque music that he loved and had in his church. When I listen to music at all, that still tends to be my choice."

Histories of the trombone in Western music mark it as the prototypical Roman war herald (as the *buccina*), as well as the first instrument allowed in the churches for its closest simulation of the human male voice. Keeping with the theme of playing the room, the 1996 Belgian CD *Pijp* captured the brothers doing another such collaboration with acoustics. This one included *Machine Gun* pianist Fred Van Hove, and two Belgian cathedrals. Van Hove was, by 1996, the cultural Ambassador of Flanders; like Hans-Gunther Wauer, he had acquired a taste for playing improvised music on the great organs of European cathedrals.

That affinity for the classical tradition extends into its current voices. "We've had here in East Berlin a very good relationship with new-music composers over the years," Johannes says.

> In the '70s, we worked a lot with pianist-composer Hermann Keller, and in recent years with Georg Katzer; and I did a composed piece by Helmut Zapf for tape and trombone, with whom I've also played a lot as an improviser while he plays the organ. This is also an area that has been very important for me; I am no interpreter, these pieces all used me as an improviser, and that worked very well. I love the second Viennese school. My favorite composer now is perhaps Lutoslawski.
>
> I think the overlap between improvised music here and the new music lies in a similarity of musical material and different approaches to how it is handled. The composer's music stems from his way of organizing the material in a personally distinctive way, while the improvised music has much more to do with the interactions between people meeting in the music. The musical material and ideas are really the same, the difference between composed and improvised playing doesn't lie there. But I've noticed that the possibilities of soundmaking are taken much farther in improvised than in interpreted music. This development of the soundworld itself is something I think improvised music does far better than composed music seems to be able to do.

Johannes was young enough when the Wall fell that he doesn't suffer from the "East German blues" as do many of his elders. His older brother is not so afflicted either, simply by dint of a philosophical personality. "I'm happy to have had this East German experience," Conrad says.

> I don't really like West Germany as it is today as much as it was twenty years ago. Capitalism in the West then was always balanced by what we had in the East; there was more of a sense then of social responsibility in the West, due to that balance, I think, than there is today. Much more. There was a good government support system then for unemployment in the West, and if you didn't work for a while you could still go to concerts and have a life. Now it's changing very quickly, and there is not so much money in the West for social support, and for support of arts and culture.
>
> I think the Westerners themselves didn't realize what they were getting into with this increase in capitalism. Last Sunday I played with Johannes in Bremen at an opening of an exhibition of East German painters there. When I was talking with the locals, they all said the same thing: you've been so overwhelmed by the changes in East Germany, but we are similarly overwhelmed by similar changes here in West Germany. Everything is about money here now, all the

power. And it pays well what interests it, but the music we have made here in the East, for example, doesn't interest it.

I feel we're in some sort of transitional phase that we don't see an end to yet. Everything we learned in the schools, Karl Marx and Lenin, gave us this sense of capitalism being an historical process that would play itself out in certain ways. We tried for the forty years since the war to play out his teachings about the opposing process of communism. It failed, but the validity of Marx's warnings, about the dangers of capitalism, is something that seems evident now around us in the problems we're having. Things are worse, not better.

The image of the new ivy on the old building comes back to mind, only now I imagine poison ivy. Capitalism was certainly having its day in America's beginnings, during Marx's moments, at the expense of its slaves in fields, women and children in factories, poor men in mines and railroads. It was now, arguably, going even stronger throughout the world at similar human costs in some quarters. But, just as arguably, the music and voices and lives of the slaves, women and children, and poor men then had made their impressions, had their effects, had improved their lots and dried up some of the poison. Having seen that in the history of my own American life, I recognized its potential to play out, with no less pain and struggle but also depth of spirit and joy, here in the Protestant heartland.

Ernst-Ludwig Petrovsky

> I am an enemy of every half-baked musical philosophy . . . and I hope that comes through in my music . . . Our "freedom" is not freedom from so much as freedom to something.
>
> – Ernst-Ludwig Petrovsky

> Petrovsky's strength lies in his willingness to take risks. Sometimes one has the impression that he is bestirring himself in a vacuum. Then one is disturbed and fascinated at how he merges this vacuum with his breath, with the gestalt of his craft's fulfillment. That he can move from the modern tradition to the avant-garde so gracefully, and subtly, fusing them together in the sovereignty of his voice.
>
> – Bert Noglik

> Jazz has fascinated me from the beginning; it was like a cry, which one wanted to answer.
>
> – Ernst-Ludwig Petrovsky[60]

Born in 1933, Petrovsky is old enough to remember flyovers and blackouts from the war, and Stalin's tanks rolling in after it to his hometown of Güstrow, in the German state of Mecklenburg. Although a student at Hochschule für Musik

"Franz Liszt" in Weimar around 1956, he says "My student time . . . was relatively short. I am essentially self-taught. From my parents I got acquainted with music in a bourgeois sense – in my case through the violin. It was a horror for me. Only later, when I learned jazz, did I also take in the classics." His first exposure to jazz was through the Voice of America broadcasts. Paul Desmond, Dave Brubeck, Cannonball Adderly, Joe Henderson, and John Coltrane were his main interests.

His first gig, with Eberhard Weise, was more a labor of love than profitable. In addition to Max Reichelt's dance-and-show orchestra and the Manfred-Ludwig Sextett, he led another important formation in those years, which continued to perform sporadically throughout the 1970s. "By 1964, I worked with this Jazz Ensemble of Radio Berlin, a sextet, in Studio IV. Things were better by then. Most of the jazz formations one would see were amateur groups, maybe half professional; this friend gave me a free hand to hire all professionals and do what I wanted with the group. It was up to me to make it stand or fall, he didn't really get involved with that process."

The musicians – virtuosi all, from Hans-Joachim Grasswurm on trumpet and flugelhorn, to Hubert Katgenbeißer on trombone, to Klaus Koch on bass, Wolfgang Winkler on drums, and the amazing Weise on piano – had paid some serious dues of frustration, repression, neglect, and persecution under Stalinism for their musical daring and intrepid indifference to political stupidity, and were now collecting on those dues as the society began to change in a direction favorable to them. "Kein Klagelied" ("No Mourning Song") and "Tagesträume" ("Daydream"), evoking Petrovsky's ancestral Russian roots, reflect something of a golden period for the art in East Germany, in terms of composing and arranging, and, especially, improvisational virtuosity and ensemble chemistry and rapport and sensitivity. The group's incorporation of Ornette Coleman tunes such as "Enfant" cast Coleman's idiosyncratic cry of minor-key sadness in an unmistakable act of Afro-Slavic soulmating. The group's reading of the tune itself features a triumphant Bach-like counterpoint between the bass and the horns, and an ending chord as nuanced and lush as Joachim Kühn might have played.

Still, the orchestrated, controlled approach to free improvisation prevailed, especially live and in public. Reichelt likens Petrovsky's work as a leader-orchestrator then to the similar projects of such artists as George Russell, Tony Williams, Sam Rivers, Bobby Hutcherson, and Don Cherry. When the band morphed into a smaller quartet version, with Koch and Winkler, and trumpeter Heinz Becker, it was still stronger on orchestrated than spontaneous gestures.

The music of Studio IV reveals an emphatic preoccupation with form and is most carefully worked out, in advance . . . There are free improvisation passages in duets or trios (winds with bass and drums), but these passages rarely were given much development in the sense of today's Free Jazz. They remain in the prescribed level of tension and are accompanied accordingly: by winds either in unison or contrapuntally by background riffs, arranged rhythmic patterns and rubato lines . . . Power-collectives do not occur in the course of the playing

but are inserted as dramatic effects — a sort of "Free Jazz on Hand Signals."
(Reichelt [1980: 20])

Some of the tastiest FMP recordings of East Germans were the *Selb-Dritt* (trio)
and *Selb-Viert* (quartet) spinoffs from this radio band. The trio featured Becker
on trumpet and Koch on bass, and the quartet added Sommer. The recordings
continued to show the strong influence of Ornette Coleman by way of West Coast
cool jazz, both in their freewheeling improvisations and a few of Coleman's tunes
(by way of Gunther Schuller's book of transcriptions of same that had found
its way into the East). Compared with their closest Western counterparts by
Brötzmann, Kowald, and von Schlippenbach small groups, they sound more
American, and more like some of those latter groups would later sound when they
started recording more with Americans.

Synopsis/Zentral Quartett started in 1973 and was gigging in Vienna during my
1997 visit. Its beginning overlapped with another professional studio band, the
Berlin Radio Dance Orchestra, active from 1970 to 1978.

Petrovsky's comparative descriptions of the two bands (to Noglik [1978: 130])
evoke, again, the difference between the formal social contract and the informal
familial code. The Berlin Radio Dance Orchestra afforded him the chance to learn
the section player's and arranger's crafts and techniques. While it did labor under
the constraints of the East German conventions, it was under the direction of a
radio official who respected rather than feared Petrovsky's brand of creativity, and
gave him more rein than usual to develop it. The way for the influence of Ornette
Coleman, especially, was paved there much as it was in America by the orchestrations of Gil Evans, or in France by those of Jef Gilson. Its improvisational
aspects were refined in the small groups. By the time Synopsis formed, it was
informed by the kind of telepathic bonds that allow family members to finish each
other's sentences, or dispense with words entirely.

Petrovsky's way of discussing discipline and expressivity suggests something key
about both in spontaneous as opposed to prescribed improvisation, and in small
groups of intimates trying to preserve their informality as they expand. As solo
statements expand to duo and trio ones, the informality remains effective, even
enhanced — much like a solitude one deems preferable to all but the company of
one or two other close friends with whom one knows one can be oneself. Each
knows the other's little ways and interests, and supports and delights in them.

> One is in the position of hearing two other lines unfolding, and of adding his
> own as a third. One more than that, in a quartet, requires stricter discipline
> and control, out of which a more artificial expression tends to emerge. Without
> players such as Klaus Koch and Baby Sommer, who understand *unformulated*
> art, and metrics, and rhythmics, and harmonics and and and . . . I could never
> come up with the spirited expressions I do. Certainly discipline is important,
> but nothing to respect divorced from emotional offerings. Such trios, where
> oneself and one's fellows receive equal amounts of one's respect, are the best
> grounds for developing as individuals in collective context. Especially when they

connect as friends, travel and live together, talk over their ideas and share critiques . . .

When we played in Synopsis there was always this very fruitful dialectic between mastery of musical craft and openness to new possibilities. Günter Sommer was of all of us the most masterful and "out" player at once, always provoking questions such as Where is this going? or Why not try this? Both rehearsals and concerts were equally valuable for answering such questions. (Noglik [1981: 337])

Noglik noted (328) that "Jazz in the East has not developed in collectives so much as individuals," and asked Petrovsky whether something wasn't lost in that. His answer indicates that, as in the West, the situation of a large ensemble rehearsing and performing regularly over a long period – such as a city symphony orchestra, or mainstream studio big band of yesteryear – would be ideal musically, but is usually not economically feasible. Yet that lack effects growth in other musical directions (ironically, in the East, away from collective and toward individual identity): "It would be much easier for me if there were more support of that sort. On the other hand, it has allowed us to develop our own identities fully."

As already seen, an important part of that identity for Petrovsky has been, also more than for his West German counterparts, the collaborations with contemporary East German composers Paul-Heinz Dittrich, Friedrich Schencker, Georg Katzer, and Hanno Rempel. Along with Schencker's *Electrization* reunion mentioned above, he was excited about a trio he had formed with its composer and Schencker's brother, who read passages from German Romantic poetry and James Joyce to his improvisations. "The area of tone-painting is the common ground I see between jazz and art music. In jazz a specific vitality plays a deciding role. Certainly there is vitality also in the playing of my art-music colleagues, but it springs from other sources, often from intellectual joy, or the joy of the academic regimen. But then there are also musicians one cannot categorize simply as in one camp or another" (Noglik 1978: 130).

Practically speaking, the spread of collaborations we saw among the West German with non-Western improvisers has not been matched to the same extent by the East Germans of the same generation, owing to the old restrictions on travel, and the new disorientations of Reunification. Sommer has been active in Greece, with Kowald; and Gumpert (like Kowald) has worked with a Japanese *butoh* dancer, but not as an improviser (he plays Satie). Conrad Bauer travels regularly to festivals in Canada, but usually plays there with fellow Europeans or Americans.

Petrovsky's work with younger player Thomas Borgmann's band *Ruf der Heimat* (*Call of the Homeland*) is his most current move onto a wider arena, with younger but not culturally or musically different voices. From his point of view, the gestures he is making to most widen the pale of his music currently are his duo with his wife, singer Uschi Brüning – something of a move to confound the strict

German lines between jazz/pop (her background) and art music, the latter now including "improvised music"[61] – and their work with electronic composer Georg Katzer, a melding of the "new" (synthesizer textures, examples of the tone painting mentioned above) and the "improvised."

> For me what matters about this music is how it has developed here, in our society and musical situation, how it reflects and what it offers that. So much that we see and hear is neither original or believable, whether it's anachronistic Dixieland, albeit played well, or Rock-Jazz – it is often just an American expression we are mouthing. And bad rock music is in a musical sense often destructive, and now it's the older generation who likes its free jazz while the youngsters have no patience with it, are brainwashed by Rock. The East is relatively more free of commercial-music trends than the West. (Noglik 1981: 322–3)

Petrovsky's post-GDR work suggests his agreement with that, as already glimpsed. Georg Katzer is an East German *Ernst-Musik* composer who collaborated with Petrovsky in 1969 by writing a "Concerto for Orchestra and Jazz Trio." As Katzer developed into electronics, he began performing live with other improvisers, most notably Wolfgang Fuchs's King Übü Orchestrü. Petrovsky's most recent collaboration with Katzer, the 1997 Konnex CD *Cooperations*, includes Brüning. This trio is a much more interactive and chamber music one than the more symphonic spectacles often staged between composers and improvisers, allowing for delicate explorations of timbre more than cathartic energy screams and runs of notes.

Brüning enjoyed celebrity in the GDR as a pop singer, then made a risky career crossover in her collaborations with Petrovsky. "I know only that improvised music will be my future; that jazz will be my future," she tells me. "There is a difference between jazz and improvised music. The struggle for the difference is where I want to work." Her career in pop included some very popular recordings of African-American-style gospel music – a music that is also popular on the grassroots level of small-town German Protestant churches, especially in the Eastern cradle of their birth. Explaining this move she says:

> I just can't, as an older woman, sing pop music any more. I can, as an older woman, sing gospel. If I had my way completely, I would only sing jazz and improvised music, because it's that music I can truly grow old with. I love the music, but that's not the only reason I would rather do it only; it's more that for me, jazz and improvised music are simply the real bearers of truth. I have the gospel material down and am presenting it now, but still, improvised music is better than that too. Because I'm German; I'm not black. I do sing gospel with much passion and joy, but in the end, it really has nothing to do with me. It speaks to me emotionally, so I wish to sing it, sincerely. But – also I'm not really in the church, and if I were a true gospel singer, I would be.

The 1992 CD's title, *Features of Usel*, refers to the neologism joining the couple's first-name initials. Its identity is obviously a spontaneous exploration of the possibilities of duo between the woman's voice and the man's instruments, which here include his own (nonverbal) voice, flute, piano, zither, clarinet, and alto and bari sax. All ten pieces are "composed by Brüning and Petrovsky" except the last one – again, Coleman's "Enfant," which has become something of a signature tune for Petrovsky. Brüning takes her place with such work in the company of the women, from Sainkho Namtchylak to Diamanda Gallas to Jeanne Lee to Urszula Dudziak to Maggie Nichols and others, who have carved out their distinctive niche in improvised music for the female voice.

When asked about his reputation as a very clever player – something I had read about, which Tony Oxley had conveyed to me also – and the difference between superficial glibness and real, grounded genius, Petrovsky tells me modestly:

> Tony Oxley is a very good friend of mine; we both share similar strong political convictions and speak our minds plainly about whatever we mean. And he is also a revolutionary in his resistance to clichés. But this means a kind of cleverness designed not to appease and please everyone but just the opposite, something people either love or hate.
>
> Tony is a superb drummer, but he's more than just a drummer, due to his overarching musical concept that extends into originality and away from cliché. He can do it all – jazz drumming, free playing, composing. I was very proud to be involved with his Celebration Orchestra and to record with them.

I ask his whether his style of free jazz in the East developed through a very well-defined direction guided by a certain musical education and discipline, or whether the musical discourse there tended to shape itself:

> Before the FMP musicians came, Jost Gebers met with us in the East. We exchanged hours and hours, days and nights, of philosophical conversations with each other. He spoke to us of things that we never would have become acquainted with apart from him. His was a very significant voice, to this day, actually. Without the FMP and Jost's influence, we would have gone in entirely different directions, I think. It wasn't just his ideas – it was the amount of work and dedication he put into his ideas to make them actual, including the idea of linking up with us in the East. He had spoken to us of the wider world he moved in in the beginning . . . but it was years before we really understood what he meant, because we had not yet – really, not until the Wall came down – become aware of it, where travel anywhere and access to all kinds of information was available.

Both in his interview with Kumpf (1975/1981) and his one American interview (Corbett 1989), Petrovsky conveyed a sense that the East had come to terms with jazz and free jazz that was comfortable enough for all concerned.[62] In discussing West-East movement (between FMP and him) before the Wall fell, he told Kumpf he encountered more difficulty with the Western than Eastern officials; and, to Corbett, he said the connections the GDR had with outside countries were better than the Soviet Union's. The initial craze of popularity in the East the decade before, boosted by the associations with rock music and liberatory cultural politics, had seemingly won free jazz's bid for social legitimacy; the state no longer banned or even ignored the music, though its relatively small audience by the '80s did not merit it much support in money or other official resources (subsidized recordings and performances). The old network of jazz "clubs" (local associations) served as the backbone of activity. To Corbett, mere months before the Wall came down, Petrovsky even said the comfort level in the GDR was a little too high, that jazz musicians "didn't have enough problems."

Jawohl, the calm before the storm.

Post-GDR Voices

The Zentral Quartett's eponymous 1990 CD and their 1994 *Plié* showcase all the different techniques and concepts, both compositional and improvisational, they developed over years of playing the four East German principals, all wrapped up for easiest, broadest access. In doing so, they show well the way improvisation and identity come together in idiom.

The first track of *Zentral Quartett* is "Synopsis." The theme reprises the joy and excitement of the youthful challenge to the totalitarian absurdity in East Germany, the eagerness to join the rest of the world in freedom, as well as the very opposite joy of generating such a movement within a potentially humane social system and having it succeed, improve things, rather than labor under crushing hostility and neglect. "Ohne Illusion" ("Without Illusion") is the one example of a spontaneous open improvisation – interesting both for showing us how that goes at this point of the game, and also as the rarest, newest flower in this idiom's new bouquet of them.

Sommer's piece "Hymnus 3" calls forth the Protestant church music at the foundation of so much African-American music and culture, kept in the East in a relatively unbroken line since Luther and Bach. It showcases the trombone, and sums up both "East German blues" and the "old song" of diatonic triadicism, in the context of this group's singular reach back to German folk and medieval roots. Finally, it resonates with the way the religious tradition and imagery survived through the atheistic dogma of Brecht and Eisler and into their heirs (friends of Gumpert et al.) in the East German theater.

The fall of the GDR deflated rather than inflated, as in Russia, its post-free scene. As noted, through the various political and musical gains made in East Berlin with the help of their Western comrades, the Zentral Quartett members and their colleagues, as in Russia, helped agent their state's official demise, but hardly by dropping out of it.

After Mangelsdorff and the Kühns and others went through doors first opened by the African Americans looking beyond America or the West entirely, interest grew within Eurasia in its own earlier and more folkish traditions. Different rhythm and pitch systems from Asia and India were interesting jazz players world-wide, and in Europe many such systems from the south and southeast – especially, for our purposes, those from the Balkans and Greece – were closer versions sharing many traits and affects with both those more exotic and the Western European ones. Instruments defined as "folk," too, became of growing interest to free-jazz players for their expansions of sound and expression.

In the GDR, when it was jazz that provoked unease in the culture and folk music that found the politically correct privilege of place,[63] the Synopsis/Zentral-Quartett big four turned that attitude around to their advantage, rather than shunning or running from it. In America, a strong general sense of jazz as an African-American expression with its heartbeat in the blues has been cultivated. But here, again, is how Ulrich Gumpert described it: "Jazz tradition for me, methodically considered, is a European tradition with an important message" (Engelhardt [1980: 33]).

The folk song, wrote Engelhardt at the GDR scene's prime, a decade before the Change, is Europe's equivalent of the blues, a means to its own such message. He argued for the GDR players' use of folk material so as successfully matching the blues bedrock in jazz in terms of its musical depth, simple profundity, and expressiveness of a people's unique time and place. It was just the backbone free improvisation needed to keep it from dissipating, as in the West, into forced exper-imentalism and the comic.[64]

Moveover, it need not endure the fate of all music in American (Fascist) culture, that of commercial appropriation and subsequent degradation as art; folk music had always been and remained in GDR free jazz "in opposition to plebian utopia and upper class abuse" (33; by rights, Albert Ayler should have been more impor-tant here, with his folkish themes, but his recordings were harder to come by than in the West). Gumpert is cited again to assert an aesthetic that engages listeners on a deep and comprehensive level, rather than one that alienates. GDR free jazz is posited as a music that can encompass all innovations from the West – libera-tion of meter, pulse, harmony, timbre, tonality, noise – as means of opening and building on traditional roots, of fulfilling rather than refuting and destroying their potential. Not only that – it can treat the imposing classical tradition, including the "artificial European state music" spawned by that tradition, with the same approach as it treated folk music: irony, and a spirit of irrepressible life tran-scending oppression and repression. Indeed, it can "tear up" American jazz so with the latter's own musical means, as jazz's version of that "artifice" becomes more the problem than the solution.

Noglik, another East German steeped in this music, looks back on the histor-ical abortion of Engelhardt's vision for Wolbert seventeen years and an era later.[65] Still, the step he takes away from that socialist-realist misstep through folk tradi-tion remains consistent with the logic of its vision:

Jazz, its background as an African-American idiom, has developed into a global musical language. That is, there are musicians now around the world who bring their own new possibilities of shape and expression to the genre. In this sense, jazz is a "world music." Although jazz is grounded in its own original identity, which thus opens all these others to their own various different identities, it is not thereby a world music in the sense of integrating (theoretically) all the world's musics into one . . . After one learns a language, one then learns to make one's own expression therein.

*   *   *

As European jazz players have turned to their own cultures to find their musical identities, they have turned more to art music than folk tradition. Not completely, but more widely and overtly, so one must dig to find the significance of the role of the folk tradition, both in its presence and absence. Most obviously, folk music has been more the rural than the urban tradition, unlike both jazz and art music; it has been driven more by social communication and ritual functions than by ideological or aesthetic considerations, also unlike them. It has developed as regional/ethnic rather than national/international expression, often with political agendas to resist the hegemony of the latter.

Where these have functioned as unproblematically with jazz as does its own African-American folk tradition (blues) has been in the Romanic, Celtic, and Scandinavian lands: Enrico Rava (with Sardinian folk musicians), André Jaume (with Corsican), Tete Monteliou (with Catelan material), Michel Portal (with Basque material); and Andalusian and Celtic presences are all examples of the national jazz scenes of Spain, France and other countries with the regional-ethnic cultures within and overlapping them.[66]

Noglik lists several criteria ruling a folk tradition's usefulness to European jazz players: is it a living part of their own social existence, or something politically and/or commercially prostituted and pimped? does it have progressive or reactionary historical associations? is it simply kitsch, by virtue of being objectified by notation, for mass-cultural consumption? The German folk tradition is so problematic on all these counts, he says, that the only way German youth of the '60s could even think about identifying with any folk music was through the folk revivals in America, Britain, Ireland, and South America. "Be vigilant, don't sing!" he cites the warning from a German author of the time to his fellows.

Indeed, the GDR's most proactive embrace of the folk tradition did not translate after the Change to its own strong version of the one that would dawn gradually in both Western Europe and the former Soviet states. Instead, insofar as the GDR players carry on their identity in a post-GDR world, it is as something like an imaginary folklore itself, that of the socialist utopia that wasn't.

The Zentral Quartett players, with their post-Change collaborators, offer aspects as different as their personalities that combine to paint a picture of an identity distinctive for their shared history. Gumpert and Petrovsky exude something like Tuvan singer Sainkho Namtchylak's professed alienation (p. 253) from a West designed more to pull them into it than to understand them or their history. Sommer and Bauer seem both more adaptable to that West, and more at home in the new East it now governs. Both pairings have unique offerings the world should not have to judge or choose between.

On the one hand, Sommer and Bauer developed careers that demonstrate, in the development of musical content and approaches as much as in extramusical aspects, the professionalism of the musician serving a function, responsibly entertaining audiences and/or teaching students. They did this in the Eastern statist society in a way that served them well with the shift to the Western marketplace society.

Gumpert and Petrovsky, on the other hand, are arguably the more sheerly musically profound by virtue of the impact they were able to have as composers and bandleaders, as well as players. Petrovsky's early studio bands and their branchings, and Gumpert's workshop bands and the material he wrote for them, ushered in the statements from the East that had the most and pithiest sway through the FMP presentations. Still, they both emerge from the Change in Berlin most at odds with society, proven masters frustrated and at a loss with the business dynamics and dilemmas of a scene that is perpetual scuffle for everyone, and rewarding for very few.

This is a study in both personality types and cultural ones. Some play the crowd better than others; both types make great music, but each thrives best under a certain set of assumptions, conditions, criteria. The culture that respects personal genius as a value of the common good supports and rewards it above the more overt abilities to give audiences, students, and business people an easy access to it; the culture that suspects personal genius, doubts it, demands such easy access – the social and practical skills of the entertainer and teacher – as proof of its worthiness.

This is not to suggest that both types of culture are clearly dichotomized by East and West – Petrovsky and Gumpert faced down their share of official hostility and neglect coming up in the East, and Sommer and Bauer reaped rewards and respect there too – but it does seem clear that Petrovsky and Gumpert enjoyed relatively more fulfillment than frustration of their gifts in the GDR, that Sommer and Bauer were more the chafers at the bit, and that the latter are having an easier time of it now that the bit is removed.

Each of the four has his own projects apart from the Zentral Quartett; all, both individually and in their group, are more the freelance musicians swimming and fishing the same waters as their Western colleagues than they are the exotic, politically sexy guests from a strong home base of support they used to be. They do not play and record with their Western colleagues as much as they did before the Wall fell, especially Gumpert and Petrovsky. What each and all together have done over that time is both part of the new world and interesting to ponder as the remaining echoes of a world they helped to reshape in their own image, and then to undo completely.

Noglik summed up the development in East Germany from the mid-1970s into the '80s with the words "differentiation," "individualization," and "increasing internationalization." He described the '80s as a solidification of gestures and concepts initiated in the '70s. At the same time, he cited Petrovsky's critique of musicians who had gotten artistically lazy after jazz had gained official acceptance, taking on the consciousness of "renters" more than creative people.[67] Of the Zentral Quartett, however, he wrote: "Insofar as the aesthetics of sound and expression are rooted in life situation, Synopsis, under its new name of the Zentral Quartett, offers the richest, truest articulation of the emancipation process of jazz in the GDR. The lament, the cry, the triumph and the reconfiguration of meaning. It is all there to hear, as it has all been lived" (1996: 220).

Since the fall of the Wall, the Zentral Quartett players offer aspects as different as their personalities that combine to paint a picture of an Eastern identity; their histories likewise spell out the features of an Eastern scene and its situation now. Those left highest and driest by history have the most incentive to dig for a new song out of their plight, such as African Americans themselves did. Hanns Eisler's vision of a musician's responsibility to make a music that not only stirs and satisfies aesthetic impulses but also sociopolitically moral and ethical ones is a vision these players not only grew up with but, arguably, fulfilled throughout their glory years in the '70s and '80s, to a greater degree of effectiveness than their Western counterparts, in terms of actually changing their society.

The radical gestures of free jazz have been either effectively marginalized or pressured back toward the mainstream in capitalist culture, much more than they were thwarted by the communist one. The East Germans teach us much about music-making from a sociopolitical vision without being co-opted by it, and about music that has the last word not only against the power-over elitism of stupid aristocrats and party bosses, but also that of stupid corporate bosses and their friends in high (political, cultural, academic) places.

Emancipation III: The Archaic Freedom

We live poised between the part and the whole . . . between, as Schiller called them, the tendency to substance and the tendency toward form . . . Between them both we find our way, giving to each its due. Schiller likened this kind of engagement with the world to true play, for only in play is one free.

– Arthur Zajonc

Nietszche defines a nihilist phase which corresponds to what you call "anarchist"; to question everything. There is a second phase which is more interesting: once you've realized what everything is and how it works, how it's going to repeat itself, endlessly, you just step out of it, and affirm other, positive values. You don't waste any more energy criticizing and destroying.

– Jack Smith[1]

Five

The Free World Beyond America

If one does use ["other"] ethnic material, one cannot do so as if one were doing what was originally done with it . . .

Finally, there remains the longstanding fact that these musical exchanges can always involve a mutual plunder. We have to be a little careful, because we are the children of white imperialism . . .[2]

World Music/Weltmusik

Following are a few representative examples of attitude and approach shared by the post-free-jazz improvisers vis-à-vis other musical traditions. They embody completely Rempel's third stage – openness, after chauvinism and liberalism – of the West's reception of and collaboration with the Rest.

In 1997, I followed Alexander von Schlippenbach around Germany and Austria, catching him in solo, duo, trio, and slightly larger groups. I also caught him leading the GUO reincarnation (the Berlin Contemporary Jazz Orchestra) and was able to speak with many of the bandmates mentioned in previous chapters. One of the most insightful such talks was with Paul Lovens, von Schlippenbach's long-time main drummer, and one of the handful of Europeans (with Dutch Han Bennink and Brit Tony Oxley) most instrumental in redefining the drumkit as a source of percussive color and texture more than metered pulse. He explained to me how free improvisation had grown in and shaped his life:

In the beginning we were still trying to crumble things away. But there were phases – not in the music in general, but in everybody's musical development – when we wondered, what the fuck should I do now? From there on, you start to play, and you play, but you realize that what you have to play has to depend on what you are hearing. So we went to scratch, zero, and started to listen to what each other was doing. Imagine the situation; nobody knows what they should do, they're all trying to listen to what the others are doing, and nobody knows what to do. [He laughed with dark glee.]

After having been able to maintain doing that for thirty years, it suddenly seems very important, in one sense, to maintain what has always been there – before Monk, before King Oliver. Because the information of what could be played as music is so overwhelming. You have tapes and CDs of everything from the Inuit to the [San] Bushmen, 12-CD box sets of it all, and so on. We heard a little bit of this spectrum in the '70s, and it inspired us in musical terms, which means in terms of the material we could use, rhythmically, sound-wise, and so on. But it also means there are all these things, and we should respect that they belong to a certain time and a certain region.

I'm totally anti-"world music." I think musics have to develop from the region. But now we are in a trap, because there is no music of the region left. You have a few special rhythmic waltzes or polkas in Bavaria; everything else has been wiped away – by the waltz in general, for instance, which came to Vienna from the Turks, and so on and so on, ending up with Michael Jackson. So we are in a very peculiar situation in terms of orientation, of where our roots are.

It seems to me that our roots are in our record players. There's nothing wrong with that, except that we should not get into the trap of copying rhythms and other things. The only way I've found for me or my colleagues to deal with it is to ignore definite styles, and perhaps become desperate.

I caught up with Günter Hampel in his New York digs during one of his treks around the globe to play his current music. He sat me in the chair his old friend and bandmate, the late Don Cherry, used to sit in while visiting him there. One of their favorite topics of conversation then, he said, was their music's links with that of the rest of the world:

I've traveled throughout India, Indonesia, Afghanistan, Iran . . . wherever I went, I played with traditional locals. They call our music free jazz, but its looser approaches are the things that make it easier for us to get together with other idioms, because we aren't bound by a system. If you play bebop, everything is already worked out for you; the style dictates the way every instrument is played, the voicings, the phrasing. But in a free band, this must be made up between the people who come together to play, according to what will work for them.

As with Albert Mangelsdorff's 1963 Asian tour and many since, the Goethe Institute sponsored an Asian tour of von Schlippenbach and the GUO in 1980, facilitating important connections with the Japanese jazz scene. The other side of this coin of officially supported outreach has been an on-off relationship with his own country for appreciation and support. (Ironically, the post-free Americans have had to go east, to Europe, to find forums for their music, while their European peers have often had to go farther east – more often than west – including East Germany, and across Eurasia toward the Pacific.)

Von Schlippenbach told Thiem:

Japan was fantastic . . . our Tokyo concert was the climax of the whole tour . . . it was a little more difficult in Malaysia and Indonesia, but . . . we scored a big success in Bandung, of all places, which was amazing because it's just a small provincial town in the jungle of Java. If we play well and the audience reacts spontaneously, understanding is possible even in places like that. In India things also varied from place to place. In Calcutta it went very well, but it was more difficult in Bombay . . . we played two concerts in Bombay. In between them we gave a "lecture demonstration" explaining aspects of the art of free improvisation with different groups of musicians from the orchestra playing and then discussing what they did with the audience. Strangely enough, that second concert in which we played a completely improvised piece got a more favorable response than the first in which we chose the same set we played in Tokyo. Maybe the instructive demonstration which took place the day before at the Rang Bhavan had a useful effect. Anyway, the whole thing was of more value than the constant suavity with which Jazz Yatra audiences especially are soaped down. (Thiem [1982: 46–7])

The speaker of the following words is William Parker, the New York bassist who started, with his close friend Peter Kowald, what is now the Vision Festival of new and improvised music, dance, and art in his East Village neighborhood. Parker has played extensively with Cecil Taylor and just about everyone else in the global network of the post-free-jazz scenes we're discussing. He told me:

What I realized is that the best musicians in any country, first of all, never leave the country, and are hardly ever recorded; and the best musicians are the ones who you can go up to in the mountains, or wherever they live, and say, let's just play. And you can play, and they can play; and it's not about, "well, we're Brazilian and you're American, let's do this beat or let's do that beat." And you can go to Japan and find their musicians, and each country has those musicians, and on the same level you can communicate.

I played with a Cuban folkloric band, and everybody in the band was over 60, and they wanted me to be a guest. I thought they'd want me to learn their *clavé* [foundational rhythm] and stuff like this, and I asked them what they wanted me to do, and they said "You just play." And I said, "well don't you want me to keep some kind of beat?" and they said, "no, just play." They did what they did, and I did my thing, and it was a complete mesh on that level. I think things on the highest level work like that.

Critical Voices

Berendt's work, both as jazz presenter and scholar, has large overlaps with both the Ethnomusicological and the Speculative-Musicological discourses.[3] The very first Jazz Days – the Berlin festival he launched in 1964, which provoked FMP's first Total Music Meeting in reaction against its perceived pandering to American stars and mainstream jazz – was called "Jazz Meets the World," with subsets such as "Jazz Meets India," "Jazz and Flamenco," "Jazz and Balinese Music," and so on.

This programming sprang directly from its director's interest in other cultures and wide travels, and took hold and has grown over the decades since, both in the very concept of a "world music" genre and in those less commercial collaborations between the post-free players and traditional musicians from non-Western cultures.

Berendt: "Only one bridge increased in strength: sexuality. These both – God Eros and Lady Music – formed the 'vehicle,' the means by which the discoverers – through the subjugation and murder, the stealing and deception – discovered the way to a humane path." Those words prefaced his essay for Wolbert ("Über Weltmusik," 1997: 269) on the process of branching out of one's home to foreign lands, of initiating contacts both positive and negative with other peoples. For the West, that process has led to the first and only civilization in world history to spread itself throughout the globe, and to make war and weapons on a global scale to do so.

If Eros is indeed the humane aspect of a process otherwise characterized by War ("conquest, murder, theft and deception"), then the Eros-full music will be the most immediately effective "world" music, one suggesting the ancient custom of marriage between rival clans to assure political and social stability.

Berendt investigates jazz as a primal and Erotic syncretism by way of his own history as a world traveler and perennial student of other cultures (and of anthropology and psychology). He cites German musicologist Georg Capellen's 1906 introduction of the concept of "world music" into that discourse.[4] Capellen's points focused on fundamental similarities between Western and non-Western music systems such as widespread use of the pentatonic scale, suggesting a common ancient *Urgrund*. He proffered non-Western expressions as the most fertile source of future Western development, exemplified by the way Impressionist painters drew on Asian, and Cubists on African, artworks.

Berendt discusses this musical interchange in the cultural terms of "contemporary ethnomusicological, anthropological, and biological research," working the idea that a bio/cultural phenomenon does not wane but rather waxes in the face of challenge (he sets this against the turn-of-the-century social-Darwinist ideals of racial and cultural purity in Germany that led to its Nazism). He refers to "anthropologist Claude Lévi-Strauss's study of the African Dogon tribe," which cast the Dogons who "succumbed" to the foreign influence of Islam as the weaker members.[5] He cites psychologists who found the opposite, that it was precisely the most active, strongest, most intelligent Dogons who tended to become Muslims. Those who held to ideals of a "pure" identity of cultures (their own and others) took on a debilitating (inflation of) self-consciousness and self-confidence. The whole idea of such "purity" is rooted in the idea of time's moment exalted at the expense of its flow, because it arises only when long familiarity with and internalization of what was originally "other" turns it to "self":

An exceptionally telling example of this questionable concept of purity in music is the Gregorian chant's history. With it – as we read in every history of music

– began so-called Western music. But if that is so, the history began much earlier: namely in the music of the Near East, with the hymns, sequences, and responses of Egypt's Coptic church (on which the early church father, Pope Gregory 1, called), and also on the music of peoples living still in the Maghreb desert – Tunisians and Algerians (who on their side played an important role in the genesis of Flamenco music). (1997: 270)

Berendt points to the overtone series as common ground not just for the world's musics as cultural expressions, but for the physical universe on the level of planets (per Johannes Kepler) and subatomic particles (per Max Planck). He cites vibraphonist Karl Berger – a German living in America, one of the more proactive thinkers and players to come out of and build on the free-jazz movement – to corroborate his vision of the musician's body as the site of such universals micro and macro: "Listen to yourself. Find all in yourself" (272).

Berendt's point is that since all cultures are grounded in the same human body, not in their differences, they can therefore be "pure" – enjoy an identity with integrity – and "mixed" in unification with all others simultaneously. Furthermore, mixing, syncretic syntheses between such "purities" are the fruit of the strongest – the most actually "pure" bodies, those with a well-defined, grounded identity and integrity in their respective pools – not the weakest.

This Erotic worldview aligns him with evolutionary biologists such as E. O. Wilson, who has recently (1998) drawn similar conclusions for culture. It is dangerous thinking for those wary of essentialism and the racist-sexist agendas it can spawn; but it is unavoidable if one will centralize the body, and geographical environment, as music and culture's source. It delivers us from the equally dangerous thinking that leads to a superficial vision of melting-pot equality in nature and culture (reflected by Communism and Capitalism both, and all their peculiar mixtures of bad art with social science), rather than the thousand-flower, cross-pollinating gardens of variously empowered hybrids examined here.

If Berendt's Erotic outlook is a little too sunny vis-à-vis the problems of power imbalance in such cultural exchanges, Jost's "Free Jazz and the Music of the Third World" (1971–2) gives us more food for that thought.

So-called "national styles" are very common in the history of Occidental Art. Even though the twentieth century with its cultural internationalism promoted by the media has leveled most of the distinctions, it is still possible to detect certain national characteristics, in the field of contemporary music . . . During the Sixties, no one would have bothered to wonder as to whether in Jazz such diverse "national" tendencies prevail. Jazz was considered the world's musical language, sedulously propagated by the Voice of America and the State Department, using the notion "world-language" in an ideologically tinted way; that term did not only maintain the international, world-wide significance of American Culture but by the same token concealed the cultural deprivation of Afro-American musicians – and it was their "language," their musical expression, Jazz dealt with primarily. Meanwhile, sometimes at festivals, it happens that during the sets of their European colleagues black Free Jazz musicians leave the concert hall, shaking their heads – and they do so not because they think the musicians on-stage are incompetent but because they cannot identify or sympathize with their music. Jazz has lost its quality of being a generally accepted binding force as the "World's Language." (62)

Jost posits the free-jazz movement as an expression of pan-African resistance and liberation. He sees it turning to non-Western cultures more for a poetic symbolism than for a deep musical connection (for example, Coltrane's *Africa, India,* or Pharoah Sanders's *Japan*). The musical contributions those musicians did offer – modalism, cyclical rather than linear progression, drones, non-Western rhythmic patterns, improvisational strategies – were necessarily subsumed in what remained a musical discourse uniquely African-Western. Jost suggests that improvisations on non-Western musical materials, and compositions from their concepts, were simply today's smaller world's versions of past fusions between, say, Congo Square and French Opera houses, or Southern rural blues and itinerant German and East European music teachers, or the "ragging of the classics" some piano-savvy house slaves and free blacks performed.

In other words, they comprised the long-cultivated unity between international expressions of whiteness and negritude. Jost's essay supplements those of his French colleagues in a way that corroborates and amplifies their own (uncharacteristic) nods to such interdependence and unity (for example, Lère's vision of black resistance to white oppression as the necessary fulfillment of Western social ideals), nods that might otherwise have been subsumed in a reification of black "otherness," a reification oscillating between hagiographic fawning and effetely "civilized" snobbery. If the music is a violent force – as might be most successfully argued in the case of free jazz as practiced both by African-American inter/nationalists in the 1960s and by their German *emanzipatorische* counterparts – its violence might just as successfully be argued as that of opposing forces deliberately pursuing their own (Erotic) clash so as to join.

Russian Freedom

Miles Davis told his biographer Quincey Troupe that he saw the future of improvised music in shorter phrases and statements, away from the byzantine structures of bop, sheets of sound, and the like. In fact, "byzantine" signals, from the Russian land of the word's origin, the opposite of Davis's vision in its belated *Emanzipation*. What we more typically see in the thousand flowers of the West, as varied as they are, is indeed a tendency toward short, restrained statements, after years of open-ended, high-energy *Kaputtspiel* catharses.[6] We see the latter continue in various forms, but no longer as the center of a European revolt against America. We see this music's postmodernity in its embrace of styles from everywhere and everywhen, including those that were "deliberately neglected" for one reason or another in the past. This is Jost's third stage of the *Emanzipation* (first mentioned in chapter two).

The jazz scenes in Soviet Russia and its neighboring republics had become staid and respectable in the 1970s. They had gained a social depth but lost their edge, through yet another generation defining the music as a youthful peccadillo going "too gentle" into the "good night" of established culture. While Czech, Polish, and (especially) East German scenes were taking on new vitality, fuelled by openness to rock and other art forms, the pre-Stalinist Russia that had launched its own most original, adventurous, and multimedia jazz scenes, with little outside help, and the post-Stalinist Russia that had managed to work it back into its official culture in a relatively healthy way, was seeing the music become old, cold, and academic.[7]

With the start of the 1980s, however, jazz was taking on a new life despite anything the Party thought about it, especially in Russian Provincial cities and capitals of non-Russian republics. The core *Emanzipation* idea that "black power" meant "white freedom" finally took hold here as it had in 1960s' Western Europe; and local talents, especially younger ones, mined local ethnicity (anti-monoculture) while rejecting racial exclusivity (black chauvinism). Bop became the epitome of Old School, just as it was revived in America so effectively by the young lions there. This embrace of the thousand-flower ethic was not universal. Many older Russians were more like West Germans in this regard, less like East Germans; discredited Stalinist culture policy still tainted for them the idea of an uncorrupted folk (now called "ethnic") music.

But, again, they were the Old being challenged by the New. Their "jazz" was out, improvisational "polystyle" and "unity in diversity" were in. And in these satellite sites, more than anywhere in the West, large compositional frameworks blossomed to bear new improvisations. They were free not only of the problems of "folk" but also of the elitism associated with the composer's tradition. It was a perfectly Braxtonian proliferation of greater freedom through greater (organic) complexity.

The premier voice of this new direction was pianist Viacheslav Ganelin. Starr placed him "by any measure . . . among the most interesting jazz musicians playing in Europe today" (1994: 311). Born near Moscow in 1944, Ganelin migrated with his parents (and many other Russians) in the early 1950s to the Baltic. He grew up in the Lithuanian capital of Vilnius, studied at the conservatory there, and formed a trio with drummer Vladimir Tarasov and reedsman Vladimir Chekasin to play in local cafés and festivals. Chekasin described the trio's approach: "Some elements we borrow from jazz, others from chamber music or the folklore of various peoples. Sometimes we also use the naive techniques of children, and this all gives rise to unheard of combinations" (322).

That description covers precisely all of the elements, including childhood, making up chapter six's theoretical framework for the centrality of free improvisation. The "unheard of combinations" go far beyond "jazz meets the world" types of mix-and-match experiments, by centralizing Western composition tradition right there with free improvisation, and all the other elements mentioned.

Chekasin's explanation of the Ganelin Trio's process resembles Conrad Bauer's of his group Fez: ideas emerge in free play and are then worked and reworked collectively into a memorized, unnotated structure. The difference lies in the musical ambition Ganelin and his colleagues follow. Mihaiu (in Feigin) describes that structure in formal terms:

> In a 1971 debate on free jazz (*Jazz Forum* 13–14) Andrzej Trzaskowski said that "actually, there are three types of form in existence: theme-and-variation form, evolutionary, and open. The first is probably the most traditional. Next, evolutionary, as in Coltrane, and last, open . . . for example, a composition that can last for two hours or two minutes, that can start or end at any given moment." With Ganelin-Tarasov-Chekasin such fine differentiations lose their meaning. The suites combine these three approaches, and obtain an ineffable new form. Indeed, there is a suggestion of openness in everything they play, the mind is never restricted to preconceived aims; there are also long "evolutionary" passages in the spirit of Coltrane's last period of creation; but on the other hand the musicians avoid any kind of self-indulgence. The actual form is dictated by the inherent energies of the content, but it is also defined by critical intelligence. The canonical theme-and-variation form, which had provided the basis of most jazz music until the *free* rebellion in the late fifties, is not neglected by Ganelin-Tarasov-Chekasin. (49–50)

Barban (also in Feigin, 1985) described the trio's "organic unity of composition and improvisation" as a "wealth of different stylistic elements . . . from folk dance and the Baroque to the aleatory and traditional jazz" (33). Interestingly here, he locates that free access to historic styles in the group's sense of musical time. His words capture perfectly the difference between the neocon preservationism of Wynton Marsalis and the quite different tributes to tradition of Anthony Braxton or (the late Art Ensemble of Chicago trumpeter) Lester Bowie. They also give a fresh touch to the issue of primal music in free improvisation. They are worth citing at length, in hopes that their author's larger untranslated work will soon join them in English translation:

> For the mainstream musician time is anachronistic, that is to say always retrospective: in every epoch of jazz the best period has always been in the past, the present is only a shadow of "the golden age of jazz" with its departed "giants." In the music of the trio time, as a metro-rhythmical phenomenon, is genuinely universal, the players being deeply aware of the relative, illusory and purely "historical" nature of time in any and every genre. This awareness obliges them constantly to go beyond the rhythmic organization associated exclusively with jazz, and enables them to move freely over the whole musico-cultural time-field, recognizing the artificiality and conventionality of all purely genre-based

limitations of time. This temporal pluralism lies at the root of the Ganelin Trio's use of widely differing styles. The dynamic equilibrium of heterogeneous temporal forms is distinctly noticeable in their music, and it explains the different systems of values in the three players' performances.

Their art is in some way akin to the original, primeval sense of music – the actual *business of "performance"* being related to "music" as philosophizing is related to philosophy. Episodes of "musical life" provide the main "plots" of their works, which are at the same time both musical "being" and musical "thinking." The old, rigid conventions of (non-free) jazz made it impossible to realize this ideal which is imminent in all types of musical improvisation.

The Ganelin Trio's approach to music-making gives music the status of a non-conceptual ontological knowledge of reality, of a system that provides an irrational explanation of being, of man's existence. It is this that raises their collective musical statements from the commonplace to the poetic, because in every artistic context "genuine speech is pre-poetry" (Heidegger).

For this reason it was natural and not difficult to understand why the Ganelin Trio were the first to cross the "borders" of jazz in the Soviet Union, for they possess that rarest of human characteristics, real originality. (37–8)

The Ganelin Trio has gotten most of its Western exposure through the recording and booking agency of London-based Leo Feigin and his Leo recording label. In turn, the Russian free scene has been well informed by that label's Western offerings, to which Braxton and his most likeminded colleagues have contributed much. Again, for my money and my real life's quests and callings, this collusion of Chicago's Great Black Music and primal Caucasia's Snow White Freedom is the most amazing example of musical thought converging from its two extreme poles.

Sergei Kuriokhin, ten years Ganelin's junior, is another pianist on a similar path. He came up through the usual Russian conservatory training in Leningrad, played rock on the side, learned jazz through the Voice of America. McCoy Tyner caught his first attention, then Coltrane, Braxton, guitarist John McLaughlin, composer Mauricio Kagel, and Thelonious Monk. He is a good example of a feature of jazz/free-jazz/*Emanzipation* history – the role of the piano – as a revolution within Western music that I have danced around since chapter one.

Kuriokhin claims (like his fellow pianist from East Germany, Ulrich Gumpert) more interest in saxophonists than in pianists, as influences. He even speaks of Russian piano tradition as sort of a "father" to be killed. In speaking this way, he speaks explicitly to an aspect of the history as explained here that has been more implicit along its course. The piano has evolved from the Pythagorean monochord and early lyres and harps as a "father," in that it (and its wind version, the organ) has functioned as the governor of the horns and percussion. It is the composer's instrument, from which the composer has worked out lines for voices to sing, horns to play, and times to keep – all in the order we saw Chailley capture with his chart, an order spelling out both the acoustic moment of tones-and-overtones and the Western-historical development of their harmonic-melodic arrangements over time.

In chapter three, I referred in a note to a film about stride pianist pioneer Willie "the Lion" Smith. It has a clip of James Reese Europe's pianist, the young Eubie Blake, demonstrating what was called the "beautification" of a tune. He played "Swanee River" in the left hand, slowly, and arpeggiated chords against the changes of the melody lines with his right, harp-like, in rubato time (something like what Günter Sommer saw Cecil Taylor doing improvisationally in their duo together, in fact, as will be discussed shortly). The reversal of that approach, effected by the stride style – rhythmic chording in the left hand, melody in the right – reflected the larger reversal of roles that took place with the rise of the wind ensembles, military and parlor, and the move of (melodic-top) strings to the (harmonic-bottom) rhythm section in jazz bands.

Interestingly, the great and definitive African-American bands were led by pianists (Fletcher Henderson, Duke Ellington, Count Basie, Teddy Wilson, Sun Ra), and their European-American counterparts (Benny Goodman, Artie Shaw, Woody Herman, Harry James, Glenn Miller, the Dorseys, Buddy Rich, Maynard Ferguson, Don Ellis) more often by horn players or drummers (Stan Kenton the glaring exception, and the most interesting white counterpoint to the black pianist/orchestrators/leaders in terms of musical thought). Also interesting is the dominance of African Americans in the jazz piano lineage (Art Tatum, Bud Powell, Monk, Andrew Hill) leading up to Cecil Taylor, in light of the latter's greater influence in the West German and pan-European *Emanzipation*, and of his saxophonist peers (Coleman, Ayler, Coltrane) on French, Russian, Scandinavian, and East German versions of it.

Both phenomena suggest that African-American music culture needed most to seize on that engine of Western musical thought to get inside it, take it apart, and redirect it to nurture rather than exploit black bodies and identity; and that white America needed rather to leave that thought behind and get in touch with its own visceral (Erotic/Martial, horn-blowing, drumming) rather than cerebral (Holy/Religious) self. This musical symbolism fits in with the history of both African-American intellectual and spiritual patrimony of the music and white power-over exploitations of it, both Martial and Erotic.

In Taylor's hands, and in those of post-bop, post-free pianists from around the world working the ground he broke, that patrimony itself has been killed, be it whitefaced or blackfaced. The Erotic and Martial power has been seized back from the drums and horns, as the piano is "deliberately neglected" as a design of Western musical thought and made rather to sound the unleash of rhythm and the sonorities of a horn's dirty timbres, themselves freed from parroting one of many lines conceived at the keyboard.

Kuriokhin articulates (in Feigin [1985: 105]) the aesthetic of sound as an extension of theater and dance, in the grand Russian tradition starting with Valentin Parnakh, kindred spirit to Sun Ra and Han Bennink. Kowald's *Jahrmarkt* project, the French projects we surveyed, the Art Ensemble of Chicago, and Braxton's most ambitious projects share this Greek *mousike* aesthetic. Kuriokhin espouses Zen Buddhism as a kind of "mythodology" of choice for the cultivation of spontaneity as a central rather than a contingent way of creating. Like Paul Lovens, he eschews the idea of a "world music soup," has rather a strong sense of Russian nationalism; but like his Siberian colleagues (see Feigin [1985: 116–17]), he also has a strong sense of the cosmic and spiritual therein, one they all recognize immediately in their colleagues and models from abroad, such as (their examples) John and Alice Coltrane, Carla Bley, Anthony Braxton, Cecil Taylor, Ravi Shankar, Roswell Rudd and others.

To summarily characterize these developments in Russia and its regional and geopolitical neighbors, one might say that bop effected an initial rescue of the individual freely roaming mind and personality from dumb state claims on it, but that it sank in too much introverted, passive cerebralism to effect larger social change. One might say that rock, conversely, broke out of that passivity and into the liberation of the dancing body and erotic communion, but that it too proved assimilable by Party containments and directions of its energies, by too little rather than too much thought.

One might also find it noteworthy that the real musical significance of the Ganelin Trio and others mentioned here lay in their total disengagement from formal system building, whether political (as the French free scene flirted with most) or musical. Rather, all such system-building is organic rather than formal, transient and fluid rather than fixed and permanent, and multicultural and multicentered rather than monocultural and totalitarian or totalizing in spirit (per Misha Mengelberg): monautarchic and panautarchic, let us say, rather than personalized in collective or collectivized impersonally. All of this came about outside the official culture entirely, as that culture's official demise came about beyond the Glasnost policy that tried to preserve by reforming it.

Mongolian Voices

Peter Kowald's words to Noglik (1981: 442–3) show how long his own sense of the global wedded to the local has held his imagination:

> There are in almost all parts of the world musicians who have come to improvisation through the new jazz we play. They bring something from their own native idioms, but musical and regional differences begin to melt together in the music. I'm not talking about some forced fusion of jazz and folk musics, but rather a common future built from the ground floor of similar essential experiences with improvisation. I am also convinced that in our time the biggest problem is no longer one of isolation, but – and this goes for other arts and culture in general, as well as music – losing ourselves in some sort of global, international scene.

His words to me sixteen years later about his group Global Village (after Marshall McLuhan) and his work with Tuvan singer Sainkho Namtchylak speak to his way around this problem.

Namtchylak's grandparents were nomads. Both of her parents were teachers, and she grew up with traditional Tuvan music in Mongolia. In her twenties, she sang Tuvan folk songs on tour with four other women. Eventually she went to Moscow where she studied *bel canto* style singing and was exposed to jazz people and left the folk song.

Kowald wrote on her FMP debut CD's liner notes (*Lost Rivers*, 1991):

> in the cultural history of the Occident (from Heraklitos to Fluxus, the exceptions prove the tendency), the image of floating and letting go is rather unpopular; instead, there is an attitude of taking apart, cutting into pieces, separating, analysing, specializing [this describes my distinction between the Holy and Religion]. I consider it good and right that there is room in us for waiving feeling and willing thinking. I find it essential that there is proper (and not properly at all) floating between these two.

This paean to holism extends to Kowald's words to me about his own recording debut with the singer. He cited as his best record *When the Sun is Out, You Don't See the Stars* (FMP 1990), featuring Namtchylak and American trumpeter Butch Morris.

> I didn't organize the music – I organized it a little more than everybody else for that record, but basically it was a collective thing and I still love that collective improvisation. And it's wonderful, because Butch and Sainkho met for the first time in that studio, and then she does her overtone things, and Butch does his kind of Rex Stewart trumpet, this traditional black trumpet music. This is wonderful to me, this is really wonderful. That's how I believe it works. It's a method that could be something of a model, of how people can come from different cultures, different areas, with different characters, with all of that, and they bring what they bring, and it's okay – just throw it together with the other stuff, and it works. After just a little bit of figuring out how it works together, then it does.

The birth of a scene took place in Siberia, through Kowald's collaboration with Namtchlyak. They did two trans-Siberian tours together by train, travelling to Tuva up to the Japanese sea. Namtchylak's husband then was an Austrian who played the bass clarinet and saxophone with them, and there was a percussionist for one tour. Kowald recalls how when they played in her home town, all her uncles and family and all the throat singers came. "As I hear now, it must have been a legendary concert, because now there are Tuva singers who play Tuva rock, and Tuva improvised music, and Sainkho gets their records and tells me, 'Yes, this one was at our concert.' Because this concert kind of did something to the whole community of musicians there. There are not so many."

Siberian drummer Sergey Belichinko is one of several of them, interviewed in Feigin, who formed a quartet called Homo Liber and made a record by the same name to share their music with the West. About that music, Belichinko said,

I live in Siberia where European and Asian musical cultures, which are very different, have intermingled. For instance, I listen to the music of Touvinians – marvelous improvised music. The Touvinians are Buddhists and their music is full of echoes of China and India. I listen to Central Asian music, particularly Uzbek. It seems to me that Siberia has in concentrated form some essence of a pre-European past, thousands of years old, untouched by professionalism. A sort of musical matrix. (Feigin [1985: 115])

In fact, this connection with Mongolian shamanism resonates with some other currents in African-American culture that have fed into jazz along with the African and European ones, currents worthy of attention here.

Primal American Voices

Namtchylak bears a striking resemblance to my daughter's Native American (Nez Perce) mother's side of her family. The film *Genghis Blues* is a fascinating account of San Francisco Creole blues musician Paul Pena's love affair with Tuvan music, and visit to its Central Asian homeland. That unlikely odyssey recalls another film, *Black Indians*, about the relatively undocumented but widespread history of inter-marriages between African and Native Americans.[8] All three (deeply personal) factoids lead me to a quick but provocative point about three pillars of American music whom I know best, all most sympathetically, one intimately.

The core issue of musical time and meter has been under consideration throughout this study, as has the famously elusive "swing" in jazz as something derivative of the Western down beat, bringing definition to its bloodless shell. This position made sense as a way to get to European jazz's problems with swing, and its relatively unswinging versions of free jazz. But it also rings true with the general reception and self-presentations of these three pillars of American music – Charlie Parker, Cecil Taylor, and Anthony Braxton – when they first threw their hats into the ring.

Charlie Parker and his bop revolution were not hailed as the swingin'-est, most "naturally rhythmic" Negro music of their New York moment; both were rather put down by musicians and press alike as cold, academic, unemotional, and unswingingly, cerebrally weird. Parker's heritage had as much Choctaw as African in its mix, and – as I said about the music of Cecil Taylor, who also claims his Native American roots with pride – Native American music does not swing, it has its own damn down beat. Parker's music was so "birdlike" precisely because it flew away from and above the beat, turned it around, displaced it, shifted its phases and periodicities in a never-ending dance around its cracking bull whip.

Wolbert's articles include two historical reprints in English, one of which, "The Chili Parlor Interview," is Michael Levin's and John S. Wilson's interview with Parker for *Down Beat*'s 9 September 1949 issue. Consider from the following citation why this interview would be of such interest to a German-language retrospective of jazz history:

"Bop is no love child of jazz," [says Charlie Parker] ". . . is something entirely separate and apart . . . The beat in a bop band . . . has no continuity of beat, no steady chug-chug. Jazz has, and that's why bop is more flexible . . ." He admits the music eventually may be atonal. Parker himself is a devout admirer of Paul Hindemith, the German neo-classicist, and raves about his *Kammermusik* and *Sonata for Viola and Cello* . . . he would like to emulate the precise, complex harmonic structures of Hindemith, but with an emotional coloring and dynamic shading that he feels modern classical lacks . . . Charlie himself has stayed away from a big band because the proper place for bop, he feels, is a small group. Big bands tend to get overscored, he says, and bop goes out the window . . . The only possibility for a big band, he feels, is to get really big, practically on a symphonic scale with loads of strings . . . "This has more chance than the standard jazz instrumentation," he says. "You can pull away some of the harshness with the strings and get a variety of coloration." (in Wolbert [1997: 187–8])[9]

Are you listening, Mr. Hanslick?

Elsewhere in the interview, Parker dismisses bop's commercial success as part of that "jazz" world that disdained him, and that he disdained: "Some guys said, 'Here's bop,' . . . Wham! They said, 'Here's something we can make money on.' Wham! 'Here's a comedian.' Wham! 'Here's a guy who talks funny talk'" (188).

Another of these passages ties back in with the idea of a primal-musical *Urgrund* shared by bop and that shamanistic culture spanning Mongolia and the Americas via the Bering Strait. In surveying the world's examples of tertial patterns in melodic construction, Curt Sachs wrote of the relatively rare pattern of quadruple thirds, "requiring the wider range of a ninth . . . In the two basic forms, *C E G B D* and *D F A C E*, they are conspicuously absent from the Pacific; they do not touch Asia save in Turkey [linguistic and ethnic kin to Tuva], and reach only a few North American tribes, including the Copper Eskimo, and also American jazz" [also interesting here: it was the Inuit people who had the most contact with the early Norse explorers and settlers of Greenland and points westward] (Sachs [1961: 150]).

In fact, it was Charlie Parker who expanded the harmonic palette into bop precisely by stacking ninths and higher thirds onto the already tertial chords used in the swing era. And, as Levin and Wilson recounted in 1949, that expansion took place on a tune called, as it happened, "Cherokee."

As for Braxton, the charges against him for not swinging, not being black enough, being too open to Europe, are a well-documented part of his career. His most recent compositions, the Ghost Trance series, stem from his fascination with Native American culture and history, and are built around the kind of variously accented quarter-note rhythm drummed under Native American chant and dance. The Native Americans were overrun and contained by Europe, but never made to "swing" their song in a strange land, as Africans were.

Back to Namtchylak. Her importance here has several reasons. Most immediately, she carries the thread of the shift toward the voice as instrument in this music – again, one pioneered mostly by women – and toward speech-and-voice-like music on the other instruments. Her particular voice is one that was, along with its throat singing and other techniques indigenous to Tuva, formally trained in the *bel canto* style in Moscow, and was also informed by the all-pervasive American jazz. As an improviser, she is important for voicing her part on the Eurasian musical continuum we are beginning to see connect with post-*Emanzipation* music in Europe, and with its American counterpart (in Butch Morris and others). Specifically, her Mongolian shamanistic roots link her to Korean and northern Japanese musicians, both groups represented in similar collaborations with European improvisers.

Speaking about her own music, Namtchylak wrote (in German, for Kowald [1998: 108–10]):

> When I learned the shamanistic and all the various singing techniques of the Siberian minority group, I noticed above all that the shamanistic rituals recorded by the early ethnological expeditions, this ancient art, that it is not simply music mixed with text and so on, but that it is more: a freedom from within. Therefore it was easy for me to be a bridge between what is called traditional music and the new improvised music, which already had the same openness. Our traditional music is not of a fixed form that one must adhere to without changing. I also discussed this in Tuva with the traditional overtone singers and singers of our other music, who convinced me that this music is not a dead or museum-bound art form that living people must not disturb. It is living, it lives with and in us, and it requires all from us to determine how we can apply it to the situations of our present. When I hear classical music, it often strikes me as missing something, because it's so fixed and rigid, and it is hard to find a freedom in it when everything is notated.
>
> The shamanistic culture has this art of being in the here and now. My dream is that people will not come up to me after a concert and tell me what a superb singer they think I am, but rather that they found some important meaning in the music. Because I strive on the stage to get so swallowed up by the music that I no longer exist. No "I," but something that is no longer discernible from the "I" of the total ensemble. I've lived in the West for four years, and I recall how fresh and enthusiastic I was at first, and how comparatively empty I feel now. I've given my all to this Western world, and feel I have yet to get a response back from it.[10]

Peter Kowald: Strings, Woods, Women

Kowald, like Don Cherry, built much of his post-1960s' career around multicultural collaborations. The complexity of being German – which is really, these days, a microcosm of the larger complexity of being a Westerner – was a prime motive behind that outreach.

Sainkho said to me "yes, everything is difficult now in my country, but my traditions are great." I can say that everything is relatively wealthy in my country,
but my tradition is not okay. I ask myself, and others have asked me, why I am
interested in the global village idea. When I play with all these people, like the
traditional Japanese *shakuhachi* player, I don't know if I am bringing a tradition with me in the way he is. I don't play like Bach, I don't play – well . . .
[he contradicts himself] . . . I can show you a review by a guy of a solo bass
concert I did a few years ago at this FMP festival in Chicago. I played a long
solo, I think fifty-five minutes, and the guy just compared it with a long Bach
piece, for the first time for me, in terms of structure. I like it myself a lot, the
way he interpreted it. So maybe let's say the formal consciousness does have
European roots.[11]

Kowald's "think-local-act-global" cosmopolitanism began with his youthful
passion for things Greek, awakened by both positive and negative aspects of
coming up German. The positive: his education at Wuppertal's "classical" high
school, where he took nine years of Latin and six years of ancient Greek languages,
through literature. The school had an exchange program with a sister school in
Athens, and Kowald's family hosted a Greek student, whose family hosted him in
turn. "Spiros came, he's a little older than me," he recalls. "Then when I was
sixteen, he invited me to his family and I fell in love with his sister. I learned Greek
very quickly," he laughs, "so when I was seventeen I could speak relatively fluent
modern Greek, and then I studied it after I finished high school. Then I translated *rebetiko* songs into German, and a lot of poetry." (Kowald studied Greek
philology at the university in Bonn, and has translated the work of modern Greek
poets for German readers, including Nobel prizewinner Odysseus Elytis and Lenin
prizewinner Yannis Ritsos, both also personal friends.[12])
    Besides this amazing genre that has been called "Greek blues,"[13] the sheerly
instrumental music of the improvising rural clarinetists caught the young musician's ear; he "would bring a record here and there for Peter [Brötzmann], because
he liked them too, these clarinet players with the kind of low, Johnny Dodds
sound." These musical affinities have led over time to an involvement with Greek
musicians with whom, along with Günter Sommer, Kowald has virtually generated an improvised music scene in Greece.
    Pyrichia is Kowald's collaboration with Greek traditional musicians Ilias
Papadopoulos playing the lyre, with a bow, and clarinetist and flutist Floros
Floridis. The sounds of this recording evoke the primal ancient base of the
Dionysian *aulos* and the Apollonian lyre at the root of Western music history. It
suggests a Greek affinity with the intensity of sound of the German free jazz, as
well as with the broader spectrum of Eurasian folk and ceremonial musics.
    What interested me was the way the history of the European free-jazz state-
ment was at first German, excluding American, and then later made connections
with Africa and Japan and Greece and Siberia and so on. What is emerging is a
real picture of how the global village works and how the local situation works with
it, as Kowald explained so well. However, it seemed to me that the more people

try to make something that is new to them, the farther back they go into the depths of time, to the old, in their own sphere. Kowald's relationship with Greek culture deserves attention simply because, in a way, Greece is the source of Western culture.

When I drew his attention to this, Kowald said:

> Greece is the bridge . . . I remember learning in school that it started in Egypt and Mesopotamia, and then it went to Greece, and then it spread out to what we call Western civilization. But since the Ottoman Empire, Greece is the bridge between Europe and the Far East. Greece is from this side the bridge, and that's what I'm interested in, because it has a lot of Eastern qualities, that extend to Japan. The whole East starts in Greece, through Turkey, Persia, India, and then it goes to China and Japan – or it doesn't go to, it came from there, but from this point the East starts in Greece.

I recall the AACM motto "Great black music, from the ancient to the future." The idea of a thing standing there in the world being itself – *Ding an sich* and *Musik an sich* – without being manipulated or mediated so much (the Holy), is still strong in ancient Greek philosophers.[14] Kowald himself favors Socrates, Heraclitus, and other pre-Platonic Greeks, for their "more Eastern, less analytical" thinking process.

> I always remembered John Cage saying that he wasn't too interested in music as a conversation. I always try to keep that in mind – but still, the way our music is . . . there is a lot of storytelling in it. Even so much as being a method of performance. All these questions are not conclusively answered, I think. We see that other cultures, when they talk about important questions of wisdom, a lot of them do it through telling a story. Europe, or, let's say, Western civilization, has developed this analytical mind where you don't necessarily have to tell a story in order to talk about something.[15]

Duos Europa, Duos USA, and Duos Japan came out in 1989 on one CD, originally conceived as a 3-LP set. Kowald did short duos with a wide variety of improvisers from jazz and other traditions throughout the world, all recorded between 1984 and 1989. The array very much has the feel of a geocultural terrain being mapped out (much as his friend Günter Sommer did in his solo music, as will be discussed), a discovery of common ground through the back door of improvisation, as it were. It also has the feel of a studio project, not least because the pieces are so short, and follow each other well within the CD's concept, which would not generally happen so live. These duos are Kowald's examples, like Fuchs's work and Sommer's miniatures, of many such short statements that came out of European improvisers who had found their free voices in the open-ended, long catharses of the first hours.

Seizan Matsuda's traditional *shakuhachi* with Kowald's bass is a rich mix of sound and expressiveness. Their timbres are equally primal, wood and wind and strings in their most natural elements together. Following it, Evan Parker turns in his usual intense performance, in the rhythm of fingers dancing out repeated phrases in a varying rhythmic flow, and breath teasing out harmonics in similar rhythms. The spontaneous stops and starts this duo executed suggest a Webern piece, or a Japanese *haiku.*

The duo with Greek singer Diamanda Gallas is startlingly evocative, again because of the rough, dirty timbre and energy both soundings draw out of each other. This woman evokes for me and many the old stories about the ancient Greek Furies of the Dionysian cult, the raging, uncivilized side of women, which played a large part in the Orphic myths about the music inherited, along with the Apollonian side, by the West from Greece.

The German–Japanese axis is once again struck up on the common postwar ground of the American jazz vocabulary, in the duo with alto saxophonist Akira Sakata. The free-jazz frenzy follows that traditional balladry. The axis continues, with Japanese trombonist Masahiko Kono. The glissando potential and the similar range of the two instruments are exploited in this duo. The chemistry of Japanese cellist Keki Midorikawa revels in the speech-like glissando and attacks of the two sibling instruments, bowed in the finest Asian style of Zen-like moment and European technique.

Back to Japan's own tradition we then go, with *koto* player Tadao Sawai. The interest here is obviously in the two plucked and glissando sounds, along with the meeting of the two iconic soundings of East and West in the improvisers' immediate rapport. Japan is evoked more distinctly, as also American jazz by the pizzicato bass, in the duo with traditional *biwa* player Junko Handa in the next duo. Kowald evokes the latter's indigenous vocal expressions with his own Mongolian-inspired drone playing and singing, moving from that initial West–East polarized duo, to more common Eurasian ground. The polarization is reclaimed for the drama of contrast, in the end. Putting Derek Bailey after this duo was a savvy choice, juxtaposing the English guitarist's famously pointillistic Western avant-garde sound world with the traditional one of Japan.

The next duo must have had a double charge for Kowald. Greek clarinetist Floros Floridis plays one of the instruments of Kowald's first big formative influence Peter Brötzmann, and does so out of the musical tradition of the culture that won his heart and mind from the same early age. The blues spirit and poetry of African-American vocalist Jeanne Lee, Gunter Hampel's wife, bring Kowald to the American "father" he had to "kill" before resurrecting him, along with himself, in the mainstream jazz discourse from America. (Notice the millennial content of the lyric – "In these last days . . . where every day is a struggle . . . there is great joy and unassailable strength in being on the way" – brought down from black gospel, to the Eurasian *Emanzipation.)*

Rhythm is the Breath of the World

Günter Sommer's most interesting recent work also includes collaborations with an important literary figure, novelist Günter Grass.[16] That, along with his body of recorded solo and group percussion music and his collaborations with various voices within and outside his local saxon/German tradition, make him uniquely relevant beyond the GDR experience.

Sommer's notion of a musical exchange of "semantic information" between cultures has shaped the way he approaches his solo percussion music, as one with both a deep and strong local identity and ears open to its counterparts around the world. Commenting on the Balkan-traditional scales and rhythms I say I detected in many of his recordings of free improvisations, he says:

> We certainly have in the East a strong influence from Balkan music. Very many Bulgarian musicians, Rumanian; and it has always fascinated me. And I must say, also Petrovsky, and Gumpert, and Bauer, we have a very great interest in all Eastern music, from Asia, for the semantic information it carried to us – the way the semantic information in African drumming always meant something more than the purely musical code of its one-and-two, three-and four-one-and-two three pattern; there is always semantic information it carries, it is not only a rhythm but also a . . .
>
> Personal expression? [I ask.]
>
> No. Well, yes, but more; it is also information about a view of the world, like a postal carrier; it is a way to send messages, news, information. It is information about a culture, and I receive it from other drummers as such, and my own drumming sends messages and information about my own culture. And this cultural information that is transmitted, one can either hear and receive it, or not. It's up to you. But my intention is to transmit it, as I see my drumming peers in other cultures doing: along with the personal voice and emotion, to transmit cultural information.
>
> All improvising musicians should be open to each system for the way it can be used. First you have to study it, but then you have to use it for your own language. When Petrovsky is playing, sometimes he is very close to clarinet players from Bulgaria. It's not so obvious at first, you have to listen for it.

Sommer's view of the Western "world music" genre expresses an Eastern view of Rempel's "openness," set against the West's "liberal" engagement of outside influences.

> In Western Europe there have always been many groups that combine jazz with Rom, or Indian, such as the group Omega, or Charlie Mariano's group. It has led to the current "world music" concept, and it is a West German phenomenon, not something that ever caught on in the East. Perhaps there is something like nostalgia in this Western mode of collaborating with these other traditions. They have become so inundated with this Western capitalist culture, I think they want to escape from it into the roots they've come to miss.
>
> My colleagues and I have drawn on African-American and European classical traditions, but it isn't that both are equal in all respects. What's missing in our tradition is the swing element; what the African-American one lacks is our sense of form – dramatic, symphonic. They had 12-bar, 8-bar, 16-bar blues

forms, the AABA form – and that's about it. The symphonic form, with its introductory prelude, and its subsequent sections to work through the material, the reprise – the entire classical tradition has developed this, and it is something that conveys real drama, like a theater piece. It doesn't come from America, it comes from here.

I ask: "In the culture here in Germany – East, or the whole country, now – what do you think is the impact of this 'semantic information?' I'm thinking of Germany's history of racism, and its assertion of its own Western music legacy as superior in the world."

People in Germany – especially in my area of Saxony, and Prussia, which you have characterized correctly – need an accessible entry point to that which happens outside of their own place in the world. I will always be German when I work with African or Asian material; I think that means they can, through me, get a true slice of life from a part of the world they may never experience in its original form.

Sommer's solo recordings comprise a series of three releases called *Hörmusik 1, 2, & 3.*[17] When he performed them in public, he did so in private. "When I would play solo concerts, people were always so preoccupied with what they saw me doing," he says. "They didn't follow the composition of the music, because to watch me was such an exotic thing, with all these strange instruments. That started to bother me, so I decided to rob them of that visual event, and to play behind a curtain."

Sommer has expanded his jazz drumkit to include more than the usual three or four pieces from biggest bass to smallest tom, with a range of drums tuneable to notes in a scaled octave. He has bells, gongs, iron bars, and brass bowls of all sizes hanging from wires, evoking the Asian part of his Eurasian stretch eastward, and south, to India. The word "Afroasiatic" haunts the listener's mind as talking drums and clanging metal paint their pictures of ritual and ceremony undistracted by the historical baggages of stringed (rational) or wind (martial) instruments.

Then, when he does let his zither-like *darabuka* speak, and various bellows-driven and mouth-blown instruments, from the bandoneon and *schalmei*[18] to medieval Western instruments such as the shawm and hackbrett, to his own PV-pipe organ-like invention the *bubamspiel* (recall the historical connections between the Western organ and its Eastern prototypes, imported a millennium ago), we begin to reconnect those roots to the church organ tradition that grew and blossomed in Bach (recall Sommer's collaborations with organist Hans Günter Wauer), to the instrument's Hammond incarnation in jazz, to the blues harp tradition.

Especially striking is the *rohrglockenspiel*, or tubular bells, which also sound on *Emanzipation*-period recordings by others, and are mentioned in the literature on the music as evocative, even iconic, of the Western European church-bell soundscape. This is not an instrument typically heard in the corresponding American instrument arrays of improvisers, which is both surprising and not. Surprising, because it is commonly found in American bands and orchestras from high schools to professional symphonies, and not surprising because it does evoke a certain Western cultural rigidity in sound, with its clean and tempered pitches and suggestion of Christian church bells, which do not prevail as publicly in America. In Sommer's hands, next to the gongs, bells, and cymbals, it evokes his Saxon home as just another patch on that quilt.

In all this, as he aspires to be for his local audience, Sommer might be the traditional ethnomusicologist's most accessible point of entry to the European improvised music scene. In other hands, such a solo project might be one of a modern person roaming through the sounds as if through one big junkyard full of treasures all divorced from their original context; or of a passionate collector of sounds avid to contextualize them all within his or her own brilliant imagination and/or strong ego, via leaps of faith. With Sommer, it feels much more like the vision of one grounded in history and world on a large and deep scale, depicting that vastness not with some microcosmic grandiosity of his own, but with the measured, calm and open curiosity of a child with a passion for order – the order of narrative – that enhances rather than stifles his wild freedom. Something like Japanese *taiko* drummers, he conveys a certain relaxation, even in his most agitated furies, that never abates, and always seems thoughtful. The joy and excitement seem to lie for him in unfolding, at his own leisurely unpressed pace, one deliberate statement after another, the traditional always serving as the touchstone for the new, and the new defined primarily through the idiosyncrasies of his instruments and his uses of them. Those new statements in fact evoke for me something primal, and do so from that unique position of the "land in the middle."

This is very different from the brinksmanship of a Han Bennink, or the mercurial texturing of a Paul Lovens or Tony Oxley, or the drive and subtleties and power of the African-American masters from Art Blakey through Tony Williams and others whom Sommer names as important influences. They might be, arguably, more virtuosic than him, more fiery in certain ways, but what he does with his array is more evocative of the Eurasian soundscape and its history, to my ears, and of Africa by way of America. His words about semantic information from Asian and Indian music traditions speak most in his solo music.

His strong attachment to and identification with his Saxon heritage comes out most clearly in the third *Hörmusik* CD, a recording called *Percussion Summit*, with Sommer on timpani, Joe Koinzer on tubular bells and marimba, American Ed Thigpen on drumkit, and another jazz drummer, Okay Temiz. It includes a piece called "Preussische Abgesang mit Sachsen Glockenklang" ("Prussian Swan Song with Saxon Bells"). Sommer explains it as a competition between Prussia, the Northern region, and Saxony, where he comes from. "Each have a nationalist pride. *Abgesang* means what they sing as they leave the battleground in defeat, and *Glockenklang* is what I, the Saxon victor, play on my bells, declaring a kind of battle, and victory over the Prussian drums, the timpanis and marching drums. This is something that is more like a mock than a real battle; both sides understand that. The people are laughing, and everyone understands that neither the Saxons nor the Prussians are the superior force, but equals."

With the first two *Hörmusik* recordings, this one works itself away from the free-jazz furor and into reconnections with traditional rhythmic and melodic worlds. As it extended logically through Sommer's solo music, it unfolded as a compositional statement as strongly as an improvisational one, Max Roach-like; and it moved through German folklore as framed and encouraged in the old GDR into a broader folkloric sort of gesture that evoked older, other civilizations as well as tribal cultures spanning the globe.

Like that of his friend and frequent collaborator Peter Kowald, Sommer's work grew into a natural overlap with the current world music scene. He has become the drummer to call on if one wants to cover that whole emergent spectrum beyond the level of pastiche or ornament. Even though he has not had the access Kowald had to travel and make as many actual contacts, he has done what he could alone, and with Kowald and the Greek musicians we met, and with French players Sylvain Kassap and Didier Levallet (on the CD *Cordes sur Ciel*) to connect with Eurasian folk roots.

The body of solo work established by the three *Hörmusik* recordings offers an interesting alternative to what postmodernist theorists – most pertinently here, Berliner Veit Erlmann (1993, 1996), drawing on American Frederic Jameson (1991) and French Jean Baudrillard (1990/1993) – see as pastiche, itself a concept forged by Adorno, and developed by Baudrillard through his concept of the simulacrum. This is an aesthetic of an artistic expression that has no real anchor in time or place, rather evokes an artificial nostalgia for an imagined time and place, always cynically, in the context of an all too real and present spirit of capitalist materialism.

Sommer's project was a real freedom forged in the ultimately artificial confinement to the time and place of the now-vanished GDR. The curtain behind which he made his solo music in public is a perfect image of the Iron Curtain, or the Berlin Wall (though I have never heard him or anyone else speak of it that way). But the soundscape made behind them topographized a Eurasian musical terrain that seems free, by virtue of its real captivity, of all charges of being the pastiche that masks hegemony.

Riobec is the CD of Cecil Taylor's 1988 duo with Sommer. It is something of a soul exchange: the African American seizing the torch of the Romantic European pianist, with his insistence on the best Bösendorfer piano in high concert situations, and his command of it; and the East German percussionist with a diatonic grounding and traditional Western music approach to harmonic structure and development, playing pitched drums and other instruments he made with his own hands, like some traditional village drummaker in Ghana.

*   *   *

Our tour of the new European players cannot be completed without another study in contrasts. Like all of the players on *Machine Gun*, Swedish drummer Sven-Åke Johansson and German saxophonist Peter Brötzmann have traveled from the classic breakthrough of European identity in this music down their own individual paths. Johansson's has been a softening diffusion into several of the different directions touched on here (theater, literature, various post-free-jazz musics), Brötzmann's more a laser beam of intensity unabated, from Germanic roots through Africa and Japan and electronics, to an unmistakeable reconnect with jazz in America. Brötzmann is not about the composer's tradition, not about theater, only marginally (in his solo music) about the word (*logos*) side of things; he is much more about the "semantic information" (per Sommer) of roots music, of primal dance, of rhythm and of timbre, of the folk tradition as filtered through Albert Ayler. Johansson is about all those things Brötzmann is not, even as both seem to get their respective energies and visions stoked by their work with younger players (trumpeter Axel Dörner for Johansson, and trombonist Johannes Bauer and drummer Willi Kellers for Brötzmann).

Sven-Åke Johansson

Johansson moved from his home in Sweden to Paris in the early 1960s. It was his forays to Germany, through Cologne and Wuppertal to Berlin, that started his work in what he describes as "improvisation free of metric strictures, more of an expressive music." That led him to a variety of different experiences with *geräusch* and *klangfarblich* music, along with what he calls "new metric music" – his own self-generated rhythmic patterns notated to provide material for improvisation[19] – all of which he has cultivated since. His musical universe holds interpretive forays into 1950s' cool jazz and American songbook classics by Noel Coward and Cole Porter; Hans Eisler's *Kampflieder* and other songs, with a small combo; improvised words and songs, with accordion and other music; and compositions commissioned by various parties. "I have always, even when I was playing the most free jazz, been making pieces and keeping my eyes open for possibilities to have them performed, simply to have that much more material than that afforded by a-thematic spontaneity.[20] Also, this expressive music that is so intertwined with improvisation is so much a self-expression, and one doesn't always want to express oneself so much as other things."

Johansson's spacious Berlin flat includes two rooms housing a large collection of percussion instruments, along with the many books and recordings and the other usual accoutrements of the casually and seriously cultured life. Among them, on an artist's work table, stands a miniature stage set, a mock-up for a theatrical-musical performance he is designing. His percussion work has evolved from his early 1960s' jazz dates with American players in Europe through the free-jazz days to the role of the percussionist as colorist and developer of *Geräuschmusik*. His word improvisations have taken the kind of spontaneous verbalizing Cecil Taylor sometimes does in his playing and expanded their potential as spontaneously improvised *Lieder*. These songs, with their images and narratives, have in turn led him into the arena of performance art and installations, and of musical experiments based on ideas relating to math or physics, in fine Pythagorean (and Alvin Lucierian) tradition. All of which makes him a perfect example of the way the free-jazz gesture has led to new expressions of old traditions, including the ancient Greek meld of bardic poetry, music, theater, and the mathematics of sound, through the German alternative to French and Italian opera, the *Singspiel*.[21]

Most unique about Johansson's work as an improviser are his word improvisations.

> Bringing words into improvised music was something that seemed to be taboo in the free jazz realm because of the weight of the history of opera and *Lieder* tradition. Vocal sounds were okay, but improvising words was too close to telling stories. It always interested me to improvise poetry in the same way I do sheer sounds. They seem so intertwined to me.
>
> During the time I played classic American jazz, I switched from my habitual right-handed to a left-handed handwriting practice. I am naturally left-handed, but in school one had to write with the right hand. So this was a way for me to become more ambidexterous as a jazz drummer. I would try this for a few hours a day for awhile, to work on a style of free-association writing. That might have something to do with what I tried to do later as an improvising poet.

The aptness of the title *Drive* can be heard in the 1979 duo LP with Alex von Schlippenbach in which Johansson plays drumkit full bore, in a sort of pulsating, wave-forming constant thrash light years beyond the almost conventional drum break of *Machine Gun*. Most of this LP is the kind of high-energy free-jazz improvisation one would expect of these two at that time, at a Total Music Meeting, and they do make a good team, both forceful and mercurial.

Toward the end, after the peak of the primary musical energy, Johansson chimes in with words. Here the irony in his fractured delivery of sentimental material – he sounds like he is trying to create a send-up of a Cole Porter ballad – is offset by von Schlippenbach's atonal wanderings. Following the word improvisation is another part of Johansson's *Spiel*, the accordion. Like many free sessions, it demonstrates how one idea or sound world can emerge from another very different one, unpredictably.

Blind aber Hungrig (*Blind but Hungry*) is subtitled *Norddeutsche Gesänge* (*North German Songs*), a rare undersized FMP LP (FMP-S 15, 1984) with words that sprang from associations with the little road-stop places off the autobahn between Hamburg and Bremen and Berlin that Johansson traveled often with von Schlippenbach. "The North German songs sprang very much from the constant exposure to words on road signs, the place names; my imagination made up scenes and stories to go with them." This process evolved in his way of working and influenced subsequent projects. "I've worked it with theater people to create scenery for me to make something like miniature operas."

The "idyllic" in the concept of one such, the *Idylle und Katastrophe* (po torch records, ptr/wd 6, 1980), seems to lie in Johansson's word pictures, and the "catastrophic" more in the instrumental music. Each short bit of wordplay is something of a verbal snapshot of a simple, everyday image. One describes a chimneysweep sitting by a chimney, the ashes, his black clothes, his bicycle. This image is described as "as true as it is free." The words are strung together, through repetition and change, as if Johansson's mind's eye were slowly scanning an inner vista, lingering here, moving there; the repetition establishes the image, makes for a musical rhythm, leads to a new image to describe. Occasionally the speaking voice breaks into song, like a prayer or a chant. "Im Taubenschlag" ("In the Pigeon House") again takes a mundane image – a little enclave of postal pigeons carrying messages that will not be read – and invests it with the suggestiveness of spontaneously improvised music, makes it a metaphor of same.

Sometimes a word is worked for its phonic mutations. "Entfernungen," or distances, works the word *flug* (the root of many words having to do with airflight); *zeug* (machine); and *zug* (concerning trains). Johansson plays with them, repeats them, works them over, alters them slightly, in order to generate his improvisation in words. Generally, these images give an unprogrammed, unprogramming element of concreteness to the abstract mystery of sheer sound sculpture. As much as this music is so suggestive of such everyday strangeness as humans engaging with the grit and grime of their own technology, or pigeons cooing together in their coop without a clue about the messages they carry, or the eerie distances in the sounds of trains and planes, it is a wonder that words such as Johansson's have not been spun out by more of its players, in a similar fashion.

Music and Johansson's wordplay work together in ways ranging a spectrum from close rhythmic and pitch interaction – for example, with the word *blumen* in the text of a song, and von Schlippenbach's pianistic echo of it – to one in which the speech stays at the same slow, measured, ritualistic cadence and affect while the music runs far ahead of it into a kind of dance around it, the energy of which seems to derive from something far more than the sonic shell – which we must ponder as lying in the visual imagery and conceptual meanings of the words, that which transcends their sonic shells.

It is this dynamic that prevails in "Kaltenkirchen," which breaks down roughly into three parts. The first, after an improvised piano introduction, is a kind of a *sprechgesang* delivery, in which each word, every pronoun and article, often each syllable, is a rest stop, a platform from which, occasionally, more syllables or words are launched in sequence. The piano is usually dancing around these verbal images and sounds, spinning from them far more musical threads than they bear alone. The picture Johansson paints develops, with that voice of the Schoenbergian *Sprechsänger*, from an image of glass and porcelain figurines in a warehouse into (the song's second part) a parody of sentimental American songbook lyrics casting a natural scene – birds, a pond, a fish jumping – in a similarly artificial way, and then into the third part, a rushing spoken ending image of a bird swooping down to catch the jumping fish, and of carp soup being served in the pub beside the train station the next day. So, again, from the idyllic to the catastrophic in nature.

Von Schlippenbach's piano improvisation, while occasionally displaying a close sync with the passing pitch or rhythmic pattern of Johansson's speech, mostly seems like an elaboration on the words, as if into musical language as the more articulate, richer one.

A culmination of this process in Johansson's recorded work saw the improvisation bloom into composition in a two-LP, 8-scene "*Singspiel* with Environment and Ballet." Entitled ". . . *über Ursache und Wirkung der Meinungsverschiedenheiten beim Turmbau zu Babel*" or ". . . cause and effect of the various meanings sprung from the building of the tower of Babel," the production pits Johansson's written text against the musical and dialogical improvisations of players such as von Schlippenbach, Paul Lovens, Fuchs, and others, doing what they always do, playing without musical scripts, here off of a semi-scripted theatrical event. The interest in this particular piece of dramaturgy lies in our knowledge of Johansson as a word improviser, extending that cultivated process into literacy.

The overall effect is less formal than something similar but through-composed, while more so than a wide-open improvisation of either words or music. The dramaturgical organization links most of the freely improvised musical content to its post-Schoenberg Western art music side when the words and drama are happening, and to the free-jazz side when only instruments are playing. In all, it is very like the Dutch branch of free-musical theater cultivated by the Willem Breuker Kollektief.

This way of words worked from a musical event both as a verbal fruit – in the way they are sung even when spoken, never glibly uttered like a reading over a musical accompaniment – and also as a seed of musical fruit that elaborates the word's potential, reflects the intimate symbiosis between the word and instrumental music as it developed in Germany and the West. We have seen its current expressions through collaborations between improvisers and poets, novelists, and playwrights, but this is the first example of one of the instrumental players of this music extending his improvisatory process into the realm of his voice not only as a soundmaker but also as an image- and thought-maker. It is, of course, precisely what black preachers have long done in their churches, much of which has informed jazz.

What might be seen as the safest radicalism of the free-jazz *Emanzipation*, then, was the primal scream, the Germanic cry, shrieked like Ayler's and Coltrane's but with different original voices and messages ("semantic information") – safest in the sense of surest returns to surest deepest roots. If we were to move up the spectrum from most to least safety in such radicalism, we might move through the same gestures of melody and harmony and pitch-system building that actually did evolve in the West, unsafe because prone to repeating the same problematical history. But surely we would be on our most treacherous ground when we attempt to find the right balance between speech and sound, because that is the juncture where God and the Devil, the Holy and Religion, can so resemble each other. With a word, the music either speaks its own truth to the whole other cosmos that belongs to language, in all language's oral and literate dimensions, or it lets itself be invaded and taken over by the force of that cosmos's independent wills and agendas. "Music is a whore," Christian Broecking wrote, "it can mean anything." Yet, finally, words may be uttered, beasts named, sheer music given poetic voice by one who knows the wordless song well enough to make the words it suggests sing.

Peter Brötzmann

Shoji Hano is a 50-year-old drummer from southern Japan who first trained and performed extensively in a rural commune of traditional *taiko* drummers. Since moving out into the improvised-music scene, he has recorded on a small independent label in Japan in collaboration with Isho Yukihiro, a celebrated player from a famous family of players of the *noukan*, the bamboo transverse flute used in *noh* and *kabuki* theater.

As wild and abandoned as his duos with Brötzmann sound, careful and complete listening to the tape I made of them reveals a very disciplined, focused attention in the drumming, a thickness that rolls and pops along smartly without an excess of bouncing, or melodramatic attacks to shock – something that locks on like a laser and does not spend itself in catharsis. Again, a duo partner particularly suited to Brötzmann's need for growth and sustained energy. Brötzmann tells me:

> I had another experience last year that I liked very much. I worked with a Moroccan guy, Mahmoud Gania, who plays the *guembri*, a kind of North African bass-stringed instrument – one of the well-known people of the *Gnawa* music. *Gnawa* is played by black Africans coming mostly from Mali, or Senegal, as slaves. The Arab people brought them and couldn't sell them, so they stayed there [he laughs] and they developed their own language and their own very interesting rhythm-oriented, very driving music. I like this kind of music because it goes; and these people, they play for hours, for nights. In my way about thinking of the timing of tunes or pieces you play – whether the European or American way, it's the same – after a time, you have to come to an end. But they never do – they get in a kind of trance. Mahmoud's wife is a dancer in a kind of dervish band with him, and it goes on for hours and hours and hours.

The Wels Concert brings us to this musical-traditional triangle with one point in Brötzmann's Northern Europe, one in the North African home of the Gnawa musicians, and the other in the African-American milieu of drummer Hamid Drake's Chicago. Again, one sees Brötzmann's impulse not to capitalize on his early breakthrough of the Germanic cry through the jazz discourse, which would have been pathetically narrow, so much as to expand his horizons in directions that make sense in terms of his limitations and strengths as a player. The net result is a musical network that links up farthest flung voices of whiteness and blackness as imaged in the representations of African-American, African traditional, and German free jazz in the music press both academic and popular, and shows them to be integral, organic parts of the same musical village.

Songlines, a trio with Chicago bassist Fred Hopkins and Coltrane-schooled drummer Rashid Ali, is notable among most of Brötzmann's others for being so in the jazz pocket of walking bass and metered rhythm, and keening hypnotic horn over a drone. Ali's pitched drums recall both Günter Sommer and Art Blakey; Hopkins's deeply pulse-rooted bass work, and traditional root-toning, timekeeping role partners up with those drums to give Brötzmann the kind of ground Ornette Coleman and Coltrane preferred to play against, something he said he missed in most of his European colleagues. Having found his voice and developed it with those colleagues, he transplanted it in African/African-American soil, where flow enveloped moment rather than the European reverse.

Despite all of this, Brötzmann takes care to point out to me his distance from the music industry's "world-music soup." "I'm not into this trend of everybody playing ethnic music. That started years ago, with Ginger Baker bringing all his African friends and women here on stage, and it was wonderful. But nowadays . . . I think it's all a terrible misunderstanding . . . a kind of commercial business way of thinking. That's not my intention here. I'm just fascinated by the way the whole thing is going, with no problems . . . mind, a body, and all of it is going in one kind of movement."

Those Who Can, Teach

Kowald and Sommer will serve as two actors in this one history who have managed to work its pedagogical implications into European music education. A comparison of their approach to American jazz performance curricula, as teachers of what they know from their experience as players, is instructive.

Kowald (who died in 2002) played his music in Tunisia, India, Singapore, Indonesia, Korea, Japan, Siberia, and Russia, as well as America and most European countries. He met musicians from many traditional cultures who influenced what he did as an improviser, and brought them to Europe to perform and record with him, and was their guest on their turfs. Several of them were guests in performances and workshops he facilitated weekly for a year in his home for any local music students and musicians interested in coming together to conceive and craft musical events collectively, as an improvised music ensemble.[22]

I choose the word "facilitate" consciously; Kowald's own path and personality would have prevented him from either spoon-feeding or dictating the musical material or approach. He did not instruct the group in the traditional jazz or classical techniques, styles, repertoires, or conventions he learned in his own youth through the usual curricular and extracurricular ways, at least not as ends in themselves. The students interested in what he was offering ranged the spectrum of skill and conceptual proficiency, and his desire was to coax out a group mind and musical situations that would reflect that range and allow everyone to thrive and grow. Similarly, guests from Mongolia, Japan, Greece, and elsewhere did not dwell on their home traditions or techniques with an intent to expose the students to new knowledge or get them to adopt, from scratch, something foreign to them so much as to inspire them to take responsibility for shaping individual and group expressions and interdynamics that are uniquely theirs, that emerge with them, from and for their community, along with their own personal voices and abilities.

The Carla Maria von Weber School of Music is a bastion of classical tradition and pedagogy. Günter Sommer inherited a department that was, to his mind, killing the spirit of jazz improvisation by teaching it as a classical discipline to be preserved in a dated and objectified repertoire, rather than as a tool for self-discovery and community definition and rejuvenation. He revamped this department with the help of his strong international personal network of improvisers coming out of other traditions.

This outreach and in-gathering of both men is the natural outcome of their histories in the two Germanies. Both histories start with a childhood immersion in European classical training in the public schools and move at an early age to a passion for another culture's music – American (especially African-American) jazz – then to an imitation of its performance out of its original context. They then develop from that to a feeling of being derivative, an imitation, however good, of something they could never really call their own – along with an alienation from their own home tradition as a total musical *Umwelt*; then experiment and find their own voice and messages, alone and with like-minded peers, shutting out the influences of their formative years (Kowald's "kill the fathers"). From there they reclaim those expressions and collaborate with those of (non-Western) others, not as aspirants seeking to master the other idioms but as Europeans who had developed their own personal/cultural idiom which could feed and be fed by others, as equals. Then they move to take responsibility for the business process of creating paid, public performance opportunities, through projects motivated and independently facilitated more by musical and social considerations than by commercial or existing conventional ones. Finally they move into the role of teaching all of this not on the margins or oppositionally, but in the mainstream of the culture.

The relationship of both men to their students honors all aspects of this path, from its early unreflective acquisition of what is home, to its later seduction by an "other," to the subsequent alienation from both home and other engendered thereby, to the personal vision quest and achievement of its goal, to the mature position of power from which they relate to both home and others (including other disciplines such as painting, literature and dance) in local and global contexts.

The picture just drawn speaks to recent literature on tertiary-level teaching issues as they relate to the role of the professional musician and to intercultural music education.[23] The examples of Kowald's and Sommer's work as educators, and of these readings about both teacher training and student training, suggest the following agenda: primary and secondary music education might best function as a performative model, a training in instruments and bodies of musical knowledge specific to a cultural tradition; whether that tradition is one's own or another's, and the details of how it might best be taught, is an issue for the primary and secondary levels. The best teacher will be one adept in organizing and conveying material, guiding students through it in a disciplined way, then assessing the outcome in a way inclined to letting go of the attitude of control and mastery as its criteria are fulfilled.

At the tertiary level of higher education, the skill and authority of the master toward the novice might be replaced by an ability to cultivate the student's own authority; to expect and encourage the students to question their own and all performative mastery, to turn it from ends into the means to seek something original and unique to their own personal and collective needs, dreams, and situations. And, instead of sending successful graduates on their own way in the world as the primary and secondary teachers do, the tertiary-level teacher will be able to assess and accept the students' results in a discernment of their internal logic and integrity, to validate and embrace them as successful, to claim them for cultural use both when they reaffirm established wisdom – as, for example, Wynton Marsalis has done with jazz and classical music in America – as well as, even especially, when they challenge or rearrange it, as Anthony Braxton has done in the same musical discourses.

This performative primary and improvisative tertiary model empowers musical professionalism with the responsibility, right, and ways to determine its own destiny. It does so in part by bestowing a flexibility within and between cultural-idiomatic expressions necessary to their balanced, egalitarian dialogue with their own pasts, and to their collaborative, or at least cooperative, futures. This transformation of West from ruler of to cooperator with the Rest is what America may have most to learn from Europe, in this music.

Six

The Marriage of Time and Archē

Music is the art of measuring well.

– Augustine of Hippo

It was music that ate up time, that froze it in its tracks. They were there. They were gone.

– Steve Lake[1]

In 1995, *New York Times* classical music reviewer Alex Ross overviewed the musical-experimentalist tradition of Berlin. After panning as tired some of its recent gestures – one example was Stockhausen's placing of the Arditti Quartet members in four different helicopters to interact with the sound of the rotor blades, and each other, over the air waves – Ross wrote:

> The dark wonder of Berlin ought to have inspired a different kind of music. It has, but the composers have so far not been German . . . Cecil Taylor, the great American free-jazz pianist, organized an epic series of concerts here in 1988, culminating in a two-hour-long orchestral improvisation named after Berlin's *Tiergarten*. (I wasn't there, but I have been listening to a phenomenal recording issued by the Berlin free-jazz label FMP . . .)

I was not there either, but I was at a similar event nine years later, not far away, with the same pianist in the same city with the same FMP producers. After the four friends who disliked him so much walked out, I gave Taylor and his band my full attention. I was tired from jet lag, unfocused, uninspired, and, in fact, myself annoyed with what I was hearing.

Initially, the music's uncalculated openness promised relief to my sleep-deprived, disoriented organism. But a few moments of this intense whimsy were enough to make me feel imposed upon by infinitely more demands than would come with more determined music. Here I was expected to indulge someone's self-indulgent gropings, repetitions, experiments; to watch and understand and care as he either succeeded or failed in constructing an essentially private experience and universe; to take up what seemed the enormous labor of bringing my own meaning, significance, pleasure, and fulfillment to material that, by itself, brought me to a chaos, boredom, irritation, and strain growing into a horror of more disorientation, even pain, as it developed and intensified. An interesting aesthetic concept, but one I would rather snarl at than embrace.

This aversion gradually gave way to a less hostile, if still uncommitted, tracking of the musical activity. Then suddenly, at a point some five minutes into my flagging patience, whatever Taylor had been doing climaxed and stopped. It felt as though he had shared my irritation and was mercifully ending its source. In that moment, the indefinition of an amorphous flow stood itself into the definition of a crystallized stillness. A little Sabbath . . .

More specifically, an audial experience of successive moments became an echo-imprint of one moment, effecting several things in a flash: a mental image, something like a Jackson Pollock painting, burned onto my inner eye like the ghost of a light bulb, giving the temporal-audial flow a moment's shape: boundaries, textures, colors, statically shifting in timeless thought, rather than flowing, developing, in time; a mental utterance, a sense of words flying unwilled from my language center to that entoptic light like moths to its bulb. "Crackle-militia-im/PLOsion" is a quick example of the kind of cadence, imagery, and sound (along with glossalalia-like words) Taylor's playing stimulated in me; a mental physic, a charging of my nervous system by the sounds in the ears and the sights in the eyes, such that I began to feel energized more than drained, alert and curious about, rather than dreading, what would happen next.

It was as though something had been alive but going nowhere, and that unpleasantly – but as soon as it died, it had gotten somewhere, and that pleasantly. Its soul somehow permeated the next musical event; the other players could not avoid some sort of relationship with it, whether through concordance, contrast, or even obliviousness. It was there, in time, framing the place where the next musical event would occur, and I kept referring to it, and referring the new event's flow to it (and I felt the musicians were doing the same) as it receded in memory to give way to something new (although – part of the fascination of all this – it would re-emerge at times, seemingly unbidden, throughout the long unbroken set).

This conversion of the real to the remembered repeated itself with successive transitions: flows and stops, each flow a process and each stop a point of definition, reflection, rejuvenation, and poise for the next flow. The overall energy level increased throughout in ebbs and flows, like a rising tide. Its points of definition were not essentially rational; insight, more than rational understanding, is perhaps the operative concept. Sometimes I felt the playing process had achieved more than others; still, whenever it ended I could see it as an entity in itself, a gesture, a statement, or a picture to which no more would be added, like a life defined by death, however well or ill lived.

That last analogy generated useful light to cast on the influx of energy and change of affect I experienced. With each of these stops, these "deaths" of the musical flow into their own definition, I experienced a shot of energy. I would use part of this energy to track the next flow, but on the whole I received more than I spent. That reminded me of the deep, ancient myths about the sacrifice of life for the generation of new life. I felt more than a metaphorical connection between my experience and such myths, remembering Attali's look at music as primal violence and murder – which, I reminded myself, must be read as an assertion (of the life of the perpetrator) as much as a negation of (the victim's) life. (Again, the assertion of God's life, of Life's life, over our own, in the Sabbath – rehearsals for real death.)

One more aspect of this experience distinguished it in my mind: after the first set, I felt undeniably sated. To return for more would have violated my biological gauge of the experience in favor of the conventionally composed and imposed clock time of someone else's idea of a "concert," two sets bracketing an intermission (with all due respect to whoever else's biological clock was truly served thereby).[2] I passed the second set at the café-bar chatting with the four friends and others who shared our choice, whatever their reasons.

I had been listening to Taylor and some of the others he played with that night long enough to feel comfortable as a listener. I had also been writing about such music as a journalist long enough to have developed ways of describing, giving opinions, and assessing it for general readers. I had also participated in it as a musician enough times – sometimes even with the bandmates playing with Taylor that night – to know how to discuss it in that context. But how to write about it as a scholar, analytically? then even further, theoretically?

Analysis: The Music's Logos

What one finds in scanning analytical studies of post-free jazz and postserial Western art music for what can and cannot be salvaged is: "not only analytical but general scholarship on improvisation is in its infancy," in the words of Australian musicologist Roger Dean;[3] the scant English-language analytical literature on jazz is virtually all on pre-free improvisation, or that prescribed by compositional premises from the Western diatonic-chromatic system, and is inscribed in conventional Western notation, sometimes with minor alterations to convey elements other than metrical and pitch relationships (timbre, inflection, etc.);[4] that these pre-free improvisations have been analyzed with a range of approaches, including literary and social scientific ones that involve no musical-transcriptive analysis; and that those more strictly musicological and music-theoretical approaches that do involve transcriptions overwhelmingly use conventional notation and associated frameworks – such as Schenkerian and pitch-class set theory – that even with pre-free jazz and twelve-tone music were acknowledged as being stretched to their limits by such applications.[5]

That stretch is much like the one an Egyptian astronomer named Ptolemy made to keep increasingly unwieldy data within the bounds of his geocentric discourse. In short, while diatonic-chromatic pitch matrices and paradigms certainly carried over from earlier jazz into the free-jazz discourse, the music itself no longer revolved around their grounds. Those grounds themselves were rather revolving around a sun that, judging by the "infancy" of the scholarship mentioned above, is still mostly too bright and/or unfiltered to look at and describe and study.

Note the "mostly." Ekkehard Jost opened his book *Europas Jazz* by asking how one could analyze a music that exhausts itself in the moment of its sounding. He did begin to answer his question in subsequent pages. With the sure instincts of a player who is as compelled to analyze as to do what he is doing, his answer identified the name of that music's sun, thus orienting the analyst to its light at the end of the tunnel of pitches. That name is Time. We will turn in a moment to an analytical lens designed to filter it. First, here, we will clarify what we hope it will illuminate, going by the names of "composition" and "improvisation."

Dean's book comprehensively addresses the inadequacies of current transcriptive analysis of (especially free) improvisation. He states that "for freely improvised music, pitch structures, with timbre/texture and rhythm, must be explored freshly for *what they reveal more than what they prove*"; and that "such explorations require equally fresh and creative transcriptive approaches, *to target and/or prioritize and define the maximum variety of information*" (1992: 204, my emphases). He also writes that "conventional Western analysis, though it has focused on harmony and motive, with rhythm subsumed therein, is probably still the focus most suited to 'jazz and freer improvisation.'"

My emphases signal what I like about his words, and what I follow in developing my own such approach. I contest his latter pronouncement, however, unless my approach might be read as a legitimate expansion on that "conventional Western" one. I also don't see the shift of that focus I want to make to be one of emphasis to rhythm, at least for the "freer improvisation," especially from Europe. Ethnomusicological and jazz studies have benefited recently from a shift to rhythmic analysis, and conventional notation used maximally and creatively can support that shift.[6] But, again, they all work with pre-free jazz, which mates African-based rhythmic cycles with Western metric frameworks for viable musical-systemic offspring. Free jazz and its branches are as free of such constraints as they are of the constraints of tonality both diatonic and chromatic. That is, they are free in the same sense I mentioned above: such elements are still kicking around in the music, but they do not constitute a framework of meaning and performance.

It is tempting at this point to hide under the "postmodern" umbrella unfurled in the previous chapter and ask what exactly the free-improvisational gesture at the heart of the music we have examined is. What does it mean? how does it mean? Nothing, everything. It blindly generates a pastiche of systems and soundings once thought to mean something, everything, but that now lie strewn across the field of time and history like marvelous machines too dangerous to operate as intended, yet too powerful and promising (and present) to leave alone.

The more responsible (and interesting) idea, however, is "metamodernism": beyond reactive irony, there is indeed a grand narrative. It is always there, at any given moment, always has been, always will be. It is just that it is never the one and only one, to prove against all others. It is both all unity and all diversity, and whether it is making War or Love with itself is up to it (us). It is a Holiness, but it is not the Religions we make of it.

Moving away from Dean's reluctant faith in convention, some other voices will aid the construction of a metamodern analytical engine. A sample study of one musical recording, "Sun," the entire B-side of *Globe Unity* (SABA 15109, 1966), will suggest a way to treat all other free improvisations. The piece is from the early days of German free jazz by the Globe Unity Orchestra.

Jost's (1987: 79–9) analysis of "Globe Unity," the entire A-side, involves two strategies: time the musical event, and describe it verbally. His blow-by-blow description marks the piece as it unfolds through a real-timeline from 0'0" to 19'58", with eighteen changes along the way. The shortest unit so described is fifteen seconds, the longest 3'53". What this method reveals, and what is the case, is a mix of tones, instrumentations, chords, and rhythms scored loosely and openly so as to serve as mutable triggers, platforms, and signals initiating free improvisations, from solo to collective and all combinations in between. Jost characterizes the end result as a composition centralizing not rational relations of pitches and pulses but "sound surfaces" (*Klangflächen*). I choose "Sun" for its proximity to "Globe Unity," to extend Jost's methodology seamlessly in the direction I want to take it, through such surfaces toward musical time.

Jost's time demarcations, as presented, also revealed something that was the case: whatever else about the piece was orchestrated, either by its sketchy graphic score or by the audially discernible decisions made by improvisers, on the fly, the times marking the piece's changes clearly were unprescribed. They were among the elements left open to chance, and they would never unfold the same way twice, even if the players repeated a given arbitrary reading of the score. That is, the musicians might decide to try and re-create the same order of solos and other decisions they originally made spontaneously, but they would never be able to make those eighteen changes at exactly the same clock times.

I make this point retrospectively. When I first tried Jost's approach on "Sun," I used the timeline as he did, for a framework to hold the music sounded as conventional analysis would use a score, with its numbered measures and alphabetical sections. I got something similar to his results: a left-hand column of seemingly arbitrary stopwatch times marking descriptions in a right-hand column of half-composed/orchestrated, half-improvised events.

What drew me into those results further was the left more than the right side. Noll's (1977) work, a decade older than Jost's, spoke most to that. He is one of many music scholars who draw on the German phenomenologists for methodological tools to add to their own kits.[7] Treating the recording as the twentieth century's new "score" to be explained, Noll applied phenomenology's founder Edmund Husserl's depiction of time to the real-time phenomenon of an unscripted musical event. This construct immediately reminded me of the experience of the Cecil Taylor performance described above:

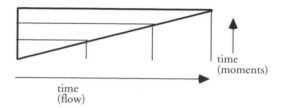

time
(moments)

time
(flow)

Fig. 6.1   Husserl's schema of time flowing into the moments of memory.

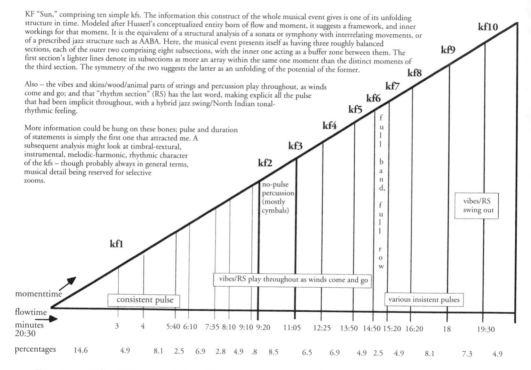

KF "Sun," comprising ten simple kfs. The information this construct of the whole musical event gives is one of its unfolding structure in time. Modeled after Husserl's conceptualized entity born of flow and moment, it suggests a framework, and inner workings for that moment. It is the equivalent of a structural analysis of a sonata or symphony with interrelating movements, or of a prescribed jazz structure such as AABA. Here, the musical event presents itself as having three roughly balanced sections, each of the outer two comprising eight subsections, with the inner one acting as a buffer zone between them. The first section's lighter lines denote its subsections as more an array within the same one moment than the distinct moments of the third section. The symmetry of the two suggests the latter as an unfolding of the potential of the former.

Also – the vibes and skins/wood/animal parts of strings and percussion play throughout, as winds come and go; and that "rhythm section" (RS) has the last word, making explicit all the pulse that had been implicit throughout, with a hybrid jazz swing/North Indian tonal-rhythmic feeling.

More information could be hung on these bones; pulse and duration of statements is simply the first one that attracted me. A subsequent analysis might look at timbral-textural, instrumental, melodic-harmonic, rhythmic character of the kfs – though probably always in general terms, musical detail being reserved for selective zooms.

kf10

kf9

kf8

kf7

kf6

kf5

f
u
l
l

b
a
n
d,

f
u
l
l

r
o
w

kf4

kf3

kf2

no-pulse
percussion
(mostly
cymbals)

vibes/RS
swing out

kf1

vibes/RS play throughout as winds come and go

momenttime

flowtime

consistent pulse

various insistent pulses

minutes
20:30

| | 3 | 4 | 5:40 | 6:10 | 7:35 | 8:10 | 9:10 | 9:20 | 11:05 | 12:25 | 13:50 | 14:50 | 15:20 | 16:20 | 18 | 19:30 |

percentages   14.6   4.9   8.1   2.5   6.9   2.8 4.9 .8 8.5   6.5   6.9   4.9 2.5 4.9   8.1   7.3   4.9

Fig. 6.2   The KF comprising kfs, my construct built from the analytical writings of Jost (1987) and Noll (1977).

   Husserl was trying to capture the experience of time passing in consciousness, from moment to moment, layering in memory; Noll put the musical information he wished to convey in a similarly growing triangle of nested moments. He called the whole a complex sound surface (*Klangfläche – KF*), and each of the single "moments" it comprised a simple one (*kf*). He described each of the latter with various graphic and verbal shorthands of their musical attributes (timbre, rhythm, volume, style, etc.)

   I altered this to have it frame "Sun." I preferred the triangle implied by its undershadow, with the moments marked by vertical rather than horizontal lines, for its more definite contrast between time both flowing (on the X axis) and stand-ing (on the Y) in a moment.[8] The result I got clearly revealed the mystery of the musical timescape. The points of interest here are immediately apparent to the eye, and confirmed by the percentage numbers. The vertical divisions – subdivisions in kf1, thus light lines; major divisions around kf2, thus heaviest; and the regular divisions of a succession of similar, separate kfs (3–10), with the normal lines – signal time windows mostly very similar in duration, with occasional halv-ings. Most fascinating, some proportions repeat virtually exactly (the 4.9s and 2.5s, which recur regularly throughout; and the 6.9, in the fifth part of kf1 and in kf4).

Without trying to parse and ponder too much, one can see at a glance that pat-terns are occurring of the sort that composers typically design and orchestrate, yet they are unfolding on the fly, unprescribed. Relationships between the similar and proportional time-windows suggest themselves in their very recurrence, and their placement within the flow. The first and longest section has the look of an intro-duction, the 4.9 has the look of a major motif, the 2.5 of a submotif, the 6.9 of a second theme, and so on.[9]

The unifying framework of the complex KF is drawn from the personal/col-lective body's own unprescribed, unconsciously willed order; it couches both its more and its less prescribed, consciously willed designs. Before focusing on exam-ples of those two aspects of the musical information in this framework, it is nec-essary to recognize that we are projecting this order onto a chaos, as well as divining it therein. The precise time demarcations have a margin of error like that of an opinion poll, because while some sections do indeed begin or end with the precise attack of a moment in time, most occur more gradually. That wiggle room is small enough to preserve an overall design the music verifies, but large enough to make the analyst more a co-creator than a mere transcriber of the event. It is a more, not a less, mysterious order if it emanates from the analyst as much as from the music.

This ambiguity polarizes when we zoom in from the complex to its simple com-ponents. On one pole, conventional analysis does best address certain aspects of the music; on the other, the analyst's co-creator role takes on even more authority. For an example of the former, fig. 6.3 transcribes the recurring appear-ance of the *Rohrglockenspiel* spelling out various clusters of non-repeating pitches, punctuated by the last such statement by unison winds, in kf7. The pitches decrease in number until just before the cymbal solo of kf2, and resume their growing trend until the end, when the wind instruments play a row just one pitch (G-flat, the C major's tritone, dead center of its octave) shy of the full chromatic scale. That is certainly there for every ear to hear, and here for every eye.

Like the timeline, this framework too reflects an order in the music not imme-diately discernible to the listening ear. It is also as clearly both as unambiguous and determined as the timeline was the opposite. The question the timeline raised about itself – is it a projection or a revelation of order? – is definitely answered here by the latter option.

But what if I add to this data a suggestion of meaning that is not there, yet also

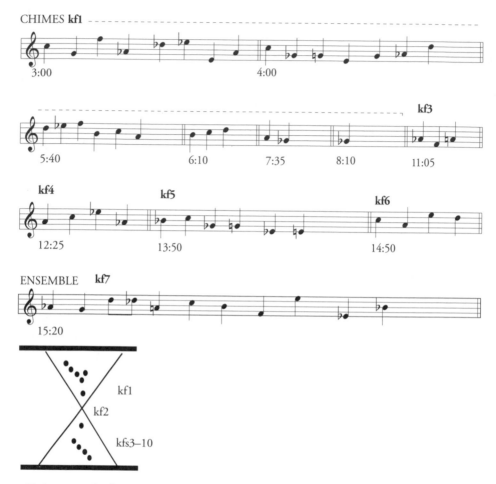

Pitches as sands of cosmic time
flowing through the no-time
point of percussion
leading to the biological time of
breathing beings (wind players)
who can only bear its flow for the
moment of life.

Fig. 6.3   This series of non-repeating pitches decreases in number by the end of kf1 until, at kf2, all pulse disappears. It picks up again at kf3 and builds to a full chromatic row stated by the full ensemble, in kf7.

not inconsistent with the logic of what is there? For example, what if I assert that the statement of all twelve pitches in the chromatic scale would have been tantamount to the death resulting in the utterance of the name of G-d (to again borrow from Hebrew theology)? Or that the deep chimes sounding them are Europe's cathedral and church bells ringing through its history and lands? What if I assert that metal sounds as metal is (that hard, cold, dead stuff of earth we mine and smelt and forge, into the wires of musical strings and the shapes of musical sound-makers), that wind sounds as wind is (something more organically us, alive in our breath, something we also catch and harness, in the air, differently)?

When we start talking like this about the simple data of fig. 6.3, we read a meaning into music beyond the physical mechanics of its vibrations, waves, and acoustics. We also come down on the projection side of the projection-vs.-revelation question raised by the timeline's elegant design. Yes, our reading may qualify as rational revelation, but clearly it is not the only one possible, and is rather one from an infinite number possible that we could choose. Which begs the next question: what is the place of such projection in our analysis?

Conscious or not, such projections already have a place in music scholarship, from its beginnings. We have seen them here, in the Greek association of modes and instruments with psychological and geographical states and social forces, in Western scholasticism's associations of pitches and meters with social and theological dynamics. We have seen them in the hermeneutical readings of historical Western music done by the "new" musicologists, the occult readings done by "speculative" musicologists, and the political and cultural readings done by comparative musicologists and their Communist and Nazi versions.

My experiences as a musician, as much as my studies of and interviews with others, have forced me to accept responsibility for this inescapable process of projection. I know the music is not generated in a vacuum of meaning, out of a sheerly physical talent on an instrument, or a blind affinity for a genre, or a genius for system-building. Each piece, session, rehearsal, event, gesture of music has a personal and transpersonal mythos it voices, has forces and ideas it sounds. Conventional transcriptions such as fig. 6.3 give us more detail than the skeletal ambiguity of fig. 6.2, but they don't put all the flesh on those bones.

The next step in developing our analysis is through the work of American musicologist Lawrence Ferrara (1991). The hallmark of his "eclectic method" of musical analysis is the use of different analytical approaches to address different aspects of a single musical event. Its ten steps are characterized by "open listenings" for each aspect, some of which are not rationally or objectively quantifiable. One is for emotional affect, and one calls on the analyst to summarize the assemblage of all musical components with a description of his own making, using his creative imagination. The analyst must do what Ferrara calls "divination"; or, as he also writes, "the analyst is a related or corresponding [to the artist] genius" (94). This open acknowledgment of subjective emotions and metaphorical imagination in musical analysis opens the door to music scholarship as a literary genre as much as to the branch of hard and soft science writing, via acoustics and anthropology, it has become.

Given all this, it is axiomatic that all analyses and theories devised with this approach are as arbitrary and authoritative at once as is the music itself (recall Dean's request for analyses to reveal rather than prove something). Things about the music are revealed in one of an infinite variety of possible ways, just as the musical event is one of an infinite variety of expressions that could have been made (Dean also corroborates this, when he notes that most music carries more information than is processed cognitively by either listeners or players, and that analysis should focus on the information so processed). Of course, each improvisation is different; likewise, it should be understood that each analysis of the same recorded event is only one of many possible from a succession of listenings.

In addition, the surface and the whole are conceived here as the primary focus, its components (of pitch or rhythmic patterns, or any other such material details) secondary. This is a return to the wholeness (Holy) of Heraclitus that preceded the (Religious) rationales of Plato, Aristotle, Augustine, and Boethius. It is a reversal of both Schenker and pitch-class theorists, who start from a detailed surface expression and purport to unearth underlying schemes that generate its various patterns. Thus (per phenomenology) the exoteric sound in time stands as primary reality, not a derivative and a veiling of a hidden esoteric reality. When we see the astonishing symmetries and balances of durations of musical statements in the kf's of our examples, we are seeing something that unfolded spontaneously from an organism's unconscious biology as much as or more than from its conscious cultural or mental maps of aesthetic truths. Whatever aesthetic or philosophical meaning these musical events have is thus ascribed to them after their facts, not prescribed by that meaning. Again, this brings the analyst/theorist – the audience, for that matter – into full participation with the player in the act of musication, rather than to the subservience of passive aspirant to, or parasitic explainer of, the esoteric knowledge.

The figures above include allusions to my own such projections of myth onto the music's rationalized patterns: the caption for fig. 6.2 contrasts the constant presence of non-wind with the transience of wind instruments, setting up a point about life and death; a similar image is evoked with the hour-glass and its caption in fig. 6.3, adding the dimension of time to said life and death. Indeed, "the compleat analysis" may come, as this approach flowers to its full potential, to require a mythologization, along with a rationalization, of the musical material. Scholarly rigor, responsibility, competence, and elegance may then be redefined to meet standards applied to artists, as well as conventional analysis's more "scientific" criteria. If such were applied to me here, I might respond that von Schlippenbach did not call his piece "Time," but I called time my sun, and I used his "Sun" to demonstrate that, without distorting or violating his work in any way, but, on the contrary, by revealing something in it that I would bet money he would like to know about himself.

In conclusion, the analytical work of Braxton (1985, 1988), Wadada Leo Smith (1995), and others in the tradition of composers and improvisers who devise verbal (albeit often more poetic than "scientific") rationales for their own works, methods, and systems (for example, John Cage, Harry Partch, Jin Hi Kim) serve as examples of the artists meeting the scholars halfway, in that same arena of "genius" Ferrara exhorts analysts to share with them, only from their other direction. As the academic comfort zone expands from its hard- and soft-scientistic base in the way suggested here, the creative artists around whom the rational scholars build their careers may be pulled into that zone with them, and out of the garrets and gilded cages that stand amidst our lovely ivory towers.

Theory: The Music's Sophos

Improvisation's postwar moves away from the Western compositional paradigm unfolded in discrete steps and stages prior to the American free-jazz movement and its later European echoes. Each such step was often through freedom from first one then another musical principle or practice, and often that in the evolution of a single artist's work. As improvisation progressed so from freedom to freedom, its journey increasingly raised the sheerly musical questions of what "free" really meant, for both improvisation and composition. If improvisation is indeed something for which nothing is provided (per citation opening chapter one) – the "unforeseen" – why is it so overwhelmingly practiced historically, even in jazz, as invention of variations on prescribed themes, by prescribed rules? If it is, rather, always reactive to and shaped by such prescriptions, how is it the "generative force" Derek Bailey called it? And if it is that, the autonomous and definitive ground of all (by implication, then, derivative) composition, why has composition been seen as a step up from it – its refinement, its fulfillment as a potential – in terms of aesthetic and social value? What is the difference, if any, between "free" improvisation and "free" (meaning "experimental" or "nonidiomatic") composition? Finally, if Western music (including jazz, I would add) was indeed based on written tradition until the 1960s (per Benítez [1986], same first-chapter citations), what is all of that we call "improvisation" in earlier Western music, and in pre-free jazz? That is, if it is not what chapter one's opening citations call it, and is rather some derivative or precursive stage of composition, what exactly is its nature?

The sample analysis above begins to answer those questions. At first glance, fig. 6.3 seems to reveal a *logos* at the root of the autonomically improvising body itself, not one imposed on it by the consciously rational mind. The analysis graphed by both figs 6.2 and 6.3 having teased out the rational and the mythical in their Erotic balance (neither improvisation nor composition enslaves the other), we can begin to identify improvisation on its own terms. A scan of that scholarship on improvisation that Dean called "in its infancy" suggests three kinds of freedom in free improvisation: freedom-from, freedom-to, and freedom-in.[10] Freedom-from is reactive, the starting point: rules and conventions once embraced as laws are stretched, challenged, broken. Freedom-to is proactive, the next step: rules, patterns, conventions – from other genres, traditions, systems, of both cultural and personally idiosyncratic origin – are embraced as gameplans and playbooks, mutable and contingent, more than as absolute laws. Finally, freedom-in is "autactive," the consummate stage: one path is chosen from among all possible, and its route, uncharted from without, has nonetheless imprinted its own order on the improvising body as a law unto itself. The process has gone full circle, mutability and contingency go away, the player is back in passive enthrallment to a (new) order that will come in its turn to be so challenged and changed.

Less abstractly, think of the process of inventing then learning to ride a bicycle. It begins by asserting freedom from the limitations of the walking body; it develops by asserting freedom (of access) to the wheel, and to a new way to conceive and use it; it ends in the construct of the bicycle and the mastery of its use, a freedom in motion that becomes automatic and unconscious, after the consciously willed trials and errors of the first two freedoms. It is on that then mentally effortless but physically taxing bicycle ride that one begins to dream of inventing the automobile . . .

None of these three kinds of freedom was new to Western music or jazz history, but all were arguably more problematic in the America that spawned them than in Europe. When we say "free improvisation," we usually mean freedom from form: no notated or mental map, no gameplan or rules – unscripted, spontaneous musication. The quick and dirty implication behind this idea is of a blank slate of consciousness ignited by the creative spark of genius, a mystery and life force born and/or breaking free of all cultural conditioning, and living in that freedom perpetually. Form then emerges from the inside out of that body uncoerced and unconditioned, rather than from an abstract imposed from the top down and/or outside in.

That picture fits the etymology of "improvisation," but few noteworthy examples of the musical process it refers to. First, starting with post-Baroque improvisation in Western music before the nineteenth century, we see a body's mastery of and integration with a tradition's system, mythos, rules, and conventions that is so thorough and deep as to leave behind all suggestion of an actor performing a script. What Schenker and other classicists would call a "fantasy," or a "free composition," is the fruit of such freedom, as are the keyboard improvisations of the Bachs, Mozart, and Beethoven. This embodiment of a paradigm is actually freedom in, not from, form – something akin to the body's match between its own genetic hardwiring and a given language's rules of grammar.

The history surveyed by the contributors to Wolbert (1997) of Europe's influences on American jazz and jazz's subsequent scenes in Europe, occupies roughly the same time period of the waning of such freedom in form in improvisation and the waxing of it in composition in European musical practice and pedagogy (the art of composition might be said to have freed itself from the vagaries and ambiguities of improvisation by seizing total control). Moore (1992) attributes the decline of improvisation in Western art music to dynamics of class largely unmentioned (owing, he suggests, to self-interest) in conventional musicology. He reminds us of the prevalence of improvisation as a crucial driving force in the Western music tradition up to the middle of the nineteenth century. He notes that improvisatory traditions are typically built on the foundation of preceding musical styles everyone understands (which includes an understanding of what to avoid in improvisations, as clichéd, tasteless, or uninventive).

Improvisation qua improvisation, therefore, is not a universal way for musicians from various situations to collaborate, any more than mastery of one language equals mastery of another. The master improvisers/composers of Western art music were so because they were comfortable and proficient in that court tradition; with the fall of the aristocracy and rise of the bourgeoisie came a view of Western culture as something to be enshrined, codified, preserved, promoted, and disseminated – the view of usurpers who had been excluded from it, saw it as the embodiment of power and nobility (the Big House), thus tried to save it, even while revolting against its masters. This, naturally, was not an impulse born of a secure grasp of the musical/cultural "language," nor an internalization of it conducive to "free" (original, creative, within mastery) improvisations on it. Modern music pedagogy sprang from this impulse – overly rigid and regulated "conservatories," too much reliance on notation and a general contextualizing of the tradition as a genre loaded down with cultural associations of "high" as opposed to "low."

Relevant here is Moore's mention of this pedagogical movement, which virtually defined nineteenth-century American music culture, as almost exclusively German. A newly wealthy class of burghers, taking their cue from intelligentsia such as Goethe, Schiller, and others, made it their mission to "save" aristocratic musical standards from collapse (remember, Germany's own aristocracy held out, with the burghers' support, against the democratic reform movements begun in Europe two centuries ago). Civic-minded societies were formed, the music was taught as *the* music, not with the curiosity and openness to other musics natural to people secure in their own, but with the siege mentality of those whose grasp tightens from lacking firmness. Folk and popular musics – also widely improvised on, yet largely immune to this cultural shift – were disdained as "low" by people who previously took unselfconscious pleasure in them. Thus, to an unprecedented degree, the musical experience became either too high or too low for the majority of people in the culture to comfortably enjoy.

Much of this phenomenon can be seen in the history of jazz in both the United States and Europe. The whole idea of the "classicization" of jazz has been problematic. Born out of an understandable human need for support and respect, as well as for contact and relationship with "the other" (whatever the power roles), it nonetheless threatens to deny an even stronger need to "musick" (per Small [1987]) in a natural and organically evolving way, free of coercively imposed conditions and expectations irrelevant and foreign to that process.

Moore casts improvisation as the heart of this process, and depicts a West in conflict about it, a conflict not even two centuries old, but one expressed in life-or-death terms, especially in Germany. Jazz was welcomed (though by no means by all) in the Weimar, then persecuted in the Nazi years – and out of both situations sprang "jazz societies," civic-minded associations with a mission to codify, canonize, preserve, and promulgate "the real music," often authenticated through a certifiably African-American origin as much as through musical elements such as "swing" and "hot." The result was, just as with the Western court-music tradition in the hands of the bourgeoisie, a culture prone to derivativeness and sycophancy (along with its other face, condescension and control) vis-à-vis the "geniuses" who made its music. This is what the *Emanzipation* players lashed out at with the emergence of their own musical identities and languages, within which they could both compose and improvise. This is also part of what their African-American predecessors had lashed out at in their own country, this (basically German) burgherization of music that appropriated real human being as something that should and must be (that can be) commodified and controlled, as "naturally" as aestheticized.

Moore's history reminds us that the conflict in jazz history is not between racially essentialized cultures so much as between a given social group and those voices of its own – prophets, shamans, creative artists – that they do not know whether to love or hate, reward or kill. That it has looked so much like the first in America stems from the racial demographic of jazz – an African-American phenomenon reaching from its beginning beyond its culture of origin to the European-American mainstream, then to the larger international arena, in each arena the same prophetic voice – which has distinguished itself not for its reintroduction of improvisation to the so-called "low" culture of its folk and popular origins (both white and black) so much as to the so-called "high" (white) culture where improvisation had died. In the process, it has continually had to shake off the impulses of that "high" culture to appropriate it as the next "classical" art form – impulses that are as internal as external to the music-making community itself, again, for deep and understandable human reasons.

Over the time Moore surveys, the notational aids that came to serve improvisation in jazz were essentially updates of those for the Baroque improviser, indicating root tones of chords (figured bass) with alphanumerics to convey their configurations and voicings, along with a melody line. The difference in the improvisational practices of the two times and places, of course, lay in the area of mythos, or identity: the improvisations of pre-jazz European masters affirmed their identity and that of their cultures, and the integrity of their composition (high, court, and church) tradition, expanding it from within. Composition was not qualitatively different from improvisation; one played spontaneously or wrote deliberately by the same rules, to the same ends, and one often composed loosely, to greater or lesser degrees, for improvisers, sketching the barest musical bones to be fleshed out in performance. Even when innovations came from the bottom up, through medieval secular, or Protestant choral, or Renaissance dance, or Romantic folk music, the classist hierarchy inscribed in the music, whether composed or improvised, remained intact in one form or another. Indeed, it is precisely why the high tradition was so "free" in its form, whether improvising or composing: it suffered no real challenges to its premises from (the less free) below, was rather supported and fueled thereby.

The nature of improvisation in jazz, while methodically similar to that, was not the same freedom in form – African-American players did not step right into the ongoing musical discourse as if to the manor born, to be welcomed, recognized, accommodated by the manor's lords – but neither was it the pure freedom from form that racially, culturally, or personally essentialist or exceptionalist readings would imply. Insofar as it was, like rhythm, a peculiarly African-American cultural process, it developed dialectically with Western composition as a challenge to the latter's musical premises, cultural mythos, and potential for self-expression. From J. R. Europe's stated intentions for improvisation as a vehicle (among others) for the development of African-American identity, to the first New Orleans gestures both "hot" and "legit" to the bands of Fletcher Henderson, Duke Ellington, Count Basie, and others, through the bop years up to those of Charles Mingus and Sun Ra, the development of the art of improvisation to and through ever greater "freedoms" was crucial to the forging of a new identity not only in but also for and of that music. That identity was increasingly informed by musical elements brought in from outside the West, elements implicating Western fundamentals as often as it ornamentally spiced them. While as vital to the arts of composing and orchestrating as it had been to earlier Western music, improvisation in jazz was imbued with a much more urgent task. Not only were Africans brought to America outsiders by virtue of African roots and slavery, they continued to be so in the other ways well documented throughout the twentieth century by black scholars and literati. This "double soul" (per Du Bois) shaped their own identity as Americans, as Westerners, at the culture's core of labor, *de jure* citizenship, language, history (over time), and musical material.

In acknowledging that African-American freedom, whatever the mastery behind it, was thus not the same freedom in in the Western paradigm as it had been for Europeans themselves, and that it was indeed freedom from more and more of that, we are faced with the question of what it has exercised its own freedom in, and whether that is something as rich and potent as that which it was freeing itself from. In part, that "something" consisted of traceable African retentions, and new African-American inventions[11] – but jazz was not the meeting of two or more equally distinct, conscious, and potent cultures exchanging their information. How, after generations of slavery and loss of original roots, then of struggle as an underclass, did this thing called "improvisation" lead to an access to the Western soul with such power and genius? How did it move the West in its turn to so much deep love and hate, beyond rational and even conscious design? Not for its clever expression of ethnic identity or local culture, nor even for its human edge of suffering and need (supplicants begging entrance, souls demanding expression), but above all for the ways it grasped, fulfilled and expanded the heart of the Western soul and mythos itself, of freedom as Eros rather than War, of rule as self-rule and Golden Rule.

The same questions can be asked about European Americans and Europeans. Starting with the Original Dixieland Jazzband and going down the line from Paul Whiteman, Bix Beiderbecke, Benny Goodman and his peers, to Stan Kenton, and the West Coast and Cool players, what distinguished their handling of the same musical process of "improvisation" from that of their African-American mentors and peers? What led to a thing called a "cool," "white" sound in the same music, and why? What constitutes its derivative position in so much of the American history and historiography of the music, and why?

Though such questions gnaw at the bones of the obvious, they point out some things about the development of the music scenes just prior to the free-jazz movement, first on one, then on the other side of the Atlantic. First, the freedom in form of the European post-Baroque improvisers was, indeed, a freedom informed by something; it was not improvisation as defined etymologically, something "unforeseen." It was no more or less mysterious a process than learning to ride a bicycle, wherein one becomes unconscious of all the necessary skills as one's body makes them automatic. Second, the freedom *from* the formal conventions of Western music, the liberties taken by African-American composers and performers, always combined with such freedom *in* those conventions, with Western rules governing the liberties of whatever their bodies had made, and continued to make, automatic-somatic in their histories and lives outside the Western cosmos.

The point here, again, is that "improvisation" is a misnomer. Something was being provided, from the two sources of European and African cultures and their manifold personal expressions in America, which the players/composers then "put together" as American, in sound, on paper. This "improvisation" is really more a composition, etymologically speaking: a "putting-together" in negotiation of two bodies of information (the traditional and something else) equal in nature and potency and definition. Freedom in and freedom from form are not so much fusion or separation of a thing called contents with or from a thing called form as they are strategies of the body to mine itself and its world. Both are Rohrshach-like tests that reveal a given body's desires, designs, even demises. An "improviser" either demonstrates immediate command of something provided, or demonstrates a freedom from that provision that is mediated by that "something else" that has been provided – or, in synthesis, demonstrates both.

My suggestion is that this is how one might explain the history of improvisation in jazz in terms of the ongoing history of composition in the West. This suggestion, however, leaves hanging for now the question of what exactly is that "something else" that "improvisation," if it truly is "composition," "puts together" with the traditional material. If it is not a derivation of a definitive, what is its own corresponding definition? If, in jazz, it is more than African retentions or African-American inventions, if it is rather a fountain of new patterns and concepts that match or counter in kind the literized concretes of the Western paradigm, what is that "more?"

As for the freedom to form signaled by the Third Stream and world-music gestures – the simple access by one body of information to another – if we do see the arts of composition and improvisation as two equal aspects of the same one music, each aspect capable of freedom both *in* and *from* itself and the other, we already grant each freedom *to* the other. Composers have unlimited access to the "improvised" bodies of information, and improvisers to the "composed." Again, provisions abound, nothing is really unforeseen, *tabula rasa*, or *ex nihilo* (which is not to say all is conscious and rational, and nothing mysterious). Recall Chailley's chart: the rational emerges from, adds to, retains the primal, it does not erase or suppress it, at least in principle, and it does revert to it. As straightforward and logical as all this reads in the abstract, its place in the music's history has been problematic all along.

Freedom-in would seem to be the least problematic – clear mastery of clear conventions, challenging no fundamentals, fulfilling their potential in new ways. But think of the examples of some who achieve it but go unrecognized, at least at first. Thelonious Monk and Herbie Nichols, Litweiler's two examples of fertile precursors and harbingers of the new "freedom principle" in the music, are classic examples of such difficulty, common to all the arts and letters in all times and places. The objective musical traits of each player did not demonstrate the "freedom principle" so much as did the centralization itself of their "originality" and "genius," their creative authorities as subjects. But such self-assertions of subjectivity, of idiosyncrasy, were not as valuable, for the most part, at first, in American as they were in European eyes (both, especially Monk, were particularly strong influences on the *Emanzipation* players). Similarly, Arnold Schoenberg and even J. S. Bach were two paragons of freedom in form whose reception and impact at the moments of their boldest reaches were nowhere near as great as later.

Likewise, experiments in freedom-from, from the first improvised "hot" breaks (cadenzas, recitatives) of early jazz to the open-ended, unscripted improvisations of Tristano, Jimmy Giuffre, Ra, or Mingus, in the 1950s, were objects of esoteric interest, even obsessive fascination, but also marginal, hardly acclaimed as bellwethers of "the shape of jazz to come" that they later became in Ornette Coleman and others. Improvisation was always more generally seen as the "outside" to composition's "inside"; the more brilliant and powerful and inexhaustible the improvisations of a Charlie Parker or a Sonny Rollins, the more their compositional constraints hung like straitjackets on their bodies of work (the constraints free jazz had to rip off). But the initial forays away from those constraints served only to show how internalized they had become. Tristano, as Jost pointed out (1974: 41), was doing little more than demonstrating his command of Western counterpoint and line construction, and bop masters such as Parker and Rollins were only showing how thoroughly they too had internalized the Western paradigm, and how competently (freely) they could re-voice and re-spin it. Conversely, shaking off the constraints also showed how much at sea, or limited, players might be without them. Mingus mostly balked at freedom as such a "principle," despite his seminal explorations; and Tristano did not make it his new-and-improved standard. Formal constraints and conventions can be hidden behind, can both milk and measure inspiration when it is either lacking or raging destructively out of control.

Freedom-to, in the light of these initial aversions to chaos, stasis, and subjectivity, would seem to have been the least controversial approach to exploration and growth, as well as the most tried and true. Although marriages of "jazz" and "classical" music, as also of jazz and various "world musics," have often been dismissed as misbegotten experiments in both musical and social hybridity, from Duke Ellington to the Modern Jazz Quartet to Anthony Braxton, they have been at the core of jazz's history all along.[12] But again, specifically to these decades, while the Third Stream movement excited some circles, it was generally received as a suggestive but awkward match, especially in the wake of the more fruitful experiments of modalism and free jazz to come. It presumed, one might say, the situation of Baroque improvisation/composition as sketched above, wherein the identity of the music was clear, uncontested, and unabashedly hierarchical in certain viable ways.

The points to glean from this sketch of the American scene just prior to the free-jazz years revolve around the ways these particular freedoms played out less problematically in Europe. Monk's harmonic and rhythmic mastery of European cabaret fare stumped American, even African-American, enthusiasts of bebop, but it inspired viscerally and decisively the European imitators of American jazz to "do their own thing."[13] Europeans saw in Monk's mastery and subjectivity not the bizarre eccentricities of blackness signifying on whiteness so much as the freedom in form they knew well from the examples of songwriters such as Hanns Eisler and Kurt Weill, of French *chanson*, of Dutch and English folk song, of the craft of both music hall and conservatory (not to mention the nineteenth-century Romantic-musical roots of them all). Monk was a major influence on the early work of the *Emanzipators* (especially Günter Hampel, Alexander von Schlippenbach, and Misha Mengelberg) for suggesting to them the possibilities of forging their own different idiosyncracies (and it is noteworthy too that the European-American who most championed Monk early on, Steve Lacy, would find more acceptance of his own work in Europe).

Moreover, the prospect of "doing their own thing" promised the recognition and affirmation of a domestic (prior to an international) audience that welcomed a distinctly European identity over a secondhand American one. This, in stark contrast to the resistance and neglect with which an American mainstream, including its successfully integrated black currents, continually greeted each new reach for both Western/American potential and black identity therein. Monk is in the tradition of art for art's sake, pure music, far from commercial popularity, thus closer to European "amateurism" (the labor of love superior, not inferior, to [crass] "professionalism") than many more popular American jazz artists.

Freedom from form was similarly less unsettling and more promising in Europe. By this time, Europeans had two historical experiences that somewhat paralleled the African-American ones of loss of original culture and adaptation to new one: they had self-destructed as world powers in their battles with each other and America, and had been reorganized under the American shadow. Like African Americans, when they turned to "free improvisation" to "signify" on their own history and their new present, they were drawing on internal and external ruins and rubble that still carried much information, and on new reconstructions of it they could cooperate with, if not carry off alone. The dialectic of old composition and new improvisation was not one of two contestants for political power or cultural cachet, as in America, in which the freedom from one by the other suggested barbaric anarchy, on the one hand, or oppressive tyranny, on the other. Freedom-from in the European context rather promised, simply, freedom from the tyranny of composition and composer – which tyranny improvisation and improviser also constitute when reified, as Europeans had done with their American models – and restoration of the self-determination, in new form, that they once had enjoyed as improvisers in their own pre-nineteenth-century practice.

Finally, the freedom to each other posited by the Third Stream's constituents of jazz and Western art music in America had a deeper and more organic counterpart in Europe. The American movement came under most fire from parties invested in keeping African-American identity sequestered idiomatically in "jazz" and "improvisation," European-American in "classical" and "composed" (whether "serious" or "popular"), and the two segregated in classist-racist intellectual hierarchy, exceptions proving the rules. Or, conversely, it was rejected for its perceived paternalistic "jazz uplift" agenda. While there were similarly superficial hybrids in Europe, their implication there was more of a homogeneous group playing around with its own cultural categories. Europe's jazz and contemporary art music were two musical discourses by the same people, players and composers usually trained in the same conservatories – divided somewhat, sometimes, by generation, politics, class, and nationality, but sharing much more undivided common histories and identities than blacks and whites owned up to in America. European classical and jazz musicians had always been interested in each other, for the most part, and when the winds of history nudged them together more than apart, they found chemistry where Americans found awkwardness and conflict.

Theory: The Music's Archē

An overarching theme of this study has been that the free-jazz decades (the 1950s to 1980s, roughly, unfolding from West to East in northern latitudes) saw both a radical deconstruction of 2000 years of Western music history and a recapitulation of many similar clashes between the West and the world, and with itself, throughout those millennia. The following sketch of that history (table 6.1), with just a page or two of explanation, will give context to the analytical abstracts and their points above in their real-world sites of culture, history, and brain.

Taken together, the middle columns (not in bold) explain the one history from Rome's first encounters with the Germanic tribes through the process of their assimilation into Mediterranean civilization, to the rise of their own Western civilization and its spread to Russia and America, with Slavic and African slaves. The narrative implied by the left–right dynamic of each coupling, and the juxtaposition of all, is that the order and power of civilization and rationality lay on the right, the challenges to it by other orders and powers on the left, and right ruled left by a mix of force, persuasion, and compromise, and occasional capitulations and changes of its order (but not its power).

The outer columns show less historical, more varied couplings of facts and ideas. With the two parenthesized sources (Attali and Hall) on the right, the other asides (racist, sexist, and so on) signal the mindset behind the coupling; thus "black" is

Table 6.1   Western music history at a poststructuralist (and conflationary) glance.

the Holy	tumbling strain	one-step melody (Sachs)	Religion
Dionysian	phrygian mode	dorian mode (McKinnon)	Apollonian
barbaric	Germanic *baritus*	Latin literature (Tacitus)	civilized
pagan eroticism	Greek *mousike*	Christian plainchant (McKinnon)	godly asceticism
northern Europe	Gallic chant	Old Roman/Gregorian (Treitler, Hiley)	Mediterranean
northern Europe	Gothic	Roman (Lang)	Mediterranean
northern Europe	Protestant	Catholic (Lang)	Mediterranean
northern Europe	Baroque	Classical (Lang)	Mediterranean
mythic/mystic, folk	Romanticism	Enlightenment	secular-rational, art music
black	Africa	Europe (Small, Baraka)	white (racist)
woman, youth	America/body	Europe/word (Mellers)	man, elder (sexist, patriarchal)
Carnival	jazz/hot	serial music/cool (Kumpf)	Lent (Attali)
rustic, body	oral	literate (Sidran)	cosmopolitan, mind (cultural/intellectual elitist)
limbic brain	improvised	composed (Bailey)	**reptile, and neocortical brains** (Hall)
	new-and-improvised-music global network	globalized music industry	

associated with "barbaric," "youth," "pagan" and all the other left-hand labels by the white racist mentality, and so on.

While most of these couplings are self-evident, it may seem counerintuituve to lump "Protestant" and the other "northern Europe" watchwords in with "pagan" and "barbaric," but in fact they were seen so by the "civilized" lights on the right when they emerged. The juxtapositions of the cultural and musical descriptors on the array tell their tale.

Tumbling Strains and One-Step Melodies

The bold cells flag special attention. The "tumbling strain" and "one-step melody," from Curt Sachs, serve as archetypes for these two faces of Western music history;

the "limbic" and "reptile/neocortical" brains, as Hall explains their musical implications, shed light on the human organism's source of those faces in culture. Much
of Sachs's work has been surpassed by subsequent better informed studies of the
various cultures he generalized from with less accurate information.[14] His discussion of tumbling strains and one-step melodies, however, stands the test of time,
and while it does not prove or disprove my own approach, it speaks suggestively
to it. It speaks especially to the reaches into mythico-historical musical paradigms
and images made by the various precursors and pioneers of the free-jazz movements in America and Europe, explaining much about the nature of their clashes
and syntheses of improvisation and composition in jazz and Western music
traditions.[15]

Sachs (1961) discusses the two musical approaches he found throughout the
tribal musics of the world:

> The most fascinating of the oldest melody patterns may be described as a "tum-
> bling strain." Its character is wild and violent: after a leap up to the highest
> available note in screaming fortissimo, the voice rattles down by jumps or steps
> or glides to a pianissimo respite on a couple of the lowest, almost inaudible
> notes; then, in a mighty leap, it resumes the highest note to repeat this cascade
> as often as necessary. In their most emotional and least "melodious" form, such
> strains recall nearly inhuman, savage shouts of joy or wails of rage and may
> derive from such unbridled outbursts . . . (51)

> Side by side with tumbling strains, we meet on the lowest cultural level an
> apparently less emotional type of melody, which in its most rudimentary form
> consists of only two pitches sung in alteration. The voice moves up and down
> and more or less describes a horizontal zigzag line . . . (59)

> Both horizontal and tumbling strains are often found within the same
> tribe and indeed within the same piece. This peaceful coexistence in so many
> cases forbids a separate attribution of either style to certain races or
> minor groups. Nor does it allow us to think of different layers of the Paleolithic.
> The way in which the two species mingle rather bares two different roots
> of singing, one derived from the violent howl, and the other, from recitation.
> (72)

Sachs details these two melody types with various examples from around the
world, arguing that they coexist in the same personal and social bodies because
they speak to different but complementary musical needs. The tumbling strain
images verticality, from a high to a low, sounding time's moment rather than its
flow. Its function is unbridled self-expression, emotional release, often the imitation of animal and other sounds from nature. It refines and formalizes itself by
contracting into cascades of thirds within the octave; indeed, it is characterized by
the octave as a working frame.

The one-step melody images rather the horizontal – the stability of culture
against nature's/time's torrential, kaleidoscopic flow – of a single, static pitch, then
another, each clearly defined and both as clearly redefined in their relationship.
It is a melody shaped by speech, by recitation of all that speech can convey,

including its own syntax and rules, and the communication of social information. "Unemotional" suggests that self-expression is not its primary function.

The two forms develop toward one another. Whereas, again, tumbling strains develop through contraction (of unpitched noise) into melodies within the octave formed with discrete intervals of thirds and fourths – leaps up and down, vertically – one-step melodies become more infused with the meaning and drama of their words as conveyed by the inflection, cadence, and meter that shapes syntax, the one step rather expanding to another, then into a sequencing and swelling of intervals not necessarily framed by the octave. When the forms meet and merge, they are the triadic meeting and merging with the diatonic.

Here are the prototypes not of contents (tumbling strain) reined in and perfected by form (one-step melody), but of two kinds of forms with contents. The octave is a physical, acoustic phenomenon, something with organic shape and proportion, manifest both inside and outside the body (the ear discerns, as a voice or string or column of air reveals, its definition); and the interval of the third, whatever meaning psyche or culture might divine in it, is similarly a distinct part of the overtone series, with unique vibrational character.

Speech, as much a neurologically hardwired as a mutable cultural pattern, is governed by a different, newer part of the brain than is music-making, and was carried beyond the body by literacy before music was.[16] The tendency of tumbling strains to formalize into octave-bound thirds might be thought of as a bottom-up assertion of nature into culture; the tendency of one-step melodies to chain and entrain themselves into music ranging free of those particular natural patterns might be seen as top-down moves by language to chain and entrain nature into new patterns – songs that may start out "unnatural," compared with the tumbling strain, but more culturally useful in some way (for example, work songs, religious or bardic chants, courtship or martial songs). Starting as an acquired taste, they enlist the body's natural desires and needs and potentials to their own designs, optimally through seduction, but optionally through force (of that part of the brain's will over one's body, and/or the bodies of others).

While it would be going too far to say that literacy (in print or electronic media) is a disembodied force with no biological ties or channels – it is generated and received by physical brains that are part of larger central nervous systems, some parts of them evolutionarily older than others – it is safe to say that literacy has come later than and out of orality in culture, rather than the other way around; has evolved to serve concepts of the transcendent and the abstract more effectively than those of the immanent and concrete, for which orality is better; and has served the agenda of power-over bodies more than orality has, insofar as civilizations have grown, and grown through, literacy. It is also obvious that literacy's relationship with music has called on the latter from beyond music's immediate physical location in the body/brain to serve literacy's agendas of speech and ratiocination, much as its part of the brain calls on the body's self-interested sexuality, work, play, and aggression to do the same.

If this sounds like an unhealthy dynamic, recall that, again, the body itself is a network of simple and complex systems, some more primal than others; it is often thus at odds with itself, and forced to resolve the conflict by constant negotiations that give first one then a conflicting need the upper hand, then both in balanced symbiosis or compromise. So too the social body; in Sachs's passages, the two approaches to music have the potential to cooperate with and shape as much as to clash with and manipulate each other. More precisely, power-over bodies typically impose their agendas on themselves as much as on others; they also have access to power-of techniques, to free themselves, with others, from their own repressions. Bodies oppressed, correlatively, collude in their own oppression, as well as resist it; and they likewise have access to power-over tactics when they want to rewrite the scripts governing their personal and social bodies.

Of all the Indo-European tribes that had moved from the Caucasian steppes into India, Europe, and both African and European sides of the Mediterranean, eventually merging with the indigenous peoples they conquered there, the most recent Germanic incursion via Scandinavia retained in northern Europe the original Aryan linguistic and cultural elements the longest; of those, the ones who settled in the northernmost lands retained them even longer, in their comparative isolation from the centers of southern culture. These elements, Sachs suggests, were more similar in fundamental ways to those in the African peoples south of the Mediterranean world than they were to the latter.

The implication of all this is that civilization – an abstract collective transcending, and coercing as much as seducing, its bodies – tended to develop through the one-step melody, the one allied with speech's forms and contents. One might call it the rise of the selfish meme (*pace* Richard Dawkins), challenging its partner the selfish gene – the partner singing in the tumbling strain its own self-sufficient emotions and life, its world's natural forces, its immanence in sex, aggression, the family-clan-tribe territory – for dominance in the game of culture-making. If this coup of meme over gene succeeds, it looks like this: the "high" music, shaped by and serving speech and the rational, lets the "low" music, shaped by and serving the whole body/nature, run on as it will (freely) until needed. High then conscripts low for high's needs, overrides low's autonomy, and nullifies it as a fellow generative form – treats it like contents in need of (high) form's governance.

That is the sense in which the tumbling strain is rendered "improvisation" by the one-step melody. The former's providential resources in nature, the body, the embodied brain, the physics of sound, are deemed as providing much animally but nothing humanly useful. They are seen as being themselves in need of high formal providence, of human validation by the abstracts of language divorced from the body immediate, language married rather to (embodied by) literate media. This is the picture of War between the two approaches, with the one-step melody dominating.

That hierarchy can be reversed to similarly demystify the word "composition." In fact, in the two inner columns of table 6.1, the right-hand column has not sustained an absolute power over the left one forever. Every revolution, negotiation, or victory through attrition that has installed a force on the left in some seat of power over that on the right is a picture of the tumbling strain's moment in the sun. Many such moments entail wholesale transfers of something from left to right column. Putting this axiom in our two musical terms, we can see composition as a mere mnemonic trigger, or suggestive abstract, of improvisation. Left to its own devices, it is meaningless intellectual doodling until conscripted by the living body's agendas of self-expression, defense, aggression, labor, procreation, and so on.

The point to this thought experiment (besides its evocations of some real historical patterns that pertain here) is to foreground what we call "improvisation" and "composition" as two similar and equal generative forces in the same one music, pushed to either complementary or conflicting roles, according to personal and social dynamics. What is conventionally called improvisation – creating music from paradigmatic, idiomatic norms and rules and materials – is the freedom in form, as defined above. It can reveal an artist's unique identity as well as its paradigm's abstract fulfilled, because it has successfully conscripted the artist's body. Within that body's unique identity, as in the mutations of a fruit fly, there may be some whorl of fingerprint that will then lead to changes in the blueprint.

Furthermore, what is more radically called improvisation – creating music from no such guidelines, spontaneously, interactively – is also still composing, "putting together" provisions organized by no mental map but certainly by mental mapping, and by physical organisms and artifacts, within both the body and its environment. This freedom from (disembodied, abstract) form serves two purposes: like freedom in, it reveals the artist's identity, but also the ways and degrees to which that identity has indeed internalized or eschewed blueprints, or is attracted to one rather than another natural affect or design. Tell one person to "just play" and the result will sound like a wounded rhino, maybe to a beat, maybe not; tell another the same thing, and he or she will produce a well-tempered string or cluster of notes Bach or Charlie Parker, or John Cage or Arnold Schoenberg might have written or played spontaneously. One of these might be the beginning of the next big public wave, the other something that had been the musical coin of the realm but is now privatized forever, to everyone's relief. The point is that neither would ever have seen the light of day if both players had gone through their days trying to repress such freedom in the service of some melting pot of conventional sound enlisting them both.

Freedom to form best describes the most fruitful and common "freedom" enjoyed between players and material in this age-old dialectic. At bottom, it is simply the healthy concourse between the two sides of the dyad, rather than their unhealthy mutual isolation, or domination of one by the other. It is their Eros rather than their War, and certainly shows itself in the examples of chapter five.

Brains Young and Old

We've touched on sexist, racist, and generational classism enough that the allusion to them in table 6.1 needs no further explanation. The other bold references, to the tripartite brain, come from out of the blue at this point. As applied to improvisation and composition by anthropologist Edward T. Hall, they enunciate here the biologic more fundamental than the sociologics of gender, race, or age to those musical issues in the cultural-historical terrain of table 6.1.

Hall's distance from the disciplines of music and musicology served him well as a guest lecturer of the Society for Ethnomusicology "illiterate in music, and even more important, ignorant of its situational dialects" (1992: 223). Music's three generative processes – performance, improvisation, composition – line up respectively with what Hall calls the reptilian, mammalian, and human brains. He is actually referring to the one tripartite human brain, with its reptilian, limbic, and neocortical layers, respectively. This is one of those examples of ontogeny recapitulating phylogeny, as reptiles are evolutionary older than and primal to mammals, and as mammals are so to humans.

Looking at improvisation (as opposed to the performance of scripted ritual) in culture, Hall says, "Seated in the old mammalian brain, improvisation is a process originating in play in mammals" (224). Noting that reptiles do not play, he writes "The limbic system is the center of emotions, parenting, social organization and play . . . And *play* is the device which not only permits all mammals to have fun, but gives them a means of mastering the skills needed for survival."[17]

To that linkage between neural and musical trinities, Hall adds another, between two other sets of three (modes of learning and levels of culture): culture is transmitted to succeeding generations via inherited, acquired, and learned knowledge of its formal, informal and technical levels, respectively. The formal is that which is defined, given, to be performed; it is inherited, inscribed on the body by rote memorization and practice, of religion, myth, ritual, convention. The technical is that which is rationalized in systems of number, notation, words – law, science, philosophy/theology, and so on. The informal is acquired, picked up by children through osmosis, as it were, from adults, the world, and each other. This is the mode and level to which Hall assigns improvisation, thus situating both as "rooted in an older part of the brain (the limbic system), rather than in the word- and number-based learning that is primarily processed in the left hemisphere of the neocortex" (225):

> improvisation appears to be more closely allied to acquisition than to learning, which is one reason why it has such an "individual" flavor. A fact that is frequently overlooked by those reared in North European cultures is the pervasiveness of rhythms, not only in nature but in the transactions between people in daily life. All of life, as well as what preceded life (if that distinction is valid) involves rhythms . . . In fact, life begins with rhythms. (227)

Hall sees childhood as the natural period for the flourishing of improvisation:

> Children before the age of six live in an acquired world and it is in the process of playing with the material of that world that they are able to master the unwritten, unspoken rules controlling their world. They go through a good deal

of improvisation, a process which we seem to lose until we have really mastered other systems as adults. Picasso's success as an artist was not due only to his great talent but to the fact that, like Mozart, he liked to play with his art. (226–7)

Sven-Åke Johansson offered one of many corroborations of this idea provided by masters of the improviser's art I have seen over the years (most famously, Miles Davis spoke to Quincy Troupe about it in regard to his musical bond with drummer Tony Williams).[18] Johansson told me that in thinking about my question of what his source of ideas or inspirations for compositions or improvisations was, he returned often to his youth, and that things took on a relevance in the improvisations as material.

> It's not so much like remembering as it is that they come out unconsciously. The conscious part lies in deciding from the infinity of possibilities – what do you do when, and why? when there's empty space, where do you go next? should the hand simply make its move? [He makes a gesture.] That's how most improvisation functions, most art, I would say – and very often it is a gesture one realizes one also spontaneously did quite often in one's youth, in play. Much of real value in the music world must come out of one's own inner resources, and I've found that much of that for me goes right back to my youth.

Interestingly, Johansson is the one of very few among our protagonists who has taken on language with the free improviser's mindset. Hall, citing linguist Charles Ferguson (1992: 226), puts language in the neocortex, but communication in the limbic brain: "Although it has been demonstrated that speech is centered in the left hemisphere of the neocortex, other communicative and adaptive behaviors are functionally related to the limbic system. In other words . . . communication in birds and mammals is centered in the limbic system, and is distinct from the left brain functions of speech" (226). This suggests that, like reptiles, humans qua humans, creatures of the neocortex, also do not play. Their limbic layer can use what their neocortex generates, namely words, but the intellection of sheerly cerebral mind (abstract system-building, Religion) is as cold and unfeeling as the rituals of survival (Eros and War) performed by the snake in the grass. When the neocortical and limbic brains are at War, systems coercively divide and contain the components of the whole (Holy), "form" tyrannizes "content," the word chokes the body, the "work" kills the play, in a single body and in a collective of bodies. When they are Erotically fused, the two brains are redeemed in symbiotic balance, power, and health.

This picture of maturity's (neocortical) Erotic fusion with its own (limbic) youth rebukes the Wars between old and young examined throughout this study. It also suggests itself as the ontological recapitulation of the phylogeny of a brain with evolutionary younger and older layers. Are those three layers at war within us, or are we governing their peaceful cooperation? Is, indeed, the war the agent of the peace (per the proper meaning of *jihad* as "spiritual struggle"), or its absolute enemy (per its connotations of "terrorism")? If the former, can we manage it consciously so as not to project it blindly; if the latter, which will prevail, and when, and why?

The questions, directed at each of us, go also to the cultures and societies we make. Are their three aspects of (evolutionary) *time* cohering and flowering Erotically, or is their War tearing their bodies and/or others down? Must youth kill its fathers to mature and live? Must those fathers then fear time, new life, as their death? Must the formal violently preserve itself against the unscripted play of the informal in a person or a collective, as if it were always reckless rather than also relevant, even redemptive? Must the technical (scientific, rational, religious, secular) be so feared by the informal (playful, irrational, magical) and the formal (holy, traditional, ritualistic), or must it leave them both behind as irrelevant or stifling?

Apropos of the free-jazz movement – which I have pictured here as having replaced harmonic-melodic with rhythmic-temporal motivic fields serving as matrices of potential for pitch-timbre expressions, and notable for its liberation of musical time from metered pulse to fields of duration – Hall traces the distinguishing factor between three neural/cultural layers to "studies of time as a nonverbal system of communication, conducted with George Trager, a well-known linguist. From the very beginning I have been deeply preoccupied with time as a basic archetypal manifestation of culture – an organizing system of behavior. Because time is a component of everything, I reasoned that it would be a good starting point for an analysis of culture" (1992: 227–8).

Hall's own anthropological studies have looked at the way different cultures experience and organize time. He speaks of his formal, informal, and technical categories as having either high or low contexts, "high" referring to communication in which so much is already assumed and shared that relatively little need be more than implied. Low contexts, by contrast, require much more information. Moving back to the relationship between music and language, he writes:

> It would seem that music is inherently higher in context than words and may even predate words in the history of our species. In the process of our shifting from musical communication produced by the vocal apparatus to words, because of lowered context, we lost some of the "music." There is no doubt that words are a cornerstone in the entire process of communicating in the Western world, *but are not nearly so important in high context Japan where they are distrusted.* (233, emphasis mine, invoking the many close West–East collaborations among the artists of our focus)

The Marriage of Former Rivals

Charles Mingus solicited Duke Ellington's opinion of the then "new thing" in jazz launched by Ornette Coleman's first recordings. Duke's answering question – "Do we really want to go back to something that primitive?" – reminded me of that phenomenon of innovations, often received and represented by the press and general public as "avant-garde," being in fact conceived by the musicians making them as reaches into some primal past, half historic, half mythic, as much as gestures looking forward in time. While it is true that we can impose an evolutionary teleology and timeline on some of the pairings in table 6.1 – for example, civilization obviously came after non-civilization in history, as did literacy after orality, composition after improvisation, Christian plainsong after Greek *mousike* and so on – it is even more true and obvious that both sides are more complementary than successive, more like a see-saw than an evolutionary ladder. When one side appears, the other does not go away; indeed, each side gives rise to and feeds the other. It therefore does not work to say that a turn to the archaic means a turn to something in the most distant past that gave way to the historical and modern, and is now being revived after having been overridden. The archaic, the arena of first principles, has never left.

Figure 6.2 captured an order in the music that suggested an ordering autonomous to the body; fig. 6.4 is my visualization of the process that makes that order unfold. Its analytical-theoretical map of the improvising body is connected with the idea of the archaic because both music and the human organism function somewhat as time machines. The ontogeny of our development from embryos recapitulates the phylogeny of our emergence from the microbiology of

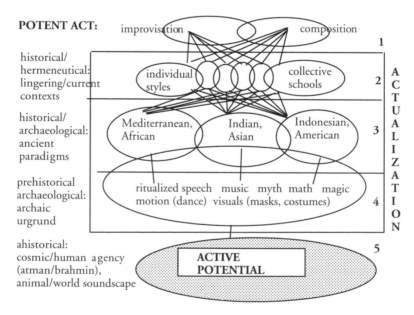

Fig. 6.4   The marriage of the former rivals.

the sea; the evolution of our species from reptilian to mammalian to human beings is recapitulated in the layers of our reptilian, limbic, and neocortical brains. Evolutionary time's flow is captured in the moment of our own bodies.

Similarly, we have looked back over the mythoi of instruments embodying different aspects of humanity, of gender infusing those instruments, and of the history of harmony encoding gender's two voices in ways reflective of social mythos and ethos. Classism begins and ends at home, between the man and the woman and their children; historical time's Loves and Wars are seeded by their bodies, to flower in their collectives, from smallest to largest.

Figure 6.4 depicts the moment of the musical creation, of either an improviser or composer. Its five layers represent levels of consciousness within the act of musical creation, something like chakras that can be either awake or asleep in the body. Each layer is discrete and distinct from the others, and can thus clash with each and all of them (War); but all also comprise a whole greater than their sum when connected by their (Erotic) fusion.

The top layer is the gesture that makes the music. If only the top layer existed, every act of creation would be from a *tabula rasa*, essentially uninformed by the past or the present outside the player's own self-contained genius, originality, and authority. This idea of the blank slate, of total and perpetual struggle against the past as dead weight, has a special place in the history not only of jazz and free jazz, but also in those of the larger (retrospectively) Western projects of Hebrew monotheism, Greek rationalism, Catholicism, Protestantism, America, Communism and the "free" world beyond America.[19] The enlightened New storms and severs the unenlightened Old, routs it without ruth, makes it a wolf in a trap chewing off its own foot.

This notion of freeplay as generative *tabula rasa* simply fits neither facts nor experience as reported by the vast majority of free improvisers, nor by other disciplines. The brain/mind system, the more it is studied by (for example) linguists, evolutionary psychologists, and sociobiologists, is seen to be as much like an array of specialized systems genetically "hardwired" for specific adaptations (to nature) as like a general-purpose computer waiting to be programmed (by nurture, or, per Hall, "acquisition"). Universal and ultimate issues and questions – what/who is humanity? what is the meaning of life? – arise viscerally in pursuit and development of the most individual, local, and conditional logics.[20]

If the action of layer one is connected with layer two, it becomes grounded in historical styles and schools other than the player's own. Thus, Beethoven and Romanticism, Bach and Baroque, Duke Ellington and Swing, Charlie Parker and Bop, Ornette Coleman and Free – any genre, and any of its non-generic stylists. The player is not only free *from* these, as in layer one alone, but now also free *to* them, as part of his or her palette for originality. In practice, accessing layer two is how musicians typically learn, as a stage prior to either building something original or settling themselves into derivative work and careers (which I would depict as moving from layer one to layer two, rather than combining them). European jazz developed in this way, imitatively, until its *Emanzipation* in the

1960s; African-Americans, for that matter, also deferred in this way to Western formal conventions until the 1960s.

Layer three brings in the overarching historical traditions that couch layer two, giving access to all formalized and historicized music everywhere and everywhen, as well as the way to discern between personal styles, local-historical styles, and global-historical styles. The point is that as we add these layers they become fodder for personal, original music, not scripts of tradition to be performed. Thus, at this point we move beyond our local-historical issues into the world and history at large (as, again, African-American culture did in the 1960s). For example, if playing the blues in a night club, or a 32-bar song in a college, become problematic contexts, I can move into musical material and its associated contexts (Sommer's "semantic information") wherever and whenever I find them, put my own spins on them, apply them to my own situations. Sun Ra, Anthony Braxton, and John and Alice Coltrane did that to broaden their music out of the American universe, as did the East German and other Soviet-ruled musicians to get out of their state-governed dance bands. They did not revive something from an earlier time, they changed their time and place by connecting with other times and places. But, again, if we stopped at this layer, all improvised and composed music would be creatable and analyzable in terms of its infinite personal variations on fixed formal schemes and systems, codified as either oral or literate tradition or both – which is what the vast majority of public, commercial music is.

The composite of these three layers is, for me, both personally and politically, an idol; it has the power and promise of an idol, and also the limits and treacheries. We fall short of our own human agency and responsibility, we serve genres and traditions as something higher rather than subject to us, and we rise and fall with, kill and die over them. While their musical materials do comprise some of what we hear in improvised music – we do hear scales, rhythms, and other such traditional material – they do not stand as its foundation. Layers four and five get us into that foundation, what I am calling the archaic as a function of the improvising body.

Layer four represents an imagined primal past of which there is no historical record, oral or literate, but which we postulate as undeniable (as we do the process of evolution from the record the earth itself is) from what music we do know, and as ongoing: the human capacity, ingrained and interacting with the environment, to generate any and all such formalized systems – of languages, arts, sciences, religions – as people and as peoples. And, in layer five, the common ground we share with the nonhuman universe from which our humanity draws its life and shape.

Braxton's work has been of such interest to me because in its demonstration of layers four and five it is rare. Its reflection of layer five is especially rare, not only because of its "shamanimalism" (for example, Braxton's instruction that "you must become the dog" of *Composition 99G*) but because it is rooted in Eros and War, back to animal "music" as mating and territorial defense strategies. How that works for him I have seen up close, but I would not presume to describe it, because the very act of description becomes judgment, thus violation, even if accurate (this is why Religion, the rationale of the Holy, can be a destructive force). However, I can articulate its process in me as a musician.

When playing, I face moments of flow, thrash, and mindplay. I work myself into a state through the music that is flirting with orgasm (Erotic pleasure trance), death or murder (War's heart attack of adrenalin, roar of rage), or robotism (mindplay) at their most logical extremes. That which guides and saves me, governs me, is the Holy, ineffable, the eye that can never see itself.

These layers are archaic in the word's true sense because they define the realm of first principles; and we get to them by mining correspondingly deep levels of our own bodies/minds, proprioceptively integrating every anatomical system from brain to loins, like practicing phenomenologists or meditating yogis, whatever end of the chakra spectrum we start at, in the process of creating a musical universe that expresses both us and the larger universe as uniquely as do our fingerprints and faces. In shifting awareness and its musical expression between neocortex, limbic, and reptilian brains, we are moving through our own little time machine from the new and improved and personal and cultural to the old and proven and impersonal and natural. In plumbing the timely moment of our bodies, we tap into a timeless organic reality, a conflict and symbiosis of systems, that is both as new as each of us is and as old as our species and, fundamentally, the world and universe itself.[21]

My suggestion is that the music we call nonidiomatic, free improvisation, with the compositional strategies designed to serve it, is characterized by its access to and integration of all these layers at once, dynamically, without getting trapped – to our financial and social benefit, or at the risk of our lives and souls, in today's world – in any of them.

Out

Now is the Time

Though they slay me, yet will I trust in them.

— Juliana of Norwich

My first hours in Berlin were spent at Dagmar Gebers's apartment. Her English is very good, as is her knowledge and understanding of much of the American jazz history and personal and professional circles of my own background. Through that common ground, and the international 1960s' countercultural coming-of-age-history and orientation we also share, she and I had a good rapport.

Dagmar was born and raised near Cologne. Her father, a Czech, suffered ostracism under the Nazis for his nationality and suspiciously leftist orientation. She moved to Berlin in 1970, and met FMP founder Jost Gebers, whom she married soon thereafter. In her professional capacity of photographer, she produced most of the realistic and unpretentious shots of European musicians in the German articles, books, and recordings informing this study. Her seventeen-year marriage with Jost ended in the late '80s, but they remained good friends and sometime-coworkers at FMP projects.

I was one of several guests in her home who came to attend with her FMP's annual series of concerts, the (1996) Total Music Meeting. Cecil Taylor's concerts and my talks with the people around them then comprised the experiences that framed the questions that drove the months of interviews with European musicians and activists to come. A couple of (German-speaking) Arab men and another German woman, all Dagmar's friends, were my fellow guests. The conversation that piques my memory still is that with Halid, one of the Arab men.

Halid was a physicist, and while neither of us spoke the other's language all that well, we too had a rapport. His comfort in Germany as a "guest" struck my American self immediately (then) as surprising, as did the depth of apprehension he expressed about ever visiting America. This system of the "guest" in Germany is, briefly stated, one through which immigrants come, often by invitation, to work and even live much or all of the time, but it is very difficult and rare for them to get citizenship, and they often remain as guests all their lives. Not only that – any children they may have, and those down through the generations indefinitely, remain guests. The result is large communities (mostly of Turks) with a younger generation largely born in Germany, speaking German, knowing less about their land of origin than about Germany, on the most primal level, and yet remaining outsiders by law.

Having come of age in a time and place when agitation for legislation against even second-class citizenship (and that too shaped by racial-cultural "otherness") seemed a human imperative – one associated directly with the music of this study – this arrangement immediately struck me as a recipe for social unrest.[1] There are certainly concerted moves to change it, primarily on the part of those from the large "guest" communities in big cities such as Berlin, but my impression, from reading and talking to people, from the news and information media, was one of a relative stability ranging from resigned pessimism about winning a bid for citizenship from the country as a whole to indifference to such a bid.

This fatalistic embrace of an intolerable was the exact opposite of the American-pluralistic tolerance and acceptance of Taylor's music I had advocated to the four friends. It put the minority group of a formally homogeneous society in the position of adjusting to the majority, rather than entreating the majority of a formally heterogeneous society to accommodate its minorities. The post-Reunification turmoil of the time included neo-Nazi youth and their violence against Turks in Berlin, which led me to expect at least a discomfort among Arabs, Turks, Greeks, and others with their hosts, perhaps even expressions of wistful sympathy for the American ideals of racial equality, equal opportunity, and multicultural enfranchisement.

But Halid's apparent comfort (and that of others I would meet) in Germany was rather matched with an impression of America as a dangerously individualistic, violent, amoral, hectic, materialistic place with no sense of social responsibility or deep culture. Just as my identity as a white rather than black American had seemed to melt away into a single Americanness when put in a European room, so, for me, as I talked to Halid, did the distinction between Germany's white Western hosts and their non-white, non-Western guests that was so stark in my initial expectation. Surely much of the resigned tolerance borne by this legislated out-caste was a matter of better-the-devil-you-know, but it also felt ominously like the accommodation of an older generation to power, an accommodation that its sons and daughters would not abide.

Five years later, on 10 September 2001, I made the usual Monday commute from my Connecticut home to my teaching job at Rutgers University in New Brunswick, New Jersey. The mix of car and train took me right through downtown Manhattan. This particular semester, my days in the classroom were Monday and Wednesday. The one before they had been Tuesday and Thursday . . .

A couple of weeks after the September 11 attacks on the city, I flew to Darmstadt to present a paper touching on some of the material and ideas presented here. Days before that conference, German composer Karlheinz Stockhausen had created a stir in the international press by comparing the attack on America to a "great work of art." He seemed to be speaking like a Leni Riefenstahl, an artist so taken with the power of beauty and the beauty of power that he completely over-looked the power of morality and the morality of power. I had to ponder his remark past its surfaces of both outrageousness and true insight, and respond to it as an opportunity to return to the questions about good and evil and art that the four friends raised at Cecil Taylor's concert, back in 1996. The Holy and Religion, and Eros and War, as I have conceived and used them, were never merely rhetorical, not historically, and not personally. And now, yet again, they were in my face as concretely entwined with music as ever, threatening and promising, begging attention and response.

Stockhausen's words struck the same nerve in me the attacks themselves did. It was a nerve conditioned by my whole adult life's engagement, now a ripe one indeed, with music (Stockhausen's included) associated with a political and philo-sophical struggle against American and Western hypocrisies and abuses of power. The burning towers brought to my mind memories of burning crosses, burning American cities (Detroit, Los Angeles), burning Buddhist monks and napalmed children in Vietnam; of children sacrificed to ancient gods, of brides and widows burned; of burning bushes, and promised lands stormed; of burning Roman crosses, of "witches" and "heretics" burnt at the stake in the millions; of Huns and Crusaders, of whites and Indians warring in America, of lynchings and their charred bodies; of Stalin's purges, Hitler's ovens, Hiroshima, Nagasaki, Dresden; of (per Malcolm X) chickens coming home to roost.

I was staring again at the same old two-faced Holy. One face spoke (words of both insiders and outsiders wanting in): "We Western powers-over are blessed with our wealth and power because we earned and deserve it, built it on hard work and good will toward all, malice toward none, and in the wisdom of Love Who is the One True God in Whom We Trust, in solid alliance with Man Who is the Measure of All Things. Those malcontents, hostiles, oppressed and impoverished among and around us are simply the collateral damage of problems we have risen above in our own strength and grace, will always try to improve and bring up with us, when possible. When not, we will govern and contain their threats and chaos as necessary, in holy self-defense."

The other face spoke (words of both outsiders and insiders wanting out): "You Western powers-over got where you are today through a history of conquest, pillage, enslavement and exploitation. Your professed love of liberty and equality is a sham, as is your profession of faith both in God and in reason, science, and universal social progress. We malcontents, hostiles, oppressed and impoverished among and around you are rising and gathering to undo your evil regime, will do so peacefully if you will listen and hear and change, but we will raze your haughty towers if you do not."

Same old Janus-faced Eros, Janus-faced War. Same old three-faced Religion, spun through stories and thoughts begun in Ur of Chaldea, in the (Iraqi) cradle of civilization, moving through Egypt, then Israel, Greece, Rome, Europe, Arabia, through the printed word. Both faces speak, at, against, past, and with each other, in the love-hate muddle of a family and growth:

Only one among the gods is *the* God, and He has chosen a Man (Abram), to stop slaughtering his own young, to stop slavishly worshiping and start shaping and governing nature, including his own, and his family's . . .

God has chosen a people, through one (Isaac) over the other (Ishmael) of the Man's sons, has made a contract with each, full of promises, full of threats, based on scripts to be performed, wars to wage, laws to observe . . .

Meanwhile, Man has developed quite well enough without this one true God, thank you, throughout the wide world bright and dark. In Greece, at Egypt's and Asia's tutelary sides, he has told and written other stories, other thoughts, lived in and with nature, including his own and his family's, in other ways. His gods were many, and no more true or false than he himself, the rational measure of them all. They included Eros and Ares, usually on separate paths, but deeply linked, and once even meeting for a wild tryste. They saw Man in a place below them, not their partner, not "chosen," not "incarnate" or "loved." They (homoerotically) saw woman as a beautiful evil, a thief of Man's power, control, and freedom. They saw Heroism as a good as monstrous as the evil it countered in the Hero's own breast; they saw it as an embrace of chance and chaos, of freedom from life's bondage. They saw it as Heroic because Fate (a three-faced woman) always lay deeper than that fog of Eros and War, was always the design that lined the Hero's glory, ensnaring his wiser age after luring his blinder youth. They saw the monstrous energy the Hero expended, in athletic prowess, in artistic prowess, through his sweating brow, as the ritual that glorified the gods. They saw the most beautiful male, the best athlete and singer, Mr. Apollo himself, as the embodiment of distance and rationality, as also the god of sexuality and love . . . as also the man no woman wanted! The women rather worshiped Dionysius with their lust, the baby boy, the drunk, the one they could both manage and never control, cooperate with only in the destruction of poor Orpheus, true lover and singer . . .

God has chosen a Man, a Son both His and Man's . . . God's woman is Man . . . God has chosen a Woman, given her primacy of place, a room of her own in the Man/Sion . . . God has chosen a babe, in a manger . . . the human family is complete, Holy now, God's power-over has become Man's power-of. Erotic love has become Romantic love, and that embedded in *agape.*

So what is the problem?

God has chosen a people, through life, beyond death, to soar with His Holy Spirit beyond the keeping (performance) of His Score. His Word is not the Law, but rather the Love, the Liberty, the truth that sets us free, improvised on the fly from on High, among and around the principalities and powers of the world . . .

God has chosen a Prophet, to finish the work begun by the first Man he chose, in Ur, and by all the other prophets; to honor the primacy of place, holy and distinct, of the Woman he chose; to scourge the Earth, if Holy Eros fails, with the War of *jihad,* to make all Holy per Religion, all War per Eros, all power-over power-of . . .

This deep history and myth is what has ensouled the music of a few little corners of the world – the fertile crescent, the northern forest, the Mediterranean, the

Arabian peninsula, the coasts of West Africa, the cities of the northern latitudes – that had ballooned through time, space, and media to become the one History, thousand-tongued, of the one world, thousand-faced. My looks into the music of my African-American teachers and peers, and then of their European protégés and peers, unearthed its soul as naturally as a good archaeological dig.

However, they told me nothing to counter Herr Bröcking's remark that "Music is a whore – it can mean anything." Like the wild proliferation of early Christian "gospels" that gave way to the order and unity of the orthodox canon over time, the *Emanzipation* impulse and its fruits have provoked many to throw out its freedom with its excess, like a baby with the bathwater.

If that is so, and I cannot deny or change it, then I am free along with everyone else to say what it means, and to let the chips fall where they may. I can say she is not a whore, she is a woman I can respect, with a mind of her own in love with mine, and a body uncovered only to me, for only mine to embrace and enter. I can say, with John Coltrane, that my music is not a neutral force, or a force for evil, but a force for good, consciously, intentionally. I cannot define good or evil, ugly or beautiful, in the abstract, but I can certainly do so, down to the last matter-of-taste detail, in the theater of my own body and its concourse with others. I can't *will* utopia alone, but I can hobble together a music and life that *does* it alone, and *with* whomever it meets on its way.

No murder here, no lying, no cheating, no hate, wherever else they may be. No pandering to power for power, no neglect of joy and peace. No splits between my body and mind and dreaming soul, nothing sick or wounded that goes unhealed. If the world says human nature will always make sacred love obscene and profane, and sacred war a bloody rather than a spiritual battle, I can say my human nature knows and does better. I can say this is not monstrously, impossibly Heroic, but simply daily human normalcy, and I can find as many bodies to prove my point as I can to disprove it.

Some called Coltrane's music an expression of chaos and hate, others tried to enlist it against their own enemies, still others tried to don it as their own so as to avoid making their own . . . but Coltrane himself said it was the fruit of his aspiration to goodness, to sainthood, nobody's whore, nobody's sword. If he can do that, so can I.

This real freedom is what safeguards the activation of layers four and five in Fig. 6.5 – the reversion to archaic ground – from the fate of the powerless primitive or the untamed chaos. I can go there in my body when layers three, two, and one – those of history's storied logics – start to make my body their meat puppet (or just their meat). I can generate my own logics and stories and feelings there, rewrite the scripts of culture, regenerate the nature itself.

The theme here has been freedom – of healthy bodies from sick minds, from slavery to other bodies, from designs of the past or some planned future. What they are free *to* is necessary to consummate those liberations *from*, to keep the same old devils from rushing into the same old vacuums, eternally recurrently. If the fight yesterday was a New World's against the injustice and tyranny of an Old, the one today will be the New's against its own such sins. If the fight yesterday was for civil rights for blacks (or other minority races, or women, or children in this country or the other), the one today will be for human civil rights worldwide. If the fight yesterday was for the moral few against the immoral many in power, the one today will be for the moral many against the immoral few holding or grabbing for power. Remember the definition of free as "friend, kin" – and the fact that the bloodiest feuds so often come from such bonds gone bad. The anarchy the music so evokes – that of Eros as well as War – is one that has always governed bodies in cultures, as much as have the hierarchies of power arrayed to enforce this or that idea, interest, vision, or tradition. No one time or place or people – certainly not the one that holds the dominance of power – holds a monopoly on this archaic freedom.

After all the images of mayhem called up by 9/11, I came across a couple of images in my background reading for this study that gave flesh to the response to Stockhausen's remark I needed. Daniel Belgrad (1998), discussing the improvisational American poet Charles Olson, wrote:

> Searching in the ruins of Copan for keys to the Maya civilization, Olson became excited about the history of Kulkulkan, the Maya priest-king. The mythical Kulkulkan symbolized to Olson the possibility of social power through cultural authority. He wrote to Creeley:
>
>> Are not the Maya the most important characters in the whole panorama . . . simply because the TOP CLASS in their society, the bosses, were a class whose daily business was KNOWLEDGE, & ITS OFFSHOOT, culture? . . . and that any such society goes down easily before a gun? . . . ((The absolute quote here, is, one prime devil, Goebbels, who sd: "When I hear the word 'kultur' I reach for my gun."))
>
> This statement of Olson's turned the myth of progress on its head. The most desirable cultures, he asserted, fell most readily before the weapons of Goebbels and his kind. The idea suggests an inversion of social Darwinism, for it implies that colonizing powers are, as a rule, inferior to the cultures they displace. (73)

And:

> Olson implied that this loss [of treasures trampled underfoot as worthless by invading Europeans] had occurred because European civilization identified its progress solely with wealth as defined by the accelerated exchange of commodities; as a result, all other standards of value faded before an accumulative desire.
>
> This voice argues that hope lies not in a radical break with the past but in a selective recovery of it – even underfoot, in the Americas, there are clues to social alternatives that suffered untimely destruction. (75)

If, suddenly, the superior but weaker culture were empowered, and the dominant and inferior one disempowered – sort of a millennial vision of the meek inheriting the earth – what would the world look like? If Eros will never trump

War by becoming it, how then will it? Some images from the news only slightly less recent than those of the Holy Terrors of either smart bombs or smart hijackers speak to me.

The New York Times reported a return of Native Americans and buffalo to the American heartland Plains, and an exodus of whites, as their farming operations failed. The gist of the article was that the agricultural practice and culture established there since 1848 or so may be turning out to be just a failed experiment, not the inevitable progress of civilization previously supposed. A little later, stories came out about the demilitarized zones in Korea and Europe, caused by the Cold War, turning from "no-man's lands" into wildlife preserves, and attracting the attention of people who would have them officially preserved as such.

When I consider the similarly unsustainable imbalances connected with current global environmental, economic, and political policies and conflicts, I find myself imagining the three top layers of my fig. 6.4 chart dissolving before my eyes. When that happens, I want those fourth and fifth layers to be awake and blazing along to generate three new ones – just like I heard Cecil Taylor do that night in 1996, with my fellow Braxton bandmate Chris Jonas and those other Northern forest wild men, after their first few moments of growling, muttering, and shrieking like beasts, when they picked up their human instruments and got down to business.

Notes

Introduction

1. Jost (1997).
2. See John Gray's bibliography of media coverage of what he calls "fire music" (the title of his book, 1991: 15–25) for the source of the headlines. Litweiler's (1984: 105) is one of many reports of Davis's smear of Coleman. Tjader's comments are from my (1979) interview with him; on Woods, see Feather (1971).
3. Nicholson (2000, 2001).
4. The jazz press picked up on the free-jazz moniker from the title of one of Coleman's early (1963) recordings. Hartmann (1991: 57) notes the record company's role in packaging Coleman's first releases with the epochal titles *Change of the Century* and *The Shape of Jazz to Come*, and Litweiler (1984: 13) cites Coleman's denial of any intention to start a movement (or even, presumably, another album title) when he named one of his pieces "Free Jazz."

   For an excellent recent study of both music and its larger cultural associations, including (centrally) those of "freedom," see Saul (2003). For major European constructions of the "free jazz" rubric when it was still fresh, see Comolli and Carles (1971/2000), Willener (1970), and Jost (1974). The first two (French) exemplify the *nouvelle critique's* (new criticism's) sociologi-cal and cultural–historical significations on the music as a gesture of

international black (Comolli and Carles) and young white (Willener) resistance and liberation. The third (German), overtly distanced from that sociological approach, focuses rather on the Western music-historical aspects the music extended, altered, or challenged. A more recent European discussion of the usage of "freedom" in the context of the music's history and development, first in America then in Europe, is in Richter's (1994) chapter "Freiheit"; it covers both the social and musical projects of "freedom" from the distance of a new generation. See also Wilson's "Pulsschlag der Freiheit: Tony Oxley" for a picture of freedom specifically from and in musical time, one of many such in the European literature on this music, and a focus especially pertinent here, as we will see.

5. For some viewpoints suggesting reasons free jazz as a style and/or movement may have *looked* dead along the way, see Liefland (1976), Attali (1977: 137–40), and Whitehead (1995). All three consider – from the German, French, and American perspectives, respectively – "free jazz's" failure to thrive either in the marketplace or as a well-supported alternative industry, though not necessarily as a countercultural musical gesture.

   Such views of "free jazz" as a dated dead end, or a perpetually marginal unanswered question, accept and build on a mainstream jazz culture at face value, dismissing the music according to the criteria of arts and entertainment, culture, and academic industries.

6. The first nineteenth-century activists for a democratically united Germany were known as the '48ers. The connection between the countercultural youth of 1848 and those of 1968 is one that haunts this study. For a bracing resonance with this spirit, see Kurlansky (2004).

7. Especially in Germany. See Potter (1998) and Dennis (1996) for a general sense of the importance of grassroots amateur music culture in Germany over the last two centuries, one with strong, if more insular, American counterparts (for example, trumpeter Bix Beiderbecke's family). See Wouters (1994: 51–71) for the research of a contemporary German sociologist with an interest in jazz's history in German youth cultures.

8. See Genarri (1991) for a substantial look at key critical voices and issues over the years of literature on jazz. His six sections cover the contrasting Eurocentric and Afrocentric explanations of Schuller (1968, 1986, 1989) and Murray (1970), respectively; of jazz as both primitivism and modernism; of jazz as America's ("uplifted," and/or "evolved") new "classical" music; of the new African-American critical literature launched by Amiri Baraka (formerly LeRoi Jones, 1963), followed up by others; and of the more current American voices, black and white, vying not so much against each other as for a wider variety of agendas. The latter, along with revisits to the earlier literature, are best represented in the editorial introductions, commentary, and conclusions of collections and histories such as Walser (1999), Porter (1997), Gottlieb (1996), Meltzer (1993, 1999), Shipton (2001), Erenberg (1998), Vincent (1995), and Sudhalter (1999). All broach a subject they presume to have traditionally been intellectually patronized, skewered toward some dated bias or another, or overlooked in some crucial way, and try to right the wrongs and/or flesh out the picture.

9. See Moody (1993) for a sense of Europe's historical hospitality to expatriate jazz musicians. See Heffley (2002b) for a snapshot of its increase since the *Emanzipation*. By contrast, see Collier (1988) for a challenge of this common view of a hostile American

and all-embracing European reception of jazz.

10. They were present in print before that, of course, but on white editorial and aesthetic terms. See Kenney, in Weiland and Buckner (1991).

11. After Jones – more a public intellectual than an academic, as also Stanley Crouch would become – came Murray (1970, 1973, 1976), Spellman (1966), Southern (1971), Cole (1976), and Thomas (1976). These were more the academic studies – mostly about individual artists who pertain here (John Coltrane, Cecil Taylor, especially) – but still offered by mainstream presses, still visibly public discourse. Gates (1988), Floyd (1995), and others, both black and white, represent a shift of American jazz discourse into academia, and academic presses.

12. Gabbard's *Jazz Among the Discourses* and *Representing Jazz*, stemming from a 1990 conference of the Modern Language Association on jazz in the media and culture, bear a relationship to jazz something like Theodor Adorno and the Frankfurt School might be said to have with their Western art music tradition. Its contributors are scholars speaking across their disciplines – virtually none from a music department – who bring a more sustained formal rigor and scope to jazz discourse than the sources mentioned above (note 8), along with the same fresh approaches and material. This kind of work goes far toward explaining the recent institution at Columbia University of a Center for Jazz Studies, the nation's first academic center devoted to exploring the role of jazz in American culture. See also Heble (2000), Ake (2002), Lewis (1996), Corbett (1994, 1995), among others mentioned ahead, for examples of this elevated discourse that also pertain here.

13. Literati such as Richard Wright, Ralph Ellison, James Baldwin and others; see Meltzer (1999).

14. As also on the German, now becoming as international as the French, in translation, especially through Adorno (1963; see Brown [1992] and Harding [1995] for pertinent discussion of Adorno's influence on English-language jazz studies), Jost (1974), and Berendt (1974).

15. Wilfrid Mellers (1964; see also "Mellers at 80" [*Popular Music* 13/2, May 1994], especially Peretti's "Caliban reheard: new voices on jazz and American consciousness" [151–64]), was probably the first European writer on American music who caught my interest, for his rich integration of literary and political theory with Western music cultures both "high" and "low," and with perennial philosophy. Comolli and Carles (1971) and Jost (1974) were both serious responses – sociological in the French authors, and musicological in the German, both from the most engaged cutting edges of their disciplines – to the free-jazz phenomenon as it was first unfolding. Brits Wilmer (1977), Carr (1973, 1982, 1991), and Lock (1985, 1999) likewise impressed me for the serious, intelligent attention they gave the African-American musicians I (unlike many American critics) thought most important and interesting, and for the same reasons. Berendt (1983/1987) brought a perspective to American jazz informed by his vital practical involvement with music and cultures from around the world, as well as with his own European tradition; and, again, with occult and religious lore, and perennial philosophy.

16. See Berlin (1999). Of course, the dark side of Romanticism was Hitler's call to arms for "blood and soil" – aversion to which informed some German and Russian scholarship's aversion to any hint of black nationalism and chauvinism during the free- jazz years, as we will see.

17. Vincent (1995: 197).

18. Historically, Chicago is also the site of the most famous activities of the nineteenth-century German anarchist forebears of the 68ers (see p. 308, n. 6). See Glassgold (2001) for a good account of the '48ers and American anarchists, and Willener (1970) for a similarly on-the-ground picture of the '68ers. See also Berman (1996) for a more international and retrospective take on the latter. Chicago has been an important American venue for many of the Europeans discussed here, thanks to journalist/critic/scholar and producer–presenter there, John Corbett.

19. Black Saint (BS 120137-2, 1991).

20. Attali's *Noise* (1977/1985) is a reading of Western music history through the eyes of one probing the connections between the art form and its larger cultural contexts (politics and economics, in his case), which conventionally specialist musicologists did not address. It provoked an American movement of "new musicology," articulated by Susan McLary, Gary Tomlinson and others. Thus we get new looks at Beethoven from a contemporary feminist perspective, at opera through queer theory, and similar spins (see Kerman [1985, 1991] and Bohlman [1993] on this trend and its voices. I have certainly drawn on both the information and approach of Attali, and the spirit of the new musicology here).

Down the jazz line, Comolli and Carles's book was largely a direct response to Baraka's (Jones's) *Blues People*, a groundbreaking probe of black American identity in jazz (see also Kofsky [1970], Backus [1978], and Jones [1970/1967]).

21. Another word out of academic discourse. See Heble (2000: 122) for the lay of "subaltern's" discursive land (also Spivak [1988]).

22. See McKinnon (1990: 3) for a picture of early Greek antiquity's meld of theater, text, and sound before late antiquity's (Platonic-Aristotelian) abstractions and divisions of those components – something similar to the Wagnerian *Gesamtkunstwerk*. I will enlist the term *mousike* throughout this study as a shorthand counterweight to the more Western phenomenon of *Musik an sich* – music as a concert art form divorced from such connections.

23. Whitehead (1998), Cotro (1999), Wickes (1999), and (both on Russia) Starr (1994), and Feigin (1985) respectively.

24. Rippley (1976: 16) mentions the common Germanic tribal stock of the white West, undistinguished by nation until the Middle Ages. Often this influence, being fundamental, is more invisible than that of others (see Budds [2002: 2–3]), which reflects the high numbers of German immigrants in America, and their proportionately low visibility as such.

25. The European press on jazz since the 1960s

has, by contrast to the American one dis-cussed above, developed down lines less polarized and politicized between academic and public culture (see Heffley [2000: 313–24] for a close comparative study of the two coverages).

26. Recall Charlie Parker's and Charles Mingus's interest in the work of Charles Darwin and Sigmund Freud in their song titles (Parker's "Anthropology," Mingus's "Pithycanthropus Erectus" and "All the Things You Could Be by Now if Sigmund Freud was your Mother"): exam-ples of a general assertion of African-Amer-ican interest in Western intellectual history that accom-panied bebop. Recall too the broad embrace of Marx (by way of C. L. R. James, Frantz Fanon, Herbert Marcuse, and others) by writers and activists such as Huey Newton, Eldridge Cleaver, Amiri Baraka, and Angela Davis. To again compare with Europe, most such American engagement with Western intellectual history in jazz has been sketchy and superficial, compared with the recent German and French literature on European jazz, both pre- and post-free.

27. The contemporary theoretical linkages that apply most to European improvised music would start with the first phenomenologists (Husserl, Heidegger, building on Hegel, rooted in Romanticism's equal and synchro-nous regard for nature as for culture) and comparative musicologists (Stumpf, Helmholtz), both for their eschewal of inherited mental maps (and mapping) and their embrace of the physical, sensory world as an unbroken whole to be divined. The spread of their influence through the Exis-tentialists to the Beat writers – who them-selves stemmed from the parallel stream of post-Romantic American writers from Walt Whitman through German-American Henry Miller – covers the terrain of the 1950s–'60s' jazz milieu that produced Ornette Coleman's American reception (see Spiegelberg [1994] for the details of this arc).

We will see in chapter six how phenom-enology's more direct development in and from Germany has developed it as a tool of international music scholarship singularly well suited for the European music of our focus.

28. See Earkin (2002) for a pithy overview of "big history" as a school of thought. See Cavalli-Sforza and Cavalli-Sforza (1995), Diamond (1999/1997), E. O. Wilson (1998), Hardt and Negri (2000), Childers (1998), Di Mont (1995), Armstrong (1993), Sachs (1961), and Taylor (2000) for the big-history sources on both nature and culture that informed the power-over/power-of abstract of this study. See also Zinn (2001) for big history's little cousin ("little history"), the most local counterpoint to the most global sweep.

29. Each broad sweep and detail chosen in my hypothetical prospectus was informed by some aspect of the music examined or by the literature on it in the light of the pre-vious note's references. For example, Gary Taylor's account of the rise of agriculture and civilization includes the domestication of animals, thus the beginning of the practice of castration, and from that the social practice of domesticating conquered peoples as beasts of burden themselves (slaves), and of castrating them – all of which contextualizes here the history of lynching in America, Theodor Adorno's infamous contempt for Louis Armstrong as a "castrated male," and Ornette Coleman's famous flirtation with castration (see Ake [2002: 79], on Coleman; and Harding [1995: 153] and Heble [2000: 175–6] on Adorno).

30. Childers (1998) presents the post-Enlight-enment political history of democracy's challenge of monarchy; Hardt and Negri (2000) explore how the sovereignty of the king was more internalized than eradicated by the new democratic state; and Conner-ton (1989) illuminates the cultural-psychological nature of that process (as col-lective bodily memory, ritual performance, not inscribed transmission – thus its rele-vance to improvised music).

31. See Ake (2002: 10–41) on early jazz's New Orleans Creole face, and Erenberg (1998: 236–7) on the "figs" – two of countless accounts of an endless running battle between personal and ethnic freedom of expression and formal civilizational codes or conventions of power over same.

Chapter One

1. See Lee's (2003) profile of Ortner, who chairs Columbia University's Department of Anthropology; and Lotringer's (2001: 250) interview with Smith.
2. Comolli (1966: 24–9).
3. Braxton (1968).
4. Berendt (1986).
5. Von Schlippenbach (1979).
6. Recall Rippley (1976), Budds (2002), and O'Connor (1968) for the way this dominance of Germans reflected the larger American demographic. See also Gushee, in Porter (1997: 99), for independent American corroboration of Joppig.
7. The monochord was a Greek experimental prototype of a stringed instrument: a single string stretched taut over a moveable bridge, which could mark the various lengths of divisions of the string that sounded the overtones. See Chanan (1994: 178–80) and Leppert (1993: xxvi) for pithy accounts of this instrumental-symbolic history. See Lomax (1993: 347) and Davis (1995: 31–2) for a related history, in their discussions of the blues instrument called the "diddley bow," a monochord conceived and used to evoke human-vocal sound and rhythm more than pitch relations.
8. See Van Nortwyck (1992: 118) for this view as derived from the primary Greek sources of the myth themselves. Interestingly, he casts "eros" as the social unifying force against "logic," the latter being that which "rationalizes," differentiates, one thing from another; his eros/logic opposition has its exact and independent match in German bassist (also a scholar of ancient Greece) Peter Kowald's liner notes on Siberian singer Sainkho Namtchylak's debut FMP CD (*Lost Rivers*, 1991). It is a short step to my equation of such "logic" with War, which enlists force to establish one such division asymmetrically – a "truth," posing as "the Holy" – over another. (Lest that smack of moral relativism, I recall the classic counter composer John Cage posed against the "truth" that one plus one equals two: one plus one equals one.)

My asymmetrical Eros is, in a nutshell, peace without justice – a classist social order, but one chosen by all (as Hobbes chose absolute monarchy, in his *Leviathan* [1651]) as strategically preferable to unmitigated War. Sigmund Freud (1930), among others, posited a dialectic between Eros and Thanatos, setting Eros-as-life against Thanatos-as-death – but my construct accounts for both life and death impulses in both Eros and War. As such, it is closest to the Greek myth of a love affair between Eros and Ares, and to subsequent literature that weights Eros's kinship with death as much as its obvious one with life – thus to the love-hate dynamics (between races, religious zealots, genders, nations, ideologues, and generations) in the "one history" explained here.

See also Berman (1996: 47, 332), on Marcuse's "sexual theories about Eros and its insurrectionary possibilities," especially against what he saw as "American totalitarianism." More graphic and grassroots examples of same are in the collection *Hatred of Capitalism* (Krause and Longere [2001]). Foucault (1988–90) ponders the big history behind the social/political power plays of Eros.

9. The "big-historical" literature backgrounding my War would include studies of aggression in animals in the competition for mates, territory, and social status, especially those focusing on the role of bodily sound and song (Wallin [1991], Attenborough [2002]); and, archetypally for the West, the root and main trunk of the literate-historical project itself, starting with the Old Testament and ancient Greeks.

Closer to this study's home, Hobbes's war of "all against all" as the default state of nature, and the absolute power of the state to counter it, sets the right tone. From it, Attali, Adorno, Hardt and Negri, Foucault, Jameson, Baudrillard, Belgrad, Mellers, Comolli/Carles, and Baraka (see Bibliography) inform the background to the War I invoke as relevant to the music we examine. What they all have in common is a vision of (internal) Western class warfare and its (outreaching) colonialist and racist faces – a War unresolved until the asymmetrical

Eros mitigating it is symmetrical, and the War sublimated away from violence, oppression, and repression into the less dire negotiations, compromises, and syncretisms of Eros and its arts.

10. Baraka (1970/1967), Backus (1978), Kofsky (1970), and Comolli and Carles (1971) are prime examples from the leftist ideologues of the time. Scan Gray on Coltrane for the many hostile reviews that came out after his recordings.

11. Some prime examples are Yusef Lateef (among many others) with Islam, George Russell (also among many others) with the mystic G. I. Gurdjieff (see Monson [1998]), Sun Ra with ancient Egyptian mythology (Szwed [1997]), John and Alice Coltrane with Hinduism (Berkman [2003]), and Anthony Braxton with occult traditions (Heffley [2002a]).

12. See Taylor (1997: 94). See also Shatz's (1999) portrait of rising young American jazz pianist Brad Mehldau for its account of the latter's serious seduction by German Romantic music and literature.

The Romantic association also grounds (in nature) the grassroots movement that shifted the music out of (low-culture) urban clubs and (high-culture) concert venues and studios to the more pastoral festival setting, a context established and cultivated in European/Canadian before (and somewhat more effectively than) American culture, especially for free jazz and other improvised music.

Isaiah Berlin's (1999) slightly more hard-boiled view is that Romanticism grew in the soil of France's conquest and occupation of Germany, a sour-grapes turn by the losers away from the game (rationalism) the winners had sewed up. Richie (1998: 238) holds a similar view of Luther's Reformation, in reaction to a southern Renaissance with which Germany was too poor and removed to compete. Such views go well enough here, resonant as they are with the position of the black and white American "underdogs" who came up with jazz.

13. Again, see Hardt and Negri (2000: 95) for their idea of the modern nation-state's sovereignty internalizing and reincarnating, rather than destroying, that of the king

and his hierarchy (much like the Catholic Church did for the Roman Empire). That notion is a perfect example of the War that is neutral to the positions of its power players, not differentiating between repression and revolution: both are similarly martial and hierarchical, over and above their differences.

McNeill (1995) brings this primal phenomenon out to the level of culture, especially military culture, and the way music functions in it. His description of marching bands pertains to everything we consider here about the roles of both martial music and dance music – War and Eros – in the rise of Germany and then the United States as world powers and, concurrently, the leading lights in Western music (the former from Bach on, the latter through jazz). He presents the synchronized rhythm of sound and dance as an (Erotic) organizer/motivator of bodies, one on a par with that of the coercive logic of words and ideas (War).

14. Engelhardt (1980: 34).

15. See Berendt's (1986) full German-language account of Mangelsdorff's history in postwar German jazz, in the context of the scene as a whole. See Hinely (1997) and Litweiler (1984: 247) for English-language profiles.

16. See Bibliography for production data of this and all subsequently mentioned recordings.

17. See www.goethe.de/eindex.htm for a sense of this organization's mission and activities. It has been an important facilitator of the spread of all German music, language, and culture outside Germany, including that studied here.

18. A quick initiation into the modal system as used in jazz: at a piano keyboard, play a C-major scale. That's the Ionian mode. Now play the same white notes, only start up a step, on D, to the next D. That's the Dorian mode. E launches Phrygian, F Lydian, and so on up to C again. The essential difference between the modal system in jazz and Common Practice harmony lies in the independence of each scale's tonal center; the Ionian holds no sway over the Lydian in the way that C holds over (its "subdominant") F and the other notes in a C-major scale. Modal jazz pieces could be composed

by rooting any of the seven scales on any of the chromatic scale's twelve tones.

For a thorough explanation of the system updated to apply to jazz – using the crux of equal temperament, the circle of fifths, to keep the diatonic system's flexibility and standards across the acoustic spectrum – see Russell (1953, 1964/1969). See also Monson (in Nettl, 1998), for the sociopolitical and philosophical-religious contexts couching the musical move.

19. Jost's point – that the shift in the concept of musical time from flow (teleological development, dialectically cognitive meaning) to moment (stasis, trance, holistic somatic meaning) is fundamental to the correlative shift from the developmental paradigm of diatonic chromaticism to the static one of modalism – is crucial to this study's concluding focus (on musical time, spelled out in the final chapter).

Apropos of that, see de Wilde (1997: 212) on pianist Thelonious Monk's treatment of musical time. Monk was one of the more significant and direct precursors of European, as much as American, free jazz, as we will see.

20. It was not, of course, the first in twentieth-century Western tradition itself. Most rationally, Debussy's centralization of the whole-tone (augmented) scale, as later Schoenberg's of the chromatic, defused scalar hierarchy of pitch. Less rationally, the collage juxtapositions of Charles Ives, and the range of experiments presented by his American colleagues from Carl Ruggles to John Cage, loosed the same Gordian knot by the sword rather than the system.

See also Litweiler (1984) on Mingus, Tristano, Monk, and Herbie Nichols as precursors of this move from harmony's scripted development to its static suspension into a sonority backgrounding other musical events.

21. One of the fathers of comparative musicology wrote that ". . . the Musical Scale is not one, not 'natural,' nor even founded necessarily on the laws of the constitution of musical sound . . . but very diverse, very artificial, and very capricious . . ." (Ellis [1885: 526]). And from Scholl and White: "From the practical point of view the pitch

intervals employed in the early stages of polyphony could have reflected either the natural pitch ranges of baritone and tenor vocal registers, the pitch or tone quality changes occurring in antiphonal singing, or the order of intervals in the natural overtone series. However, once in practice, the chosen intervals were integrated into the thought process of the Middle Ages as though no other choices were possible. Thus the pitch distances or intervals of the octave, fifth, and fourth became 'perfect' intervals reflecting the mathematical ratios that govern the movements of the planets and regulate cosmic forces" (1970: 62). See Chanan (1994: 59–69) to bring this history up to our moments.

For a vision of the global musical cosmos of scales and scalar systems stretching from pentatonicism to modern twelve-tone systems – all as a timely and timeless palette for the serious jazz musician, along the lines of Coltrane's favorite practice fodder, Slonimsky's *Thesaurus of Scales and Melodic Patterns* (1947), only less narrowly Western – see Yusef Lateef's (1981) *Repository of Scales and Melodic Patterns*.

22. Chailley (1986: 26).

23. Although, as Gennari notes (1991: 465), when Picasso worked the "primitive," he was still a high-culture player; when Louis Armstrong played the trumpet in his modern "hot" style, he was labeled not primitivist, but simply (noble-savage) primitive.

24. Gundarsson's (1993) New-Agey but informed presentation of *Teutonic Religion: Folk Beliefs and Practices of the Northern Tradition* emphasizes the equality between the sexes, and the generally democratic and nature-friendly thrust of the tribal society. (Indeed, unusually in the world then, the deity for the sun was female [thus *die Sonne*], that for the moon [*der Mond*] male.) See also Fox (1987) and Newman (1987) for details of the Marian revival as it impacted the work of German medieval composer Hildegard of Bingen and others; and Bogin (1980) on the women troubadors of the twelfth century.

From Scholl and White: "The German poet-musicians did not conform to the stock situations and characters of their French forebears. These *Minnesingers* added an individual frame of reference and often wrote on such themes as their personal religious experience" (1970: 76). I would emphasize the radical breakthrough to the ideal of romantic love, in stories such as *Tristan und Iseuld*, as uniquely Western/northern European liberatory impulses of eros and individuality – resonant with Luther's concerns, on the more pious side – against Middle Eastern and Mediterranean impositions of hierarchical social rules governing both (and favoring both men and celibacy).

25. See Lang (1941: 128) for examples from northern Europe.

26. See Sachs (1961: 150–52, 154–5, 179) for the historic details of that four-point summary; Berendt (1983/1987: 112–13) for a description of the transformation, through the fourteenth-century Troubadors, of the interval of the third from Satanic dissonance to the consonance of courtly love; Chanan's (1994: 59–69) "The Rise of the Triad," for an integrated discussion of the socio-philosophical implications (and later, contemporary results) of this shift from melodic motion to harmonic stasis in Western musical thought; and Schuller (1968: 52) for a glimpse of African "thirdness" meeting its Northern European match in North America.

27. Such connection of musical with social information may seem a fanciful stretch to anyone who cares to dispute it. It is known discursively as "structural homology," "the insistence on structural resonances, or more precisely, on homologous relationships between music and social structures" (Guilbault [1993: 210]). My particular stretch here is informed by a classroom session I enjoyed at Wesleyan, led by the late South Indian master musician T. Vishwanathan. To introduce us to the Indian raga system of scales, he described the tones in terms of social hierarchy – king, queen, viceroy, etc. His tradition, I recalled, is rooted in the most primal Aryanism, one that spawned the caste system, brideburning, and other such Warfare resonant with my own later Western legacy.

I have no problems with Guilbault's point that creolization, an example of which was jazz, can reinscribe the social implications of a musical system without rearranging it. Indeed, I have read here such reinscription myself, in the European free players. The interesting truth in structural homology lies not any rigid fixing of, but in the mutable metaphorical resonances between, social and musical phenomena. One history, many explanations.

28. Cited by Szwed (2002: 323–4) from Tingen (2001: 132–3). Davis on this: "I had gotten into the musical theories of Karlheinz Stockhausen . . . Paul was into Bach, and so I started paying attention to Bach while Paul was around . . . I had begun to realize that some of the things Ornette Coleman had said about things being played three or four ways, independently of each other, were true because Bach had also composed that way. And it could be real funky and down . . . The music was about spacing, about free association of musical ideas to a core kind of rhythm and vamps of the bass line . . . So that was the concept, the attitude I tried to get into the music in *On the Corner*" (Walser [1999: 374]).

29. Shipton (1997: 789).

30. Besides Coleman's already mentioned origination of the term "free jazz," see Gray (1991: 146–63). The pre-eminence and content of the press generated internationally by Coleman, documented by Gray, presents him as the groundbreaking voice of both musical and black liberation in jazz.

31. Examples from this study's sources: Wickes (1999), Cotro (1999), Willener (1970), Whitehead (1998), and Jost (1987) and other Wolbert authors on the various European national scenes. As we will glimpse next chapter, Coleman's European reception also compares to Beethoven's (per Dennis [1996]), in the sense that various parts of the aesthetical and political spectrum projected their own agendas onto his music.

32. Jost (1974: 44–65).

33. See Schuller's (1961) transcriptions of Coleman compositions. They, like the occasional Coleman piece in a jazz "fake" book

(of lead sheets), have chord symbols *à la* conventional song forms, permitting improvisations on a metered, chorded form rather than forcing free ones. See Charry (1997–8) for Coleman's own bows to such convention on his earliest recorded work.

34. Shipton (2001: 789). Note the nature of the liberation of melody from harmony – ie., per above analysis of Western music history, of the male motion from the female stasis, and vice versa.

35. Brownell's (1994) survey of "Analytical Models of Jazz Improvisation" opens with a citation from seventeenth-century English musicologist Christopher Simpson's *The Division Viol; or the Art of Playing Ex Tempore Upon a Ground Bass* (1665), claiming that "if we take Christopher Simpson's advice to aspiring 17th-century improvisers on the viola da gamba and replace the terms '*Ground, Subject,* or *Bass*' with 'standard tune'; '*Viol*' with 'saxophone'; and '*Descant* or *Division*' with 'improvised solos,' we will be left with advice (though in somewhat archaic language) that would be well taken by contemporary performers of jazz music" (9).

36. See also Forte's definitive (1973) work on Schoenberg's system.

37. See Fields (2001). Again, note the implications for gender roles in the light of my conversation with Chailley, above: from subservient lessers or threats to patriarchy, women rose through the figure of Mary to their Medieval pedestal of transcendence to male immanence. Pendulum of power swinging, seeking its balance . . .

38. See Meltzer (1999: 239–40) for the 1982 citation, and Shipton (1997: 789) for the second. Noteworthy in these sketchy words is simply the idea of corralling the chromatic scale not linearly but vertically, within the three (melody-rooted, Chailley's male/bass clef) separate stacks of four (triadic seventh chords, Chailley's female/treble clef). The idea that the four static chords on the three moving roots could cover chromatic rather than only diatonic terrain dovetails with Coleman's fascination with adjustable clefs, which can put any pitch anywhere on the staff (something Braxton, very much the

Coleman aficionado, has worked into his notated music). It also corroborates Stanley Crouch's description (cited in Richter [1995: 94]) of the blues as chromatic rather than diatonic because of the blue notes themselves, which sound outside the major scale.

In other words, add blue notes (flatted thirds, sevenths, and fifths) to the three scales of the I-IV-V root motion – an intervallic equivalent of Coleman's II-V-I version – and you get all twelve chromatic pitches.

Among such theoretical engines pertaining here, the most primal example of this fusion of flow and moment is found in Sachs's description of the relationship between the one-step melody and the tumbling strain (1961: 51, 59, 72); the most recent includes the pitch-class set theory of Allen Forte (1973, a linear approach) and the (vertical) approach called the "combinatoriality of complementary hexachords" (the two augmented scales, a half-tone apart, that the chromatic scale comprises).

Sachs's, Coleman's, and Forte's such pairings of horizontal and vertical serve to illustrate their nonhierarchical axiality prior to, parallel to, and beyond, respectively, the hierarchical system of Common Practice.

39. Recent research on the role of the emotions and their biology in the shaping of rational thought (Nussbaum [2001], Pinker [2002], Damasio [1994, 1999], and Sansonese [1994], especially those parts specific to music and bodily sound) speaks to this crucial aspect of the whole that jazz embodies vis-à-vis the rest of Western music tradition, especially in the persons of Coleman, Taylor, and the other pioneers of this post-free part of that tradition.

40. See Shipton (2001: 778). This contrasts with the often very circumscribed universes even of those composers of new music who incorporate chance operations and wide interpretive berth. Improvisation generally struck John Cage as ego indulgence, and Stockhausen kept his own reins on the "intuition" he granted his pieces' players (see Globokar [1998: 10]). See Peter Kowald's (1998) account of his local German improvising group members bristling at American trumpeter-"conduc-

tioner" Butch Morris, for presuming to direct their free expressions in any way (something Kowald had clearly managed to avoid in his own process of initiating them into free improvisation).

41. This point also recalls our look at Fux and Schenker for their testimonies to the primacy of melody in the Western harmonic system, and at that melody as an immediate issue of the improvising body.

   Benjamin's (1981) general exposition on Schenker's ongoing relevance to Western music scholarship speaks also to his relevance here. "Schenker . . . regarded the ability to improvise coherently as a prerequisite for using his theories . . . the creative user of his theory . . . must share to some degree in the master composer's capacity for 'aural flight,' or *improvisatory, long-range hearing* (160, my emphasis; see Potter's [1992] mention of just such long-range planning in the improvisations of John Coltrane and pianist Bill Evans). Of Schenker's own book *Free Composition*, Benjamin says it "is not primarily an intellectual approach; it does not demand an unusual capacity for logical thought, a prodigious grasp of abstractions, or a way with words, and it certainly does not call for interdisciplinary competence. The things it most requires are a deeply rooted, almost visceral sense for tonal continuity, long-range aural memory, the gifted musician's talent for mimicry, extended here to include the imitation of analytical and notational style, and, as is true for all artistic enterprise, a highly developed need to communicate in concrete ways" (161).

   These and similar statements (many asserting the importance of improvisatory skill as a prerequisite of real mastery of any idiom; see Rink [1993]) establish Schenker as a role model more than a prescriptive figure, and Schenkerianism as potentially universal as much as Western-parochial.

42. Grolier (1996), "Baroque Art and Architecture."

43. Lewis (1998) provides an incisive look at the "Historical Roots of Racism" that is as sweeping as it is timely, thus resonant here; more specifically, it resonates with the irony of the worst tyrannies and evils occurring at a time when the ideals of universal justice and equality are also on the rise. One begins to get a sense of leaps of faith into both light and dark, and the latter, however abysmal, as shallower rather than deeper than the former.

44. Zakaria (1999) calls it the "deadliest conflict in history until then," and its concluding treaty, the Peace of Westphalia, "probably the most important treaty of the millennium. It ushered in the modern state system that governs our world – the very system that is now, 350 years later, being undermined by transnational forces such as the euro, the Internet and Amnesty International." (After 9/11, he might have added stateless fundamentalism.)

45. Lang (1941: 56).

46. Compare Lang's (1941: 489–514) description of Bach's *Fromm* (piety) and family life with Jost's (1974: 44–65) of Coleman's country-bluesy, childlike sound of joy and sadness – both decidedly innocent, as opposed to cosmopolitan worldly, voices.

47. See Lang (1941: 434, 436–40, 529, 585).

48. See Hartman (1991) and Shipton (2001), for two transatlantic examples. Litweiler (1984: 50) presents Coleman's own words on the subject: "I'm very sympathetic to non-tempered instruments. They seem to be able to arouse an emotion that isn't in Western music. I mean, I think that European music is very beautiful, but the people . . . playing it don't always get a chance to express it that way because they have spent most of their energy perfecting the unisons of playing together by saying, 'You're a little flat,' or '. . . a little sharp.' . . . A tempered note is like eating with a fork, where that if you don't have a fork the food isn't going to taste any different."

49. See Tomlinson (1993: 67–100) for a discussion of "Modes and Planetary Song." John Coltrane was fascinated by the occult lore surrounding specific vibrational frequencies.

50. It was Jean Philippe Rameau who codified this gathering of loose ends into what we know as Common Practice, or "functional" harmony today (again, see Brownell [1994] for the relevance to jazz; also Lang [1941: 543–7], Chanan [1994: 61–2] and Scholl and White [1970: 120–21]). See also

McLary, in Attali (1985: 150–52), for her interesting description of the third (functional harmony's basic unit) as a static, or "inert" interval.

51. Instrumental music developed from the array of instruments dating to medieval times to those we know today; wind instruments were more popular in Germany than elsewhere in Europe. Individualism manifested in the rise of solo and trio sonatas. The dance suite gave form to this instrumental burgeoning, exalting fugal counterpoint over the melodic lyricism of the Mediterranean lands. The spirit and potential of polyphony now served the "Germanic urge for immersion in the ultimate secrets of music" (Lang, [1941: 488]). Bach's main development of his system took place on the organ, a keyboard instrument that featured different timbres and tone colors, as well as the capacity for horizontal and vertical polyphony.

52. See Jost (1974: 59, 84) for details of personnel. The point to make here about both projects is that each departed from the more typical (even to Coleman and Coltrane, before and after these recordings) format of star with sidemen to one of diverse and equal voices pursuing a collective sound. The personnel on each comprised a merger of two core groups, a strategy commonly employed by the European free-jazz collectives that followed.

53. Jost (1974: 89–90).

54. Albert Mangelsdorff, Jost Gebers, and Peter Brötzmann are only a few of other Europeans who expressed their puzzlement to me over Coleman's reputation for being so radically "free." Few mentioned his influence (though Alexander von Schlippenbach did) as being as important as Cecil Taylor's, or Coltrane's later work. Brötzmann actually said, "Americans have a completely different view on the so-called free music. It has never been free. Maybe the only one is Cecil Taylor . . ." (Turi [1988: 48]).

55. Szwed's (1997) portrait of Sun Ra reveals that artist's admiration for what he saw as the hierarchical, regimented discipline and organization of Western civilization, a model he often urged African-Americans to emulate.

56. Coleman played in pianist Paul Bley's band before forming his own, and included pianist Walter Norris on *Something Else!* After that, he was piano-free until later decades, when he collaborated with Geri Allen and Kühn.

57. Schoenberg (1954: 193).

58. Seiber was the instructor at the world's first conservatory courses in jazz, during the Weimar years (see Bowers, in Budds [2002]).

59. See Hunkemöller (in Wolbert [1997: 535–44]).

60. Rempel's overview of "Jazz in Europe" observes three types of European response to foreign cultural influences: resistance, a Eurocentric chauvinism that would repress them; liberalism, which would accept surface elements but appropriate them for existing European contexts (an interesting indictment of the word's history in politics and culture); and openness, which would explore the implications of fundamental change.

Pfleiderer's (1998) examination of the area ("between exoticism and universal music") of the intersections of jazz with Asian- and African-traditional music in the 1960s and '70s extends this sort of West/Rest mingling to the times and players outside the small circle of European art music. He also depicts it as more the spiritual quest (to escape "white" religions) than the worldly expansions of earlier colonialist and later commercial ("world music") ventures.

61. Jazz lore is full of the importance of graceful comportment, from Duke Ellington on. Miles Davis was famous for his sense not only of clothing style but of everything visual about his presentation – his posture, the way he held and played his horn, and the expectations along such lines he had for his bandmates (he articulated this as crucial in an interview on Dick Cavett's television show; his erstwhile pianist Bill Evans has demonstrated as much "posture with attitude" at the piano as Davis has with his trumpet. See also Smith, in Nettl [1998: 261–90]). Trombonist Roswell Rudd, in a private conversation, praised his long-time bandmate Archie Shepp for the latter's sense of theater in presenting his music, and

Rudd himself has aspired to develop such a delivery.

62. See Stockhausen (1989), Maconie (1976), Morgan (1991), Griffiths (1978/1994), DeLio (1984), Schoenberg (1969/1954), and Rich (1995) for a thorough grounding in twentieth-century European and American art music. Globokar (1998: 235) offers a pithy account of the fusions of free jazz and contemporary composition from about 1970 to 1997. The book of essays and interviews, as a whole, is an exceptionally valuable source of insight and information covering the issues of composition and improvisation as they interfaced in Globokar's own history-making activities.

63. *Postserielle Musik und Free Jazz: Wechselwirkungen und Parallelen: Berichte, Analysen, Werkstattgespräche.* The broader influence, specifically of Webern, on the German/International new-music scene – "'Neue Musik,' 'Avantgarde Musik,' 'Freie Musik,' 'Avancierte Musik,' 'Zwölftonmusik,' 'Akustische Kunst,' 'Elektronische Musik,' 'Improvisiertes Zusammenspiel' bzw. 'Kollektives Musizieren'" – is described in an article published in the German new-music magazine *Spex* while I was in Berlin, "Alle Spuren führen zu Webern: Über das Revival der Neuen Musik" ("All Roads Lead To Webern: On the Revival of New Music" [Ody 1997]).

64. Kumpf himself is another one of those avid players (a clarinetist) who writes. See his website at www.jazzpages.com/hkumpf.htm.

65. Although it was the *tactus* (pulse) in medieval music that was determined by the heartbeat of the group member the others perceived as the most consistently even-tempered – the well-tempered conductor; and the Baroque shift from vocal to instrumental music was also one from music-as-text (speech is also a function of breath) to music-for-dance (rhythmic), as already discussed.

66. See Schoenberg (1969/1954): 192–6).

67. When Evan Parker spoke to me of the impact Peter Brötzmann had on him in the *Machine Gun* period, it was clear that the German energy and volume was subsuming the introverted English delicacy, as well as the Dutch playfulness and theatricality. That dynamic reversed itself in Germany through the rise of Wolfgang Fuchs and his King Übü Orchestrü. The expert among American jazz critics on the post-free European scenes, John Corbett (1989: 20) has called King Übü the latest word in European collective improvisation, a sort of elevator of the Globe Unity Orchestra bar. Like von Schlippenbach, Fuchs conceives and crafts his group's musical events, but "composer" seems even less appropriate a moniker for what he does with King Übü than it does for von Schlippenbach with the GUO.

King Übü can be described as a collective extension of what Fuchs does as a solo instrumentalist. Taking his cue from what Corbett calls "Evan Parker's paradigm-shift," Fuchs has built a vocabulary of his own on his saxophones from the bottom up, sound by sound. His extension of that vocabulary beyond the solo to the collective also reflects the project of Anthony Braxton, who first and most famously launched the approach. Fuchs's distinction therefrom is that he did not extend into scored compositional statements to conduct and be read and interpreted by his collective, but into a collective process of improvisation guided only by ear and interaction within the unscripted moment. The result is something like what Webern was to Schoenberg: instances of short, static statements rather than long and winding cathartic ones, plumbing the moment more than the flow.

Trumpeter Axel Dörner, whose diverse handlings of the Monk legacy, the English style of "sound sculpture," the overlap with rock, and the newer practice of *Geräuschmusik* and its theatrical elements, further and refine the use of those areas as parts of a single palette for the improviser.

I would place Dörner, like Fuchs, on a continuum with von Schlippenbach. He grew up near Cologne, where he went for his early formal music education, at (after von Schlippenbach) "the first school for jazz in Europe"; like von Schlippenbach, he was exposed then to the latest developments in new music, studying with teachers who had worked with Stockhausen and other composers; like von Schlippenbach, he developed an abiding passion for Thelonious Monk's music; like von Schlippenbach, he made pieces on which to improvise, as well as improvising freely and in pre-free jazz styles; finally, his professional associations with elders in Berlin were thickest with both Sven-Åke Johansson and von Schlippenbach, both of whom themselves have a thick musical bond.

Dörner's FMP dates include featured spots in the large groups of von Schlippenbach (FMP–CD 61), Sam Rivers (FMP–CD 75), and Fred Van Hove (FMP–CD 88); he's also recorded with peers closer to his age on other labels, including the double LP arrangement of Monk tunes. The latter was his calling card to von Schlippenbach in 1997, when the band they formed with him was presenting an all-Monk program at Podewil and the Bb-Club. Dörner's more new-music, performance-art aspects found outlet in his work with Johansson, as did his post-electric-Miles/Punk-Rock forays at the East German club Anorak, and his delicate *Geräuschmusik* collaborations with young British improvisers at the 213 Club, all of which I saw and recorded.

See Heffley (2000: 1009–1182) on both these artists, and on drummer Willi Kellers, percussionist-composer Sven-Åke Johansson, and reedsman Thomas Borgmann.

68. We will see the significance of the descriptor "utopian" in the peculiarly French context of "free" in the next chapter. The way Globokar contrasts it to "truth" here resonates with my counterpoint between "the Holy" and "Religion."

69. "Substreams" (in Wolbert [1997: 526–32]).

70. Stravinsky stated that composition was frozen improvisation; Pierre Boulez stated that, given different versions of the same performance, one will always take the best one. Stravinsky's composerly use of improvisation is described in Asaf'yev (1982: 226). Boulez articulates fully his problem with improvisation in Attali (1977: 145–6), essentially expressing the critique of it that ripples throughout the literature on and by other composers and critics as various as Stravinsky, Boulez, and Adorno (1963);

Cage (in Revill [1992: 158–9]), Stockhausen (in Morgan [1991: 417]) and Anthony Davis (in Dean [1992: 143]); and Anthony Braxton (in Dean [1992: 133]).

The common gist of their various complaints comes from the assumption that, either always or sometimes, (improvisation's) process's purpose is product (at least) as much as expression or communication; and that composition is the only way to turn process (improvisation) into product (or even, we might add, product into process, in the case of composition for improvisers). Considering the later careers of Glenn Gould and the Beatles, as examples, that product need not be a score, can also be a recording.

71. See Damasio (1994) for the neurobiological answers to this rhetorical question.

72. See Jeffrey (1992) for a Western-historical example of such a service. Braxton's use of musical notation and written instructions, despite their notorious complexity, have always struck me as another such example.

73. See Lord's classic (1960) account of this history. Blacking's (1971) view of music as a primary modeling structure on a par with language – something nature hardwires into the psyche as much as nurture conditions it – moves us into the terrain that pertains.

Just as ethnic and identity studies, and literary and art criticism, have overlapped with music scholarship, so have studies in language and linguistics. Their particular promise here lies in the relatively recent awakening of, again, literate and oral traditions to each other as equals serving complementary aspects of the collective and individual psyche – Lord (1960), Rouget (1985), Sidran (1981), Suhor (1986), Perlman and Greenblatt (1981), Levman (1992), Sansonese (1994), Deleuze and Guatarri (1975/1986), Raffman (1993), Gill (1994), and Hartman (1981) are all widely disparate examples from interdisciplinary and music scholarship of this shared awakening that do pertain here – and to the revelation of nature the gesture of free improvisation inevitably offers in its willful eschewal of nurture (socially acquired musical conventions).

Chapter Two

1. The musicians were Chris Matthay, trumpet; Chris Jonas, soprano saxophone; Harri Sjostrom, soprano saxophone; Elliot Levin, tenor saxophone, flutes; Jeff Hoyer, trombone; Tristan Honsinger, cello; Dominic Duval, double bass; and Jackson Krall, drums, percussion. Drummer Sunny Murray was listed on the program, but did not play.

2. The most balanced and concise of several recent retrospectives on Fluxus is the British journal *Art and Design*'s "Profile No. 28" (1993). Fluxus was largely a German-based movement, in the beginning. Korean artist Nam June Paik, one of it major figures, names its March 1962 "exhibition" at the Galerie Parnass in Wuppertal the "first Fluxus Manifestation in the world" (Peter Brötzmann, then more the painter than saxophonist, was Paik's assistant in the project). As a movement-cum-organization, it was founder George Maciunas's baby; as an attitude and approach to creativity, its importance to the free-jazz movement in Europe, through the aesthetic forged over time by Brötzmann, lay more generally in its anarchistic (see John Cage, *Art and Design* XVIII) and interdisciplinary (visual art, theater) vision. For a sense of the more cynical (but still strong) Dutch counterpoint to the German enthusiasm for Fluxus, see Whitehead (1998: 36).

3. The *butoh* dancers are particularly interesting artistic allies. Their movement emerged, somewhat like the '68ers, as a gesture against American cultural and military hegemony. See the video documentary *Butoh: Body on the Edge of Crisis* (Blackwood [1990]) for an excellent overview of the movement and its leading figures.

4. Hardt and Negri speak of Empire's "inclusion" of this power-that-challenges, preceding "differentiation" and "management" – a strategy to assimilate and even profit from potential threats. Braxton has written and spoken often about the "spectacle" of "the sweating brow" of the "jazz" musician in the throes of improvisation; and Edward Said (1991) has spoken of the ritual of the Romantic concert as a classist construct, of "nobles" who can afford to be passive (an "audience") while "performers" do their work for them. The similarity of these modern images to the ancient Greek *katharsis* of the theater, and even more so to the Roman spectacles of fights to the death, is striking.

5. Resonant with this proposition are Foucault's (1977) "genealogy" of power; Attali's (1977) "repetition" of power relations; Connerton's (1989) reinstatement, in other forms, of such relations by those who overthrow it; and, again, much of Hardt and Negri (2000). All are explanations of power-over's history as one of a subtle manipulation of and insinuation into power-of bodies, more than of a perpetually clenched iron fist ruling them from above.

6. Some examples of the second, bigger wave of "free" include the German recordings *Voices* and *WERGO-Jazz*, by Manfred Schoof; *Free Action*, by Wolfgang Dauner; *Gesprächsfetzen* and *In Sommerhausen*, by Günter Hampel; and *Transfiguration* and *Impressions of New York*, by Joachim Kühn – all slightly earlier and/or less widely known outside Europe than the German recordings examined later. Those from elsewhere in Europe were by drummer John Stevens (*Challenge* and *Karyōbin*) and pianist Howard Riley (*Angle*), in England; by Gruppo Romano Free Jazz (*Tendenziale"*), in Italy; by Vlodziemierz Nohorny (*Heart*), in Poland; and, in France, by Jef Gilson (*New Call from France*) and François Tusques (*Free Jazz*).

7. See Gilroy (1993). Rose's more recent (than Harriott's time) article (1988) shows this African presence in England to be still alive and well in the generation after Harriott, in post-free collectives such as Abibi Jazz Arts.

8. See Wickes (1999: 13–15) for details of Harriott's history, and (26) for an informed discussion of the commercial pressures in Britain working against him, unmitigated by the stronger solidarity of the African-American community in the States.

9. See Wickes (1999: 21) on Britain's Indo-Jazz groups and recordings of the 1960s.

10. Steve Lake's (1973) "Free For All: Are We Ignoring a Musical Revolution or Is It

Undisciplined Anarchy?" is rich for its insights into the players' consciousness of their identities both as Brits and as Europeans, and for their hostile view of American society. Its theme – both the in-feuding and solid front against an American commodification of blackness that caused black rage, and for a purer, deeper Europe – would surface in interviews with European free players throughout this time. England's particularly adamant aversion to America reads in retrospect like a contempt made all the keener by its greater familiarity – that is, an underscoring of England's close connection to dominant American culture, linguistically, ethnically, commercially, and politically (both were recent world powers with domestic democratic charters).

11. The Belgian-born Rom guitarist Reinhardt was famous as Europe's one true original voice in early jazz.

12. See Carr (1973) and Wickes (1999) on England, and Whitehead on Holland (1998).

13. *Eugene (1989)*, mentioned above, produced by Giovanni Bonandrini; and *Small Ensemble Music (Wesleyan) 1994* (Splasc[h] Records CDH 801.2, 1999), produced by Francesco Martinelli.

14. In Wolbert (1997: 472). See also Heffley's (1996) index entries on Gaslini.

15. These terms resonate respectively (and counterintuitively) with my "improvising body" and "mental maps," perhaps shifting my emphasis from the individual to the social body.

16. "It is no accident," Cerchiari writes (1997: 474), "that wind instruments, for their nearness to the human voice, play a special role in Italian jazz." Recall (from chapter one) Leppert's association of winds with the feminine, and the human voice; and the greater tradition of Chanan's *homo rationalis* on the strings, especially keyboards, along with the winds as "low," in the more Nordic countries.

17. Fox, in Wolbert (1997: 435–46), discusses the Swing Era orchestrations of Ray Noble and others as part of an English tradition of dance band arranging that retained elements of the classical orchestra we saw (in Joppig) the wind bands blow away.

Gil Evans, influenced by this tradition, extended it in American jazz. Wickes's accounts of conservatory-trained jazz innovators such as John Dankworth (1999: 4) and others, and those of the blues, folk, and rock impacts on the 1960s' free scene (1999: 25–39), coupled with the anti-elitism of what would be the '68ers, convey a sense of why a formal "classical" aesthetic would be too politically incorrect to dominate any Western European *Emanzipation*. This would change, over time, through the course of the music in the Eastern bloc.

As for Italy's less problematic adherence to such an aesthetic (much like Vienna's Vienna Art Orchestra), see Corbett (1998) on the Instabile Orchestra.

18. Bannister (1992: 14).

19. See Garbarek's ECM website http://www.ecmrecords.com/ecm-cgi-bin/bio?68.

20. See http://www.annekoski.fi, aic.se, dkjazz.dk, and jazzbasen.no for current information on Scandinavian jazz scenes. They suggest that the time is right for an English-language book devoted to Scandinavia, to go on the shelf next to Wickes on England, Whitehead on Holland, Starr and Feigin on Russia, and Heffley on Germany.

21. Mengelberg had "a Stravinsky education, so funny chords were something I found a lot of fun in ... Brubeck's being a pupil of Darius Milhaud had some positive effect; sometimes his harmonies were more daring than in most jazz music I listened to" (Whitehead [1998: 12]). He also said he liked Art Tatum, but thought him "harmonically wanting."

22. This blurring was as practical as it was aesthetical. All European official cultural support privileged the composed over the improvised, so the free improvisers who wanted gigs and grants were pressed to present themselves as composers. Variations of the strategy played out in each country.

23. I use the word "Germanic" to recall the roots of several nations, including France (the Franks) and England (the Angles) and the majority of European America, in their common tribal-linguistic ground. Indeed, the tribal descriptor "Anglo-Saxon" maintains the continuity of the discussion begun here, with Hanslick's suggestion of Saxon as

"low" to Viennese "highness." See Leppert (1993) for a thorough discussion of the English influence on (high) American musical culture.

24. For a big-historical reflection on distinctions of identity between Continent and British Isles, recall France and Germany as the site of the bulk of the witch burnings, set against England as that of the first of the European women regnants (Mary Tudor); the recent-historical women's movement (from the turn of the eighteenth century, preceding and directly spawning its American version some fifty years later, a movement intertwined, albeit not always cooperatively, with Abolitionism); and even a modern-day revival of the "witch's" reputation (via Wicca as a contemporary neo-pagan religion). See Loesser (1954) and Chanan (1994: 27, 202–5, 208–10, 215) on the nineteenth-century history of the piano in America and Europe, and Heble (with Siddall [2000: 148]) for connections between that history and women in jazz.

Having pondered the blues last chapter in the male/analytical framework of acoustical-musical science, several sources on the genre combine to offer this chapter a rich bouquet of its more female/mythological aspects. Interesting in our context is a scan of a few recent (European-) American and European histories of the blues, with an eye on what their shifts of emphasis and nuance contribute to a sense of what the blues means to the white West, specifically in relation to jazz and especially free jazz.

Lomax (1993), the closest to European/American folk music traditions, finds metaphorical power in a comparison of black preachers to populist English balladeers and European fairy tales (57), and ancient Greek bards (265) for their similar invectives against the (often collective) monsters of tyranny and injustice, and for (the usually individual) heroism against them; and he finds something more like roots than links or reflections in his association of (both the vocal style and the stringed accompaniments of) the blues with classism "from the Far East to Ireland" (233; elsewhere on that page he includes parts of

Africa, the Mediterranean, and the Middle East; see Mellers's [1964] discussion of the "culture of the word" and the "culture of the body" for a similar big-historical ground of the blues).

Francis Davis (1995: 23, 35, 41, 42, 88), drawing on his own poor Irish-American background, asserts more personal, even intimate, synchrony between African and Irish cultures in America and the blues. When we shift our scan to the Brits (one of whom, Paul Oliver, Davis [1995: 19] calls the world's foremost authority on the blues), we get a take on the Southern plantation system as a microcosm of European classism (Oakley 1997: 17); on the blues as a prodigal cousin of British folk music (Wickes [1999: 10]; this glance, in the context of a long look at British free jazz, is part of Wickes's larger reminder that there were deep-rooted musical-cultural reasons that America would be so susceptible to such a thing as a "British Invasion" onto its so-American turf of rock music, around the same time as free jazz started); and on the blues as an extension of the vocal (as opposed to instrumental) side of the English music-hall tradition in America (Shipton [2001: 40–61]) and of that tradition's dance side in England (Fox [1997: 435–8]). Closest to our subject here, Lock (1999) invokes the genre as a template for the musical projects of three of the most Western-savvy musical mythologizers of American blackness (Duke Ellington, Sun Ra, and Anthony Braxton), two of whom are post-free-jazz figures.

Again, these writers are more concerned with the import of the genre on Western, even more specifically European national, issues of musical discourse than with creating some ethnograph of a black expression sufficient to itself in its mastery and extension of Western forms, as if the latter were value-neutral.

Miller and Richter, two contemporary Germans, do most to tie the blues into both Western music history and the very local and personal histories of free jazz in America and Europe. Miller (1997: 63–78) builds his narrative on the idea that the blues expresses the human condition –

specifically, awareness of mortality – that is universal, not "black," but is also frightening and thus avoided and denied, when possible, through projects and projections of power (the pharaoh or king as god, immortal; the slave as sacrifice, expendable, with all the lesser hierarchical degrees of social status in between that inhere to this day). The blues, when impossible to deny, provide honest and useful confrontations with the death in life, and give undeniable voice to life's two most crucial requirements: food (that is, in all songs about money problems, second in frequency) and sex (the topic of the majority of the songs). The Western forms and aesthetics discussed in the last chapter are shorthand sketches, often fictions (such as "blue notes" sung as emphases and heard as expressions of sadness); but they are not the only Western aspects of the music.

Richter (1995) adds to the discussion a focus on the preeminence of the free and post-free artists and issues at the center of this study, and on their central relevance to the blues, pre-free jazz, and German philosophers on art such as Hegel and Heidegger, thus suggesting an alternate universe to the American one that relegates (ghettoizes) blues to racist oppression, jazz to American modernism, and free jazz to American margins.

25. Not a few of these helped launch the careers of the important men in the music. Armstrong did so for her husband Louis, and Mamie Smith for Coleman Hawkins, for example. See Teish (1985) on Marie Laveau's forceful influence on the development of the New Orleans Congo Square events that would seed the spirit of jazz in the city with Africanisms quenched or dissolved elsewhere. Also: Lomax (1993: 48), Davis (1995: 80), Oakley (1976: 29).

26. Mentioned are Carla Bley, Diamanda Galas, Jutta Hipp, Irène Schweitzer, Jeanne Lee, Maggie Nichols, Lindsay Cooper, the Feminist Improvisers' Group, Julie Tippett, Norma Winstone, Urszula Dudziak, Lauren Newton; not mentioned are Sainkho Namtchylak, Jin Hi Kim, Uschi Brüning, Aki Takase, and Joëlle Léandre.

27. This is my contention. I ran it by Mangels-

dorff, who did not agree with it, citing the American trombonists he admired; and Johannes Bauer, who did, noting that the instrument was better suited, with its tonal-timbral flexibility – a slide instead of valves, a mouthpiece sized just right for both loose and tight embouchures – for the expanded vocabulary and palette of post-tonal music.

28. Marian McPartland is one of several examples of the confluence of English, woman, and piano-or-voice achieving influential impact on American pre-free mainstream jazz, and presaging the prominence of women pianists and singers (especially singers) in both American and European (especially English) post-free improvised music: Norma Winstone, one of the pioneers of the latter category, a jazz-grounded but innovative and adventurous improviser; Annie Ross, with her big success in Lambert, Hendricks, and Ross as a lyricizer of transcribed improvisations; and Cleo Laine, who brought John Dankworth's band from its cerebral to a more popular appeal. Swiss pianist Irène Schweitzer – the one woman in Europe's *Emanzipation* history with as much stature as any of the men – founded the Feminist Improvisers' Group, in the early 1980s, with two English women, saxophonist Lindsay Cooper and singer Maggie Nichols. See Heble (2000: 141–66) for a discussion of gender in jazz resonant with this one.

29. See D'Souza (1995: 167) for a sense of how classism is the reality underlying racism, which the former implicates as a red herring.

30. See Dizikes (1993: 86–8).

31. Lomax (1993: 356–7), interestingly, sees in this Romantic Hero's solo role a double-edged sword: it neutralizes the power of the collective by splitting it into a mute, passive audience and an impotent individual voice; but it gives that voice the power to critique, like the (also impotent but also protected) court fool, the power-over systems and agents.

32. See Leppert (1993: 227).

33. See Poiger (2000: 143) and Heble (2000: 167–98).

34. See Heble (2000: 152–3).

35. See Szwed (1997: 41, 45, 46, 106, 346–7) on

Ra, Ake (2002: 62–82) on Coleman. Taylor is especially pertinent here, for his primary role in the European scenes.

36. See Poiger (2000: 139) for Berendt's interesting take on both twelve-tone music and jazz as defusions of sexual tension, thus conduits to the androgynous, the former by relaxing, the latter by indulging, both utterly, those tensions.

37. Again, a scan of Wickes's and Whitehead's index entries for American free-jazz luminaries conveys a sense of their influence on English and Dutch scenes. McRae's retrospective (1983) sketch of the British free-jazz scene starts by mentioning the influence of Ornette Coleman and Cecil Taylor only as background, foregrounding that of McGregor's Brotherhood of Breath. Ansell (1985) nods to the South African influence for its infusion of rhythmic and melodic energy in a scene that might have paled without it, and Wickes shows the interactions between the South Africans and the other voices forging English "freedom" then. See *Leonardo* music journal CD series "Not necessarily 'English music:' A collection of experimental music from Great Britain, 1960–1977" (Cambridge, Mass.: Leonardo/ISAST, 2001, v. 11) for a substantial and representative cross section of the English scene.

38. Drummer John Stevens, saxophonist Trevor Watts, trombonist Paul Rutherford, trumpeter Kenny Wheeler, guitarist Derek Bailey, and bassists Barry Guy and David Holland were principal among the SME members.

39. Indeed, the gist of one German report on the British free-jazz scene (Rüsenberg [1972], closely preceding Carr) is the same as Carr's, with an even keener sense of scandal. I encountered similar critiques of America as neglectful of its major innovators (Braxton, Taylor, the usual suspects) in my more recent interviews.

40. Going to Gray (1991) for a comparison of free-jazz scenes by country, omitting the United States, we see the largest number of groups, artists, and collectives (fifty-two) in Great Britain, with Germany running a rather distant second (with eighteen). As for the rest of Europe, Gray lists eleven groups or artists in France, seven in the

Netherlands, and one to three each in Greece, Italy, Switzerland, Finland, Denmark, Belgium, and Austria. The number of media entries corresponds roughly to those proportions, tipping exponentially upward as the numbers increase (that is, the media attention devoted to each of the most visible and active English and German players is much larger than that devoted to their other European counterparts).

Again, this reflects the larger neglect of English-language scholarship, compared with French and German, on the music. Historical retrospectives and comprehensive surveys of the present did not appear until the 1980s (Wilmer [1981], Litweiler and Smith [both 1985]; and articles by McRae [1983] and Ansell [1983, 1985]), and only in the 1990s did anything close to theoretical musings appear (Bailey [1993], Corbett [1994, 1995], and Baskerville [1994]).

41. Peter Kowald stressed to me the importance of the overlap of jazz and experimental art music, especially post-Ives. See "Forum: Improvisation" (*Perspectives of New Music*, September 1982) for readings reflecting on the history and issues of AMM and other European and American free scenes (by Larry Austin, Larry Solomon, Eddie Prevost, Keith Rowe, Derek Bailey, Lee Kaplan, Vinny Golia, John Silber, Davey Williams, Malcolm Goldstein, and Pauline Oliveros).

42. See Wickes for details on all these. Oddly, he does not have a headed section or index entry on Incus, but much information on its principals and their connections to FMP and similar European counterparts (1999: 96–104).

43. The current American structure of the volunteer association is the nonprofit corporation, which, government cuts in arts funding notwithstanding, promises a practical socioeconomic context for many noncommercial artists, though its full potential has yet to be tapped. Also, its history since the 1965 inception of the National Endowment for the Arts is controversial from the point of view both of conservatives unsympathetic to many of its beneficiaries and of some of those potential beneficiaries themselves (for example, composer/saxophonist

Fred Wei-han Ho), for being a form of welfare serving its own bureaucracies and agendas more than its recipients. See Rothstein (1997) for another voice not against, but from, the arts community that is critical of the NEA, as an idea that – like free enterprise and communism – looks good on paper but is tainted and debased in practice by both power politics and petty politics, and by a wrongheaded application of the idea of political democracy to aesthetics.

44. Most have been short-lived, owing either to dissolution or assimilation, but hope for the approach remains alive. Riley lists some of the most significant precedents started in Europe (FMP, ICP) and America (Sun Ra/Saturn, Don Pullen and Milford Graves's SRP, JCOA, Jihad, New Music Ensemble, and Harry Partch's Gate 5 label; see also Gray's chapter "The Jazz Collectives," [1991: 41–58]).

45. Jost (1979: 165–95) has identified the collective as something more characteristic of European than American free-jazz groups, though Gray kept that more embedded than highlit in his presentation. See also Jost (1994: 239–41) for bassist David Holland's account of the problems he and fellow Circle group members (Anthony Braxton, Chick Corea, Barry Altschul) had with conducting the group's business as a collective rather than a leader (Corea) with sidemen.

Such clashes paralyzed FMP for seven "dreadful" years, to cite Jost Gebers's term for the dysfunction, prompting the group to turn its management over to him and free its musicians to put their individual careers before that of the group. (This was the classic post-1960s' syndrome of non-hierarchical collectivist experiments failing and turning back to conventional divisions of labor and power.) Similar attempts to coalesce the loose network of pan-European labels and collectives – primarily Incus, ICP, BVHAAST, Bead, Matchless, sound aspects, hat Hut, Intakt, Creative Works, Po Torch, Claxton, Nato, Leo, Enja, and ECM – proved equally impractical.

46. See Benjamin (1968) and director Peter Greenaway's interview with Cage in *4 American Composers* (1989). Anthony Braxton, to again mention an example I am close to, is as obsessed with recording as documentation – both for him and his musicians and for the listeners – as he is with playing, and, similarly, as obsessed with composing and notation as he is with improvising freely.

47. See Bailey (1993: 146) for an example of an oft-recurring debate over whether the optimal condition for collective free improvisation is with intimates or strangers.

48. Cotro, in fact, did compile his own such chronology (1999: 71–6), covering the years from 1966 to 1976. It highlights significant new labels, venues, and groups furthering the improvised musical explorations in Europe as a whole, and in France more specifically. Its 1966–7 entries show some music events as part of anti-Vietnam war rallies. Willener (1970) spells out such connections in fuller detail (see especially his chapter "Free Jazz," one of ten in five parts that frame the '68ers ethnographically, analytically, theoretically, cultural-politically, and sociologically, in that order). Berman (1996) contextualizes the mostly French movement's international influence.

49. See Ake (2002: 15–16) for the way the "black code" shaped the dynamic between the early Creole (formally trained, "legit") players and their "hot" ("blacker") counterparts.

50. For an English-language slice of Cotro's subject, see Looker (2001) on BAG in Paris circa 1968–72.

51. Both *Jazz Hot* and *Jazz Magazine* had a richer, less polarized mix of fan-journalistic and scholarly voices on the music than their main American counterpart *Down Beat*. *Le Cahiers*, and in 1968, *Actuel*, founded by French drummer Claude Delcloo, lean even more to the academic-interdisciplinary, farther from the music-specialist fanzine (see Cotro [1999: 49, 77–9]). *Le Cahier* showcased pieces by Jean Cocteau, Claude Lévi-Strauss, Alain Gerber, and others (see also Meltzer [1993], Walser [1999], and Porter [2002] for their European voices on jazz, especially those of Boris Vian, Darius Milhaud, Simone de Beauvoir, Hugues Panassié, André Hodeir, Roger Pryor Dodge, Philip Larkin, and Eric Hobsbawm). Both *Le*

Cahiers and *Actuel,* says Cotro (79), encompassed five categories of "La Critique du Free Jazz:" sociopolitical, conceptual/philosophical/aesthetic, historical, musical-technical, and subjective-personal. They show how quickly the music was absorbed and turned to French concerns.

52. See Berendt's (1986) book's chapter "Jazz and the New Fascism."

53. See Cotro (1999: 57–8). All of this resonates with the impulse behind the *butoh* and Fluxus movements, to restore gritty natural life to an overly refined culture. Signaling the prevalence of the "beauty" aesthetic in the United States, Willener relates a poignant anecdote from Ornette Coleman: "Once I played . . . for a conference of the American Architects' Association – it was for a discussion entitled 'Beauty and Ugliness' . . . they told me that I represented ugliness'" (1970: 251, n6). He also cites Boris Vian, a player and writer, who eschews rational understanding and asserts immediate grasp of the source, as one accepts a person. "One doesn't like free jazz, one realizes one fine day . . . that it is," displeasure, beauty and all; Willener cites psychologist and jazz critic Alain Gerber (1970: 234). All of this goes to my experience with the four friends who hated Cecil Taylor, and to the idea of comportment (per Globokar, Miles Davis, and Roswell Rudd on Shepp) as a sign of a player's music as important as its sound.

54. Released in 1966 on the German SABA label, it was France's first free-jazz record released outside the country, and the one most representing its scene as a whole for a while.

55. For example, *Hommage à Guy Lux* (1967) was an ironic reference to a popular television personality, as well as to a composition by Luciano Berio called *Omaggio a Joyce.*

56. Wilen was a pioneer in flexing electronics along the improvisational lines of AMM in England, Michel Waisviz in Holland, and Richard Teitelbaum and George Lewis in America, and that in the land of their most composed, thanks to Francis Schaffer, Pierre Boulez, and IRCAM. His prerecorded sounds were not the *concrète* center of his piece, but part of the improvisational mix, in the spirit then of Stockhausen's *Kontakte* and Jean-Claude Risset's mixes of electronic and acoustic sounds.

57. Jost's (1974) closer look at these first major African-American voices of the free distanced itself from the French "nouvelle critique" and from "a Panassié kind of purism," in the author's declaration that he chose to write about his subjects for their musical preeminence, not their blackness (12). He accepted Baraka's definition of free jazz as a singularly black expression, but he saw the German relationship to it as much the same as that of eighteenth-century German composers with the "Italian" operas they wrote.

58. See Cotro (1999: 166). Elsewhere in Europe, others voiced similar complaints. Stockhausen (in Morgan [1991: 417]) voiced his at the peak of free jazz's European debut (early 1970s), echoed a few years later by Attali (1977: 137, 138–40). Thiem (1982) and Berkowitz (1995) are only two examples of other European (mostly French, German, and English) articles that convey much the same message in terms of their own national scenes.

   Anthony Davis (in Dean 1992: 143) – a pianist and composer celebrated for his mastery and originality in so-called free improvisation as well as other post-1960s developments in jazz and its interfaces with contemporary Western art music – called free improvisation "a musical dead end." Dean (133) also cites similar remarks by Anthony Braxton, who has never dismissed free improvisation as a dead end, but has often said it does not suffice as a total aesthetic.

59. The trend of small groups coming together to form large ones with, accordingly, unusual doublings and triplings of instruments, was rather unique to the European free jazz scene at the time. One did see it happening in the States at the time; groups led by Coltrane, Coleman, and Sun Ra, for example, would have two drummers, or two bassists, but rarely, and usually it happened as the group's one leader putting the band together that way. It made for group identity problems when the doubled players were clashing more than complementing

each other, such as happened between Elvin Jones and Rashid Ali in Coltrane's group. *Ascension* and *Free Jazz* were exceptions, and studio rather than touring dates.

60. See Cotro (1999: 207). The group, called the Eternal Rhythm Orchestra, comprised Jacques Thollot and Barney Wilen, the only French players; other Europeans Joachim Kühn, Albert Mangelsdorff, Karl Berger (all three German), Eje Thelin (Swedish), Muffy Fallay (Turkish), and Americans Sonny Sharrock and Pharoah Sanders.

61. See Cotro (1999: 208–11, 253) for a complete roster, with instruments and recording data.

62. *A Love Supreme* is a saxophone melody shaped to the text of Coltrane's prayer, printed as liner notes; and he plays the title's riff in all twelve keys, with an improvisational palette that, within and between all his modes and scales, includes all chromatic pitches. Hear Rowland (2001) radio documentary, and see Richter (1995: 77) and Porter (1985, 1998) on this.

Chapter Three

1. See Brown (1991) for a discussion of Hodeir's attempt to locate "jazz" in "swing" – something as understandable (and untenable) as Panassié's to locate it in "black."

2. Two books on jazz by German scholars (one by a professional jazz pianist) appeared in the 1920s (see Cook [1989: 39]). The latter included chapters on rhythm, syncopation, and tempi; on instrumental roles; and on harmonic and melodic matters. Its final chapter was on improvisation, or how to *verjazzen* ("jazz up") existing melodies. Paul Bernhard's *Jazz: Ein Musikalische Zeitfrage* (1927) also covered practical musical matters, and situated the music as a crucial resource to the European composing tradition.

Robinson (1991) makes the case that German jazz developed in large part – certainly in larger part than in other European countries, most notably France and England – from its own pedagogical texts on the music. This is interesting in the light of the central role played by itinerant German music teachers and their theory and exercise books in the musical training of African-Americans around the turn of the century in the South (some oral history for which I am indebted to my friend and colleague Malinké Robert Elliot, cofounder with Julius Hemphill of St. Louis' Black Artists Group [BAG], whose older St. Louis relatives bore this out).

3. France, by comparison, was an "ardent but ultimately fickle lover," says Cook (1989), in much the same language as Jost characterized the later French free scenes. This particular contrast, between femme-French and butch-German, has occurred many times in the accounts of both cultures as identified by their music histories: French *trouvères*/German *Minnesänger*, opera/*Singspiel*, Debussy/Wagner, Impressionism/Expressionism, lady liberty and the fatherland, for example.

4. It is interesting to note that "energy music" in American free jazz was associated with an infusion of spirituality and health into the music (see Berendt's [1986] chapter "Jazz and the New Religiosity"), and that the German sources in my research have alluded to that much more specifically than a number of others (such as the French, and the Dutch, who have been similarly fascinated by the sociological, intellectual, and/or philosophical implications of the music).

5. Recalling the reference in the introduction to the subaltern voice, it is again noteworthy that the major voices of the music itself had been speaking in print all along, but always on the terms and turf of that medium. See Heble's essay "Performing Identity: Jazz Autobiography and the Politics of Literary Improvisation" (2000: 89–116) for a sense of the problem of the dominated speaking the language of the dominators.

6. "Whiteness" has been put to good use in cultural studies (Gordon and Newfield [1994]) and sociology (Lipsitz [1995a,b]) as a tool to ferret out and hold up to the light subtleties of racism previously nuanced under even the best intentions; between 1990 and 1995 it has served (mostly American studies of) "literary criticism,

history, cultural studies, anthropology, popular culture, communication studies, music history, art history, dance history, humor studies, philosophy, linguistics, and folklore" (Fishkin [1995: 428]) to cut through the fog of denial the self/other construct puts over the deepest and thickest tangle of human connections and intimacies between whites and "others," such as (pertinent here) "blacks."

7. See Charry (1997–8).

8. It also seems significant and obvious that the African-American middle class, including its "jazz" face in the United States, has pulled back from that point, to stake its claim on that American ground. Indeed, Wynton Marsalis and Stanley Crouch might be seen as recent American voices of what might be called blackness-as-whiteness, a project extending from J. R. Europe through Louis Armstrong, Duke Ellington, Lester Young, Charlie Parker, Miles Davis, and Charles Mingus. Again, the subaltern voice beating the sword of the dominant language into a ploughshare.

9. See Corbett (1994), and Elworth in Gabbard (1995). Schwendener's (1989) musings over Art Pepper and Bill Evans depict a "sadness" in whiteness (of which Chet Baker could have been another classic example), associated also with the beat writers and their way with jazz, that is emptier, less vigorous, less spiritual than its black counterpart in the blues. Perhaps the closest European kin to this spirit lies in the tradition of the dissipative melancholy of English and German Romantics, though it is also similar to the tribal shaman who lets himself waste away in sickness (figuratively, to die) as part of the process of expanding the force of his life (and his power over sickness and death).

10. As have Jones (1970), Kofsky (1970), Comolli and Carles (1971), and Sidran (1981), to name only some early groundbreakers who centralize blackness with their very titles. More recently, Hersch (1995–6), Lewis (1996), and Frith (1989: 164–75) have looked back on free jazz, historically and cursorily, in the same light of ethnicity.

11. Lotz, in Wolbert (1997: 296–7).

12. See Bergmeier and Lotz (1996) on this

Nazi-sanctioned band, and Fackler (1996) on the Ghetto Swingers (of Theresienstadt concentration camp). See Kater (1992) and Zwerin (1987) for the best English-language looks at jazz under the Nazis.

13. See Szwed's (1997) index entries for Baxter and Disney.

14. See Pollard (2001).

15. Noglik: "Some of the Berlin players were of a decidedly American caliber, others less so. But the fact alone that 15 German soloists, after working together through a decade of oppression for the sheer love of it, were still able to play the music at all, was news and a source of astonishment to Rex and his band" (1996: 207). Trumpeter Axel Dörner cited Stewart to me as seminal to his own concept of no-time, no-pitch *Geräuschmusik* (noise music) because of the extremes of vocal effects in Stewart's playing.

16. See Cuscuna (1988: i–xviii) and Watrous (1999: AR37) for a brief history and an update of Blue Note; see Cook (2003) for full details. Berendt interviews "an older Berliner" for his personal reminiscence about an international show business network of Jewish impresarios, of which Berlin was only a part. Berendt corroborates his source by citing famous Americans – George Wein, Norman Granz, Martha Glaser, Albert Grossman, Sol Hurok, Bill Graham – still (then) part of this network in the jazz, rock, and pop world.

17. See Burde (1978: 26) on the "teutonic spirit" in Brötzmann that so offended German guitarist Attila Zoller.

18. Berendt was *Heartplant*'s producer, and also an internationally established European jazz critic, journalist, and promoter – thus well positioned to help define his own product as of general significance.

19. I owe much of this insight to pianist Borah Bergman, who pointed out Taylor's pianisms to me in private conversation. It is an approach I also see in Anthony Braxton's treatments of time and meter in his compositions.

20. See Brauer (1978), Lindenmaier (1978), Rusch (1977), Shoemaker (1985), and Vickery (1995) for the Canadian and American coverage that most promoted

these recordings in North America. Canada, perhaps because of its closer ties with its European cultural sources, has provided a better environment of (mostly festival) venues, recording opportunities, and sensitive press for European players than has the United States, for the most part.

21. See Heffley (2001). Lewis is a veteran trombonist-cum-scholar from the Chicago base of the American-cum-European improvised music scene; he currently teaches at Columbia University.

22. Michael Cuscuna, an American record producer with a thick professional and personal investment in mainstreaming the cutting-edge jazz of the time, wrote an early (1969) piece on the German jazz scene as a whole that suggested such a bias. He called the Globe Unity Orchestra the "first successful new-music big band," mentioning FMP artists von Schlippenbach, Schoof, Brötzmann, and Wolfgang Dauner, along with American emigré vibist Karl Berger, Albert Mangelsdorff, clarinetist Rolf Kühn (Joachim's brother), and Günter Hampel. Cuscuna characterized the Germans collectively as having "an understanding of the essence of jazz, a creativeness, a freshness in their work and an *uncanny sense of musical form*. They have absorbed many of *America's rough innovations*, made during the avant garde's revolutionary years, and been able to formulate an *identifiable, cohesive music*," and Germany as "growing into as strong a creative center for jazz as it has been for classical music for so many eras. These musicians are proof of that for they possess the articulation, creativeness in solo and conception, idea of form and technique of the best American artists" (1969: 25–6; my emphasis, on Cuscuna's echoes of the old "jazz uplift" syndrome).

23. The literal translation is "broken-playing phase." In private conversation, Peter Kowald expressed regret over ever introducing the term. He had thrown it out casually as an offhand description of the dialectical process of "killing the fathers," but the critics and journalists seized upon it as a definitive discursive term, much as they did the term "free jazz" in America, for that matter. As such, it endured.

24. *For Adolphe Sax*, cut in 1963, was also after Coleman's *Free Jazz* but before *Ascension*. Ayler's first two (1962, 1963) but not his most important (from 1964 to 1967) were also just out, but not as accessible.

25. This double-edged reception, of course, echoed the responses to the emergence of free jazz in America – mostly white responses to black music, but not entirely so – documented by Gray: John Coltrane was charged with expressing "hate" in his music, and Ornette Coleman, Cecil Taylor, Anthony Braxton, and others were denounced as frauds by American critics and musicians as much as Brötzmann was by some of their European counterparts.

26. Peter Kowald's sense of his German roots is typical. "When I grew up in the '50s, as a boy – more consciously, after the early '60s – I had a broken tradition, because all of German culture had been abused by the fascism of Hitler," he told me. "So I didn't want to sing any German songs. All of us felt that way . . . I could never be proud of my own history . . . My father was in the war, and so was his father, and now all these things are coming out to be talked about in Germany that weren't for years, because the old people are gone. Now they are talking fifty years later about things they should have talked about in the late '40s or '50s."

27. An irony worth mentioning is that the free-jazz gestures of both Ornette Coleman and Albert Ayler (after the modalism of Miles Davis and Coltrane) rested in large part on a reassertion of melody's primacy in a tradition that (by implication) had become overly laden with harmony. While the most obvious centralizations of melody lay in the more Mediterranean French and Italian scenes, the East German scene, surveyed ahead, is also notable in this regard, as is much of the work of the West Germans, to varying degrees of overtness and nuance. An interesting musical study could be built from instances of "quotations" of culturally charged melodies within "free" improvisations (for example, Brötzmann's of *Deutschland Über Alles*) and from the spins ranging from irony and satire to poignant reverence thereon. (See also the discussion in chapter

one of Western harmonic theory as driven by melody.) The point is that if harmony distinguishes Western music from the rest of world, to go to melodic ground is thus to reconnect with that rest/world, through the "first principles" (*archē*).

28. In Whitehead (1998: 46).

29. To trace this back a step to *Emanzipation* stage one, a conversation Hampel had with his friend Thelonious Monk about Coltrane suggests Hampel's peculiarly German interest in one aspect of the saxophonist's influence. While visiting in Monk's apartment and listening to Coltrane records, Hampel related, Monk's wife Nellie commented that "'Coltrane plays the sound of the trains outside, of the cars squeaking, and all the notes that aren't there, that aren't really notes.' Then Monk would be sitting there smiling, and he would only say, 'Trane can play,' you know. What he meant was that if a man hears all these sounds, he integrates them into his music, because it's the sound of the time he's living in. To us, at that time, any and every sound was part of the musical palette."

This anecdote speaks to the fondness in the European improvised music scene for what Germans call *Geräuschmusik*, or noise music, something cultivated especially by English and German players. *Geräuschmusik* overlaps with the ensembles of improvisers influenced by John Cage, such as the English group AMM and its current offspring, informing the younger groups of people improvising live with electronics.

30. Brötzmann is only one of many European improvisers deeply involved with painting. Some musicians, like some filmmakers, are more literary, others more visual. The Western composer's tradition is arguably more literary, from chant to opera to even the narratives and dramaturgy underlying the Romantic *Musik an sich*. I would characterize post-*Emanzipation* improvised music as decidedly more visual than literary in concept, the exceptions (explored ahead) proving the rule.

31. Such identities – titled pieces, implying a static whole with a beginning, middle, end,

and overarching structural concept – he says are most often imposed on a recorded improvisation after the fact, in deference to the conventional needs of packaging and labeling.

32. Corbett (1989).

33. In interview.

34. Named after the student section of Paris where the strikes and riots that shut down the city in May 1968 began.

35. See Panke (1972) for a sense of this as it emerged.

36. In Noglik (1981: 100).

37. Lovens told me: "I'm one of the believers in true love, and working marriages, stable situations, and relationships with people. So we've been lucky to have this combination of Evan Parker, Alex Schlippenbach, and me, and it's turned out to be a lasting thing. I mean, ask any woman who wants to marry her man whether she knows before what's going to happen." Evan Parker told me, on the subject of this trio and other long-standing musical relationships: ". . . it's a big community, family kind of thing; that sounds a bit sentimental, but the whole thing is driven by love, I suppose, in the end, the same kind of love you do get in a family when the family's really working well, you know, people tolerate one another's idiosyncracies, even what you might call weaknesses, character defects . . ."

38. Cook (1986: 48).

39. He has resumed it since then, as I saw at least twice in the 1997 live performances I caught.

Chapter Four

1. Adorno cited in Willener (1970: 260).

2. From a private conversation.

3. See McKinnon (1990), Hiley (1993), and Sachs (1961) on Gregorianism and its relationships to Byzantium and to northern Germanic cultures.

4. See Grun (1946/1975: 135). Scholl and White (1970) also stress the key role of classical poetic meters centralizing groupings of three beats as themselves classic examples of Trinitarian symbolism grafted into the new

device of musical meter; and the implications of pitch symbolism as similarly cosmic in scope, with the intervals of the fifth and fourth designated "perfect" by virtue of their supposed association with the ratios of the distances between planets.

5. The CD *Musique de la Grèce Antique* (Paniagua, 1979), of modern interpretations of ancient Greek music texts, opens with an explosion of such noise. Anthony Braxton's syllabus for his History of African-American Music class at Wesleyan University started with such music and worked its way through Western music history, along with traditional African musical examples. In this context, Chicago's predominance of Eastern over Western European immigrants seems noteworthy, with, again, its history of anarchism.

6. Michael Danzi (1986) wrote a memoir about his experience as a professional jazz musician in Europe. "People have forgotten that, after World War One, the greatest concentration of intellectuals and cultural innovators was not in Paris, and certainly not in London or New York – but in Berlin. The reason was really quite simple. The revolution in Russia saw getting on for half-a-million immigrants from there, and others from Poland, Hungary, and the eastern countries. These famous violinists, pianists, cellists, composers, scientists, philosophers, theatrical artists, and men of medicine, came to Berlin to start a new life. A few Italians, French, and English-Americans also came to Berlin, whose atmosphere in the 1920s was conducive to good living, to research, and investigation in all fields of knowledge. All manner of ideas were considered. Take just one example in music. Composers were writing in the chromatic twelve tone scale; in 1926 there was a broadcast of the quartertone, by four musicians, one playing in Berlin, one in Rome, one in Paris, and one in London. Quite some feat for 1926, and never to be repeated" (45–6).

7. Jef Gilson's homage to this piece has already been noted; hear also Alice Coltrane's remarkable realization of the same piece (2001 [1976]), Warner Bros, 9362-47899-2

CD). The influences of Aleksandr Scriabin and Sergei Prokofiev loom as large as those of Schoenberg and Stockhausen in Anthony Braxton's ouevre.

8. Lilla (1998) makes an effective argument for a difference between the European and American brand of late 1960s' student protest movements that accounts for two separate histories (and presents) thereof. Despite their surface overlaps of style and concerns, he says, the political orientation in America turned early on to a cultural one – say, from tactical protests targeting the Vietnam war to the more strategically fundamental challenge of the women's movement. That cultural orientation has endured in America, through aging baby boomers who have developed it in academia, journalism, and identity politics.

The European students, on the other hand, were heirs to a leftist tradition, the abuses of which by both fascists and communists made the (white) American student movement look naively idealistic and disengaged, by comparison. The '68ers (in Europe) evolved away from that tradition, after a much more prolonged and violent confrontation that lasted into the 1980s, opting for a fruitful engagement with the establishment, coming in time to bring about real socialist and environmentalist reforms. Moreover, their versions of cultural reform (in women's rights, gay rights, family roles, education) proceeded without the often obsessive identity politics Americans carried in to lighten the load of their melting-pot and Puritanic baggage.

9. Erenberg (1998) and Vincent (1995) do highlight the leftist activism often couching, sometimes driving, the spirit of American jazz before the 1960s. Black activists such as (Chicago-based) Marcus Garvey and Paul Robeson, W. E. B. Du Bois and others had such connections with Soviet Communism, famously. Still, they did not comprise a subcurrent with noticeable impact on the business and aesthetic conventions of the music per se, as came about in the 1960s, via Max Roach, Charles Mingus, and others following.

10. See MacKillop's (1950) *Down Beat* coverage

of the Schillinger system. This mix of engineering, music, mathematics, avant-garde, and the ancient and occult was formative in setting me up so perfectly for Braxton's universe, I'm sure.

11. See also Ake (2002: 10–41) for complements to and corroborations of this view.

12. See Oakley (1976: 55), Lomax (1993: 360–66, 374–5), and Davis (1955: 85) for the contours of this narrative.

13. Attali uses the image of Carnival (the body unrestrained) for energies "normally" restrained by Lent, allowed to vent for a while before resuming their roles in repressive hierarchy. Again, see Kraus and Lotringer (2001) for essays that suggest the notion of sexual freedom, post-1968, as more politicized in Europe than America. Poiger (2000) centralizes gender identity and its social-erotic roles in her assessments of East German music scenes, as does Starr (1997) for Russian, both foregrounding the investment of the state in defining and controlling those identities and roles for young bodies.

14. Wolbert presents those darker sides of the less-repressive-than-America European receptions of race and eros in jazz history. As nineteenth-century internationalism and liberalism gave way to twentieth-century nationalism, fascism, and communism, thence to an official view of certain racial and sexual profiles as degenerately hedonistic, a repression correspondingly more extreme and official than anything America had hatched then came to the fore.

A 1931 account by a German student in Paris describing a *bal Négre* bears citing, for its resonance with the reactions to Cecil Taylor, John Coltrane, Ornette Coleman, Anthony Braxton, and others seen here. The student describes a stage with a small ensemble of Western instruments, which to his Western ears are sounded in a "frightfully shocking, repulsive and also fascinating" way. He then describes a "bubbling, musically unorganized sound mass in which one can detect a piece of melody here and there, ripped from all context and meaning to become a flaming ornament. An actual playing of organized sound can absolutely

not be the intent here. It would be drowned in the strong throbbing pulse that completely enthralls the musicians and dancers. Every instrumentalist is playing to himself in his own possessed way, sometimes vanishing into the sound mass, then re-emerging for a shrill declamation. The medium for all this cacophony throughout is the regular vibrating energy of the rhythm, including that from the piano, which indeed here, in a radical sense, has become a drum . . . Out of the bodies [of the collective], through the beating vibrations of the rhythm, comes the wildest and most primal expression. The measured orchestrations of modern popular dances have no place here. Bodies rather interact vehemently in place, shifting only gradually about the room. Their interaction takes place mostly through the hips, expressing an overt sexuality. Only after all such energy has been spent does exhaustion itself demand a pause.

"What is happening here is obvious: the genuine and vehement invasion of a foreign race through the outer skin of European civilization. The organization of their own balls is a specific expression of this general phenomenon" (Emsheimer 1997: 333–4; note the depiction of "European civilization" as having a "skin" – part of the body-based rhetoric the Nazis would push to such inflammatory heights).

15. Cited in Brodowski (1997: 451).

16. See Brodowski (1997: 453–4) for more names of interest to Poland's jazz scene.

17. See Brown (1992), Harding (1995), and Proiger (2000: 21, 142–5, 149) on Adorno and jazz.

18. For more jazz-pertinent discussion of Schoenberg's lineage through Webern, and Stockhausen, see passages on Hans Kumpf in chapter one. For analysis of their radical innovations as returns to ancient roots as much as reaches toward the future, see Heffley (1996: 118–30).

19. The fuzzy line between the Fascist and the more thoughtful European critiques of jazz suggests itself here. Adorno's famous critiques of jazz as shallow compulsion and Stockhausen's aversion to its pulse as too reminiscent of Fascist march music

(Maconie [1976]) are actually closer in spirit to the free-jazz pioneers in America and Europe who had similar complaints, albeit in more musical terms. Elvin Jones's, and then Tony Williams's, way of confounding the steady beat in the drums opened up the door to the complete "no-time" percussive colorisms of Paul Lovens and Tony Oxley in the view of several FMP players I spoke with; and a discussion about rap music I had with the four East German Zentral Quartett players ran down lines similar to Adorno's on jazz: simple, repetitive rhyme and rhythm used to pump up the most superficial, lowest, mass impulses in people (saxophonist Ernst-Ludwig Petrovsky compared rock music's beat with Hitler's brownshirts). A similar conversation among thoughtful white Americans would be awkward because of the sensitivity to racism; here it was clearly cast in a resistance to any music that appeals to base, shallow instincts in order to manipulate for power, whether through political or commercial minstrelsies.

20. By Eisler, most publicly (see Betz [1982: 39–44]). Again, of interest here is Eisler's view of Schoenberg: ". . . the manifestation of nervousness, hysteria, panic, confusion, the lost, the terror . . . the base character of Schoenberg's music is Angst" (Richie [1998: 342]). Eisler's dogmatically but also deftly functional tonalism had as big an influence on the East German FMP musicians as the idea of socialism and communism has always had on certain people, even when disastrously imposed from the top down. Like Eisler as opposed to Schoenberg, the Eastern musicians never renounced tonal tradition as radically as their Western counterparts, who also were heard, as Schoenberg's aloofness from the siren call of overt political agendas was read, as nervous and unmoored.

21. *Gebrauchmusik* ("useful music") was a movement generated by musical collaborators with playwright Bertolt Brecht, composers Paul Hindemith, Kurt Weill, and Eisler, among others. It was conceived in a social-utilitarian spirit as a corrective response to a music industry polarized between an overly insular art music culture that rendered its audience too passive, and a popular-music culture that was little more than boilerplate ("paper music" – something like that produced by academic-careerist composers these days). See Chanan (1994: 25).

22. Adorno's original words were in *Zeitlose Mode* (1953). Kumpf's 1975 book (with an updated second edition in 1981; see chapter one) is indeed an exploration of the notion that the music Adorno championed (in Schoenberg) is enjoying a happy and fruitful marriage with the jazz Adorno abhorred.

23. Hanns Eisler, "On Jazz," *Materialien zu einer Dialektik der Musik* (Leipzig [1973: 248]), in Noglik (1996: 209). Eisler's antipathy to jazz, like his friend Theodor Adorno's, lay in his distaste for its cultural context, not its practitioners' talents. "I don't believe that jazz and swing music is entirely bad. Men like Duke Ellington and Benny Goodman are really talented musicians. But Duke Ellington makes his fortune in night clubs, and his development as an artist is therefore handicapped. Benny Goodman, a very fine clarinetist, has made stupid and boring movies in Hollywood, and ruins his real craftmanship by such methods" (Eisler 1973: 422).

24. See Petrovsky and Brüning (1996).

25. See Linzer (1980).

26. *Dramaturgie* is an oft-used way of describing harmonic-melodic development in East Germany, and a telling one, given the larger Eastern propensity for the theatrical and literary in its music culture. It captures the East German scene's links with the theater, and Russia's version of the *Emanzipation*, as described next chapter.

27. Like Wilson, Kumpf, and Jost, Rempel is one of those many Germans who also make the music they write about.

28. Jost (1987: 233).

29. Engelhardt's (1980) fix on two elements of the GDR aesthetic reflects this easier Eastern acceptance of the roots of American music: the folk song, and "methods of montage, parody, alienation as they were developed (in the '20s) in the socially involved, anti-romantic art which itself was a response to the First World War"

(34). Drawing from the work of (mostly) Gumpert and Sommer in the 1970s, Engelhardt focuses on the turn from diatonicism to modalism, and on the polyrhythmic nature, similar to that of African music's, emerging from the hocketing approaches of early Western music. His choice of words reflects his sense of Europe's match of Africa's depth in American jazz: "Only the 'blunt' archaic malleability which radiates from the melody line is important and it is just as important that ecclesiastic tunes are accepted in the original in jazz at the right geographic and historic place, namely Middle Europe" (34).

The early influences of Weise, Schulze, Schönfeld, and even Kühn stand as Western European-oriented cul-de-sacs from which the Synopsis players would turn back to the original (Holy) spirit of that "Eisler-Weill-Monk-folk" syndrome, to redeem it from its taint of (Religious) ideological dogmatism. Eisler's was an influence akin to John Philip Sousa's on early jazz, or Thelonious Monk's on forward-looking innovators to come after him, or Kurt Weill's on popular music and jazz – a musical craftsmanship in a lean, focused style that cut right to the quick of the matter at hand, with a simplicity and elegance that transcended its own deep roots in its local expression and its original social function. Engelhardt nods to West German and American jazz players' forays into Eisler mentioned above, but he is quick to peg them as an expression of a Western avant-garde, a dilettante flirtation compared to the abiding passion of the East Germans.

30. The various Gumpert workshop bands all started out at the "Kammer"; and Gumpert went on to become the musical director of many projects in the strong GDR theater scene that grew in this house, where Brecht and then Heiner Müller were resident playwrights (discussed in more detail later).

31. Cited from Conrad Bauer interview. Original GDR broadcasts include *Just for Fun*, *In der Elbe schwimmt ein rosa Krokodil*, *Tango für Gitti*, and *Echoes von Karolienhof.*

32. Günter Sommer: "In East Germany, by comparison, the influence of the Russians

was really negligible. They stayed to themselves in their camps. So we had no influence from either Russian or American culture, we were only poor East German musicians." Fisher's (1995) themes and thesis revolve around the idea that the whole of Germany, West and East both, did not truly begin coming to terms with its Nazi past until Reunification took it beyond the agendas of Cold War superpowers in both places, forcing it to trust in its capacity to govern itself (29).

33. Mangelsdorff's *Es sungen drei Engel* and the Kühns's *Sie gleicht wohl einem Rosenstock*, both in 1964.

34. The Elbe River flows through Dresden. Sommer, who wrote the piece, showed me from its banks the (now restored) bridge Napoleon destroyed behind him when fleeing the Russians.

35. In context, this remark resonates with the suspicion of *beauté* as a tool of Fascism explored by Berendt's problem with German filmmaker Leni Riefenstahl, and with the Romantic ideal in general.

36. In German, these terms "new" and "contemporary" (*zeitgenossischen*) are well-chosen to evoke the music culture in East Germany, in which the "new" and "contemporary" had an official place of honor and understanding in the society, one untarnished by the problematic history of "jazz" or "improvised" in the official mind.

37. See my discussion of this in Heffley (1996: 445–60). Again, here, it goes to the difference between Romantic and Enlightenment spirits in the examples.

38. Wolf Biermann was a popular topical folk singer, sort of an East German Bob Dylan, whose lyrics provoked the government to expel him. "First you must know that there wasn't a real press. You couldn't read in the newspaper any real reflections or discussions or critiques about political issues and decisions that affected your daily life. What Wolf Biermann's lyrics did was name, directly, the false positions and errors he saw in the government, without beating around the bush. What happened yesterday, last week, what is the situation with the Party, the government, the Stasi, his own

situation with the authorities. And all these things were things that could have happened with any one of us" (Sommer to me). See also Fisher (1995: 115–16) on Wolf Biermann. *Echoes von Karolienhoff,* an FMP recording of the Gumpert Workshop Band, alludes to evenings of music and camaraderie shared by the musicians at Biermann's apartment in Berlin's Karolien-hoff district.

39. See Midgette (1998) for an account of the Berliner Ensemble's recent (and first) American performance of Brecht.
40. See Blake (1995).
41. He's referring to Charlie Haden's *Liberation Music Orchestra* (Impulse! 1973), which included Eisler's "Song of the United Front." Haden is one of Ornette Coleman's early bassists.
42. It was this wave of exposure that also made American gospel music so popular on the grassroots level. Amateur gospel choirs are almost as common in Eastern churches – where Protestantism was born – as they are in African-American ones.
43. Indeed, the Gumpert Workshop Band – with Heinz Becker on trumpet, Manfred Hering on alto and tenor, Petrovsky on reeds, Helmut Forsthoff on tenor, Johannes Bauer on trombone, Gumpert on piano, Klaus Koch bass, Günter Sommer drums – takes up eleven minutes of side two with a fiery rendition of Mingus's "O Lord, Please Don't Let Them Drop That Atomic Bomb on Me/Mingus," arranged by Gumpert and Sommer. Again reflecting the Western influence by now, it was fully as wild and crazy as anything the GUO might have done, in the raw intensity and reach of its open improvisations. Consider the prayer expressed by the title from the point of view of someone living in Berlin, East or West, throughout the Cold War years.
44. An interesting aside: the *München Kammerspiele* commissioned Gumpert in the 1980s to write a tango; "theater people, including Heiner Müller, got absolutely obsessed with the tango," he says. (The accordion-like *bandoneon,* Argentinean Astor Piazolla's instrument, as well as the central one of this genre, is of German origin.) See Kalb (1996) for an informed

American's take on Müller's importance, and of America's relative ignorance of same.
45. See Brasch (1977). *Hahnenkopf* means "rooster's crest," a phallic imagery enlisted to evoke the poems' characters and themes.
46. Hear Carter's (1988) recordings *Roots and Folklore: Episodes in the Development of American Folk Music Fields.*
47. *Die Engel (The Angels* – Steidl Verlag, in Göttingen), with text by Jochen Berg and a painting for each short opera's set supplied by painter A. R. Penck. Briefly, it is a med-itation on the cosmic dimensions (in the figures of four angels) of human love (an issue of the most bloody organ, the heart, says Berg in the CD documentation), the arrogance of Europe as the world colonizer, the limitations of the higher forces (angels, gods) in helping humanity, and the power humanity has to go beyond them into something new. It premiered in 1988.

   See Marc Silberman's (1995: 129–50) translation of Berg's *Strangers in the Night* for what David Robinson (1995: 4) calls "a fascinating look at how the Brecht/Müller dramatic tradition has survived the fall of the GDR."
48. Kowald received the highest honor for a German jazz artist, the Albert Mangelsdorff Prize for "best German jazz musician," in 1996. Von Schlippenbach was its first recip-ient, in 1995.
49. See Watson (1992: 133–98), Friedman (1999), Miller (1999), and Gray (1998). Kristof (1999) notes that our economies, our labor, and capital were actually more global in the last century, and that the rise of nationalism disrupted a level of inter-connection we have yet to regain. Barber's excellent book *Jihad vs. McWorld: How the Planet is both Falling Apart and Coming Together and What This Means for Democracy* (1995 – the title says it all) has a pithy gem of a chapter on East Germany that captures everything I saw and sensed in my months there.
50. In this process, Sommer mirrored that of one of the African-American masters of the idiom, Albert Ayler, whose links to the same European folk and marching band tradi-tion are obvious and well documented.

Drummer Art Blakey, one of Sommer's primary American influences, corroborated the idea of such borrowing (Gerard [1998: 57, 63]). See Gerard generally for his thoughtful and informative meditation on racial identity in American jazz – the "white" side of which parallels much about Sommer's and his European colleagues' own struggles with identity.

51. Gerard (1998: 63) again presents Sommer's main influence, Art Blakey, as corroborating his concept: "The way [Blakey] tuned his drums created the effect of a drum ensemble. Blakey pioneered the technique of bending drum pitch." Sommer told Noglik (1978: 180): "I see drums – perhaps surprisingly – as at times even more strongly melodic than melodic instruments, because I discover a strong measure of melodicism in rhythmic passages. Some so much so that they have the expressive and meaningful quality of human speech." Cecil Taylor has described the piano as eighty-eight tuned bongos (Wilmer [1977: 45]).

52. See, for example, Eisler (1975, 1986) and Adorno and Eisler (1947), the writings Sommer would have read. Betz (1982) and Blake (1995) offer wide windows onto Eisler in English.

53. In addition to his highly popular duets with Günter Grass, Sommer's similar collaboration with actor Friedrich-Wilhelm Junge around a text by writer Johannes Bobrowski (*Alles auf Hoffnung. Mehr ist nicht zu sagen*, or *Everything in hope. Nothing more to say*) is another of the publisher Steidl Verlag's elegant book-with-recording-and-fine-art-illustrations packages (1987).

54. See Noglik (1978: 173).

55. From Grass's West German point of view, Germany's past dictates caution about the very idea of once again unifying it under a central power, especially one that is heavy-handedly (now pro-capitalist) anti-leftist.

56. A church that housed a film archive during the war. No bomb exploded it, but the heat of the firebombing ignited the films and caused the building to implode. Sommer and others feel it should be left half-destroyed as a potent war memorial, like Berlin's *Gedächniskirche*.

57. *Fez* roughly translates as "just a lark" in English.

58. DoppelMoppel ("double nonsense") is an interesting case study for several of the musical submotifs apparent in the West German scene: it is yet another example of two small entities coming together to form a larger one; it throws the same instruments together, offering a group sound based on their doubling rather than on a variety of different instruments; and it is an example of the younger/older-player alchemy that has always been more a part of the European than the American mix in this music in Germany.

59. Indeed, the move from the most publicly accessible guitar-and-voice to one of the least mass-appealing instruments is intrinsically shaped by their differences: "It is more often said that trombone is too awkward and clumsy to really suit jazz. I can no longer feel that way, even if I do have a few more problems in genuinely expressing myself on the horn. If I pick up the guitar now, I note immediately that I've already gone much further on the trombone. But it did take time to get there." In light of this, too, it is interesting that his public development on the horn has included the long associations with guitarists (Kropinski and Sasche).

60. From Noglik (1981: 317, 316, 323).

61. See Corbett (1989).

62. Both tone and content of these interviews resonates with literature on and from areas of the GDR other than Petrovsky's musical one – for example, Lukens and Rosenberg (1993) – all of which share a common theme that many aspects of the "bad old days" were not so bad, certainly not as bad as the heavy-handed, abrupt demises and dismissals of them imposed by the government in Bonn after the Wall fell.

63. Wolfgang Steinitz's award-winning book *Six Centuries of German Folk Songs with Democratic Character* and Hanns Eisler's *New German Folk Songs* were examples of this attitude.

64. Joachim Kühn's lack of this interest in folk music, combined with one in both Bach's Baroque and Ornette Coleman's blues, is an interesting counterpoint to this scene he ignited then fled.

65. "Jazz Music and Euro-Folk: Comments on a Problematic Relationship" (Wolbert [1997: 513–14]).

66. Knauer (1994b: 7–11) also places successful and earlier mergers in Eastern European countries, generally. For more on this issue, see the "Jazz und Folklore" section of *Jazz in Europa* (Darmstadt Jazzforum 3, 1994). Most pertinent therefrom here is Knauer's (1994a: 185–200) use of the concept of "productivity" from German linguistics – the capacity a language can exhibit for change and growth through the more flexible elements of its own internal dynamics – as a way to think about jazz's transformation from an oral to a literate musical tradition (or rather its spanning of both traditions, from the former); and Jost's use of the term "imaginary folklore," to discuss integrations of Basque traditional elements with jazz as played by saxophonist Michel Portal. Briefly, imaginary folklore is Europe's version of African-American mythohistorical evocations of Africa in the 1960s and since: something less than concrete musical exchanges and mutual influences, but clearly something more (at least potentially) than Western appropriation, given the ethnic lineage of the player and his personal intent with the material.

67. See Wicke (in Garofalo [1992: 84]) for a pithy summary of this situation as it played out among rock musicians, with whom the Eastern free players shared much common ground, both musical and sociopolitical.

Chapter Five

1. Zajonc (1993: 290) and Smith (in Kraus and Lotringer [2001: 257]).

2. Cited by Noglik in "Jazzmusik und Euro-Folk" (Wolbert [1997:517]), musicians Stuart Jones and Clive Bell, respectively.

3. "Speculative musicology" – the study of the occult as well as the psychological and social principles music mirrors – was pioneered by the German Marius Schneider (see Godwin, 1989) and borne along by one of my primary German sources here, Joachim-Ernst Berendt (1983/87). See especially the 3-CD set *Voices* (1990) and its booklet, his presentation of choirs from around the world; his liner notes for the CD *Percussion Summit* (Moers Music [1984]); and *Der Welt is Klang* (*The World is Sound* [1987]), his exploration of mystical and occult-traditional views of music.

4. Since the current usage of "world music" began to emerge in the literature in the 1960s (for example, Wesleyan University's World Music Program, one of the first and best such in the world), the nuance in English has been oriented toward "the diverse musics of the world." The German *Weltmusik* suggests more the idea of a synthesis between them that magnifies their common universals. It has also been much discussed (Feld, Erlmann, Jameson) as a global-industrial marketing ploy in the "liberal" (per Rempel) tradition of superficial exoticism. Pfleiderer (1998) mentions Stockhausen and Schnebel for their respective additions of the utopic to the rubric, an angle obviously pertaining here.

5. Lévi-Strauss never did work with the Dogons. Berendt may be referring to a study by someone else – probably Marcel Griaule – for which Lévi-Strauss wrote an introduction.

6. John Zorn is the now-classic example of this in improvised music. In our purview here, Wolfgang Fuchs, Axel Dörner, and Sven-Åke Johansson are similar masters of brevity as the soul of soul. Space constrains their inclusion, but a comprehensive look at their work, and at more of the musicians discussed here, is in Heffley (2000).

7. There were exceptions. Starr mentions Moscow saxophonist Alexei Kozlov, who won some popularity by moving from an amateur bop to a professional jazz-rock fusion show. He argued his political correctness to the Party by claiming rock to be more the "music for the masses" than the folk music old-school Stalinists were stuck on. Still, his popularity was as harmless (indeed, as helpful) to the latter as Miles Davis's was to the "free world" of capitalism at the time.

8. See Belic (2000) and Richie (2000). The scene showcasing the way the Tuvans lived

collectively on their shared land, in the modern context of their motorcycles and housing, was a startling glimpse of what America might be like had it developed modernity in the context of native cultures here. See Staples (2003) for an informative complement to *Black Indians*, one that is still a shock from the unknown to most white Americans.

9. See Erenberg (1998: 230) for a more general take on the boppers as high artists disdaining "jazz" as the low entertainment of classism.

10. Namtchylak has, since those words, expanded into the World Music/New Age market, with her CD *Tearing Down Borders* (Musicworks CD68, 1997).

11. The reviewer was Howard Reich ("Master of Invention," *Chicago Tribune/Metro Chicago* 11/20/95). We can add his immediate perception of Baroque formalism in free improvisations far beyond the pitch pale of Bach to our corroborations of German free jazz's music-historical roots.

12. Keeley (1999) offers Greek studies a timely look at their body of work, conveying its update of the spirit of ancient Greek myth as well as its move from the shadow of same – a view that resonates with mine of Kowald's work.

13. Created by war refugees, it is depicted dramatically in *Rembetiko: The Birth of Greek Blues* (director Costa Ferris, 1983, New York Film Annex), winner of Filmfest Berlin's 1984 Silver Bear Award.

14. See Heidegger's musings on Greece (in Heidegger [1975]), and Spiegelberg's (1994: 336–424) musings on those.

15. See "For the Birds," an interview with Cage in Kraus and Lotringer (2001: 161–71) that captures his East-born philosophy as a way of engaging the Holy without resorting to Religion (see also Retallack [1996] and Revill [1991]). Cage's proposition that "one plus one equals one" stands against all the ancient Greek parsing of logic, as also against Western music-making as an engagement with relationships between hierarchical divisions of that "one." Cage's philosophy also casts him more into the visual than the literary sort of composer, to recall categories discussed above: into time's

moment more than its flow. Kowald is admitting here to a Western penchant for narrative (*Dramaturgie, musicalité*, as we have seen them both) that the *Emanzipators* have not been able to shake away even when they have tried.

16. The two have put out a popular series of readings by the author accompanied by Sommer's improvisations on his various percussion and wind instruments, through Steidl Verlag (Göttingen). The publisher of Gumpert's *Die Engel* (with Berg's libretto and A. R. Penck's art) has a line of products put out under the motto "Hören und Lesen," or "hearing and reading." *Da sagte der Butt* (*So Says the Flounder*, 1993) is a CD/book of poems and vignettes.

17. The first was released on FMP (1979), the second on the Swiss label Intakt (*Saschische Schatulle*, 1993), and the third (*Percussion Summit*) on Moers (1984).

18. Also known as Martin's horns, these are double-reed metal horns invented by the same man who invented the oscillating German police siren (two pitches sounding the interval of a fourth) made infamous by Second World War movies. They were conceived as a sort of poor man's instrument, to enable the proletarian masses to make music.

19. These are similar to Braxton's "pulse tracks"; see Heffley (1996: 54).

20. Among the materials he gave me were copies of commissioned pieces, graphic notations he devised to denote variable pools of rhythmic patterns, time windows, and phrasings from which specified instruments (some "found," like rakes and shovels) were to construct actions and interactions. Again, something similar to some of Braxton's, or Christian Wolff's work, or the improvisations of Nexus (something that would fit right in with the post-Cage Wesleyan University music department). His *MusikTexte* (1993) article "Musik in Raum" ("Music in Space") is a pithy summation of his philosophy of music as a function of specific environments, both temporal and spatial.

21. A musical theater form dating from the eighteenth century, one more historically primal and grassroots, albeit later, than

opera, which was conceived originally as courtly spectacle and diversion.

22. Kowald's (1998) *Ort* and *Sehen Sehen* are CD-accompanied books of text, photos, and art documenting this year's events.

23. See Spruce (1996) and Lieth-Philipp and Gutzwiller (1995). Spruce (1996) includes an essay by one of Kowald's and Sommer's English colleagues and friends, guitarist Derek Bailey. The picture Bailey's "Classroom Improvisation" draws suggests, like the work of Kowald and Sommer, a music education designed around performative mastery of skills and systems on the primary levels, followed on the tertiary levels by improvisative creativity with the tools gained by that mastery. Other explorations of issues such as creative thinking (Webster), assessment strategies (Spruce), and aural as well as literate proficiency (Priest), while not designed to contribute to this suggestion, serve it well. Lieth-Philipp and Gutzwiller's collection complements Spruce's Western pedagogical and curricular orientation with a more global one.

Particularly relevant to the agenda of Kowald and Sommer is Bor's critique of the ethnomusicological tradition, right up to its present moment, as inherently flawed in its assumptions and approach (one that is either not hands-on enough, or too inappropriately so, leading to intellectual imperialism in the first case, and cheap imitation in the second).

Chapter Six

1. From liner notes for Cecil Taylor's 1988 FMP CD (8/9) *Alms/Tiergarten (Spree)*.
2. I use the term "biological clock" advisedly. As Kramer (1988: 345) notes, the term faded from use as hard currency in discussing human experience of time in music and in general, as no "time-sensing organ" (such as the eye is a light-sensing organ) really exists. For my purposes, the term is still valid if understood simply as a reminder that the human experience of time is directly bodily in some way, as opposed to, say, our experience of the objective, extra-corporeal

phenomena of light or sound or space with frequencies or dimensions beyond our sensory capacity to register. The literature on musical time perception on which I draw is more recent than Kramer's sources, and will clear up any confusion about what "biological clock" means.

3. See Dean (1989: 204); also Solomon (1982: 77).
4. Berliner (1994) is a good example of such work.
5. I examine them elsewhere (Heffley 2000: 1206–81).
6. Keil (1966, 1995), Berliner (1994), and Monson (1996) are examples of good, solid work in this area.
7. German phenomenology has served music scholarship for some time now, as well as the scholarship on society and culture, crucial to ethnomusicology. Its appeal has been one of a grounding, a reorientation to the fundamental experience of perception and conception during those early twentieth-century historical moments that challenged deep and longheld assumptions about such things. It is an eminently suitable philosophy for informing analysis of German free jazz, because it was born in the same culture out of the same stream of pressures and impulses, if we look at the challenges to German identity from its defeat by Napoleon to the fall of the Berlin Wall as on a continuum. It is equally familiar to the ethnomusicological approach, with its Berlin legacy (Carl Stumpf, one of the discipline's forefathers, was part of its formative years), and its ongoing quest to open Western history and culture to real engagement with the rest of the world. Finally, it is also suited to artists who also analyze and theorize about what they do, or to "participant observers," with their hands-on, open-minded, and imaginative engagements.
8. See Bartholomew (1989: 35) for his own fresh and edifying variation on Husserl's initial diagram. His triangle descends rather than rises, accreting new moments as contingencies of the first one, suggesting memory's construction of a present as a deepening into the subconscious, as my rising triangle suggests it as a rising into consciousness.

9. Kramer's work (1978, 1988; the former, a paper, is incorporated into the latter, a book) speaks to this data. He sees in the end of tonality a concurrent end of teleological motion in Western art music, thus a shift from flow to moment, horizontal to vertical in musical time, a shift leading to musical holism: every moment contains the piece's totality of information/identity, rather than only part of it unfolding through its time.

His book's final chapter, "Time and Timelessness," summarizes its thrust: twentieth-century Western art music, starting with Debussy, Satie, and Schoenberg and his students, is characterized by a move from a preoccupation with time as teleological flow to time as an extended present that denies both past and future, swallowing them both in its moment.

Kramer's book's expansion of the article thoroughly expounds and exemplifies concretely his thesis that duration, and proportion in sequences of durations, are crucial to musical meaning in the same way that timing and pacing are important to a finite organism. Too much time is oppressive, too little is frustrating, and just enough of one time is the perfect setup for just enough (which may mean somewhat more or less) of another. The organism feeds on variety, for stimulus, as well as on repetition, for efficient organization of chaos ("It is a well-documented fact that, in the absence of clearly articulated meter, we impose it in the process of listening or performing," he writes [1988: 347]).

A passage from Arnold Hauser caps Kramer's article, and speaks as pointedly of Western art music's concern with time as the French biographer of Thelonious Monk (de Wilde [1997: 212]) speak of jazz's, and of Monk's: "The time experience of the present age consists above all in an awareness of the moment in which we find ourselves: in an awareness of the present ... Is one not in every situation of life the person capable of experiencing this and that, who possesses, in the recurring features of his experience, the one protection against the passage of time? Do not all our experiences take place as it were at the same time? And is this simultaneity not really the negation of time? And

this negation, is it not a struggle for the recovery of that inwardness of which physical space and time deprive us?" (193–4).

10. Powers (1980, 1982, 1988, 1992), Nettl (1974, 1998), Moore (1992), Pressing (1988), Bailey (1993/1980), Solomon (1982), Sloboda (1988), Dean (1989, 1992), Smith and Dean (1997), and Belgrad (1998) are the sources on improvisation most informing this study. The way their data and theoretical concerns speak to the accounts of the American and European free-jazz histories I draw on informs my from-to-in construct.

11. Waterman and Herskovits (in Tax, 1952) both take us back to the beginnings of modern African-American studies by white Western anthropologists. They are notable for their strong sense of similarity of that cultural "other" to their own cultural "self." African music, especially West African music, writes Waterman (echoing others considered here), had areas of both clear distinction from and broad similarity to (especially West) European folk music. In addition, African cultures preserved in America more kinship than commonly thought. See Mintz and Price (1976) for the turn toward thinking in this field that takes issue with this retention notion, arguing the problems with assuming it and the stronger likelihood that what looked retained from Africa was rather rooted in and unique to Africans in America.

12. See Shipton (2001: 336, 350, 544) for pre-Third Stream examples; also Ake (2002: 20–24) on Jelly Roll Morton.

13. So says Berendt (1997a) about the many African-American jazz musicians in Europe during the 1950s. See de Wilde (1997) for a comprehensive European (French) take specifically on Monk.

14. See Kubik (1994) for more current data from, and thought about, sub-Saharan African music.

15. My experience with players of this music is that the most serious and intellectually curious, and virtually all of the most influential, feel a direct connection to and timely relevance in such ancient ancestry. A fascinating example from the literature (which I came across on the most public shelves of Wesleyan University's Olin Library) testifies to this fascination of practitioners: *Roots and Branches*

of Jazz, an un-bylined study published in 1987 by the Society for Preservation and Propagation of Eastern Arts, based in Utah, is a case in point. Obviously written by local players, probably Mormon-influenced, its research is undocumented, and its presentation short of conventional professional standards of printing and language usage. But its results are not undocumentable, and it traces the genealogy of jazz in America through its West African and Eurasian lines, in sound historical detail and informed speculation, as far back as I am doing here.

16. In recent years scholars have posited the relationship between music and language in various ways. Levman (1992) is a good source from the ethnomusicology discourse, summating and choosing one of these ways. He defines them (147) as comprising three positions: that language and music developed along separate paths and are in effect two completely different faculties; that music developed out of language, or at least was chronologically later than language; and that language developed out of music, or both developed from a common "proto-faculty." His own argument is for the last, building on the work of Wallaschek (1891), Newman (1905), and Nadel (1930). More recent scholarship (Sachs [1948] and Blacking [1973]) has shrugged off the question as speculative, though Nettl (1956) lends scholarly credence to the sketchy but intriguing suggestions of McKenna (1994) and of Levman's own position, that musical and speech faculties are more similar than different, and have developed from a common protolanguage that was more musical than linguistic – its sounds directly expressed their meanings, linguistic codes developing therefrom later – and that evidence for this is found through disciplines as various as biology, ethology, anthropology, neurology, psychology, linguistics, and acoustics.

17. Recall Derek Bailey's words, opening chapter two: "Improvisation is a basic instinct, an essential force in sustaining life. Without it nothing survives."

18. Berendt's (1996: 261–79) "Wandel und Widerstand" ("Change and Opposition") is a sagacious muse on the latter as agent of the former (the German word *Widerstand* connotes in this context social resistance, protest, to a status quo). He sees society experiencing its artists as agents of change and conflict, but the artists themselves experiencing the same process as joy, fun, ecstasy, childlike play, even (in the case of the first New Orleans jazz players) in the face of discrimination, hardship, neglect – expressions of wholeness and life rather than protest and pain and frustration.

The other side of Berendt's compliment, of course, is the racist condescensions of "blacks," not to mention "jazz musicians," as charming or mischievous children, at their core, relative to "whites" and "serious musicians." Such condescension recalls the whole history of Western culture's containment of women, lower classes, and slaves and their descendants as childlike subjects, at best, and dangerous threats to social order, at worst.

See also Hardt and Negri's conclusion, for the figure of Francis of Assisi as the model of childlike utopianism they draw from the past as a guiding light for the future, after their thorough excavation of the same sociopolitical history mined here through music.

19. See Pinker (2002) for a thorough review and critique of the blank slate idea.

20. See Damasio (1994, 1999) and Edelman (1987, 1992, 2000) for a rich course in neurobiology. Edelman (a self-professed amateur musician who makes insightful connections between music-making and his own scientific work) especially presents a picture of how the brain generates the traits we call "originality" and "genius" in the arts.

21. See Sansonese (1994) for a fascinating account of how the rational, mystical, historical, mythical, and personal converge in the "sacred geography" of the body.

Out: Now is the Time

1. As it did Henry Louis Gates, Jr., who came through Berlin to lecture about African-American issues while I was there. It struck him immediately as the natural first focus of activism when asked by an audience member what people of color living in Germany should do about their own social situation.

Bibliography

Texts

Untranslated French and German sources are identified by their untranslated titles, to indicate which have been translated by the author when cited. Sources unmentioned in text are mentioned here as background information important to the author's interpretations of his material.

1996 Grolier Multimedia Encyclopedia. Novato, Calif.: Grolier/Mindscape.

Addis, Laird. 1999. *Of Mind and Music*. Ithaca and London: Cornell University Press.

Adorno, T. W. 1967. "Vers une musique informelle." In *La Musique et ses problémes contemporains*. Paris: Juilliard.

Adorno, Theodor, and Hanns Eisler. 1994 [1947]. *Composing for the Films*. New York and Oxford: Oxford University Press.

Adorno, Theodor. 1963. "Perennial Fashion – Jazz." In *Prisms*. Cambridge, Mass.: MIT Press.

——. 1973. *Philosophy of Modern Music*. New York: The Seabury Press.

Ake, David. 2002. *Jazz Cultures*. Berkeley, Los Angeles, and London: University of California Press.

Anderson, Warren D. 1994. *Music and Musicians in Ancient Greece*. Ithaca and London: Cornell University Press.

Ansell, Kenneth. 1985a. "AMM: The Sound as Music." *The Wire* 11, January: 21–7.

——. 1985b. "Free Jazz in Britain." *The Wire* 14, April: 26–7, 29.

——. 1985c. "Derek Bailey and Company." *The Wire* 15, May: 33–5.

——. 1985d. "Incus for the Record." *The Wire* 15, May: 42–3.

Apel, Willi. 1958. *Gregorian Chant*. Bloomington, Ind.: Indiana University Press.

——. 1961. *The Notation of Polyphonic Music 900–1600*. Cambridge, Mass.: The Medieval Academy of America.

Armstrong, Karen. 1993. *A History of God: The 4000-Year Quest of Judaism, Christianity, and Islam*. New York: A. A. Knopf.

Art and Design. 1993. "Profile No. 28."

Asaf'yev, Boris. 1982. *A Book about Stravinsky*. Ann Arbor, Mich.: UMI Research Press.

Attali, Jacques. 1977/1985. *Noise: The Political Economy of Music*. Minneapolis: University of Minnesota Press.

Attenborough, David. 2002. *Song of the Earth* (videorecording, for *Nature*). New York and London: Thirteen/WNET and BBC.

Ayto, John. 1990. *Dictionary of Word Origins*. New York: Arcade Publishing.

Backus, Rob. 1978. *Fire Music: A Political History of Jazz*. Chicago: Vanguard Books.

Badger, R. Reid. 1989. "James Reese Europe and the Prehistory of Jazz." *American Music*, Spring, 48–66.

Bailey, Derek. 1993 [1980]. *Improvisation: Its Nature and Practice in Music.* New York: Da Capo Press.

———. 1996. "Classroom Improvisation." In Gary Spruce (ed.). *Teaching Music.* New York: Routledge: 227–32.

Bannister, Gary. 1992. "Eugene 1989." *Earshot Jazz*, September.

Baraka, Amiri (LeRoi Jones). 1970/1967. *Black Music.* New York: W. Morrow.

———. 1963. *Blues People: Negro Music in White America.* New York: William and Morrow.

Barber, Benjamin R. 1995. *Jihad vs. McWorld: How the Planet is both Falling Apart and Coming Together and What This Means for Democracy.* New York: Random House.

Bartholomew, Douglas. 1989. In *Understanding the Musical Experience*, edited by F. Joseph Smith. New York: Gordon and Breach.

Baskerville, John D. 1994. "Free Jazz: a Reflection of Black Power Ideology." *Journal of Black Studies* 24, no. 4, June: 484–97.

Bastien, David T., and Todd J. Hostager. 1991. "Jazz as Social Structure, Process, and Outcome." In Reginald T. Buckner and Steven Weiland (eds.). *Jazz in Mind: Essays on the History and Meanings of Jazz.* Detroit: Wayne State University Press.

Batel, G. 1978. "Free Jazz als intensive Form soziomusikalischer Kommunikation." *Melos/NZ; Neue Zeitschrift fur Musik,* 4/6 (1/8): 507–11.

Baudrillard, Jean. 1990/1993. *The Transparency of Evil: Essays on Extreme Phenomenon.* London/New York: Verso.

Belgrad, Daniel. 1998. *The Culture of Spontaneity: Improvisation and the Arts in Postwar America.* Chicago and London: The University of Chicago Press.

Belic, Roko. 2000. *Genghis Blues* (videorecording). New Video Group.

Benítez, Joaquim M. 1986. "Collective Improvisation in contemporary Western art music." In Yamaguti Osamu (ed.). *The oral and the literate in music.* Tokyo: Academic Music Ltd.

Benjamin, Walter. 1968. *The Work of Art in the Age of Mechanical Reproduction.* In *Illuminations.* New York: Harcourt, Brace and World.

Benjamin, William E. 1981. "Schenker's Theory and the Future of Music." *Journal of Music Theory,* 25/1: 155–73.

Berendt, Joachim Ernst. 1967. "Free Jazz – der neue Jazz der sechziger Jahre." *Melos; Zeitschrift für Neue Musik.* October: 345–51.

———. 1975. *The Jazz Book: From New Orleans to Rock and Free Jazz.* Translated by Daniel Morgenstern and Helmut and Barbara Bredigkeit. New York: L. Hill/Independent Publishers Group.

———. 1983/1987. *The World is Sound, Nada Brahma: Music and the Landscape of Consciousness.* Foreword by Fritjof Capra. Rochester, Vt.: Destiny Books.

———. 1986. *Ein Fenster aus Jazz: Essays, Portraits, Reflexionen.* Frankfurt am Main, Germany: Fischer Taschenbuch Verlag.

———. 1990. *Voices: A Compilation of the World's Greatest Choirs.* West Germany: Mesa Records.

———. 1996. "Wandel und Widerstand." *Jazz in Deutschland.* Jazz-Insitut Darmstadt: 261–79.

———. 1997a. "Expatriates." In Wolbert (1997: 305–12).

———. 1997b. "Exposition für eine Exposition." In Wolbert (1997: xiii–xv).

———. 1997c. "Über Weltmusik." In Wolbert (1997: 269–76).

Berg, Jochen. 1995. "Strangers in the Night." In "No Man's Land: East German Drama After the Wall." *Contemporary Theatre Review* 4/2: 129–50.

Bergmeier, Horst, and Rainer Lotz. 1996. "Ein obskures Kapitel der deutschen Jazz-geschichte." In *Jazz in Deutschland.* Hofheim, Germany: Wolke Verlag: 13–48.

Berkman, Franya. 2004. "Divine Songs: The Music of Alice Coltrane." Ph.D. dissertation. Middletown, Conn.: Wesleyan University.

Berkowitz, Kenny. 1995. "Up and Crumbling: German Jazz After the Fall." *Option*, November: 76–81.

Berlin, Sir Isaiah. 1999. Henry Hardy (ed.). *The Roots of Romanticism.* Princeton, N. J.: Princeton University Press.

Berliner, Paul. 1994. *Thinking In Jazz: The Infinite Art of Improvisation.* Chicago and London: University of Chicago Press.

Berman, Paul. 1996. *A Tale of Two Utopias: The Political Journey of the Generation of 1968*. New York and London: W. W. Norton and Company.

Bernstein, Leonard. 1973. *The Unanswered Question. The Norton Lectures*. Columbia M4X 33032.

Betz, Albrecht. 1982. *Hanns Eisler: Political Musician*. Cambridge and New York: Cambridge University Press.

Bielawski, Ludwik. 1985. "History in Ethnomusicology." *Yearbook for Traditional Music* 17: 8–15.

Blacking, John. 1971. "The Value of Music in Human Experience." *Yearbook of the International Folk Music Council* 1.

——. 1973. *How Musical is Man?* Seattle: University of Washington Press.

Blackwood, Michael. 1990. *Butoh: Body on the Edge of Crisis*. Videocassette/Michael Blackwood Productions, Inc.

Blake, David, (ed.). 1995. *Hanns Eisler: A Miscellany*. Australia and New York: Harwood Academic Publishers.

Block, Steven. 1993. "Organized Sound: Pitch-Class Relations in the Music of Ornette Coleman." *Annual Review of Jazz Studies* 6: 229–52.

Bogin, Meg. 1980. *The Women Troubadors*. New York and London: W. W. Norton.

Bohlman, Philip V. 1993. "Musicology as a Political Act." *The Journal of Musicology*. 11: 4.

Bowers, Kathryn Smith. 2002. "East Meets West: Contributions of Mátyás Seiber to Jazz in Germany." In Michael J. Budds (ed.), *Jazz and the Germans: Essay on the Influence of "Hot" American Idioms on 20th-Century German Music*. Hillsdale, N.Y.: Pendragon Press.

Brasch, Thomas. 1977. "Hahnenkopf." In *Kargo*. Frankfurt am Main: Suhrkamp Verlag.

Braudy, Leo. 2003. *From Chivalry to Terrorism: War and the Changing Nature of Masculinity*. New York: Alfred A. Knopf.

Brauer, Carl. 1978. "Still More FMP." *Cadence*, March: 24–5.

Braxton, Anthony. 1968. *Three Compositions of New Jazz*. Delmark DS-415.

——. 1985. *Tri-Axium Writings 1, 2, and 3*. Hanover, N.H.: Tree Frog Music.

——. 1988. *Composition Notes A, B, C, D*, and *E*. Hanover, N.H.: Tree Frog Music.

Brodowski, Pawel. 1997. "Jazz in Polen." In Wolbert (1997: 449–54).

Brown Jr., Marion. 1976. "Faces and Places: The Music and Travels of a Contemporary Jazz Musician." Ph.D. dissertation. Middletown Conn.: Wesleyan University.

Brown, Lee B. 1991. "The Theory of Jazz Music: 'It Don't Mean a Thing . . .'" *The Journal of Aesthetics and Art Criticism* 49: 2 Spring: 15–127.

——. 1992. "Adorno's Critique of Popular Culture: The Case of Jazz Music." *Journal of Aesthetic Education*. 26: 1.

Brownell, John. 1994. "Analytical Models of Jazz Improvisation." *Jazzforschung* 26: 9–31.

Budds, Michael J., ed. 2002. *Jazz and the Germans: Essay on the Influence of "Hot" American Idioms on 20th-Century German Music*. Hillsdale, N.Y.: Pendragon Press.

Burde, Wolfgang. 1978. "A Discussion of European Free Jazz." In *For Example*. Berlin: FMP.

Burns, Ken. 2000. *Jazz*. PBS Home Video/Warner Home Video.

Carr, Ian. 1973. *Music Outside*. London: Latimer New Dimensions.

——. 1982. *Miles Davis: A Biography*. New York: W. Morrow.

——. 1991. *Keith Jarrett: The Man and His Music*. London: Grafton.

Cavalli-Sforza, Luigi Luca, and Francesco Cavalli-Sforza. 1995. *The Great Human Diasporas: The History of Diversity and Evolution*. Cambridge, Mass.: Helix Books/Perseus Books.

Cerchiari, Luca. 1997. "Jazz in Italien." In Wolbert (1997: 469–78).

Chailley, Jacques. 1986 [1951, 1977]. *Historical Treatise of Harmonic Analysis*. Paris: Alphonse Leduc.

Chanan, Michael. 1994. *Musica Practica: The Social Practice of Western Music from Gregorian Chant to Postmodernism*. London and New York: Verso.

Charry, Eric. 1997–8. "Freedom and Form in Ornette Coleman's Early Atlantic Recordings." *Annual Review of Jazz Studies* 9.

Childers, Thomas. 1998. *Europe and Western Civilization in the Modern Age*. Springfield, Va.: The Teaching Company.

Clarke, Eric F. 1992. "Improvisation, Cognition and Education." In John Paynter, Tim Howell, Richard Orton, and Peter Seymour (eds.). *Companion to Contemporary Musical Thought*, II. London and New York: Routledge: 787–802.

Cohn, Richard L., and Douglas J. Dempster. 1992. "Hierarchical Unity, Plural Unities: Toward a Reconciliation." In *Disciplining Music: Musicology and its Canons*. Chicago: University of Chicago: 156–81.

Cole, Bill. 1974. *Miles Davis: A Musical Biography*. New York: W. Morrow.

——. 1976. *John Coltrane*. New York: Schirmer Books.

Coleman, Ornette. 1968. *A Collection of 26 Ornette Coleman Compositions*. New York: MJQ Music.

Collier, James Lincoln. 1988. *The Reception of Jazz in America: A New View*. I.S.A.M. Monographs, no. 27. Brooklyn: Institute for Studies in American Music. Brooklyn College of the City University of New York.

Comolli, Jean Louis. 1966. "Voyage au Bout de la New Thing." *Jazz Magazine*. no. 129, April: 24–9.

Comolli, Jean-Louis, and Philippe Carles. 2000 [1971, 1979]. *Free Jazz, Black Power*. Paris: Folio.

Connerton, Paul. 1989. *How Societies Remember*. Cambridge: Cambridge University Press.

Cook, Richard. 1986. "Alex von Schlippenbach: The Indispensable Focus." *The Wire* 30, August: 10, 48.

——. 2003. *Blue Note Records: A Biography*. Justin, Charles and Company.

Cook, Susan C. 1989. "Jazz as Deliverance: The Reception and Institution of American Jazz during the Weimar Republic." *American Music*, Spring: 30–47.

Corbett, John. 1989. "Ernst-Ludwig Petrowsky: Interview. *Cadence* 15/9, September: 16–18, 20.

——. 1994. "Peter Brötzmann: Machine Gun Etiquette." In *Extended play: sounding off from John Cage to Dr. Funkenstein*. Durham and London: Duke University Press: 247–59.

——. 1995. "Ephemera Underscored: Writing Around Free Improvisation." In Krin Gabbard (ed.). *Jazz Among the Discourses*, Durham and London: Duke University Press: 217–42.

——. 1998. "Band With a Mission." *Down Beat*, June: 38–40.

——. "An open letter to FMP." Undated, part of FMP's fundraising kit.

Cotro, Vincent. 1999. *Chants Libres: Le free jazz en France, 1960–1975*. Paris: Outre Mesure.

Cowell, Alan. 1997. "Germany the Unloved Just Wants to Be Normal." *The New York Times*, 23 November: WK3.

Crouch, Stanley. 1995. *The All-American Skin Game, or, The Decoy of Race: the Long and Short of It, 1990–1994*. New York: Pantheon Books.

Cuscuna, Michael. 1969. "A New Front; the creative reservoir of German jazz artists." *Jazz and Pop*, July: 25–6.

Cuscuna, Michael, and Michael Ruppli. 1988. *The Blue Note Label: A Discography*, New York: Greenwood Press.

D'Souza, Dinesh. 1995. *The End of Racism*. New York, London, Toronto, Sydney, Tokyo, and Singapore: The Free Press.

Dalhaus, Carl. 1983. *Foundations of Music History*. Cambridge: Cambridge University Press.

Damasio, Antonio. 1994. *Descartes' Error: Emotion, Reason, and the Human Brain*. New York: Quill/Penguin Putnam.

——. 1999. *The Feeling of What Happens: Body and Emotion in the Making of Consciousness*. San Diego, New York, and London: Harvest/Harcourt, Inc.

Danzi, Michael. 1986. *American Musician in Germany 1924–1939*. As told to Rainer E. Lotz. Frankfurt: Nexus Verlag.

Davidson, Archibald T., and Willi Apel. 1946. *Historical Anthology of Music: Oriental, Medieval and Renaissance Music*. Cambridge Mass.: Harvard University Press.

Davidson, Basil. 1987. "The Ancient World and Africa: Whose Roots?" *Race and Class*, 29: 2.

Davis, Francis. 1986. *In the Moment: Jazz in the 1980s*. New York and Oxford: Oxford University Press.

——. 1990. *Outcats: Jazz Composers, Instrumentalists, and Singers.* New York and Oxford: Oxford University Press.

——. 1995. *The History of the Blues: The Roots, the Music, the People from Charley Patton to Robert Cray.* New York: Hyperion.

De Ruyter, Michiel. 1997. "Jazz in der Niederlanden." In Wolbert (1997: 477–82).

De Wilde, Laurent. 1997. *Monk.* New York: Marlowe and Company.

Dean, R. T. 1989. *Creative Improvisation: Jazz, Contemporary Music, and Beyond: How to Develop Techniques of Improvisation for any Musical Context.* Milton Keynes and Philadelphia: Open University Press.

——. 1992. *New Structures in Jazz and Improvised Music Since 1960.* Milton Keynes and Philadelphia: Open University Press.

Deleuze, Gilles, and Félix Guattari. 1975/1986. *Kafka: Toward a Minor Literature.* Minneapolis: University of Minnesota Press.

DeLio, Thomas. 1984. *Circumscribing the Open Universe.* Lanham, New York, and London: University Press of America.

Dennis, David B. 1996. *Beethoven in German Politics, 1870–1989.* New Haven and London: Yale University Press.

DeVeaux, Scott. 1989. "The Emergence of the Jazz Concert, 1935–1945." *American Music,* Spring: 6–31.

——. 1997. *The Birth of Bebop: A Social and Musical History.* Berkeley, Los Angeles, and London: University of California Press.

Diamond, Jared. 1999 [1997]. *Guns, Germs, and Steel: The Fates of Human Societies.* New York and London: W. W. Norton and Company.

Dimont, Max. 1995. *Jews, God, and History.* New York: Mentor Books.

Dizikes, John. 1993. *Opera in America: A Cultural History.* New Haven and London: Yale University Press.

Doru žka, Lubomir. 1997. "Jazz in der Tschechoslowakei." In Wolbert (1997: 455–62).

Earkin, Emily. 2002. "For Big History, the Past Begins at the Beginning." *The New York Times,* 12 January: B7.

Edelman, Gerald M. 1987. *Neural Darwinism: The Theory of Neuronal Group Selection.* New York: Basic Books/HarperCollins.

——. 1992. *Bright Air, Brilliant Fire: On the Matter of the Mind.* New York: Basic Books/HarperCollins.

Edelman, Gerald M., and Giolio Tononi. 2000. *A Universe of Consciousness: How Matter Becomes Imagination.* New York: Basic Books/Perseus.

Ehrman, Baird. 1994. *The Letters of Hildegard of Bingen,* II New York and Oxford: Oxford University Press.

Eisler, Hanns. 1973. *Musik und Politik: Schriften 1924–1948.* Leipzig: VEB Deutscher Verlag für Musik.

——. 1975. *Das Argument As 5.* Berlin: Argument-Verlag.

——. 1986. *Fragen Sie mehr über Brecht: Gespräche mit Hans Bunge.* Darmstadt: Luchterhand.

Ellis, Alexander J. 1885. "On the Musical Scales of Various Nations." *Journal of the Society of Arts* 33: 526.

Elworth, Steven B. 1995. "Jazz in Crisis, 1948–1958: Ideology and Representation." In Krin Gabbard (ed.). *Jazz Among the Discourses,* Durham and London: Duke University Press: 57–75.

Emsheimer, Ernst. 1997. "Gesellschaftsmusik im Großstadtzentrum Frankreich – Bal Nègre in Paris." In Wolbert (1997: 333–4).

Engelhardt, Jürgen (trans. Ruth B. Williams). 1980. "Einige Anmerkungen zur Ästhetik des DDR Jazz/A Few Comments about the Esthetics of GDR-Jazz." *Snapshot: Jazz aus DDR.* FMP LP booklet: 33–44.

Epstein, David. 1995. *Shaping Time: Music, the Brain, and Performance.* New York: Schirmer Books.

Erenberg, Lewis A. 1998. *Swingin' the Dream: Big Band Jazz and the Rebirth of American Culture.* Chicago and London: University of Chicago Press.

Erlmann, Veit. 1993. "The Politics and Aesthetics of Transnational Musics." *The World of Music* 35/2: 3–15.

——. 1996. "The Aesthetics of the Global Imagination: Reflections on World Music in the 1990s." *Public Culture* 8: 467–87.

Fackler, Guido. 1996. "Jazz im KZ. Ein Forschungsbericht." In *Jazz in Deutschland.* Hofheim, Germany: Wolke Verlag: 49–92.

Fanon, Frantz. 1966. *The Wretched of the Earth.* New York: Grove Press.

——. (trans. by Charles Lam Markmann) 1991 [1967]. *Black Skin, White Masks.* New York: Grove Press.

Feather, Leonard. 1962. "Feather's Nest." *Down Beat.* 15 February: 40.

——. 1971. "Blindfold Test: Phil Woods." *Down Beat.* 24 June: 18.

Feigin, Leo (ed.). 1985. *Russian Jazz: New Identity.* London, Melbourne, and New York: Quartet Books.

Ferrara, Lawrence. 1991. *Philosophy and the Analysis of Music.* Westport Conn.: Greenwood Press.

Fields, Marc (writer/director/producer). 2001. *Willie the Lion* (videorecording). Trenton, N.J.: NJN Public Television.

Fisher, Marc. 1995. *After the Wall: Germany, the Germans and the Burdens of History.* New York: Simon and Schuster.

Fishkin, Shelley Fisher. 1995. "Interrogating 'Whiteness,' Complicating 'Blackness': Remapping American Culture." *American Quarterly* 47/3: 428–66.

Flower, Nick. 1995. *Hildegard von Bingen: Heavenly Revelations.* Munich: MVD Music and Video Distribution/Naxos CD 8.550998, liner notes.

Floyd, Samuel A., Jr. 1995. *The Power of Black Music: Interpreting its History from Africa to the United States.* New York and Oxford: Oxford University Press.

Forst, Achim (ed.). 1983. *Free Music Production: Records. Informations.* Berlin: Free Music Production.

Forte, Allen. 1973. *The Structure of Atonal Music.* New Haven and London: Yale University Press.

——. 1988. "Schenker, Friedrich." *The Grove Dictionary of Music and Musicians.* London: Macmillan; Washington DC: Groves Dictionaries of Music: 627–8.

Forte, Allen, and Steven E. Gilbert. 1982. *Introduction to Schenkerian Analysis.* New York: W. W. Norton and Company.

Foucault, Michel. 1977. "Nietzsche, Genealogy, History." In Donald Bouchard (ed.). *Michel Foucault: Language, Counter-Memory, Practice.* Ithaca: Cornell University Press.

——. 1988–1990. *The History of Sexuality.* New York: Vintage Books.

Foucault, Michel, and Pierre Boulez. 1986. "Contemporary Music and the Public." *Perspectives of New Music* (Fall–Winter).

Fox, Charles. 1997. "Jazz in England." In Wolbert (1997: 435–48).

Fox, Matthew (ed.). 1987. *Hildegard of Bingen's Book of Divine Works.* Santa Fe, N. Mex.: Bear and Company.

Fraser, J. T. 1987. *Time, the Familiar Stranger.* Amherst: University of Massachusetts Press.

——. 1990/1975. *Of Time, Passion, and Knowledge: Reflections on the Strategy of Existence.* Princeton, N.J.: Princeton University Press.

Freud, Sigmund (trans. David McLintock). 2002 [1930]. *Civilization and its Discontents* (*Unbehagen in der Kultur*). London: Penguin (orig. London: Hogarth Press).

Frith, Simon (ed.). 1989. *World Music, Politics and Social Change: Papers from the International Association for the Study of Popular Music.* Manchester and New York: Manchester University Press.

Gabbard, Krin (ed.). 1995. *Jazz Among the Discourses,* Durham and London: Duke University Press.

——. 1995. *Representing Jazz,* Durham and London: Duke University Press.

Gates, Henry Louis. 1988. *The Signifying Monkey: A Theory of Afro-American Literary Criticism.* New York and Oxford: Oxford University Press.

Gendron, Bernard. 1995. "'Moldy Figs' and Modernists: Jazz at War (1942–1946)." In Krin Gabbard (ed.). *Jazz Among the Discourses.* Durham and London: Duke University Press.

Gennari, John. 1991. "Jazz Criticism: Its Development and Ideologies." In *Black American Literature Forum* 25, no. 3, Fall: 449–523.

Gerard, Charles. 1998. *Jazz in Black and White*. Westport, Conn.: Praeger.

Giddins, Gary. 1981. *Riding on a Blue Note: Jazz and American Pop*. New York and Oxford: Oxford University Press.

———. 1985. *Rhythm-a-Ning: Jazz Tradition and Innovation in the '80s*. New York and Oxford: Oxford University Press.

Gill, Jerry H. 1994. "Langer, Language, and Art." *International Philosophical Quarterly* 34: 4, 136.

Gilroy, Paul. 1993. *The Black Atlantic: Modernity and Double Consciousness*. Cambridge, Mass.: Harvard University Press.

Gioia, Ted. 1987. "Jazz: The Aesthetics of Imperfection." *The Hudson Review* 39, Winter: 585–600.

Glassgold, Peter (ed.). 2001. *Anarchy! An Anthology of Emma Goldman's Mother Earth*. Washington D.C.: Counterpoint/Perseus Books.

Globokar, Vinko. 1998. *Laboratorium: Texte zur Musik 1967–1997*. Saarbrucken: Pfau Verlag.

Godwin, Joscelyn. 1989. *Cosmic Music*. Rochester, Vt.: Inner Traditions.

Goodwin, Andrew, and Joe Gore. 1990. "World Beat and the Cultural Imperialism Debate." *Socialist Review* 20/3: 63–80.

Gordon, Avery, and Christopher Newfield. 1994. "White Philosophy." *Critical Inquiry* 20, Summer: 737–57.

Gordon, William A. 1967. *The Mind and Art of Henry Miller*. Baton Rouge, La.: Louisiana State University Press.

Gottlieb, Robert (ed.). 1996. *Reading Jazz: A Gathering of Autobiography, Reportage, and Criticism from 1919 to Now*. New York: Pantheon Books.

Gray, John. 1991. *Fire Music: A Bibliography of the New Jazz, 1959–1990*. New York, Westport, Conn., and London: Greenwood Press.

Gray, John. 1998. *False Dawn: The Delusions of Global Capitalism*. New York: The New Press.

Greene, Jack P. 1993. *The Intellectual Construction of America: Exceptionalism and Identity from 1492 to 1800*. Chapel Hill and London: The University of North Carolina Press.

Greider, William. 2003. *The Soul of Capitalism: Opening Paths to a Moral Economy*. New York: Simon and Schuster.

Gridley, Mark, Robert Maxham, and Robert Hoff. 1989. "Three Approaches to Defining Jazz." *The Musical Quarterly* 73/4: 513–31.

Griffiths, Paul. 1994/1978. *Modern Music: A Concise History*. New York and London: Thames and Hudson.

———. 1996. "From the Edge of Experience, a New Sound." *The New York Times* 1 December: H31.

———. 1998. "How Music Spins a Web of Meaning." *The New York Times*, 1 February: AR43.

The Grove Dictionary of Music and Musicians. 1980. London: Macmillan; Washington D.C.: Groves Dictionaries of Music.

Grun, Bernard. 1975. *The Timetables of History: A Horizontal Linkage of People and Events*. New York: Simon and Schuster.

Guilbault, Jocelyne. 1993. "On Redefining the 'Local' through World Music." *The World of Music* 35/2: 33–47.

———. 1993. *Zouk: World Music in the West Indies*. Chicago: University of Chicago Press.

Gushee, Lawrence. 2002. "The Nineteenth-Century Origins of Jazz." In Lewis Porter (ed.). *A Century of Change: Readings and New Essays*. New York: Schirmer Books.

Hale, John. 1994. *The Civilization of Europe in the Renaissance*. New York: Atheneum.

Hall, Edward T. 1992. "Improvisation as an Acquired, Multilevel Process." *Ethnomusicology* 36, no. 2, Spring/Summer: 223–35.

Hanslick, Eduard. 1885. *The Beautiful in Music*. New York: The Bobbs-Merrill Co. 1974.

Harding, James M. 1995. "Adorno, Ellison, and the Critique of Jazz." In *Cultural Critique*. Fall: 129–58.

Hardt, Michael, and Antonio Negri. 2000. *Empire*. Cambridge, Mass., and London: Harvard University Press.

Hartman, Charles O. 1991. *Jazz Text: Voice and Improvisation in Poetry, Jazz, and Song.* Princeton, N.J.: Princeton University Press.

Hauber, Annette, and Dr. Dietrich Schulz-Köhn. 1997a. "Jazz im besetzen Frankreich (1940–1945)." In Wolbert (1997: 335–44).

——. 1997b. "Frauen im Jazz." In Wolbert (1997: 699–718).

Hebdige, Dick. 2001. "Even unto Death: Improvisation, Edging, and Enframement." *Critical Inquiry* 27, Winter.

Heble, Ajay. 2000. *Landing on the Wrong Note: Jazz Dissonance and Critical Practice.* New York and London: Routledge.

Heffley, Mike. 1979. "Cal Tjader Interview: Latin/Jazz Pioneer." *Willamette Valley Observer* 3/79: Eugene, Oregon.

——. 1996. *The Music of Anthony Braxton.* Westport, Conn.: Greenwood, hardback; New York: Excelsior, softback.

——. 2000. *Northern Sun, Southern Moon: Improvisation, Identity, and Idiom in* Freie Musik Produktion. Ph.D. dissertation. Middletown, Conn.: Wesleyan University.

——. 2001. *Music in the Free World 1950–1970* (conference symposium, 17–18 February). Archived in Olin Library, Wesleyan University, Middletown, Conn.

——. 2002a. "The Tri-Centric Transcripts." *signal to noise* 24, Winter: 39–47.

——. 2002b. "Joe Fonda: Transcontinental Connection." *signal to noise* 25, Spring: 12.

Heidegger, Martin (trans. David Farrell Krell and Frank A. Capuzzi). 1975. *Early Greek Thinking.* New York: Harper and Row.

Hersch, Charles. 1996. "'Let Freedom Ring!': Free Jazz and African-American Politics." *Cultural Critique* 32, Winter: 97–123.

Herskovits, Melville J. 1952. "Some Psychological Implications of Afroamerican Studies." In Sol Tax (ed.), *Acculturation in the Americas: Proceedings and Selected Papers of the XXIXth International Congress of Americanists.* Chicago: The University of Chicago Press.

Hildegard von Bingen (trans. and ed. Adelgundis Führkötter). 1965. *Briefwechsel.* Salzburg: Otto Müller Verlag.

—— (trans. Bruce Hozeski). 1986. *Scivias.* Santa Fe, N. Mex.: Bear and Company.

Hiley, David. 1993. *Western Plainchant: A Handbook.* Oxford: Clarendon Press.

Hinely, Patrick. 1997. "Albert Mangelsdorff: Atmospheric Conditions Permitting." *Coda Magazine*, 271: 8–11.

Hodeir, André. 1956. *Jazz: Its Evolution and Essence.* New York: Grove Press.

Hoffmann, Bernd. 1996. "Die *Mitteilungen*–Anmerkungen zu einer 'verbotenen' Fanpostile." In *Jazz in Deutschland.* Hofheim, Germany: Wolke Verlag: 93–102.

Holland, Bernard. 1995. "Playing Fast and Loose with Time." *The New York Times,* 29 October: H33.

Horowitz, Irving Louis. 1982. "On Seeing and Hearing Music: Nine Propositions in Search of Explanation." *Annual Review of Jazz Studies* 1: 72–8.

Huebener, Theodore. 1962. *The Germans in America.* Philadelphia: Chilton Co., Book Division.

Huesmann, Günther. 1997. "Geburt und Werdegang des Jazzfestivals." In Wolbert (1997: 667–84).

Hunkemöller, Jürgen. 1997. "Die Rolle der Schallplatte im Jazz." In Wolbert (1997: 547–56).

——. 1997. "Jazz in der Neuen Musik Europas." In Wolbert (1997: 535–46).

Iannapollo, Robert J. 1988. "Brötzmann, Peter." In *The New Grove Dictionary of Jazz.* London: Macmillan; New York: Groves Dictionaries of Music: 155.

Jackson, Timothy L. 1992. "Current Issues in Schenkerian Analysis." *The Musical Quarterly* 76: 242–63.

James, C. L. R. (ed. Anna Grimshaw and Keith Hart). 1993. *American Civilization.* Cambridge, Mass.: Blackwell.

—— (ed. Martin Glaberman). 1999. *Marxism for our Times: C.L.R. James on Revolutionary Organization.* Jackson, Miss.: University Press of Mississippi.

—— (ed. Scott McLemee). 1996. *C. L. R. James on the "Negro Question".* Jackson, Miss.: University Press of Mississippi.

James, Jamie. 1993. *The Music of the Spheres: Music, Science and the Natural Order of the Universe.* New York: Grove Press.

Jameson, Fredric. 1991. *Postmodernism: Or, The Cultural Logic of Late Capitalism.* Durham and London: Duke University Press.

Jeffrey, Peter. 1992. *Re-Envisioning Past Musical Cultures: Ethnomusicology in the Study of Gregorian Chant.* Chicago: University of Chicago.

Jeudy, Henri Pierre. 1991. "Die Transparenz des Objekts." In Florian Rötzer (ed.). *Digitaler Schein. Ästhetik der elektronischen Medien.* Frankfurt am Main: Suhrkamp: 171–82.

Johansson, Sven-Åke. 1993. "Musik im Raum." *Musik Texte* 48, February: 13.

Johnston, Ian. 1989. *Measured Tones: The Interplay of Physics and Music.* New York: Adam Hilger.

Jones, Le Roi. See Baraka, Amiri.

Joppig, Gunther. 1997. "Vom Bläserquintett zur Big Band." In Wolbert (1997: 9–22).

Jost, Ekkehard. 1971–1972. "Free Jazz und die Musik der Dritten Welt." *Jazz Research/ Jazzforschung,* No. 3/4: 141.

———. 1994 [1975]. *Free Jazz.* New York: Da Capo Press.

———. 1976. "Musikalisches Theater und Free Jazz." *Musik und Bildung,* March: 160–61.

———. 1979. "Europaische Jazz-Avantgarde – Emanzipation Wohin?" *Jazzforschung* 11: 165–95.

———. 1987. *Europas Jazz 1960–1980.* Frankfurt am Main: Fischer Taschenbuch Verlag.

———. 1988. "Instant Composing as Body Language." In booklet accompanying 2-CD set *Alms/Tiergarten (Spree).* Berlin: FMP.

———. 1989. "Ist der Free Jazz tot? Anmerkungen zu einer windigen parole." *Jazz Podium,* January, 16–19.

———. 1994. "Über das Europäische im europäischen Jazz." In *Jazz in Europa.* Hofheim, Germany: Wolke Verlag: 233–49.

———. 1997a. "Free Jazz." In Wolbert (1997: 241–54).

———. 1997b. "Die europäische Jazz-Emanziapation." In Wolbert (1997: 501–12).

———. 1997c. "Jazz in Deutschland – Von der Weimarer Republik zur Adenauer-Ära." In Wolbert (1997: 357–76).

———. 1997d. "Jazz in Europa – Die frühen Jahre." In Wolbert (1997: 299–304).

———. 1997e. "Le Jazz en France." In Wolbert (1997: 313–28).

———. 1997f. "Reflexionen über Jazzgeschichte." In Wolbert (1997: xi–xii).

Kalb, Jonathan. 1996. "On the Becoming Death of Poor H.M." *Theater* 27/1: 65–73.

Kater, Michael H. 1989. "Forbidden fruit? Jazz in the Third Reich." *The American Historical Review* 94, February: 11–43.

———. 1992. *Different Drummers: Jazz in the Culture of Nazi Germany.* New York and Oxford: Oxford University Press.

Keil, Charles. 1966. "Motion and Feeling Through Music." *Journal of Aesthetics and Art Criticism* 24/3: 337–49.

———. 1987. "Participatory Discrepancies and the Power of Music." *Cultural Anthropology* 2/3: 275–83.

———. 1995. "The Theory of Participatory Discrepancies: A Progress Report." *Ethnomusicology* 39, Winter: 1–19, 73–100.

Kennedy, Randall. 2002. *Nigger: The Strange Career of a Troublesome Word.* New York: Pantheon Books.

Kenney III, William H. 1991. "Negotiating the Color Line: Louis Armstrong's Autobiographies." In Reginald T. Buckner and Steven Weiland (eds.). *Jazz in Mind: Essays on the History and Meanings of Jazz.* Detroit: Wayne State University Press.

Kerman, Joseph. 1985. *Contemplating Music: Challenges to Musicology.* Cambridge, Mass.: Harvard University Press.

———. 1991. "American Musicology in the 1990s." *The Journal of Musicology* 9, no. 2, Spring: 131–43.

Kernfeld, Barry. 1983. "Two Coltranes." *Annual Review of Jazz Studies* 2: 7–66.

Kippen, James. 1987. "An ethnomusicological approach to the analysis of musical cognition." *Music Perception* 5, 2: 173–96.

Kiroff, Matthew J. 1998. *Caseworks as Performed by Cecil Taylor and the Art Ensemble of Chicago: A Musical Analysis and Sociopolitical History*. Ann Arbor, Mich.: UMI Dissertation Services.

Klopotek, Felix. 1997. "Retro als Subversion: Über Anthony Braxton's Jazzpianoexkursionen and andere Marginalitäten." *Spex*, August: 167–72.

Knauer, Wolfram. 1994a. "'Musicianers' oder: Der Jazzmusiker als Musikant. Anmerkungen zum Verhältnis von Jazz und Folklore." In *Jazz in Europa*. Hofheim, Germany: Wolke Verlag: 185–200.

——. 1994b. "Vorwort." In *Jazz in Europa*. Hofheim, Germany: Wolke Verlag: 7–11.

——. 1996. "Emanzipation wovon? Zum Verhältnis des amerikanischen und des deutschen Jazz in den 50er und 60er Jahren." In *Jazz in Deutschland*. Hofheim, Germany: Wolke Verlag: 141–58.

Kofsky, Frank. 1970. *Black Nationalism and the Revolution in Music*. New York: Pathfinder Press.

Kohl, Jerome. "Time and Light." *Contemporary Music Review* 7, 2: 203–20.

Köhler, Peter. 1997. "Die 'Ghetto Swingers' im Konzentrationslager Theresienstadt." In Wolbert (1997: 389–90).

Kopelowicz, Guy. 1967. "Le Nouveau Jazz et la Réalité/Americain." *Jazz Hot*, no. 231, May: 18–23.

Kopotek, Felix. 1997. "One Man Walked Alone." *Jazzthetik* 9, 97: 53–5.

Kowald, Peter. 1998. *Almanach der "365 Tage am Ort"*. Cologne: Verlag der Buchhandlung Walter König.

Kramer, Jane. 1996. *The Politics of Memory: Looking for Germany in the New Germany*. New York: Random House.

Kramer, Jonathan D. 1978. "Moment Form in Twentieth Century Music." *Musical Quarterly* 64, 2, April: 177–94.

——. 1988. *The Time of Music: New Meanings, New Temporalities, New Listening Strategies*. New York: Schirmer Books; London: Collier Macmillan.

Kraus, Chris, and Sylvère Lotringer. 2001. *Hatred of Capitalism: A Semiotext(e) Reader*. Los Angeles and New York: Semiotext(e)/MIT Press.

Krell, David Farrell. 1977/1993. *Martin Heidegger: Basic Writings*. San Francisco: Harper.

Kristof, Nicholas D. 1999. "The World: A Better System in the 19th Century? At This Rate, We'll Be Global in Another Hundred Years." *New York Times*, 23 May, Section 4, 5.

Kubik, Gerhard. 1994. *Theory of African Music*. Wilhelmshaven: F. Noetzel.

Kumpf, Hans. 1981a. "Ernst-Ludwig Petrovsky." *Jazz Podium* 7, January: 14–16.

——. 1981b [1975]. *Postserielle Musik und Free Jazz: Wechselwirkungen und Parallelen: Berichte, Analysen, Werkstattgesprache*. 2nd ed. Rohrdorf: Rohrdorfer Musikverlag.

Kurlansky, Mark. 2004. *1968: The Year that Rocked the World*. Ballantine Books: New York.

Kurth, Ulrich. 1996. "Kurzew Geschichten: Die 90er Jahre." In *Jazz in Deutschland*. Hofheim, Germany: Wolke Verlag: 245–60.

Lake, Steve. 1991. Untitled FMP press kit essay.

Lake, Steve, and Chris Welch. 1973. "Free For All! – Are We Ignoring a Musical Revolution or is it Undisciplined Anarchy?" *Melody Maker*, 15 December: 40–2.

Lang, Paul Henry. 1941. *Music in Western Civilization*. New York: W. W. Norton and Company.

Lange, Horst. 1960/1996. *Jazz in Deutschland: Die Deutsche Jazz-Chronik bis 1960*. Hildesheim: Olms Presse.

——. 1997. "'Artfremde Kunst und Musik unerwünscht' – Jazz im Dritten Reich." In Wolbert (1997: 391–404).

Lateef, Yusef. 1981. *Repository of Scales and Melodic Patterns*. Amherst, Mass.: Fana Music.

Le Mée, Katharine. 1994. *Chant: The Origin, Form, Practice and Healing Power of Gregorian Chant*. New York: Bell Tower.

Lee, Felicia R. 2003. "Newark to Nepal and Back." *New York Times*, 16 August, A15, A17.

Leonard, Neil. 1986. "The Jazzman's Verbal Usage." *Black American Literature Forum* 20, Spring/Summer, 151–60.

Leppert, Richard. 1993. *The Sight of Sound: Music, Representation, and the History of the Body*. Berkeley: University of California Press.

Lère, Pierre. 1970. "Free Jazz: Evolution ou Revolution." *Revue d'Esthetique* 23, no. 3/4: 313–25.

Levin, David Michael. 1985. *The Body's Recollection of Being: Phenomenological Psychology and the Deconstruction of Nihilism*. London: Routledge and Kegan Paul.

Levin, Michael, and John S. Wilson. "The Chili Parlor Interview." In Wolbert (1997: 187–92).

Levman, Bryan G. 1992. "The Genesis of Music and Language." *Ethnomusicology* 36, Spring/Summer, no. 2: 147–70.

Levy, Kenneth. 1998. *Gregorian Chant and the Carolingians*. Princeton, N.J.: Princeton University Press.

Lewis, Bernard. 1998. "The Historical Roots of Racism." *The American Scholar*, 67/1, Winter: 17–25.

Lewis, George. 1996. "Improvised Music After 1950: Afrological and Eurological Perspectives." *Black Music Research Journal* 16/1, Spring: 91–122.

Liebeschütz, Hans. 1964. *Das Allegorische Weltbild der Heiligen Hildegard von Bingen*. Darmstadt: Wissenschaftliche Buchgesellschaft.

Liefland, W. E. 1976. "Free Jazz – nur eine Geschichtsdelle?" *Jazz Podium* June: 10–12.

—— (trans. Rosemarie Jung and Geoffrey Roberts [poem]). 1980. "Grenzänge – Grenz-gesänge" ("Transit Walk–Transit Talk"). *Snapshot: Jazz aus DDR*. FMP LP booklet: 6–14.

Lieth-Philipp, Margot and Andreas Gutzwiller. 1995. *Teaching Musics of the World*. Affalterbach, Germany: Philip Verlag.

Lilla, Mark. 1998. "Still Living With '68." *New York Times Magazine*, 16 August: 34–7.

——. 1999. "An Idea Whose Time Has Gone" (on François Furet's *The Passing of an Illusion: The Idea of Communism in the Twentieth Century*). In *The New York Times Book Review*, 25 July: 12–13.

Lindenmaier, Lukas. 1978. "Peter Brötzmann: interview." *Cadence*, 3–7, 20, 22.

Linzer, Martin (trans. Rosemarie Jung). 1980. "Jazz in der DDR: 10 Punkte zur Entwicklung einer Szene" ("Jazz in the German Democratic Republic (GDR): 10 Remarks on the Development of a Scene"). *Snapshot: Jazz aus DDR*. FMP LP booklet: 15–18.

Lipsitz, George. 1994. *Dangerous Crossroads: Popular Music, Postmodernism, and the Poetics of Place*. London and New York: Verso.

——. 1995a. "The Possessive Investment in Whiteness: Racialized Social Democracy and the 'White' Problem in American Studies." *American Quarterly* 47/3: 369–87.

——. 1995b. "Toxic Racism." *American Quarterly* 47/3: 416–27.

Lissa, Zofia. 1965. "On the Evolution of Musical Perception." *The Journal of Aesthetics and Art Criticism*, Winter: 273–93.

Litweiler, John. 1984. *The Freedom Principle: Jazz After 1958*. New York: W. Morrow.

Lochhead, Judy, and Joseph Auner (eds.). 2002. *Postmodern Music, Postmodern Thought*. New York and London: Routledge.

Lock, Graham. 1985. *Forces in Motion: Anthony Braxton and the Meta-Reality of Creative Music*. London: Quartet Books.

——. 1999. *Blutopia: Visions of the Future and Revisions of the Past in the Work of Sun Ra, Duke Ellington, and Anthony Braxton*. Durham and London: Duke University Press.

Loesser, Arthur. 1954. *Men, Women and Pianos: A Social History*. New York: Simon and Schuster.

Lomax, Alan. 1993. *The Land Where the Blues Began*. New York: Delta/Dell.

Looker, Ben. 2001. "Poets of Action: The St. Louis Black Artist's Group, 1968–1972." *Gateway Heritage* 22, Summer, no. 1.

Lord, Albert B. 1960. *The Singer of Tales*. Cambridge, Mass., and London: Harvard University Press.

Lotz, Rainer E. 1997. "Amerikaner in Europa." In Wolbert (1997: 291–8).

Luebke, Frederick C. 1990. *Germans in the New World: Essays in the History of Immigration*. Urbana and Chicago: University of Illinois Press.

Lukens, Nancy, and Dorothy Rosenberg (trans. and ed.). 1993. *Daughters of Eve: Women's Writing from the German Democratic Republic*. Lincoln, Nebr., and London: University of Nebraska Press.

MacKillop, Kenneth. 1950. "The Schillinger System." *Down Beat* 9/22: 18; 12/4: 8.

Maconie, Robin. 1976. *The Works of Karlheinz Stockhausen*. New York and Oxford: Oxford University Press: 8–9.

———. 1990. *The Concept of Music*. Oxford: Clarendon Press.

Manniche, Lise. 1991. *Music and Musicians in Ancient Egypt*. London: British Museum Press.

Margüll, Fritze. "25 Years of Improvised Music 1969–1994." FMP promotional brochure, 1994.

Mayr, Albert. 1993. "New and Rediscovered Zeitgebers in Recent Music." *Contemporary Music Review* 7/2: 79–90.

McClain, Ernest G. 1978. *The Myth of Invariance: The Origin of the Gods, Mathematics and Music from the Rg Veda to Plato*. Boulder and London: Shambhala.

McKenna, Terrence. 1991. *The Archaic Revival*. San Francisco: Harper.

McKinnon, James. 1987. *Music in Early Christian Literature*. Cambridge: Cambridge University Press.

—— (ed.). 1990. *Music and Society: Antiquity and the Middle Ages from Ancient Greece to the 15th Century*. Englewood Cliffs, N.J.: Prentice-Hall.

McMahon, James V. 1990. *The Music of Early Minnesang*. Columbia, S.C.: Camden House.

McNeill, William H. 1995. *Keeping Together in Time: Dance and Drill in Human History*. Cambridge, Mass.: Harvard University Press.

McRae, Barry. 1983. "The British Free Jazz Movement." *Jazz Forum*, No. 81: 40–4.

Mecklenburg, Carl Gregor Herzog zu. 1979. "Stilformen des modernen Jazz." *Collection d'Études Musicologiques Sammlung Musikwissenschaftlicher Abhandlungen*. Baden-Baden: Verlag Valentin Koerner.

Mellers, Wilfrid. 1964. *Music in a New Found Land*. New York: Hillstone.

Meltzer, David (ed.). 1993. *Reading Jazz*. San Francisco: Mercury House.

———. 1999. *Writing Jazz*. San Francisco: Mercury House.

Merriam, Alan. 1967. "Use of Music in Reconstructing Culture History." In Creighton Gabel and Norman Bennet (eds.). *Reconstructing African Culture History*. Boston: Boston University Press: 85–114.

Midgette, Anne. 1998. "A Cultural Ward of the State Becomes an Orphan." *New York Times*, 7 June: AR38, 45.

Miller, D. W. 1999. "Lessons From the Laboratory of Eastern Europe." *The Chronicle of Higher Education*, 3 September: A23.

Miller, Manfred. 1966. "Free Jazz: Eine New Thing Analyse." *Jazz Podium*, May: 128–30; June: 156–9; July: 182–4.

———. 1997. "Everyday I have the Blues – Notizen zur Geschichte un Funktion des Blues." In Wolbert (1997: 63–78).

Mintz, Sidney W. and Richard Price. 1976. *The Birth of African-American Culture: An Anthropological Perspective*. Boston: Beacon Press.

Moisala, Pirrko. 1995. "Cognitive Study of Music as Culture – Basic Premises for 'Cognitive Ethnomusicology.'" *Journal of New Music Research* 24, 1: 10–20.

Monson, Ingrid. 1995. "The Problem with White Hipness: Race, Gender, and Cultural Conceptions in Jazz Historical Discourse." *Journal of American Musicological Society* 48, 3: 396–422.

———. 1996. *Saying Something: Jazz Improvisation and Interaction*. Chicago and London: University of Chicago Press.

———. 1998. "On Freedom: George Russell, John Coltrane, and Modal Jazz." In Bruno Nettl, (ed.), with Melinda Russell. *In the Course of Performance: Studies in the World of Musical Improvisation*. Chicago and London: University of Chicago Press: 149–68.

Moody, Bill. 1993. *The Jazz Exiles: American Musicians Abroad*. Reno: University of Nevada Press.

Moore, Robin. 1992. "The Decline of Improvisation in Western Art Music: An Interpretation of Change." *IRASM* 23: 1.

Morgan, Robert P. 1991. *Twentieth-Century Music*. New York: W. W. Norton and Company.

Müller, Markus. 1994. "25 Years 'The Living Music.'" FMP presskit sheet.

Müller, Thorsten. 1997. "Feindliche Bewegung." In Wolbert (1997: 379–88).

Murray, Albert. 1970. *The Omni-Americans: Black Experience and American Culture*. New York: Vintage.

——. 1973. *The Hero and the Blues*. Columbia: University of Missouri Press.

——. 1976. *Stomping the Blues*. New York: Da Capo Press/Plenum Publishing.

Naura, Michael. 1997. "Im Untertagebau der Jazzkeller." In Wolbert (1997: 405–10).

Naura, Michael and Wolfram Knauer. 1996. "Musikergespräch mit Michael Naura: Es war ein lustiges Völkchen." In *Jazz in Deutschland*. Hofheim, Germany: Wolke Verlag: 159–74.

Nettl, Bruno. 1958. "Historical Aspects of Ethnomusicology." *American Anthropologist* 60: 518–32.

——. 1974. "Thoughts on Improvisation, a Comparative Approach." *Musical Quarterly* 60: 1–19.

——. 1986. "Some Historical Thoughts on the Character of Ethnomusicology." In Charlotte Frisbie (ed.). *Exploration in Ethnomusicology: Essays in Honor of David P. McAllester*. Detroit: Information Coordinators, 35–46.

——. (ed.), with Melinda Russell. 1998. *In the Course of Performance: Studies in the World of Musical Improvisation*. Chicago and London: University of Chicago Press.

The New Grove Dictionary of Jazz. 1988. London: Macmillan; New York: Groves Dictionaries of Music.

Newman, Barbara. 1987. *Sister of Wisdom: St. Hildegard's Theology of the Feminine*. Berkeley: University of California Press.

Nicholson, Stuart. 1995. *Jazz: The 1980s Resurgence*. New York: DaCapo Press.

——. 2000. "The Sound of Sameness: Why European Jazz Musicians No Longer Turn to America for Inspiration." *JazzTimes* 12: 44–9.

——. 2001. "Europeans Cut In With a New Jazz Sound And Beat." *New York Times*, 3 June: Section 2: 1, 28.

Nisenson, Eric. 1997. *Blue: The Murder of Jazz*. New York: St. Martin's Press.

Noglik, Bert. 1979. "Europäische Jazz-Avantgarde: Emanzipation wohin?" *Jazzforschung* 11: 165–95.

——. 1981. *Jazzwerkstatt International*. Berlin: Verlag Neue Musik.

——. 1987. "Aktuelle Aspekte der Identität von Jazz und 'Improvisierter Musik' in Europa: Differenziertes Selbstverstandnis und Internationalisierung." *Jazzforschung* 19: 177–86.

——. 1988. "A Light Ignited in the Open." In booklet accompanying 2-CD set *Alms/Tiergarten (Spree)*. Berlin: FMP.

——. 1989. *Twenty Years Free Music Production*. FMP promotional brochure.

——. 1990. "Horizontverschiebungen: Über die Bewegung der Begriffe und die Prozesse des Hörens." *Klangspuren: Wege improvisierter Musik*. Berlin: Verlag Neue Musik.

——. 1990. *Klangspuren: Wege improvisierter Musik*. Berlin: Verlag Neue Musik.

——. 1991. "Komposition und Improvisation – Anmerkungen zu einem spannungsreichen Verhältnis." In Wolfram Knauer (ed.). *Jazz und Komposition*. Jazz-Institut Darmstadt, Germany: 203–20.

——. 1994. "Osteuropäischer Jazz im Umbruch der Verhältnisse." In *Jazz in Europa*. Hofheim, Germany: Wolke Verlag: 147–62.

——. 1996. "Hürdenlauf zum freien Spiel. Ein Rückblick auf den Jazz der DDR." In *Jazz in Deutschland*. Hofheim, Germany: Wolke Verlag: 205–22.

——. 1997a. "Jazzmusik und Euro-Folk – Anmerkungen zu einem problematischen Verhältnis." In Wolbert (1997: 513–24).

——. 1997b. "Substreams – Die verborgene Moderne in der improvisierten Musik Europas." In Wolbert (1997: 525–34).

——. 1997c. "Vom Linden-Blues zum Zentralquartett – Fragmentarisches zur Entwicklung des Jazz in Der DDR." In Wolbert (1997: 421–34).

Noglik, Bert, and Heinz-Jurgen Lindner. 1978. *Jazz im Gesprach*. Berlin: Verlag Neue Musik.

Noll, Dietrich J. 1973. "Musik als kommunicatives Teamwork." *Jazz Podium*, May: 15–16.

——. 1977. *Zur Improvisation im Deutschen Free Jazz: Unters, zur Asthetik frei improvisierter Klangflächen*. Imburg: Verlag der Musikalienhandlung Wagner.

Nussbaum, Martha C. 2001. *Upheavals of Thought: The Intelligence of Emotions*. Cambridge: Cambridge University Press.

Oakley, Giles. 1976/1983/1997. *The Devil's Music: A History of the Blues*. New York: DaCapo Press.

O'Connor, Richard. 1968. *The German-Americans: An Informal History.* New York: Little, Brown and Company.

Ody, Joachim. 1997. "Alle Spuren führen zu Webern: Übe das Revival der Neuen Musik." *Spex,* August: 156–65.

Palisca, Claude V. (ed.). 1996. *Norton Anthology of Western Music,* I, *Ancient to Baroque.* New York: W. W. Norton and Company.

Panassié, Hugues. 1936. *Hot Jazz: The Guide to Swing Music.* New York: M. Witmark and Sons.

Paynter, John, Tim Howell, Richard Orton, and Peter Seymour (eds.). 1992. *Companion to Contemporary Musical Thought,* II. London and New York: Routledge.

Paysan, Marko. 1994. "Transatlantic Rhythm: Jazzkontakte zwischen Deutschland und den USA vor 1945." In *Jazz in Europa.* Hofheim, Germany: Wolke Verlag: 13–41.

Peretti, Burton W. 1992. *The Creation of Jazz: Music, Race, and Culture in Urban America.* Urbana and Chicago: University of Illinois Press.

——. 1994. "Caliban reheard: new voices on jazz and American consciousness." *Popular Music* 13, 2, May: 151–64.

Perlman, Alan M., and Daniel Greenblatt. 1981. "Miles Davis meets Noam Chomsky: Some Observations on Jazz Improvisation and Language Structure." In Wendy Steiner (ed.). *The Sign in Music and Literature.* Austin: University of Texas Press: 169–83.

Petrovsky, Ernst-Ludwig and Uschi Brüning. 1996. "Gedanken eines Menschen aus Güstrow, der zwischen Nazi-Märchen, Stalin-Panzern und FDJ-Liedern der Faszination des Jazz erlag." *Jazz in Deutschland.* Darmstadt: Jazz-Institut Darmstadt: 223–44.

Pfankuch, Gert. 1997. "Amateurjazz in den fünfziger Jahren." In Wolbert (1997: 411–20).

Pfleiderer, Martin. 1998. *Zwischen Exotismus und Weltmusik: Zur Rezeption asiatischer und afrikanischer Musik im Jazz der 6oer und 7oer Jahre.* CODA, Musikservice and Verlag.

Phelps, Reginald H., and Jack M. Stein (eds.). 1970. *The German Heritage,* third edition. New York: Holt, Rinehart, and Winston.

Phillips, Caryl. 1987. *The European Tribe.* Boston, and London: Faber and Faber.

Pinker, Steven. 2002. *The Blank Slate: The Modern Denial of Human Nature.* New York and London: Viking and Penguin.

Poiger, Uta G. 2000. *Jazz, Rock, and Rebels: Cold War Politics and American Culture in a Divided Germany.* Berkeley, Los Angeles, and London: University of California Press.

Pollard, Sam (ed.). 2001. *American Roots Music* (videorecording). Palmer Pictures.

Porter, Lewis. 1985. "John Coltrane's *A Love Supreme*: Jazz Improvisation as Composition." *Journal of American Musicological Society* 38: 593–621.

——. 1998. *John Coltrane: His Life and Music.* Ann Arbor: University of Michigan Press.

—— (ed.). 2002. *A Century of Change: Readings and New Essays.* New York: Schirmer Books.

Potter, Gary. 1992. "Analyzing Improvised Jazz (Reprint)." *College Music Symposium* 32: 143–60.

Potter, Pamela. 1998. *Most German of the Arts: Musicology and Society from the Weimar Republic to the End of Hitler's Reich.* New Haven and London: Yale University Press.

Powers, Harry. 1980. "Improvisation." *The Grove Dictionary of Music and Musicians.* London: Macmillan; Washington D.C.: Groves Dictionaries of Music.

——. 1992. "The Genesis of Language and Music," *Ethnomusicology* 36: 147–70.

Pressing, Jeff. 1982. "Pitch Class Set Structures in Contemporary Jazz." *Jazzforschung* 14: 133–72.

——. 1988. "Improvisation: Methods and Models." In John A. Sloboda (ed.). *Generative Processes in Music: the Psychology of Performance, Improvisation, and Composition.* Oxford: Clarendon Press; New York: Oxford University Press: 129–78.

Priest, Philip. 1996. "Putting Listening First: A Case of Priorities," In Gary Spruce (ed.). *Teaching Music.* New York: Routledge: 206–15.

Pritchett, James. 1993. *The Music of John Cage.* Cambridge and New York: Cambridge University Press.

Prögler, J. A. 1995. "Searching for Swing: Participatory Discrepancies in the Jazz Rhythm Section." *Ethnomusicology* 39, 1: 21–54.

Quinke, R. 1977. "Die Berliner Free Music Production." *Musik und Bildung*, Bd. 9, October: 556–9.

Raffman, Diana. 1993. *Language, Music, and Mind*. Cambridge, Mass.: MIT Press.

Redding, Arthur F. 1998. *Raids on Human Consciousness: Writing, Anarchism, and Violence*. Columbia s.c.: University of South Carolina Press.

Reichelt, Rolf (trans. John Evarts). 1980. "Einige Aspekte der Entwicklung des Free Jazz in DDR" ("A Few Aspects of the Development of Free Jazz in the German Democratic Republic"). *Snapshot: Jazz aus DDR*. FMP LP booklet: 19–28.

Rempel, Hans (trans. Elizabeth Johnston). 1980. "Jazz in Europa" ("Jazz in Europe"). *Snapshot: Jazz aus DDR*. FMP LP booklet: 29–32.

Retallack, Joan (ed.). 1996. *Musicage: Cage Muses on Words, Art, Music*. Middletown, Conn.: Wesleyan University Press.

Revill, David. 1992. *The Roaring Silence: John Cage: A Life*. New York: Arcade Publishing.

Rich, Alan. 1995. *American Pioneers: Ives to Cage and Beyond*. London: Phaidon Press Limited.

Richie, Alexandra. 1998. *Faust's Metropolis: A History of Berlin*. New York: Carroll and Graf Publishers, Inc.

Richie, Chip. 2000. *Black Indians: an American story*. Dallas, Tex.: Rich-Heape Films.

Richter, Stephan. 1995. *Zu einer Ästhetik des Jazz*. Frankfurt am Main, Berlin, Bern, New York, Paris, and Vienna: Peter Lang, Europäischer Verlag der Wissenschaften.

Riley, Peter. 1979. "Incus Records." *Coda*. No. 167, June: 3–8.

Rink, John. 1993. "Schenker and Improvisation." *Music Theory* 37: 1–54.

Rippley, La Vern J. 1976. *The German-Americans*. Boston: Twayne Publishers.

Ritscher, M. *Immaculata*. 1994. Hildegard von Bingen. Bietigheim, Germany: Bayer Records BR 100 116 CD, liner notes.

Robinson, David W. 1995. "Introduction." In "No Man's Land: East German Drama After the Wall." *Contemporary Theatre Review* 4, 2: 1–6.

Robinson, J. Bradford. 1991. "Zur 'Jazz'-Rezeption der Weimarer Periode: Eine stilhistorische Jagd nach einer Rhythmus-Floskel." In Wolfram Knauer (ed.). *Jazz und Komposition*. Jazz-Institut Darmstadt, Germany: 11–25.

Roots and Branches of Jazz. Salt Lake City, Utah: The Society for Preservation and Propagation of Eastern Arts.

Rose, Cynthia. 1988. "New Wave Jazzers." *New Statesman and Society*, 25 November: 13–15.

Rosenfield, Israel. 1986. "Neural Darwinism: A New Approach to Memory and Perception." *The New York Review* 9 October: 21–5.

Ross, Alex. 1995. "In Flux, Berlin Remaps, Reminds." *New York Times*, 13 August: Section 2, 25.

Rothstein, Edward. 1994. "Music On Their Minds." *New York Times*, 17 November: AR 31.

——. 1997. "Where a Democracy and its Money Have No Place." *New York Times*, 26 October: AR1, 39.

Rouget, Gilbert. 1985. *Music and Trance: A Theory of the Relations Between Music and Possession*. Chicago and London: University of Chicago Press.

Rouy, Gérard. 1976. "Globe Unity sur le carreau de la mine." *Jazz Magazine*, no. 241, February: 16–19.

——. 1977. "Incus; ou, la force tranquille." *Jazz Magazine*, no. 254, May: 20–21.

Rusch, Bob. 1977. "FMP Music Production Summer Releases." *Cadence* 2, no. 8, July: 12–16.

——. 1977. "Zerbam! Gerberfoibleschelter!" *Cadence* 2, no. 6/7, March: 7–12.

Russell, George. 1953. *The Lydian Concept of Tonal Organization*. New York: Russ-Hix Publishing.

——. 1964[1959]. *The Lydian Chromatic Concept of Tonal Organization for Improvisation*. Reprint, with appendix. Cambridge, Mass.: Concept Publishing Company.

Rutter, Larry. 1966. "Avantgarde: Perspektive einer revolution." *Jazz Podium*, October: 266–8, 270.

Sachs, Curt (ed. Jaap Kunst). 1961. *The Wellsprings of Music*. New York and Toronto: McGraw-Hill Book Co.

Said, Edward. 1991. *Musical Elaborations*. New York: Columbia University Press.

Sandner, Wolfgang. 1997. "Vorformen des Jazz – Minstrel und Ragtime." In Wolpert (1997: 45–58).

Sansonese, J. Nigro. 1994. *The Body of Myth: Mythology, Shamanic Trance, and the Sacred Geography of the Body.* Rochester Vt.: Inner Traditions International.

Saul, Scott. 2003. *Freedom Is, Freedom Ain't: Jazz and the Making of the Sixties.* Cambridge, Mass., Harvard University Press.

Schafer, Murray. 1980. *The Tuning of the World: Toward a Theory of Soundscape Design.* Philadelphia: University of Pennsylvania Press.

Schechner, Richard. 1977. *Essays on Performance Theory, 1970–1976.* New York: Drama Book Specialists.

Schiff, David. 1999. "Schoenberg's Cool Eye For the Erotic." *New York Times,* 8 August: AR 29–30.

Schlippenbach, Alexander von. 1975. "Potenzierung Musikalischer Energien: Das Globe Unity Orchester." *Jazz Podium,* March: 11–13.

——. 1979. "Free Jazz." *Neue Zeitschrift fur Musik,* May/June: 244–9.

Schmidt-Joos, Siegfried. 1972. "Free Jazz ohne Publikum?" *Jazz Podium,* September: 15–17.

Schneider, Peter. 1991. *The German Comedy: Scenes of Life After the Wall.* New York: Farar Straus Giroux.

Schoenberg, Arnold. 1969/1954. *Structural Functions of Harmony.* New York and London: W. W. Norton and Company.

——. 1995. *The Book of The Hanging Gardens and Other Songs, for Voice and Piano.* New York: Dover Publications.

Scholl, Sharon, and Sylvia White. 1970. *Music and the Culture of Man.* New York: Holt, Rinehart, and Winston.

Schopenhauer, Arthur. 1966. *The World as Will and Representation.* New York: Dover Publications.

Schuller, Gunther. 1968. *Early Jazz: Its Roots and Musical Development.* New York and Oxford: Oxford University Press.

——. 1986. *Musings: The Musical Worlds of Gunther Schuller.* New York and Oxford: Oxford University Press.

——. 1989. *The Swing Era: The Development of Jazz, 1930–1945.* New York and Oxford: Oxford University Press.

Schwendener, Peter. 1989. "The Sad White Jazz Man." Review of Art Pepper, *Straight Life. TriQuarterly* 74, Winter: 247–54.

Seay, Albert. 1975. *Music in the Medieval World.* Englewood Cliffs, N.J.: Prentice-Hall.

Seeger, Charles. 1940. "Folk Music as a Source of Social History." In Caroline Ware (ed.). *The Cultural Approach to History.* New York: Columbia University Press, 316–23.

Senghor, Leopold. 1968. *Negritude and Germanism.* Tübingen: H. Erdmann.

Servos, Norbert, and Gert Weigelt (photography). 1984. *Pina Bausch – Wuppertal Dance Theater, or The Art of Training a Goldfish: Excursions into Dance.* Cologne: Ballet-Bühnen-Verlag.

Shatz, Adam. 1999. "A Jazz Pianist With a Brahmsian Bent." *New York Times,* 25 July: 31.

Shelemay, Kay Kaufman (ed.). 1990. *The Garland Library of Readings in Ethnomusicology: A Core Collection of Important Ethnomusicological Articles in Seven Volumes.* New York: Garland.

Shepherd, John. 1994. "Music, Culture and Interdisciplinarity: Reflections on Relationships." *Popular Music* 13: 2.

Shipton, Alyn. 2001. *A New History of Jazz.* London and New York: Continuum.

Shoemaker, Bill. 1985. "Free Music Productions." *Coda* 201: 4–5, 22–3.

Sidran, Ben. 1981. *Black Talk.* New York: Da Capo Press.

Sinclair, John, and Robert Levin. 1971. *Music and Politics.* New York: The World Publishing Co.

Slobin, Mark. 1993. *Subcultural Sounds: Micromusics of the West.* Middletown, Conn.: Wesleyan University Press.

Sloboda, John A. (ed.). *Generative Processes in Music: the Psychology of Performance, Improvisation, and Composition.* Oxford: Clarendon Press; New York: Oxford University Press, 1988.

Slonimsky, Nicolas. 1947. *Thesaurus of scales and melodic patterns.* New York: Scribner.

Small, Christopher. 1987. *Music of the Common Tongue: Survival and Celebration in Afro-American Music.* London and New York: John Calder and Riverrun Press.

Smith, Bill. *Imagine the Sound No. 5: The Book*. Nightwood Editions, 1985.

Smith, F. Joseph (ed.). 1989. *Understanding Musical Experience*. New York: Gordon and Breach.

Smith, Hazel, and Roger Dean. 1997. *Improvisation, Hypermedia, and the Arts since 1945*. London: Harwood Academic Publishers.

Smith, Wadada Leo. 1995. "An Ankrahsmation Analysis: Anthony Braxton's 'Composition 113' (1983)." In Graham Lock, (ed.). *Mixtery: A Festschrift for Anthony Braxton*. London: Stride Publications, 93–102.

Solomon, Larry. 1982. From "Forum: Improvisation." *Perspectives in New Music*, September: 77.

Southern, Eileen. 1971/1983/1997. *The Music of Black Americans: A History*. New York: W. W. Norton and Company.

Spellman, A. B. 1966. *Four lives in the bebop business*. New York: Pantheon Books.

Spiegelberg, Herbert. 1994. *The Phenomenological Movement: A Historical Introduction*. Dordrecht, Boston, and London: Kluwer Academic Publishers.

Spivak, Gayatri Chakravorty. 1988. "Can the Subaltern Speak?" In Lawrence Grossberg and Cary Nelson (eds.). *Marxist Interpretations of Literature and Culture: Limits, Frontiers, Boundaries*. Urbana: University of Illinois Press, 271–313.

Spoerri, Bruno. 1972. "Neue Formen – Freies Spiel; Grundlagen der Jazzpraxis." *Jazz Podium*, August: 50.

Spruce, Gary. 1996. "Assessment in the Arts: Issues of Objectivity." In Gary Spruce (ed.). *Teaching Music*. New York: Routledge: 168–82.

Staples, Brent. 2003. "When Racial Discrimination is Not Just Black and White." *New York Times*, 12 September: A30.

Starr, Frederick S. 1994. *Red and Hot: The Fate of Jazz in the Soviet Union, With a New Chapter on the Final Years*. New York: Limelight Editions.

——. 1997a. "Jazz in der UdSSR." In Wolbert (1997: 463–8).

——. 1997b. "Früher New Orleans Jazz – Legende und Wirklichkeit." In Wolbert (1997: 79–102).

Stevens, Charles. 1994. "Traditions and Innovations in Jazz." *Popular Music and Society* 18, 2, Summer: 61–78.

Stockhausen, Karlheinz. 1978. "Weltmusik." In *Texte zur Musik 1970–77*. Cologne: DuMont, 468–76.

——. 1989. *Towards a Cosmic Music*. Shaftesbury, Dorset: Element Books.

Strogatz, Steven. 2003. *Sync: The Emerging Science of Spontaneous Order*. New York: Theia/Hyperion.

Such, David G. 1993. *Avant-Garde Jazz Musicians: Performing 'Out There'*. Iowa City: University of Iowa Press.

Sudnow, David. 1978. *Ways of the Hand: The Organization of Improvised Conduct*. Cambridge, Mass.: Harvard University Press.

Suhor, Charles. 1986. "Jazz Improvisation and Language Performance: Parallel Competencies." *Etc.* 43, Summer: 133–40.

Suppan, Wolfgang. 1973. "Free Jazz: Negation aesthetischer Kategorien – Rueckkehr zur funktionalen musik." *Musikerziehung* 26, no. 5: 206–8.

Szwed, John F. 1997. *Space is the Place: The Lives and Times of Sun Ra*. New York: Pantheon Books.

——. 2002. *So What: The Life of Miles Davis*. New York: Simon and Schuster.

Taubert, Ray, and David Radlauer. 1985. "Jazz in Germany: A Survey of Hot Dance, Swing, and Traditional Jazz in Germany, 1924 to Present" (produced for and broadcast on KALW-FM, San Francisco, by David Radlauer and Ray Taubert).

Taylor, Gary. 2000. *Castration: An Abbreviated History of Western Manhood*. New York and London: Routledge.

Taylor, Ronald. 1997. *Berlin and its Culture*. New Haven and London: Yale University Press.

Teish, Luisah. 1985. *Jambalaya: The Natural Woman's Book of Personal Charms and Practical Rituals*. San Francisco: Harper and Row.

Tenney, James, and Larry Polansky. 1980. "Temporal Gestalt Perception in Music." *Journal of Music Theory* 24, 2: 205–42.

Thiem, Michael. 1982. "Alexander von Schlippenbach." *Jazz Forum*, no. 77: 44–7.

Thomas, J. C. 1976. *Chasin' the Trane: The Music and Mystique of John Coltrane*. New York: Da Capo Press.

Tingen, Paul. 2001. *Miles beyond: the electric explorations of Miles Davis, 1967–1991*. New York: Billboard Books.

Tomlinson, Gary. 1993. *Music in Renaissance Magic: Toward a Historiography of Others*. Chicago: University of Chicago Press.

———. 1995. "Ideologies in Aztec Song." *Journal of American Musicological Society* 48, 3: 343–79.

Troupe, Quincey. 1989. *Miles Davis: The Autobiography*. New York: Simon and Schuster.

Turi, Gabor. 1988. "Peter Brötzmann: Music from the Stomach." *Jazz Forum* 115: 46–9.

Van Nortwick, Thomas. 1992. *Oedipus: The Meaning of a Masculine Life*. Norman Okla.: University of Oklahoma Press.

Ventura, Michael. 1987. "Hear That Long Snake Moan." *Whole Earth Review*, no. 54, Spring: 28.

Vickery, Steve. 1994. "Leo and F. M. P. Independence." *Coda*, no. 258, November/December: 22–5.

Viera, Joe. 1974. *Der Free Jazz: Formen und Modelle*. Vienna: Universal Edition.

Vincent, Ted. 1995. *Keep Cool: The Black Activists who Built the Jazz Age*. London and East Haven, Conn.: Pluto Press.

Virilio, Paul. 1980. *Esthétique de la disparation*. Paris: Editions Balland.

Wallin, Nils L. 1991. *Biomusicology: Neurophysiological, Neuropsychological, and Evolutionary Perspectives on the Origins and Purposes of Music*. Stuyvesant, N.Y.: Pendragon Press.

Walser, Robert (ed.). 1999. *Keeping Time: Readings in Jazz History*. New York and Oxford: Oxford University Press.

Waterman, Richard Alan. 1952. "African Influence on the Music of the Americas." In Sol Tax (ed.). *Acculturation in the Americas: Proceedings and Selected Papers of the XXIXth International Congress of Americanists*. Chicago: The University of Chicago Press.

Watrous, Peter. 1999. "Jazz's Best-Known Label at 60." *New York Times*, 10 January: AR 37.

Watson, Alan. 1992. *The Germans: Who Are They Now?* London: Methuen.

Webster, Peter, 1996. "Creativity as Creative Thinking." In Gary Spruce (ed.). *Teaching Music*. New York: Routledge.

Werts, Daniel. 1988. "Pitch Organization in Cecil Taylor's *Legba Crossing*." In booklet accompanying 2-CD set *Alms/Tiergarten (Spree)*. Berlin: FMP.

Westendorf, Lynette. 1994. "Analyzing Free Jazz." University of Washington, Ph.D. dissertation.

Westin, Lars. 1997. "Jazz in Schweden." In Wolbert (1997: 489–500).

Whitehead, Kevin. 1995. "Death to 'the Avant-Garde.'" *Village Voice*, March 21.

———. 1998. *New Dutch Swing*. New York: Billboard Books.

Wicke, Peter. 1992. "The Times They Are A-Changin': Rock Music and Political Change in East Germany." In Reebee Garofalo (ed.). *Rockin' the Boat: Mass Music and Mass Movements*. Boston: South End Press.

Wickes, John. 1999. *Innovations in British Jazz, I, 1960–1980*. Chelmsford: Soundworld Publishers.

Wiedemann, Erik. 1997. "Jazz in Dänemark." In Wolbert (1997: 483–8).

Willener, Alfred. 1970. *The Action-Image of Society: On Cultural Politicization*. New York: Pantheon Books.

Williams, Martin. 1992. "What Kind of Composer was Thelonious Monk?" *The Musical Quarterly* 76, 3, Fall: 433–41.

Wilmer, Valerie. 1977. *As Serious As Your Life: The Story of the New Jazz*. London: Quartet Books.

Wilson, Edmund O. 1998. *Consilience: The Unity of Knowledge*. New York: Knopf.

Wilson, Peter Niklas. 1993. *Anthony Braxton: Sein Leben, Seine Musik, Seine Schallplatten*. Waakirchen, Germany: OREOS Verlag.

———. 1999. *Hear and Now: Gedanken zur Improvisierten Musik*. Hofheim, Germany: Wolke Verlag.

Winter, Keith. 1979. "Communication Analysis in Jazz." *Jazzforschung* 11: 93–134.

Wise, Michael Z. 1998. *Capital Dilemma: Germany's Search for a New Architecture of Democracy*. New York: Princeton Architectural Press.

———. 1998. "Where the Past Haunts, Berlin Embraces the New." *New York Times*, 7 June: AR38, 42.

Witherden, Barry. 1990. "Low Life Giant." *Wire* 73, March: 38–41.

Wolbert, Klaus (ed.). 1997. *That's Jazz: Der Sound des 20. Jahrhunderts.* Darmstadt, Germany: Verlag Jürgen Häusser.

Wood, Anthony. 1983. "FMP." *Wire*, No. 4 (Summer): 30–32, 42.

Woodward, Richard. 1994. "A Rage Supreme." *Village Voice*, August: 9.

Wouters, Kees. 1994. "Von den Wandervögeln zum Wanderers Hotclub." In *Jazz in Europa.* Hofheim: Wolke Verlag: 51–71.

Zajonc, Arthur. 1993. *Catching the Light: The Entwined History of Light and Mind.* New York and Oxford: Oxford University Press: 290.

Zakaria, Fareed. 1999. "The Empire Strikes Out: The Unholy Emergence of the Nation-State." *New York Times Magazine*, 18 April: 99.

Zinn, Howard. 2001. *A People's History of the United States, 1492–Present.* New York: Perennial Classics.

Zucker, A. E. 1950. *The Forty-Eighters: Political Refugees of 1848.* New York: Columbia University Press.

Zwerin, Michael. 1987. *La Tristesse de Saint Louis: Jazz Under the Nazis.* New York: W. Morrow.

Interviews

My interviews took place (in 1997, unless otherwise indicated) as follows: Günter Sommer, on the road from Dresden to Konstanz, 7/30, and in Konstanz, 8/1; Axel Dörner, in his Berlin apartment, 8/7, and backstage at Berlin's 213 Club, 8/15; Vinko Globokar, at his Berlin apartment, 9/20; Peter Kowald, at his home in Wuppertal, 8/19–20; Peter Brötzmann, at his home in Wuppertal, 8/18; Dagmar Gebers, at her Berlin apartment, 8/10; Alexander von Schlippenbach, at his Berlin apartment, 8/9; Wolfgang Fuchs, at his Berlin apartment, 9/15; Dieter Hahne, at FMP's Berlin office, 11/13/96, and 6/20; Ulrich Gumpert, at his Berlin apartment, 8/13; Albert Mangelsdorff, at Berlin's Adlon Hotel, 9/6; Jost Gebers, at various Berlin restaurants, 6/14, 6/15, 6/23, 9/20; Paul Lovens, at the annual *Konfrontationen* festival in Nickelsdorff, Austria, 7/20; Evan Parker, at the annual *Konfrontationen* festival in Nickelsdorff, Austria, 7/21; Sven-Åke Johansson, at his Berlin apartment, 9/15; Gunter Hampel, at his New York apartment, 9/1/98; Joachim Kühn, in his New York lodgings during studio session with Ornette Coleman, 2/10/98; Johannes Bauer, at his Berlin apartment, 9/7; Willi Kellers, in a Berlin restaurant, 9/19; Conrad Bauer, at his Berlin apartment, 9/1, and Ernst-Ludwig Petrovsky, on the road from Dresden to Vienna, 9/22, at Hotel Franz Josef in Vienna, 9/23, and backstage at a Berlin school performance, 9/29; Uschi Bruning, backstage at a Berlin school performance, 9/29; Anthony Braxton, 12/2001, at Red Lobster restaurant near Middletown, Conn.

Recordings

Ayler, Albert. 1964. *New York Eye and Ear Control.* ESP 1061.

Braxton, Anthony. 1993. *Eugene (1989).* Black Saint BS 120137–2.

——. 1999. *Small Ensemble Music (Wesleyan) 1994.* Splasc[h] Records CDH 801.2.

Bauer, Conrad. 1986. *Reflections.* FMP CD 74.

——. 1993. *The Konrad Bauer Trio.* Victo CD 023.

——. 1995. *Bauer Bauer.* Intakt CD 040.

Bauer, Johannes. 1992. *Organo Pleno.* FMP CD 56.

——. *Pijp.* 1996/7. WIMprovier CD 140497.

Brötzmann, Peter. 1967. *For Adolphe Sax.* FMP 0080.

——. 1968. *Machine Gun.* FMP CD 24.

——. 1976. *Brötzmann/Solo.* FMP 0360.

——. 1977. *Schwarzewaldfahrt.* FMP 0440

——. 1977. *Ein halber Hund kann nicht pinkeln.* FMP 0420.

——. 1979. *The Nearer the Bone, the Sweeter the Meat.* FMP 0690.

——. 1979. *Three Points and a Mountain.* FMP 0670.

——. 1980. *Brötzmann/Kellers.* FMP 0800.

——. 1981. *Kellers-Brötzmann.* FMP 0800.

——. 1982. *Andrew Cyrille Meets Peter Brötzmann in Berlin.* FMP 1000.

——. 1984. *Berlin Djungle.* FMP 1120.

——. 1984. *14 Love Poems.* FMP 1060.

——. 1986. *Last Exit.* Enemy Records. EMY 101–2.

——. 1989. *Reserve.* FMP CD 17.

——. 1991. *Funny Rat.* E-G-G 89002 (Japan).

——. 1991. *Songlines.* FMP CD 53.

——. 1992. *März Combo Live in Wuppertal.* FMP CD 47.

——. 1993. *Die Like a Dog.* FMP CD 64.

——. 1997. *Exhilaration.* Soul Note 121330–2.

——. 1997. *The Wels Concert.* Okkadisk OD 12013.

——. 1999. *Little Birds Have Fast Hearts.* FMP CD 101.

Carter, John. 1988. *Roots and Folklore: Episodes in the Development of American Folk Music Fields.* New York: Gramavision.

Coleman, Ornette. 1958. *Something Else.* Contemporary S 7551.

——. 1959. *Change of the Century.* Atlantic 1327.

——. 1959. *The Shape of Jazz to Come.* Atlantic 1317.

Coltrane, John. 1964. *A Love Supreme.* Impulse AS-66.

——. 1965. *Ascension.* Impulse AS-95.

Dörner, Axel. 1993. *The Remedy.* Jazz Haus Musik CD 69.

——. 1994. *Die Enttauschung.* 219 Red 001.

Fuchs, Wolfgang. 1979. *Momente.* FMP 0610.

——. 1983. *Berliner Austausch Dienst.* Uhlklang 3.

——. 1983. *Berliner Begegnungen.* SAJ-47.

——. 1983. *Frogman's View.* Uhlklang 9.

——. 1985. *King Übü Örchestrü.* Uhlklang 6.

——. 1985. *So-und? So!* Uhlklang 7.

——. 1987. *The Berlin Station.* SAJ-57.

——. 1991. *Live in Berlin '71.* FMP CD 34/35.

——. 1993. *Binaurality.* FMP CD 49.

——. 1996. *Bits and Pieces.* FMP OWN-90004.

Globe Unity Orchestra. 1966. *Globe Unity.* SABA 15109.

——. 1973. *Globe Unity '73 Live in Wuppertal.* FMP 0160.

——. 1974. *Hamburg '74.* FMP 0650.

——. 1975. *Evidence.* FMP 0220.

——. 1975. *Into the Valley.* FMP 0270.

——. 1975–76. *Jahrmarkt.* Po Torch JWD 2.

——. 1975. *Pearls.* FMP 0380.

——. 1986. *20th Anniversary, Globe Unity Orchestra.* FMP CD 45.

Globokar, Vinko. 1987. *5, die sich nicht ertragen können.* FMP 1180.

——. 1992. *Globokar by Globokar.* Harmonia Mundi CD 905214.

——. 1991. *Les Émigrés.* Harmonia Mundi 905212.

Gumpert, Ulrich. 1978. *Unter Anderem: 'N Tango für Gitti.* FMP 0600.

——. 1979. *Echoes von Karolienhoff.* FMP 0710.

——. 1979. *Ulrich Gumpert Workshop Band.* Amiga 8 55 753.

——. 1991. *Die Engel.* Steidl Verlag CD 3-88243-197-0/1, 0/2.

———. Compositions/improvisations with Thomas Brasch, Heiner Müller, and Jochen Berg texts (from Berliner Ensemble productions, private tape from Gumpert's collection).

———. 1991. *The Secret Concert.* ITM 1461.

Hampel, Günter. 1969. *The 8th of July 1969.* Birth Records CD 001.

———. 1998. *The 27th of May 1997.* Birth CD 045.

———. 1999. *Heartplants.* SABA/MPS 1965; Japanese reissue POCJ-2672.

Hipp, Jutta, *First Ladies of Jazz* (with Hans Koller, 1952; ZDS 1202 Savoy Jazz, 1989)

Johannson, Sven-Åke. 1980. *Idylle und Katastrophen.* po torch records, ptr/wd 6.

———. 1984. *Blind aber Hungrig.* FMP-S 15.

———. 1986. *. . . über Ursache und Wirkung der Meinungsverschiedenheiten beim Turmbau zu Babel.* FMP-S 20/21.

———. 1997. With Rüdiger Carl at 1997 Total Music Meeting (private tape from Johansson).

Kowald, Peter. 1966. *The Early Quintett.* FMP 0540.

———. 1972. *Peter Kowald Quintet.* FMP 0070.

———. 1975. *Carpathes.* FMP 0250.

———. 1979. *Die Jungen: Random Generators.* FMP 0680.

———. 1980. *The Family.* FMP 0940.

———. 1982. *Two Making a Triangle.* FMP 0990.

———. 1984–89. *Duos Europa, Duos USA, and Duos Japan.* FMP CD 21.

———. 1988. *Open Secrets.* FMP 1190.

———. 1991. *Pyrichia.* Ano Kato Records CD-P 3.

———. 1991. *When the Sun is Out, You Don't See Stars.* FMP CD 38.

———. 1998. Peter Kowald solo concert (1998 Total Music Meeting, private tape from Kowald).

———. 1998. *Cuts: Ort Ensemble Wuppertal.* FMP CD 94.

Kühn, Joachim. 1997. *Generations from East Germany.* Klangräume CD 30320.

Mangelsdorff, Albert. 1984. *Pica Pica.* FMP 1050.

———. 1993. (1980, 1964). *Jazz Now Ramwong.* Bellaphon Records CDLR 71001.

———. 1993. (1979, 1963). *Tension!* Bellaphon Records CDLR 71002.

Namtchylak, Sainkho. 1991. *Lost Rivers.* FMP CD 42.

Paniagua, Gregorio. 1979. *Musique de la Grèce Antique.* Arles: Harmonia Mundi.

Petrovsky, Ernst-Ludwig. 1969. *Jazz mit dem Ensemble Studio 4.* Amiga 8 55 187.

———. 1978. *Ernst-Ludwig Petrovsky.* Amiga 8 55 621.

———. 1979. *Selb-Viert.* FMP 0760.

———. 1980. *Selb-Dritt.* FMP 0890.

———. 1982. *Dedication.* FMP LP 0900.

———. 1986. *Electrization.* Ernst-Ludwig Petrovsky with Frederick Schenker and Berlin Sinfonie Orchester, private tape.

———. 1992. *Features of Usel.* FMP OWN-90001.

———. 1995. *Ruf der Heimat.* Konnex CD 5067.

———. 1995. *Ride into the Blue.* Konnex CD 5069.

———. 1997. *Cooperations.* Konnex CD 5079.

Rempel, Hans. 1976. *Number Six: Two Compositions for Improvisers.* FMP 0490.

Rowland, Steve (producer) and Larry Abrams (writer/co-producer). 2001. *Tell Me How Long Trane's Been Gone* (radio documentary, 5 CDs). Chicago: WFMT Fine Arts Network.

Sommer, Gunther. 1965. *Manfred Krug und die Modern Jazz Big Band 65.* VEB Deutsche Schallplatten 8 50 054.

———. 1968. *Jazz: Jazz-Gedichte von Jens Gerlach.* Amiga 8 50 149.

———. 1979. *Hörmusik.* FMP 0790.

———. 1984. *Percussion Summit.* Moers.

———. 1989. *Riobec.* FMP CD 2.

———. 1990. *Cordes sur Ciel.* European Music Production: EPC 883.

———. 1993. *Da sagte der Butt* (with Günter Grass). Göttingen: Steidl Verlag.

———. 1993. *Sachsische Schatulle.* Intakt CD 027.

———. 1997. *Aphorisms* (private tape from Günter Sommer's collection).

———. 1997. *Touch the Earth – Break the Shells.* FMP 67.

Spontaneous Music Ensemble. 1995. *Spontaneous Music Ensemble.* Emanem 4005.

Synopsis. 1973. *Just For Fun.* FMP 0140.

———. 1973. *The Old Song.* FMP 0170.

———. 1974. *Synopsis.* Amiga 8 55 395.

———. 1974. *Auf der Elbe Schwimmt ein Rosa Krokodil.* FMP 0240.

———. 1978. *Jetzt Geht's Kloss!* FMP 0620.

———. 1979. *Versäumnisse.* FMP 0740.

———. 1996. *Smell a Rat.* AHO CD 1025.

———. 1996 (1977). *Synopsis '77.* SYN CD 01.

(Zentral Quartett.) 1990. *Zentral Quartett.* Zong CD 2170 019.

———. 1994. *Plié.* Intakt CD 037.

Taylor, Cecil. 1958. *Looking Ahead.* Contemporary 3562.

———. Tentet, 1996. Total Music Meeting, 11/2–3 (rough-mix cassette).

Various artists. 1979. *Snapshot: Jazz Aus DDR.* FMP.

———. 1985. *Jazz in Germany: A Survey of Hot Dance, Swing and Traditional Jazz in Germany, 1924 to Present,* produced for and broadcast on KALW FM, San Francisco, by Dave Radlauer and Ray Taubert.

———. 1997. *Jazz in Deutschland aus dem Amiga-Archiv 1947–1965.* Amiga 74321433802.

———. 2001. "Not necessarily 'English music:' A collection of experimental music from Great Britain, 1960–1977." *Leonardo* music journal CD series (Cambridge, Mass.: Leonardo/ISAST, 2001, v. 11).

Von Schlippenbach, Alexander. 1969. *European Echoes.* FMP 0010.

———. 1969. *The Living Music.* FMP 0100.

———. 1974. *Three Nails Left.* FMP 0210.

———. 1977. *Piano Solo.* FMP 0430.

———. 1979. *Drive.* FMP 0810.

———. 1982. *Anticlockwise.* FMP 1020.

———. 1982. *Rondo Brilliante.* FMP 1040.

———. 1989. *Smoke.* FMP CD 23.

———. 1990. *Elf Bagatellen.* FMP CD 27.

———. 1991. *Physics.* FMP CD 50.

———. 1993/94. *Aki Takase, Alex von Schlippenbach Piano Duets Live in Berlin 93/93.* FMP OWN-90002.

———. 1997. *Light Blue.* Enja CD 9104–2.

Index